The Masterpiece

Philip Drew is an internationally renowned architectural writer who has published monographs on Frei Otto, Harry Seidler, Arata Isozaki, Tadao Ando and many others. His book *Leaves of Iron*, the first account in 1985 of Glenn Murcutt's architecture, has become a classic. Drew has been a senior lecturer in architectural history and theory at the University of Newcastle and has lectured widely in architectural history in Australia and the United States.

By the same author

Third Generation
Frei Otto
Tensile Architecture
Two Towers
The Architecture of Arata Isozaki
Leaves of Iron
Harry Seidler (*with Kenneth Frampton*)
Veranda
Real Space
The Coast Dwellers
Sydney Opera House
Edward Suzuki
Tadao Anado: Church on the Water, Church of the Light
Gunma Prefectural Museum of Modern Art
Touch This Earth Lightly

Philip Drew

The Masterpiece
Jørn Utzon

A Secret Life

Hardie Grant Books

New edition published in 2001
by Hardie Grant Books
12 Claremont St
South Yarra Victoria 3141
Australia
www.hardiegrant.com.au
First published in 1999

Copyright © Philip Drew, 1999

All rights reserved. No part of this publication
may be reproduced, stored in a retrieval
system or transmitted in any form by any
means, electronic, mechanical, photocopying,
recording or otherwise, without the prior
written permission of the publishers and
copyright holders.

National Library of Australia
Cataloguing-in-Publication Data:
Drew, Philip, 1943-
The masterpiece: Jørn Utzon: a secret life
Bibliography
Includes Index

ISBN 1 876719 34 6

1. Utzon, Jørn, 1918-, 2. Sydney Opera
House – History. 3. Sydney Opera House –
design and construction. 4. Architects –
Biography. 5. Architecture, Modern – 20th
century – New South Wales – Sydney. 6.
Sydney (N.S.W.) – Buildings, structures, etc.
I. Title.

725.822099441

Cover design by David Rosemeyer
Cover photo of Utzon © Lene Utzon
Cover photo of Opera House © Philip Quirk,
Wildlight Photo Agency
Text design by Luisa Laino
Typeset by Mike Kuszla
Produced by Griffin Press
Printed and bound in Australia

Haven't you ever noticed that the people who live by the open sea are like a race apart? It's almost as if the sea were part of their lives; there are surges – yes, and ebbs and flows too – in all their thoughts and feelings. They can never bear to be separated from it – oh, I should have thought about that before.

Henrik Ibsen, *The Lady from the Sea* (1888)

He is the quintessential Dane, the fear, the iron resolve to repress what's happening around him. The untameable optimism.

Peter Høeg, *Miss Smilla's Feeling for Snow* (1992)

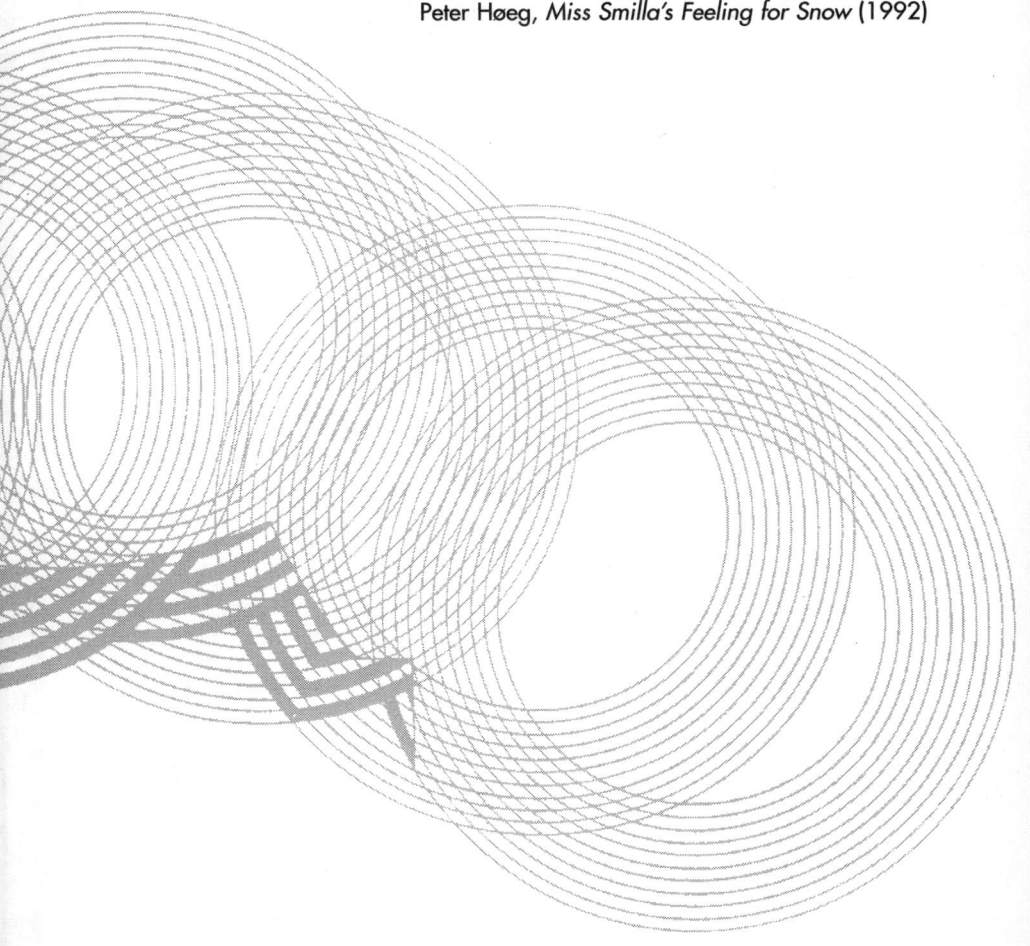

Contents

Preface	The Search for Utzon	ix
1	A Country Youth *Jutland, to 1936*	1
2	Snow Sleeping *Copenhagen and Stockholm, 1937–1945*	23
3	Drawing Dreams *Copenhagen, 1945–1948*	43
4	Architecture Without Signatures *Morocco and Mexico, 1948–1950*	67
5	The Beech Forest *Hellebæk, 1950–1955*	79
6	A Cathedral in the Air *Hellebæk, 1956*	95
7	Men of Vision *Sydney, 1947–1956*	119
8	The Tough Political Questions *Hellebæk and Sydney, 1957–1959*	141
9	Following *Sputnik*'s Trajectory *Hellebæk, 1959–1962*	175
10	Terraced Sanctuaries *Hellebæk, 1957–1963*	209
11	A Big Exotic Bird *Hellebæk, 1962*	221
12	Maturing the Vision *Sydney, 1963–1964*	243
13	A Hammer Blow *Sydney, 1964*	269
14	A White Radiance Rising *Höganäs and Sydney, 1958–1967*	289

15	Ballot-box Despot *Sydney, 1965*	**299**
16	A Conspiracy of Nobodies *Sydney, January–April 1966*	**333**
17	Tangles in the Web *The Opera House After Utzon, 1966–1973*	**369**
18	Back in Denmark *Hellebæk, 1966–1970*	**399**
19	Laying Low *Denmark, Hawaii, Mallorca, 1971–1972*	**417**
20	Flowers of Light *Mallorca, 1973–1976*	**431**
21	'It isn't necessary' *Mallorca, 1977–1983*	**447**
22	Solitude *Mallorca, 1984–*	**469**

Reflections **493**

Appendices

    Appendix A: Sydney Opera House: architectural and secretarial staff **499**

    Appendix B: Works and projects, 1944–98 **500**

    Appendix C: Awards and prizes **503**

    Abbreviations **504**

Bibliography **506**

Acknowledgements **510**

Notes **512**

Index **564**

Preface
The Search for Utzon

Reaching the end of the twentieth century is a little like climbing a mountain peak; besides the sense of achievement, there is also the satisfaction of being able to see the century spread out with the most important and crucial events made more visible. The Sydney Opera House was one of the crucial architectural events. In its 8 June 1998 issue, *Time* magazine included it in its 'Five for the Ages' selection of this century's greatest buildings.

Utzon, the Opera House's creator, has in a sense been overwhelmed by its fame, by the curiosity in him which has been the result. In the years after 1966, he tried to escape its renown and to move on with his life, but the more he ran from it, the more it lengthened its shadow. His story and the story of his building are coupled, the man and his work are inseparable. Hence this book is effectively two stories: a biography of Jørn Utzon, and a biography of his most famous creation, which I have endeavoured to place in perspective in terms of its relationship to his earlier architectural development and influences, and his subsequent career.

No one can doubt Utzon's importance to this century's architecture. Nor should his appreciation of what is enduring and valuable to us as sensuous, tactile beings be underestimated, insofar as it enabled him to produce a series of buildings which are open and optimistic creations and impress us with their unparalleled generosity of spirit.

Utzon never asked me to write about him. He is such an iceberg; most of him is hidden, the parts which we might believe we know rest on another, much more sizeable chunk below the surface. My task has been to chart the unseen mass of Utzon's life and, wherever possible, to understand how it impinges on the more visible parts of his public behaviour and architecture.

Utzon places great value on remaining anonymous. When cornered, he will sometimes oblige with a casual, unreflective interview in which he can select and present things the way he likes. This situation is unsatisfactory, not only for today, but for posterity. History requires that we know more than just the bare outlines of his life. We should know about the human side of Utzon, because, without that understanding, we cannot fully appreciate his architecture. So many of the presumed facts are incorrect or only half true.

One of Utzon's greatest gifts to the twentieth century was to give architecture back to ordinary people after a time, during the first half of the century, when Modern architecture was increasingly owned by a small, educated art elite. The prevailing view was that only the initiated could properly understand Modern architecture's sources and its transformation from nineteenth-century engineering and the avant-garde art movements of the early twentieth century.

In the 1940s, Utzon turned to the anonymous buildings of Morocco, Mexico, China and Iran, among other countries, for inspiration in a search for a popular architecture without signatures, and without boundaries around its appreciation. He pioneered a new awareness of vernacular architecture and, in turn, created his own industrial version, which, while it was quite remote from vernacular architecture technologically, was equally accessible. By bridging the gap between the modern and the primitive, Utzon gave architecture back to a wider audience so it could again contribute to the wider common culture as it had once done. It was perhaps the most enriching gift of all.

This alone would have been sufficient to justify his place in architectural history, but Utzon is also a remarkable person. I first became interested in Utzon in the winter of 1963 when a fellow student, who was a nightwatchman at the Opera House site, took me for a tour late one Saturday night. We crept through the inky black corridors into the grand volumes of the under-stage areas, which were filled with a soaring silvery light, then clambered up onto the moonlit floor of the theatres. It was an unforgettable experience. Like an ancient tomb complex, it was deserted and eerily empty. Even at this very early stage, when so much yet remained to be built, the structure possessed a presence that no one could possibly miss.

In August 1970, I visited Utzon's home at Hellebæk to seek his co-operation for a book about his architecture. The Stuttgart art book publisher Gerd Hatje had agreed to take on my proposed book about Utzon. Utzon put me off with the excuse that it was too soon after the Opera House fiasco. It would be better, he suggested, to wait until he completed a few more buildings. Disappointed, I wrote *Third Generation*, which surveyed the generation of architects in the United States, Japan and Europe who were beginning to make their mark and included Utzon and Australia's John Andrews. I was excited by Utzon's work and the new ideas that were arising around the world at the end of the 1960s, during a time of crisis for Modern architecture. Utzon liked the book very much.

Over the years, however, Utzon has rejected every author's approach, with the result that to date there is no substantial publication about him, only an occasional, isolated chapter or magazine feature published each time he completed a new project. In this way he has maintained the mystery. I was not the only architectural historian to try, for Utzon also turned away Tobias Faber, a long-time friend, and the English architectural academic and critic Kenneth Frampton, currently a professor of architecture at Columbia University.

I visited Utzon again in February 1990 at his home on Mallorca, when he kindly took me to his favourite restaurant, Sa Barraca. He was charming and relaxed. This time I did not press the point, it seemed much better to let him speak. He appeared happy and contented that, after all that had occurred, Australians now loved his Sydney Opera House. Utzon regarded it as some kind of gift to Australia and its people, and he was relieved that Australians were at long last able to accept it.

Concerning books, the truth probably is he will never be ready. That is why I decided to write *The Masterpiece* now before it was too late.

Each generation has a responsibility to question the past and explore the core events; without asking difficult, unsettling questions, we can never hope to understand Utzon or the sources of his ideas for his buildings. I find it inconceivable that, deep down, Utzon actually wishes everyone should remain ignorant about his ideas and intentions. Yet his actions suggest otherwise.

We must know how a person lived if we are to properly interpret and understand their work, not as some critics would give it, cut off from the living context. We should be familiar with the circumstances of a life to be in a position to connect the work with the life experiences and what they discovered, in order to see the work in a more meaningful context. Utzon appears to want to control what we know, so we only learn sections of the complete story. My intention, when setting out, was to locate all the pieces of the jigsaw, and to reconstruct a more complete picture of his life.

Any genuinely meaningful criticism must be informed by facts, not by myths, hearsay, or make believe. Without a foundation of truth, it cannot have any weight or authority.

Jørn Utzon is an enigma. His refusal to talk to us, his penchant for hiding, only makes him more tantalising. On first encounter, he seems so tremendously charming – everyone remembers him that way. The beautiful engaging smile, the warm interest he displays in others, his ability to make even the most unremarkable things seem extraordinary, set him apart as a special person. The charm, however, can be a blind.

There are many parts to him: he is an actor and an accomplished mimic who loves to take off other people and poke fun at their foibles. And despite his intelligence and acute sensitivity, he made some terrible blunders which all but ruined his career.

He continues to be a very private person. There are reasons – some understandable, some that elude explanation – which will emerge later. His intense, lifelong quest for anonymity, a life removed from the limelight, can only be seen as eminently sane, if exceptional, given the crazy world we live in. It runs counter to the trend for over-exposure and public self-confession. At first encounter, it strikes us as old fashioned. But Utzon is extremely shy at heart. To borrow Peter Høeg's description of the character Adonis, Utzon is best summed up as 'the quintessential Dane, the fear, the iron resolve to repress what's happening around him'. 'Untameable optimism' is a particularly apt epithet applied to Utzon.

The need to properly evaluate the Sydney Opera House calamity has become more urgent with the passing of time. It grew out of the politics of the era but it was equally a tragedy of character. Many of the people who were involved are now in their late seventies and early eighties; Utzon himself celebrated his eightieth birthday on 9 April 1998. The three architects who replaced Jørn Utzon after 1966 – Peter Hall, Lionel Todd and David Littlemore – are all dead. To have delayed writing this book any longer would have risked losing the valuable memories and opinions of those people who shared in the events of Utzon's life. As such people die we lose the chance of discovering many of the critical details of Utzon's life and work. This would represent a huge loss as we would also miss the chance to discover what really happened during the Sydney Opera House crisis.

This is only a fraction of the entire story. Utzon is a key player in a fundamental change that led to a broadened agenda for Modern architecture after the 1950s. At the time of its inception, the Sydney Opera House challenged many cherished and fundamental tenets of Modern architecture. By tracing Utzon's progress we gain new insights into how, aided by his close identification with Scandinavian traditions and Alvar Aalto, Utzon humanised and opened up Modernism to include ideas about organic form, without abandoning its commitment to standardisation or the industrialisation of the building process.

In hindsight, we can see that the mantle of failure foisted on Jørn Utzon, which pursued him long after Sydney and bedevilled his career, was a considerable tragedy for Utzon and a loss for Denmark as well. Danish architecture and design peaked in the mid-1950s, then flat-lined from lack of a fresh impetus in the 1980s and '90s. If Jørn Utzon had returned from Australia an architectural hero, he would undoubtedly have been offered important public projects in Denmark. Not only would this have been marvellous for Utzon, it would have given Danish architecture a new start, and possibly have changed its course. The Danes regrettably turned out to be as timid and parsimonious as their Australian counterparts.

There is a fairytale and fantastic thread running through Utzon's life. It is present in his buildings and his dreamlike personality. The fact that it persists demonstrates that there is something basic underlying it; whatever that may be, something within Utzon, drawn from the character of Denmark itself, exercises a universal appeal.

Who is the real Utzon? Is it the person we encounter in a multitude of public interviews in the press and recorded on film? How does this public persona square with the private persona we are seldom permitted to glimpse? Like another Scandinavian recluse, the Swedish-born Hollywood actress Greta Garbo, Utzon has guarded his privacy.

The mystery of Utzon provokes us. There are so many secrets that we return to again and again, in the hope of finding even the smallest clue. With the passing years, his blunt refusal to be more open, his hiding away, has added to rather than diminished the intrigue.

The Sydney Opera House presents a similar riddle. It remains indifferent to our questions and prying fingers with the result that we keep returning to it, in the hope that we will accidentally stumble on its core and it will all mysteriously fall into place. We are still enthralled by it, just as the judging panel in January 1957 was the instant they laid eyes on Utzon's elegant competition sketches.

In the 1990s, the world is in an unseemly hurry to make up for its earlier neglect of Utzon. It has showered him with honours, such as the Wolf Prize in 1992 from Israel. On 17 April 1998, Utzon received the Sonning Prize and prize money of 500,000 kroner from the Rector of Copenhagen University, Kjeld Møllgård, before an august assembly which included the Danish Minister for Culture, Elsebeth Gerner Nielsen. Utzon was embarrassed by so much attention. The last time a Dane had received the prize was in 1961 when it was given to Niels Bohr. The previous recipients included such names as Bertrand Russell, Alvar Aalto, Laurence Olivier, Karl Popper, Ingmar Bergman and Vaclav Havel. From the lectern, Utzon spoke in a low voice about the power behind the Australian people's wish for the Opera House in Sydney and his team's joy in doing the work. Regrettably, the prize coincided with Utzon's announcement that he no longer builds anymore. A week earlier, Utzon had accepted the keys of the City of Sydney.

On 11 August 1999, Utzon agreed to prepare design guidelines for future work on the Opera House after the appointment of Mr Richard Johnson (a principal of Denton Corker Marshall), to work on the brief for a second proposed A$66.5 million upgrade. The nomination to UNESCO in Paris (prepared in 1996) for listing on the World Heritage Register still had not been forwarded. It was anticipated Utzon, with son Jan, would submit the design guidelines by June 2000.

Utzon's agreement is an extremely positive development which brings to a close his 33 year estrangement from the House and places him at the centre of future plans. Worries arise about the outcome because Utzon is 82, has never visited and seen the House, much less experienced the deficient acoustics of the Concert Hall.

Henrik Ibsen explained that in *The Lady from the Sea* in 1888 he was exploring the mysterious tidal pull the sea exerts on a certain kind of person. Although it is an extremely Norwegian play it says universal things. It tells us something important about Utzon, who has never been cut off from the sea, either physically or mentally, for any length of time. Like the Ibsen character, he feels lost away from it. By accident, Ibsen wrote his play at Sæby on the east coast of Jutland, not far from Ålborg where Utzon grew up 'by the soft quiet Danish sea'. 'Soft' and 'quiet' also describe Utzon.

The sea is intertwined in Utzon's architecture, in his thought, in so many aspects of his life and activities. He is only truly happy when he is near water. It is his most profound connection with nature, and one of the strongest clues we have about him. The sea possessed him, just as it possessed the Lady from the Sea.

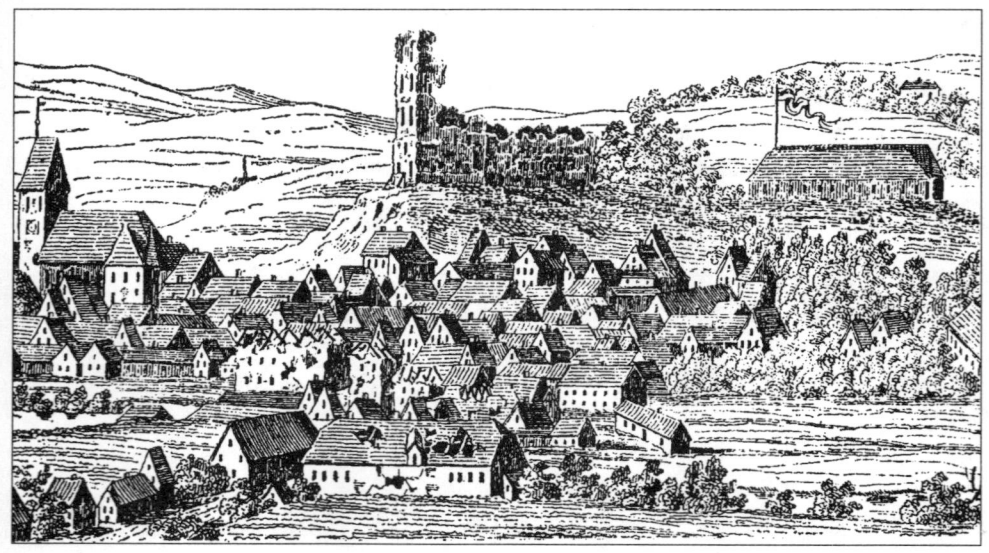

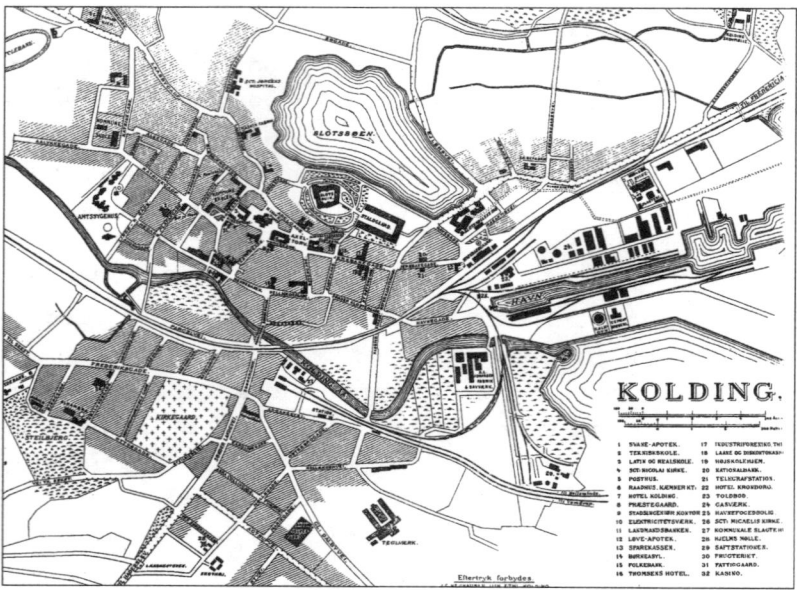

Above: Kolding after bombardment on 23 April 1849. Utzon dyeworks (middle left) was destroyed.
Below: Nineteenth century Kolding: ruined castle and lake (centre top); Utzon dyeworks (lower centre) on Søndergade, not shown, stood beside Kolding AA (river).
From *Det Gamle og Nyere Kolding*, p. 444, 490.

1

A Country Youth
Jutland, to 1936

Names are more than mere tags that identify us as individuals. They have the power to shape a person's self-image, to set up expectations. In time, names acquire a special magic, running through people's lives like ripples in water. They can mean nothing, or they can signify a great deal. In the case of Jørn Utzon, his name almost defines him. His name is very nearly the story, from which arises its magic – for it contains some undisclosed mystery.

'Ud' was a rather common first name in Denmark in former times.[1] Utzon originally meant 'son of Ude', and was formed the way so many other Scandinavian surnames are, following the practice of giving the father's first name to the son. Its meaning is more elusive. 'Ud' is equivalent to 'out' or 'exit'. In Denmark the 'Udgang' signs placed next to the highway and in public buildings indicate 'way out' or 'exit'. It may be merely a coincidence that Utzon is an outsider, that a certain amount of 'ud' or 'out' is present in Jørn Utzon. This is evident from his desire to live away from others in comparative isolation on the edge of the city. 'Ud' may have been the name applied to someone who did not fit in or belong, but this seems unlikely.

Jørn Utzon is descended from Ude Pedersen of Kolding (1578–1641).[2] Ude Pedersen belonged to the superior class of merchants and was a leading citizen and an adviser or councillor in Kolding. He had four children and began the use of Udsen as a family name when he called his eldest son Peder Udsen (1616–59), or Peder son of Ude. Peder Udsen is represented with his wife and their children in a large painting in Kolding church.[3] Morten Udsen, Peder Udsen's eldest son, took over the family business on his father's death, and conducted a considerable trade from which he amassed a small fortune and so obtained a prominent position in Kolding. Peder's youngest son, Ude Pedersen (d. 1707), studied theology and became the parish priest for Gosmer and Halling, and his son, Lauritz Udsen (1679–1735) – from whom Utzon's family is descended – followed his father and filled a similar ecclesiastical benefice as a curate.

The youngest of Lauritz Udsen's three children, Peder Udsen (1727–92), proved to be the most interesting and of all the Utzon ancestors more is recorded about him. His past was shrouded in 'secretive darkness', and such was his reputation that even while he lived many questions arose about him. Was he an embezzler? Did he speculate wildly in the hope of quick money to repay his debts, only to flounder? He was head clerk at Estrup and Skodborghus properties and on 8 April 1761 purchased the position of regimental quartermaster in the Ist Fynen Cavalry Regiment from Rasmus Brun for 2000 Rdl.[4] Peder Udsen travelled extensively in southern Jutland in his role as regimental quartermaster for the Fynen Dragoon Regiment, a post which, if it failed to cover its incumbent in glory, multiplied his debts. Throughout an intermittent career his fortunes fluctuated and he suffered a series of financial failures: at one moment he was rich and successful, in the next, he was plunged into debt and financial ruin. After resigning from the Schleswigean Regimental Cavalry on 25 June 1774, he occupied Beckmarch manor on the west coast of northern Jutland at the end of 1774, then sold it twelve years later. He spent his final declining years, after the death of his wife, living with his son-in-law. One senses a tremendous effort in Peder Udsen's life, to raise himself and supply his family with the material trappings of a solid middle-class existence which actuated his desperate grasping of every opportunity.

Quartermaster Peder Udsen was a plump, though handsome man with a strong round face. A picture of Udsen shows tidy hair brushed back across his skull and unsmiling piercing eyes. His wife, Ane Birgitte Udsen (1740–85, née Høstmarch), looks determined. She has long plaits and wears a dress with a low, lace-trimmed bodice. Her face is framed by a tiara of flowers. She must have endured a great deal in the course of her husband's fluctuating fortunes. When she was 45, her health failed and she died suddenly.

It was during the period from 1760 to 1780 that the name changed from *Udsen* to *Utzen* and *Utzon*.[5] In legal documents dated May 1775 and August 1792, Peder Udsen adopted the style Utzen. The first official use of Utzon occurs in December 1806 in a document executed by Peder Udsen's son, Michael Lausen Utzon, drawn up to effect the transfer of a dye works in Kolding from its owner, Jens Jacobsen.[6] Thereafter, Utzon becomes the customary spelling. At the beginning of the nineteenth century, the Utzon family was connected with the traditional trade of farver, or colour dyer, in south-eastern Jutland. The dyeworks which the family owned at Søndergade was burnt to the ground during a bombardment of Kolding on 23 April 1849 during the First Schleswig War of 1848–50. The destruction of the dyeworks reversed the family fortunes and Jørn Utzon's great-grandfather, Nicolaj Peder Utzon (1805–80) moved to the ancient medieval town of Ribe on the west coast of Jutland. Ribe projects out of the low, flat expanses of marshland surrounding it much like a spike hammered through a plank. With its access to the North Sea, Ribe prospered through its valuable sea connections with England, Germany and Flanders. Nicolaj Utzon built a thriving business trading as a dyer of wool cloth and was prosperous enough to support an apprentice and three maids.

Nicolaj's second son, Hans Jørgen Utzon (1845–1922), and his wife Anette Marie Christine Oberg (1846–1912), who was from Sønderborg, moved to the distant village of Hellebæk at the opposite end of Denmark. Lying on the beautiful exposed north coast of Zealand, Hellebæk became a refuge for Hans Jørgen. He obtained work as a watchman, or *opsynmand*, at the Hellebæk

Fabrik after the birth of the second child Elisabeth Christine in 1877, and before Jørn Utzon's father, Aage Oberg Utzon, was born.[7] At the time the factory produced clothing.

The small village of Hellebæk overlooks Øre Sound (Øresund). The nineteenth-century poet Carsten Hauch was so impressed by the beauty of its setting he claimed:

> *Everything that is spread out in front of the wanderer's eye,*
> *Round about in our country, is gathered here,*
> *Grain rich valleys with green hills,*
> *Lakes with ocean and the loveliest trees;*[8]

Like many towns in the region, its name recognised the local brook, 'bæk', while 'helle', from *helge*, means sainted or sacred. The picturesque village was established in 1597 to accommodate workers employed at King Christian IV's hammermill which was built to produce weapons. It functioned first as a copper mill, then a gun factory, and later as a foundry until 1870, when it was converted to a clothing factory. The straight main street, Bøssemagergade, has gun maker's rowhouses lining it on both sides and resembles a large red-brick gun barrel pointed at the Sound.

When Hans Jørgen Utzon arrived in Hellebæk with his wife and their two children, the making of weapons in the factory had ceased and been replaced by the manufacture of clothes and carpets. He became a watchman or keeper and abandoned his trade as a farver. During the February 1890 national census, he acted as the count superintendent (*Tællingskommissærens*) for the Hellebæk district, which indicates that he must have been well enough educated to be entrusted with the task of recording names, family details, and keeping an accurate tally.[9]

Aage Oberg Utzon was born on 16 November 1885, at Hellebæk, the youngest of the three children born to Marie

Christine.[10] He was 12 years younger than his brother, Nicolaj Peder Utzon, who was born at Ribe, and later became a forester or *skovfagdeler*. The Utzon attachment to the local forest began with Nikolaj Utzon.

For centuries, Øresund (so named because it is shaped like an ear), has been a heavily trafficked sea route, plied by vessels of many flags seeking a fast direct route to the Baltic from the North Sea via the Kattegat. At any time, the waters off Hellebæk are crowded with ships heading for or out of the Baltic, or on their way to eastern Danish ports. During the summer months, this bustling sea traffic is joined by fleets of small yachts and local working watercraft. It is hardly possible to avoid the tremendous volume and variety of ships passing Hellebæk so it was not surprising that Aage, from his earliest years, developed a keen interest in ships and navigation. At the end of high school, Aage Utzon trained as a ships' engineer at nearby Helsingør. After this, he crossed to England for further study as a naval architect at Armstrong College, Newcastle.[11]

In Newcastle, Aage Utzon formed a number of friendships which he kept up throughout his life. English engineering and civilisation made a strong impression on him, and this admiration of things English was later passed on to Jørn.[12]

On his return to Denmark, Aage Utzon worked briefly at the large Burmeister & Wain shipyard at Copenhagen, but he evidently saw few opportunities for advancement there. On 24 May 1915, he married Estrid Marin Valeska Halina Olsen (1894–1951). She came from Ålsgårde near Hellebæk. Her family came originally from Riga, on the Baltic in what is today Latvia but was part of the Russian Empire until 1918, in recognition of which her middle name was Valeska.[13] Aage Utzon was nearly 30 when they married. His bride was 20. They make a handsome pair: he was tall with clean-cut features and strong cheek bones, clear intelligent eyes under bushy, upswept eyebrows, and a solid chin that suggests a determined nature. His forehead was high under a swept-back thatch of fine dark hair which had turned grey early, but even at 70, photographs reveal an athletic, strong man devoted to physical fitness. Estrid Utzon appears much softer than Aage. She was an attractive brunette with a disarmingly innocent smile whose image radiates warmth. It is impossible not to feel that Utzon owes his generous and, at least on the surface, hedonistic disposition to his mother.

A year after they married, Leif (1916–64) was born, followed two years later, on 9 April 1918, by Jørn Oberg Utzon. Six years separate Jørn from his younger brother, Erik, who was born in 1924 while they were living at Ålborg. All the children have the same middle name, Oberg, to honour their grandmother Anette Christine Oberg. Jørn, a modern contraction of Jørgen, is the Danish equivalent of George and recalled his grandfather, Hans Jørgen Utzon.[14]

Jørn Utzon inherited his mother's warmth, her relaxed charm which overlaid his extreme sensitivity, and generous disposition. To this was added the physical build and stamina of his father, and his father's determination and persistence. Physically, Utzon was quite similar to his father, yet in some attributes his endowments outstripped Aage's. He was taller and better-looking, though less energetic and athletic. He also inherited Aage's wit and fondness for jokes, and his tendency to satirise the foibles of others. As he grew to manhood, Jørn developed a similar love of yachts and sailing. Both father and son were also much more complex than they appeared at first glance.

Jørn Utzon gained an additional layer of complexity from his mother. She contributed the softer, creative side in him, and the tendency to be anxious, shy and reclusive. When confronted by an obstruction, instead of gritting his teeth and hurling himself at it, Utzon would more often than not seek to evade it. Utzon is essentially a shy person who is only completely at ease in the company of close friends and family.

In Ålborg Utzon's parents rented a flat in a large four-storey yellow-brick block on the corner of Vendelbog 8 and Strand Vejen, which is parallel to the waterfront of Limfjord Sound, west of the present road bridge that connects Ålborg with Nørresundby on the north shore. Walled in behind the L-shaped block was a small squalid courtyard where children could play in safety.

The flat was in Ålborg's industrial district, jammed between the old town and the main northern Frederikshavn railway line. The shipyard was on the opposite side of the city, at East Harbour (*Østre Havn*), five kilometres away. The Utzon neighbourhood was dominated by the Dansk Sprit factory, maker of Ålborg's famous aquavit, and the Obels Tobacco factory, whose unmistakable tobacco smell permeated the area as a constant reminder of industry.

Ålborg sits on the skewed shoulder of the Jutland Peninsula, below its head. It is an important regional city dating from 1340. In English its name translates as eel-castle, a reference to the local toll castle, Ålborg Manor (1555), which is the only lord lieutenant's manor left in Denmark. The city started as a trading centre serving other towns on Limfjorden and in the very early days, its wealth arose from its trade in herring. Until the nineteenth century, Ålborg was the second largest city in Denmark. It was twice burnt down in the sixteenth century, and consequently, with the exception of the toll castle which is of fine half-timbered construction built around a courtyard, little of the old city has survived. In addition to the toll castle, there is the richly decorated Jens Bangs Stenhus at Østergåde 9, built from 1623 to 1624. Bodofil Cathedral, from 1400, not far distant from Vendelbog, has a superbly austere white tower and sharply pointed spire, which was used as a navigation landmark by mariners out on Limfjorden.

Despite its attractive location, framed at the back by a high wooded hill, with Limfjorden supplying a water frontage and outlook, Ålborg had a reputation for being a grim industrial town. Sited at the narrowest point on the fjord, Ålborg huddles behind its waterfront. In winter, the front walls of factories and houses lining Limfjorden are slammed by salty blasts from the north. The fjord presents a hostile emptiness beneath a dense pewter sky.

At the shipyard Aage Utzon earned a reputation as an engineer skilled in responding to any situation which called for a novel approach or new shipbuilding technique — anything, in fact, which was a departure from standard technical routine. He delighted in trying out new ideas, especially where they involved theory. His fascination with theory affected his approach on many levels.

Shipbuilding in those years was a large and economically significant activity. Aage Utzon, therefore, was assured of a prominent social position in the town. The family, for instance, had a telephone at a time when this was unusual. Aage worked on yacht designs at night during the week, and sailed on the weekends. Life was satisfying.

Together with George Berg from Flensberg, Aage Utzon had designed his first boat in 1915. This was a modest dinghy later described as a *kragejolle*.[15] Shortly after this, Aage Utzon fell out with Berg because of a dispute over who originated the *spidsgattere* design. The *spidsgattere* type is a double-ended craft, pointed at both stern and bow, with a full heavy form, straight keel, and is derived from the traditional herring and plaice fishing craft of a century or more ago that worked the Danish inshore fisheries. It is similar to boats found at Skovshoved not far from Hornbæk, near Hellebæk where Aage Utzon grew up.[16] The hull shape is beautiful in its own right and resembles a fish that has been cut in half lengthwise above the vertebrae.

Berg was an experienced sailor who based his boat designs on his sailing experience, whereas much of what Aage Utzon did stemmed from theory, or an experimental idea he wished to test. Utzon considered that a boat should possess a full or plump foreship to give it an effective streamlined shape that would brush aside the waves as it moved ahead.[17] In applying the dictum, Aage Utzon succeeded in designing boats that slipped through the water smoothly and with seemingly effortless ease.

In 1918, working alone, Aage Utzon designed the *Shamrock* for the local Ålborg harbourmaster, Molbach. It was the first in an extensive line of *spidsgattere*, or double-ended boats. With its distinctive pointed stern, it eventually became synonymous with the Utzon name and helped to established his reputation worldwide as a yacht designer. By the 1950s, Aage Utzon's fame as a yacht designer had spread as far afield as England and the West Coast of the USA. A party of Japanese once presented themselves at Jørn Utzon's Hellebæk office and asked for an interview with Mr Utzon. They were told that Mr Utzon was in Sydney. They did not appear to understand and repeated their request, this time with greater insistence. This brought the same negative reply. Finally, the exasperated Japanese spokesperson explained that it was the famous yacht designer Aage Utzon, not his son, they wished to see. Even at the height of interest in the Sydney Opera House, Aage Utzon was more famous in some circles than his son.

The *Shamrock* was a large 5-tonne displacement *spidsgattere* and carried 60 square metres of sail. Utzon and Molbach successfully sailed it in the local Jutland regattas and up the west Swedish coast.[18] The routine of shipyard work during the day and designing yachts at night established a pattern that persisted throughout Aage Utzon's working life.

All these years, Aage Utzon was a dedicated sportsman who encouraged his teenage sons to come along with him on hunting expeditions to the wilds of North Jutland. Aage enjoyed making things with his hands. He also had a destructive side to him inasmuch as he was what might be termed *homo ludens*, or a playful man, someone who engaged in irresponsible pranks. In addition to the swimming and running, he was a clay pigeon shooter.

Aage was a skilled model maker who took special pleasure in making exact and beautiful timber half-models of his yachts.[19] These would later influence Jørn Utzon's development of the hall shapes of the Sydney Opera House. The auditorium shells resembled inverted boat hulls, so it was natural for Utzon to make half-models for the Opera House halls using the same technique. During his 47 years as a yacht designer, from *Shamrock* to his last boat, *Nautica*, in 1965, Aage Utzon developed more than 25 yachts. He was idealistic as well as practical – and actuated by a genuine concern to help others. In the early 1940s, for example, in response to letters from sailing enthusiasts in Denmark and Sweden, Aage sent out free of charge hundreds of sets of drawings of his Ålborg dinghy. He did this to promote the sport of sailing and encourage a healthy outdoors way of life.[20]

The improvement of a yacht type occurs in a series of steps. Any improvement occurs as a separate small adjustment and can be tested and assessed in terms of sailing performance. It has much to teach other designers. It is the ability to relate sailing experience to theory, through a combination of standardisation and practical experiment based on established sets of rules, that is so valuable to a yacht designer.

Aage impressed on Jørn Utzon the need to set aside an early solution if a new or better one presented itself. In yacht design, because of continuous competition, old designs are continually being modified. In designing the Sydney Opera House, the practice which caused the most friction with his consultants, notably Ove Arup & Partners, was Utzon's willingness to set aside a previously agreed solution and to replace it with a superior one. The search for perfection, which Jørn Utzon repeatedly stated as his goal, is no different in principle from his father's yacht designs. Utzon seldom wavered from his conviction that perfection is found in the next solution.[21] When Utzon refers to perfection in architecture, this is what he means.

It is rare for such a reiterative approach leading to the improvement and refinement of a standard to be applied to architecture. Yet it has the potential to yield striking and impressive results. It must be recognised that it is only suitable for certain types of repeatable buildings. Having been exposed to yacht design from an early age, it was inevitable that Utzon should absorb some of its lessons and come to see the advantage of standardisation and incremental improvements. A similar approach can be seen at work in Jørn Utzon's evolution of the courtyard house type. The courtyard house is an equivalent for Jørn Utzon to his father's work on the *spidsgattere* boat. Once you have a basic type, you are in a position to introduce small improvements without disturbing the basic pattern.

Utzon was exposed by Aage to a design regimen that was neither abstract nor distant from experience, and which combined work with theory and tested the outcome. First and foremost, it involved a deliberate series of steps starting with a theory or a type, which was subsequently built and trial sailed. Designing a yacht involved analysing its performance, then finding solutions in order to make further improvements. Each new model was sailed to see how it measured up against the previous model. The goal was perfection. At some point the designer would recognise whether a new boat could be improved any further. If instead of winning races it lost, it was clearly a failure. Irrespective of how appealing a theory might be, the result showed it either worked or did not work.

Reflecting on his father's work as a yacht designer, the feature that impressed Jørn Utzon most and stayed with him long afterwards was his father's aim to make everything on a boat to the right dimensions and with the right material. Each part was not to be too thick or too thin, whether it was a fender on the deck, a mast, or was made of metal or other material. It all had to be just right. Utzon felt the same way about architecture, which he considered should be just as exacting and perfect in its standards as a finely crafted boat. Because everything is right in a boat, there is a distinctly comfortable, reassuring feeling about it. Everything is in the right place and has been correctly made. The years of watching his father's work in the shipyards at Ålborg and Helsingør instructed Utzon in the logic of making things and increased his feeling for the beauty evident in practical objects.

Leif and Jørn were sent to a private school, Klostermarksskolen elementary school at Dronning Christines Vej 6. It was in a quiet, middle-class suburb surrounded by trees and gardens. The building is a pleasant, if plain, two-storeyed block in red brick on the east side of the main north–south railway line, looking across the tracks which divide Ålborg in two. It is bare, with what decoration there is confined to a single arched gable above the entrance porch.

Klostermarksskolen may have been a short distance from the Utzon flat at Vendelbog 8, but the social divide was considerable. To reach the school in the posh suburbs of the east side from the working-class industrial neighbourhood where they lived, the Utzon boys passed under the elevated railway viaduct that marked the social boundary.

Jørn Utzon spent five years at Klostermarksskolen. His interest in nature made itself apparent even at this early stage. This is evident from the series of small gifts he and his brother gave to the school. In 1925 he presented the school with a stuffed bird, the following year it was a mineral specimen, and in 1927 a buffalo horn and a shark's jaw – presumably it was not from a very large shark.[22] These objects reflected Jørn and Leif's interest in hunting and biology. The bird and animals were probably trophies from Aage's hunting trips in the wilds of northern Jutland beyond Nørresundby.

In a photograph taken shortly after the end of the Second World War, Jørn Utzon and his two brothers pose beside their father in a field near Hellebæk. They look aristocratic in their formal hunting attire and with their upright and commanding bearing. Jørn is the tallest. Aage, his arms crossed, wears a heavy coat and a buttoned shirt with tie, beret and jodhpurs. They hold broken double-barrel shotguns which they cradle under their arms. It is a very manly group, very English, with Aage's dog adding the final touch.

Class photographs taken of Utzon at Klostermarksskolen reveal a radically different person to the adult Utzon. In his 1925, 1b class photo, Utzon stands behind a girl, in the middle row, third from the end. His face is round and well formed, with a firm chin line, full lips held in a pout, and the eyes somewhat deeply set and shadowed. He has a neat but abundant thatch of dark hair brushed forward to the front to cover his high hairline. He peers intently at the camera. There is a certain grim unhappiness in his expression. These were difficult economic times. The other boys have similar, unhappy and bewildered expressions. Utzon's class supervisor, Miss Muller, her dark hair pulled back behind in a tight bun, cuts a large, matronly but not unsympathetic figure.

Danish was not spoken uniformly throughout the country. In the various regions people spoke their own dialect, which was not readily understood in Copenhagen. Utzon's parents grew up on the north coast of Zealand, west of Helsingør, and spoke that local dialect. In Ålborg Jysk, the Jutland dialect, was spoken. Utzon's speech would have stood out from the local children at school and made him the target of bullying in the early years. As an adult Utzon speaks a standard, neutral Danish similar to that on the radio, which is more widely understood and is relatively free of traces of the Jutland dialect.

In the later 1929, 5b class photo, Utzon had matured considerably and is easily recognised. He has on a wool cardigan and a tie and appears more relaxed now. The corners of his mouth are curled up in the beginning of a smile. His smile, like his mother's, is warm and generous. His face has lengthened since 1925 and the structure of his adult face is now well established. The dark hair is brushed forwards as before and hides his forehead; sideburns round out the oval outline and his facial features seem flatter in the overcast daylight. Even at 11, he is handsome. He also appears to be more self-assured and confident than before, and more ready for life. Jørn Utzon the adult has begun to emerge.

When Jørn was eight years old, and soon after the birth of the third son, Erik, the family moved into a detached cottage in a new suburb on the south-eastern outskirts of Ålborg, at Vejgård. It was outside the Ålborg municipality in an area formerly occupied by market gardens. The neat two-storey brick and tile-roofed cottage at Nørre Tranders Vej 65 is by today's standards small and cramped, but compared to their city flat at Vendelbog it was a palace and even had its own garden. Nørre Tranders Vej wound through open farmland from Limfjord to the ancient village of Nr Tranders, made famous by its church.

The houses along Nørre Tranders Vej were all new and the development imitated the English ideal garden suburb, each house set in its own garden. The newly prosperous middle class now had the opportunity to escape from their overcrowded city apartment blocks, standing cheek by jowl with industry, to the relatively salubrious conditions of country living. That, in combination with the birth of their third son, probably precipitated the Utzon parents' move. There was a further advantage – the cottage was quite close to the shipyard, allowing Aage to cycle to work.

The Utzon house at number 65 is a narrow, neat, brown-brick cottage with a shallow bay-front containing two large windows. Above it, a prominent, steeply raked red-tiled roof shelters the bedrooms on the second floor. A single dormer breaks through on the south. The roof is finished by a pinched hip that lends it an oddly Tyrolean appearance. At the rear, a low single-storey wing is attached to the main body of the cottage as a tail. This provided extra space which the family must have been grateful for since the new baby had to be accommodated as well as the two older boys.

Years later, Jørn Utzon recalled that his father grew vegetables in the front nursery garden and their neighbours all had their gardens with sheds.[23] It was a hard-working community in which people kept rabbits or poultry, while others built boats in their spare time.

At the end of his elementary schooling, Jørn was enrolled, as was his brother Leif, in the mathematics–natural science stream at high school. In 1927, a new municipal high school on nearby Christen Kolds Vej had opened, but Aage sent his two oldest boys to a private high school on the opposite side of the city instead. Whereas Leif excelled at school, Jørn was a very ordinary student. It soon became obvious that Jørn was weak in mathematics, which was essential if he was to become an engineer. At school his work was also affected by dyslexia.[24] These were minor problems and did not hold him back at school, and there is no evidence that he felt disadvantaged. Like so many children at this age he was totally absorbed in his own world, playing boys' games and discovering under his father's watchful eye a part of the wild unspoiled nature north of Ålborg.

The private high school to which Jørn Utzon was sent on Sankt Jørgens Gade operated both as a middle school covering the four intermediate years and as a gymnasium. In Denmark, the middle school or Mellemskoleklasse was succeeded by three years of gymnasium classes (Gymnasiekklasse) leading to the General Certificate of Secondary Education exam (GCSE), making a total of seven years of secondary schooling. Although the cathedral school on Sankt Jørgens Gade was founded in 1540, the present building is more recent and dates from 1889. It is a grand classical edifice of strictly symmetrical design. Like other school buildings in Denmark, it recalls a sturdy brick warehouse more than it does a school, and its austere ordinariness bears down upon rather than raises up the human spirit.

Inside it is symmetrical, being divided by a monumental entry hall that leads directly from the street to a wide imposing central staircase; before it is reached, two hallways branch off on either side. The main staircase is embellished with a selection of large plaster of Paris casts, ranging from the Apollo Belvedere, Diana from Versailles and Venus from Arles – on the half-landing and wherever a ledge presents itself. The Ålborg Katedralskole is crammed with copies of copies, classical sculpture that lacks both the quality and authenticity of the originals. These plaster classical gods and goddesses writhe in the chilly light of the large central window. The atmosphere is imbued with nostalgia that is unconnected to Ålborg; instead of the life around them, the students are presented with second-hand versions of ancient Greece, which radiate none of the spiritual warmth they require to grow intellectually. What the school had seized upon was a classical ideal, too remote, too disengaged to bear on the present century.

However, the school exposed Utzon to, and created an awareness in him of, classical sculpture. It seems inevitable that, years later, Utzon would approach architecture as a province of sculpture. Monumentality rests with the temple, they are close companions with the gods. This was spelled out to Utzon in these high-school corridors, by the plaster simulacrums of deity which excluded the Ålborg outside its walls.

Utzon did poorly in his final, fourth year at middle school. To improve his academic average he repeated the year before commencing gymnasium. At the second attempt his 1933 results showed a modest improvement, but not enough to make any real difference. Jørn Utzon completed his final year at Ålborg Katedralskole in mid-1937 and sat for his *eksaminer* in July 1937, passing with an aggregate average score of 6.16. This placed him fifth from the bottom of his class of 17 in the mathematics–natural science (*Matematisk–Naturvidensk Retning*) stream.[25] The result was slightly worse than for previous years. Utzon suffered his first real setback because his poor academic showing now prevented him from entering naval officer school.[26]

Prior to this, the possibility of becoming an architect had not entered Utzon's head. Jørn Utzon was a capable sailor and loved everything about sailing and the sea, so the navy seemed the obvious choice for him. The high school result therefore came as a serious disappointment. In his senior years at high school he often visited his father at the Østre Havn shipyard to examine Aage's latest yacht designs. His father encouraged him by enlisting Jørn's aid in drawing the final plans for new types, and Jørn also worked on the models. Another possibility therefore was for Utzon to study naval architecture instead. Unfortunately his poor GCSE result, particularly in maths, ruled this out as well as his results were insufficient to get him into a polytechnic high school to begin initial training in naval architecture.

By temperament, Jørn Utzon was happy and easygoing, and he was unaccustomed to dealing with setbacks. This was his first serious reversal and his response – of pushing the problem to one side, assuming that everything would take care of itself in time – contained portents for the future. Being an inveterate optimist, he did not question how this would happen, he simply assumed that it would. Instead of actively fighting to reverse the outcome, which in any case was impossible, he sensibly accepted the situation and looked around for alternatives.

The Utzon household was a conventional middle-class one. All this was changed in 1930, when Jørn was 12, as a result of visiting the great 'Stockholmsutstalingen', the Swedish Exhibition at Stockholm. Until then the cottage on Nørre Tranders Vej had been furnished with heavy Victorian furniture. Inside the house was dark and depressing, and there was a notable absence of art on the walls. This environment, together with the decision that Jørn should pursue the mathematics–natural science stream in his middle-school and gymnasium classes, accorded with his father's scientific outlook at this time, into which art hardly entered. The nearest approach to anything artistic in Jørn's life was assisting his father with his yacht drawings. These were technical drawings which were notable for their precision and their clear accurate linework, which predisposed Utzon's own, later architectural style of drawing. The goal was accuracy rather than artistic expression.

In the summer of 1930, Aage Utzon took his family to see the great Stockholm Exhibition. It was a remarkable adventure travelling first to Copenhagen, then across Sweden north to Stockholm. The exhibition had an enormous impact all across Scandinavia, where it was regarded as an official endorsement of the new social democratic culture.[27] The intention of the exhibition was to radically modernise the Swedish economy by replacing older, craft methods of production with modern industrial practices. It was little short of revolutionary, but it did not solely seek acceptance for the new mass-produced articles that had begun to appear. Even more importantly, the exhibition sought to affirm the advent of the new culture of industrialism. It set out to renovate the entire Swedish culture – how everyone lived, worked and spent their leisure hours. This entailed a great deal more than merely substituting craft with industrial methods; this by itself would count for very little if the values and outlook of general society were unaffected.

The Swedish government was endeavouring to foster a domestic market for the new industrial products, in order to underpin its export drive. To achieve this it required a base of local consumers to buy the new goods and to succeed the government needed to re-educate public taste; this was the task set the exhibition.

Aage Utzon was the exhibition's best customer. He was enthralled by almost everything – the new domestic interiors, the new furniture … As a naval engineer, he was accustomed to thinking in terms of function and industrial standardisation; however, the sober way in which the new functionalism was presented – with its clean, well-engineered forms – lifted function onto a new, lyrically expressive plane he had not encountered before. The exhibition experience transformed his outlook on life and design – and the life of his family. Aage Utzon became a convert to the new functionalism and modern design.

The exhibition was comprehensive in its breadth and convincing in its detail. It presented model flats and houses furnished with the most advanced fittings and furniture. There was a fully furnished two-storey apartment and other model interiors to illustrate the advantages of sensibly planned cubic storage units and open modular shelving. There was even lightweight furniture, including practical chairs and lounges which housewives could lift and shift about easily. Marcel Breuer's chrome steel and leather chairs, designed only four years before, were on display alongside elegant dining settings and new lamps. There were sun terraces where the health conscious could sunbake on reclining settees. The bedrooms were equipped with functional desks with writing shelves that pulled out, and the kitchens had the most modern appliances. The living rooms, in contrast to the Utzon house at Ålborg, were large and uncluttered, with plenty of daylight admitted through large, south-facing windows.

Impressive as it was, the most inspiring feature of the exhibition was the architecture. It integrated the other aspects of the exhibits as well as being novel. In a totally convincing way it suggested that the new industrial utopia, far from being a pipedream, was really just around the corner. Many years later Jørn Utzon recalled:

> *My parents returned home completely carried away by the new ideas and thoughts. They soon commenced redoing our home [at Vejgård, outside Ålborg]. The concept was space and light. All of the heavy, unpractical furniture was moved out and simple things were brought in. We developed new eating habits: healthy, green and lean. We began to exercise, get fresh air, cultivate light and the direct, so-called natural way of doing things. We were made to sit upright on good, practical furniture. We children had a swimming pool we could visit each day and use our bodies like fish in water. We got bicycles so we could get out in the fresh air and see what nature had to offer. We learned to admire the working man. Decent, well-done work was emphasised. Conventions were dropped, it was a question of us as people. There were no longer rules and sets of manners. I believe at this time we learned to see, and this quite naturally was of great importance. The empty, dead museum-like feeling about architecture disappeared and it became a living reality.*[28]

Jørn Utzon may be overstating the exhibition's impact, but there is no doubt as to the comprehensive nature of the revolution in living habits it caused on their return to Ålborg. The old was quickly swept aside and replaced by the new, sensible way of doing things.

The Utzon family fostered an attitude of natural simplicity, an honest openness and directness and total absence of artificiality. This explains a great deal about Utzon's personality and outlook, his unaffectedness and straightforward, natural way of behaving. This change affected not only how the family lived, but shaped innumerable personal factors that conditioned Utzon's attitudes and behaviour, almost as much as it afterwards affected his architectural orientation. The preference for the qualities of simplicity and naturalness – indeed, Utzon's lifelong admiration of vernacular-building practices – were an extension of this shift in values occasioned by the Stockholm Exhibition.[29] Swedish restraint in its crafts was prompted by a certain Swedish poverty that underlies Scandinavian taste in general. The factors of austerity, together with a celebration of natural simplicity, prepared the way for the widespread acceptance of the new Functionalism.

The second event in his teens which profoundly affected Jørn Utzon was his discovery of art. In the mid-1930s he met two artists at Ålsgårde. Martha Olsen, his grandmother, maintained a large house on Nørdre Strandvej 226, west of Ålsgårde overlooking Øresund. Utzon and Leif spent the summer holidays there. The backyard and garden looked out across the Kattegat towards the Kullen cliffs of Sweden. Nearby was a pretty jetty with an elaborate glazed pavilion at its end, carved and painted in the Nordic style. Immediately behind the jetty lived the Danish artist Poul Schrøder (1894–1957). Staying with him one year was the Swedish painter Carl Kylberg (1878–1952).[30] This was the first time Utzon had met an artist and as a result of the contact he became aware of art's possibilities.[31] Poul Schrøder taught Jørn Utzon how to draw, not in the way Utzon's father drew, with precise lines, but using soft pencils and charcoal that freely expressed his response to the world around him.

Utzon renewed Schrøder's acquaintance some years after he moved to Copenhagen, in 1941. Kai Christensen, a fellow student at the Royal Danish Academy of Fine Arts who commenced his architectural studies in 1939, had recently married and lived at Østerport, next door to a friend of Poul Schrøder's. Poul Schrøder used to visit them for reading sessions and Utzon joined their reading group.[32]

When Utzon moved to Stockholm during the Second World War, he met Carl Kylberg for the second time. By then Kylberg's wife had established a fitness club, but Kylberg, now in his mid-sixties, was gripped by delusions of artistic grandeur. He felt unappreciated and neglected. No one recognised his true artistic genius. Utzon seems not to have noticed the symptoms of raging megalomania in his friend and only saw good things:

> *for me it was a great inspiration to speak with Carl Kylberg. He taught me about the introspection of nature that he knew so well. He constantly dealt with this theme in his work: longing and expectation. I repeat it again to myself, that Kylberg found a source of great wealth in his inner being, as can anyone who dares to open themselves up. There was a sense of timelessness in him like that of water and life.*[33]

The role his family played in his life is central to Utzon. With him, everything begins and ends in the family, which is much more than a protective nest sustaining him against a hostile world and a wall to shut out adversity's sting. It supplied a secure emotional anchorage – one that has proved crucial to his creativity. At school, his older brother Leif protected and smoothed out the wrinkles for Jørn. By isolating Jørn from life's difficulties early on, his parents may have deprived him of the resilience and toughness some less fortunate children acquire, that enables them to overcome obstacles and bounce back with fewer bruises. He approached life in the expectation that his desires and wishes would be met. As a second child, less was demanded of him than Leif, so he naturally took life easier and was less robust as a consequence.

Utzon is a hedonist who sees life as something to be enjoyed and savoured. His hedonism is a strength and a weakness: because he expects life to supply him with his needs he is devoid of any sense of struggle; but when life disappoints him, he is ill-equipped to get what he wants. This explains in part the role that charm plays: it is his chief means for beguiling others into co-operating so his needs are ultimately met. Some people who are used to adversity approach life as a continuous battle; Utzon approaches it the way a courtier might, coaxing and tickling it until it yields to his will. Charm can be a very formidable weapon and should never be underestimated, but it has definite limits in what it can achieve. Making up for this, Jørn Utzon has an enormous capacity to enjoy the simple pleasures of everyday life. This has sustained him under the most difficult and trying circumstances.

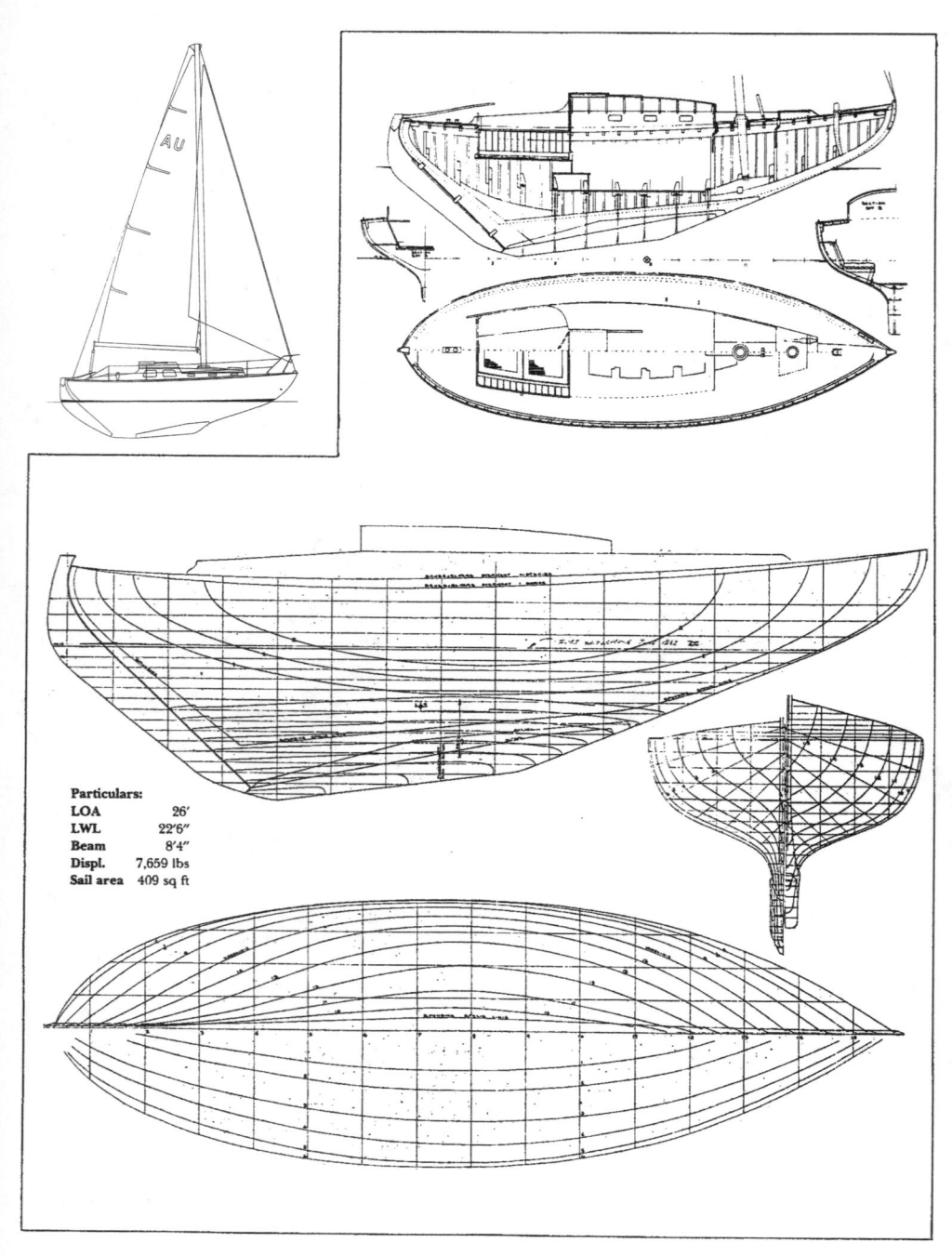

Particulars:
LOA 26'
LWL 22'6"
Beam 8'4"
Displ. 7,659 lbs
Sail area 409 sq ft

Aage Utzon *spittsgatter* design SKOAL, a Solrosen ('Sunflower'), built in Copenhagen by Kai Schwartz in 1939. Above left: 'Lene'.

2

Snow Sleeping

Copenhagen and Stockholm, 1937–1945

In 1936 everything changed. Mygind, the director of the Ålborg shipyard and Aage Utzon's superior, left to take up a new position at Göteborg, Sweden. Later the same year Aage received a telegram inviting him to take over as manager of the Helsingør shipyard.[1]

Jørn Utzon completed the final year of high school in June 1937. Two years earlier, Leif had begun his engineering studies in Copenhagen. With the two boys' schooling out of the way, the move was at once provident and well timed. As the new director, Aage Utzon was responsible for the entire shipbuilding operation, not just the engineering side, as had been the case at Ålborg.

At 18, Jørn Utzon was unsure about a career but Aksel Einar Utzon-Frank (1888–1955), the youngest son of Hans Jørgen's (Aage Utzon's father) sister, Ane Cathrine Utzon (1845–1922) stepped in with advice. Einar Utzon-Frank was a renowned and highly respected sculptor in Copenhagen, and a professor of sculpture at the Royal Danish Academy of Fine Arts.[2] His work can be found all over the city: at the Royal Theatre adorning the bridge above Tordenskjoldsgade; within the sombre triangle-shaped Police Headquarters block where he created a Mannerist serpent-killer statue in memory of policemen killed on duty; and, in Utzon's day, in the courtyard of the original elegant seventeenth-century Charlottenborg Palace off Kongens Nytorv, which housed the Royal Academy. Utzon-Frank recommended that Jørn should study architecture because, as he wisely pointed out, this was safer than the artist's vocation which was Utzon's first choice, but was, in Einar Utzon-Frank's experience and opinion, far too insecure financially.

Jørn Utzon accepted the advice. In late 1937 he enrolled in architecture at the Royal Academy school. In doing so, he may still have been following his original idea of becoming a naval officer by an indirect path, since acceptance by the Royal Academy was an alternative way to enter naval officer training school. Later, as Utzon became more engrossed in his architectural studies, he abandoned the earlier plan.

Tobias Faber, who enrolled at the Academy in 1935, ahead of Utzon, and who subsequently became a lifelong friend of Utzon's, has stated that Utzon really wanted to become an artist as a result of his meeting with the Swedish artist Carl Kylberg.[3] Utzon's mediocre GCSE Eksaminer result was less important at the Royal Academy architecture school, where his professors were more interested in his freehand drawing ability than his maths score.

Jørn Utzon joined a group of a hundred candidates who presented themselves to the Academy in September 1937, and competed for places in the intensive month-long examination for admission. Out of the 25 on the list of those who were admitted that year, Utzon's name was last.[4] At 19, he was also the youngest and least mature. Some of the students were around 30 years old, with the average age about 25. The first and second years of study were full time. In the summer break it was usual for students to work as tradesmen or labourers on building sites.

Jørn Utzon did not stand out in the early years. He only began to be noticed later, after he caught the eye of Kay Fisker, a professor at the Academy, and a renowned architect. Fisker invited Utzon to assist him on some of his competition projects. He also introduced Utzon to the famous Finnish architect, Alvar Aalto, who visited Copenhagen regularly to give lectures. Aalto was a notorious alcoholic who took advantage of these frequent visits to go on marathon drinking sprees.

In 1940, the leading professors at the Academy were Kay Fisker and Steen Eiler Rasmussen. Fisker was an inspired lecturer and enjoyed an international reputation as an architect, while Rasmussen, who was a mediocre architect, was more famed as a writer. Fisker's lectures were extremely popular. Utzon studied town planning as a specialised field with Steen Eiler Rasmussen for two years; this sharpened his appreciation of environmental design matters — in the decade after 1948, Utzon won five town-planning competitions in Sweden. Rasmussen was especially interested in English craft production, largely because of the many illustrations it contained of the perfection of standard types.

In 1959, Rasmussen published a delightful little book called *Experiencing Architecture*. In it, he discussed how people experience buildings: how a building is sculpture and art with the added complication of function; how buildings depend for their effect on the contrast of solids and cavities; the effects of daylight, colour, sound, texture, rhythm, scale and proportion on them. Utzon's views on architecture are, not surprisingly, similar to those of his teacher. Rasmussen's account is a means of understanding Utzon's emphasis on the spontaneous impact which buildings have on our senses.

Utzon kept to himself at first at the Academy. He had grown up in a large country town with the inviting name 'eel-castle', which, while it possessed a shipyard and other industries such as a distillery, could offer little in the way of culture. To his new city acquaintances he must have seemed a country bumpkin. Copenhagen was culturally sophisticated and Utzon must have felt ill-at-ease and lost. Student life revolved around the Academy canteen, which competed in importance with the formal studio classes. For the students, the exchange of ideas, winning an argument and learning to express an opinion, took place in bars and the Academy canteen more than in class. Much of a student's critical intellectual development occurred outside lectures. Utzon wasn't unfriendly, his reticence was more to do with his shyness and being overawed. A few years later, Jørn Utzon came out of his shell. But initially his circle was limited to a few friends such as Halldor Gunnløgsson, Poul Schouboe, who started the course in the same year, and Tobias Faber. A number of other friends he made in this period, namely Peer Abben, Kai Christensen and Mogens Irming, later collaborated with Utzon, and some even became lifelong friends.

Halldor Gunnløgsson especially fascinated Utzon. Gunnløgsson's mother was an actress from Iceland, recently divorced; she had money and was independent. Halldor inherited his mother's smouldering volatility and there was also something of the Viking *berserkr* in him, so quickly did his personality shift at times. When he drank to excess he appeared to go berserk. Halldor Gunnløgsson also possessed a quick intellectual brilliance and this drew Utzon to him. Both were outsiders and, whilst he appeared to be brashly confident, Gunnløgsson like Utzon had few close friends. With his bearish personality and quicksilver intellect Gunnløgsson soon dominated Utzon. The contrary happened with Tobias Faber, whom Utzon led and inspired and dominated. This is all the more surprising considering that Faber was two years older than he was.

Gunnløgsson was just a month older than Utzon, and the closeness in their birthdays no doubt provided a further bond. Both Poul Schouboe and Gunnløgsson's mothers were actresses and this added to their aura a cosmopolitan sophistication that Utzon, who came from the provinces, felt he lacked. As a mere engineer's son he seems to have been uncomfortable, and the contrast of his country gaucheness increased his awareness of his distance from the other middle-class students.

Faber recalled Utzon was like a peasant boy compared to the city intellectuals who surrounded him, and not all the enthusiasm he could muster could hide this fact. Utzon was aware that it showed and this further increased his unease. Utzon distrusted anyone who was his intellectual superior or was more knowledgeable professionally. The early encounter with sophistication may have affected him in other ways, for instance in his reticence to academic critics and ambivalence to intellectual analysis and theory. Outwardly he rejected the bookish approach, while secretly he was greatly influenced by the books he came in contact with.

Although Utzon has given many interviews to journalists, he has avoided talking about his work to properly informed architectural critics and historians (with the exception of the dead Swiss historian Sigfried Giedion, whose support, in any case, he desperately needed in 1966). He gives the appearance of being afraid – perhaps of betraying himself in some way – yet when he does manage to speak, it is with passion, conviction and tremendous sincerity.

Gunnløgsson's drinking interposed a considerable obstacle to Utzon's friendship with him. When he was drunk, his language and behaviour became sordid and objectionable. Utzon was susceptible to alcohol and became intoxicated after only a few beers. He was a social drinker who limited himself to a few glasses at most. Utzon admired Gunnløgsson's other qualities: along with his sharp intellect he had a rapier wit, and was ruthless in pursuing his goals. Utzon lacked Gunnløgsson's focus and intensity, his shyness continually got in the way. The contrast between the voraciously intellectual Gunnløgsson and the practical joker Utzon, who put a humorous spin on everything, could not have been more stark.

Utzon relied on his sensitivity, drawing on his emotional intelligence more than on his intellect for his discoveries. His thoughts came slowly and depended to a great extent on his acute observation of the things around him. Gunnløgsson relied on his intellect and reading. Ideas issued from him like explosive sparks. Utzon's ideas were deeper, more intuitive, instead of cerebral or bookish. Utzon is more easily overlooked compared with Gunnløgsson, because he possessed a more original and profound talent. His creative struggle was much harder. The qualities Utzon admired in Gunnløgsson, which he singled out and sought to emulate, were the very ones he lacked. If he aspired to Gunnløgsson's intellectual brilliance, it was beyond his reach. Over the years the Gunnløgsson friendship, which was a mixture of attraction and repulsion, would splutter, falter, revive, only to die finally.

Utzon was not an intellectual. He looked around him at nature and architecture, choosing examples that caught his eye which he could appropriate and use. At the same time, he removed the sharp edges, rounded what he touched so it is less harsh on the spirit, and gave it an organic wholeness. He is romantic in attaching so much importance to nature and nature's forms. The range of his selection is surprisingly limited, yet it is at once poetic in its search for natural rhythms and ruthlessly deterministic in what at first must appear a contradiction, for Utzon never abandoned his commitment to using repetitive industrial processes and types. His architectural determinism mirrors the ruthless species determinism in nature. To Utzon, the trunks, branches and canopy of a beech forest are things to be imaginatively applied to the precast columns, brackets and roof of a furniture showroom in Copenhagen; clouds riding the trade winds at Hawaii reappear in the sculptured ceiling of Bagsværd Church.

While they were students in Copenhagen, Leif and Jørn Utzon shared a large flat at Nyhavn which was owned by a rich uncle. Most architecture students lived near the Academy if they could, because it was a requirement to attend studio daily. The flat at Nyhavn was convenient and close. Utzon's parents, in the meantime, had moved into a house on Strandvej 42, at Helsingør.[5]

Each of Utzon's teachers left their mark. Kaare Klint, who started the furniture design school in 1924, and went on to train many of Denmark's leading furniture designers, was one such teacher.[6] He was the great-grandson of Peter Vilhelm Jensen Klint (1853–1930), the designer of the Grundvig Church in Copenhagen. Gunnar Biilman Petersen, a graphic artist and designer, was another of Utzon's teachers. He was the first professor of Graphic Arts at the Royal Academy and the designer of the Danish currency. Petersen was a marvellous draughtsman who made freehand birthday cards full of facetious allusions that were so convincing it was difficult to distinguish them from real bank notes.

For a short time, Jørn Utzon worked in Petersen's office[7]

where his devotion to precise drawing standards – acquired from Aage – was reinforced, and he gained some office experience of sorts. Petersen was as demanding of himself as he was of others, and possessed a splendidly dry sense of humour. He helped Utzon set his own exacting drafting standards based on what he taught him. Utzon hated the practice of crossing lines at corners and preferred the crisp precision and impersonality associated with Petersen's engraved bank notes. The bank note lines stopped where they intersected. Utzon's drafting is delicate and uniform, like a bank note.

Utzon developed a variety of drawing styles: formal drafted drawings in the crisp Petersen mode, soft artistic pencil sketches for preliminary ideas influenced by Poul Schrøder, and the accepted Academy freehand drawing style characterised by fine, wiggly lines that rippled like a seismograph pen registering small shocks of energy, giving a feeling of life to the drawing.

Lines register mood. The way they are drawn – if they are sharp or smudgy, delicate or thick, spontaneous and unpredictable or deliberate and controlled – reveal what is in the artist's mind. Jørn Utzon's drawings also express what are his intentions. The thick smudges of the 6B pencil were reserved for early first thoughts when his ideas are forming and are still tentative. They whirl around in grainy constellations, vague and unstructured and expressive. These preliminary sketches are explorations, they contain accidental suggestions, a small clue, start of a principle. Utzon delighted in picking up a salt shaker (the need to express himself could happen anywhere), and drawing with it on a restaurant tablecloth. At such moments, the salt would spill out in careless, magnificent, free-ranging tracks across the cloth. These salt-shaker sketches, executed for friends on tablecloths, resemble his soft pencil sketches translocated into a more fleeting medium.

There are many different ways to draw. Utzon perfected two: one spontaneous and exploratory, the other, delicate, machine-like and weightless in its precision. Each serving a different purpose. The first flowed down his shoulder to his fingertip and emerged as a dribble of salt, the second was delicate and light and considered, gave a fine exactitude to the forms that were under consideration and therefore in the process of development. The first is about spontaneity, like a hand groping in the dark seeking something, the second is like an engraved bank note or a naval architect's plans, which can be trusted because they are exact.

The first building by Utzon was erected on the sea-wall at Ålsgårde below his grandmother's house at Nørdre Strandvej 226 in 1940. He was its designer, supervised the work, and participated directly in its construction, aided by a carpenter who was employed by his family. It was done to satisfy an eight-month practical building requirement in building trades for his degree. Unlike his classmates, who worked as tradesmen or labourers on building sites and learnt about practical building the hard way, Utzon's grandmother paid a carpenter to do the building work and so Jørn avoided any hardship.[8]

Utzon worked alongside the carpenter and assisted him to build the modest little skillion-roofed cabin.[9] Utzon has claimed that the Ålsgårde cabin has no significance. While it is true that the cabin is small and not very architectural, it says much about Utzon's values and approach, which, even at the beginning stage, revealed themselves. Not only did Utzon plan and design it, he was directly involved in its realisation. This is the way he likes to do things: working with tradesmen; giving instructions and watching the progress; correcting and adjusting along the way. Utzon has always distrusted large organisations – he prefers to work closely with people. This enables Utzon immediately to catch anything that is not quite what he had in mind and correct it. Drawings are too remote; they have a role only after the architect knows what he wants.

The cabin was, in fact, a shed and consisted of a living room with a door at one end, and a 2.95 m long window divided into 24 small lights, on the north looking across the Kattegat towards the Swedish coast. The small 8.24 x 3.9 m wide shed has an exposed brick chimney on the seaward side and a simple kitchen adjoining the living room at the far end, opposite the entry. In front of the fireplace is an intimate area for sitting. The roof slanted back from the shore and made the shed appear to stare at the sea. It looks like a snug sailor's home clad in plain pine weatherboard on a stud-frame, with a tar paper roof. It may not be much, but it says a great deal about Utzon. Utzon made no attempt to inflate the shed or make it into something it is not. He avoids any architectural rhetoric. It has one note, and that note is its anonymity. Nothing has been embellished or added for effect; every part is useful. These days it forms an accepted feature of the shoreline. For that reason, if perhaps for no other, it should be considered a true indicator of Utzon's intentions as an architect – in his choice of the humble and honest instead of the grand, pretentious, or high-styled fake.

Germany's sudden invasion of Denmark took everyone by surprise. Even though events across Europe at the start of 1940 looked ominous, Danes continued to hope that they would be able to remain neutral as they had done in the First World War. This was impossible, for Denmark was a bridge to Norway and Germany needed Norway for strategic reasons. Without warning, early on the morning of Tuesday 9 April 1940, German troops crossed the frontier into Denmark, and the Luftwaffe circled low over the King's residence to signal that the occupation of Denmark had begun.

The Occupation was harsh, but less brutal than it was in many other countries. The German authorities considered that the Danes were more Aryan than they were themselves, and generally, at least in the early years of the Occupation, Danes were well treated. The Occupation eventually forced the Royal Academy architecture school to close down in mid-1943 but in 1942 classes were continued in Copenhagen and Århus; thus Utzon's class was split into two groups of 12. Half dispersed around Copenhagen, while the other half was sent to Århus, where they completed identical projects under a coordinated programme.[10]

Defiant Danes drove around Copenhagen with RAF

roundels painted on their car doors as a protest against the German claim that they were there to protect Denmark from a British attack. In the same vein, Jørn Utzon and some of his friends caught pigeons in Kongens Nytorv square and painted British roundels on their wings before releasing them. So in addition to the British bombing, the German Occupation troops were threatened by low-level attacks from Danish pigeons carrying Royal Air Force insignia emblazoned on their grey wings.

The Occupation united Danes against a common enemy, but it also caused divisions over the vexatious question of whether to resist or to co-operate with the occupying power. When the Royal Academy in Charlottenborg Palace was occupied by Nazi troops a member of the Academy staff, the architectural historian Vilhelm Wanscher, supported the Nazis. When it became known, students boycotted his lectures; he was forced to leave and eventually ended in Rome.

Under the Occupation, Denmark was quickly and efficiently converted into a farm and factory to provision Germany. There was a night curfew, and people could not venture out after 6 p.m. A shortage of domestic fuel meant that people huddled in their blacked-out rooms at night and shivered in the freezing cold. To pass the time during the evenings, they formed reading groups. But conditions were far worse elsewhere.

Despite the seriousness of the situation, Jørn Utzon was not deterred from his practical jokes. On one occasion a student friend of Utzon's, Knud Rohbrandt, returned from a visit to his mother carrying a large and much-prized sausage. Jørn and Halldor Gunnløgsson stole it, climbed the facade of the building where Rohbrandt was staying and left the sausage dangling high up on the gable. It took Rohbrandt the best part of a day to retrieve the sausage. In retaliation, Rohbrandt stole Gunnløgsson's heavy winter overcoat and left it draped over a sculpture high on the Charlottenborg mansion which housed the Academy.

In the early 1940s, Utzon and Gunnløgsson lived for a time in the Christiansborg district of Copenhagen. They spent most days at school. Like the other architecture students, they ate at the Royal Academy canteen, much as students do today. One day Madame Svensson, who managed the canteen and was small, fat and bossy, objected to their carryings-on. In retaliation, they decided to play a prank on her. They went out and bought cheap plates then returned to the canteen. In the middle of what appeared to be a furious argument, Jørn and Halldor began hurling the plates on the floor and leaping on them. It may have been harmless, but Madame Svensson concluded they were engaged in smashing canteen property. She rushed at the pair, her fist upraised and her face flushed with rage, and exclaimed, 'You have more words than any painter.' There was no insult more calculated to humiliate a budding architect than to be compared to an artist. The plate smashing stopped in an instant.

Such behaviour was prevalent amongst architectural students, who competed to see which one of them could come up with the most outrageous practical joke. Utzon won first prize one year. The best jokes were talked about years afterwards. This behaviour belonged to the period prior to the war, when architects made a point of distancing themselves from other professions by the way they dressed, by practical jokes and by displays of levity. In a number of ways architecture students set out to demonstrate they were not conformists, unlike the engineers who were always overly serious.

Jørn Utzon met Lis Fenger for the first time on 8 April 1940, when Tobias Faber invited Utzon to Lis's twenty-first birthday party. It was a pivotal moment for Denmark, as well as Lis and Jørn. The following morning, Denmark was occupied. Tuesday the 9th was Jørn Utzon's birthday.

For most people, life now assumed a grim earnestness. Jørn Utzon was determined not to let this uncalled-for accident interrupt his life. Possibly it was his gaiety and defiance that Lis found attractive. Utzon found ways to enjoy himself. People liked him for that.

Jørn was funny and amusing, irreverent and immature – traits that seemed to co-exist – but he was also full of life, if somewhat spoilt and over-indulged and used to getting his way. Possessed of a lively, effervescent nature, Lis Fenger found the moral gravity of her family stifling. People were attracted to her because she was spontaneous and natural. She captivated others simply by being herself. She was devoid of artificiality or pretence. Tobias Faber had been a friend of Lis Fenger's before she met Utzon and he continued to be a friend of both when they became a pair.

The Fenger family came from Hjørring, a small town in Jutland about an hour's train ride north of Ålborg. Lis was the second child, one of eight girls, in a large family of 11 children. Her mother was devoutly religious. The youngest child, a son, was intellectually impaired, and this caused her mother considerable distress because she blamed herself. Her father, Mogens Fenger (1889–1955), married Anne Malthea Schmiegelow (1891–), in 1916.[11] Lis's mother was the daughter of another medical man, Professor Ernst Schmiegelow. Mogens Fenger completed his medical degree in 1913 and was a visiting surgeon at the Kommune Hospital from 1924 to 1928, before transferring to Hjørring Hospital in 1929 as Head Surgeon. In 1939 he was placed in charge of diagnostics. Dr Fenger had a long, distinguished medical career and served the Danish medical profession widely.

Lis Fenger was born on 8 April 1919, a day earlier and one year later than Utzon. The closeness of their birthdays may have thrown them together and established a bond initially, but they soon found they shared other interests. Both Lis and Jørn had grown up and gone to school in northern Jutland and they now found themselves in Copenhagen, cut off from their friends. Lis was studying to be a commercial artist and was intensely interested in art, which further cemented their attachment.

After he completed his thesis at the Royal Academy, on 4 July 1942, Utzon abruptly left Denmark for Stockholm to join Halldor Gunnløgsson. A few days before this, he met Tobias Faber outside the massive brick Copenhagen Town Hall, to arrange for Faber to join him in Sweden. With Gunnløgsson's assistance, Utzon soon found a job in Sweden with the same firm that employed his friend. This, in turn, enabled him to work there legally. Finding a position in the office of Hakon Ahlberg was a stroke of good fortune. Ahlberg had recently finished writing an account of Utzon's hero, Gunnar Asplund, which was published as a book in 1943.[12] After this, Utzon spent almost three years with Poul Hedquist who continued the architectural practice started by Gunnar Asplund following Asplund's early death in 1940 at the age of 55.

Utzon and Faber both admired Gunnar Asplund. Utzon, like many of his generation, was wary of architectural history and considered the best way to design was to start from zero. This was consistent with modern architectural attitudes to the past, but in Asplund's case, his attempt to deny history was misplaced inasmuch as Asplund had been greatly influenced by a visit to Italy and Greece in 1913–14. Utzon did not see the contradiction. He was selective and took only ideas that interested him. Imitating Asplund, Utzon would reduce a project to its essence and seek to elevate the primacy of a leading idea. What is a library? What is a school? Utzon would ask himself, as he began a design.

Asplund had been dead for two years by the time Utzon arrived in Stockholm so he could not talk to Asplund, but had to be content with reading about his ideas and looking at his buildings instead, which he and Faber did at every opportunity. Utzon visited Asplund's grave with some friends to pay his respects, but although the night started solemnly it ended in ribald revelry. Faced with a problem, Utzon would ask, 'What would Asplund have done?' In the end he adopted Asplund's way of thinking but not Asplund's style.

Asplund and Sigurd Lewerentz had won the competition for the Woodland Cemetery at Sockenvägen with an informal romantic plan in 1915. Progress on the Forest Crematorium was slow and when disagreements arose, Asplund resigned. After each resignation, the client would recall Asplund and accept his terms. This particular tactic of Asplund impressed itself on Utzon, to the extent that he later repeated the story to his office staff at Hellebæk.

The crematorium chapel, Asplund's most famous work, is on the outskirts of Stockholm. A large cross stands alone on a low eminence surrounded by sombre pines, with the crematorium chapel off to one side. The main chapel was a variation on a squared Greek temple modelled in a very simple classical yet modern way. Just as Praxiteles in the fourth century BC showed the 'hinges' of the body in his sculptures, in architecture the ancient Greeks showed a special regard for the articulation points in their temples, which are also sculptures – of a special kind. Asplund set out to do something similar, to make a crematorium which was sacred, apart, yet marvellously alive and in harmony with its surroundings. It has a primitive dignity, an aliveness that recalls Greek sculpture.

At the front, there is a covered court with a bronze-and-glass door behind it which could be retracted into the ground to open the crematorium's interior to the forest beyond it. By retracting the wall, Asplund could incorporate the court in the interior and thereby enlarge it, but there was an added benefit. The dark became light and the interior, once closed, was laid open to the outside. Nature, which was held back, is brought forward. Asplund stretched the chapel further than the limits of its walls, to suggest the continuation of the spirit past the disintegration of the body. The spirit of the deceased is released into the pine forest. The external cross was another reminder, and a symbol of the resurrection. Asplund was able to symbolise the belief that death was not the end of everything, rather that it was a further stage in the journey of the soul.

In early sketches for the external glass walls surrounding the Sydney Opera House theatres, Utzon at first made them retract upwards under the shells, perhaps not exactly as Asplund did in his crematorium chapel, but with the same principle in mind. Reflecting on Asplund's crematorium, Utzon said, 'He [Asplund] takes such good care of the people burying their beloved. There is a feeling of relief and calmness.'[13]

While he was in Sweden Utzon heard the story of Ragnar Östberg, who had designed Stockholm's Town Hall, completed 20 years earlier. Östberg was still living at the time. In an interview with Professor Ashworth and Jack Zunz some time after this,[14] Utzon recalled that Ragnar Östberg had become so engrossed in the project that at the end of the work he had become a forgotten man. Repeating the story in April 1962, Utzon may have interpreted it in a very personal way and anticipated that a similar fate awaited himself if he allowed the Sydney Opera House to dominate his professional horizon to the exclusion of all else.

Utzon worked largely on schools whilst he was employed by Professor Poul Hedquist. He rarely spoke about his work to his friends, and, when he occasionally did, it was to say how efficient Hedquist was. Other than that, the work held little interest for him. Stockholm was important to him for other reasons. While there he started his investigation into Chinese architecture in earnest. In Stockholm, Utzon made a present to Tobias Faber of books on Chinese architecture by Osvald Siren and J. Prip-Møller, along with a catalogue from the 1937 Milan Triennale on rural vernacular buildings.[15] Before that, the range of his interests hardly extended beyond anonymous vernacular buildings and micro-photographic enlargements of biological structures in German photographic publications.

When Utzon left Copenhagen he went alone, but Lis Fenger joined him in Stockholm later in 1942. Lis and Jørn were married on Friday, 4 December 1942. Both sets of parents made the arduous journey to Stockholm to be present at the ceremony, which was attended by the Gunnløgssons, Tobias Faber and other expatriate Danish friends.

At the beginning of his stay in Stockholm Utzon shared a flat with Gunnløgsson and his wife Celia (née Lund) and the arrangement continued after the wedding. It was an upstairs apartment in a pretty two-storey timber house on the outskirts of Drottingholm, in an idyllic country setting with a bridge and stream of clear water nearby and trees and pastures on which cattle grazed in the distance. The contrast between Drottingholm's peaceful, arcadian scenery and the bleakness of occupied Denmark was extreme.

Sharing the crowded white weatherboard house at Drottingholm had its drawbacks. The living arrangements in the apartment, in common with flats in many old buildings, were inconvenient and lacked privacy. To reach the living room, the Utzons were forced to traipse through the Gunnløgsson bedroom. The Gunnløgssons were equally inconvenienced, as to get to the bathroom they had to pass through the Utzon bedroom. Considering that this was wartime, the four were lucky to have found a flat, but living on top of one another proved most difficult for the two women. Celia Gunnløgsson was a quiet homebody who retreated to the kitchen, where she performed wonders, but she appeared lost outside it. Lis was outgoing and vivacious, and became the natural focus of fun and attention at parties. Celia was pushed to the sidelines by the more glamorous Lis. Without stopping to think, Lis would take the credit for the splendid table, while Celia, who did all the hard work behind the scenes in a cramped kitchen, silently fumed with repressed anger. The relationship between the two became strained, but had to be endured because apartments were scarce.

In mid-1943, however, Jørn and Lis moved to a flat in Stockholm's old quarter known as Gamla Stan. Gamla Stan was chosen in the thirteenth century as the site of a city and became Sweden's capital a century later. Österlånggatan Street, on which the Utzons lived, followed the original island shoreline before it had been extended on reclaimed land, and ended at the Royal Palace on the spot where the old royal castle had once been. In winter the wind howled along the street. Many of the buildings on the medieval waterline were severely damaged and were badly in need of restoration by 1943.

A certain amount of remedial work had been carried out in the second half of the 1930s, but this stopped during the Second World War, leaving the island's buildings to fall into further disrepair.[16] Gamla Stan was notable for its picturesque squalor and age. Many of the buildings were in imminent danger of collapse because they rested on unreliable old fill and the timber piles under them on the reclaimed perimeter were rotten. Walls inclined in every direction, cracks abounded, windows were unsealed and let in the wind in winter. There was no avoiding the damp and the lack of proper bathrooms or kitchens. Conditions were primitive in Gamla Stan.

Making up for this, the quarter was surrounded by sea and it was in a section of Stockholm that had a rich past and which had not been ruined by the cleansing hand of modern Swedish urban renewal.

When others back in Denmark heard of Utzon and Faber's success in finding jobs in Stockholm, a minor exodus of young architects quickly ensued. By 1943, a sizeable Danish contingent was established in Stockholm. Because they were young, they had fewer encumbrances. When they could afford it, they would gather at the Kateleu restaurant for company and news. Besides Jørn and Lis Utzon, the Gunnløgssons, and Tobias Faber, Stockholm attracted Nils and Eva Koppel, Ebbe and Karen Clemmensen, Ole Holweg, Erik Asuussen, Erik Christian Sørensen and others, who moved to Sweden for the duration of the Occupation until the liberation of Denmark.

During winter, there were opportunities for the couples to go skiing. Areas near the Norwegian border were forbidden to Danes to prevent them crossing and joining the Norwegian resistance. This left the central highlands. The Utzons and Gunnløgssons skied in central Sweden in 1943 and 1944. Their first ski holiday was spent at Hoglehardelan and Sloglikaidalan. The following year, at the beginning of April 1944, they went to Hoakervalen and Bydalen, which involved a long and tiring train journey north to Mattmar station on Lake Storsjön. The Jämtland highland west of Hallen with its rolling terrain and absence of mountains was ideally suited to cross-country skiing.

The Utzon party skied from one location to the next during daylight, stopping at night to shelter in the rough timber huts provided for this purpose. After being shut up indoors for so long, gliding along over the snowfields under brilliant skies in the sparkling spring sunshine felt intensely liberating. All their cares seemed to drop away behind them. At midday, they would stop to rest. Where there was a hut, they would clamber up onto the roof, skylark there and eat their picnic lunch. It was so warm on occasions that Jørn and Lis stripped off their clothes and jumped into a small lake to prove how hardy they were. The Gunnløgssons were more circumspect and chose a site well away from the main party. With bathrooms in such short supply, bathing was a universal problem.

Sometimes, when the sun was out, the men would strip to the waist and sit in the snow. They all enjoyed the horsing around and the holidays were a carefree time. Jørn and a few of the men indulged in mock 'snow sleeping': stripping down to their underpants, they sat or lay down on the snow while they read a newspaper. It was very Scandinavian in its mixture of discomfit and the absurd. When Tobias Faber broke a ski, Jørn shared one of his skis and the pair slithered along erratically, like a drunken three-legged stick insect.

By 1945 it was apparent that the Second World War was coming to an end and they should all soon return to Denmark. In April, Utzon, Tobias Faber and Ebbe Clemmensen joined the Danish Brigade force in Sweden at Tingsryd in Skane, to undergo training in preparation for ending the Occupation of Denmark. April and May were bitterly cold. They were accommodated in barracks, but later, after they moved to Genarp, the entire Danforce Brigade of eight to ten separate camps slept in tents for two weeks.

At 8.34 p.m. on 4 May at Genarp, Utzon heard the news from London on the BBC that the German armed forces in Holland, north-western Germany and Denmark had unconditionally surrendered to the 21st Allied Army Group commanded by Field Marshal Montgomery. Although there were 150,000 German military personnel trapped in Denmark they did not pose a significant danger, the real threat came from the 2500 Danish Nazis. Most of the casualties in the days that followed were caused by these local Nazi sympathisers. As drivers, Utzon and Faber were prime targets for Nazi sharpshooters who might seek to immobilise the Danforce truck columns on their slow progress towards Copenhagen.

On the night of Saturday 5 May, Utzon and the first Danish troops crossed the Sound at Helsingborg on the Swedish side. They drove south to Copenhagen and were greeted by a tumultuous welcome on their entry to the capital. Tobias Faber followed a day later.

The war was over. Millions of people whose lives had been

disrupted began to return to a more normal existence. Eight months earlier, on 27 September 1944, Jørn and Lis Utzon's first child, Jan, had been born in Stockholm. He symbolised the new future, a new life they dreamed and yearned for. Now, with their return home, they could begin to build their future.

Satirical self-portrait on Utzon's business card.

3

Drawing Dreams
Copenhagen, 1945–1948

Although in general Denmark had fared much better than the rest of Europe during the war, and Danes were largely unaffected by Allied bombing, its economy lay in ruins. Whereas in America industries and technology had developed in great leaps and bounds under the stimulus of wartime demands, Danish industry emerged hopelessly antiquated and out-of-date. Denmark had to wait until 1948 for the arrival of Marshall Aid from the US before there was any marked improvement in its economy.

Building activity had been at a standstill during the Occupation. Important civic buildings which had been started before 1940 were deliberately allowed to languish or were stopped to prevent them being completed. The Danes refused to allow symbolically important structures, such as the Århus Town Hall and Copenhagen's Radio House (Radiohus), to open under the Nazis. With the war over, these nationally significant projects were rushed forward to completion. Utzon arrived back to a society eager to make up for the wasted years, but found he could do little in the climate of economic stagnation.

On his return, Utzon moved into a flat at Rosenørns Alle 57 in a big, grim four-storeyed block, a short distance beyond H.C. Ørsteds Vej. The block, which had three entrances, was bleak and anonymous. Rows of identical windows stretched across the grey-rendered, yellow-brick, northern street facade in bands and were separated at each floor by moulded string courses. Trams rattled past the Utzons' flat on the first floor, which was large by 1945 standards and conveniently located not far from the city centre. Rosenørns Alle is a broad east–west thoroughfare that crosses the southern section of the Copenhagen Lakes and continues on to the City Hall. The new Radiohus building by Vilhelm Lauritzen, one of Denmark's leading exponents of Modernism, was only a few blocks away from Utzon's flat. It would have been impossible for Utzon not to have seen it. Additionally, Tobias Faber was employed at the time in Lauritzen's office supervising its completion and would certainly have been familiar with its details and the important structural and acoustic experiments that Lauritzen had had carried out. An acoustics expert, Vilhelm Lassen Jordan, had made a 1:50 scale model in gypsum plaster – a precursor of his later major project using model testing in the two large halls of the Sydney Opera House – to resolve problems in the 1093-seat concert studio. This was an early attempt to apply model techniques to investigate acoustic problems in auditoria.

The victory in Europe heightened everyone's material expectations. One indicator of this was the number of architectural competitions. For all the destruction, people believed anything was possible. For some time, Utzon was totally absorbed in the post-war flurry of Scandinavian competitions. Competitions provided an avenue for winning large or prestigious jobs and helped young architects starting out to become better known. In England and America, and even more so in Australia, such opportunities to win prestigious commissions were generally given to the senior and politically astute, or powerful players and movers within the architectural profession, who had the requisite political or business connections. The Scandinavian competition system was more enlightened, being based on design talent rather than political savvy.

Since few competition projects were ever built in practice, they exploited the participants. Entering competitions was strenuous and exhausting. Because of the frequency of competitions in Scandinavian countries including Denmark, architects soon developed a simplified competition presentation style, which showed only the most basic essentials of the proposed building, knowing that all the details could be worked out later. The drawings were frequently sketchy and concentrated on the main qualities the competitor wished to emphasise.[1] This minimised the drawing task and permitted a designer to concentrate his or her attention on enhancing the architectural qualities of the scheme. Furthermore, many competitions were held for political reasons or to avoid making a decision. In these instances, the minimum sketch approach reduced the amount of work and was more economical.

In time, Utzon became very adept at competitions. He had begun entering them even before the war ended. At Tingsryd barracks in Skane, where he and Faber were doing military training, they entered the Bellahøj Development competition, which involved a large-scale housing development to be built at Bellahøjvej in Copenhagen. The Faber and Utzon proposal was radical for the time, but was placed fourth, beaten by conventional proposals based on large slab blocks. They would have fared better if they had chosen to follow the Modernist approach then in vogue, of concentrating the housing in a few tall tower blocks. The planning wisdom in 1945 dictated residential tower blocks because this freed the ground for parks and open space. The second-place scheme – by Utzon's friend, Peer Abben, which he carried out with Otto Frankild – included 14 rectangular slab blocks broken into two groups of seven on either side of the community facilities, and isolated in a featureless island of parkland.

The Faber–Utzon scheme was very Danish in the way it aligned the housing with the land's contour lines and allowed the terrain to dictate the housing arrangement. Rather than follow the rationalist approach of a few large units, they adopted a more traditional rural approach of burrowing the buildings into the land, like a farmhouse that snuggles up to a hill for protection. Their instinctive feeling for scale allowed them explore a freer grouping that was far less alienating and avoided the deadly geometric formalism of the higher-placed designs. Their greater sensitivity in this regard is apparent in the deliberate relationship of the housing to the landforms, which imparts an identity based on the landscape itself. The naturalistic park surroundings were isolated from the expressway traffic by the provision of a long winding road access which circled around the site edge.

It was not until the mid-1960s that town planners began to recognise that housing people in tower blocks resulted in severe social problems, loneliness and depression, so Utzon and Faber were much in advance of their time in anticipating the social pitfalls of tower-based mass-housing schemes. They endeavoured to reduce the scale of the housing at Bellahøj by placing it in smaller units to create a more intimate scale, thereby reducing the sense of alienation. They spread these smaller units in irregular chains of rowhouses that meander and step around the contours in a manner not all that different from the later Fredensborg terrace housing, which Utzon implemented at the beginning of the 1960s.

A decade after this competition, in 1951–4, the Københavns Almennyttige Boligselskab realised the Bellahøj estate with 25 or so multi-storey tower blocks.

In 1945, Utzon and another architect, Henning Helger, were both awarded a minor or lesser Gold Medal (*mindre Guldmedaille*) from the Royal Academy of Fine Arts for their Academy of Music projects.[2] Utzon explained later that the medal was awarded: '... by participation in an annually arranged competition for architects under the age of 35. In 1944 the subject was an academy of music with concert hall.'[3] The Music Academy project for Copenhagen comprised a concert hall, music school and practice rooms, supposedly to be located on the corner of the old Garrison church at Østerbrogade and Kristianiagade at the northern end of the Copenhagen lakes, on land actually used as a graveyard. The project required relocation of the headstones to turn the land into a park.

Utzon's scheme was muted and tentative, a feeling that was reinforced by the lack of detail as though he was not fully convinced about the design. His technique at this stage lacked sureness. This may explain why he received only a minor instead of a full medal. There is much that is interesting, not only because of the musical function which Utzon has tackled, but because, even at such an early stage, well before he travelled to Mexico and China, important and enduring themes are announced. Foremost is the terrace. A terrace is a raised level platform made of earth, with a sloping or vertical front and sides faced with masonry or turf. It was used in Europe for walking and viewing the garden. Although less important and less developed at this stage, because it involved a complex for the performance of music, the terrace in the scheme invites comparisons with Utzon's Sydney Opera House scheme 11 years later. It would, however, be a mistake to see the project as a forerunner of the Sydney scheme, even taking into account its youthful tentativeness.

The source of Utzon's terrace is unclear. More than likely it arose from his absorption in Chinese imperial architecture, because in ancient China terraces served as platforms for important buildings. They performed two functions: they protected the timber structure from the weather and they enhanced the building's grandeur by elevating it, thereby emphasising the horizontal plane and increasing the importance of the building in relation to its immediate surroundings by lifting people up above them.

Utzon designed his Academy of Music using simple rectangular shapes held together under a strong horizontal roof. The classrooms have unequally pitched roofs which conflict with the softly rounded, sloping, acoustic shell roof above the concert hall.

An important ingredient of Utzon's presentation was his delicate pencil perspectives of the enclosed courtyard overlaid with light watercolour washes. The classical restraint of the courtyards was borrowed directly from Gunnar Asplund.

Most noteworthy is Utzon's use of a broad, linking platform to unify the individual buildings. The platform was clad in large slabs of a white bush-hammered limestone with staggered vertical joints that emphasise the horizontality of the base and the platform's edge. The platform was kept low except at the concert hall, where it was carried up to the underside of the curved concert shell roof, which sat directly on it. For all Utzon's hesitancy, this was a promising work for someone who had just turned 27. It convincingly explored sculptural ideas derived from the Swiss architect Le Corbusier and from Utzon's Swedish hero Asplund, without attempting to imitate them.

It contains an early intimation of Utzon's special capacity which persisted throughout his career: his capacity to draw on a number of distinct sources simultaneously – many admittedly anonymous – and restate them in a new way so they do not appear in the least bit hackneyed. Utzon inherited from Modernist dogma the compulsion to be original and cancel all previous debts. This is largely impossible, since cultures are built up over time from the interweaving of a variety of contributions and influences. But because of his worry about not being original, Utzon hid his architectural influences, which partly accounts for his concentration on nature and vernacular buildings, since these are universal things that do not belong to any individual and are therefore free of copyright.

Whereas Le Corbusier had proceeded in the 1920s to liberate architecture with forms that hover in the air above the ground, the terrace does the exact opposite. By lifting his forms so they stand on slim pilotis, or columns, Le Corbusier set about expressing the new architecture as autonomous and turned it into a symbol of twentieth-century machine civilisation. The terrace was diametrically opposed to the spirit of Le Corbusier.

Although there are enormous differences, Utzon is far closer in his intentions to the great American architect Frank Lloyd Wright in this regard. Whereas Wright carried walls beyond the roof eaves into the landscape, in order to suggest unlimited extension towards an invisible horizon, Utzon's plateaus or terraces confine his buildings behind a boundary line that limits their extent and separates them from their surroundings. This is more akin to Asplund, and the classical Greek temple standing on its stylobate from which its columns rise, than Wright. Paradoxically, Utzon's intention was clearly to relate the buildings to nature, not the opposite. The relationship is more empathetic in content than spatial. This makes Utzon different to Wright, who relied on a series of characteristic mannerisms that are readily recognised and idiosyncratic, and entirely given over to his buildings developing a dialogue with nature. Utzon is a typical European who looks with longing towards the freedoms of America but must establish his own safe limits nevertheless.

To understand Utzon's ambivalence to Wright we need to understand what his encounter with Chinese architecture taught him during his stay in Sweden. Even though there are obvious similarities between Utzon's work and the Chinese placement of imperial palaces and temples on terraces faced with brick or stone, Utzon gave the artificial plateau a very twentieth-century interpretation and assigned a new set of quite distinct roles to the ancient Chinese terrace.

The reinforced concrete concert hall roof of his Copenhagen scheme was supported on concrete beams resting on the load-bearing walls at either side. It was covered on the outside with copper sheets and had a profile identical to the acoustic profile underneath, which was shaped to reflect sound into the audience. Hence the external shell profile expressed exactly the acoustic function of the auditorium. The idea is similar to Le Corbusier's competition design for an acoustic shell in his 1927 League of Nations Palace at Geneva. Timber was widely used in Utzon's scheme: the ceiling was lined with pear tree wood and he asked that the external timber be treated with a colourless impregnating solution to show its grain. There were a number of similarities with the concert studio of Radiohus, which was unfinished at this time. Lauritzen had enclosed the concert studio with a thin concrete shell from which he suspended a secondary, thinner, ripple-wave profiled acoustic shell to diffuse sound waves. Lauritzen's acoustic ceiling gently dived to the front stage in a flattened arc which anticipated the curvature of Utzon's ceiling. Later, the Sydney Opera House also adopted a similar arrangement of an outer structural shell spanning the space from which an inner acoustic shell was hung.

In 1945 Utzon entered another competition, to design a crematorium consisting of three chapels on a small hilltop. His scheme created a contrast between the quiet Danish landscape and a violent shell burst of splintered brick walls that spilled out in all directions from the ruptured hill. Whilst Danish landscape is crowded with minor incidents, it lacks mountains to match the romantic nineteenth-century ideal of the sublime exemplified by the physical grandeur of the Swiss Alps. It is uneventful and, although well supplied with lakes, it does not even possess the modest equivalent of England's Lake District. Instead of striking up a quiet harmony, Utzon capped the hill with an architectural explosion, which erupted into the surrounding landscape.[4]

The shattering of the hill disturbs the nature around it and reminds us how shocking death is. The chapels were to be placed at the epicentres of three separate explosions, which shoot outwards down the slope. This main movement was opposed by the backward tilt of the chapel roofs. Starting at the chapels, blades of brick fanned out radially from the hilltop. Of varying heights, they would thrust out from a centre point inside the mass of the hill. From above, these planes darted in all directions.

The explosion motif gives the impression that an intense energy discharge has torn the hill apart and caused it to fly outwards. As sculpture, the composition of Utzon's proposed crematorium suggests something of the nightmare of disintegration and things ending and falling apart, which we are powerless to prevent.

Perhaps some residual violence left over from the recent war detonated this sculptural hillside explosion. The crematorium scheme makes us think that Utzon is concerned primarily with making iconic sculptures. It is a reminder of his ability to convert architecture into memorable sculpture. While he demonstrated his sensitivity to Danish nature, he refused to be bound by it and to be limited by its pacific qualities. He prefers instead to shatter our expectations of harmony and peace with his exploding sculpture.

Jørn Utzon is a contradiction: deeply nationalistic and aware of tradition, he nevertheless always looks outside Denmark for his ideas. He is unusually international compared to his Danish contemporaries. This manifested itself in his work very early. The explanation may lie in his father and mother's very different backgrounds; his father's middle-class origins in central Jutland clashed with his mother's Baltic heritage, thus inclining Utzon to look outwards instead of inwards.

Five months after his return to Copenhagen from Sweden, Utzon set off for Finland with Lis and Jan, having secured work in Alvar Aalto's office in Helsinki. Earlier that year, on 15 August 1945, Utzon wrote to Alvar Aalto and mentioned his gold medal.[5] After the Utzons' departure on 2 October, Tobias Faber moved into the now vacant flat at Rosenørns Allé 57.

Although he intended to stay in Finland for a year, Utzon was forced to cut short his visit to Aalto and returned to Copenhagen at the beginning of December, after just nine weeks away, in time to celebrate Faber's birthday on the 12th. The Aalto office records indicate that Utzon was there from 25 October until 5 December 1945, or about six weeks. He had been given the job on the recommendation of Erhard Lorenz.[6] It is not known for certain what he worked on while he was in Helsinki – but considering the short duration of his stay this cannot have been substantial. Utzon has stated in a letter that he worked on town plans and reconstruction schemes in Finland.[7] His unexpected return to Copenhagen created difficulties for Faber, who had moved into Utzon's flat on the understanding that the family would be away some time, and he was forced to find new accommodation at short notice.

Burying his disappointment, Utzon made new plans to visit Finland in 1946. But in the third trimester of her pregnancy Lis became ill, and on 11 March 1946 Utzon sent a telegram to the Aalto office to say he would not be coming. Lin Oberg Utzon was born on 21 May 1946 and, for a time, Utzon was forced to cancel any plans for travel to Finland or elsewhere.

On his return to Copenhagen, Utzon met Faber and they discussed the advantages of going into partnership. No formal arrangement was ever finalised, but the discussions were significant because they marked the beginning of a new and productive collaboration between the men, in the main devoted to entering competitions. The most important was the International Crystal Palace Competition in 1946. Like the crematorium chapels, the Crystal Palace occupied a hill site, but on a much grander scale.

Although ten years later Utzon included it in his list of competition prizes, Faber and Utzon's submission was unplaced and did not receive so much as an honourable mention.[8]

'The Crystal Palace is no more.' With these few dramatic words, on the evening of 30 November 1936, the BBC had broken the shocking news that fire had completely destroyed the Crystal Palace. With the war over in 1945, the suggestion to rebuild Sir Joseph Paxton's great 1850–1 Crystal Palace exhibition structure at Sydenham was set in motion.

This was carried out by means of an international competition sponsored jointly by the Crystal Palace Trust and the Arts Council of Great Britain, with the intention of creating a real centre for culture in Britain that would exert a profound effect on the national life. It was hoped the National Recreation Centre would serve as a symbol of the new Britannia emerging victorious from the harrowing experience of the war.

The competition programme was extremely ambitious – perhaps too ambitious in view of the severe economic problems faced by Britain at the time. Besides a huge mixed-use recreational venue equipped with exhibition halls, a sporting complex for ice hockey, swimming, gymnastics, dancing, and a major stadium for 100,000 people, the competition brief demanded an important cultural component, including an opera house to seat 2500, a large concert hall for 4000 and a smaller concert hall to seat 1500, and a 1500-seat theatre, plus restaurants and the like.

The competition created enormous excitement amongst architects in Europe. This was partly because of its huge size and national prestige, but mostly because of the historical associations with the old Crystal Palace, which had been a major pioneering demonstration of the use of standard industrial components. Many foreign architects entered.

Because Utzon's flat at Rosenørns 57 was the only available space large enough, Tobias Faber, Mogens Irming and Jørn Utzon worked on the competition there. They made an early start on 29 December, but no serious design was done until 10 March, prior to Faber moving out on the 20th to Rosenørns Alle 58, across the street. The drawings for the Crystal Palace were completed and dispatched to London on 5 April, three weeks later. Admittedly this speed was not unusual in competitions, but it left them little time considering that their submission also included a model.

The results were announced on Friday 3 May by Lord Ammon.[9] The first prize of £2000 went to a scheme based on the ancient Roman Thermae of Caracalla, with a viewing tower added to bring the design up-to-date and give it a more modern touch.[10] A caustic Le Corbusier labelled it 'pseudo-modern architecture from 1925'. The winning proposal was grandiose, in the spirit of Francois Mitterrand's monuments for Paris in the 1980s, but premature in 1946 at the beginning of the Cold War. The timing was wrong, Britain and Europe were still struggling out of the ruins of the war and the British found themselves in no position to pay for such a hugely expensive undertaking in a period of acute post-war shortages.

Britain's attempt to establish its post-war cultural ascendancy and position at the head of the British Empire by rebuilding the Crystal Palace soon collapsed, and the project did not proceed much beyond the competition stage. Although it failed it left a legacy – the idea of a major cultural centre – which was eventually realised on London's South Bank. Perhaps it was not an accident that Herbert Jackson and Reginald Edmonds's stale Neo-classical Roman baths employed the worn-out symbols of an earlier empire in decline, but it was irrelevant in the context of the new industrial super-state. There was a further paradox in a victorious Britain celebrating that victory using exactly the same Roman imagery as the Nazis they had just defeated. Albert Speer's 1937 plan for Berlin, which was intended to be the capital of a new united Europe, called for an enormous grotesquely over-scaled 251 m diameter dome as its centrepiece. There was not much difference between this and what Jackson and Edmonds proposed; what they lacked was Albert Speer's obvious flair and easy familiarity with such a stark Neo-classical vocabulary.

Sir Kenneth Clark, on behalf of the assessors, strove without much success to justify their appalling decision, but only succeeded in making it appear even more silly and reactionary: 'The assessors have not awarded the prize to a great pioneer work or to a great masterpiece of architecture. A number of pioneer works have been submitted, but they were not workable.' Since the pioneering works to which he referred were clearly workable and Clark must have known this, his use of function as an argument was self-defeating.

Among the 'pioneer works' the most remarkable was from the partnership Clive Entwistle and Ove Arup. More than the others, it recaptured the innovative and adventurous spirit of Paxton's original Crystal Palace. Le Corbusier praised its 'eminent sense of architecture'. A large measure of the scheme's success was due to two Danish consulting engineers: Ove Arup had developed the structural scheme for Entwistle, and J. Varming supplied the suggestions on the heating and ventilation principles. Ove Arup had earlier achieved a name for himself with his contribution to the British Mulberry harbours for the D-Day landings at Normandy in June 1944. Sir Kenneth Clark's real objection is contained in his comment on the unconventional nature of the Entwistle glass-and-concrete pyramid which, he admitted, '... probably works beautifully and is certainly no more fantastic than Mulberry. But it is not conventional. It is an idea, a very beautiful one, that would undoubtedly invoke its response were it to be built'.[11] In objecting to beautiful expressive ideas that work superbly but were too modern and unconventional Clark revealed the conservative side of his pre-1920 aesthetics, which made it impossible for him to approve such avant-garde ideas.

In describing the three-dimensional effect of the reinforced concrete-and-glass pyramid, Clive Entwistle noted, 'The Hellenic sculptor had a saying, "The Gods see from all sides." Today man himself sees from all sides.' He added:

> *The roof has become the fifth facade, and seen from this point of view the ambiguity of the pyramid is of particular interest; it faces the sky as much as it does the horizon. Not only does the new architecture need sculpture, it is itself re-becoming sculpture.*
>
> *The forms of the new architecture have a special character. Reminiscent of pure geometry, crystals, histological and skeletal structures, aerodynamic forms, even elements of*

machinery, they yet remain aloof from close resemblance to or imitation of any of these categories of form ... they alone attain a lawful significance.[12]

This was published in 1947. In April 1965, Jørn Utzon used much the same words to describe his concept for the Sydney Opera House and even went so far as to appropriate Entwistle's use of the term 'fifth facade' in his *Zodiac 14* article.

The Utzon, Faber, Irming entry (no. 85) for the Crystal Palace was submitted at the last moment. It is important for a variety of reasons, not the least of which is that its ideas it resurfaced, though in a notably more mature way, in Utzon's 1956 Sydney Opera House design.

The road up Westwood Hill from Sydenham railway station staggers and lurches up to Crystal Palace Parade. The street names are all that remain as reminders of the once magnificent Crystal Palace. The site straddled an exposed muddy ridge, littered with the tents of campers, and was dominated at the east end by a single metal radio broadcast tower. Opposite Crystal Palace Parade, which follows the line of the ridge, it had been levelled where the Palace had once stood; below that, the hill fell away steeply to the south.

The Faber–Utzon entry grouped the main body of buildings along the ridge. Here the architects unified them by arranging them on a large elevated terrace, also making the most of the only flat area in the site with easy road access. A large platform was placed along the ridge and extended down the hill at the ends on two sides to enclose an open area in the middle. The terrace-deck thus framed the site on three sides and isolated it from its immediate surroundings. This gave the group an interior focus.

A large stadium was to be excavated into the hillside below the platform, farther down the hill and well clear of it. The Faber–Utzon scheme had one significant advantage: all its facilities, which would otherwise have lacked legibility, were assembled and linked by the common platform base. As a monumental terrace for all the principal buildings to stand on, it successfully unified the disparate parts of the group. It was a clever piece of bridge-work at a large scale; in one stroke it facilitated horizontal movement by eliminating barriers and placing pedestrians on a common level, and reduced changes of level due to the hill to a minimum, and this in turn would have contributed considerably to ease of movement.

The Crystal Palace terrace is a precursor of the Sydney Opera House platform. Utzon's 1946 sketches are notably similar to ones that he produced in 1956 for the Opera House, and included a view of the interspace between the two Crystal Palace concert halls which showed a staircase leading from the terrace down into the park. Maxwell Fry, a leading English proponent of Modern architecture and former partner of the architect Walter Gropius, perceptively observed: 'No. 85 I mention because it represents a point of view and is homogeneous; but it is dreamy and emotional, completely un-vulgar, which is something, but far too resigned to be real'.[13] 'Dreamy and emotional' sums Utzon up, as does Fry's suggestion that the scheme is 'too resigned to be real'. His remarks are worth pondering. Fry detected in the drawings an ambivalence to reality that profoundly affected Utzon later, as though he was unwilling to live in the real world. He noticed a mood of hesitation, as if Utzon found it difficult to separate dreams from reality. Dreams interweave self-absorption, narcissism, self-reflection and story telling. These are things Utzon enjoyed and, for the artist, it is important not to dismiss them, but to draw on them and use them. Sometimes it is difficult to maintain the balance between imagination and the practical.

The Crystal Palace competition revealed Utzon's early ideas on how terraces could be used to separate pedestrians from motor vehicles. It represented a clever adaptation of the ancient Chinese terrace to meet the unprecedented problem of traffic in the modern age. It made use of the flexible underspace created by lifting the pedestrian above the natural ground plane on elevated, reinforced concrete decks supported on slender columns. The practice of vertically separating different types of traffic is now a standard town planning procedure, but in 1945 it was still very new.

The grand terrace split Utzon's form into a duality: the monumental base was expressed as an elegant horizontal concrete parasol. Above it were the theatres, concert halls and the like, which, much as in the Academy of Music entry the previous year, were covered by distinctively shaped, sculptural, shell roof structures. On the four levels of terraces adjacent to Crystal Palace Parade, Utzon, Faber and Irming would have constructed courtyards and balconies so as to resemble rice terraces of East Asia. Crowning this, and to attract everyone's attention, would have been a light radio mast with central vertebrae stabilised by three outwardly inclined struts.

In a series of delicate pencil sketches, Utzon likened the repetition of cylindrical slender concrete columns beneath the terrace floors to trees in a forest, where light filters weakly between breaks in the leaf canopy. There were further interesting comparisons with the Arab bazaar or *souk*, and Italian squares filled with coloured umbrellas.

Impelled by the increased weight of family responsibilities, Utzon set up his own architectural office. Lacking an established clientele, he was forced to enter numerous architectural competitions, both in Denmark and southern Sweden. He did not limit himself to Scandinavia, as witnessed by his submission with Faber and Irming in the Crystal Palace competition. It was soon apparent that he had a talent for competitions, not so much because of his drawing skills, but because his imagination led him to explore unconventional possibilities ignored by other contestants. In competitions, success is a matter of ideas. Utzon excelled because he spent most of his time thinking and this gave his solutions an original quality. Freed to a considerable extent from client demands which might have hamstrung his creativity, his participation in competitions helped him to develop his own architectural vision. The more competitions he entered, the better at them he became.

Competitions took up much of Utzon's time in 1946. There was a community centre and theatre at Falköping and a town plan for Boras in Sweden; the Architectural Association's one-family houses and town planning competition in which he received both first and second prizes; the Næstved sports park;[14] and a Hobro restaurant and community centre forest pavilion on Jutland.[15] While he was placed in these competitions, none resulted in a solid commission of any kind.

The water tower and maritime signal outside Svaneke, at the eastern tip of the island of Bornholm in the eastern Baltic, is the one exception.[16] It demonstrated that he could make an object that was modern and elegant according to its own lights, and which could co-exist happily beside tradition. Bornholm was very fresh in the minds of the Danes. Its two main towns, Rønne and Nexø, had been bombed by Russian aircraft after the German commander of the Bornholm garrison refused to capitulate to the Russians because he insisted on surrendering to the British. The Russians retaliated by occupying the island for almost a year before handing it back officially to Denmark on 5 April 1946. Jørn Utzon's water tower was part of the reconstruction effort; it took many years to build and was not completed until 1952.

Usually water towers are cylindrical or spherical. At Svaneke, Utzon inverted the customary golf-tee shaped water tower so that the conical tank formed an elegant concrete teepee. It consists of a tall tetrahedron comprising three inclined, reinforced-concrete, rectangular-section corner poles, the upper side of which was enclosed by horizontal timber boards concealing the water tank. A horizontal gap was left for the lookout, with the timber boarding continued above it to the apex.

Utzon contrasted the openings and the solid infilled side sections in between the three concrete poles so that the landscape is framed by the structural supports and is entwined with it, evoking a sense of the intense isolation and loneliness of the place – at the easternmost point of Bornholm. The pyramid is at once figurative and abstract and surprisingly animated. From a distance, the silhouette of the tower might almost be mistaken for a giant human figure from Miguel Cervantes.

Utzon renewed his acquaintance with the architect Arne Korsmo in September 1946. He had met Korsmo for the first time in

Stockholm in 1944 when Korsmo fled there from his home in Norway. The pair took an instant liking to each other. Korsmo has left this account of their meeting:

> *In Jørn Utzon's room in the old part of Stockholm, where according to him he lived among thieves and rogues, and newly married, I got a new look at life – a younger, freer, more unconventional outlook. It was not long before we, on one of our summer outings to Sandhamn in the Stockholm skerries, could really talk to each other. Everything we found on the beach – stones, bits of glass and glistening black charcoal – was put together into our first poem about our mutual pleasure at spatial perception. And once we realised that we spoke the same language as regards architecture and other experiences, it was clear that the logical consequences was for us to work together.*[17]

Korsmo, who also worked for Poul Hedquist in Stockholm, was 18 years older than Utzon and a far more experienced architect. Korsmo liked the company of young people because he found their company stimulated him, but with Utzon he found someone who was closely attuned to his own way of thinking and who could also offer him new and quite unusual insights and ways of reading nature.

Utzon and Korsmo both regarded nature as the one great inspiration of the designer. Its ruthless functionalism and rich diversity demonstrated that there was a connection somehow mixed in with natural selection that produced a fabulous beauty of form which seemed to be boundless. Natural processes were at once remarkably economical and efficient and chillingly beautiful. Nature, it appeared, invariably made the most of the materials at its disposal, producing from the most minimal, unattractive ingredients a wealth of colour and form that was truly breathtaking. Beauty, it seemed, could be conjured from almost anything.

As well as their shared devotion to nature, Utzon was deeply impressed by Arne Korsmo's way of viewing things. His father, Emil Korsmo, was a retired professor of botany who had trained Arne to see that nature writes a clear, logical structure in its forms.

All natural things have to adapt themselves to the vicissitudes of life, to find balance and grow in harmony with their local environment. Emil Korsmo made photographic enlargements of weeds to demonstrate this very point about nature's bias for logical structures.[18] His most important conclusion was that nothing is ever truly finished – nature is trapped forever in the unending chain of becoming. Therefore no form in nature should be regarded as final, but instead should be seen as a further stage in the ruthless struggle to survive. For Utzon and Arne Korsmo the implication was obvious and far reaching: nothing which is tied to life is ever finished. Architecture, which is related organically to life, must express growth and change.

Some designers strive to produce a final perfect object. When finished, it should not be possible to add or subtract anything without disturbing the harmony of the form. This type of formal perfection was promulgated by Leon Battista Alberti during the Renaissance in fifteenth-century Italy, and was the opposite of Gothic extemporisation. It held little appeal for Utzon. He does not appear to have ever subscribed to such a belief in the aesthetic completeness of art as a kind of perfect creation. If he did, Arne Korsmo persuaded him otherwise. It is easy to understand where Utzon's idea of additive architecture originated. Constructing a form by adding extra identical units may be viewed as the architectural equivalent of cellular replication in biology.

In the same way that a plant adjusts to its locale, architecture should respond to place and deal with the particular. Utzon saw architecture as needing to express a similar uniqueness to a plant species that adapts itself to the specific physical conditions where it is found.

Arne Korsmo delighted in turning everything on its head. With his long face, aquiline nose, clump of unruly dark hair leaping off his right forehead and lips that half twisted in a smile, Korsmo looked a bit like a rabbit. He possessed a similar quick nervousness in his body movements.

Jørn and Lis Utzon journeyed north to visit Arne Korsmo and his second wife Grete in the Norwegian mountains in September 1946. Korsmo always enjoyed a joke. When a man knocked on Korsmo's door selling game licences for the grouse-hunting season which ended the next day, Korsmo leapt up and shouted at him: 'Are you crazy! Do you think you have the right to sell death certificates for birds? What do you think the grouse would say! Get out!'[19]

Arne Korsmo loved opposites: poetry and logic. Utzon was similar to him in this respect. Korsmo continually sought to make his creations flow with the stream of life. It was his fondness for poetry and his bright intelligence that attracted Utzon. Korsmo supported Utzon's own developing perceptions and gave him confidence that he was not alone.

Their first work together was the entry for a furniture competition arranged by the Museum of Modern Art, New York, in 1946.[20] The chair they designed was a complex, bow-like structure with backrest and arm supports supported by interwoven, leaf-shaped, curved, laminated timber legs. It was thoroughly organic and looked like something made from twiglets-and-leaves casually plucked from the forest floor. Its delicate leaf-like aspect was combined with sensuous flamboyant Baroque shapes that also had a quintessentially Scandinavian quality. Simplicity was wedded to a wild voluptuousness. The free, curved lines of the chair pointed forward to the shells of the Sydney Opera House. The Korsmo–Utzon chair received a mention and was illustrated in the museum catalogue.

It is not clear who was the more dominant and creative of the pair, and who influenced whom. What seems to have happened is that they produced a spark, fired by differences of temperament and experience, which were more complementary than similar. This led to quite remarkable results. The impetus may have come from Utzon or, equally plausibly, Korsmo may have given rise to ideas dormant in Utzon which he did not recognise himself. A friend of Korsmo's, the Norwegian architectural historian Christian Norberg-Schulz, contended later that it was Utzon who acted as the catalyst.

However it happened, it is clear the projects they worked on jointly – namely, the competition for the Oslo Central Railway Station (1947), the Business School for Gothenburg (1948), their plan for Vestre Vika in Oslo (1948), and the Civic Centre for Falköping (1949) – were entirely new and differ considerably in approach from Korsmo's previous productions in the 1930s. They became organic. Utzon and Korsmo's plan for Vestre Vika is just such an instance, stressing the unfinished nature of the development and approaching urban renewal as a further stage. The organic intent expressed itself in several ways: in the selection of materials; the importance of modules; and choice of colours to allow further building units to be added later. The incompleteness arose as a direct response to the undulating terrain of Oslo. This, in turn, led to the formulation of an additive architecture concept, which was intended to grow like an organism, multiplying or shedding cells, depending on its needs and the environment.

Nineteen-forty-seven ended in disaster for Utzon and Faber. They had written a joint article in the summer, subsequently published in the Danish architectural journal *Arkitekten*,[21] which was meant to be a statement of architectural belief for both. Today it has a special status as one of the few early statements by Utzon which clearly spells out his architectural views. Regrettably, neither author acknowledged the source of the main bulk of the ideas and their plagiarism was quickly detected.

When published in September it was immediately criticised because a large part of the essay had been taken from a 1939 book by Albert Frey published in New York. Frey had produced an elegant design primer from the Modern architectural standpoint which exactly anticipated Utzon and Faber eight years later.[22] Their article, 'Tendencies in present-day architecture', began with a general introduction and was illustrated with some 28 examples. Extended captions at the foot of each illustration acted as a second supplementary text. Seven illustrations[23] and large sections of the text were lifted direct from the Frey book without acknowledgement.

The next issue of *Arkitekten*[24] carried an ironic exposure of Faber and Utzon written by Knud Lautrup-Larsen[25] who pointed out the similarities between the two texts and documented each plagiarism picture for picture. He asked them why, if they were willing to acknowledge their indebtedness to Frank Lloyd Wright, Le Corbusier and Alvar Aalto, they omitted Albert Frey, to whom their debt was much greater.

In their reply, Utzon and Faber lamely conceded that not acknowledging Frey was a mistake and admitted their plagiarism. No apology could entirely erase the damage. Fortunately, the damage to their reputations was temporary and was quickly put behind them. Utzon and Faber should have known better, but both were young and impatient to make their mark professionally. It is hard to apportion blame in this case, but Tobias Faber as an architectural historian and a future leading architectural writer should have known better. Their friendship, in any case, survived intact — if somewhat bruised.

It would not be the last occasion that Utzon would present other people's ideas as his own. He made such a fetish of originality, he found it difficult to openly acknowledge external intellectual or creative debts. This may account for his attachment to such anonymous sources as nature and vernacular buildings, and Chinese and Mayan architecture, which are much less recognisable or distinctive than Western sources. On the 1947 occasion, it was not so much what Utzon said as what he did not say that was revealing. In some ways this is very indicative, it is the omissions, the things that are left unsaid, that are most revealing.

The article developed two strong themes: first, it recognised the importance of vernacular architecture as a model; and second, it drew attention to the inspiration afforded by observing the unity in nature between an organism's life cycle and its structure and form. The thrust of Faber and Utzon's argument was the need to establish a direct and coherent connection between the life form — what they referred to as 'the forms of existence' — and the architectonic feeling which accompanies it and is its manifestation. To explain the connection, Faber and Utzon introduced the phrase '*arkitektonisk fornemmelse*'. Its equivalent in nature was '*naturens arkitektur*'.

The argument was terribly simple — almost too simple given the complexity of the phenomena it claimed to deal with. Their view, in essence, requires that character in architecture should derive from, or be the result of, an 'out-pressing of inner spirit'. It cannot arise from outside the organism as an imposition; instead, it must be intimately connected with the architectonic expression. Faber and Utzon strongly condemned formalism:

> *Others [who have reverted to functionalism] try to carry functionalism further but are unable to do so without ending up with formalistic results. One might call them motifists, in that they assemble the form of their architecture out of motifs torn loose from their origins; motifs with which they are infatuated. Their architecture becomes unclear, just as language without a grammar.*

This was Faber speaking, but clearly Utzon agreed with him. The 'Tendencies' essay completely rejected the concept of style. Faber and Utzon envisioned their architecture as developing from nature and vernacular forms rather than from high culture, which meant a succession of styles. Their point of view is amply demonstrated by the illustrations in the essay: of a total of 28 images, 11 were of natural forms and nine of vernacular sources, while a further five were drawn from the organic architecture of Wright and Aalto.

What most concerned them was the imposition of an obsolete, *a priori* formalism in contemporary architecture, which pre-empted the results of expression based on and linked to technique. At stake was the demand that a proper organic connection should exist between cause and form, as between the style of life and architectural expression. Both Faber and Utzon asked for the two to be related and clearly expressed. The concluding paragraph of the essay encapsulated this point:

> *Finally, there are architects who are in complete contact with today's lifestyle and who come from a school of thought that holds that architecture should embody the framework of that lifestyle – that first and foremost one has to live in it. They base their work on the people's fundamental feeling for architecture, a feeling which through the ages has always been the foundation of a true architecture. The notion of architectural*

feeling is employed here in a dual sense; that is, the feeling that allows us both to experience architecture and make it.

This conclusion about the necessary unity of life and expression has dominated nearly everything Utzon has done since.

One of their most telling observations was that to create architecture, it is first necessary to experience the connection of architecture to life. The architect must know the feeling behind the architecture, which, in a sense, gave rise to it. For Utzon, this required that he travel to the architecture and experience it directly, so his knowledge was based on seeing, touching, knowing buildings in their local physical and cultural settings.

In the essay, Utzon implied, this was how anyone who wished to be informed must approach an understanding of architecture. It is only by such profound encounters that we grasp the inherent organic connection between content and form. The underlining premise was a rejection of book learning coming second-hand. Utzon travelled extensively in the process of making his discoveries. For him to trust his conclusions, he refused to allow any extraneous intermediate connections to interfere. He bases his architecture on what he sees and feels, on the full sensuous impression with objects. Utzon emphasises the anonymous in order to avoid what he considered was idiosyncratic expressions or manifestations of personal caprice. His aim is a deep harmonious connection with all things and with the universal. In this sense his work might be called religious. It was for this reason that he turned to anonymous vernacular and indigenous buildings for inspiration, and went to regions such as North Africa and Mexico, which supplied magnificent living examples of the organic. The vernacular offered him a further parallel with nature – an architecture closely connected to nature. Utzon regarded these sources as his great teachers.

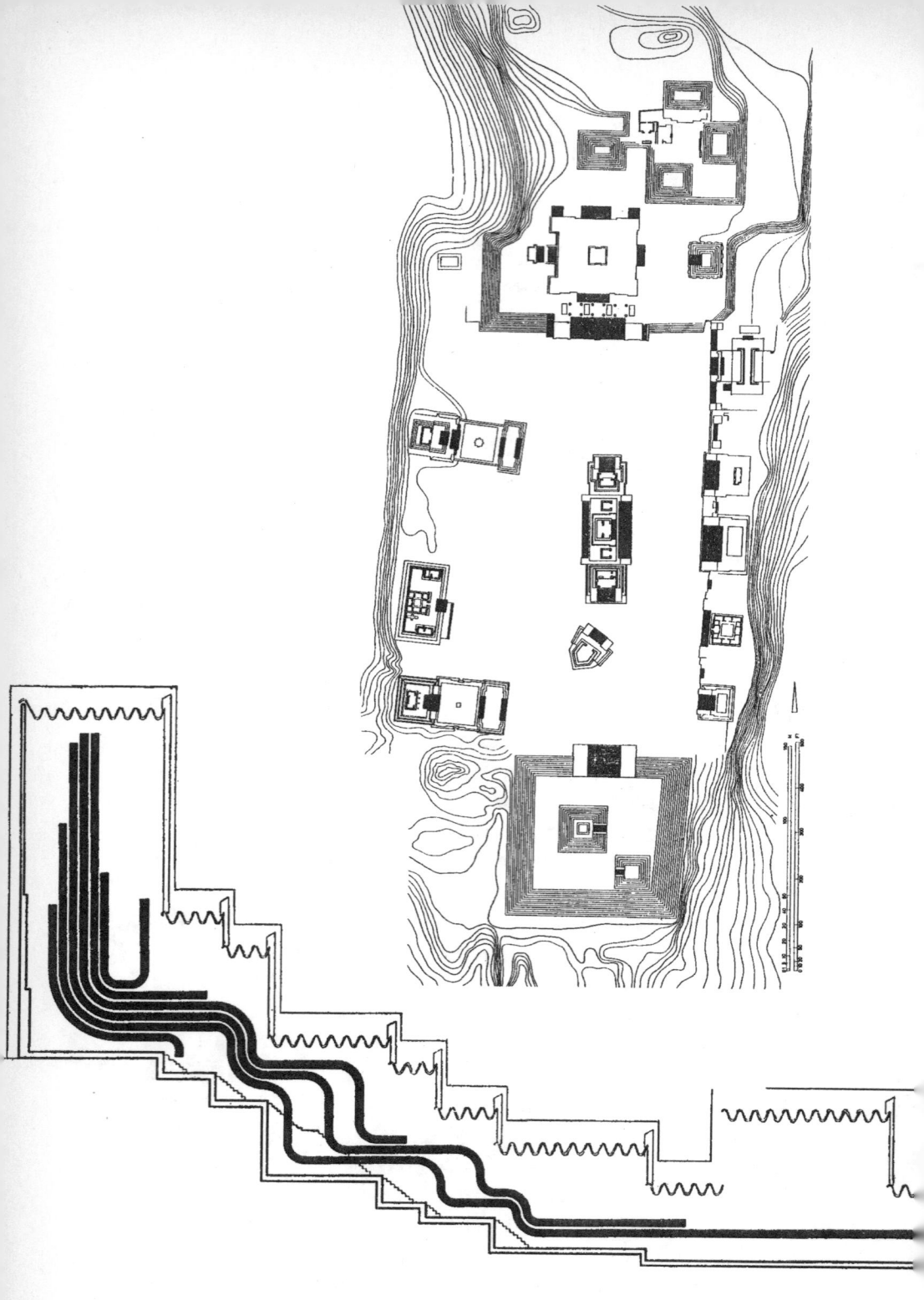

Above: The Sacred complex at Monte Alban: south platform (bottom), three pyramids group (centre). From Henri Stierlin, *Ancient Mexico*.
Below: Project for paper factory, Mexico, 1947. Section.

4

Architecture Without Signatures

Morocco and Mexico, 1948–1950

Utzon's involvement in competitions was as great in 1948 as it had been the previous year. In particular, he entered the Århus sports centre competition and many others. As a living, however, the competition work was insufficient to support a family. Looking for new opportunities, in the previous year, 1947, Utzon had turned his attention to Morocco.

While he was absent, Lis and the babies returned for the time being to stay with her parents at Helsingør. Utzon prepared designs for three factory projects and a housing scheme in Morocco: of these, one was to manufacture cement, another prefabricated elements, and the last was for the manufacture of paper. None of the projects was ever built.

The paper factory scheme was the most interesting of the three, largely because it introduced a motif that Utzon developed 12 years later for the Melli Bank in Teheran. Utzon's solution was sketchy and diagrammatic and got no farther than an elementary representation of the paper-manufacturing process as fundamentally a linear one. In his sketches, the various stages of paper manufacture were represented diagrammatically by a series of thick black horizontal lines that flowed down seven steps in the floor. Each step was matched by deep vertical beams in the roof immediately above, to punctuate the changes of floor level. The architectural cross-section developed a visual poetry that resembled an improvised jazz score. There was also a distinctly regional flavour that emerged from the graphic imagery which recalled modern Arabic script. The section definitely looks like Arab writing and may have been a deliberate joke by Utzon.

While the design may have begun with function, Utzon is dreaming; and far from being strictly architectural, it acquired further allusions that extended beyond architecture and embraced the local Moroccan culture. The paper factory roof consisted of a row of large standard 'V' teeth, whose profile in section suggests a horizontal screw or a continuous sine curve. The floor plan is equally fascinating and was based on the linear production process that flows between and was contained by two long parallel side walls, which Utzon strengthened at intervals with vertical nib buttresses that vary in height and thickness. The highest nib occurred at the back, and stepped in with each height increase, to express the accumulated load at its base.

The paper factory sketch from 1947, with its peculiar amalgam of poetry and rationalism, is an early demonstration of Jørn Utzon's predilection for architectural sculpture.

In 1949, Jørn and Lis travelled to the USA and Mexico. Utzon purchased a used car and, travelling with Arne and Grete Korsmo for much of the time, they traversed the length and breadth of the United States.[1] Arne Korsmo arrived in the USA on a Fulbright Scholarship. The timing of Utzon's trip was very fortunate. He called on Eero Saarinen at his office outside Detroit and had an interview with Mies van der Rohe in Chicago. Utzon made quite an impression on Saarinen; asked in 1957, eight years later, if he knew anything about Utzon, Saarinen said:

> *Utzon is a man about 42 or 44 years old. I met him several years ago. Well, he is a tall, very handsome Dane with blond hair, as most Danes have. I've seen quite a bit of his work, some time ago. I saw several of his competition drawings*

which he has won, and there is a very fine quality about his work.[2]

The two couples spent a weekend with Frank Lloyd Wright at Taliesin East, then they set off on the long and tiring drive across the south-west to visit Charles and Ray Eames at Pacific Palisades in California. Next, Utzon and Lis struck out for Taliesin West at Scottsdale, outside Phoenix in the Arizona desert. Their ultimate goal was Monte Alban in the valley of Oaxaca, 350 km south-east of Mexico City, and Uxmal and Chichén Itzá on the slightly rolling limestone plain of northern Yucatan. They treated the journey as an adventure, and seem to have thought nothing of the terrible roads and primitive conditions. Simply getting there was a feat in 1949.

While he was in Chicago, Utzon spoke to the famous German architect Ludwig Mies van der Rohe, who had been the last director of the Berlin Bauhaus before it was closed in 1933 by the Nazis. When Utzon arrived for his meeting with Mies, the great man was sitting in a large room, alone except for his secretary. He was huge and irascible. His stolid bulk drew everything in his vicinity into his gravitational field. Dressed in a black suit and smoking a cigar, he contemplated the large empty table in front of him, hardly glancing at his secretary across the room. Utzon approached and introduced himself to the secretary, who then turned to Mies and relayed Utzon's message – which Mies van der Rohe had pretended not to hear when Utzon spoke. Mies sat impassively sucking his cigar and ignored Utzon's presence. The interview proceeded in the same bizarre fashion: Mies's secretary acted as interlocutor, relaying what each said to the other; Mies neither looked at nor spoke to Utzon directly. It was a curious piece of theatre. A conversation on the telephone would have been more intimate. The point, if there was one, was that Utzon hardly existed. Like nearly everything that Mies did, his impersonal communication with Utzon was the perfect minimalist interview.[3]

Utzon's abasement paid off. Surprisingly, Utzon and Arne and Grete Korsmo received permission to visit Mies van der Rohe's newly completed Farnsworth House on the Fox River at

Plano, outside Chicago. What struck them most about it was its wholly unexpected combination of a strict sense of order with a new spatial freedom that was palpably sensuous. Arne Korsmo reported later:

> *Natural space pervades the entire house to the enclosed core at the centre. The stirring branches and leaves of the great trees, the shifting light and drifting clouds, the heaviness of the overcast sky – all this penetrates the glass and is reflected back. The river runs past, the trees stand in clusters, forming pockets of space. The steel columns rise from the ground, and stretched between them are three floating planes. The light is absorbed into the travertine floor, the white plaster of the ceiling reflects all the light without added colour, the yellowish grey silk of the shantung curtains quietly gives back the rich, shifting light. At night the shantung silk enfolds you like a tent ...*[4]

Utzon never forgot what he absorbed at Plano. Evidence of this can be found in his own house at Hellebæk built less than two years later.

Utzon was pulled in two directions: towards Wright's organic synthesis and infatuation with landscape and, equally powerfully but opposed to this, towards Mies's recasting of the steel and glass pavilion as a classical temple, with its echoes of Asplund, whose simplicity and minimalism acquired almost theological overtones of absolutism. As people, Mies and Wright could not have been more different and this is reflected in their architecture. Utzon found himself in sympathy with Wright's inspired horizontality, with the generous expansiveness of his space, and the exhilarating way Wright expressed the hugeness and endless rhythms of the American prairie. Wright engaged nature and this excited Utzon immensely. Wright described his removal of boundaries and limits as 'smashing the box'.[5] The new liberated sense of American space and landscape was one of its most precious contributions to the twentieth century. Wright shook Europe. America would never again be accused of aping Europe. The previous century's view of it, as the brash untutored child of Europe, was outmoded.

To someone such as Utzon, who had grown up confined by the smallness of Denmark, where the sea alone offered a glimpse of the infinite and where nature was circumscribed by the human, the contrast the American West offered must have come as a tremendous shock, with its explosion of space in the Great Plains and the natural grandeur of the Rocky Mountains.

Utzon discovered in Wright's forms, and the freedom of his space, support for his belief in organic architecture, especially in the harmony with nature of Wright's two houses. At Taliesin East in Spring Green, Wisconsin, and Taliesin West in Arizona, Wright supplied a vital connection with nature, a kind of catalyst enhanced by its gestures. His architecture was deeply spiritual in its own way, because it opened its occupants to experiences of nature that were quite profound.

Utzon arrived at Taliesin East bearing a greeting from Professor Kay Fisker in Denmark and he also presented Wright with a U 4860 pendant lamp he had designed for Kemp & Lauritzen. It is not known what Wright thought of his light. Their visit was short – Utzon did not intend to enrol as a paying student and apprentice, but came as a young architect paying homage to an older, much admired master.[6] In 1957, eight years later, when Wright was 90, he claimed that Utzon had never visited him at Taliesin East. With so many famous people arriving at his door in his final years, it is not surprising that Wright did not remember Utzon.

For Jørn Utzon, meeting Charles Eames took on the quality of a pilgrimage.[7] In 1949 Eames had completed a marvellous house assembled from stock mass-produced materials he ordered from manufacturers' catalogues. Each bit of it was standard – the doors and windows, for instance, were produced for use in factory construction. Enclosed with a mixture of transparent and translucent glass, and stucco, the result looked strikingly Japanese.

Eames built his Pacific Palisades house and adjoining studio on the ground to avoid building a bridge across the eucalypt-covered site as he had originally intended. Next to the two-storey house, on the other side of a courtyard, was the smaller studio. Later, at Hellebæk, in his own house, Utzon adopted a similar arrangement with the garage opposed at 90 degrees and separated from the body of the house. Unlike the Eames house, Utzon's house was entirely single-storeyed.

The Eames house was a brilliant object lesson in the application of anonymous ready-made industrial products to domestic construction. It was one of the most significant and influential buildings in the era immediately after the Second World War. Much like the Eames's extraordinary collection of toys and bric-à-brac, the house was an ingenious application of a select-and-arrange technique. Charles Eames had achieved a reputation in the early 1940s for his furniture, which employed moulded plywood shells. In his later work, Utzon adapted Eames's approach. Instead of relying on ready-made components from standard industrial catalogues, as Eames did, Utzon developed his own special standard elements, a 'kit of parts' as he called them, which he designed and had specially made. The connection between this and Eames's assemblies of standard industrial components was direct.

In the wake of his modest 1946 success in the Museum of Modern Art furniture competition, Jørn Utzon looked forward to discussing with Charles Eames how he could place his furniture designs before the manufacturer, Herman Miller Inc. of Zeeland, Michigan. Eames was important for another reason: he used moulded plywood shells in his furniture and in other applications as well and this made a lasting impression on Utzon. The later solution to the Sydney Opera House auditoria – using plywood mullions for the glass walls and their plywood fittings and furniture – adopted a similar path to that pioneered by Eames.[8]

Utzon was impressed by buildings as systems, whether the example was the ancient Sung Chinese building system or systems such as Lego blocks, which offer a wide range of possibilities. Utzon's American journey enlarged upon his Moroccan discoveries of traditional Arab building. Utzon was searching for an anonymous organic architecture without any signatures, in harmony with nature. This was more than a philosophical commitment and orientation; it involved something in Utzon's own make-up that demanded he eliminate the idiosyncratic, an urge to purge all individual and personal traces from a work and submerge it in the universal.

Anonymous means without any name acknowledged as that

of author, or the like. It was precisely this quality that Utzon wanted for his architecture: buildings without a signature that were distinguished by their quality of rightness and by how well they fitted in, and that possessed the same qualities of fitness, economy and appropriateness of form as his father's yachts. This was much more important to Utzon than having his own name identified with a particular work.

Indigenous buildings are to architecture what folk and fairy-tales are to literature, and folk song is to music. They are a shared expression, one that preserves continuity within a culture as they pass from one generation to the next. Utzon's great interest in anonymous building led him to the organic conception of architecture. Organic architecture presents considerable difficulties of definition because it can mean so many things. Not even Frank Lloyd Wright, its most celebrated proponent, could satisfactorily explain what he meant by organic. Roughly, it refers to the quality in any artificial object whereby all its parts are so well integrated into the whole it strikes us as being comparable to a natural organism. Wright came closest to explaining it when he said it was a 'ten-fingered grasp of reality'.[9]

Arne Korsmo had reaffirmed the argument from nature; now Utzon enlarged it to include vernacular building. Anonymous folk building connected humans to nature at a more instinctive, basic level. Consequently, folk building was less forced and cerebral than Modern architecture with its idolisation of the machine.

For Utzon, architecture should possess a fundamental societal reference, one that grew and changed as society changed and did not hold society back. Utzon looked for ways to extend architecture beyond the human and into the cosmic sphere. This cosmic dimension was perhaps best exemplified by the Mayan sites of Monte Alban, Uxmal and Chichén Itzá. These possessed monumental stone platforms and wide stairs which rose up and broke through the rainforest canopy of the trees. From the tops of such stairs, the forest spread out like an unending green ocean.

Monte Alban, the sacred capital of the southern Mexican Zapotecs, is on top of a mesa at the junction of three fertile plains, 396 m above the city of Oaxaca. It stands in splendid isolation on its hilltop. Of the many sites Utzon visited in Mexico, Monte Alban, with its huge esplanade surrounding a central building aligned north–south and following the line of the hill, seems closest to his Opera House in Sydney.

It is not difficult to imagine Monte Alban's flat esplanade as the waters of Sydney Harbour, with the east and west line of buildings around the edges as the harbour foreshore, and the three pyramids in the central group and the skewed observatory building as the primitive equivalents of the two Opera House halls and the restaurant. Both the Monte Alban acropolis and the Sydney Opera House can be seen from all sides. The Monte Alban composition, like the Sydney Opera House one, is centripetal – with the main buildings grouped at the centre. From inside the composition, near the centre, the centripetal movement is reversed and directed outwards.[10] The Sydney Opera House is similar: from the harbour, the city turns towards it seeking a focus; but standing on the podium base the inward attraction suddenly about faces – and the Opera House halls and restaurant spaces radiate out towards the harbour and the city. The spatial movement reverses itself. Setting aside the differences in their surroundings, the Sydney Opera House follows Monte Alban's spatial model to a surprising extent.

From his visit to Monte Alban Utzon also learned how powerful and sublime the terrace can be. The Mayan terrace connected rather than isolated buildings from landscape.[11] Utzon sketched the mountain and its series of buildings on the abrupt east and west edges. The clarity of the edge resulted from the terracing and bold retaining walls and, whilst they enhanced the isolation of the sacred platform, they also drew the surrounding mountains closer to the sanctuary by helping to eliminate the middle ground in between.

On the hilltop, the terrace connected the temples visually with their surroundings so they appear to sit gloriously suspended between sky and valley. The isolation of the terrace levels was broken by wide stairways, which incite a flowing interplay of broad perspectives. The levels slide over one another in steps, each successive terrace resting on the next. The staircases lead each terrace up to the one above it, in an ascending hierarchy which culminates in a monumental temple building. The rhythmic progression developed until it reached a stage where a grand climax was called for to end the sequence, some suitably powerful terminus which concentrated all the gathered energy of the journey in a single powerful node.

A few Mayan temples, including the Observatory at Monte Alban, were oriented differently to the main complex. Instead of complying with the north–south axis like the rest of the buildings, the long axis of the central Observatory rotated at a 35-degree angle to the other buildings.[12] This twist, like the inward angling of the Main and Minor halls of the Sydney Opera House, comes as a surprise and greatly enhances the spatial movement and interest. Rotating the form introduced a new dynamic into the composition, which would have been relatively static without it.

The pyramids, temples and observatories constitute a marvellous sculptural ensemble. So much is dependent on the elaborate and extremely subtle interplay of horizontal planes produced by the superimposed terraces rising serially one upon the other. There are many similarities with the Sydney Opera House: the north pyramid is approached by a 70 m wide and 10 m high staircase, not greatly different in size to the main staircase of the Opera House. The south platform, in particular its two pyramids which are on a raised, square, terraced platform at the southern end of the esplanade, recalls the Opera House's three shell roofs on a sculptured terrain of terraces. Monte Alban not only provides specific answers to subsequent problems Utzon would face, it offers a more general insight into the sources of Jørn Utzon's inspiration. Evidence for this is contained in the striking photographs Utzon took there.[13]

A century after Monte Alban was built, Chichén Itzá was founded by the Itzá, in 600 AD. The early Indians were trapped by the jungle; it was all around them on every side. High stone platforms and great staircases provided the only means to escape the jungle's stranglehold. The Mayan platform gave a new, cosmic dimension to the terrace by placing the Indians in touch with the sky and an expanded universe above the jungle. Looking out over the rolling jungle towards the distant horizon from such platforms was akin to looking at the sea. Pyramids were monumental pedestals: some were a sacred culmination point and could not be climbed while others could be climbed. The climbable pyramids were springboards bouncing the eye out into nature, on which the priests ascended to meet the gods.

As instruments that connected different parts of the landscape, the Mexican pyramids held a special meaning for Utzon. His photographs of Chichén Itzá capture the interplay between the Caracol Observatory and the tall Castillo pyramid some distance away. Utzon was fascinated by the two monuments, which resemble giants conversing to one another across the jungle.

To reach the Yucatan in 1949 involved a journey which was no mean feat. The hardships seem to have heightened Utzon's appreciation of what he found and the value he attached to his discoveries:

> *In this jungle the Mayans lived in their villages with small pieces of land cleared for cultivation, and their surrounding, background as well as roof, was the hot, damp, green jungle ... By introducing the platform with its level at the same height as the jungle top, these people suddenly obtained a new dimension of life worthy of their devotion to their Gods ... They had from here the sky, the clouds and the breeze, and suddenly the jungle roof had been converted into a great open plain. By this architectural trick they had completely changed the landscape and supplied the visual life with a greatness corresponding to the greatness of their Gods.*[14]

It was Utzon's conclusion that such stone jungle platforms were instruments for restoring the lost horizon.

The temple complex at Uxmal, with its many terraces and monumental stairways, comes closest in scale to the monumental terraced platform of the Sydney Opera House. The essence of Uxmal's broad horizontal platforms on different levels has been repeated in Sydney. Here Utzon rediscovered an earlier experience. Breaking through the canopy of the jungle into the intense sunlight reminded him of Denmark when, after weeks of rain, clouds and darkness, the sun broke through. The intense exhilaration he felt climbing the staircases and emerging above the jungle was indescribable.

For Utzon, the attraction of an anonymous architecture may arise from a peculiar reticence in the Danish psyche. Jørn Utzon set out to wipe architecture clean of personal signatures. Modernism had aspired to a similar kind of anonymous industrial expression in the 1920s, but somehow this was soon overtaken by the cult of the great artist. In Utzon's terms, a building succeeded if it reflected the processes of life. Only in this way did a work become a touchstone of community identity. It was not sufficient for it to draw attention to its designer, for affirming the common things binding people was a far greater purpose. In a deep and unchanging commitment, Utzon wanted the very opposite of the Renaissance idea of an artist-hero.

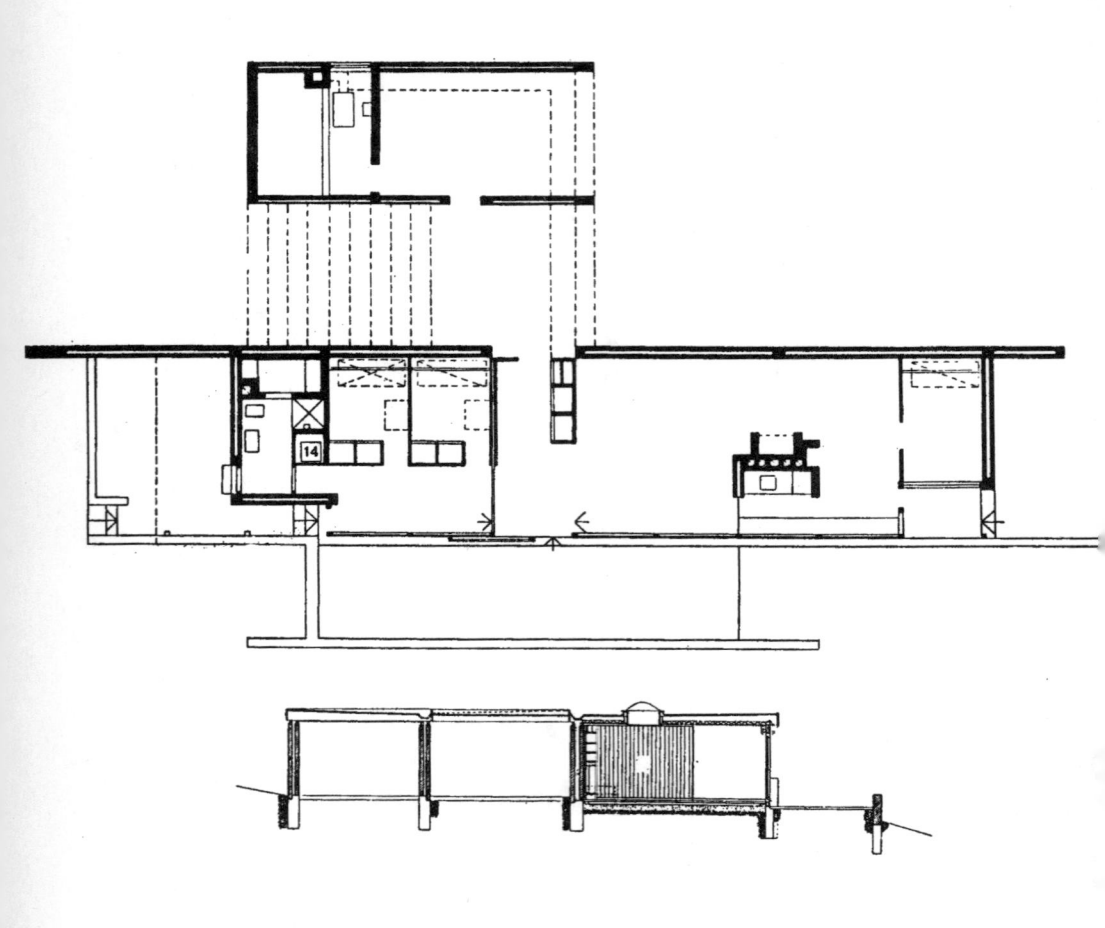

Utzon family house, Hammermill Wood, Hellebæk, April 1952. Above: Plan. Below: Section.

5

The Beech Forest
Hellebæk, 1950–1955

Adonis is always on the outside. He never holds a position of authority, is never a subordinate; whenever trouble is brewing his back is already turned, as he heads off into the sunlight. His life is like a dream; the dream of the individual hovering above the crowd, and this dream is part of the truth. But at the same time I am quite certain that this hovering has not come cheap. It exacts its price.

Peter Høeg, The History of Danish Dreams, 1995[1]

The decision to settle at Hellebæk was not surprising: Utzon's father lived there with his grandmother nearby, it was after all one of the most enchanting and beautiful areas of Denmark, and it was close to the sea.

Utzon appears destined to live on the fringes, at a distance outside the main centre. This was no accident; it was deliberate on his part, for it happened not once, but repeatedly. Although based on Utzon's love of nature and his desire to be in daily contact with it, other factors — such as his social phobia — may have been involved.

Hellebæk is about an hour's drive north of Copenhagen. Between them the gently rolling chocolate farmland is interspersed with dense thickets of trees, an occasional glassy lake is tucked furtively into a fold and white cubic farmhouses stand alone; all have a satisfying rhythm. Such random openness curtailed by the woods is gently reassuring. It is intimate, almost personal, in the way the windy prairie could never be. Nearing the coast, the dagger-like spires on Frederiksborg Castle stab the pale blue sky from the opposite shore of Lake Esrum.

Amongst his Academy year, Jørn Utzon was first to build his own house. It was some years later before his friends Erik Christian Sørensen and Halldor Gunnløgsson caught up.[2] This early start contributed to his reputation and boosted his career.

The forest bordering Strand Vej was newly planted when the house was built. Later, as the trees matured and the tree canopy thickened, Utzon's house was enveloped by the forest. To reach it meant following a winding forest trail for over a kilometre in and out among the beech trees. The beech forest occupies a very special region in the Danish psyche. The appearance of new leaves on the beech at the end of April is welcomed as the first sign that winter is over. It is associated with mushrooming in the autumn and quiet Sunday family strolls; it is a place for lovers to dream, but it also offers a refuge for solitary and lonely souls away from the oppressive crowding in the towns.

A beech forest is quite architectural, with its vertical smooth trunks serving as columns in a careless, endless, Gothic nave and open forest floor carpeted with decaying leaves. The long, extended arms of the outstretched branches explode into glorious spreading fans of translucent green that hover overhead and produce endlessly repeating, brilliant vaults. The fortuitous succession of open clearings and glades comes to resemble a large, green, fairy palace, whose meandering rooms and galleries flow from one to the next.

The dirt road to Utzon's house from the coast road continues for about a kilometre before it crosses the Hornbæk railway line, then it divides, and shortly after that on the left is Utzon's house. Breaking forth from the forest, it sits lit by sunlight in its own clearing. Against the dark green backdrop of foliage, its roof is a horizontal slash of black stained timber resting on yellow-brick walls. The yellow bricks give out a golden radiance like blocks of compressed sunlight.

The entrance is hidden under a connecting pergola. One arrives at the back — the front of the house faces south and is on the opposite side. From the approach to the entry, the sunlit walls under the dark-stained timber pergola beams are striated by a pattern of dark shadows brushed in diagonal stripes. The house is thrust back hard against the low rise. On the south side, away from the entrance, the ground falls gently into a small stream choked by giant spongy water lilies, which drains into a nearby pond.

Finding the house for the first time is an adventure in itself. You stumble unexpectedly upon it, as if by accident. It feels so strange, all by itself surrounded by the forest. This is the stuff of which fairytales are told. For all its modernity, the Utzon house suggests the woodcutter's cottage in a forest clearing. There are faint echoes from the world of childhood and fairytale and Hansel and Gretel's parental home 'hard by the great forest'. This is due almost entirely to the enchanting forest setting.

The remoteness of Utzon's house is an illusion. Although it appears to be surrounded by the Hammermill Wood, it is really located at the edge of the forest. The site forms the corner of a large land parcel beside Hellebækgaard Close.[3] Utzon acquired the 1.27 ha site in two stages, first buying a lot in 1952 on which he built his house, then adding a second block adjoining it on the west side in 1958.[4]

In this and other subsequent deals, Utzon demonstrated he was an excellent judge of real estate value. His ability to drive a bargain may derive from his merchant forefathers, but his guiding principle was always aesthetic. Utzon valued sites for their beauty, not as commodities.

Around this time, at the beginning of the 1950s, Utzon was affected by two family tragedies; his mother died suddenly and not long afterwards his brother Leif lost a child in tragic circumstances. Jørn Utzon's mother, Estrid Valeska Utzon, died on 6 October 1951, six months before Utzon completed his new forest house. His older brother, Leif, was so troubled by the loss of his son he moved to France in 1952 to make a new start. Leif Utzon had married Annie Christensen in October 1943. He was a chemical engineer attached to Louens Kemiske Fabrik, which operated a large laboratory on the outskirts of Paris. Leif was placed in charge of a plant producing penicillin.

Although Jørn Utzon began work on his house in early 1950, it was not finished until April 1952.[5] Utzon was staying temporarily at Hornbæk, and he and his family needed a permanent place to live. At the time, its completion somehow added further to the poignancy and sadness of his loss.

Jørn Utzon's house was a further application of Aage Utzon's ideas on healthy living. Even making allowances for the severe material shortages of the 1950s, the house's amenities were extremely spartan. Utzon spent almost two years finalising the plan.[6] He kept the toilet and bedrooms, in particular, simple and practical – almost too much so, compared to the large family room and extensive outdoor terraces. The forest surrounding the house was incorporated as a sort of outdoor exercise extension for Utzon and his family to wander about in. The bathroom had a shower recess and the children's bedrooms lacked windows. A single ventilated skylight in the roof supplied daylight to them. Adjoining the dining area, the main bedroom was labelled as a study drawing-studio and doubled as a workroom. The food preparation area next to the glass wall was also reduced to a short galley kitchen and equipped with a single bench-cupboard and cooking alcove at the back of the fireplace.

Utzon explored a number of schemes before coming to a decision. The first scheme was based upon a Wright-inspired cruciform arrangement of two intersecting roofs. The second, influenced by Mies van der Rohe's Farnsworth House, became more open and pavilion-like. The final scheme was neither Wrightian nor Miesian, but a mixture. Instead of Mies's ultimate floating glass box with floor-to-ceiling glass walls on all four sides, Utzon stretched the pavilion volume sideways, and anchored it firmly to the ground.

The previous Wrightian concept was now simplified. Wright's thesis of the house as a dark protective cave was modified into a fluid vessel loosely framed by horizontal and vertical planar elements that effectively converted into a large sculpture.

The architectural composition was reduced to only three brick walls, which increased in height with each step back from the front; these were laid out on the ground one in front of the other so they overlap; they are of different lengths and are separated by two horizontal terraced platforms – one inside, one outside. The terrace-decks were staggered in the same manner as the walls, the floor inside forming one terrace, with the other overlooking the garden in front. The outdoor terrace was slightly lower and provided an outdoor extension of the day living area. The two terraces were connected by large sliding timber doors. At right angles to the wall at the back, the garage was enclosed by a separate fourth wall.

In simplifying his house into just a few vertical and horizontal planes – unlike Mies van der Rohe whose designs took on a pure elementary abstract expression that was removed from the human – Utzon introduced the idea of elemental planar spaces – his brick and timber planes are made from real materials. Utzon's house carries a human imprint because he has retained a Danish commitment to craft. The character and the individuality of each material matter very much to Utzon.

Utzon's Hellebæk house forms a stretched horizontal rectangle. It is hardened at the back and protected from the forest on the north by a high, continuous, yellow-brick wall. It appears visually larger than it actually is. By pressing the volume of the house against the back wall Utzon made the interior longer and hence shallower. The main south elevation is exaggerated in length compared to its depth and this makes it seem bigger. The spaces spill outwards, an effect that is enhanced further by carrying the back wall and the terrace-wall beyond the ends of the roof into the landscape.

The sculptural arrangement of the three walls combined with the two overlapping terraces repeated Mies van der Rohe's Farnsworth House at Plano, Illinois. The precise composition is withheld from visitors arriving by way of the forest to the north. Even from a short distance Utzon gives very little away. The inside is masked on the outside by the two opposed walls at either side of the entrance and by the carport.

Utzon's interior is much more psychologically secure than Mies's glass Farnsworth pavilion. Utzon is concerned with people's privacy. He overdoes this in the two bedrooms for the children, which are completely enclosed and have no windows. These bedroom cells were altogether too introverted and prison-like. Jørn Utzon recalled many years afterwards that his son Kim,

> *began by making holes in the walls with anything he could get his hands on, and as he grew older and could handle various tools, he made more elaborate holes ... but the holes made him very happy because he could use his imagination with them. Sometimes they were a snowfield with skiers, or a harbour with boats. And he dreamed up all kinds of little animals living in the holes.*[7]

The Utzon house represented a type of subdued rationalism. Whereas Mies van der Rohe suspended the floor and roof decks at Plano above the ground, and concealed the overhead structure by expressing the roof as a pure plane, Utzon excavated into the earth and threw up horizontal terraces that anchored his brick walls. His terraces produce a level base separate from nature, but still tied to the ground. Mies did the opposite by severing the physical connections to the site. His house floats in the air as if suspended there by magic.

Utzon's house opens to the south with the dining space and living room united in a large unfettered space which is interrupted at one end by the mass of a brick fireplace behind the kitchen. This blocked it from the dining area and the adjoining but separate study–main bedroom at the far end. At the opposite end of the open living area, the two children's bedrooms and play area could be isolated by a large sliding door. Next to them was the bathroom, toilet and sauna. The garage and furnace room were in a separate block.

The long living room is divided by blade walls which extend out from the lengthy back wall as perpendicular fingers. These have different lengths and terminate well before they reach the southern, glass wall. The back wall and the low retaining wall outside assist to frame the long garden terrace, which continued on past the roof eaves as a means of emphasising the horizontality of the house. Pine ceiling boards run the length of the house, both inside and out, and similar Oregon lining boards, fixed vertically, line the internal walls. The house was warmed by a system installed under the coir-fibre matting.

For simplicity, Utzon chose to use only a few materials throughout. They were yellow-grey brick, Oregon pine, built-up bituminous roof, and thick timber window frames and fascias all stained black. Utzon applied the principle he had observed in indigenous buildings, which use only a few materials. The result is a wonderful consistency.

Today Utzon's house is neglected and in need of maintenance. It was a key work which helped to open up the Danish house in the 1950s, and while it certainly was not the first, it was without doubt one of the finest examples of the open-plan principle at this time.

In 1952 Jørn Utzon took steps to place his professional life on a more secure footing. He began a partnership with two brothers in their building company, Erik and Henry Andersson, SAR,[8] at Helsingborg. The Anderssons' office was quite near Utzon, on the opposite side of Øresund, although it was in Sweden. The Andersson brothers had studied architecture at Gothenburg and came from a long line of Swedish master builders. Under this new arrangement, Jørn Utzon would produce designs for architectural competitions in association with their company, on the undertaking that where he was successful, the Anderssons would build the scheme. In the 1950s, an agreement such as this between an architect and a building contractor was still novel. It led to problems later on, though, after Utzon won the Opera House competition and found himself saddled with the Andersson brothers. Well before this, he had begun to find the association onerous because of the unsatisfactory way his ideas were translated into bricks and mortar. Initially, however, it gave him some measure of financial security.

Utzon continued to work with Arne Korsmo; in 1950, for instance, they designed a stool together and participated in a plan for Skoyen Upsala in Oslo (1952), but the relationship was more sporadic than continuous.

Utzon's two most memorable designs in 1953 were his third-prize entry for a pavilion at Langelinie in Copenhagen port, which looked like a tower of stacked champagne glasses, and his single-family house beside Lake Fure (Fure Sø) at Holte, in Zealand, immediately north of Copenhagen. Both schemes were near the water.

Langelinie Pavilion was similar to the tree-like Laboratory Tower which Frank Lloyd Wright had designed for the Johnson Wax Co. at Racine in Wisconsin, USA. However, in contrast to Wright's tower, the diameter of Utzon's circular floor plates diminished with height while the Laboratory Tower was assembled from alternating large and small plates. Utzon's tower had an eccentric silhouette that tapered upwards away from the water on the land side, but it presented a nearly vertical face to the harbour. The floor plates were supported by a central core consisting of two cylinders, one inside the other. The personal elevators and dumb waiters were in the smaller inner cylinder and around it wound a circular stair linking the floors, which was surrounded in turn by a second, structural, cellular concrete core containing the toilets.

The floor plates, of precast reinforced concrete, were supported on their underside by a system of circular and radial beams cantilevered from the slip-form core. The restaurants on the smaller mezzanine floors were connected to the lower main floors by a semi-circular stair on the perimeter edge. Plants were massed around each mezzanine floor perimeter to prevent diners accidentally falling over the edge. Each floor was stepped to divide the space into smaller, intimate areas suitable for party groups.

Utzon was extremely interested in the family house at this time. A year after he built his house at Hellebæk, he completed a second house at Holte (1952–3). His most challenging problem at Holte was to build a house using only a limited kit of pre-constructed units which could be brought onto the site and erected speedily. With its uniform roof width, Utzon's Hellebæk house anticipated the Holte house, but at Holte he took this approach much further. The Holte house has sturdy concrete piers which raise it stork-fashion, one storey above the marshy ground of Fure Sø. The principal volume of the house consists of a long open space, which is quite narrow, much the same as Utzon's own house. Its post-and-frame structure was new and was the first application by Utzon of his concept of basing a building on a limited kit of ready-made standard parts.

For the basic skeleton, Utzon used compound precast concrete pillars having an inside, single-storey-height pillar coupled to a double-storey one on the outside. The step registered the load from the main, second floor. It also provided a seat for the long concrete perimeter beams which sat side by side on the short inside pillars. This was repeated with the long edge-beams framing the roof. Once the basic precast concrete construction kit was erected, pre-cut lengths of timber floor and roof joists were quickly lifted in position between the two lines of supports. As a building method it was very straightforward.

On the ground floor are the entry hall, staircase and incidental areas such as a cupboard and heating room, storage for bicycles and the family motor car. The living areas, including the kitchen, and the bedrooms are on the upper floor. The plan is linear, similar to a railway carriage, with rooms lined up side by side. The main living area is open, with the enclosed four bedrooms ranged along the back. At the lake end, the living area is extended outside onto a veranda. To stiffen the frame, Utzon placed the kitchen in the middle next to the staircase. Structurally, the house has five bays each subdivided into 12 by a 4 × 3 grid, which determined the placement of walls and modulated the fenestration.

The walls on the lake side were double-glazed for additional insulation. In the large gap between the glass, Utzon experimented with sodium silicate waterglass to absorb condensation. Away from the lake, facing the street, the walls were lined outside with golden larch vertical boards treated to enhance their natural texture. The structural and infill elements were picked out and accentuated with strong colour: black for the reinforced concrete pillars and red for the beams to distinguish the active structure more readily from the remaining passive, non-structural, supported elements.

The frame reads clearly from a distance. There is no confusion about how the house has been made, for its match-stick construction has been accentuated by the strong black-and-red colour scheme to distinguish it from a cellular collection of brick boxes. The entire building has a child-like simplicity that makes it easy to comprehend in a glance. It stands comfortably beside the dark waters of the lake, shielded by a belt of russet reeds, its transparent glass wall catching and mirroring the reflection of a leaning tree in the water. A small clinker rowing skiff moored at a jetty increases the rustic charm. There is a softened quality in Utzon's application of Modernism, and a simplicity which, despite the modular expression of the structure and the rationalism of his daring use of bold colour, has an irrefutable Danish character – one that perhaps arose from Utzon's response to such details as the lake and the boat. The Holte house may contain debts to Mies van der Rohe, but it is very Danish in its way, and instantly recognisable as an Utzon work.

Utzon designed a number of other private, single-family houses at this time. These include Villa Arnung at Nærum (1953), completed with another graduate from the Royal Academy, Bent Alstrup, two villas at Rungsted, followed two years later by the Villa Lillesoe at Furesoen (1955) and Villa Frank at Vedbæk (1955), also with Bent Alstrup. Rungsted and Vedbæk are situated along Øresund north of Copenhagen. The Villa Frank house was a long, low, horizontal house with a flat roof, quite similar to Utzon's own house at Hellebæk.

These years were financially difficult for Jørn Utzon. Entering competitions was expensive, and even when he was successful the prize money barely covered the cost of submitting a design. Competitions alone did not pay the household bills and a family cannot dine on glory for long. Utzon hoped that one of the competitions would result in a building commission. In the meantime, his reputation as a designer was growing.

By 1955 Utzon's children were growing older, Jan was nine and had started school. Meanwhile Aage, his father, was 70 and was living alone in the gate-keeper's cottage at Bøssemagergade 72. This was a pretty cottage with white walls and thickly thatched roof, at the top end of Bøssemagergade next to the lake. It had been built in 1735 and was reputed to be the oldest dwelling in Hellebæk, a fact that must have reinforced Aage Utzon's perception of his family's history. It was old like himself, but was only a short distance from Utzon's modern forest house. Aage lived there surrounded by boat models and drawings and his large collection of family portraits. In return for the use of the cottage, Aage acted as the gate-keeper for the nearby forest. The duties were not strenuous and gave him access to the fishing in the lake.

Jørn Utzon was determined to remain independent and work by himself. Wherever possible, he preferred to work on projects in association with other architects in an informal rather than in a permanent arrangement. He could easily have secured a position in a large office, but he refused to surrender his independent architectural status.

The 1953 Skaanske low-cost housing competition was directed at a new family house prototype to be constructed on the edge of existing towns. Utzon won first prize, but as usual no commission came from it. Utzon's scheme is important because it contains the earliest demonstration of his concept of the courtyard-house type which later became a feature of his group housing projects, such as the Kingo houses (1957–60) outside Helsingør, and his Fredensborg terrace houses (1962–3). The Skaanske house in Scania introduced Utzon's concept of the house as a distinct refuge and realm for the family. It marks the beginning of his almost obsessive emphasis on personal privacy at the expense of communality.

Much the way that the forest insulated and gave his Hellebæk house its privacy, in the Skaanske design a 3 m high wall surrounded the dwellings on every side. This gave the courtyard houses a prison-like aspect, and was in fact extremely introverted and inhospitable seen from the outside. Utzon visualised the family as a unit that has to be protected on the outside to preserve its independence, which might explain this aspect of the design.

A free realm around the family is achieved, but only at the expense of imprisoning the family. The enclosing, outside walls not only shut the world out, they also shut the family in. Privacy is undoubtedly achieved, but at considerable cost to the family by severing its outside connections with the community at large and its neighbours. Utzon's courtyard house restates his own choices and is based on a hermetic model of the family.

From the time they were introduced in the 1920s, one-and-a-half and two-storey rowhouses proved very popular in Denmark. This was in spite of the impossibility of ensuring outdoor privacy in these houses because all outdoor areas were invariably overlooked by neighbouring houses. In 1953 the courtyard house as a self-contained family unit was a relatively new idea.

Scania, in the south-western corner of Sweden, was originally a part of Denmark prior to being lost in 1685, and shared many cultural similarities. It is a flat, bleak, windswept country. In the 1950s, the population of Scania grew rapidly by enlarging its existing towns, principally around the town edges. The question arose of how best to deal with the population increase without destroying the countryside near the towns. Also, in such an exposed landscape protection from the wind was of paramount importance. One obvious way to accomplish this was to transform the dwelling into a sun trap by adopting courtyards which excluded the wind in winter.

The *firlænge*-type farmhouse, with four wings around a courtyard, was common to both Scania and Denmark. Such farmhouses existed around Ålborg when Utzon was a boy and on much of the west coast of Jutland, four-winged traditional Danish courtyard examples were very typical.[9] But Utzon's actual inspiration for his Skaanske design was not immediately Danish, but Chinese. The Chinese house was a refuge, surrounded by a wall that segregated it completely from adjoining houses. This pattern of building the house around a courtyard developed during the Han period in the third century BC. In ensuing centuries it became the customary type of Chinese domestic architecture. Like so many of Utzon's borrowings, he did not take the idea directly but adapted it to take into account contemporary social factors and technical considerations.

In his Scania courtyard-house sketches, Utzon set out to demonstrate how the basic walled-house could be grouped compactly along streets in towns, producing a formal, monolithic appearance. This could be varied in the country, where he proposed a staggered arrangement so the housing was irregular and the single-house units read more distinctly. The individual skillion roofs rest on the outside perimeter wall and could either be continuous or interrupted in sections, depending on the number and disposition of rooms. Where there were no abutting rooms, the wall height was lowered to expose the courtyard to the outside.

The Chinese courtyard house had evolved to deal with an extremely harsh winter climate, far more intense than in either Denmark or Scania. Culturally the Danes had very little in common with the Chinese, and Danes found this total exclusion to be very alien. Not surprisingly, the Kingo houses were heavily criticised when they appeared, being called 'Arab houses'.

The courtyard-and-terrace idea had considerable merit and Utzon persevered with it. The customary placement of a detached house at the middle of an allotment causes a range of problems that is not easily resolved. For instance, it is extremely uneconomic and inefficient in its consumption of land and services. In the courtyard arrangement Utzon proposed, the kitchen, bathrooms and core services were located near the street mains and this reduced the site development costs. In addition, the 3 m high wall enabled home owners to develop their houses individually when it suited them. Furthermore, pushing the house to the site boundary avoided squabbles between neighbours over hedge-cutting or overshadowing by trees and such like.

The primary benefit of the courtyard model was its efficiency and its flexibility. It allowed each owner to add rooms as the family grew in size, and simultaneously it left the central area free to be used according to the owners' wishes. To explain all this, Jørn Utzon invented a series of stories to illustrate the development alternatives. He started with the grandfather who lives with his relatives; another family lives in a perpetual mess; while another followed the story of a young couple who build a single bedroom and kitchen in a walled-off enclosed rectangle. In this last scenario, the husband left soon after the house was finished, and the wife then added an extra section and opened a small bakery to support herself.[10]

Utzon explained the advantages of the courtyard house in terms of its flexibility. His stories explored the individual history of each dwelling and stressed how each could develop independently of the others. As an architect, Utzon liked to imagine future possibilities. If organic architecture meant anything this was it: a building must grow in response to life. He saw architecture as something that is mutable, and an immutable architecture as the very antithesis of organic. Architecture should be forever unfinished, exactly as life is never finished.

The Chinese courtyard plan enabled Utzon to cope with enormous variety, and simultaneously to deal with external chaos by isolating the house inside a hard outer shell. Seen from outside, his housing groups are unified and ordered, each unit expressing minor differences that are only visible on the inside.

The chief limitation of the courtyard house was the initial high cost of the wall, which could be as much as the completed house. If the cost was amortised over several centuries or many generations, as in China, the cost was not prohibitive. But in Denmark such a design involved a considerable financial burden that could not be lessened without reducing the wall.

Utzon designed a house for his family in Morocco in the early 1950s but eventually decided not to proceed. Four years after his mother's death, on 12 February 1955, Erik, Utzon's younger brother, died in Morocco. He had just turned 30 the previous October. Erik studied forestry and sat for his exams as a forest manager in 1953 before taking up a casual position as assistant on one of Ostasiatisk Kompagni's (East Asiatic Company) large plantations on the coast of Africa. He had been living there for only two years. His death may have been suicide, however the circumstances remain unclear to this day. Erik was reported to be drinking heavily at the time and this may have been a factor in his drowning. Certainly, if Erik was as easily affected by alcohol as Jørn, alcohol may have contributed to the tragedy.

Above: Sketch of clouds over the sea. Utzon emphasises the firm horizontal line of the water, coincidentally matched by the underside of the hovering clouds.
Below: Preliminary sketch for the vaults of the Sydney Opera House. This indicates his intention of dynamic floating forms above an artificial plateau.

6

A Cathedral in the Air
Hellebæk, 1956

> *Everything that is planned for the Opera House is based on the desire to take people from their daily routine into a world of fantasy, a world which they can share with the musicians and actors.*
>
> Jørn Utzon, July 1964[1]

The Sydney Opera House unites dream with reality. It excites wonder, which is unusual for a modern work of architecture. To build it was a prodigious engineering feat which, in turn, resulted in one of the great artistic sagas of the twentieth century. That it happened at all was largely an accident. It was also due in no small measure to the visionaries who conceived the idea, and to Utzon, whose dogged determination and imagination in the first instance made it happen.

In the years from 1944 to 1956 Jørn Utzon participated in more than 18 competitions from which he won seven first prizes, four second prizes, three third prizes and four fourth places, plus three honourable mentions. This was an impressive result, but it was no more than that since it did not land him any commissions. Denmark's economy was improving slowly, however what few architectural opportunities existed were keenly contested.

Early in 1956 Utzon received a commission for 20 or so

rowhouses outside Skjern, in south-west Jutland, which he shared with his friend Bent Alstrup. There had been few opportunities till then for Jørn Utzon to apply his courtyard-house concept; even so, he was forced to dilute it at Skjern to the extent that the development was nearly indistinguishable from the neighbouring conventional rowhouses. Examined closely, aspects of the courtyard arrangement can be detected, but at a very embryonic, tentative stage. This was achieved by placing a detached shed in front of each house to create a semi-enclosed court. The modified rowhouses at Skjern demonstrate the difficulties Utzon encountered in applying his courtyard concept.

The second half of 1956 was occupied by the Sydney Opera House competition. Even so, Utzon faced other distractions, including the Louisiana museum.

Knud W. Jensen, a wholesaler and literati who had accompanied the writer Baroness Karen Blixen on a trip to Greece, purchased the old Louisiana manor house on a magnificent site at Humlebæk overlooking Øresund. He held a house-warming for friends there at Christmas in 1955. Jensen set about looking for an architect in his thirties, about the same age as himself, to design a new type of art museum on his property. He decided to approach Utzon in 1956. When he telephoned him, Utzon protested, 'I don't have time', and warned Jensen that he could not look at anything for a year. Undeterred, Jensen responded by offering to come and see Utzon because he had heard so much about his house. On hearing this, Utzon agreed that Jensen could come, but cautioned him that he was hardly ever home, and suggested he 'just walk around and look in the windows as much as you like'.[2] Later, when Jensen heard that Utzon had been given the Opera House project in Sydney, he asked Vilhelm Wohlert to be the architect; the latter brought in Jørgen Bo, and together they completed the art museum in 1958.

Utzon missed a magnificent opportunity at Humlebæk. It was one of many such sacrifices he would make on the way to completing the Opera House in Sydney.

Well into the Opera House competition, in October 1956,

Jørn Utzon received a further offer of work: 'I was asked to accept a post by UNESCO in Egypt involving planning of rural communities in the valley of the Nile'.[3] It was just as well he did not accept the offer. Egypt chose this moment to launch a war against Britain and France over Suez. At around the same time, Israeli troops invaded the Sinai on 29 October, following the withdrawal of the last British troops from the Suez Canal zone four months earlier on 13 June. Two days later, French and British aircraft were strafing and bombing Egyptian airfields. Denmark did not have much to offer, but at least it was not in a war zone.

Utzon was undeterred. His year was fully taken up with participating in the international competition for the design of the Sydney Opera House. The competition had been advertised on 6 December 1955, registration was invited by 15 March 1956, and 3 December was nominated as the closing date for submissions. This left competitors less than nine months to formulate a design. With the Melbourne Olympic Games in the news, the competition attracted a staggering 881 registrations.[4] So Utzon had already committed himself to the Sydney Opera House competition when he received the offer of the UNESCO job in Egypt. Also, by October Lis was six months pregnant with their third child. Egypt was hardly an ideal place to take the newborn Kim.

The Sydney Opera House competition coincided with the 1956 Olympic Games in Melbourne. Politically, it was Sydney's response to the Melbourne Games, which were throwing the international spotlight on Australia. There was an important difference in the world's perception of the two cities, for although in Melbourne the focus was exclusively sporting, in Sydney the emphasis shifted to culture and music. As demonstrated by the large number of entrants, the competition attracted enormous international interest.

Utzon could not afford to concentrate exclusively on his competition entry. He made a start in May and spent six months working on it whenever he could find the time. In between, he earned income from routine projects. Erik

Andersson, a Swedish architect and his unofficial business partner, who lived and worked 30 minutes away by ferry on the other side of the Sound at Helsingborg, assisted Utzon in the early stages with practical construction advice. Later, when Utzon assumed the more dominant role and the concept took shape, the entry was submitted under Utzon's name alone.

Utzon devoted a far greater proportion of his time to thinking about the problem than to actual drawing. The longer than usual time allowed for the competition was an advantage, because it gave him the necessary time to develop his thoughts.

Like many of the other foreign entrants, Jørn Utzon had never visited Sydney. The competition programme was released in mid-February along with the competition booklet, known as the *Brown Book,* which set out the conditions and contained ten black and white photographs of the Bennelong Point site from various viewpoints around the city and the harbour foreshore. These were supplemented by a large site plan. However, it was impossible to get any feeling of the scale of the site from this information. Bennelong Point, at the bottom of Macquarie Street, was a tangle of tramlines which terminated at the crenellated, pseudo-Gothic brick tram shed. On the northern tip of the Point was a park with a semi-circular avenue of fig trees. On both the east and west sides of the site, the existing wharves were in varying states of disrepair.

The conditions of the competition, which stated the building requirements and priorities for the use of each space, made it abundantly clear that concerts were to take priority over opera in the large hall. This was later confused by the use of the word 'opera' in the title of the competition, 'National Opera House'. The maximum height of any proposed building was restricted to 45.7 m (150 ft) to comply with Sydney's existing heights of buildings regulations.

Appendix 4 of the conditions added such further requirements as a landscaped forecourt or square with extensive paving – presumably on the Italian model – to provide an attractive approach and setting for the proposed building. This was matched by a similar landscaped area on the northern tip of

Bennelong Point facing the harbour. A boulevard was proposed along the western edge of the point outside the site in order to link Circular Quay to the Opera House. It was these later requirements which excited Utzon's interest; he disliked having to consider a building in isolation and was stimulated by the prospect of treating all of Bennelong Point as a single entity.

Jørn Utzon's entry embodied some of his key discoveries from before 1956. But it is not enough to analyse the design in terms of Utzon's previous work; to do so leaves much of its originality unaccounted for. The design was the result of a soaring leap of the imagination. It was very daring and took many risks. In its way it was comparable to the launch of the first Russian *Sputnik*, which orbited the earth on 4 October 1957. It has not been stressed strongly enough in the past how brilliant and well-conceived Utzon's original proposal was. Looking back, the other entries were almost comic, not to be taken seriously on such a magnificent site. Utzon's design was so much superior it stood out from the competition. There really was no comparison. If doubts arose later on, this occurred because the public, the politicians and quite a few architects were stunned by Utzon's audacity and inventiveness. The Opera House in Sydney was an undertaking on a scale and complexity few people properly appreciated. Indeed, few politicians understood the implications of this complexity in terms of budget, time and planning. New South Wales's bickering politicians, whose first priority was their own re-election, were not equipped, either intellectually or in terms of providing leadership, to cope with the challenge.

The requirements of the competition called for a large hall accommodating 3000 to 3500 people that was to be devoted primarily to symphony concerts, with large-scale opera as a secondary use, followed by ballet and dance. There was to be a second, smaller hall seating 1200 people for dramatic presentations, intimate opera, chamber music, concerts, recitals and even lectures. The auditoria had to be designed to suit each of these uses, and the conditions listed the various uses in their order of priority.

The building was to be much more than an opera house; it was a performing arts centre after the 1950s mould, then a popular trend. By bringing a major theatre, concert hall and opera and ballet venue under one roof, it was hoped that the cost of providing administration, workshops, rehearsal rooms, restaurants, broadcasting and media facilities, and publicity could be pooled and result in a saving to the overall budget. There was also an expectation that such arts centres would be more efficient and cost-effective than dispersed facilities in individual theatres. Additionally, it was hoped that creating a single omnibus centre for the performing arts in a city would result in greater visibility and community focus for these arts.

As well as the large and small halls, which were the key facilities in the complex, the competition brief asked for a restaurant to seat about 250 people; lounge; cloakrooms; other bars and refreshment areas to serve the theatre patrons; plus two meeting rooms for 100 and 200 people respectively. The brief appeared to be very comprehensive and well considered, at least superficially. However, there were many unforeseen snags.

Today, it is customary to assess how feasible the requirements are – in short, whether the project can be realised practically – before announcing a competition. No one thought to do this with the Opera House competition. There was no calculation of the minimum volumes needed in the two large auditoria to satisfy accepted acoustic criteria and no check on whether the multi-use concept for the major hall would work acoustically.

The critical decision in the Opera House competition was the placement of the two main auditoria on Bennelong Point. The site dimensions, especially the minimum 97.5 m width of Bennelong Point, restricted the range of possible arrangements – the site was approximately twice as long as it was wide. Most competitors arranged the main theatres longitudinally, either back to back with a shared stage tower in the middle, or front to front. As an alternative, a few even placed the two theatres across the Point so that their foyers faced the proposed boulevard along the western Circular Quay edge. Utzon was the only competitor to locate the two large auditoria side by side, facing the city.

Utzon resisted drawing a line around the Opera House that would separate it from its surroundings. His concept was of a building interacting with and providing a focus for its setting. He realised, as few others did,

> that this peninsula popping out in a harbour would mean that it would be looked upon from all sides and even might be looked upon from above. Furthermore, because the site was rather small, I came to the conclusion that I would have to make one architectural unity out of this whole peninsula. Everything had to be planned, nothing left to circumstances. The rim of the cape, the original view and my building had to be a unity.[5]

His conclusion, as in the Crystal Palace competition a decade earlier, seemed self-evident: 'The Gods see from all sides'. As a sailor, Utzon was more used than most to seeing things from every side.

If the site had been in the heart of the city surrounded by neighbouring buildings, this would have dictated the usual conventional urban solution. That was not so. Utzon was able to take advantage of the splendid scenic possibilities offered by Bennelong Point to free the theatres of the blank-box that was invariably built in central-city sites to house the fly-towers. Sydney's heart was its harbour. Utzon, as a Dane who had grown up beside a fjord, understood that implicitly. Conventionally, the prominent stage tower rising to 30 m or more would be relegated to the back of a site, on a back street, where it would not be noticed. On Bennelong Point this approach was out of the question. Everything would be visible. Utzon commented later that his scheme contained 'five elevations'. It had water on three sides, which necessitated jettisoning the standard urban solution. As he later remarked, 'If you build a normal theatre it will look like a boot with the stage-house as the top part of the boot, and if you put two boots here you do not see the plateau, you will actually destroy it.'⁶

Visualising the site required a tremendous feat of imagination on the part of the non-Australian participants in the competition. Utzon recalled:

> *There was quite a lot of information, but as it so often goes with programs and rules like these they have been made by people who knew everything about the questions, and they could not know what the competitors as architects specially wanted to know ... They could not know the importance of the colour of the sea or about the shades of light ... These were things one had to find out for oneself.*⁷

Utzon devoured everything he could about Sydney, including descriptions from Australian literature. The material in Denmark was scarce; in frustration he turned to sea charts obtained in Copenhagen and from these he was able to measure the distances and gauge how far apart Circular Quay and the Sydney Harbour Bridge were, to gain a proper sense of scale. His appreciation may have been rudimentary, but it gave him a better feel for Sydney and its harbour.

For the duration of the competition period, Utzon was totally absorbed by the project. He derived a lot of pleasure from the work and the question of whether he won or lost soon ceased to be important. He reflected later:

> *You feel during a work like this, that everything you are doing has something to do with this special project ... If you go for a walk in the woods or stroll along the beach you look at things with new eyes in relation to your project.*

And look with new eyes he did. Years afterwards, Utzon recalled his initial inspiration:

> *I stood looking at clouds over a low coastline, and I had a look at Kronborg Castle at Elsinore, and at Gothic churches. There you have forms against a horizontal line*

like the sea or the clouds without a single vertical line, nothing constituting a weight, and with forms that are different from all angles.[8]

Kronborg Castle guards the northern gateway of Øresund – the passage leading into the Baltic between Denmark and Sweden – at its narrowest. As a shape, Kronborg unites the horizontal and the vertical: the horizontality of the bastions and terraces across the seafront is opposed by the emphatic vertical thrust of the castle. The dual nature of Kronborg's horizontal base and vertical mass impressed Utzon.

Kronborg provided Utzon with something concrete which set him thinking. He had sailed around it many times and it was very familiar to him. More importantly, it was something he could return to and consult. He was fascinated by the way the castle changed depending on where he viewed it. The gun terraces supplied a solid base for the rectangular palace above. This assisted Utzon to visualise Bennelong Point and how his opera house might look.

It also helped him in other ways. Many of the competition entries housed the theatres inside bulky square boxes. In desperation, some looked for ways to camouflage the ugly theatre stage towers by tilting walls or sculpting them, often with clumsy or unsatisfactory results. Kronborg Castle proved conclusively how a large, isolated building might be placed on a point. It helped Utzon decide about the best way to deal with such an exposed form. Although the castle's massive, light-grey, sandstone walls on four sides around the central courtyard possessed little by way of decoration, the overall starkness was relieved by the thrilling individuality of its spires and towers. These introduced an unexpected, whimsical note on top that diverted attention away from the generally sombre appearance, by pointing to the sky. The extensive grass terraces opposite the Sound anchored the castle firmly to the earth. Kronborg Castle has a disturbing theatricality that is hard to miss and which is heightened by the occasional presence of dark storm clouds. The best time to look at it is in the morning with the sun behind it. In the early dawn, its massive bulk and erect spires shiver in the chilly golden light. At the end of the Helsingør marina seawall, the castle looms in the distance, a dark black rectangle outlined against a luminous curtain of fugitive light, its jagged outline rearing from the sun-flecked sea.

For Utzon, the conclusion from Kronborg must have been irrefutable – the main thing to avoid was any suggestion of a rectangular box. His aim should be to turn the Sydney Opera House into a sculpture-in-the-round. Like Kronborg, one part would grow out of the solid rock; the other part, the theatres, like a low cloud, would merge with the sky. There were to be just these two elements – an earth platform and a roof leaping into the air from it – contrasting passive and active.

Utzon's interest in sailing influenced his work in a multitude of ways. He never forgot what he saw when sailing. To steer a yacht, the helmsman has to peer through the gap between the foot of the sail and the gunwale. A similar gap exists between the underside of the shell roofs of the Opera House and the terraced base. Concealing or framing a view in this fashion draws the eye deeper through the tear in the visual fabric.

There is an early photograph of Leif and Jørn racing off Helsinbørg in a sailing skiff: Jørn stretches out and balances on the bulwark; the two young men seem close and there is an obvious familiarity to gestures as they share a moment of excitement. After the war ended, Jørn and Leif Utzon once went sailing in the Kattegat. Inadvertently they forgot their passports and wandered into Swedish waters. While it was an understandable mistake, the Swedish patrol which intercepted them was not amused. It arrested them and held them until they could verify their identities.

When Utzon opened up the auditorium interiors around the sides and back in his design by incorporating movable glass walls, they assumed a similar appearance to an ancient Greek amphitheatre in a hillside. Everything – music, audience, architecture, the natural physical setting – was meant to be open from the inside to the outside and in direct physical contact with its surroundings.

Seated in either of the auditoria, audiences would look across the harbour and feel the wet sea breeze on their faces while they listened. It would be like Delphi, but it would be better in some ways because the audience was protected overhead by a wonderful suspended acoustic shell of timber. Utzon's aim was to recreate the ancient primitive connection between music and water and earth and sky. If his vision faltered because of practical concerns, Utzon could not quite let go of it and persisted with it in his later drawings.

It was not an entirely new idea. The old Concert Hall at Tivoli in Copenhagen, which the Nazis destroyed in the summer of 1944, also had glass walls.[9] This Arabian-style Concert Hall was designed to allow the audience to see the gardens while they listened to the music, which produced a very special magic by enhancing the illusion that the concert was taking place in the open air. Architecture and music and landscape interacted and merged into one experience, much the way that we imagine it did in the ancient Greek amphitheatre. The gesture was a reminder of the lost roots of music in dance and magic ritual. The Danes loved the Old Tivoli Theatre so much that when the new theatre was rebuilt in 1956, it used glass walls in the same Tivoli-style as the earlier theatre.

In his competition scheme Utzon included a system of inclined tilt-a-wall panels that could be raised out of sight between the auditorium ceiling and the roof shells. This represented a considerable advance over the old Tivoli Concert Hall but the idea was the same. Whereas the Tivoli Concert Hall used two glass walls, one inside to enclose the auditoria and another outside one, in his Opera House scheme Utzon suggested inner 'overhead' Oregon pine doors between the floor and theatre's timber acoustic ceiling which could be closed or opened at will. In the foyer and hallways outside, there was a second series of matching 'overhead glass doors'. This would have permitted audiences during intermissions to enjoy the harbour without getting up from their seats, while sheltering under the suspended wooden acoustic shell.[10]

When Utzon did his drawings, he was keenly aware that the judging panel consisted solely of architects who were trained to read technical architectural drawings. This allowed him to simplify his information:

> You could stress certain things very clearly, and in a very simple way, and leave out certain details, because you knew that the project would be judged by experts. In my designs I have done everything to underline the idea and to leave out everything which could disturb the general idea.[11]

There may be a degree of hindsight in this statement, an attempt by Utzon to answer subsequent criticism in the panel's report that his schematic submission was incomplete, in which it was stated, 'The drawings submitted are simple to the point of being diagrammatic.'[12]

Utzon did the competition drawings alone without the extensive resources of a large commercial office, which forced him to simplify and eliminate extra detail where it was not needed. Utzon also wished to stress the main idea, therefore a more diagrammatic approach suited his intention. He made a virtue out of his limited means.

The drawings were executed in soft pencil on a flimsy yellow butter paper with a minimum of elaboration.[13] The lines are generally firm and confident but in places they have a faintly tremulous movement that gives them life. This also reminds us that they were drawn by a human hand, not a machine. The base of the building, which was to be clad in large slabs of natural stone, was lightly shaded in pencil to make it more three-dimensional. The soffit of the shells was also lightly shaded to distinguish the upper- from the under-surfaces. Surprisingly, Utzon failed to show the external glass walls between the base and the roof shells – perhaps because he wished to indicate how the auditorium shells would nestle inside them. In all of the elevations (side views), the shell roofs were drawn completely open, and this gave them a somewhat surreal quality.

Utzon sought a sculptural solution; to achieve it, he worked directly in three dimensions. In a 1992 interview, Utzon explained:

> *I wanted to get it right. This was a job that was very important to me. In principle it was very simple. I wanted something that looked like it would grow, as Australia was growing. It was just like sculpture. I worked like a sculptor; I tried to shape the things and I made many models. It came from model work, more than from paper work. You couldn't have [done] this on paper because it would not be alive.*[14]

The drawings record the outcome of the model-making process. It is impossible to produce such complex shapes as these on paper – this can only be accomplished by working with a model initially, and later recording the results in a drawing. Erich Mendelsohn – an influential German architect whose Expressionist forms are based on curves – produced a series of fantastic sketches after 1914 which at first seem very similar to the Opera House shape. These, however, possess a decidedly two-dimensional graphic quality, unlike Utzon's drawings which are intrinsically three-dimensional.[15] Utzon could not have derived the shapes any other way. The extreme subtlety of the roof shapes confirm this. Such a result was inconceivable based only on 'paper work', as Utzon no doubt discovered from his visit to Alvar Aalto's office in Finland. They also demonstrated Utzon's ongoing commitment to an ideal organic form:

> *instead of making a square form, I have made a sculpture – a sculpture covering the necessary functions, in other words, the rooms express themselves, the size of the rooms is expressed in these roofs. If you think of a Gothic church, you are closer to what I have been aiming at.*
>
> *Looking at a Gothic church, you will never be finished with it – when you pass around it or see it against the sky. It is as if something new goes on all the time and it is so important – this interplay is so important that together with the sun, the light and the clouds, it makes it a living thing.*[16]

No words could be clearer or more succinct in conveying Utzon's aims. He rarely strayed from it even under the most intense political pressure. Over 30 years later, we hear echoes of the same organic ideal, when he compares the idea of an Australian identity with nature as forever changing. The incompleteness of the roof forms make us aware that they are but incomplete fragments removed from a sphere that is whole.

Utzon separated the theatre performance spaces (the halls, foyers, ticketing areas and public toilets), from the service functions, which he housed out of sight in the solid plateau base. This was an important decision that influenced the rest of the design. The wedge-shaped platform occupied the full width of the site, began at the southern extremity and rose in a series of terraces towards the north end of Bennelong Point. Utzon placed the two halls on top of the platform. They are next to one another, with their axes inclined inwards so they intersect at the commencement of the monumental concourse stairway. The western broadwalk extended from the platform over the water on concrete piers. Thus the platform was widest at its northern end, where it had to accommodate the two fan-shaped auditoria.

In older, traditional opera houses, the side- and backstage areas were normally much larger than the auditorium itself. This presented what must have seemed an insoluble problem for Utzon because he lacked the space for side- and backstages at the same level. Instead, he discovered an ingenious way around this involving the use of a system of stage lifts known as paternosters. This is akin to the arrangement on aircraft carriers for lifting aircraft kept below up onto the flight deck. When a stage set was needed, it could be hoisted vertically onto the stage by means of a lift. The stage scenery and props are loaded on wagons, rolled onto the large lifts, and then lifted to the stage level. This had the advantage that it left the stage tidy and free of clutter. Utzon's plan concentrated the lifts in two groups in each circular revolving stage, with a further lift at the rear behind, giving each auditorium a total of three lifts.[17]

The terraces and stairs effectively constituted the roof over the stage- and prop-work areas, which were underneath. The

Vienna State Opera House was the only working example of such stage machinery at the time of Utzon's design.[18] The implementation of his scheme depended entirely on this new approach to stage technique. Utzon maintained that he introduced the two halls side by side from the start because it seemed right to him, and he did not investigate alternatives, even though his scheme was untenable without stage lifts because the restricted width of Bennelong Point prevented him from introducing side-stages.

In addition to these technical issues, Utzon was also anxious about the external effect of the building. He pictured the staircase adorned with flowers. In the report attached to the site plan, Utzon requested that the entrance staircase should be filled with 'flowers and plants in big boxes and jars' to supplement and increase the festive atmosphere initiated by the balustrade planter boxes:

> *The spectators will enter from a level about 15 m (50 ft) above the ground level, and even if they descend they will still have the feeling of being near the upper part. There are two stages and there will be an acoustic shell above the audience and the whole thing is then covered by a sort of rain-coat.*

This rather special rain-coat, as Utzon termed it, was hoisted over the stage towers and covered the amphitheatre seating areas. The semi-circular raked seating of the auditoria, harking back to Greek amphitheatre, were scooped out of the podium platform as if from a hillside, stepped up to the north, back wall where the platform was highest. The podium section and the theatre floor profiles were identical. The steps in each auditorium swept across the podium from one side past the limit of the auditorium seats to the edge of the platform. At the ends of each row of seats, the steps splayed backwards before they reached the outside staircases, which also doubled as fire-stairs. This was brilliant because it eliminated any need to provide space-consuming fire-stairs.

Utzon emphasised the powerful sculptural continuity of the terraces and steps by suppressing from the auditorium sketches all suggestions of individual seats.[19] The outline of each step was hatched in pencil and strengthened by a shadow line, to increase the unity of the platform, punctured by indentations and voids. Utzon rendered the design in such a way as to increase the similarities with the Yucatan temple complexes he had previously visited, which rose in a series of powerful, connected terraces. Patrons entered each foyer from underneath, behind the stage towers, by covered stairway tunnels leading from the ground level. These secondary staircases were smaller internal variations of the outside main concourse stairway, and as such they were treated as extensions of the main upper terrace, which further increased the unity of the monolithic platform.

The two halls had attenuated stages, which had been compressed to fit them in. As a consequence, they were much too narrow. The radial placement of the halls side by side with intersecting axes dictated that the halls would be widest on the north and narrowest at the stages – the position, in traditional auditoria, where the width is usually greatest. This was the price Utzon had to pay for placing the halls side by side across Bennelong Point.

In the 'main section' – an imaginary cut through the vertical plane on the long axis – of the Major Hall, Utzon indicated a nest of roof shells. There was a low shell to begin with about 14 m high covering the southern foyer of the hall; immediately behind it stood the highest shell, climbing 45 m over the stage area and stage tower; further on and north of it were two smaller shells. These were much lower than the main shell and rose a modest 26 m and 14 m respectively above the base. The larger roof protected the auditorium, while part of the smaller, northernmost one fitted snugly inside its open mouth. This final shell was cantilevered over the balcony and bar refreshment areas, which have views of the harbour.

Although the roof shells were of different sizes, they had the same basic shape and so could all be fitted one within the other in the same manner as a nest of tables. Each consisted of a pair of unequal smaller shells resting against the other for stability; the triangular openings at their feet were bridged by two smaller side-shells. These formed a convex bridge between the main pair and were welded together so they are a single continuous roof unit. Each shell unit is a chair. The similarity with furniture may be purely coincidental, but it is as well to remember that Utzon, in common with many Danish contemporaries, took a keen and active interest in furniture design.

The three groups of roofs also resemble a swan family, two adults led by the cygnet in front. Such was the symbolic ambiguity of the three-element composition it evoked such divergent comparisons as ships' hulls, sails, nuns' habits and copulating turtles.

Except for the largest shell over the stage tower, whose ridge is steep, the outlines of the other roofs are generally prostrate and almost horizontal. The horizontal expression of the roofs recalls Frank Lloyd Wright's cantilevered roof overhangs. Utzon outdid Wright on this occasion. His cantilevered shell roof hoods stretch out 20 m, 25 m and 30 m. The overall horizontal expression of Utzon's competition shells indicate that, at least initially, he was inspired along similar organic lines to Wright.

The south elevation at the city end is more successful than the north elevation. Seen from the south, the ascent of the roofs and their interplay inside and out is both dramatic and satisfying. This rhythmic effect was accentuated by the flaring roof skirts at the base of each roof, which spread out around the edges. The grand staircase on which the roofs stand reaches a climax at the far northern end. The verticality of the stage housing was expressed externally by the largest shell, which Utzon drew without walls to emphasise the hand-in-glove relationship between the two. The roofs leap from terrace to terrace. To protect pedestrians, Utzon introduced a wide balustrade at the edge of the platform which incorporated a planter box. The size and number of openings in the walls of the platform were kept small and horizontal to strengthen the solidity and homogeneity of the base. Utzon at first intended to clad it with stone slabs, possibly limestone, and drew the window and air-conditioning grills as long, horizontal slits two courses high. The masonry facing was chosen to make it appear as a natural extension of Bennelong Point.

The north elevation facing the harbour was clumsy in comparison to the southern one: seen from this direction on the plans the stacked concrete shells look very much like a row of Conquistador helmets. They give the appearance of being flattened and squashed as a result of perspective, which foreshortened the shells so they seem depressed instead of rising step by step with the platform terraces towards the opposite end.

The surfaces of the roof shells are rounded, smooth and swollen in appearance like a tyre's inner-tube. They press outwards like a yacht's sail when it is filled by a breeze. The shell surface billows and swells. To Utzon, the roofs were concrete clouds. They were meant to float and appear weightless.

Utzon visualised the Opera House as a duality: there was a heavy load-carrying base, contrasting with a series of light roofs; one was anchored in the earth, the other hovered above the base and belonged inspirationally to the sky. Between, in the zone of greatest tension, Utzon left everything empty. The audience was seated there and the entertainment takes place in the gap. This inclined void above the base is the energy focus of the entire building composition.

The glass walls helped to maintain the feeling of the void. This was especially critical along the sides and ends. It explains why Utzon proposed retractable rather than fixed walls, so they could be withdrawn into the roof space out of the way and out of sight. In his competition drawings, Utzon showed the shells open. This way, the space above the platform is extended into its surroundings, namely the harbour and nearby foreshore.

Architecturally, thin roof shells were not new. When a thin sheet is folded its strength is increased. Some of the important early experimental work on shell concrete roofs was carried out in Copenhagen in the 1930s. In the Radiohus building, designed by Vilhelm Lauritzen, a 12 cm (5 in) thick concrete shell spanned the 40 m wide concert hall auditorium. This represented an exciting new development in building technology, which later inspired Felix Candela, a Spanish architect who moved to Mexico in 1939, to build using thin shells. Candela's early calculations were based on the mathematics used on Lauritzen's concert hall.[20] Candela's structures may look free, but their shape was prescribed by complex geometry. Utzon's Opera House shells were not geometry-determined, they were free sculptural shapes, and this later caused severe problems.

Utzon's idea for his auditorium shells presents a series of parallels with Lauritzen's Radiohus concert hall – namely, it too had an internal acoustic ceiling suspended from a thin outer concrete roof shell. Lauritzen subdivided the inner acoustic ceiling of the 6 cm thick concrete shell with small corrugations to which were fixed narrow Oregon pine slats.[21] The chairs were covered with oxhide, the same as those selected by Utzon for the Opera House. Utzon's materials echo Lauritzen's, for Utzon's plan lined the auditorium ceiling with a sequence of standard-width Oregon pine panels which spanned the auditorium and followed an arc section that was highest in the middle and fell gently towards the stage opening. The same Oregon ceiling shapes were repeated across the northern balcony areas and the entry tunnel openings for the southern foyers. The Oregon timber, both inside and out, was to be painted red to reinforce the same compelling idea of homogeneity.

Because Utzon's competition drawings are so simple it was relatively easy to follow the ideas contained in his main section.[22] The base, or 'plateau', of the building is really little more than a great reinforced concrete box held up by pairs of slender columns, starting at ground level at the southern end and rising in stages in a series of terraces until the third level of the two halls is reached. At this point, the base recommenced its climb in a great flight of steps which, like the Spanish Steps in Rome, spread out across the platform. The amphitheatre curved around until it met the 9 m deep balcony terraces at the rear, there it stops, steps down 1 m near the edge, and allows patrons to look out at the harbour without being obstructed by the wide planter-balustrade.

Underneath Utzon's thin concrete 'rain-coat', the internal auditorium shells were to be suspended from the concrete roofs above the amphitheatre seating. In his drawings, Utzon failed to show how he proposed to do this. The gap around the edge between the bottom line of the auditorium ceiling and the floor was less than 2.5 m. The suspended ceiling is shown on the elevation as a series of steps that match the floor section and stop at the stage. The stage tower is indicated very diagrammatically without any detail. It is also stepped in the same manner to accommodate the stage smoke extract and louvres that infill the empty ends of the large shells.

Instead of drawing a perspective of the Opera House as was required by the competition conditions, Jørn Utzon provided a view from the staircase of the space between the two halls. This was the most spatially exciting area of the entire design. His drawing possesses a flatness and linear expression similar to a Japanese woodblock print. The roof edges push out like questing tendrils, then pull back in a curled pout, advance and retreat, in a single fluid motion. The two facing roofs draw the horizontal terrace sideways. The tension is palpable, like two people kissing. The energy spills off the roofs and collects like rainwater in the great cleavage framed by the long passage. The two sets of roofs compress the intervening space, much the same as do the vertical rock walls of an outback gorge. At the last minute, almost as an afterthought and submitted as a perspective view, Utzon applied gold leaf to the soffit areas – the underneath – of the shells and pasted on thin pieces of white-painted card to represent the white-tiled upper surface of the roofs.

Of all the drawings he submitted, this delicate, pencil-drawn sketch tells us the most. It is apparent that the leading thought in Utzon's mind was opening the interiors to the outside by eliminating walls, so the space could flow freely and spread across the full width of the platform. In place of an enclosed box-like container with the theatres tucked away and hidden from the outside, Utzon transformed his Opera House into a magnificent monumental staircase from which spring up delicate, thin-stemmed white flowers. On either side of the staircase, which was shown completely open along the passageways outside each auditorium, people stroll towards the theatres. A few pause and look, as if distracted by the beauty of the scene. The curved roof shells with their funnel stems look like giant arum lilies.

In his notes on the final drawing Utzon nominated the materials to be used. It is short and includes such things as the Oregon pine acoustic panel walls and roofs, oxhide chairs and white rubber floor for inside the large and small halls. For the side passages he indicated wooden red-painted ceiling panels and shade panels with the overhead glass doors to match the solid overhead Oregon doors around the auditoria. There were white ceramic tiles externally on the concrete shells and gold leaf or colour on the roof underside. The copper hoods of the retractable walls were also painted red. Natural stone was to be used for the steps and as cladding on the platform walls. Utzon limited his choice of colour to red on a white background – white tiles, white rubber floor inside, with red chairs, red doors and ceilings. Perhaps it was a coincidence, but Utzon's red-on-white colour scheme reversed the Danish flag's white cross on a red ground.[23]

Jørn Utzon had a reputation for failing to complete competitions on time. He tended to become too involved and, as a consequence, often worked past the submission date. In the Oslo Central Railway competition entry in 1947, and the plan for Vestre Vika also in Oslo, the following year, which he entered with his Norwegian friend Arne Korsmo, his entries were sent in late.[24] In 1956 Utzon had to balance a number of competing demands. This forced him to ration his time on the Sydney Opera House competition to meet his day-to-day work and family commitments – far from easy, since inspiration does not follow a timetable.

Utzon did finish in time, but only just, as the allotted number, 218, on the scheme shows. The titles on his drawings, which were added hastily in black ink at the very end, reveal just how hard-pressed he was. The perspective was not set up properly. His submission contains many telltale indications that the drawings were produced in a great rush. His detail drawings required under the competition conditions contain little substantive information and lacked dimensions. However, whether this was deliberate or was forced on him by a lack of time is impossible to say.

The chief characteristic of clouds is their mutability and apparent absence of any structure. They continually change their shape. Perhaps this explains why clouds are seen as expressing creativity and why their turbulent transformation suggests the fight to wrest order from chaos. The saying, 'to have one's head in the clouds', is suggestive of Utzon, with his reliance on his imagination. His early sketches strive for the same cloud-like imprecision and fluidity which refuses to be pinned down or fixed in any way. Utzon's use of clouds may be little more than a metaphor for his own creativity.

In a humorous self-portrait sketch on the back of his business card,[25] Jørn Utzon drew a long stick-like figure to represent himself; his right arm is raised, holding a pen that he dips into the ink well of his brain cavity, which has a hinged lid, and writes his name. The sketch was an Utzon joke, but it also has a serious message. Utzon knew how arduous it is to be creative; he laughs at himself while pointing out how terribly difficult it is to pull thoughts out of one's own head. While he does not say so explicitly, the sketch implies that to have one's head in the clouds is not all that bad.

Utzon was a very tall man, so possibly, unconsciously, the sketch is a self-accusation. A number of his favourite metaphors, notably beech trees and clouds, could reflect a degree of self-consciousness about his own height.

The source of the Sydney Opera House's appeal to so many people is that it is so out of the ordinary, so flamboyant it verges on the Baroque. It exists on a plane by itself, like a unique gilded royal carriage. Its appeal depends on a great many things: on its wonderful soaring roof lines, the seeming freedom of the roofs, their bubbling loveliness, swollen pregnant roundness – so seductive is their incompleteness that it sweeps us up in its own fantastic realm. It takes us out of the ordinary everyday world, as though we have stumbled through a green door into an enchanted garden where anything is possible. Its fantasy pulls us back to the magic fairytale world of our childhood, a world just as improbable as mad Ludwig II's dream castle Neuschwanstein. Everything to do with its realisation was improbable. The Opera House might never have happened, yet it did, against the most extraordinary odds.

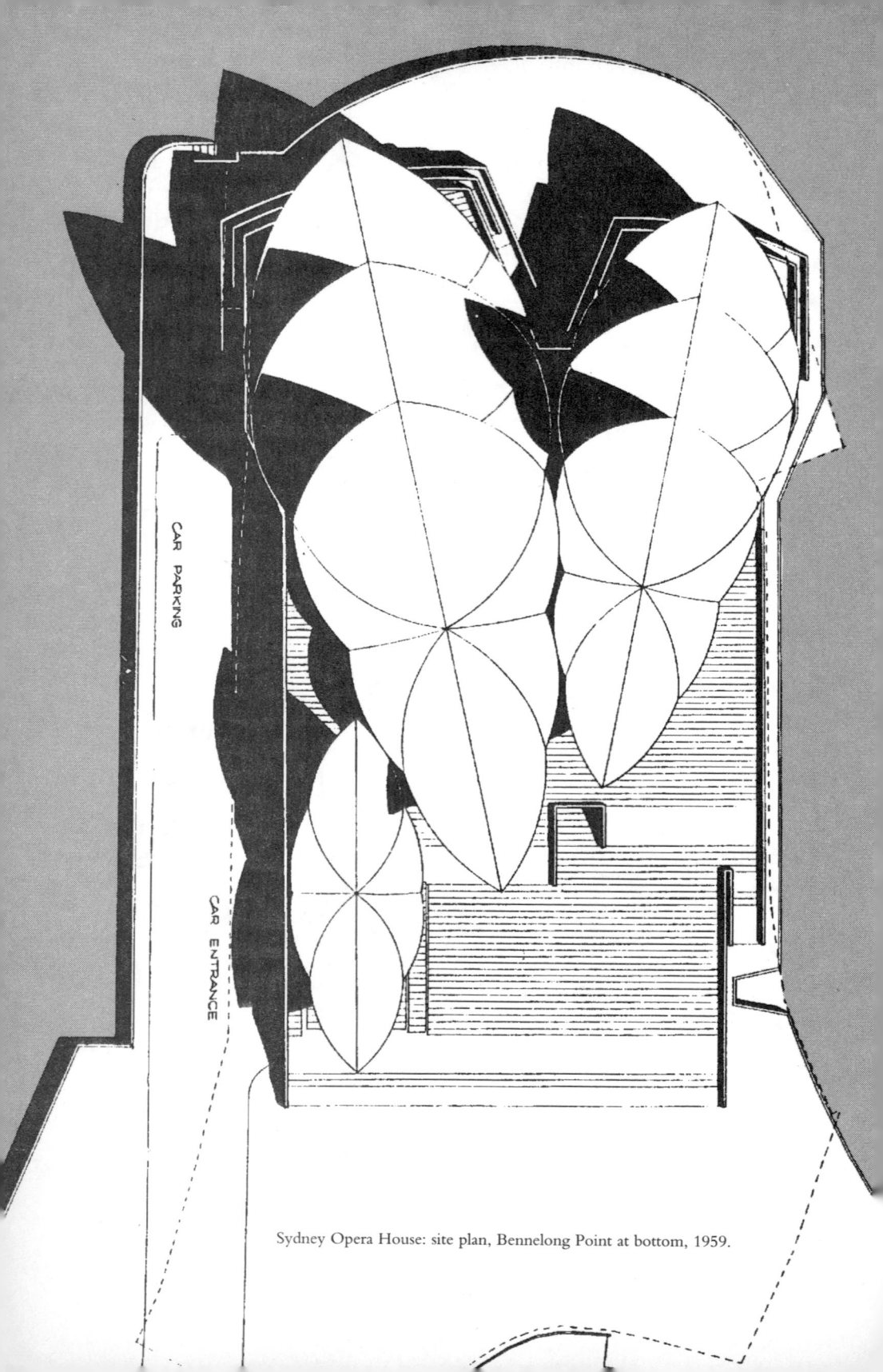

Sydney Opera House: site plan, Bennelong Point at bottom, 1959.

7

Men of Vision
Sydney, 1947–1956

> *I'm starting an 'opera house' and a 'concert hall' movement. The Town Hall in a city of one and a half million is quite inadequate, though it possesses probably the finest organ in the world. It holds about 2500 and I want a hall holding 3600 at least. The spirit and enthusiasm behind this public is immense but it needs constant kindling.*
>
> Eugene Goossens, July 1947[1]

The Goossens family originally came from Bruges in Belgium. In 1873 Eugene's grandfather crossed to England, where Eugene's father married Annie Cook, a contralto in the Carl Rosa Opera Company in which he was conductor. Goossens, the eldest of five children, was born in London on 26 May 1893. After a promising start as a brilliant young violinist, Eugene Goossens soon established himself as a conductor, and by 1922 was recognised as a leader of Britain's musical avant-garde. His development, after 1915, of a musical post-impressionist style of composition led to his recognition as a composer. Delius applauded his 'Phantasy Quartet', saying, 'it is the best thing I have seen coming from an English pen and full of emotion'.[2] During the 1920s and early 1930s, Goossens wrote his most creative work, which included the two operas *Judith* (1929) and *Don Juan de Mãnara* (1939) that still rate among his major achievements.

In 1923 Eugene Goossens was invited to America for an inaugural concert series. Two years later, in 1925, he was appointed sole Musical Director of the Rochester Philharmonic Orchestra by George Eastman, head of the Eastman Kodak photographic empire. Eastman, playing the role of philanthropist, had recently built a magnificent 3500-seat theatre, and wished to see it put to proper use. Goossens proved an instant success with his American audience. At Rochester he brought music of the highest calibre to a broad listening public. His success there influenced his thinking about what he should aim for in Australia a quarter of a century later. In considering what type of auditorium would be required for the new mass music audience, he invariably returned to the familiar Eastman theatre model with a large seating capacity. Theatres such as the Eastman type were indispensable to Goossens if he was to bring new music plus a wide classical repertoire and opera to the public.

Eugene Goossens was born with a defective heart, and a further illness in 1934 forced him to rein in his conducting style. He was an unsentimental bohemian who suffered from a heart defect in an emotional as well as strictly medical sense. He appeared incapable of communicating affection. His three marriages all failed, partly because of his constant philandering, but largely as a result of his lack of genuine affection. It made no difference that he overlooked his wives' infidelities in exchange for their acceptance of his sexual adventures. If anything, this only confirmed the problem.

Goossens was a big, pink, slow-moving fellow with large ears, a long pointed nose and bulging forehead. He was an enormously likeable person with immense reserves of charm, who spoke with a soft, north-country English accent. The same lack of emotional intensity that dogged Goossens's personal relationships with women was reflected in his music and conducting — precision and virtuosity of technique eclipsed emotional colouring. His 1934 illness lowered the emotional pitch and slowed him further. His career, which had raced ahead initially, was flagging by 1945 and needed a boost.

After 15 years as conductor in Cincinnati, Goossens was

ready for new pastures. It was time to move on, the question was where?

In 1945 he accepted an invitation from the Australian Broadcasting Commission to do a series of concerts in Australia. In late May 1946, he arrived in Brisbane for a three-month tour of 22 concerts, accompanied by his new American wife, Marjorie. At the end of it he was made an offer, which he took up in July 1947, of a three-year contract to conduct the Sydney Symphony Orchestra.

Goossens brought to Australia a fund of experience from the Rochester orchestra, where he had succeeded in bringing the best music to enthusiastic audiences in a large purpose-designed hall, an achievement he had repeated at Cincinnati. This now determined his approach in Sydney; he would be satisfied with nothing less. On his arrival, he was confronted by Sydney Town Hall which held only 2500, but Goossens wanted a hall seating at minimum 3600. Confronting the problem without delay, Goossens announced that he wished to found an Australian opera and ballet company housed in its own auditorium. 'One of my biggest castles-in-the-air is an opera house for Sydney,' he announced. 'There should be one in a city of this size for opera, ballet, theatre and concerts. A home for music is of vital concern to me, because the community should be kept in touch with contemporary thought and feeling in music.'[3]

Goossens was not alone. He acknowledged in 1954 that the idea was first suggested to him by Dr Karl Langer, who had included it in a list of proposed architectural additions to Sydney's cultural life.[4] Karl Langer was a planner from Brisbane who was employed part-time by the Cumberland County Council in Sydney. He is reported to have said to Goossens, 'How would you like to have an opera house there [on Bennelong Point]?'[5] In his report to the Cumberland Council on 21 August 1947 Karl Langer reviewed the entire Circular Quay precinct and its future. He recommended, amongst other things, the creation of an elevated piazza over the recently proposed railway station and expressway at Circular Quay large enough for 50,000–100,000 people, and with parking beneath it for 1000 cars![6]

From Vienna originally, Langer was a visionary with a keen eye for landscape. He postulated that Circular Quay would make a superb gate for his St Mark's Square-in-the-air. In the midst of considering the Quay, Langer turned his attention to Bennelong Point. Commanding the harbour and providing a natural focus and gateway for the city – which swivelled eastward towards the harbour entrance – the site was wasted as a ramshackle tram depot.

In preliminary discussions, Goossens and Langer identified Bennelong Point as offering the best site for the new Opera House. It took a further eight years, until May 1955, to persuade the State Cabinet to finally give approval to this site. The passage of time sharpened Goossens's determination. Stung by the lack of progress in his negotiations after three years of lobbying, Goossens threatened to resign in an interview in Paris given to the *Sunday Telegraph* in February 1950, 'Either we start a Sydney Opera House now – or I leave.'[7] He had done as much as anyone could to galvanise the New South Wales Government. He was so desperate that for a while he advocated that the Capitol Theatre near Central Railway Station, at the south end of the business district, be used. When this was ruled out by the Railways Department, he switched to Carrington Street, Wynyard Park, above the ramp approach to Wynyard Station in the centre of the city. Throughout these manoeuvres, Goossens never lost sight of Bennelong Point, which he described as 'the ideal place'. At one time, there were as many as 21 sites under consideration.

On his first trip to Australia, Goossens, a keen photographer who enjoyed drawing and painting in his spare time, was struck by the wild beauty of Australia's coast. He responded enthusiastically to the mystery and unlimited space of its interior and the piercing quality of its light. Goossens was especially impressed by Sydney Harbour, with its great sweeps of water and network of secluded bays and wooded coves. He admired it all the more because the busy shipping traffic reminded him of his childhood in Liverpool, England. Goossens later remarked to his secretary at the Conservatorium on one of their lunch-time walks down Macquarie Street to the tram shed at

Bennelong Point: 'This is where the Opera House is to be!'[8]

The large multi-purpose San Francisco War Memorial Opera House hall was still fresh in Goossens's memory from a visit in May 1945 when he conducted a programme of four concerts there.[9] He had been most impressed by its flexibility. This was due to the use of special stage rostrums and a removable concert shell which was dismantled during opera. What Goossens did not seem to have realised was that while it may be possible to convert an opera house into an auditorium for concerts, to go from a concert hall to an opera theatre is difficult because of the additional volume per seat required acoustically for concerts. He also underestimated the considerable advantage which the unusually high, 17 m proscenium opening gave the San Francisco Opera House. In an article written in 1949,[10] Goossens also mentioned a concert hall with adjustable interior walls that permitted it to be used both for opera and concerts. Most likely he was referring to the new Opera House at Malmö, Sweden, which was equipped with travelling walls that enabled the main hall, seating 1800, to be converted to a theatre for 1200 or a hall seating 800, suitable for recitals. Attached to it was a small hall for 220 patrons of chamber music and intimate recitals.[11] As Goossens viewed it, his proposed opera house was chiefly to house the Sydney Symphony Orchestra. In addition, however, its hall would have to satisfy the dual demands of opera and theatre. He listed the main functions as concerts, opera and spoken drama, in that order, and asked for auditoria with 3600, 2800 and 1120 seats respectively. These requirements formed the basis for the International Competition brief in 1956.

There was one critical omission. The competition conditions failed to mention travelling walls to vary the seating capacity and room size, which were essential if the different acoustic criteria for opera and concerts were to be met in one hall. Without such moving walls to alter the volume of the hall and the quantity of sound absorbed by the total area of walls and ceiling, the opera and orchestral functions were incompatible. No one seems to have had sufficient acoustic knowledge to distinguish between the two distinct approaches: a multi-purpose hall which, in the main, would be a failure acoustically; and the convertible (or multi-form) type, which held the key to success because it made it possible to substantially vary the hall acoustics.

It was imperative for Goossens to attract influential allies to his cause. 'Without it,' he said darkly, in a reference to his opera house, 'we'll stagnate in outer darkness.' And stagnate in outer darkness Sydney did most nights, especially Saturday and Sunday. Its desolation and emptiness was relieved only by the breathy tremolo of dead leaves under dim street lights, as the wind shrilly played on the overhanging cornices and statuary of the old sandstone Victorian government buildings. The Sydney of the 1950s was a graveyard after dark. Goossens demanded that an immediate start should be made to attract 'the international spotlight of culture', to dispel the cultural darkness.

One of Goossens's earliest admirers was John Joseph Cahill. Cahill was the State Minister for Local Government when the idea of an opera house was first mooted in 1948. He was an unlikely ally. Considering the political risks it entailed, his interest in Goossens's project is hard to understand but his support was crucial. Cahill acted more out of a concern for the quality of life and less as a politician in urging others to back the project. Ultimately, Cahill's political ups and downs decided the Opera House's future prospects. Soon after becoming the new Labor Premier of New South Wales, on 3 April 1952, Cahill did not hesitate to announce that Sydney would get its Opera House. The project was close to his heart and he was in a hurry.

Cahill was a practical builder. As a former Minister for Public Works, he was responsible for much of the new power and transport infrastructure in the state. But he was also sufficiently enlightened to see that material progress by itself was insufficient and ought to be matched by a similar investment in cultural progress to make life truly valuable and meaningful. Like Goossens, he was a visionary. Both hoped to improve Sydney. The Labor Party in Australia had dedicated itself to improving the lot of ordinary working people, and what Cahill now did was a continuation of that policy. Cahill epitomised the constructive side of the Labor Party. At an early stage, he decided to make the Opera House the centrepiece of his vision for Sydney. In many ways this represented a very personal commitment.

The alliance between Cahill and Goossens was based less on their personalities than idealism, and a deep-seated belief that life could be made better for everyone. Cahill was the opposite of Goossens – he was a strictly back-room politician who disliked the limelight – yet somehow they managed to function together. Goossens was a flamboyant figure: he drove in the engine of the Newcastle express train; picked out John Antill's orchestral score, *Corroboree*, for performance in 1946; and plucked Joan Sutherland from obscurity. He revelled in his celebrity status. What allowed them to work together was Goossens's vehement belief that access to music should be the right of every individual, irrespective of class or condition. This must have appealed to Cahill, so the two, in spite of their obvious differences, were able to share the same great ambition for Sydney.

Goossens soon acquired new allies, notably H. Ingham Ashworth. Ashworth, who had been a lieutenant-colonel in India and Burma during the Second World War, arrived in Sydney in 1949, a little after Goossens, to take up the chair in architecture at Sydney University. He was a short corpulent Englishman with dark curly hair and a gravelly stentorian delivery that self-consciously imitated the melodramatic rhetorical flourishes of Winston Churchill as he defied the Nazis hordes. Arrogant and deeply imbued with a sense of his English superiority, Ashworth was, nevertheless, a skilful chairman of committees. He was also, as Utzon quickly discovered, wholly ignorant about good design, but made up for this shortcoming by his unflagging support and adeptness in social matters. Like Churchill, once he was committed to an idea he did not give up easily. One of his earliest and most important contributions was to host a dinner party to discuss the fledgling Opera House project, which brought Goossens and Cahill together.

There was very little progress prior to 1954. Then out of the blue, it all began to happen. Early that year, students in

Ashworth's fifth-year studio were given an opera house to design for Bennelong Point. Goossens, for his part, offered advice and acted as a consultant in technical matters.[12]

The students' project resulted in a crude rehash of the Royal Festival Hall in London, a not very encouraging beginning, since the Festival Hall had already attracted criticism for its dry acoustics and unattractive box aesthetics. The students added an extra restaurant wing under a corrugated shell concrete roof, which they plugged into one side next to the hall's large, curtain-walled lobby. They also provided a small separate shelter for ferry arrivals.

It was an unpromising start, but it was a start nevertheless. The task of determining the requirements for the project and writing the design programme fell to George Molnar, a Hungarian lecturer in architecture at Ashworth's school, who achieved a name with his starkly modern cartoons and ironic observations on current events published in the *Sydney Morning Herald* newspaper. For his part, Ingham Ashworth looked on and supervised what in effect was a trial competition brief. From the public to politicians, few understood the technically complex requirements of a modern opera house and performing arts centre. Centres such as this were an entirely new phenomenon, and there were very few existing examples that could be studied as a guide. The absolute first requirement was a very large site: 75 m wide by 105 m long was regarded as a bare minimum. Size alone eliminated many potential sites, such as the corner of College and Liverpool streets at the south end of Hyde Park – ruled out because of its shape and inadequate dimensions. An opera house also needed to be close to mass public transport for convenient access by patrons, but access might be obstructed if it was too close to a busy roadway. Proponents looked for a prominent location within the city at the terminus of a major civic axis with plenty of space around it. There was an expectation that the new building should provide a symbol of the city – though exactly how no one could say. There was no shortage of suggestions in 1954 and few sites fulfilled all of the criteria.[13] Bennelong Point was the obvious choice, but the Sydney public had yet to be persuaded.

It soon became apparent that a mechanism was needed to involve the community. The Labor Premier, Joseph Cahill, took the initiative by calling a conference on 30 November 1954 in the Lecture Room of the Sydney Public Library to which he invited a representative cross-section of Sydney's leading business and civic leaders and others involved in the performing arts. Its purpose was the approval of the general idea of building an opera house.[14] The week before, Eugene Goossens had premiered his oratorio *Apocalypse* in the Sydney Town Hall to tumultuous applause and critical acclaim. It marked the high point in his Australian career and guaranteed broad community support for the conference objective.

Mid-way through his Conference address Cahill referred to the establishment of a small working committee to examine matters in detail on the Government's behalf and to submit recommendations – this was to be the forerunner of the Sydney Opera House Executive Committee.[15] Among the government leaders who attended in force was Mr Renshaw, whose Department of Public Works expected it would be asked to undertake the project. Their attendance was a clear indication that the Government was backing the initiative. Cahill also wanted to gauge community attitudes before committing his Government or assuming financial responsibility. What he looked for was some assurance of popular community support.

Cahill opened the conference with a strong offer of support. He soberly acknowledged, 'Unquestionably the major portion of the cost will have to be borne by the Government.' In the Legislative Assembly of the State Parliament later that same day, the Premier pleaded for the establishment of the Opera House to be exempted from party political attacks and inter-party rivalry.

Goossens followed Cahill's opening address with a short justification of the Sydney Symphony Orchestra's need to have a home of its own and presented the case for building a large hall with 3500 to 4000 seats, devoted largely to orchestral concerts, to minimise the number of repeat performances.[16] He used the occasion to reject the incorporation of the Conservatorium of Music in the Opera House, and pointed out that this was not the practice anywhere else in the world and flew in the face of international precedent. Goossens was extremely persuasive. As the representative of the Australian Elizabethan Trust, H.C. (Nugget) Coombs suggested the cost should be shared equally between the State Government, Sydney City Council and public subscriptions. One of the other delegates described the financial arrangements introduced by the Board of Governors of the San Francisco Opera House, under which 1000 guarantors individually pledged US$500.

Many of those who attended the conference were worried about how the building would be financed. Mrs Gale from the Workers' Educational Association raised the issue of the potential hostility of country people: this might be avoided, but only if ways were found to actively gain their support. She cautioned, 'The antagonism of those in the country areas towards the city railway must be seen to be believed, and we do not want a repetition of this sort of thing.'[17] Later developments were to prove her correct. However, almost everyone at the time underestimated the depth of country feeling towards the city, and extent to which the Opera House would provide a new focus for this animus.

At the end of 1954, the Cumberland County Council forwarded its report to the Government. In it R.D.L. Fraser, the Chief County Planner, recommended a site in Macquarie Street at the head of Martin Place, in the heart of the Sydney's business district, for the new Opera House. His recommendation was the culmination of a lengthy deliberation on the merits of nine possible sites and their assessment according to two factors – accessibility and prominence.[18]

In early February 1955, a committee of the Council of the NSW Chapter of the Royal Australian Institute of Architects, chaired by Professor Ashworth, nominated Bennelong Point as the site. The Institute report narrowed the choice to two of the previously suggested sites – Bennelong Point and the Domain site in Macquarie Street.[19] Besides its magnificent natural assets, which alone made Bennelong Point the desirable choice, it enjoyed the further advantage that the tram shed could be replaced relatively cheaply by an industrial building anywhere along the tram line. Buses were then under consideration as replacements for the trams, but either way presented no insurmountable difficulty. Bennelong Point was easily the least expensive site and the best in terms of its potential for an opera house expressing the essence of Sydney and its harbourside location.

The selection of Bennelong Point emphasised Sydney's most important civic axis, from the Anzac Memorial north through Hyde Park via the government precinct in Macquarie Street in front of the State Parliament. This axis ran along the eastern ridge of Sydney for over 2.5 km, through Hyde Park, which in the previous century had been the city common, a raceground, and site of gallows for hanging criminals. Beyond the magnificent Archibald fountain by the French sculptor François Sicard, it then continued as Macquarie Street down to the harbour edge.

Soon afterwards, the reference committee convened by Premier Cahill reported its findings on the site and other matters related to the establishment of an opera house.[20] It noted that public financial support would be greatest if, besides being able to say where the building would be sited, the Government could show what it would be like. Consequently, the committee focused its attention on the former site question and recommended to the Premier the adoption of Bennelong Point. In total, 21 sites were reviewed before the committee unanimously approved Bennelong Point as 'the outstandingly suitable site'. The report added: 'Above all, the site being on a predominant headland of Sydney's magnificent waterway will provide a setting unique in the world for a building of such monumental character as an opera house.'[21] Soon afterwards the Opera House Committee presented its recommendation to the Premier, and State Cabinet approved it on 17 May 1955.

It took the committee a year to decide what facilities the Opera House should contain and to begin making preparations for calling an international competition in mid-1956. Many of the issues which have since plagued the Opera House were examined at this time: questions such as the conflict of housing and hospitals versus expenditure on the Opera House during a period of fiscal stringency; the persistent intense rivalry between country and city; and the allocation of public funds for the Opera House, which was automatically ruled out by both major political parties.

To further complicate matters, local Australian architects rejected the suggestion to hold an international competition open to all comers. From the outset, the Public Works Department (which had considered that it should be given the task of designing and carrying out the project) and many members of the Royal Australian Institute of Architects expected that the competition would be restricted to Australian citizens. The influential Sydney architect and planner Walter Bunning was the loudest opponent of the international competition proposal. He later became an obsessive critic and attacked Utzon at every opportunity. Bunning was not alone in his criticism.

The split between new and old Australia had an important bearing on what later happened with the Opera House competition. At the end of the Second World War Australia had commenced a massive intake of migrants. These newcomers agreed with Goossens's assessment that Sydney lacked anything of cultural significance and welcomed the plan to build the Opera House. Goossens, Ashworth, to a lesser degree Sir Charles Moses at the Australian Broadcasting Commission and Karl Langer, were middle-class professionals from Great Britain and Austria. They brought with them a strong conviction about the importance of culture and they endeavoured, insofar as they were able, to change Australia. Other Australians who had been in the country for one or more generations, especially working-class and country people, resented these newly arrived upstarts. The Opera House project became a source of division between an old conservative Australia satisfied with how things were and the new, migrant Australia. In practice, the battle lines were less clear than this suggests and there were plenty of exceptions, but in the main, support was strongest among the Central Europeans and newly arrived middle-class English migrants. To a considerable degree, political support centred on these newer social groupings. Joe Cahill, the New South Wales Premier, was a first-generation Australian whose working-class parents had immigrated from Ireland. His support for the Opera House was based on national pride and a desire to see something worthwhile and lasting accomplished for his state. This explains why Cahill was so remarkable and something of an enigma – not simply because he fought to make the Opera House a reality, but because his commitment placed him in direct conflict with a sizeable faction within his own party. In many respects the Opera House, with its elitist appeal, was more of a Liberal Party project.

In March 1956, the Cahill Government went to the polls and was returned with a slim majority. The final result was decided by late vote counting in four city seats. Soon afterwards, Sir Eugene Goossens set off a scandal when he was stopped at Sydney's Mascot airport while entering Australia. Customs officers searching his bags discovered 1166 items of allegedly pornographic material, including photographs, books and rubber masks. Shortly before this Sir Charles Moses, a close friend of Goossens, was tipped off by an anonymous telephone caller who warned him that Goossens's luggage would be searched.[22] Goossens later claimed that he had been 'forced' by blackmailers to bring the prohibited material into Australia, but the damage was done and no one believed him. It is conceivable that he was blackmailed, but this was never proved.

In the event, Moses failed to pass on the warning to Goossens. On 22 March Goossens pleaded guilty and was fined the maximum penalty of £100 for having imported prohibited goods in his possession. He resigned as conductor of the Sydney Symphony Orchestra and from his post as director of the NSW Conservatorium of Music on 11 April. The public obloquy broke Goossens, who returned to England and died there on 13 June 1962 at Hillingdon, eight years later.

His departure was a devastating blow to the Opera House movement which he had started and vigorously led since 1947. His fall came out of the same darkness he had worked to dispel. It was not the first time this had happened, and it would not be the last. The worrying thing was that it cast the die for a spineless Sydney Opera House Committee, which abandoned Goossens at the first sign of trouble. Goossens was cast adrift with the same expedient slickness that was meted out to Utzon a decade later. In practice, Goossens had effectively been the project's client. He and the Sydney Symphony Orchestra, plus a few other groups, were the users of the Opera House. The Government did not know anything about the project's needs and Ashworth, on the Technical Panel, and the committee were part-time advisers who translated Goossens's requirements and passed them on to the Government.

The project had acquired too much momentum of its own to collapse in the wake of Goossens's departure. All the same, Goossens was the only person who knew what was wanted, who possessed the necessary dedication and tenacity to overcome the hazards ahead, and who, in any case, passionately cared how it turned out because he had a direct stake in the outcome. Neither the committee, nor Ashworth or Cahill, possessed the necessary musical background or the knowledge to master the complex artistic and technical matters the completion of the Opera House would entail. With him gone, the project lost its direction at a critical moment in its inception. This loaded a further burden on Premier Cahill – and he already had his hands full dealing with all its political repercussions. No one fully appreciated in 1956 that Goossens was truly indispensable.

The trip to Europe which led to Goossens's arrest illustrates this point. While Goossens was away, he visited two of Europe's most recently completed opera houses, at Hamburg and Vienna. His report gave valuable details about the reconstruction of the Hamburg Opera House and the Vienna State Opera, both of which had been severely damaged during the war. The Hamburg theatre was enlarged in the rebuilding with new hydraulic lifts controlling the orchestra levels to increase its size for full-sized Strauss or Wagner orchestras, or to reduce it for smaller Mozart orchestras. Besides looking at the orchestra pits, Goossens measured the Vienna Opera stage, which could be lowered or raised in eight different sections by powerful hydraulic-electric machinery. His account leaves one in no doubt about his enthusiasm: 'A visit to the enormous space below-stage with its lift mechanisms impresses by the sense of power and height, because of the stark functionalism of the machinery.'[23]

By a striking coincidence, at nearly the same time, Utzon based his design approach on this same under-stage lift system. If Goossens had remained in Sydney, the Opera House might well have turned out very differently. One thing appears incontestable: the prime mover, the sole individual who understood what was required, who was up-to-date technically as well as musically, was forced out even before the project started. Goossens had worked tirelessly to whip up public enthusiasm and was personally interested in architecture. Utzon and the man who would have become his client never met. Goossens disappeared even before Utzon was named as the project's architect.

The architectural competition was more successful and attracted more international attention than anyone could possibly have imagined. Professor Ashworth had attempted to limit the number of assessors to three, consisting of an Australian – himself – and two others from overseas; the committee however rejected this. On 4 August 1955, the Opera House Committee decided there should be four assessors, two from Australia and two from overseas, with the chairman to exercise the casting vote.[24] Ashworth, Goossens and Moses dominated these deliberations. If Ashworth had won the argument, there would not have been even a single native-born Australian assessor on the judging panel.

H. Ingham Ashworth and Cobden Parkes, the NSW Government Architect, as the token Australian, were the local assessors. Cobden Parkes was included as an afterthought. Well meaning, but completely old-fashioned and lacking any real design discernment, his inclusion was a gesture to placate the Government interest. Ashworth's aesthetic judgement was only slightly better than Parkes. He had laboured hard behind the scenes to set the terms for the competition and felt therefore he had earned his role as chairman. One of the overseas judges was a fellow Englishman, Dr J. Leslie Martin. He was Chief Architect to the London County Council from 1953 to 1956 and had been responsible in 1951, with Peter Moro, for the

Royal Festival Hall on London's South Bank. The final assessor was Eero Saarinen, an American of Finnish descent. If these two architects were unavailable, Basil Spence, who had won the competition to rebuild Coventry Cathedral, and Pietro Bellushi, an American architect, were named as alternatives.

None of the competition assessors was an architectural acoustician or had a background which would have equipped him to expertly assess the musical, performance and technical effectiveness (other than in the most general terms) of the competition submissions. In specifying a multi-purpose main hall for concerts and opera, Professor Ashworth exposed how limited was his knowledge of acoustic matters. He seems never to have realised that the two sets of acoustic requirements for opera and orchestra were incompatible and incapable of being fulfilled without some fundamental compromise. The only workable alternative was to design the Major Hall auditorium to suit opera with a stage that could be quickly and easily converted into the front part of the concert hall. By implication, the competitors were being asked to devise a system that would permit the front of the stage to be pushed backwards so the stage area could be incorporated within the same volume as the hall. Ashworth failed to warn competitors or mention these difficult and complex technical issues, one imagines because he was totally unaware they existed. Worse still, no precise acoustical performance criteria for the two main halls were specified, neither were the necessary minimal hall volumes ever calculated or taken into account during the assessment and selection of the winning schemes. Ashworth was concerned primarily with politics, not acoustics, and with ensuring that the competition was international.

Eero Saarinen towered over the other judges. In July 1956 *Time* magazine put him on its front cover and followed with a glowing account of his life and prodigious achievements in an essay entitled 'The maturing modern'.[25] The article attributed his natural competitiveness to 'Sire and Sisu', *sisu* being Finnish for 'guts'. Eero Saarinen had no shortage of *sisu*. His sire was Eliel Saarinen, a Finnish architect of international renown who had permanently settled in the United States in 1923. In 1948, at the age of 38, Eero Saarinen won the St Louis Jefferson National Expansion Memorial with an audacious, 180 m stainless steel arch which resembled a bent pipe cleaner. The design was at first credited to his father, Eliel, until the mistake was uncovered a few days later. The US$100 million General Motors Technical Centre clinched Saarinen's ranking as America's top architect. In Sydney, there was no confusion about who was the star – Saarinen clearly outshone the other assessors.

The *Time* article quoted Saarinen as saying: 'There is a whole question of how to relate buildings to earth and sky. Is the sharp horizontal really the best answer? We must have an emotional reason as well as a logical end to everything we do.' This could easily have been a quote from Jørn Utzon, so close in spirit are their ideas.

The Opera House competition coincided with a major shift in direction by Saarinen. Previous designs had been based on a refined vocabulary of cubes, but more recently Saarinen had chosen non-rectangular shapes in a quest for more sculptural outcomes. In his most recent work at that time, MIT's new auditorium at Cambridge, he replaced the standard shoe-box hall with a billowing white shell of concrete, which rested daintily on three slender stiletto points. Saarinen was an intense man who reacted enthusiastically to ideas that coincided with his own. At breakfast Saarinen once casually turned over his grapefruit and carved out elliptical parabolic arches to see if they would suit his eagle-shaped TWA Terminal at J.F. Kennedy Airport.[26] Architecture was a 24-hour-a-day obsession with Saarinen.

By 15 March, 881 competitors had registered; out of this number, 772 went on to pay their deposits. In planning the competition, Professor Ashworth and the committee did not expect more than 150 to register. The actual figure was five times that. This overwhelming response entirely vindicated the decision to hold an international competition. By 3 December, the closing date of the competition, 230 competitors had sent in schemes. Predictably, the majority of submissions came from English-speaking countries, but Germany, Switzerland and

France were also strongly represented, stimulated no doubt by the prestige and exciting nature of the project. A quarter of the registrations, 232 entries, came from the UK, followed by Australia in equal second ranking with the USA, both with 113 registrations. In all, 45 countries participated.[27] Later, when the registered competitors' names were recorded, they included such famous names as the Smithsons in England and Richard Neutra and Robert E. Alexander from Los Angeles. Among the Sydney entrants were Harry Seidler and Walter Bunning, and George Molnar in the second Stephenson & Turner entry.

The judging took place in the Art Gallery of New South Wales. This is a pretentious Classical sandstone monument from 1909 with reliefs outside in the sandstone depicting such great artists as Raphael, Donatello and other European masters to enhance its impact. The director of the gallery, Hal Missingham, agreed to the judging only on condition that the gallery was not put to the expense of hanging the drawings.

It was widely believed at the time that Saarinen arrived late and retrieved Utzon's scheme from the reject pile, after which he is supposed to have said to the other assessors: 'Gentlemen! Here is your Opera House!'[28] Such was his reputation he browbeat the other assessors who, so the story went, had earlier rejected Utzon's submission. Saarinen's unstinting praise of the Utzon scheme later persuaded many of the truth of this account. He was quoted in *Time*: 'So many opera houses look like boots. There is the high proscenium arch, then the low part for the audience. Utzon has solved the problem.'[29]

Years later, Ashworth dismissed it as nonsense and while he conceded that Saarinen did arrive a day-and-a-half late in Sydney, after the jury had begun its initial sorting of the submissions, he insisted that Dr Martin had initially been impressed by Utzon's entry and was supported by the rest of the jury. Furthermore, he stated that Utzon's scheme was selected from the very beginning for consideration.[30]

The story is ambiguous, and it can be interpreted several ways to suggest that Utzon's design should never have been considered, much less received first prize, since it did not satisfy the competition conditions. Alternatively, it could be used to prove that Ashworth, Parkes and Martin were fools who were only prevented from making a historic blunder by the timely arrival of Saarinen, who alone possessed the acumen needed to pick the one worthy scheme. There is more than a grain of truth in its suggestion that Ashworth and Parkes were out of their depth. This may explain why the story has persisted so long.[31] Whichever way it is approached, the conclusion is the same – all the judges, with the exception of Saarinen, were ill equipped. The story had the merit that it rendered a complex process more understandable by reducing it to a simple tale of genius triumphing over mediocrity. This would account for Ashworth's denial. There was a further disgraceful aspect to the proceedings: that the drawings were never hung, either during the judging or afterwards.

Ashworth, Parkes and Martin began work on Monday 7 January 1957 without Saarinen. The only break occurred when Saarinen and Martin went on an excursion to Palm Beach the following Sunday. The judging was completed the next Wednesday, the 16th, and the following Friday the assessors handed in their report and their selection to Mr S. Haviland of the Opera House Committee.[32] Saarinen actually flew into Sydney early morning on Friday 11th, on a Pan American flight from Nadi, not one-and-a-half days late, as claimed by Ashworth, but five days late. He left Sydney late Saturday night 19 January eight days later with his second wife Aline on the return leg of their journey via Indonesia, India, Rome and London.[33] The other assessors could hardly have waited from Monday to Friday, nearly five days, for Saarinen to appear before commencing their deliberations. The Ashworth version is clearly incorrect.

Politicians adore openings and public ceremonial. The competition results were announced in the New South Wales Art Gallery on Tuesday afternoon, 29 January 1957.[34] For minutes Premier J.J. Cahill played out the drama of who was the winner. At the last moment he tripped up but instead of killing the moment it sent the suspense rocketing to new heights.

It was 3 p.m. when the chairman of the Art Gallery, Mr B.J. Waterhouse, began, 'One of the great charms of an architectural competition is that one never knows at all what the result will be.' Although news journalists had been given the assessors' report it only referred to each scheme by a number. George Molnar ducked behind the dais and reconnoitred the competition drawings in the gallery. He was the only person in the room besides the judges who knew the result, but all he managed to blurt out was, 'If it hasn't got wings, it hasn't won!'

Stanley Haviland, the chairman of the Opera House Committee, bored everyone by describing how the four assessors studied 2000 drawings. At 3.15 p.m. he passed two drawings by Saarinen of the winning design to the Premier. A movie camera started whirring and a press photographer dashed across in front of the dais. Mr Haviland then handed the envelope with the results to the Premier, who regaled the waiting throng of news media with the story of how the closeted assessors amused themselves by guessing the nationality of the winner, whom they believed to be English because there were no spelling mistakes.

Showing signs of perturbation, the Premier waved the unopened envelope in the air. At 3.22 p.m. Cahill paused … resumed speaking … it was not yet time … at 3.27 p.m. he paused again. His filibuster had lasted long enough. At 3.29 p.m. Cahill stopped for the last time, delaying no longer, then he tore the envelope open and solemnly read to the assembled: 'The design awarded the first premium is Scheme number 218; the design awarded the second premium is Scheme number 28; and the third premium is Scheme number 62.' Everyone stared blankly at the Premier. Disconcerted, he attempted to explain, 'These are the numbers I'm afraid, I haven't the name, I wonder whether someone will tell me.' The crowd gasped, people shuffled. The Premier looked around uncertainly. Mr Haviland pushed forward, rummaged in the envelope and drew out a second sheet. 'Design awarded first premium,' Mr Cahill resumed, 'Scheme number 218, submitted by Joern Utzon.' It was over – Sydney had a winner! There was an audible sucking in of air as people resumed breathing.

In an interview before he left Sydney, Saarinen remarked: 'During the judging of the competition, many times we said that this was really the work of a genius and were very very impressed with the result.'[35] Cahill was greatly impressed by Saarinen and Leslie Martin's comments on Utzon's design – that it was the most exciting building they had seen. Their confidence in the design reassured Cahill and convinced him that here was something special worth fighting for.

Sydney Opera House: conceptual sketch by Utzon, 1957.

8

The Tough Political Questions

Hellebæk and Sydney, 1957–1959

In winter, the beech forest loses its roof, the sky becomes an insistent presence and the forest takes on a melancholy, wistful atmosphere. Whereas before it was a series of delicate, shimmering, green screens and chambers, casual vistas that parted and closed behind you as you walked, it now revealed itself, throwing open all its secret hidden parts. It became a sleeping memorial of gaunt sighing trunks.

In late January, winter gripped the forest in earnest. The beech trees stood apart framed against the heavy sky, their upraised limbs casting a delicate net of shadow across the unyielding frozen ground. Utzon ventured out of the house, walking briskly across the mottled carpet of snow. In parts where the sun reached it, the snow had melted. The forest creatures were in hiding and the forest was enveloped in a brittle silence which amplified every sound.

Suddenly, in the distance, Lin, Utzon's ten-year-old daughter, materialised on her bicycle, her blonde hair streaming out behind and her feet pumping up and down like miniature train pistons as she pedalled furiously towards him. Coming abreast of him she braked, alighted and thrust the bicycle sideways into the ditch beside the road. Utzon was startled, frightened lest there had been an accident at the house. Her happy smile reassured him — it was good news.

After first informing Utzon of his Sydney win, and making the most of his surprise, she demanded, 'Now can I have my horse?'

It was the second miracle that month. Kim Utzon had been born on New Year's Day, four weeks earlier. Utzon was numbed, he felt a wave of disbelief sweep over him. Perhaps there had been a mistake, someone was playing a joke on him? He had never seriously considered the possibility he might win.

Reality took on a new clarity and sharpness and the forest around him shed its bleakness. The world looked suddenly brighter. He felt his heart beat faster. Søren Kierkegaard had once suggested that life was a choice between eight forest roads leading in different directions: eight roads posed eight choices, each one a different future. In the forest the eight roads now converged into a single road for Utzon: one future and one destination — Sydney, wherever that led.

Utzon was still shaking with excitement as he entered the house. In the meantime, the feeling had grown rather than diminished: 'This news from Australia is almost as good as the news of his arrival,' he gasped, making reference to Kim's birth. 'It was a miracle for me that I won that contest, it was fabulous,' he repeated later.[1] An Australian reporter talked over the radio telephone; bubbling with excitement, Utzon began talking about his plans to settle in Australia. Not having as yet been officially notified, Utzon struggled to rein in his enthusiasm, 'It depends on what they [the Sydney Opera House Committee] can advise me how soon I can emigrate.'[2] He said he expected a cable to arrive at any moment.

Winning an architectural competition is different to a lottery. In a competition, the big prize — doing the building — is never fully guaranteed. Often what follows is filled with disappointment and bitterness. Utzon acknowledged this deep down. He was elated notwithstanding. The Sydney win set him on a fresh course which, once embarked upon, he would not be able to abort, whatever its later trials and disappointments. Kierkegaard's enigmatic road through the forest of life permitted no such detours or excursions.

In Sydney, the result was greeted with astonishment. The decision to award Utzon's unusual design first prize sparked an enormous controversy. Many people could not fathom Utzon's scheme because there was nothing in the world to compare it to. It was unique, unprecedented in architectural history. To encourage public acceptance, Arthur Baldwinson, an associate of Professor Ashworth at the University of Sydney, hastily produced a realistic watercolour perspective rendering or 'artist's view' which was published immediately with notes to indicate the position of the foyers, stage areas, theatre auditoria, liquor bars and restaurant, to assist the public visualise the location of the various components.

Harry Seidler, who had submitted an entry, greeted Utzon's design with the comment it was 'pure poetry', adding, 'It is magnificent'.[3] Not all agreed. Opinion was strongly divided: one woman called it, 'a piece of Danish pastry', to a Lindfield man it was a 'clean refreshing breeze', others compared it to 'something which might have crawled up from the ocean'.[4] Regardless of whether it was seen as 'poetry' or 'pastry', everyone had an opinion, it had created a tireless new talking point.

Approaching 90, two years before his death, Frank Lloyd Wright rattled everyone by accusing Utzon of sensationalism. Wright, who had never set foot in Australia, declared, 'Nothing but sensationalism! This design is not characteristic of Australia or opera ... A whim, that's all it is, a whim.'[5]

Few people were quite as blistering in their criticism as Wright: several equated Utzon's proposal with the pioneering Australian spirit and saw it as inspired by the future, which they considered appropriate for a young country. One letter writer called it 'an immortal piece of architecture to arouse the latent talent of Australian people'. Most agreed with the assessors:

> *The white sail-like forms of the shell vaults relate as naturally to the Harbour as the sails of its yachts. It is difficult to think of a better silhouette for this peninsula. The dynamic form of this vaulted shape contrasts with the buildings which form its background and gives a special significance to the project in the total landscape of the Harbour.*[6]

The torrent of pro and anti opinions roared and thundered for ten days before abating. Ashworth judged such opposition was more general in nature and was less to do with the design than the politics of expending a large sum of public money on a project many considered was not essential. Ashworth concluded that the people who opposed it did so because they believed an opera house was unnecessary and should not be built at all. According to this view, houses and hospitals should be given priority ahead of an opera house.

The other schemes in the competition may have been easier to understand, but they were also a great deal less interesting. Utzon's design towered above them. The second prize design, from America by Joseph Marzella, Leon Loschetter *et alii*, concentrated the stage areas at the centre and placed the two main auditoria in a spiral around them on the outside. It resembled a giant corrugated hat box which a Kansas twister had tossed into the air and dropped onto a spiral spike in the middle of Bennelong Point.[7] The circular plan created a simple, strong, easily read form, which, although it was well worked out in detail, unduly restricted and limited the future range of possibilities in the plan. The spiral geometry was much too rigid and inflexible. The assessors were of two minds: they attacked it as too 'heavy and massive'[8] then, seeking to add something favourable, declared it would 'form a total mass well suited to its position on Bennelong Point'. Outside, the cylinder facade had splayed reveals and slits between vertical fins to enhance its brute sculptural power.

The third prize, by Boissevain and Osmond, England, was more to Dr Martin's liking. It placed the two halls in two differently sized boxes with a square between them. Its theatres were timidly conventional; the larger one containing the main hall was located at the far north end of Bennelong Point, with its stage tower blocking the harbour view. The main entry and foyer was arranged at the opposite, southern city end where it opened onto a large piazza. The second box, containing the smaller auditorium, was turned sideways at right angles across the peninsula with its entrance foyer facing west. The scheme separated the two auditoria, which was considered a disadvantage by the assessors who commented that it would, 'involve a duplication of backstage arrangements, many of which can be used in a flexible way when the stages are brought into closer proximity'.[9] They did see other advantages and praised it for sidestepping the problems of 'a single massive building and because it forms ... a simple arrangement of buildings designed with a human scale and well placed around a pedestrian promenade'.[10]

Utzon surprised everyone with his ingenious idea of segregating the two theatre service areas within the building podium and placing the halls separately on top, thereby ensuring the stage areas were near the auditoria but avoiding bulky towers that might be considered too massive and unsympathetic. Each auditorium has its own identity and yet is similar. The three groups of roofs suggested a family group in which each individual is unique yet has characteristics that relate to the others. In order to achieve this result, Utzon had to inflate the importance of the main restaurant.

Utzon split his building into two sections, the one resting on the other, based on a division into the categories of public entertainment and functional servicing such as the workshops and practice areas. The broad platform or base, with a minimum number of window openings, built in a conventional way with inexpensive finishes, permitted Utzon to allocate more money on the public and performance areas where it would be noticed. The relatively economical base structure, in combination with the more costly performance areas on top, gave an overall cost saving compared to a conventional structure built to the same standard throughout. This is met often in modern design: in a motor car, for example, no one expects the engine compartment to be finished to the same exacting standards as the passenger capsule. The two things are vastly different, so the quality reflects the different standards and requirements. Utzon approached the Opera House much the same way.

At the conclusion of their remarks, the assessors put on record the fact that they,

> *had approximate estimates made for all the schemes which have been given places and several others in addition. The*

> *scheme which we now recommend for the first premium is, in fact, the most economical scheme on the basis of our estimates.*[11]

This is often overlooked. Utzon's scheme was rated significantly cheaper than the other finalists. In a further comment, the assessors observed that the shell construction proposed by Utzon had already been used in a number of countries, including the United States, Italy, England, Germany and Brazil, and it was a form of construction which they viewed as especially appropriate in this instance.

Behind the scenes, Dr Martin and Eero Saarinen acted swiftly to place the Opera House on a sound architectural footing. On 5 February, Utzon flew to London from Copenhagen for a meeting with Martin and Saarinen. Saarinen was in London on his return from Sydney to check on his new US Embassy at Grosvenor Square and to make a side trip to Oslo. Because Dr Martin and Eero Saarinen had strongly endorsed Utzon, they felt a keen responsibility to assure themselves of his professional fitness for the task. Many important questions required answers: should Utzon, for example, have sole responsibility? Should he be asked to form an association with an established architect in Sydney? From the outset, Utzon impressed Martin: 'In the first place we [Saarinen & Martin] would both like to say that we feel that Utzon is a charming person. We are sure that he will be both enthusiastic and helpful in developing the project with the committee ...'[12] Martin went on to say that he thought Utzon should have responsibility for working with the committee in developing the programme, adding that Utzon was 'admirably equipped to deal with all matters of design'.

Saarinen and Martin both agreed Utzon would need support on the technical side to calculate and build the complicated shell-vault system. To ensure that this happened, they recommended Utzon work with a consulting engineering firm of some standing such as Ove Arup & Partners of London, or Christiani & Nielsen, a Danish company famed for its pioneering work in reinforced concrete design and construction.[13] Surprisingly, they omitted the name of the famous Italian engineer and shell designer and builder Pier Luigi Nervi.

Arup did not waste time and wrote to Utzon immediately he read the news of the competition result with his congratulations and an offer of professional assistance.[14] While he was in London, Utzon was introduced to Ove Arup, who expressed enthusiasm for Utzon's structural shells and praised the constructional clarity of the competition proposal. Utzon was naturally pleased by Arup's positive opinion.

Within weeks of their first meeting, Ove Arup visited Utzon's Hellebæk office to begin discussions. Initially, they talked in very broad terms about the structural implications of Utzon's design. Ove Arup quickly formed a high opinion of Utzon's architectural ability, which, in view of his extensive experience as a consulting engineer, is not to be taken lightly — even more so, because it weathered the great crisis over the Opera House roof design. In 1963, Arup wrote this glowing estimate of Utzon:

> *He is a brilliant designer — one of the best, and probably the best I have come across in my long experience of working with architects — and has a remarkable grasp of or ability to quickly understand the essence of other technical disciplines as they impinge on his architectural conception ... He is no ordinary architect, and this is no ordinary job ...*[15]

This was high praise indeed coming after six years working with Utzon.

To gain the wide public support that was needed, the Sydney Committee immediately asked Utzon to develop his scheme. Utzon responded magnificently. Within two weeks of the announcement, he arranged for a model built at the same 1:200 scale as the competition drawings.[16]

Much of the communication between Utzon, the assessors and the committee was channelled through Professor Ashworth. It was a lively and informal correspondence, so much so that at times it is difficult to decide whether Ashworth is writing to a friend or in an official capacity. In late February, he confirmed to Utzon the key recommendation, that Utzon should consider working with Ove Arup as his consulting engineer. At the same time, Ashworth tactfully warned Utzon that there was growing political opposition in some quarters to building the Opera House. Ashworth was encouraged by the positive overseas reaction to the competition result, which he thought might materially assist them when the public appeal was launched.

At Eero Saarinen's suggestion, in March Utzon informed Ashworth he would visit five new opera houses and concert halls in Europe to study their facilities and operation and gather technical details, data on room sizes, planning etc.[17]

By 17 April, the model was ready. Utzon was worried about its display and safety in Sydney and sent his ideas on how he would like this done. No detail was too finicky to escape his attention: 'I should prefer a room with a flight of steps,' then added, 'I would like to place the model in the remotest part of the room from the entrance at [against] a dark background, for instance of bunting.'[18] The large size of the model worried him: 'The model is very fragile, the gilt underside of the shells must under no circumstances be touched, so it is imperative that we provide for a glass show-case.' As world interest in the project grew, Utzon was swamped by requests for photographs of the model from magazines in the USA and Europe.[19]

The critical question at this time was how much support Cahill could count on within his own Labor Party. To succeed, it was essential that Cahill consulted party membership and carried them along with him so they felt included in the final decision. On this issue, Cahill needed to drive the whole party forward – and this included a great number of people outside the much smaller parliamentary caucus. Cahill's challenge was to convince the local branch membership.

On 21 January 1957, Cahill celebrated his sixty-sixth birthday. The Premier's age now became an issue and led to press speculation that he might retire before the next general election, due in 1959. But Cahill still had the unfinished business of the Opera House before him, besides which, he was not ready to retire.

Under pressure from within his own party, in March 1957 Cahill appeared to retreat when he admitted that the State Government had not taken any firm decision on building the Bennelong Point Opera House. At the same time, in the Legislative Assembly, Cahill came under strenuous attack from the Liberal Member for Collaroy, Mr Robert Askin. Askin enjoyed robust debate and was not one to shrink from a fight. He now made the Opera House his issue. It is significant that the first attack and political point-scoring over the Opera House originated with Askin and not the Country Party Opposition.

Askin set out to divide the Government on the Opera House by posing the housing question: 'Is the present the right time to push ahead with this desirable but lavish venture?' which was followed by, 'And how does the Government propose to finance it?' Sensing the danger, Cahill played for time.

In his reply, the Premier appeared to be of two minds: 'Building the opera house will involve the expenditure of a good deal of money ... We will have to make up our minds whether we are prepared to do it.'[20] Having conceded this, and duly acknowledging the manifest difficulties, Cahill challenged the House to look beyond the present, 'In a young country like this we ought to be courageous ... We should pledge the future if need be.' Cahill flatly rejected that any conflict existed between the provision of housing and building the Opera House; support for one did not rule out support for the other. Both were possible.

The battle over the Opera House was fought not before, but after the international competition. The decisive clash came at the annual conference of the Women's ALP Organising Committee at the end of April. Initially, as he had done previously, Cahill seemed to give ground and waver by opening with a statement to the effect that homes should come before opera houses. Having said this, he turned to the delegates and asked them for their understanding for not recognising earlier how expensive the Opera House would be. Further into the speech, he stressed his determination not to disregard the immediate wants of the people, especially housing. Cahill retreated in order to advance. The following day he pressed forward, 'We are anxious to build this opera house if we can. We have to be prudent, keep our balance and have regard to the views of the people.'[21] In essence, he asserted that spending on the Opera House and spending on housing were separate and unrelated matters. Support for one did not preclude doing the other as well. By presenting the issue this way, Cahill carried the conference convincingly.

By early April, opposition within the parliamentary caucus was substantial and mounting. The problem was sufficiently serious, and opposition to spending on the Opera House within caucus so widespread as to force Cahill to postpone the caucus vote. On 2 April, six caucus members opposed the plan; by caucus's next meeting on 8 May, the number had risen to 17. Cahill won approval, but only by the narrow margin of 24 to 17 votes, to launch a public appeal for the early construction of the Opera House.[22] Cahill was still not in the clear. The Member for Monaro, Mr J. Seiffert, gave notice of a recision motion. The closeness of the vote shocked the Premier because it indicated that there was a substantial split in caucus. Cahill decided to take no further action to finance the building until after the NSW Labor Party's annual conference on 15 June. This shelved the Opera House issue temporarily.

Cahill soon found an answer to Mr Askin's question about financing. He confounded his critics by proposing the novel expedient of holding four lotteries per year, each with a first prize of A£50,000 and tickets costing 30 shillings, to run until the Opera House was paid for. The Government estimated that this would raise approximately A£240,000 (A$480,000) a year.[23] Today, when governments routinely sell off public assets and raise taxes from casinos, the protest over using gambling to finance the Opera House seems misdirected. In 1957, however, it was unthinkable that a government should countenance the diversion of public money into a non-government project such as a performing arts centre, which many in the community regarded as not essential.

Irrespective of the means used to fund it, one thing was clear: the money could not be provided directly by the government. Askin knew this and said so in his attack on the project's finances. To nearly everyone's great surprise and delight, Cahill's lottery plan cleverly sidestepped the issue and left Askin without a target. It was a brilliant political counterstroke.

At its weekend conference on 15–16 June, the state Labor Party, voting on the voices, gave Cahill a majority on the Opera House issue.[24] It was a magnificent tactical as well as personal victory for Cahill, who had placed his political prestige on the line and risked everything. In response, the party gave him its full backing. Utzon and Sir Bernard Heinze both sent Cahill telegrams of congratulation. They were elated by this political victory. But if the 16 June vote overcame an important obstacle, it nevertheless did not guarantee the Opera House's future.

Utzon's photographs of the new Opera House model reached Cahill the next day.[25] His timing was impeccable. The National Opera House was out of the barrier and running. This was the first of many such political obstacles. The project now moved to the next stage: the launching of a public appeal; development of the design; and Utzon's first visit to Sydney.

Everything had depended on final political approval. Now that it was secured, Utzon and the committee could start work in earnest. On 7 July Utzon despatched the model by air carrier with the warning; 'Please! I have to warn you, that the mere touch of a [finger] nail is enough to destroy the gold on the shells!'[26]

Six weeks later, Utzon arrived in Sydney on 29 July with his Swedish partner, Erik Andersson, for a three-and-a-half-week visit. This was the first opportunity for Sydney to see its new architect-hero. Most people instantly liked him: he was extremely handsome and reminded them of Gary Cooper and had a reassuring honesty in his manner. With his steady blue–grey eyes and easy, friendly smile under a high sun-tanned forehead, capped by his fit healthy appearance and quiet Danish reticence, even the most critical could find little to fault. Utzon's English was adequate though frequently clumsy, he made up for this by the vividness and originality of his imagery. There was something engaging about the way he spoke, using feelings to direct his words in a way that was most expressive and memorable. He possessed a rare ability to appear sympathetic.

The newspapers flatteringly compared him to Sir Edmund Hillary, famous for conquering Mt Everest, and the Duke of Edinburgh. Sydney society was soon lionising him, much to his embarrassment.[27]

Utzon and Andersson formed an odd couple, mismatched in nearly every way, from their height to their demeanour – Utzon at 194 cm towered over the diminutive reddish-haired Andersson at 157 cm. The men were met at the airport by the Danish Consul General, Mr F. Henning Hergel. On a stopover at Los Angeles to break the tedium of the long flight, Utzon called on the brilliant Viennese Modernist architect, Richard Neutra, who explained how impressed he was with the Opera House design and reassured Utzon by saying he hoped it would get built.

Utzon's most immediate concern was the model. In the company of Andersson, he unpacked it in the basement of the Sydney Town Hall and checked for damage. The next day, Friday, the men visited Bennelong Point. 'It's right!' Utzon exclaimed, on seeing it for the first time. 'It's okay! This is the way they placed temples in the old days!'[28] Sydney Harbour was quite different from Kronborg Castle and the Sound. It was more convoluted, harder to take in at a single glance; the foreshore, with its fern shape and overlapping peninsulas that concealed its full extent, was more intricate and picturesque. Thinking aloud, Utzon recalled how Kronborg Castle's towers moved behind each other as the ferry crossed in front. He anticipated the same would happen to the Opera House's shell roofs, that they would also slide past each other at different rates depending on the observer's position. In a similar way, the Opera House would not be static, but would change constantly. This observation is typical of the way Utzon approached buildings in terms of their effect. To Utzon, how we experience architecture is fundamental. Half an hour later, Utzon and Andersson were sitting down relaxing in the lounge of the Australia Club.

The appeal launch at the Sydney Town Hall on the following Wednesday, 7 August, came as the climax at the end of Utzon's stay. The model, which was exactly like the competition drawings, was the principal prop used to promote the Opera House project. Its role was similar to the Baldwinson watercolour perspective – it had to explain and create enthusiasm. The model was set up in the vestibule of the Town Hall. Utzon visualised people reaching it at the end of a procession in the same way he visualised the approach to the Opera House itself, beginning with a climb up a long flight of stairs. The Sydney Town Hall's succession of rooms threaded along its central axis was just about right. The drably ornate high-Victorian vestibule, with pink and green panels and gilded pilasters under a miniature imitation Bernini dome and massive chandelier, paid homage to the absent Imperial presence. It was dowdy. The contrast between its pretentiousness and Utzon's futuristic model made it the perfect foil. The model was placed on a pedestal by itself in the middle of the vestibule to allow people to view it from all sides.

Utzon's Opera House was everything Sydney's ornate Town Hall was not. Its round, aerofoil-shaped roofs contrasted with the stilted historicism of the Town Hall. The model's podium was formed from a tan-coloured plastic. On it rested the elegant white cast-plastic roof shells, their underside covered in gold leaf, which gave a precious delicate effect to their forms. The building was surrounded on three sides by blue plastic representing the harbour.

Aage Utzon had carved the wood moulds used to cast the plastic shells.[29] The press of the day, which knew absolutely nothing about architecture, was hugely puzzled by the unfamiliar roof shapes. To them, this was not architecture, at least, not any known architecture. Criticised in an interview, Utzon defended his concept: 'We ride in automobiles and fire rockets, why should we build in Victorian style today? This is our time's style.'[30]

Walking in off the street into the darkened vestibule, the small model was almost invisible in the gloom. Except for the hanging black horizontal louvre-wall infills that enclosed the ends of each shell, the model was identical to the competition scheme. Wire-and-sponge trees were scattered around the harbour broadwalk. Utzon had had to struggle hard to fit the two auditorium shells on the base, as the width was so restricted the main shells almost touched in the middle. The long window bands on the north elevation were subdivided by closely spaced vertical louvres. The triangular hoods over the windows and entrances at ground level had not been invented at this time. Utzon did not bother to show the glass walls in the sides and rear of the two halls under the black louvre-walls at the ends of each shell. In the model, the restaurant was so long and narrow it looked like an outstretched racing greyhound.

Despite its success in inviting community participation – 2500 people attended – the launch proved a financial flop. It was one of the most emotional public meetings anyone had yet witnessed in the Town Hall, and it raised A£235,500, of which A£100,000 was donated by the State Government.[31] After speeches by the Premier, Sir Richard Boyer for the ABC and Jørn Utzon, four artists presented a short music programme.[32] At the party afterwards in the Lord Mayor's reception room, singers raised a further £295 by selling kisses at the going rate of £10 to £50 a kiss. Mr Andersson paid £50 for Miss Joan Hammond, but was soon overtaken by Utzon who paid Miss Elaine Shaffer and Mrs Ruggeriero Ricci £100.

For all the enthusiasm and the vigorous commerce in kisses, the appeal fell well short of its target. This confirmed to Cahill and the Government that it would have to raise the bulk of the funds needed for the project from lotteries rather than directly from public donations.

At the Opera House Committee's meeting on 16 August,[33] Utzon requested that his firm Arton – of which he, Erik Andersson and Andersson's brother were principals – be appointed as the architect to carry out the Opera House project. Stanley Haviland, writing on behalf of the committee, rejected his request. This made Utzon the sole architect.

The Arton proposal contained a number of advantages for Utzon: it limited his financial liability and placed at his disposal the services of Erik Andersson's firm of 18 architects at its Helsingborg office. Erik Andersson was trying to insist on Utzon complying with the earlier 1952 agreement to use his company, to carry out the Opera House contract. Prior to this, for five years or so, Utzon had been employed by the Andersson brothers to enter competitions for them. Utzon had not invited Andersson to come to Sydney, but Andersson had insisted. Utzon had put on a brave face to avoid embarrassment. The committee's decision ended the Andersson connection and by 1959 Utzon's association with Erik Andersson was over and the latter withdrew, never again visiting Utzon at his Hellebæk office.

In its role as promoter, the committee appointed Ove Arup & Partners under a separate agreement, which removed the responsibility for paying the consulting engineer's fees from Utzon's hands. It was a bad decision that flew in the face of well-established professional procedure. Ove Arup & Partners, as the structural consultant, had a direct contract with the client, the Premier of NSW, and were appointed as co-principal agents with the architect. The specialist engineering consultants were to be responsible to the structural consultant, not Utzon. This arrangement effectively deprived Utzon of control of his consultants. One of the reasons the Government and the committee were keen on this arrangement was that they felt it desirable that Utzon, who was a comparatively young architect, should have the support of a more experienced firm.[34] This led to many problems and was a source of confusion about who Ove Arups answered to, and where its loyalty ultimately lay. There are sound professional reasons why architects, and not clients, employ and co-ordinate consultants.

Utzon should have resisted the change, which diminished his authority and was inimical to his interest. He did not, and instead chose to go along with what was an inherently unsound and dangerous practice that would lead to grave problems. By depriving him of his authority to handle payments or sack consultants, Utzon relinquished control of the work. That power became vested in the client.

The issue of fees was raised, but it would be many months before a formal contract of engagement between Utzon and the Government was agreed and signed.[35] Before leaving Australia, Utzon promised to return in February 1958 with a set of the final drawings of the Opera House. Twelve months after that, he planned to complete the detailed working drawings in time to lay the foundation stone.

Utzon flew out of Sydney on 22 August for Japan, then stopped at St Louis, Chicago and New York. He was an avid traveller and used the journey to gather additional information on the design of shell structures and the glass walls. Utzon was still in the process of formulating his ideas. On his stopovers in Japan and the USA he learned a number of valuable lessons:

> *Japan offered many opportunities to see staircases and piazzas in relation to big roofs and to people. It was very interesting to me to put the size of the temples in relation to the opera house. What struck me was the variation and shading of the elements and colours. Several shell-constructions and a lot of modern concert constructions are being built in Japan in the most skilled way and always with the finest craftsmanship ... In US I visited theatres, concert halls and saw Yamasaki's airport in St Louis, beautiful inside, but too heavy outside. The glass wall destroys the feeling of shell because of its vertical posts and lack of sufficient overhang.*[36]

Since his time with Steen Eiler Rasmussen at the Royal Academy, the experiential dimension of architecture had been a passionate concern for Utzon. It is easy to explain: what mattered most to him was the way people experience buildings. What intrigued Utzon was which aspects pleased people, and his curiosity led him to explore the nature of the architectural experience itself, to note which faculties – the senses as well as the intellectual mind – were most intensely involved. Drawings could never replace an actual experience, and he thought it wrong to treat them as an end in themselves.

The real measure of good architecture, Utzon thought, was its effect on people, how we see it and the feeling it engenders, are sheltered by it and made to feel safe, and in the multitude of ways it enriches our lives daily. He was much less interested in frozen architecture, as recorded in photographs, in monuments severed from people. Architecture for Utzon was intimately related to life; to say a building was 'alive' was the highest praise because it implied a closeness to the life experience.

In Chicago, Utzon visited Mies van der Rohe for a second

time. The famous German architect sat enthroned in his newly finished school, which accommodated all the students from first year to final year in one huge hall. The lights were on even though it was in the middle of the day and bright and sunny outside. Mies was displeased to see Utzon and declined to talk. Disappointed by this turn of events, as he left Utzon asked to use the toilet. Two symmetrical stairways led to the toilet; on his way down Utzon glanced across and spied Mies on the opposite, matching stair. Seeing Utzon, Mies turned abruptly and went back up.[37]

Mies detested Utzon's Opera House with a passion, because its sensuous expressive shapes were the antithesis of his own precise, minimal, steel-and-glass cages, and everything Mies van der Rohe had dedicated his life to. Utzon offered in place of his austere minimalist premise one that was liberating and sensuous and expressive. In view of Mies's large physical bulk, this was a rejection not easily ignored.

Next, Utzon called on Eero Saarinen in his Birmingham office outside Detroit on 17 September.[38] At the time, Saarinen was preoccupied in the design of the large concrete vaults for his new TWA airport terminal. He was worried about the effect of the exterior glass wall on the roof, which might destroy the delicacy of the roof forms if not handled sensitively. Consequently, he ordered a series of large 1:10 scale study models to be constructed to investigate the problem. There was a lesson in this for Utzon, who faced a similar problem with his Opera House shells: how to retain the light shell effect?

On his return to Hellebæk, it was full speed ahead. Utzon normally worked at home. To accommodate the extra staff he now needed he rented the manager's house at Fordamsvej 1 from the factory. It was a big, yellow, two-storey villa with a steeply sloping, orange-tiled roof and windows on the second floor. Visitors entered through a small, western, gabled porch at the front and were led upstairs to a large room which looked out across the Sound and had been adapted for use as a design studio. The villa was set well back from Bøssemagergade with a grassed yard in front. At the back was a patio terrace facing a small lake on which lived a family of swans.

The walls of Utzon's office were lined with Opera House job files. Later, even the floors were stacked with models of the famous 'sail' roof and wood half-models of the auditorium acoustic shells.

With its six architects, Utzon's office was relatively small, which was common in many architectural offices throughout Scandinavia, including Alvar Aalto's office. Utzon's method of working was also typically Scandinavian: he assigned each architect a separate area of the job to study and master. Utzon provided the design solutions and maintained control of the whole. The speed with which a job progressed depended entirely on Utzon himself. If he came up against a problem and slowed down, the others were held back and had to wait for him to brief them. The chief advantage of working this way, however, was that it involved Utzon in every decision and gave him total aesthetic control. This enabled him to supervise the project's development at all times and ensured an overall consistency.

Utzon knew all the people individually and could direct what they did. In November 1957, Utzon sent two staff to study the State Opera and Burgtheatre in Vienna, and the Festival Hall at Salzburg.

When the Melli Bank project came into the office and needed to be developed concurrently with the Opera House, Utzon assigned Hans Munk Hansen to carry out the work. Munk Hansen was appointed because he was an expert on Islamic architecture. Their shared interest in this had brought them together initially.

In the wake of the publicity after the Sydney Opera House competition, many tempting opportunities were presented to Utzon, but most were declined. He did not have any time to spare. This way he maintained his primary focus on the Opera House.

The mood in the office was extremely positive and full of high expectations. Everybody was buoyed up and keen. The Opera House was not just any building, it was a very rare thing in architecture, a work which from its inception carried the stamp of a masterpiece. All his staff recognised that the Opera House was one of those once-in-a-century buildings. It was so remarkable, so out-of-the-ordinary, it would never be repeated.

The office at Fordamsvej 1 had two floors. The ground floor was assigned to the technical people, while the designers, housed on the level above, enjoyed the view across Øresund to the high cliffs of Sweden, not much more than 5 km away. It was very cramped and people worked on top of one another. When the sun came out, yachts with white outstretched butterfly wings fluttered across the Sound's grey waters. Utzon was a demanding taskmaster who required his staff to work long into the night, and to be around just in case he felt inspired. This was difficult for married architects, on whom the late nights and weekends away from their families took their toll. By way of compensation, Utzon was very spontaneous and would vary the daily routine to avoid it becoming too boring. When a day proved sunny, Utzon might suggest they have a party. At such times, smoked salmon and wine were purchased and the office assembled on the back patio beside the swan lake.

Utzon's father, now retired and on a pension, helped with the architectural models. Taking advantage of his father's professional connections, a number of the half-models for the auditoria, including the spherical geometry model of the roof, were constructed at the Helsingør shipyard. The Opera House fascinated Aage Utzon. Now living by himself and 70, it gave Aage an absorbing interest, while his involvement in the model making, after a lifetime spent designing yachts, introduced a subtle nautical inflexion to the shapes, both to the inside as well as the outside.

Model making was an important feature of Utzon's work, which, while it improved the quality of the forms and helped to refine the shapes, was slow and expensive. Models were produced in addition to drawings and did not replace them. In November, Utzon wrote to Ashworth:

> *The shell-vault models will prove too complicated. We are making half models in scale 1:20 of the auditoriums here at*

the office anyhow. This is the only way of realising both the main form and the different connections between the ceiling and walls, walls and floor.[39]

Utzon was a natural teacher and frequently talked to his staff about his ideas during the lunch break. Besides keeping his staff informed about his current thinking, these monologues also enabled Utzon to clarify his ideas. The favoured topic was nature. He liked to explain how observing nature, exploring and touching a natural object, gave him a sense of its character. His other consuming topic of interest was light and, after light, texture.

Utzon demanded sharp drawings with neat, exact corners and refused to accept any drawing with lines crossed. Each drawing had to be properly composed and every piece of information properly arranged on the sheet. It was a case of do as the master says.

On 28 June 1957, Ove Arup visited Utzon at Hellebæk. Utzon showed his work to Arup, who was impressed and later expressed the highest opinion of Utzon as an architect. A month later Arup returned, accompanied by his partner Ronald Jenkins, a brilliant mathematician, and two other staff. Jenkins had designed the 7.5 cm (3 in) shell domes for the Brynmawr Rubber Factory shell roof completed in 1951, which was the first post-war building in England to command world attention.[40] They all spent a week at Hellebæk going over the competition drawings and analysing Utzon's structure. On these visits, the first thing Ove Arup would do after he arrived was go upstairs and play on the piano used for practice by Utzon's daughter, Lin. Ove Arup prided himself on his wide culture and music had been an important part of his life since childhood.[41]

Ove Arup had studied philosophy and mathematics before qualifying as an engineer. The way he approached a problem, therefore, was akin to the intellectual mode of a philosopher. Ideas interested Arup; his mind jumped from one idea like a wren between branches. He would throw a discussion wide open and often appeared oblivious to the need to find specific answers. He could be annoyingly vague, discursive and indirect, his mind darting this way and that as he piled idea on idea in a string of unfinished sentences. His thoughts ranged far ahead of his actual words and he was always in a hurry to catch up. To anyone unused to this, he could be extremely disconcerting.

Arup brought a special commitment to 'total design'. This involved integrating the various architectural and engineering strands so they became part of the one thing. 'Total design' was his most important and enduring contribution as an engineer. Arup preferred to work alongside architects, helping them and educating them simultaneously, while he absorbed and interpreted the aesthetic.

Ove Arup had joined the Hamburg office of the civil engineers, Christiani & Nielsen (also recommended as shell consultants for the Sydney Opera House by Dr Martin), in 1922. A year later, he moved to London. Arup established his name in English Modern architectural circles with his design of the concrete structure for a block of apartments by the avant-garde Russian emigre architect Berthold Lubetkin, known as Highpoint One, Highgate, built in 1935. At Highgate, Arup replaced columns with walls which he made a little thicker to carry the loads. Arup regarded the slab as the natural form for reinforced concrete placed in situ and embodied this idea to great effect in the Gorilla House and Penguin Pool at Regent's Park Zoo, both of which deservedly attracted much attention. For many years, Arup ran a construction and contracting company, which led to his interest in shuttering systems for concrete. In 1946 he wound up the business, and two years later established the firm Ove Arup & Partners, which has since become one of the pre-eminent engineering consulting offices in the world.

Ove Arup never lost his philosopher's outlook. This sympathetic openness was largely responsible for his remarkable achievements as an engineer. The Sydney Opera House severely tested Arup, though: a crisis point arose in mid-1961, when Arup, for all his flexibility, reached an impasse and the project looked like collapsing. Arup's interests extended far beyond engineering. It was his breadth of outlook that enabled him to work so productively with the pioneers of modern architecture in Britain during the 1930s. Completed in 1963, the Kingsgate Footbridge over the River Wear at Durham in England was Arup's deceptively modest final attempt to reconcile elegance and logic with ease of construction using a strict economy of means. This acutely intelligent structure was built when Arup was 68. It brought all the important, often conflicting, demands in its production together so they become more than a simple addition of the parts, but formed a whole that was at once beautiful and truthful.

The completion of the Opera House sketch plans in time for presentation to the New South Wales Government in early 1958 required an enormous effort by Utzon. The large plan drawings were supplemented by individual reports on such technical matters as acoustics and an updated estimate.[42] To do this, Utzon enlarged his staff from six to ten. Pushed by the extra demands, he had little time for anything else. Teething problems arose in 1958 with the Opera House Committee. The method of payment to Utzon through the Agent-General in London was a source of a seemingly endless series of embarrassing delays.[43] Utzon did not receive the A£5000 prize money owed him from the competition for more than a year. Even so, work continued to mount up. Around the same time an engineer acquaintance, Mr Jørgen Saxild, contacted Utzon to ask him to design the Melli Bank for his construction company in Teheran, Iran. Much of the Melli Bank work was delegated to Hans Munk Hansen, then in his late twenties.

This was not the only diversion: the Danish Union of Trade Unions (LO) competition for a college to train trade unionists in 1957 came at a time when Utzon was waiting for a decision on the Opera House. The LO College competition caught his attention because it was to be built very near him on the western outskirts of Helsingør. It gave him something to occupy himself with in the meantime. A short time after he was hired for the Opera House it was announced that he had also won the LO College.

Under the circumstances, he was left with no choice but to withdraw and the project was given to the second-place winners, Jarl Heger and Karen and Ebbe Clemmensen, two friends of Utzon from his stay in Sweden. They replaced his high-rise solution with an attractive range of low buildings, with tiled, single-pitched roofs and white walls.

During Utzon's visit to Sydney in August 1957, it had been agreed that the large hall must seat 3000 people. At Utzon's instigation, the best possible provision in either the large or small hall for opera would be an audience of not less than 1700 and a maximum of 2000, the most distant seat to be no farther than 26 m from the stage. Seating in the small hall for drama was not to exceed 1200.[44] Steensen & Varming of Copenhagen was asked to design the services for the Opera House, and Utzon persuaded the Höganäs clayworks, in Sweden, to build a full-sized prototype shell support. Sandro Malmquist, a Swede, was engaged to advise on theatre technique. Greater flexibility was achieved in the big hall by small adjustments in the size of the shell roofs. These changes were incorporated in a model to help Ove Arup and his staff begin their calculations. The roofs were lifted: the tall, largest shell of the Major Hall and Minor Hall by 10 m, while the restaurant was made 6 m higher. Starting with prostrate, horizontally spreading shells, by degrees the roofs rise and assume a more erect vertical posture.

In March 1958 Utzon presented the Executive Committee with the *Red Book*. It included a complete set of plans, sections, elevations, at imperial 1/32 in = 1 ft (1:384) scale. Supplementing this was Ove Arup's folded-plate scheme for the pre-stressed, long-span concrete floors and a tentative demonstration of a parabolic system of geometry for the roof shells. Dr Lassen Jordan wrote a report on the acoustic design of the halls in which he recommended a programme of acoustic model testing — the first major programme of its kind. Sandro Malmquist contributed a general essay on staging theatre in the Minor Hall. Interspersed between the individual reports were beautiful freehand drawings by Utzon. These brought a sense of excitement and anticipation to the presentation.

The book was an impressive achievement in terms of its broad scope and its attempt to relate all the various practical demands. Its printing alone – by Atelier Electra, Copenhagen – cost Kr 39,822 (A£2600).[45] Besides finalising the design, the *Red Book* was intended as a prospectus.

The *Red Book* involved a powerful act of synthesis by Utzon, who was handicapped by the committee's failure to pay him on time. In a little over four months, Utzon abruptly pulled the project into sharp focus so that what is described at this time is still clearly recognisable today. In most respects the Opera House on Bennelong Point is the same as the one found in the *Red Book*. Some room functions were changed and rooms shifted, but these changes were by way of improvements. In a single giant step the project acquired a convincing credibility. This was precisely what the Premier and the committee had been hoping for. It was essential at that stage to sweep aside lingering doubts and inject a new certainty into the politically charged atmosphere. Two months earlier, on 10 January 1958, the first Opera House Lottery had been drawn and with it the project's financial viability and independence from government money was no longer in doubt. The two most difficult hurdles, finance and a design, appeared to be solved. It was now up to Utzon.

From the lack of detail and padding by some of the consultants, it is evident that the *Red Book* was produced under considerable pressure. Utzon was rapidly catching up with the lack of detail in the original competition design. Each consultant depended on Utzon for his instructions, but until Utzon fully resolved the basic planning of the Opera House, and the client agreed to the changes, it was pointless for the consultants to begin making elaborate calculations. Each consultant worked concurrently and together. At this early stage, the most they could do was to confine their remarks to very general, in-principle statements.

In the *Red Book*, fine radial ribs were indicated on the underside of the shell roofs, to reinforce them against the anticipated heavy wind loadings. On advice from the assessors, Utzon removed the retractable glass walls at the sides and replaced them with static glass sheets folded into angled planes across the open shell ends. Utzon still hesitated to correct the congestion of the roof shells in the centre where they were pressed hard up against one another. This crowding was most noticeable between the two main hall roofs. On the south, the shell roof supports were less than 5 m apart. The skirt edges along the shell sides pushed forward, leaving the space feeling uncomfortable and constricted. The site was basically not wide enough for the two theatres side by side.[46] For it to begin to work, the peninsula would need an extra 10–15 m width.

Bennelong Point's narrowness also constricted the hall seating. In the *Red Book* Utzon showed 2675 seats for concerts, 1826 for opera, 1125 for theatre and 1011 for ballet.[47] The main concern was the limited capacity of the Major Hall. Ashworth estimated it was 325 seats under. For opera, Utzon sat the audience in two tiers in front of the stage. During concerts, the orchestra pit could be raised to bring it level with the stage, adding an additional 800 seats on the stage. At the back of the stage, above the orchestra, there was a horizontal canopy which could move vertically; its function was to reflect the orchestra sound into the audience.

The Major Hall was originally intended to be multi-purpose. To maintain the number of seats for concerts, for the time being, Utzon abandoned the multi-purpose hall concept, which in the *Red Book* scheme provided at best 1800 seats, and replaced it with a convertible hall having an opera stage that could be converted for use as the front part of the concert hall. This gained a further 900 seats, but caused the hall to be stretched so the farthest seat was 200 ft from the orchestra.[48] The new arrangement was made possible by introducing a demountable acoustic enclosure of a much greater size than before. Later, Utzon attempted to return to this solution but failed.

At the back of his report, Utzon included alternative floor plans showing balconies at the rear of the Major and Minor halls with the intent of increasing seat numbers by 230 and 180 respectively. With a rear balcony, the Major Hall could seat 2905, still 95 short of the 3000 demanded by the client. No matter how

Utzon tackled it, the seating problem in the large auditorium resisted solution.

Utzon's acoustics consultant, Dr Vilhelm Lassen Jordan, was famed in Denmark for his pioneering work on Copenhagen's Radiohus building. The walls of the auditorium acoustic shell inside the Sydney Opera House's roof vaults tilted inwards slightly and formed a gently rounded ceiling 109.7 m in radius. The stage tower rested on the Major Hall outside the main volume and differed from the Minor Hall, where the stage tower was separated from the auditorium by the proscenium opening. Jordan asked for the upper part of the side and back walls to be covered with panels to permit changes to the total sound absorption. Because of the Opera House's double-fan shape in plan, the greatest width and hence the largest seating area was in the middle. The auditorium retained its original shape with the ceiling broken up into smaller transverse panels whose undersurface was tilted to reflect the sound equally over the audience. It was Jordan's opinion that the volume of the two principal halls could be considered more than adequate.[49]

Almost immediately on his arrival in Sydney, Utzon spoke with the Premier who expressed the wish that work should start in February 1959. With a State election due in March 1959, Cahill wanted to pre-empt the result by commencing building a month earlier. Since the full design and documentation would take much longer than one year, the Premier agreed to Ove Arup's suggestion to divide the building into three stages: the first stage would comprise the building base; the second would see the completion of the roof shells; while the third and final stage would involve the fit-out of the theatres, the enclosure of the roof shells with glass walls, the interiors and the installation of all the building services. Many of the Opera House's later problems can be traced to Cahill's precipitous decision to begin construction before the building was fully planned.

At this early stage very little work had been carried out on designing the structure, heating or services.[50] Adding to Utzon's troubles, the April meeting of the committee materially altered the sketch scheme. Ove Arup, with the advantage of hindsight, said later that it was madness to start work so prematurely, however the political situation left them with no other choice – either they made an early start or there might be no start at all.

The NSW Government adopted a revised estimate of A£4,812,000 (A$9,624,000), and accepted an increase of one-third over the original estimate. At its meeting on 11 April, the Opera House Committee decided to let the Stage I contract, fully aware that in absence of complete working drawings, it was impossible to fix a price for the work. It would have been logical to wait until the design of the shells was solved and their weight was known, because the structural design of the base was governed by their superimposed loading. Time did not allow it.

Forced to start before he had sufficient detailed information, Ove Arup adopted an arbitrary loading for the roof shells equivalent to a 61 cm (2 ft) thick slab of concrete. This seemed more than adequate if, as he expected, the light roof shells were no more than 10 cm thick. If he was wrong, the sub-structure would have to be strengthened later to bear the increased loads imposed by the roof.

The April estimate set off a wave of adverse political criticism. Anticipating Ashworth's reaction, Utzon wrote to reassure him, 'We are all aware of keeping costs down and we are doing everything to simplify constructions, installations and every single detail.'

On the journey back to Denmark, Jørn Utzon ventured into China from Hong Kong. He was extremely fortunate to be allowed in and it was only through a chance encounter with Johannes Prip-Møller,[51] who had established the Buddhist–Christian Institute, that he managed to obtain a visa:

> it was a great experience for me to see the old architecture of China, especially Peking, it gave me a valuable experience to study the innumerable beautiful staircases and the variation of roof constructions (floating roofs).[52]

On his return to Denmark, Utzon began revising the drawings. In the wake of the March–April 1958 Sydney visit, a number of major revisions were necessary. Acting on a suggestion from Professor Denis Winston (a town planner and colleague of

Ashworth's), who thought the restaurant would be improved by placing it higher than the piazza, Utzon, for example, undertook to redesign the restaurant area.[53] When he did so the result was a better view from the tables, added to which it enriched the piazza detail.

To start the Stage I contract early in 1959, Utzon had to complete his final sketches by June 1958 to give his consultants sufficient time to complete their work. He did not complete the revised drawings until November 1958, five months after Ove Arup had called for them. Even so, the drawings were still not finalised and contained tentative intimations in lieu of the unalterable plans the mechanical and electrical engineers needed.[54]

Jørn Utzon was by now fully occupied by Sandro Malmquist, from Malmo, who was advising him on the small theatre. The same month, Mr Ralph Symonds called from London with an offer to provide larger-scale models of the Opera House. Utzon consented, since all that it involved were half-models of the auditoria interiors.

On an earlier visit to the Players' House in London, Utzon had been enchanted by the intimate relationship created between bar and auditorium in this small theatre-club. He hoped to reproduce the feeling in the Experimental Theatre. In revised drawings which Utzon sent to the committee on 3 June, he shifted the Experimental Theatre from the east side and placed it under the Major Hall so it would be accessible from the carpark, and enlarged it to seat 409; the Major Hall was revised to seat 2800 for concerts and 1703 people for opera, and the stage opening was re-arranged. This was made possible by introducing a small balcony of 11 rows, which projected forward of the rear of the Major Hall by only four rows of seats.

Utzon rearranged the Minor Hall stage opening to permit 1100 seats and declared he was now '... quite happy with this new scheme with three very different halls'. He liked the revised solution because it shared the same feeling as the original competition amphitheatre scheme. Moreover, during opera, the distance from the rearmost seat to the stage was considerably shorter than in the previous design. Utzon now worked closely with Lassen Jordan on the exact shape the interiors for the three principal halls should take. With this out of the way, he could then fix the position of the walls and the base of the shells. At its meeting in August the Executive Committee endorsed Utzon's revised drawings and approved a payment of A£33,120, bringing his total to A£48,120, or one per cent of the estimate. The work of demolishing the tram shed began on 18 August.

In Sydney, Utzon was an exotic curiosity. Hellebæk was so far away in every sense. Fred Turner, a Sydney architect, provided some insights into Utzon's office and his methods after a visit to Denmark in mid-1958:

> *Utzon is in many ways a perfectionist, and does not even consider the time which may be spent in study, trial and error of countless ways of doing a thing — but he must be convinced that whatever is finally done is right. Models have been and are being made of everything ... Doubts were expressed as to the very intricate support-points and intersections of roofing-shells at bases, particularly as to the shapes of covering tiles — so this section has actually been built, to full size in Sweden. The double-curves of the roofing-shells presented many aesthetic problems — many varying radii and curves were tried out, and scale models made in plastic. Moulds for these were fabricated to detail by a shipbuilding firm in Helsingør (Elsinore), from which the plastics were made in Copenhagen; Utzon then further studied each shell-shape in relation, one to the other, from the models until satisfied ...*[55]

By now, Utzon's office had completed the one-tenth full scale models, which Jordan needed for further research into the hall acoustics. In September, two of Ove Arup's staff spent several weeks with Utzon at Hellebæk deciding on the final structural system.

Hugh Hunt, the administrator of the Elizabethan Theatre Trust who was visiting Copenhagen on behalf of the committee, checked the drawings on stage technique. His intervention was a disaster. Thereafter, Utzon's plans for the small hall were largely dictated by Hugh Hunt, who insisted on a number of significant changes. These included the construction of a built-in revolving stage for the large hall and resulted in an absurdly shaped orchestra pit that was much too small. The mistake was later rectified when the stage machinery drawings were modified and the pit in the larger hall enlarged to improve its shape and capacity. Hunt also insisted on the inclusion of a built-in revolving stage in the smaller hall because in his opinion it would be used almost exclusively for drama. He did agree to make some provision for intimate opera by providing for an orchestra of up to 35 players. Hunt also reduced the Minor Hall stage opening from 12.2 m to 10.6 m, and instructed Utzon that no less than 390 seats were to be provided in the Experimental Theatre.[56]

The Stage I tender was considered by the Executive Committee at its 30 January 1959 meeting. Civil & Civic's bid was lowest at A£1,397,929. On the advice of the engineers who inspected the tender, it was accepted. There was a certain amount of concern because Civil & Civic's price was substantially lower than the next tender, and the firm had a reputation for deliberately underpricing their competitors.[57] Once the Stage I tender was accepted, Jørn Utzon returned to Sydney on 27 February accompanied by Lis. They brought with them a large bronze plaque to be used at the inauguration ceremony.

Utzon's visit to Sydney was quite short, due to the increasing pressure to finalise the concrete shell drawings, so Arups' Ronald Jenkins could complete his shell calculations within the set 21-month period.

Lis and Utzon arrived in Sydney late Friday evening, 27 February 1959, after a three-day stopover at the Reef Hotel, Honolulu, where they soaked up the sunshine and did some swimming. Even though it was the end of summer, they checked in to the Hotel Astra on Bondi Beach. The trip was a break from routine for Lis and they made the most of it. That Saturday evening they were entertained by Professor Ashworth, his wife Ella and their children at their home. True to her word about emigrating to Australia, Lis asked to see houses in preparation for the family moving to Australia, and the next day she was escorted around Sydney's northern beaches by the wives of two professors, Mrs Joan Winston and Mrs Ena Towndrow. Lis was delighted and Jørn Utzon later wrote to Ashworth to say that Lis felt '... she has got some very nice friends so she will be very happy when the time comes and she shall settle down in Sydney.'[58]

Four hundred or more people showed up for the commencement ceremony at Bennelong Point on Monday 2 March. The day began wet and overcast with people being forced to huddle in groups under umbrellas wearing dripping raincoats. Amid the general discomfort, the ceremony was delayed by the late arrival of the Deputy Leader of the Opposition, Mr Askin, who was busy campaigning for the upcoming State poll, less than three weeks away. Regardless of party, politicians can be relied on to forget lesser mortals such as the architect. Utzon had anticipated this. At the end of a speech that was interrupted by rain, Premier Cahill walked from the official dais to a large sandstone tablet to lay the inaugural plaque. The plaque had been designed by a young Japanese architect, Yuzo Mikami, and fabricated at the Helsingør Shipyard at the last moment two days before Utzon left for Australia. It was an intriguing circular object of ingenious construction and symbolism. When laid out, it looked like a miniature Japanese kimono.[59]

Bending over the plaque, people notice Cahill suddenly stiffen. Utzon had been waiting for this moment. Recognising Cahill's perplexity, he removed a long bolt from a cylindrical container, walked across to Cahill and showed him how to insert it into a groove in the plaque. The grooved cross marked the exact point where the longitudinal axes of the two halls met and served as a datum for all construction measurements. Utzon may have been only number seven on the dais but he was indispensable. He then demonstrated to Cahill how to tap a key into the bolt to prevent it rotating. Cahill lifted his arm in the air, a siren on a nearby police car blasted and was quickly drowned out by the roar of jackhammers. The work had started.

Speaking after Cahill, Deputy Leader of the Opposition Askin promised, 'the time for controversy is over ... It only remains for us to work together in a spirit of goodwill, and raise the necessary finance to bring this magnificent concept into being.' His assurance was shortlived. The Prime Minister of Australia, Mr Robert Menzies, sent a message of support that said he hoped this great project would be carried through in good speed. Mr Davis Hughes, NSW Leader of the Country Party, was noticeably absent. Standing in for him was the Deputy Leader, Charles Cutler, who spoke enthusiastically and encouragingly of the many ways the new building would enrich the cultural life of New South Wales.[60]

At the Museum of Modern Art in New York, Utzon's Opera House model went on display alongside Eero Saarinen's TWA airport terminal model. The Museum's exhibition demonstrated the enormous interest which the opera house design in Sydney had sparked around the world. People liked to think of Australia as a new country striking out on its own and doing unprecedented and challenging things. Sydney's Opera House pioneered the cultural frontier and seemed to be a harbinger of a new, more expressive kind of architecture that offered to sweep aside Modernism's harsh, austere look and rigid rationalism. Like other examples in the exhibition, it transformed concrete by introducing fancifully curved shapes that departed from the ordinary. A leading US architect remarked after seeing Sydney's Opera House model, that it was an 'architectural triumph' and 'superb engineering'. This sounded tremendously encouraging to Cahill, but he was only too well aware that such acclamation did not win elections. Contrary to what Askin said at the ceremony, the future of the Opera House hung on the election outcome.

At the Premiers' Conference on 4 March, Cahill put forward a proposal to establish a national housing corporation, but was flatly rejected by the Commonwealth Government. Cahill refused to drop his plan for a national housing body.

The mood of the electorate during the poll was subdued. Early newspaper reports boasted a swing to the opposition parties and predicted a deadlocked parliament. The movement away from the Government was more pronounced in the country. In an unexpected twist, the new leader of the Country Party and the Member for Armidale, Mr Davis Hughes, suffered an early swing against him but retained his seat.[61] Soon afterwards, he resigned the party leadership.

Cahill survived with a five-seat majority and announced his new ministry on 31 March. The election had been close, but was a victory nonetheless. The fate of the Opera House and the Labor Party were inseparable. The March 1959 election decided the Opera House issue for the time being.

Cahill's uncompromising stand on the Opera House appeared to be vindicated by the election. For Cahill the Opera House was much more than a personal monument. He fervently believed that Sydney and New South Wales deserved an opera house, and that it was worth fighting for, even if it meant risking his leadership. It was worth all the risks because it gave something back to the people that was lasting and would endure. [62]

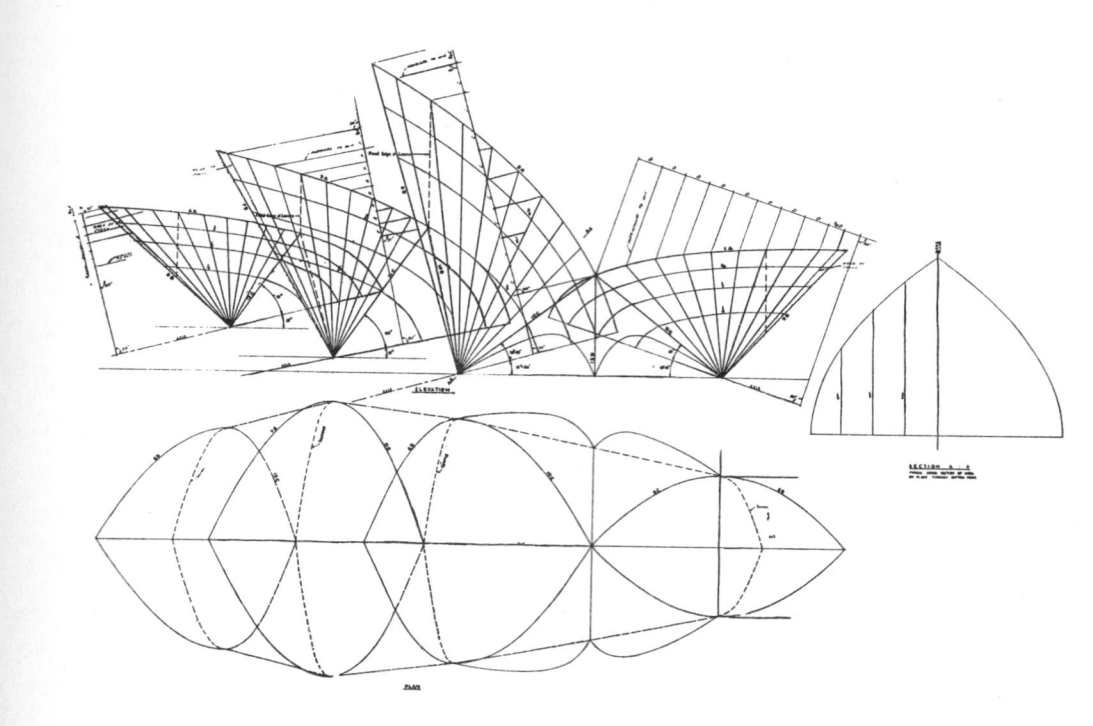

Preliminary layout of Sydney Opera House shells. Diagrams as designed by Ove Arup and Partners, engineers, 1957. Above: West elevation and plan. Below: Roof composition plan.

9

Following *Sputnik*'s Trajectory
Hellebæk, 1959–1962

Hellebæk was sunny, in Sydney it was raining. The office telegrammed its congratulations to Utzon and Lis in Australia: 'We are celebrating the day in sunshine with inaugural cake and champagne.'

The office party, attended by children and wives, was a birthday party of sorts for the Opera House replete with a large round cake whose icing duplicated the inaugural plaque. The Hellebæk confectioner made a literal copy of Mikami's drawing, including the dimension lines, arrows and numbers. While everyone relaxed by the lakeside, biting into generous slices of the sponge inaugural plaque, the actual plaque in Sydney was being screwed to a block of sandstone.

On the return journey, Utzon and Lis flew from Rome to Teheran, Iran, arriving on 28 March. Jørgen Saxild, a Danish engineer Utzon knew who owned a construction company that operated in Teheran, had earlier approached Utzon to design the Melli Bank.[1] Discussions on the Melli Bank had begun in 1958, the previous year. The project was a package deal: Utzon would be responsible for the design, while Jørgen Saxild's company, Kampsax A/S, would carry out its construction.[2] Although Utzon's fee had not yet been agreed with Saxild,

Utzon was unconcerned. He jumped at the chance to see Iran. His departure from Teheran was delayed till 4 April by a cold. Utzon received the news that he had won yet another competition – the town plan of Frederiksburg – in his sickbed.

The Melli Bank brief was extremely simple; there was to be just one large banking hall, top-lit through the roof. On his excursions to Teheran's bazaars and caravanserais, Utzon had been impressed by the use of natural light. Again and again, he returned to the bazaars to inspect their muted daylight. His observations convinced him he should avoid direct sunlight and reduce the overall intensity of indoor light, on the principle that strong direct light makes everything feel hot; soft indirect light has the opposite effect. In front of the Melli Bank, Utzon decided to create a piazza, to serve as an introduction and also as a buffer zone of insulated calm between the bank and the hubbub in the street.

Utzon later provided carparking under the building at the client's request. There were no trees outside in the street, which was extremely busy, dusty and noisy. To deal with all this, Utzon introduced a further transition after the custom of Islamic planning. The threshold is low and dark, to heighten the contrast with the main banking chamber. Anyone entering would feel compressed by the low ceiling at the entrance. Past it, steps led down to the main floor, and the roof flew up in a series of plunging transverse shells spanning the width of the chamber. Between them, Utzon formed narrow slits to admit light.

The spatial scheme was simple and dramatic and has been reused by Utzon many times since. It was not entirely original, as can be observed in any number of Frank Lloyd Wright houses. On this occasion, the originality of the idea is less important than the way it has been used. In Teheran, Utzon controlled the light and the movement of people to produce a varied sequence. Much of the Melli Bank's inspiration is derived from the local architecture. Utzon returned to Teheran a year later, in 1960. On this second visit to make some further changes, he was accompanied by Munk Hansen.

The Utzon family house in Hellebæk was small even in

Aage Utzon in 1960. Supplied by *Lene Utzon*

Utzon's mother, Estrid, circa 1937. Supplied by *Lene Utzon*

The hunting party, left to right, Erik, Leif, Jørn and Aage. Supplied by *Lene Utzon*

Two skiffs racing off Helsingør, with the Swedish coast in the distance; Leif and Jørn outstretched to the left. Supplied by *Lene Utzon*

The two Utzon families on the front terrace of Jørn and Lis Utzon's Hellebæk house, 1960. Left to right: back, Jørn and Leif; middle, Lis and Annie; front, Utzon children, including Kim Utzon (boy on knee), Lin Utzon (in white cardigan), Jan Utzon (last on the right). Supplied by *Lene Utzon*

The Utzons' house in Hammermill Wood, Hellebæk, 1952. *Keld Helmer-Petersen*

Kingo courtyard housing, Helsingør, 1957–60.

Above: The Opera House platform nears completion, 1963. *Raymond Brownell*

Below: Underside of folded concourse beams. *Raymond Brownell*

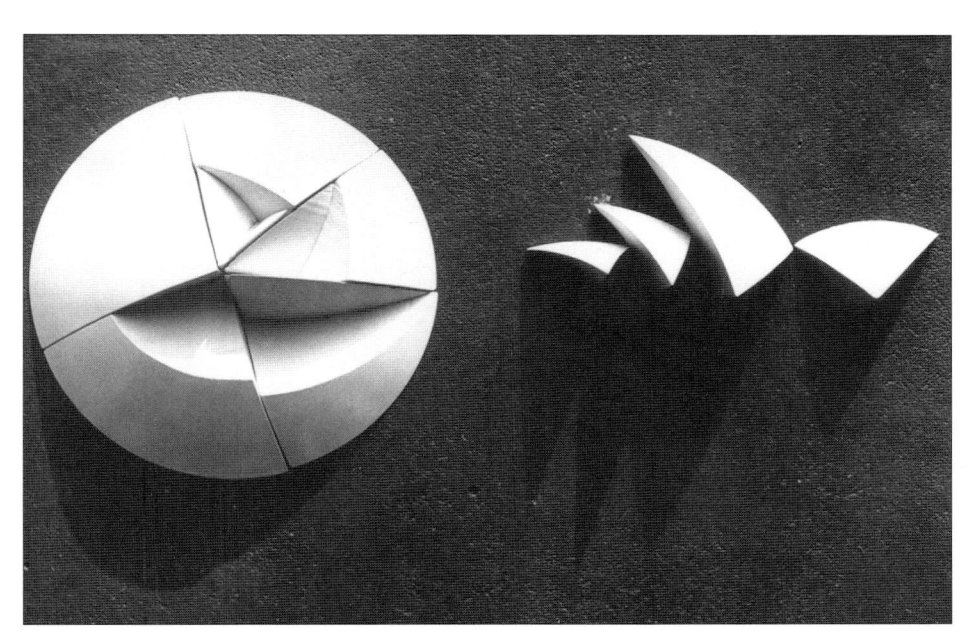

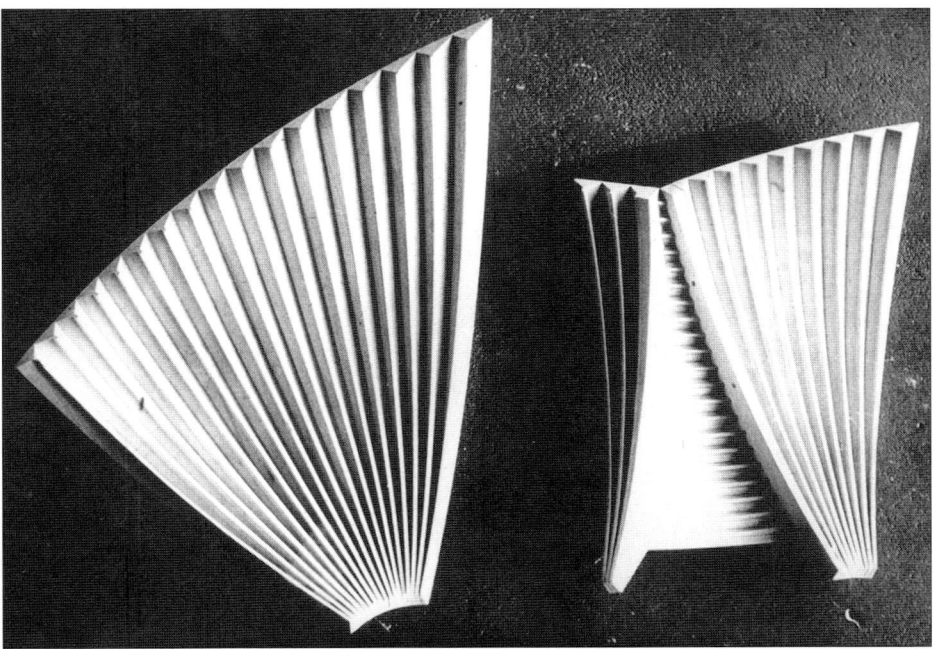

Above: Model demonstrating the spherical derivation of the geometry for the roof shells, October 1961. *Mitchell Library*

Below: Final spherical scheme, 1962–63. The underside of vault shows the Great Circle rib profile, precast partly in situ. *Mitchell Library*

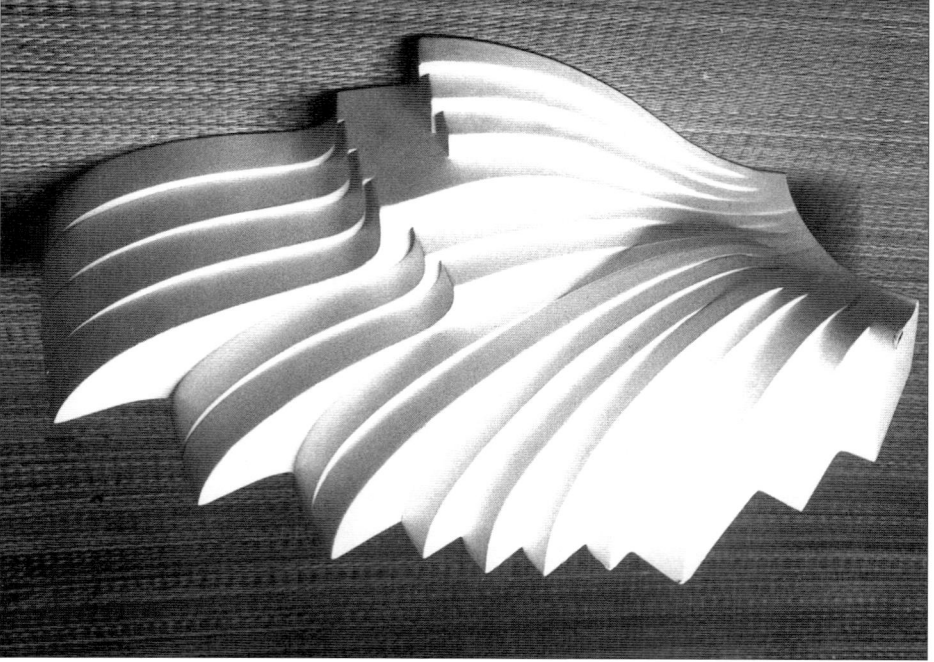

Above: Stepped auditorium view: Minor Hall amphitheatre in foreground, orchestra pit and stage. *Raymond Brownell*

Below: Plaster half-model of the Minor Hall ceiling, with concave radial profiled ribs, the final development of the 'Stepped Cloud' scheme, February 1962. *Raymond Brownell*

Above: The roof goes up: mobile rib-arch support.
Mitchell Library

Left: An octopus arch and pedestal of the Major Hall shell.
Raymond Brownell

Below right: Carpenter inside a hollow roof rib.
Raymond Brownell

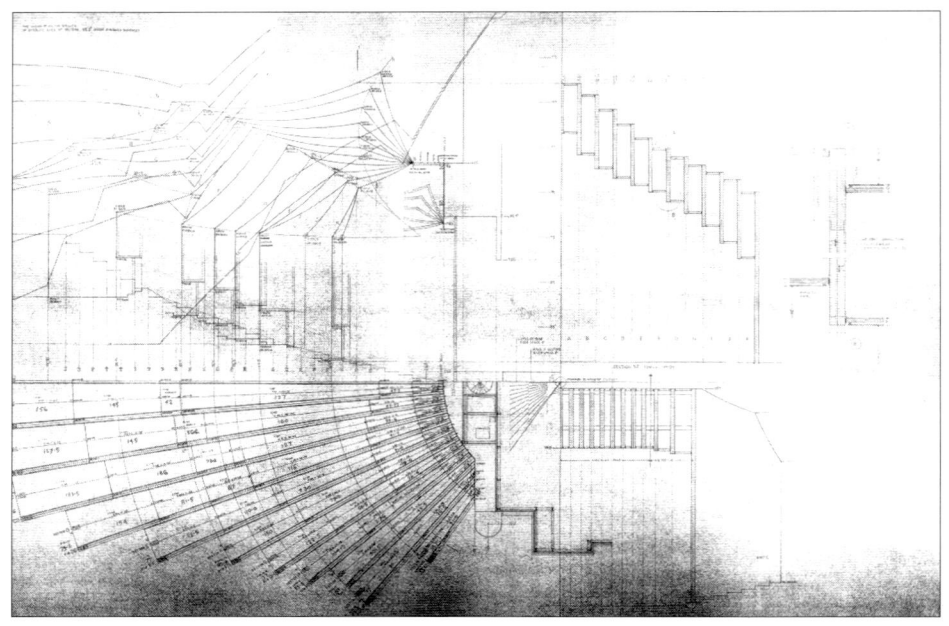

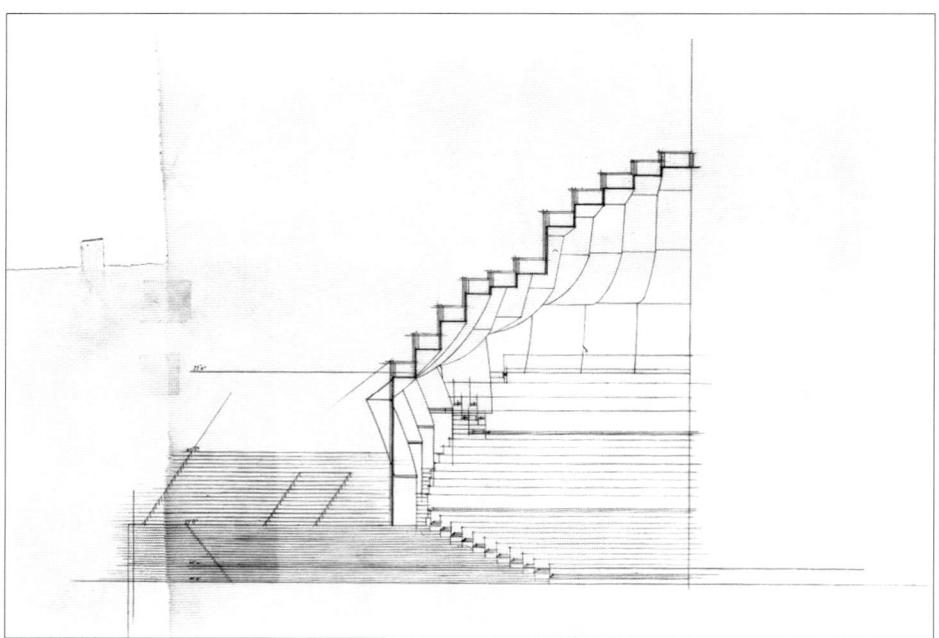

Above: Plan and sections of external contours, Minor Hall ceiling, July 1964 (SOH-1094). *Mitchell Library*

Below: Cross-section, rear of Minor Hall auditorium, plywood tube and rib system, November 1965. *Mitchell Library*

Above: Pencil perspective, southwest view across the new Heimplatz Square framed by the Kunsthaus, left; the steps lead to the theatre.

Left: Zürich Schauspielhaus theatre, longitudinal section, above, and floor plan, below. *Zodiac 14*

Above: National Assembly Building, Kuwait, 1971–83. A 1992 aerial view with main entrance in foreground, Main Meeting Hall right of central 'street'. *Moslet O. al-Sopeai*

Middle: Main Meeting Hall completed by Utzon with teak finishes, 1983. *National Assembly Secretariat, Kuwait*

Below: National Assembly Building, the central 'street'. *Moslet O. al-Sopeai*

1952. Now Utzon needed more space for his work. Demands to entertain after work increased with the Sydney Opera House and together with the arrival of Kim Utzon, the original house no longer sufficed. Furthermore, it was no longer appropriate for Utzon to work in the study–bedroom or the annexe. When important visitors, such as Ove Arup, Ronald Jenkins, Sandro Malmquist, Professor Walter Unruh, or any of a host of consultants visited, there was nowhere suitable in the village of Hellebæk for them to stay. In April 1958, such was the urgency of the task, Utzon handed over the job of enlarging his house to his friend Bent Alstrup, who prepared the drawings and obtained approvals.[3]

By building a second pavilion across the rear, Utzon more than doubled the area of the existing house.[4] At the same time, he purchased a second 0.68 ha parcel of land, for Kr 15,000, from his neighbour Mrs Pullich. The two parallel wings were connected by a narrow glazed gallery at right angles into the dining area. This new gallery divided the space at the back into two courtyards, on the west, opposite what formerly had been the garage was one courtyard, on the east side, a second courtyard extended out into a small orchard, enclosed by forest. Utzon excavated the earth bank behind the existing house to make room for the new wing. Drawing on his recent travels in Japan, Utzon adapted the idea of the traditional Japanese shoji rice-paper sliding wall and increased the privacy using slender vertical wood battens. The second building was almost invisible, hidden by the hill behind, and by the original pavilion at the front.

Utzon spent a considerable amount of 1959 working out the Opera House platform details and the services requirements for Ove Arup & Partners. Providing this data was essential to stay in front of the contractor in Sydney and so avoid delays. Not everything was realised as planned; there were frequent delays by Arups, whose staff found themselves constantly altering finished reinforcement drawings at the last moment. The result was a standard of work which the engineers deplored.

Vilhelm Lassen Jordan completed his acoustic model of the Major Hall in April. Professor Walter Unruh, the stage technique consultant from Berlin, recommended modifications to the stage lifts and the orchestra pit. Because of its significant effect on the platform, owing to its heavy weight, the stage machinery for the main hall had to be designed at this time. To deal with this, Utzon assigned his Norwegian assistant, Jon Lundberg, who was hired in September 1959, to oversee the stage machinery work. Utzon was left with no alternative except to design the stage technique in his office. This became the subject of a bitter wrangle with the Minister for Public Works on 28 October 1965, when the Minister denied Utzon's fee claim for the work.

An earlier decision by the NSW Government now began to cause embarrassment. No one had questioned the Premier's action in setting up the competition and authorising expenditures; however, what had been an interim expedient was carried over into the long term. Without parliamentary assent and an enabling Act of Parliament, the signing of Stage I of the Opera House contract by the Premier – indeed, any expenditure on the Opera House – was illegal. On 8 September 1959, Cabinet approved the preparation of legislation to sanction and provide for the construction of the Sydney Opera House.[5] The Opera House contract was deemed to fall within the meaning of the *Public Works Act, 1912*. It was backdated to 1 January 1957, and designated the Minister for Public Works to be the constructing authority with power to enter into the necessary contracts. Before the bill could be passed the Premier, J.J. Cahill, died suddenly on 22 October 1959 of myocardial infarction and was succeeded by R.J. Heffron. The legal position was not corrected until the following year, on 19 April, with the assent of the *Sydney Opera House Act, 1960*.[6]

Many later difficulties can be attributed to weaknesses in the legislation. If, instead of authorising the Opera House under the *Public Works Act, 1912*, the NSW Government had established a separate Sydney Opera House Corporation or separate authority, these subsequent problems might have been avoided or would not have had the severe consequences that they did. The new Act named the Minister for Public Works as the constructing authority, and empowered him to supervise the work. In the view of Cabinet, the Sydney Opera House Executive Committee, 'will function much as it has in the past notwithstanding that the legal authority will be vested in the Minister for Public Works.'[7] Simultaneously, it deprived the Sydney Opera House Executive Committee of its existing quasi-executive powers. The Act also appointed and named the architect and engineer, and limited the cost to A£4,880,000 (A$9,760,000) and specified that this amount could not, under any circumstances, be exceeded by more than 10 per cent. The Act also ratified the international competition retrospectively. The chief danger was the Act's inflexibility, as it made no provision for any adjustments without Parliament's consent. This proved to be inconvenient and politically devastating for the Government.

Furthermore, while the Act put the Minister for Works nominally in charge, it did not specify adequately how this would operate. Worse still, it failed to define the respective powers of the Minister and the Opera House Executive Committee, or set out rules to enable them to work together.[8] Indeed it avoided any mention of the function and authority of the committee. The Act lessened the authority of the architect and engineer considerably by handing responsibility for supervision over to the Minister. The Act was designed primarily to protect the Government from further attacks by the Opposition. As legislation, it failed completely to define the powers and duties vis-à-vis the Minister and the committee.

Without realising it at the time, the Government had created a rod for the Opposition to beat it with. This the Opposition did with each new estimate of cost which exceeded the original amount by 10 per cent, requiring the original Act to be debated and amended by the Parliament. The Minster was empowered to appoint new members to the Opera House Executive Committee or, if he so chose, he could abolish it. The committee's powers were effectively set by the Minister. It could hold discussions, call for reports, take decisions and make changes to the project, only while the Minister continued to agree with its acts.[9] In 1959, the Minister for Public Works was Mr Norman Ryan. Ryan had been appointed before Cahill's death and, by his own admission, did not understand the Opera House – yet he was ultimately responsible. Under the benign direction of a Minister for Public Works such as P.N. Ryan, the Sydney Opera House Committee was permitted to preserve the fiction that it was in charge; this situation could last only so long, and once a strong interventionist Minister came on the scene, intent on fully exercising the powers provided for under the Act, the Committee ceased to have a role.

The implications of this did not immediately affect Utzon. For many years, the Act's potential powers lay dormant and unused. It took a crisis, more particularly, a series of crises, to bring into the open the dangerous flaws in the 1960 *Opera House Act*.

Not surprisingly, the version of events that we have today is the politicians' version. Their actions and decisions have never been challenged or scrutinised properly. A complaisant press failed to look further, and assumed that the politicians on both sides were the victims of a giant architectural conspiracy, yet all the time it was the politicians who sat in the driver's seat. They, and no one else, were able to control events. If they failed to do that, they were to blame. The mistakes, the errors of judgement, were largely political, not architectural. It was political decisions that drove Jørn Utzon and Ove Arup down paths neither men would have chosen of their own volition.

Contrary to what a later Coalition Minister for Public Works, Davis Hughes, asserted in 1963, the Labor Party did not act corruptly. His accusations were without foundation. Labor's failure was one of comprehension: it did not understand how to create a performing arts centre for Sydney; furthermore, it failed to understand the magnitude of the task and the true financial cost of creating one of the great works of architecture of the century. If Labor acted courageously and decently after Utzon was removed, it must also take some of the blame for its dilatoriness and thickheadedness. The reality is that neither the Labor Government, nor the Liberal–Country Party Opposition which succeeded Labor, managed the project well. The task was beyond them.

In 1959, Utzon concentrated on the stage area of the Opera House. By the end of the year he had completed the drawings of the stage for the Major Hall. Utzon and Knud Lautrup-Larsen, his closest associate, left early in January 1960 to inspect progress at Bennelong Point and to discuss the new detailed seating plans and stage layouts with the Opera House Committee. The design of the roofs was still only exploratory, still at the stage of Utzon's suggestion for a roof 'made of netted wire and sprayed with reinforced concrete and later tiled'.

At its Friday 22 January meeting in Sydney, the Technical Panel of the Opera House Committee congratulated Utzon on his proposals for the Major Hall, which it considered satisfied all the basic demands of the panel. As well, it commended him for presenting alternative suggestions for the hall's use and asked him to instruct his engineer to design these sections of the work. Completion of the building was set for 1963. In order to achieve that goal, Utzon explained, it was critical for the stage machinery and lighting to be designed and detailed immediately and partly constructed, prior to the appointment of the contractor for the roof in Stage II. The roof would be involved and full details would have to be known by the engineers well in advance.

Utzon had at first selected sandstone to pave and clad the base; the stone, however, proved to be soft and prone to flaws. While it looked attractive, it was weak, and he was having second thoughts and preferred to substitute granite for the steps and an artificial material for paving, but still wished to retain sandstone as a facing.

At Ove Arup & Partners, Ronald Jenkins had completed a substantial portion of the experimental wind tunnel testing and structural tests on the two major Opera House shells at Southampton University. At this juncture, he decided to abandon the proposal to build the roofs as a single shell. Instead, he suggested using two skins, each approximately 7.62 cm thick, with a space between. Each skin was connected to the other by an interlocking cellular construction filled with holes for ease of access to the roof space. Arups also considered a type of rubber solution on the upper surface of the inner shell as an additional safeguard against the penetration of damp and condensation. Jenkins said he had satisfied himself in his own mind as to how the shells would be constructed.[10] It was a brave, if premature, announcement.

The next Tuesday Utzon inspected the site and left on the Friday, after a short eight-day stay. Before going, he promised to be back in December 1960 or January 1961. Utzon returned by way of San Francisco, breaking the journey at New York for an evening with George Nelson and his wife.[11] Utzon hoped to see his Opera House furniture manufactured by the Herman Miller company in Michigan. Herman Miller, the most progressive of the large US furniture manufacturers, employed George Nelson as its chief critic. Utzon had previously approached Nelson with a preliminary proposal for a special Opera House furniture line, which he wanted to have mass-produced, because it would reduce unit cost and guarantee a high quality.[12] George Nelson later wrote to Utzon in May, following their meeting, to reassure Utzon of his continuing interest.

Utzon, like many Danish architects, liked to be involved in furniture design. For a while, in 1958, he had employed a young furniture designer, Charlotte la Cour, a friend of Mogens Prip-Buus – an architect employed by Utzon – and when she left, she was replaced by Knud Vodder.[13]

Back in Denmark, Balslev, the electrical engineering consultant, forwarded to Utzon the drawings for the sub-stage machinery in the Major Hall and the orchestra pit in the Minor Hall. Then, in early March, Jenkins and H. Mollman from Arups slipped across the water to Hellebæk to study the stage areas. By August Utzon was ready to discuss the Maschinenfabrik Wiesbaden GMBH (MAN) tender for the stage machinery.

In June the office broke for the summer vacation. Utzon

spent his holidays at Strömstad below Oslo on the west coast of Sweden, among the islands.[14] The office resumed work on 16 July in readiness for the visit by Professor Ashworth to Europe. Ostensibly, Ashworth's visit was to finalise the requirements for the stage machinery and to ensure that the complete scheme was ready by the end of September in time for the appointment of the stage machinery contractor. The actual reason for Ashworth's presence was anxiety over the large increase in the cost of the stage machinery over the previous estimate, which had been based on the MAN drawings.[15] This escalation shocked the committee, which asked Ashworth to delve into its causes. The visit provided Ashworth with an excuse to check Utzon's progress as well and to see the latest and most advanced opera house and concert hall designs in Germany, which led the world in this field. Ashworth made a short stop in New York on 22 August, then proceeded to London. In New York, he visited the Metropolitan Opera House and talked to Jack Hennessy of Syska & Hennessy, the consulting engineers for the Lincoln Center, which had also engaged Professor Walter Unruh to supervise stage planning and machinery. Ashworth arrived in London on 24 August and immediately launched into a long series of meetings with Ove Arup & Partners at their offices in Fitzroy Street.

As a welcome gesture for Ashworth, Ronald Jenkins arranged a dinner party at his house. Utzon and his expert on theatre design and stage techniques, Poul Schouboe, also attended.[16] For all his brilliance as a mathematician, Jenkins, with his receding hair and ragged goatee, was an aloof, awkward figure. The party proved to be something of a trial for him. In Denmark, it was customary in the old days for men to stand at attention during toasts and click their heels as a mark of respect. When the toasts arrived, Poul Schouboe automatically rose, turned and faced his wife and slammed his heels together with a resounding bang heard by everyone, then promptly downed his wine. Breaking the silence, Jenkins spoke in a pained whisper: 'Not here, thank you, we had enough of that during the war.'

Ove Arup took the opportunity while Ashworth was in

London to stress that it was critical to the project that the work continued to be carried out in Denmark and England.[17] At the meetings, Ashworth, for his part, emphasised the political difficulties which would arise if the stipulated estimate of A£4.8 million (A$9.6 million) was exceeded. Ashworth knew this was extremely probable, having already advised the Chairman of the Opera House Committee, Mr Haviland, the new cost would be A£6.5 million (A$13 million), up A£1.7 million. Ashworth advised Utzon and Arup to adopt the strategy of approaching the NSW Government only when there was a large increase and to ignore small increases.

The stage tower was a critical cost factor. It rested on the platform base and also supported the roof – hence both the roof and platform were affected by any change in the size, weight and placement of the tower. For this reason, the stage machinery was important to the roof engineering design for Stage II and consequently the Arups engineers needed a decision on the stage machinery contract as a matter of urgency.

With all this in mind, a provisional date was established for the commencement of Stage II of 1 October 1961. Ove Arup & Partners, fearful of the mistakes in Stage I that were now coming to light, recommended that Stage II should not be let as a competitive tender. Instead, the work should be carried out by a selected contractor under a negotiated contract. Such an arrangement would not exclude an Australian company from consideration.

After further discussion, Ashworth visited the Royal Opera House at Covent Garden, whose stage machinery provided a sharp lesson on what not to do, and the Coliseum Theatre to see its antiquated stage machinery. He then set off on his Grand Tour of continental opera houses.[18] The first he visited, on 29 August, was the National Theatre of Mannheim, which comprised two halls – a minor hall seating 800 and a major hall for 1700 people. Ashworth was accompanied by Jørn Utzon and Poul Schouboe. All participated in the discussions with theatre managements. It was a valuable, if strenuous, programme: Germany was in the throes of rebuilding its musical performance halls destroyed in the war and led the world. These new halls featured some of the most advanced designs to be found anywhere. After two days in Mannheim, the three men visited Vienna for technical discussions at the office of the stage machinery engineers Waagner-Biro, with tours of the Burgtheatre and Vienna State Opera. The Burgtheatre boasted a large revolving stage with built-in podiums and a cyclorama. Of particular interest were the stage facilities at the Vienna State Opera, which seated 2300. This was 700 fewer than Sydney required for the Opera House's main hall. Rebuilt five years earlier, Vienna had six lifts which could move up or down singly, or in groups of three. The system was made possible by a paternoster movement that allowed big sets to be moved simultaneously using 25 cm (10 in) high stage wagons on slides stacked on top of one another which were lowered beneath the stage floor and could be moved over the entire stage area. This was exactly the arrangement Utzon had envisioned for his main hall in Sydney. There were two cycloramas, one white and one blue.

Waagner-Biro was keen to win the stage contract and arranged some night diversions. Utzon attended Wagner's *Rheingold* at the State Opera; the next evening it was Ferdinand Raimund's *Moisaseurs Zauberfluch* at the Burgtheatre. Seemingly by accident, a Viennese beauty was presented to Ashworth. When his temptress endeavoured to sit on his lap, the ever-vigilant Ashworth blocked her path and prevented her approaching closer by swiftly cocking a fat thigh and leg. He could not have made his rejection plainer had he been a guard lowering the boom across a border crossing. The rebuff was duly noted. At Salzburg, a further attempt was made, this time with Utzon as the target, but with the same result. Neither Utzon nor Ashworth were susceptible to such blandishments.

From Vienna, Ashworth, Utzon and Schouboe paid a quick visit to the Salzburg Festival Hall, which operated a short one-and-a-half month season in August and September. The stage machinery of the Festival Hall, which seated 2200, was serviced by five podiums capable of rising up to 3 m above the stage. There was one cyclorama, as well as a back projection screen of transparent canvas and an orchestra pit subdivided into three lifts for greater flexibility.

The party reached Hellebæk on 4 September, and was joined there by Vilhelm Lassen Jordan, the Danish acoustic consultant, and Professor Unruh from Berlin. Utzon then had discussions with Unruh on the revised stage arrangements and its working and met Goddard and Mason, from Rider Hunt & Partners, the quantity surveyors, who arrived to discuss the implications of the stage tenders and the concrete shell roofs.

At Hellebæk, Ashworth was most impressed by the model shop. This was located in an abandoned Hellebæk clothing factory behind the hotel on Strandvej street on the Helsingør side. It was a sturdy reinforced concrete factory structure with plain white-painted walls, high ceilings and exposed beams. The lofty industrial windows let in a tolerable amount of daylight, but best of all, it provided unlimited room to work. Utzon hung a large Fernand Léger with figures on one of the walls to soften the space.

Pushed for time, Utzon's staff assembled the exhibition of Opera House models inside the factory a few days before Ashworth's arrival.[19] The fact that it was improvised was not apparent, indeed, the exhibition proved a great success. Nothing could disguise the originality of the work, whose unprecedented nature spoke for itself. News of the exhibition spread quickly far and wide.[20] When word reached Copenhagen, the office was inundated by telephone calls from people requesting permission to visit Utzon's Opera House model exhibition. The situation became so hectic Utzon had to instruct his secretary to say that the exhibition had been dismantled to prevent further interruptions to the work of the office. Ashworth was so overwhelmed by Utzon's use of models in the design process he requested the Australian Broadcasting Commission to make a documentary film about it.

Some of the models were very large. Ashworth was photographed sitting inside one model of the main concert hall. Yuzo Mikami, the Japanese member of Utzon's staff, crawled into a large model to take photographs and while he was lying prone on the floor another architect slipped a stiff roll of cartridge paper up a trouser's leg, to prevent him bending his knee, leaving Mikami stranded inside and unable to crawl back out. After a while someone took pity and he wriggled free.

Because the Opera House represented such a complex, three-dimensional challenge, models of various kinds proved indispensable as aids. Ashworth noticed that everyone on Utzon's staff constantly referred to models in the shop. This was especially true of the interiors. Utzon had produced a design for the Major Hall that Ashworth later described as resembling a suspended tent ceiling. The smaller Minor Hall, which was more advanced than the Major Hall, received an equal amount of attention and looked very exciting.

Jørn Utzon could be very demanding. Once Jon Lundberg worked 14 days and nights straight without seeing his family. The arrival of Ashworth and other visitors signalled a break in the office routine and a chance to relax. Following the intense preparations for the exhibition, Utzon's staff was accompanied by Jordan, the acoustics expert, on a tour of Vilhelm Lauritzen's Concert Hall, or studio 1, at Broadcasting House, and the Tivoli Concert Hall in Copenhagen. Unruh also came along. Yuzo Mikami, revelling in his role as office photographer, snapped the party in front of the Little Mermaid and lunching in Langelinie Pavilion restaurant.

In the meantime, Utzon was busy on several other fronts: a competition in Spain for the Mediterranean town of Elvira and a scheme for a shopping centre at Eline Berge in Halsingborg, Sweden. Under duress, Utzon would suddenly break off and turn his attention temporarily elsewhere, to something entirely unrelated to the Opera House. Both schemes incorporated plateaus and platforms.[21]

At the insistence of the Sydney Opera House Committee, Utzon sent Skipper Nielsen to Australia as his site representative.[22] Meanwhile, the finalisation of the electrical consultant was becoming urgent, following the resignation of Balslev & Partners on 19 September because of problems coping with the changes to the job, in order that their replacement, Zeuthen & Sørensen, Consulting Electrical Engineers, could start.[23] Jenkins arrived in Hellebæk on 31 October to discuss the selection of an electrical consultant and with this resolved the job returned to normal. At the end of November, Jenkins confidently reassured Ashworth, after having tried two complete designs for the gallery in the Major Hall, that a gallery would not be needed. Instead, he proposed extending the general seating and using it to support the suspended rear ceiling.

For the moment, Jenkins was very happy about his collaboration with Utzon:

> I am sure you [Ashworth], like us, are very impressed by the competence of the architectural assistants. We believe the maximum number of assistants of this calibre are being employed. Mr Utzon has kept himself free of other engagements so that he can concentrate on guiding the architectural development, and personally making all the decisions. This is what we want since it is the only way to get details in keeping with the general conception.[24]

Up until then, the stage machinery and halls had been Utzon's main concern. With these settled, he turned to the outstanding problem of finding a solution for the roof shells. Fundamentally, as conceived, the shells were not viable as structures. This necessitated a search for alternative shell designs to eliminate the large bending moments produced by the roof shapes. Instead of rejecting what Utzon had drawn, Ove Arup endeavoured to find a suitable geometry that would preserve the original shape. If he had been less sympathetic and had rejected the original structural scheme, he would have avoided at least two years of wasted effort. His persistence with Utzon's unsatisfactory roof shapes cost the engineer dearly in design time and affected the construction of the roofs.[25] The task of analysing the shells and finding a suitable geometry fell to Ronald Jenkins, Ove Arup's associate partner. He pointed this unwelcome truth out to Utzon at the very beginning. In 1961, his pent-up frustration spilled over in a brutally frank admission, 'We went to all this trouble because of the shells being the wrong shape as we pointed out to you right at the beginning.'[26]

The main objection to the original Utzon roof shapes was that every shell was different. This lack of a defining geometry made it impossible to reuse formwork, which was essential for an economical construction. In contrast Pier Luigi Nervi, the great Italian shell builder, invariably made certain that his domes and hangar structures were constructed with the same repetitive precast units. Ronald Jenkins searched for a geometry to allow repetition in the formwork which would also permit him to keep the original roof shape. The alternative to this was to imitate what Eero Saarinen was doing in his TWA terminal at Idlewild Airport. Here, the vault was formed with one-off formwork in what was effectively a huge lump of poured-in-place concrete sculpture. The TWA terminal was the exact opposite of a uniformly thin concrete shell, which made it far from optimal structurally as it needed massively thick concrete leg-supports. The additional weight that resulted from a freely formed roof had to be carried by the base. That was the catch for Utzon. The platform of the Opera House had already been designed on the assumption that it would carry a lightweight concrete shell roof. If there was a substantial change, the footings and the entire base structure above them would need to be enlarged and strengthened to carry the extra weight of the roof.

In order to analyse a shell and predict the stresses in it, the engineer must first describe the shell shapes mathematically. Utzon, as he freely confessed, was no good at mathematics. Ronald Jenkins was a gifted mathematician and so was given the task of mathematically prescribing the Opera House's free-form shells.[27] In principle, shells must be very thin in relation to their span. This is because the factors that produce bending in the structure have to be eliminated, so that the shell can act like a membrane in which all forces are tangential to the surfaces. They have to be so thin to make them incapable of resisting any forces other than those acting in tangential directions. Where, as happens most often at the supports, there is a disturbance to the stress pattern and a uniform shell thickness is impossible, that part of the shell has to be thickened. The range of possible modern shell forms is very limited. Utzon was little aware of these limitations when he made his design.

The aim in the Opera House was to find a geometry to define the shell shapes which would permit Utzon's roofs to be constructed economically with the least departure from the original sculptural shape. Any great departure was likely to result in a political storm and lead to accusations by unsuccessful competitors that Utzon had altered his design.

Utzon's free-form shells in his competition scheme were unrelated to any pure compression shape that might be required structurally and concentrated the forces at the bottom. What Utzon had produced was sculpture, not a structure with any known geometry. In that sense, it was structurally naive.[28] The first task of the engineers was to give Utzon's shells a precise geometry. To accomplish this, they needed to investigate all the potential load conditions. Then, from a consideration of these, they would attempt to define shell geometries that avoided, or at least minimised, bending moments on the shell roof surfaces.

Jenkins considered a wide range of possibilities, from non-pointed arches to doubly curved shells over each hall, and a single roof without discontinuities over both halls. However, he set his sights on a structure that would preserve the original roof silhouette.

As a start, Jenkins asked Utzon to accurately draw a typical shell profile. Up till then, the profile had not been fixed; it was not a known curve but only a freehand shape.

On 4 October 1957 the Russians launched *Sputnik*, the first artificial satellite to orbit the Earth. It streaked across the night sky, a small pinpoint of moving light emitting a continuous beeping signal. Around the world, people were amazed and entranced. Till then, the sky had belonged to the gods. Now humans had stepped into this new unexplored realm, sending objects up which raced around the earth every 96 minutes.

'It goes forever, and never comes back,' Utzon exclaimed, a little optimistically as it turned out. *Sputnik* simplified the problem of the Opera House for him; his roofs would follow the satellite. The trajectory of *Sputnik* was a parabola that started by climbing vertically then gradually rolled over as it gained altitude. This, Utzon decided, was the curve he was searching for, the curve leading across a new frontier. At its base on the platform, the roof surface had to be vertical like the ascending *Sputnik* rocket, but further up it would curve until it stopped climbing and began to descend.

Utzon wasn't sure how to draw a parabola precisely, so he improvised. Taking a slender 4 mm square Perspex rod used on landscape plans, Utzon fixed it on the table edge so it stood vertically and pushed its tip with his finger, forcing it sideways so that it curved away from him. This gave him the curve he was after. He sent the profile to London with a note saying this was the shape he wanted. When the engineers at Ove Arups in London analysed the profile, Utzon's curve turned out to be almost exactly a parabola. The Opera House roofs joined the new Space Age on the tail of *Sputnik*'s parabolic trajectory.

Jenkins soon became convinced that a parabolic approach would deliver the correct result eventually. Based on the 1958 scheme in the *Red Book*, he produced a new proposal in December 1960 with the same parabolic roof profile and the same parabolic rib profile as before, but using a double skin of concrete and two-way ribs and structural louvre walls in the ends tying the sides of the shells together. In this scheme, all the shells were connected. Using the louvre wall which Utzon placed in the open ends of the shells, Jenkins tied both sides of the roof together. The total thickness of the revised construction, including the tiles, was about 15 cm compared to the distance between the outer and the inner shells of about 1.8 m.[29] The louvre walls closed the open shells and made it impossible to see into the ends from outside. For Utzon this was very disappointing but Jenkins needed the louvre wall to tie the open ends together and make the roof more stable. Utzon hoped the form of the roof would explain itself, but instead he was offered a crippled shell held together by a cross-member. Utzon objected strongly to the shell surface being met by an ordinary wall at this point.[30]

What Utzon wanted was to be able to see inside the shell

ends from outside. Only in this way would the eye be able to follow the structural story.

By early 1961, Ove Arup & Partners was under heavy pressure to find a workable solution. Jenkins had now divided the roof into three separate structures closed at the open ends by Utzon's louvre walls, which he turned into a solid membrane. Between April and June he developed three additional solutions using a combination of circular-rib and parabolic-ridge profile geometry. The first comprised a steel space-frame of varying thicknesses between two reinforced concrete skins which was thickened at the points where the louvre walls had once been. It was a transitional solution which required further work. In May, Jenkins refined it by including a series of possible structural tie-connections through the louvre walls. The whole thing was extremely clumsy and even less promising than the previous scheme. Jenkins seemed to be running out of ideas. A month later, in June, he tried replacing the double concrete skin space-frame structure with triangular precast concrete ribs which he held up by using the stage tower walls as supports. It was a definite advance, but Jenkins failed to capitalise on what he had achieved.

Around this time, he exchanged the earlier parabolic profile for a rival ellipsoid scheme with an elliptical ridge and ribs, and with the two concrete skins mounted on a slim steel space-frame. The composite steel-and-concrete construction was left unaltered.

The absence of a controlling roof geometry for the shells now brought on a major crisis. If Ove Arup & Partners failed to find an answer, the entire project would be in jeopardy. Without the roofs in the form they had been proposed, the Opera House would be a failure.

Everything depended on Ronald Jenkins but in late June 1961 Jenkins announced at a partners' meeting that he was quitting. The situation looked bleak, not only for the engineers' office, but for Utzon as well. The feeling of intense crisis was heightened by the earlier scrapping of the first scheme for the shells.[31] The mounting tension in the partnership – Hugo

Mollman, a Danish associate, had resigned in protest at the departure from a parabolic shell geometry – combined with the insurmountable difficulty presented by the shells, had proved too much for Jenkins. To fill Jenkins's place, Jack Zunz,[32] a South African engineer, was brought in.

Zunz was Jenkins's superior in one important respect – he was an astute judge of people and their capacities. After travelling extensively with Utzon, Zunz concluded that Utzon was much more complex than he appeared on the surface. Zunz saw past the charming handsome exterior, the irresistible charisma which led people to accept his ideas. There was another side to Utzon few people were privy to. Zunz recognised this and used it later to advantage.[33]

After the Jenkins crisis, Ove Arup, who was not directly involved in the roof problem, presented two options to Utzon. Instead of building the roofs with two skins separated by a steel framework, he suggested an alternative: each rib should have a 'V' fold underneath. In principle, this was the same as the folded-slab concourse beams, however, for the roofs the folded beams would be curved in two directions which made them more complex. The structure would be concrete, both inside and outside.[34] Utzon, on hearing the proposition, cried out: 'I don't care what it costs, I don't care what scandal it causes, I don't care how long it takes, that is what I want.'[35]

Utzon thought the steel frame hidden between two external concrete skins was structurally dishonest and was thrilled to be rid of it. The folded-rib solution was explicit: from underneath, each rib and line of load would be visible. For the first time since they started, the roof now possessed real integrity – the eye readily worked its way down from the ridge to each pedestal on the base; the line of the ribs followed the path of the load. The ribs drew everything together.[36] No wonder Utzon reacted with such enthusiasm. Arup's folded concrete ribs represented a logical progression from the small ribbed shells in the *Red Book* that took the folded beams of the concourse at the front and stood them upright so they radiated outwards in a giant fan-like structure comparable to a palm frond. The ribbed vaults were not only logical and clear, they also visually expressed their load-carrying function.

The breakthrough came suddenly. As is so often the case, it was preceded by a long thorough examination and testing of the alternatives. Jørn Utzon has provided an anecdotal account.[37] It is unlikely that Utzon by himself would ever have arrived at this solution without Ove Arup's insistence on the need for a controlling geometry to standardise the ribs. In the absence of Arup's harping, Utzon might never have made the leap to a spherical geometry. Even so, Utzon's discovery was an accident. Without the preparatory tutoring, it is doubtful whether he would have realised the significance of what he had found. Put another way, to state a problem correctly is to advance its solution. Arup correctly stated the problem for Utzon in terms of standardisation and geometry. Even with that, it took Utzon two years to make the final breakthrough.

Utzon had been working on several possibilities all along because he felt an in situ cast concrete structure was unsatisfactory. When Jenkins stated to Utzon that he couldn't come up with a workable scheme based on an elliptical geometry, Utzon was forced to look at other possibilities. It was Utzon who first suggested that the roof ribs be prefabricated in sections, because of his previous experience with the shell surfaces in the Höganäs mock-ups in Sweden.

Utzon felt hampered by the lack of progress in the structural design. By mid-1961 it was beginning to look like the roof would never be built. One day, deeply discouraged, he went into the model shop, and began to break up the shell roof models. Starting with the smallest roof he casually stacked each on top of the other as he tore it from the base. When he finished, he looked at the stack and was surprised to find how neatly they fitted inside one another. The curvature of the shells was similar. Thinking about this for a moment, Utzon asked himself why it was not possible to cut out the curvature from the same template. He then asked himself, 'What is the curvature which has the same radius? It is the sphere.' He had his answer. The shells could be cut from a common sphere.

Utzon was tremendously excited by his discovery. The next step was to discover what shapes you can cut from the surface of a sphere. Not being a geometrician, he took a large rubber beach ball and experimented. Utzon found he could draw very accurately on the ball with water. When wetted, the water mark stood out as a shiny wet surface against the dry areas. He took the ball and placed it in a bathtub of water. By revolving the ball, he could make a series of different spherical shapes based on the same sphere.[38]

If you replace the beach ball with the earth, the vertical lines of longitude radiating from the North Pole describe the edges of each shell, other circular arcs cut across them from the side and establish the height and ridge profile of each shell. It was all quite simple. Utzon rushed to the Helsingør shipyard to construct a wood spherical model illustrating his discovery. He was tremendously excited and worked through the night building the model, not stopping until it was finished. At his next meeting with Ove Arup it was a straightforward matter to give the sphere a radius of about 80 m (246 ft) which was the distance to the outer face of the ribs. The spine of each roof against the sky would describe a completely regular curve.

Utzon now placed his architecture in the same futuristic perspective with *Sputnik* and space exploration. He tackled the problem of the shells by looking down from outside, much the way an astronaut views the earth from outer space. Hence the geometry of the shells echoed our new perspective of earth from outer space, which had profoundly altered mankind's geocentric universe. The spherical geometry of the shells converted each shell surface into a fragment of a large, imaginary sphere.

The inspiration for the spherical geometry came from Utzon's familiarity with the fabrication of large steel ships' hulls, which he knew first at Ålborg, and later at the Helsingør shipyard:

> *I've grown up in big steel shipyards and I had at Elsinore, close to my office, all the possibilities I wanted for studying the production of big curved shapes ... Also I had developed*

various systems for prefabrication in the building industry before the opera house.[39]

Because he was so involved with the idea of prefabrication, it was natural for Utzon to want to apply it to the shells. Ove Arup did not have to be persuaded on this, he always asked how something would be built. Making the spherical roofs of precast segmental ribs would also avoid problems such as tiling the outside of the shells.

The orange-peel account, which claimed that Utzon was inspired by the shape of an orange, provided a convenient way to explain the spherical geometry. Explanations about scientific discoveries made with fruit are as old as Isaac Newton. The orange story was an instance of post-rationalisation since the orange was a smaller, more portable replacement for the beach ball.

In 1961 Jon Lundberg rented a cottage close by Utzon's house in the forest. He sometimes looked after the Utzon children and remembers Utzon's son Kim, then four years old, peeling an orange. By his account, Kim is supposed to have said, 'What about this dad?' or something similar, while holding the orange peel for his father to inspect. Lundberg recalled that the office was desperate to find a solution. The orange peel demonstrated how a curved surface could be obtained from a sphere. This may have supplied Utzon with a basic concept for analysing the roof into standard elements. Memories vary: Mogens Prip-Buus thought the breakthrough occurred at the end of lunch when everyone had drunk wine. Jørn is supposed to have said, 'It is a big sphere, with bits cut out of it just like an orange.' Then he went to the shop opposite and returned with an orange to demonstrate his idea.

There are other possible explanations: the North Atlantic mussel shells which litter the beaches at Hellebæk and Hornbæk after storms are roughly spherical and the shell is subdivided by ribs that radiate from the hinge. The two halves form tiny perfect replicas of the Opera House roof shells.

Utzon's accounts of his inspiration for the roofs varied enormously. Over the years he has repeated the story of the segmented orange.[40] In 1994, when interviewed by the Danmarks Radio journalist Pi Michael, he introduced an entirely new account: 'If you take a palm leaf – and that is exactly what inspired me ...'[41] Utzon seems to have been very confused, for one thing a palm leaf does not explain the geometry, only the pattern of ribs, and while palm trees abound in Mallorca, where he was living at the time of this interview, there are none in Hellebæk, where he was working. In design parlance it sounds suspiciously like a case of post-design rationalisation.

The common thread running through these accounts is their shared explanation for the geometry of the roofs, which represented a complex problem that Utzon was incapable of solving mathematically. So the stories present the solution in terms of a pragmatic model which was within his limited grasp conceptually. These accounts made something which was incomprehensible to most people easy to understand.

The discovery had an important and immediate practical consequence: Utzon telephoned Ove Arup in London with the news that they could cut the shells from a sphere. Ove Arup has given his own account, which deserves to be quoted at length:

> *The design of the so-called shells has been beset by difficulties. As you [H.I. Ashworth] know, when Ronald [Jenkins] last visited Sydney he had arrived at a fairly definite scheme for the construction of these shells which involved the erection of a framework in steel which would be covered by an external and internal concrete skin. There were, however, a number of outstanding architectural and structural problems which proved rather difficult to resolve. The former mostly revolved around the manner of closing the shells at the open end – the 'louvre walls'. Jørn has the whole time objected to an ordinary wall meeting the shell surface at this point and I feel certain that from an architectural point of view he is right ... but our calculations proved that we could expect very high – in fact too high – stresses at certain points unless we were prepared to abandon*

> the demand that the shells should spring vertically from the foundations, and Jørn readily agreed to this ...
>
> Some months ago Utzon made a suggestion which seemed to be a clue to a possible solution of our difficulties. As you know, one of the things which made the construction of these shells extremely difficult was that all the surfaces were different, so that there was no possibility of repetition, which is always the key to economical construction. If you examine Nervi's structures and domes or hangars they are all based on the repetition of precast units, and we had all discussed the possibility of using such a method with Utzon, but the fact that all the shells were different seemed to preclude this. However, in the course of our discussion Utzon came up with an idea for making all the shells of a uniform curvature throughout in both directions – in other words they are all cut from the same sphere. This would mean that every segment of the shell was identical.
>
> This is only a very short description of what happened ... As a result of these studies we have now produced a scheme, at any rate sketch scheme, which promises to solve all Jørn's architectural problems. He at least is wildly enthusiastic about it. It would also facilitate both construction and calculations.[42]

For Arup, the spherical breakthrough enabled all the main shells to be made from identical precast units which could be calculated. Even so, a great deal more needed to be done before Utzon could be confident he had found a workable solution. To do this, Utzon had to telescope what would normally have taken more than a year to work out into a few short months in the northern autumn of 1961.

Rafael Moneo arrived in Utzon's office in September 1961, quite soon after Utzon discovered that the shells could be built with a combination of triangular pieces taken from a sphere. Moneo was a brilliant 24-year-old from Tudela, Navarra, in north-eastern Spain. He had completed his architecture studies at Madrid's Escuela de Arquitectura earlier in 1961. It was to

Moneo that Utzon turned to derive the roof shell surfaces from a generic sphere. The wonderful drawings that survive of this were produced by the young Spaniard.

The next step was to calculate the coordinates which would properly locate the triangles on the sphere's surface. This entailed a strenuous search of the sphere to match each triangle with the shape and profile of each shell. Ove Arup provided a descriptive geometry-based procedure which, in general terms, set out the search method to be followed. Because Moneo was more familiar with descriptive geometry than anyone else, he was chosen to do the work. 'Running in the sphere' was a very laborious and time-consuming procedure and it took months to find the precise profile and locate the specific coordinates for each triangle, which defined each 'shell' in the Opera House roof.[43]

Rafael Moneo had three meetings with Ove Arup in London while he worked on the roofs. He subsequently recalled Arup as a wise engineer and a person of considerable warmth. Moneo was tremendously flattered by the position he found himself in. The geometry was his responsibility and he worked assiduously completing the geometry of the shells and the partitioning of the separate radial ribs forming the shells in February or, at the latest, March 1962. When it was done, Moneo next established the shape of the beams along the common edges shared by the upright shells and the smaller side shells. These beam-transition surfaces, visible on the outside, were formed into the complex twisted surfaces of the triangular legs which support the big shells. With the geometry of these twisted surfaces known, the major problem of the form of the shells was solved.

Even so, many intermediate steps had to be completed before the final roof shapes were determined. The results were reproduced in the *Yellow Book*, which although it was dated January 1962, in reality was not ready until March. Moneo returned to Spain by way of Scandinavia in the summer of 1962.[44]

The roofs had elliptical ridge and rib profiles which persisted till October 1961 when they were replaced by the circular geometry. During the transition, Jack Zunz experimented with larger rib folds at the points opposite where the smaller shell-heel overlapped, for greater shell stiffness. But by October, when the spherical geometry made its appearance, the ribs all had the same uniform depth. The last and final change involved the small side shells. These still retained their original bulging convex shapes from Utzon's first model in August 1957. They were now straightened, first as two folded triangular planes in January 1962, and a little later the inner, sharply folded plates were replaced by a vertical inclined prop-member supporting the two large shells, with smaller spherical segments between which were extracted from the same large sphere. The triangular side openings, which were filled by shells originally, were replaced by horizontal concrete beams held at their edges by Rafael Moneo's twisted octopus arches and a single sturdy prop in the middle on each side. The entire thing was called an octopus arch because of its many legs. The result appears quite logical and sensible in retrospect, but at the time Zunz and his engineering team were finding their way. For them, nothing was in the least bit obvious. It all had to be checked and checked again.

Standing under the roof today, beneath the huge radial fans of concrete ribs overhead, there is little direct feeling of gravity or the spherical geometry ruling the structure. It was a mighty human feat just to throw so many thousands of tons of concrete up in the air and keep it there. The fact that it stands should not cause us to overlook how over-designed and ultra-conservative it really is. There does not seem to be much doubt that the Italian engineer and contractor, Pier Luigi Nervi, with his long experience of building shells, could have done it better with far less material and without resorting to what is a mixture of beam and rib construction. Possibly it is just coincidental, but the breakthrough happened soon after the worldwide publicity that attended the superb games structures by Nervi for the Rome Olympics in August 1960, which featured extremely economical folded shell domes assembled from precast elements.[45]

Nervi demonstrated the many advantages – economic as

well as aesthetic – of lightness in shell design in his magnificent Large Sports Palace in August 1960. This had a 100 m diameter dome assembled from precast concrete V-shaped ribs that were only 9 cm thick spanning a stadium holding 16,000 spectators, with concrete one-third the thickness used in Sydney. Moreover, the stadium roof did not have to be prestressed. In his effort to shed weight from the roof, Nervi even cast holes in the hollow upper V-ribs; this also improved sound absorption and housed the air-conditioning ducts and neon tubes used for artificial lighting. As well as being daring and dramatic, Nervi's design was far in advance of Ove Arup's ribbed vault for the Opera House. Not only was his structure more elegant, it was tremendously cheaper and faster to build.[46]

Utzon probably recognised he was not receiving the most state-of-the-art advice, but there was not much he could do to change this.[47] Ove Arup & Partners were employed by the New South Wales Government and it was not only impossible but out of character for Utzon to seek to involve himself in a dispute over the engineer. Ultimately, no amount of wind-tunnel tests could make up for the lack of practical knowledge and experience in building shells which contractors such as Nervi, Esquillan and Candela possessed in abundance. Pier Luigi Nervi knew how to build light economical shells; Arup and his group had designed the Brynmawr Rubber Factory in 1951, but this was insufficient compared to the challenge they faced in Sydney.[48] They were doing everything for the first time, and they could not afford for anything to go wrong. What Sydney ended up with were massive ribbed vaults. The ribbed vaults used in the Opera House are nearly identical to Nervi's Rome Olympic structures, except for one important and decisive difference – they are many times heavier. The additional weight added enormously to the ultimate cost and was structurally inefficient. The extra weight of the roof structure multiplied the final construction cost because the lower supports and footings had to be strengthened accordingly.

Jørn Utzon and Jack Zunz were both booked to fly to Sydney at the beginning of March 1962 for the presentation of

Stage II, the roof, to the Sydney Opera House Trust, which had replaced the Executive Committee.[49] This coincided with the publication of the *Yellow Book*.

Because Arups' engineering drawings were a week late, Utzon and Zunz's flight booking was re-scheduled for a fortnight later. The delay saved their lives. All 95 passengers and crew on the American Airlines flight One on which Utzon and Zunz were originally booked to Los Angeles died when their Boeing 707-123B airliner plunged into Jamaica Bay minutes after take-off on Thursday 1 March from New York's Idlewild International Airport.[50] The Sydney Opera House dream might have ended there and then in the charred wreckage and mud of Jamaica Bay. On Wednesday 14 March, Utzon and Zunz arrived safely in Sydney for a four-week stay.

They were confronted by a number of tough decisions: Civil & Civic was insisting it be paid an extraordinary A£1.2 million (A$2.4 million) extra for below-standard concrete work. The Stage II contract was ready for signing, plus the terms for the start of Stage III needed to be settled, along with the tile contract and negotiations with R.S. Symonds for the plywood to be used for the acoustic shells in the main auditoria. Utzon brought with him the new *Yellow Book* that superseded the *Red Book* of March 1958, by now four years out of date. The *Yellow Book* was a celebration of Utzon's new roof geometry. Overcoming this problem had meant an enormous amount to Utzon personally. He felt handicapped by his inadequate maths, yet somehow he had triumphed where an engineer of unquestioned intellectual brilliance like Jenkins had failed.

Like Utzon's previous Opera House document, the *Yellow Book* was large and lavish. For the front-cover illustration, Utzon chose Rafael Moneo's diagram showing the complete geometrical construction and derivation of the Major Hall shells in elevation. The *Yellow Book* was about Utzon's solution to the roof problem.

Although the book contains 39 pages of plans, these do little more than update the external roof forms and illustrate recent design developments in the solution of the interiors. The plans were still a long way off being finalised, including the sections through the long axes of the two main halls. The glass walls had not even been tackled. Utzon offered a tentative solution, but in principle only. Whereas considerable progress was made in regard to the stage areas, which had benefited greatly from Utzon's intense collaboration with Waagner-Biro in Vienna, the Major and Minor Halls were still inadequate in seating numbers. The Experimental Theatre was undeveloped. The total number of seats provided in the Major Hall stood at around 1718.[51] In a subsequent drawing, a higher figure of 1811 seats was achieved. However it was looked at, Utzon needed to provide a further 1000 to 1100 extra seats on stage for concerts. The Minor Hall had fallen to 933 seats, also well below the number needed.

To deal with the concert seating problem in the Major Hall, Utzon developed eight alternative seating scenarios to exploit the area adjacent to the rear wall of the stage, which divided the audience into two, one part occupying the opera auditorium, the other the level space used by the orchestra for operas, including the main stage. For concerts, conferences or theatre-in-the-round the rear stage area could be elevated in tiers to provide for a part of the audience behind the musicians.

The *Yellow Book* gives the impression that while Utzon was intensively involved and was making headway, he still had a long way to go with the interiors. After five years, Utzon's progress was slow, too slow for his impatient client. The solution to the shells, though welcome and a personal triumph for Utzon, did not adequately compensate for his tardiness in other areas, notably in the Major and Minor Halls. The design of the interiors was still in the future. Utzon was delaying making a decision about them. He held back, waiting for a decisive breakthrough, and remained uncertain what to do in the interiors. The auditoria interiors had, in their way, become a test of authenticity. In the meantime the client, frustrated by the lack of some tangible indication of progress, moved the completion date from Australia Day 1963 to 1965.

For all the elegance of its graphic presentation – and the drawings were extremely beautiful – far too many of the plans contained in the *Yellow Book* merely repeated existing information. In some instances, such as where Utzon showed 1.8 m x 1.2 m x 7.6 cm thick sawn granite, this information was already obsolete. By now, Utzon proposed to use precast concrete panels externally in lieu of sandstone, his first choice. Five years into the project, Utzon was still resisting coming to grips with the structural and construction issues in practical detail.

For a while, Utzon would concentrate on an area that caught his attention, such as the tiles or the plywood, and left the rest trailing behind. He concerned himself most with the poetry of the forms, their sculptural expression; this held his exclusive attention while he explored successive ideas at an abstract level and opened up new design vistas. The inclusion of earlier roof proposals in the *Yellow Book* was not only unnecessary, it further emphasised the paucity of development since the breakthrough in the geometrical solution of the roofs.

In Sydney, in the meantime, there were more immediate questions demanding practical decisions. On Bennelong Point, only a small portion of the ribbed folded concrete slabs had been poured. Problems had arisen with the contractor carrying out this work, Civil & Civic, because of a dispute over the quality of the concrete and their extra claims, which, if warranted, would add a further A£1,232,000 to the cost of Stage I. The Sydney Opera House base was a reinforced concrete monolith surrounded on the east, north and west by a broadwalk. This was approached from the south by a large prestressed concrete concourse. The structural elements of the base were mostly walls and slabs. Where the spans were too great for flat slabs, in areas such as the backstage over the workshops, a ribbed system was being used instead. Bennelong Point had been an island in the early days, but later a seawall had been constructed of heavy open-jointed sandstone blocks on three sides and the area within the wall was filled. Before any work could start, Civil & Civic built the foundations, which consisted of bored piers 90 cm in diameter, to support the building towards the north and all around the perimeter of the site where the rock fell away steeply into the harbour. Allied with these concrete piers were mass concrete foundations, either in strip or pad form, in the central area of the building. These were required to replace fill and unsound rock. The site conditions were unpredictable and caused huge difficulties, but none of this was an excuse for the major defects and generally unsatisfactory concrete work.

On 31 March, Utzon and Zunz toured the work and ended their inspection in the upper area of the Major Hall, where there were some blatant blemishes to the concrete walls which had been recently stripped. The worst of it was in the north bar areas where Utzon had asked for the off-form finish to be of a quality suitable to be exposed as the final finish.

Mr G.J. Dusseldorp, founder director of Lend Lease – the parent company of Civil & Civic – was demanding an 88 per cent increase on the A£1,397,929 January 1959 Stage I tender amount, lifting it to A£2,630,000, under a claim for additional work.[52] He had some justification on his side, as the area of 'C' class formwork had increased five-fold, but he was also endeavouring to recover from a disastrously low tender. When Jack Zunz offered him A£15,000, this provoked a severe session of sneezing by Dusseldorp. Utzon and Zunz spent considerable time going over the job with Dusseldorp in an attempt to sort out the bad concrete work. The underside of the folded concourse beams, which were better than the bar areas, contained numerous defects. It took Italian workers years to patch up all the holes. Skipper Nielsen, Utzon's resident site architect, had repeatedly informed Arups about the sub-standard concrete but his complaints were ignored. In other areas, walls to staircases were set out incorrectly. The extent of the defects worried Utzon. He wanted a smooth, blemish-free result in the stripped concrete that would not require anything further to be done to it.

These inspections took a great amount of time and heightened Utzon's frustration about the shortcomings of a public tender system based on bills of quantities which allowed a contractor such as Civil & Civic to underprice its tender. An important philosophical point was also involved, because Utzon was strongly committed to the honest expression of materials. This was not possible with such a contractor on the site. In practice, Utzon's approach meant exposing the finished concrete, rather than hiding mistakes beneath render or paint. The quality of the Civil & Civic concrete formwork was so bad some walls and folded beams were up to 5 cm out of position.

This bolstered Utzon in his belief that the best and most effective way to achieve work at an acceptable price was by a negotiated contract instead of competitive tenders. Quite surprisingly, Utzon was supported by his consultant engineer, Ove Arup, who was in the midst of setting up the Stage II contract for the construction of the roofs with M.R. Hornibrook (NSW) Pty Ltd. Ove Arup & Partners recommended that the contractor for Stage II of the work be appointed on the basis of a negotiated contract on a cost plus basis, not by competitive tender. They gave two main reasons: many tenderers who were equipped to undertake the work were unlikely to submit bids because there were too many unknown factors and, even if they did, they would most likely load their tenders; secondly, in some cases, because of the nature of the work, it was possible that some might not bother to submit a price at all. Arups needed a contractor who would join the engineering team and act in a more flexible way than would ever be the case where the contract was let by competitive public tender.[53]

The negotiations with Civil & Civic descended into legal farce.[54] During the arbitration on 1 March 1963, John Kerr, later Sir John Kerr, was the barrister representing Ove Arup. He was a large man with a large grey shock of hair and a florid face who was much given to legal theatrics – especially when he had not had time to read his brief properly. In a question to Mr W.M. Leavey, the Managing Director of Civil & Civic, Kerr asked: 'Mr Leavey, when you tendered for this project, did you make allowance for ship jacking these beams [in the concourse]?'[55] When there was no reply, Kerr tossed his hair and repeated the question to Mr Leavey, who duly replied that he did not understand the question. At this point, Kerr tossed his hair again and repeated the question for a third time, only to be given the same answer. Frustrated, Kerr turned to the arbitrator and said: 'Mr Arbitrator, would you please explain to Mr Leavey what ship jacking these beams means.' To which the arbitrator replied, 'Sorry Mr Kerr, I don't know what you're talking about.' Kerr once again shook his hair and said, 'Mr Arbitrator, if you don't know what ship jacking means, and Mr Leavey doesn't know, how do you expect me to know what it means!'[56] In the end, nothing was agreed and the matter was sent to the Government. John Kerr might not know what he was talking about, and might not even know that he did not know, but who could forget John Kerr? That seemed to be the real purpose of the performance. Australia had not heard the last of John Kerr.

Kingo houses near Helsingør, Denmark, 1956. Site plan.

10

Terraced Sanctuaries
Hellebæk, 1957–1963

Happiness, however, I thought then and still do now, is inconceivable without a terrace, and by a terrace I mean something very different from the European rooftops that Cousin Zin described after visiting Blad Teldj, or Snowland. He said that the houses up there did not have the neatly whitewashed, and sometimes sumptuously paved, flat terraces like our own, with sofas and plants and flowering shrubs. In contrast, their roofs were triangular and pointed because they had to shelter the houses from the snow, and you couldn't possibly stretch out on them because you would slide off.
Fatima Mernissi, 1994[1]

Not even the extra demands of the Sydney Opera House could dampen Jørn Utzon's keen interest in houses. Over more than half a century, it would deepen and grow, almost as a reflection of his solitary nature.

In the years immediately following the Sydney success, Utzon competed in further competitions. Among his most notable successes were the Labour Organisation College at Helsingør, the Birkehøj project for a small town in North Zealand, a town plan for Frederiksburg in 1959, an entry in the Elvira competition in Spain and a housing scheme for Eline Berg in Halsingborg, Sweden, one year later. It is a mystery how he found the time.

Utzon relished the stimulation of competitions, but he was less enamoured by the detailed research that they frequently required.

No architectural office can stake its future solely on one great commission. It must spread the risk, for otherwise, when the work was done, the office would be left with nothing to follow on with. Possibly Utzon was looking ahead; more likely, he needed a distraction. In addition to the competitions, Utzon designed a number of houses, two in the village of Hittap north of Halsingborg were built in 1962, and in 1959–60 he extended his own house. Not including the Melli Bank, the two other most important projects were a group of 63 L-shaped Kingo houses outside Helsingør (1957–61), and a smaller, though no less significant commission, at Fredensborg (1962–3) consisting of 47 terraced houses for the Danish Co-operative Building Company, Danske Samvirke. Also at Helsingør Utzon built the Hammershøj high house, which later came under threat of demolition in 1998.

The Kingo houses are evidence of Utzon's persuasiveness. For some time he had been convinced there was a better way of designing houses to cater for family privacy which would permit families to pursue their own interests in safety. The Kingo and Fredensborg house-type originated from an earlier collaboration with Ib Mogelvang in 1953 in the Scania house competition. When this failed to go ahead, Utzon searched for a new opportunity to try out his theory.

The Danish Government had set up a state-loan scheme aimed at assisting people on low incomes to acquire their own homes. A condition of the loan was that the house did not exceed a specified, small, size. This ensured that building costs stayed low. The architectural outcomes matched the budgets. Utzon thought that it could all be done much better. For his part, Utzon photographed examples of loan-scheme housing and showed them, together with his Swedish project, to the Mayor of Helsingør, duly explaining that a much better result could be achieved. The mayor resisted at first, but was eventually persuaded to set aside a vacant site of approximately 3.65 ha west of Helsingør for Utzon's housing experiment.

The Roman Houses (Romer Husene), as they are sometimes

called because they had courtyards which reminded people of an ancient Roman atrium, were built in three stages from 1957 to 1961. The client and owner was the Kingo Housing Society, which employed the lawyer Asger Berning as its administrator, and Ebbe Langaard as its engineer. Utzon persuaded a local builder to erect the first demonstration house on Carl Plougsvej 51. The house was poorly received by journalists.[2] Possibly this was because it disregarded the street and was self-contained around its courtyard. The demonstration house was completely bare and this, combined with its unconventional plan, may have startled journalists. There was little Utzon could do about the criticism.

When journalists next visited the Kingo pilot house, Utzon marked out the position of imaginary pieces of furniture on the floor with trails of lollies so they could visualise how each room might be used. In desperation, he even wrote fictitious comments in the Visitors' Book vigorously praising the house, and left the book open near the entrance so the media could read the comments as they left. It worked this time, and the newspaper reports were favourable. Utzon had learned a valuable lesson – good publicity can frequently make all the difference between failure or success.

The loan conditions for the Kingo development permitted only one living room, a master bedroom and two small bedrooms, totalling no more than 104 m^2 in area, and set a maximum cost of Kr 60,000 (A£3950 or A$7900). The conditions were intended to assist low- and modest-income families, such as workers and poorly paid teachers. Several of Utzon's architectural staff occupied Kingo houses.[3] Each family was required to contribute a deposit of Kr 5000 (A£329, A$658), and the state advanced a loan of Kr 55,000 (A£3620, A$7240) at an interest rate of 2.2 per cent. The amount allocated for the first display house was set at Kr 35,000 (A£2303, A$4605).[4]

A first stage of 17 houses was approved at this low price.[5] To keep the costs down, the builder worked on the houses in his spare time at the end of the day when he had finished working on other contracts. The work progressed slowly. While it may have taken longer this way, the finished Kingo houses cost less than any other scheme for that period. Because Utzon was involved, the houses have more character than any other comparable group.[6] Utzon has often been charged with extravagance and waste — the truth is quite the opposite. For this reason alone, the Kingo housing is especially noteworthy because it demonstrated that Utzon could keep his costs low and produce an adventurous design with character.

By the time Utzon came to design the Kingo houses, his ideas had already matured. They were a romantic blend of Mediterranean villages and the old single-storey residential housing of Beijing, fortified by the addition of Utzon's own rich sculptural contribution. The solid strength of the outside walls excludes the world nearly entirely. From a distance, the Kingo estate takes on the appearance of a small walled medieval town, with its tall brick tower chimneys rising above the wriggly coping and the sloping, yellow-tiled roofs. The focus of the houses is predominantly internal.

The outside appearance of the houses, with their blank, yellow-brown, nearly windowless brick facades, was as much indebted to Morocco as it was to China. The houses look like a North African village in the Atlas Mountains with their stepped brick walls capped by tiles. They belong in a sunny blue Mediterranean climate and seem a little out of place presided over by Helsingør's stony grey sky. Utzon, who chose in later life to live in the sun, preferred architecture which reminded him of the south with all its easy suggestion of freedom. He is less comfortable remembering the drifting clouds casting their first shadows over Nordic fjords.[7]

At Helsingør, the houses were strung out in chains around a small lake, unlike Fredensborg, where they were disposed around and enclosed two grassed commons. In both places the inward orientation is absolute. Utzon sometimes lowered a section of courtyard wall opposite the living area to provide a view out and borrow a piece of nearby landscape. But for this, the houses would be completely introverted — psychologically as well as architecturally.

The Kingo housing occupies a site west of Helsingør that is undulating with a small lake on the western side, trapped between the elbow of Kingosvej and Carl Plougsvej. On its south, a crescent-shaped spur ran through the middle dividing the site in two; on the east, opposite Gurrevej, it formed an elevated table which subsided across the western half into the saucer-like depression filled by the lake. The 63 houses intertwined in three groups. This arrangement allowed them to be constructed in three stages. Half the houses are on the northern, Carl Plougsvej boundary and act as a buffer to the wind in winter. The L-shaped plan is turned either west or east so the glass walls of the living areas can face south towards the sun. Wherever possible, the houses, especially those on the north, were arranged to overlook the lake.[8]

The two southern groups of houses are smaller and have their own separate vehicular access off Gurrevej. They, like those on the eastern boundary, are more isolated because of their southern location. The middle south-eastern section is reached by a narrow branch road.

The housing constitutes a solid, irregular frame, with occasional breaks allowing vistas to the outside, around a central pond that gives it its focus. The ground falls gently to this tiny lake which has a thick encircling collar of rust-coloured, swaying reeds on its edge. From all directions, reflections of walls and tile roofs are picked out in its dark waters. People gravitate to it. Its asymmetrical location on the site dictated the irregular stepped arrangement of the houses, which form a loose, giant, yellow brick and tile picture frame around it to cut off the city streets. This framing concentrates everything within it and repeats at a larger scale the inward orientation of the individual courtyard-houses.

The gently sloped yellow-tiled roofs and stepped walls, tiled on top, rise picturesquely from behind the thick wall of reeds surrounding the lake foreshore. The scene has a serene innocence that brings people closer to nature and, like any farm pond, the lake serves as a reminder of the rural village and countryside. A child was drowned there some years back and the lake has since been fenced off to prevent any further accidents. The fence now isolates the housing around the lake and shuts out the landscape.

Despite the initial resistance and its many setbacks, Utzon's

Kingo housing scheme marked the revival of the Danish single-family house which was afterwards imitated around Denmark – but not, it should be added, with the same architectural skill or with the equivalent sculptural effect.[9] The fact that Utzon succeeded against the odds provides a powerful vindication of his ideas.

Utzon's housing achievements at Helsingør and Fredensborg were widely admired. According to the editor of *Arkitektur* magazine, Kim Dirkinck-Holmfeld, they left their mark on Danish domestic building in a number of important later housing developments.[10]

The Kingo housing was a low-budget precursor of the more expensive terrace houses at Fredensborg in 1962, which offer a more luxurious and expansive interpretation of the same themes.

Kingo provided the chance to build Fredensborg when the Kingo houses were noticed by Valdemar Hvid, a lawyer for the support organisation Danske Samvirke, which aided Danish citizens returning home after a long stay away on business as technical advisers or in the Foreign Service. The Danske Samvirke management committee was considering creating a community that Danes who had been overseas for lengthy periods of time could return to, and mix with people from similar backgrounds, to help them readjust. Danske Samvirke did not have a site, nor had it decided any of the details for the new buildings. Utzon was therefore asked to develop a building programme as well as design the buildings.

The site he found was at Fredensborg. Fredensborg is renowned for its palace which was built in 1724 because of King Frederick IV's admiration of the beautiful surroundings of Lake Esrum. The palace is dominated by a lofty dome and is approached by a treed avenue from the south.[11] It stands on the eastern shore of Lake Esrum, Denmark's second largest lake, some 50 km north of Copenhagen in North Zealand. It was called Fredensborg, meaning 'peace castle', to commemorate the end of the Great Northern War with Sweden. It is used as the summer residence of Denmark's royal family.

The lake and its surroundings are quite magnificent. The park was laid out at the same time as the palace, making use of the former beech forest area with long Baroque Versailles-like avenues radiating out from the palace towards the lake. Utzon's site was a large cleared south-facing hillside between the palace and Lake Esrum, isolated by high woods on three sides and entered off Slotsgade, the axial approach to the palace, through a connecting area of forest.

The forested north-western portion of the site was part of a conservation area which left only the remaining cleared hillside to the south-east for housing. Utzon negotiated the land purchase in 1959. He persuaded the local authority, which had earlier approved a conventional suburban development comprised of single-storey houses, to reverse its decision and agree to his new plan, even though this meant pushing fingers of courtyard houses into the northern conservation zone.[12] He convinced the authorities that the linked, square, courtyard houses would make the most of the special qualities of the site, unlike the previous proposal for conventional detached houses on single plots.

The Danske Samvirke committee wanted a centre to be built in the midst of the housing where the residents could hold meetings and socialise. The centre would have a dining room and kitchen, a lounge and area for parties and weddings, and would need office space to carry out administration. After some discussion, it was also agreed to provide 12 small rooms in the centre to accommodate residents' guests in a mini-hotel.

Utzon's work was purely speculative. Only if the project went ahead could he expect to be appointed architect. It was up to Samvirke and its members to decide whether it should proceed. This depended on money being forthcoming. There was an immediate positive response to the proposal from members of Danske Samvirke; money started flowing in from members and outside institutions. Utzon finished his drawings and obtained quotes from builders.

One obstacle still remained: what to do with a small elongated parcel of land on the north-east corner of the site which connected the housing main area to Slotsgade? Utzon was at first inclined to consider three storeys, but since this looked awkward beside the single-storey courtyard houses, he opted for 30 small terrace houses grouped around a square in staggered blocks of three. These were one-and-a-half storeys and faced either west or south, and had small courtyard gardens adjoining each living room. It was finally agreed that the development would consist of 47 courtyard and 30 terrace houses.

Having ventured this far, new difficulties presented themselves. It was said the estimate was too low; the bricklayers went on strike and the master builder refused to proceed. Work stopped completely for three weeks and the project looked like folding.

At this crucial moment Utzon's friend Jørgen Saxild, who had commissioned Utzon to design the Melli Bank and was on the Samvirke committee, rescued the project by providing the extra money. Even so, the committee ran into new difficulties when it failed to find enough buyers for the houses who satisfied the conditions. To overcome this further obstacle, Jørgen Saxild bought a number of the houses himself and turned them over to members of Danske Samvirke.[13] Four years later, in 1963, the project was ready. Its completion was due in good part to Utzon's entrepreneurial skills and his ability to work with people, but it might never have been realised without Jørgen Saxild. Saxild believed in Utzon and this made the difference between success or failure.[14]

The terrace features more prominently in Fredensborg than in Helsingør. Utzon cut a series of steps in the hillside to form platforms for each dwelling. Whereas the Kingo houses are grouped around the edge of the site and follow the ground contours to enclose the edge, only swinging in towards the centre in the middle of the site, at Fredensborg the serpentine fingers of houses run up and down the slope across the contour lines in a much more open and inclusive fashion. The Fredensborg housing forms a large, yellow, brick trident whose hollow prongs meander downhill and trap long wedges of meadow between them. This sloping green meadow is surrounded on every side except one by the high bare walls of the houses, which appear almost as the walls of a medieval town. At the bottom of the hillside the enclosed green spaces open onto a flat vista of cultivated farmland. Each house and its private area of garden is shut in by its perimeter of wall. On the lowest corner, the houses stand perhaps two to three metres or more above the ground outside.

Fredensborg mixes past and present. The blank walls rise precipitously from the verdant green of the meadow, to isolate the houses which resemble islands rising out of the sea. Their isolation is as complete and perfect as the fortified monastery of Mont-St-Michel in France with its walls surrounded by tidal flats. It is strikingly, if self-consciously, picturesque.[15] The walls of the houses wander in and out as if by accident, in a kind of haphazard medieval chaos.

Fredensborg must be considered one of Utzon's most successful projects. It is such wonderful sculpture, because it approaches so closely in spirit the meadow and forest that surround it. When we are there we feel we are in a different realm separate from the rest of the world outside. It is at once hermetic and hypnotic with only the blue sky and scattered clouds, the ancient beech forest in the distance, to remind us of another life beyond its walls. The housing has that anonymous quality that Utzon values so highly: we do not think to ask who made it, any more than we would ask who designed a particular beech tree. Fredensborg expresses all that Utzon wished to say about anonymous vernacular building.

We cannot see into the houses, which close themselves to our curious eyes and draw back. Now and then, from its hiding place, an isolated pine tree or flowering bush breaks the skyline, and wisps of curling smoke issue from tower-like chimneys to remind us of the very private lives tucked away inside.

Steen Eiler Rasmussen wrote: 'In olden days the entire community took part in forming the dwellings and implements they used. The individual was in fruitful contact with these things; the anonymous houses were built with a natural feeling for place, materials and use and the result was a remarkable comeliness.'[16] This is exactly the feeling of the Fredensborg housing. It is a kind of Danish Fez in which only the meeting centre raises a mild finger of dissent.

The houses are tethered to their own private courtyard gardens. The basic house plan is reminiscent of Utzon's 1952

Hellebæk house, but he bent it in the middle at right angles, to fit around the two sides of the square enclosure. The kitchen has been placed on one side of the entrance for convenience, beyond it is the dining area, shielded by a screen. The lounge next to it spreads out to catch as much of the southern winter sunlight as possible. At the far end, there is a small lumber room accessible from the courtyard. The bedroom and bathroom wing is on the other side of the entrance, on either the east or west walls. Past the last bedroom is a garage, this gives access from the outside to the courtyard. The planning is practical, straightforward and direct. The basic L-shape allowed Utzon to alter each house by adding more rooms or a study at the end as required, so it can grow or shrink in size. The focus of each house is the courtyard, with each one different to reflect the personality of its owner. Danes love their garden lots. The enclosed gardens are symbols of each household, which, if they are invisible externally, clearly express the goings-on inside.[17]

In the club centre, the space is calm, restrained, placid. Almost too placid, too accepting, too restrained. Utzon could have done more in the larger rooms. Instead, typically, he held back, and kept everything in the centre understated. It takes its character from the warm tones of the timber balustrade and stair and the ceiling trim, which Utzon used to establish a strong quiet rhythm across the entry hall. Utzon didn't attempt to overwhelm visitors by his architecture because he wanted them to feel comfortable.

He has behaved, in Rasmussen's words, as a sort of theatrical producer, the man who plans the setting for our lives and who is like a perfect host in that he provides every comfort for his guests, to make living a happy experience.

By car, the visitor to the centre is greeted by a sloping tile roof on the porte-cochere. Little else can be seen from the outside. The building consists of a main U-shaped head that caps the neck of the east meadow, and is extended down at the sides by two wings and service courts on the outside. The main tiled skillion roof follows the slope of the hill: at its lowest point, on the south opposite the large courtyard, it climbs gently two storeys over the open mezzanine level which overlooks the main lounge area opposite the entrance. This double-height mezzanine bleeds into the dining room on the left side. The same materials are used throughout: yellow brick, yellow tiles and timber for windows with closely spaced vertical bars over the outside windows. Softly muted yellow brick and red wood are juxtaposed against the luminous green of the meadow.

In response to the Fredensborg landscape, Utzon selected only one species of plant: beech trees and beech bushes in tight pillows. As in architecture, he prefers to use the same material everywhere, whether it is yellow brick and yellow tiles, or beeches for the planting, to strengthen the aesthetic impact and emphasise the homogeneity and continuity of the design. The internal woodwork consists of untreated deal boards, with white gypsum boards and unplanned mouldings for the ceilings and white Höganäs tiles on the floors. Utzon designed all the timber bench seats and the furniture for the club house.

The entry hall level extends forward past the windows in a large, brick-paved terrace. Low brick planters surround the paving on three sides and thick vertically panelled timber doors partly obscure the view. These doors lead out and a short flight of steps take us down onto the terrace; this is surrounded on all three sides by the centre's low roof. On the south side, across the open end, a simple horizontal dark-stained timber pergola frames the distant view of the farmland below. Walking towards the pergola on the level of the terrace, brick steps lead down to the grassed area between the lines of houses. The walls softly press forward, views open up, and we emerge from shadow into sunlight – not all at once, but in stages. Utzon is a wonderful theatrical director who oversees this like some invisible presence, leading the visitor to explore his walls and roofs and changes of floor level.

Tranquillity has its price. Utzon's courtyard house is encased within a blank brick shell. This was also Utzon's choice in a life spent apart from others. For Utzon, the inner enclosed garden, like the inner terrace, is an inviolable sanctuary, part haven, part prison.

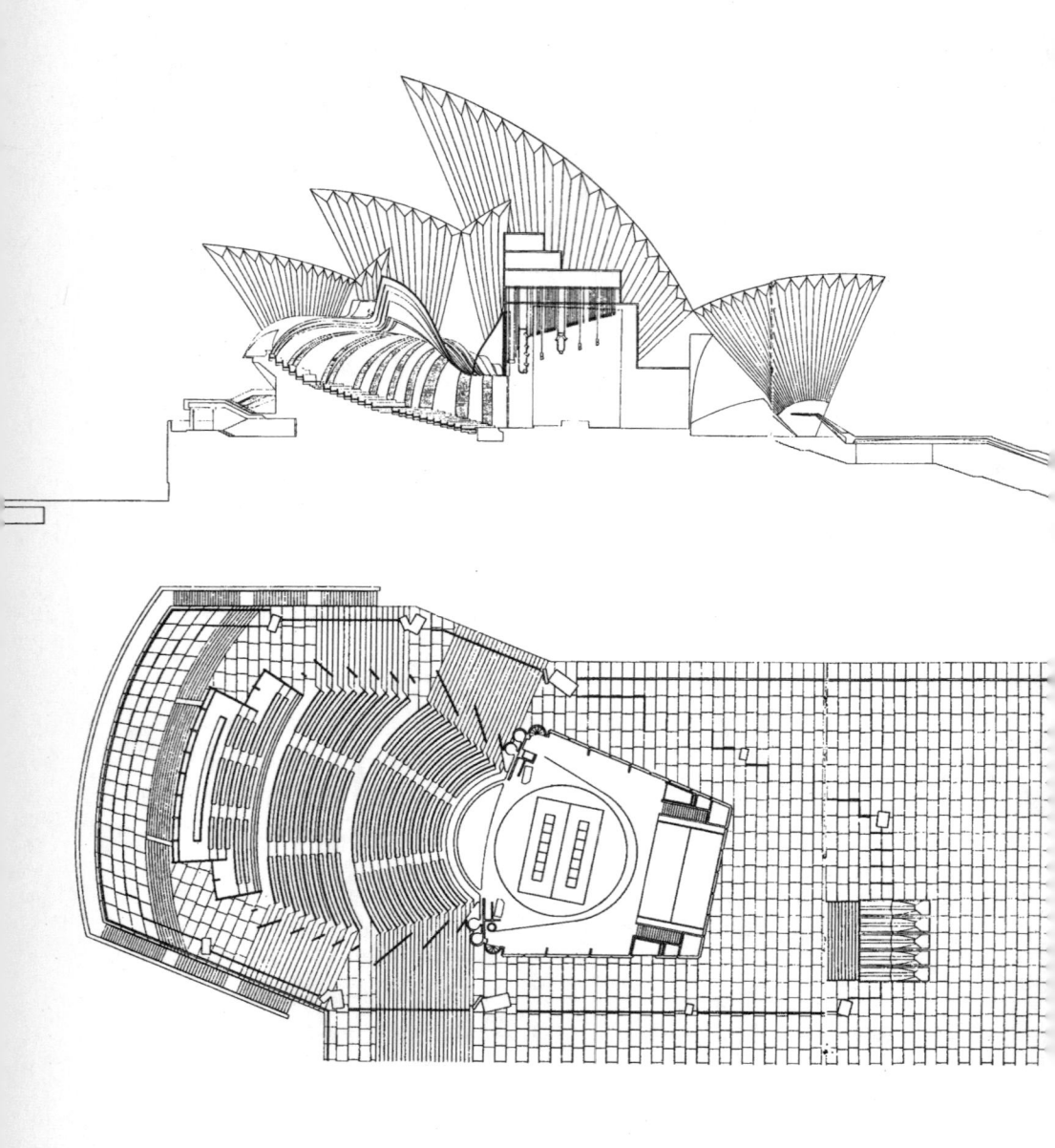

Sydney Opera House. Above: Longitudinal section through Minor Hall. Below: Plan of Minor Hall.

11

A Big Exotic Bird
Hellebæk, 1962

So the architecture, in its colour and its details has been formed to support the meeting between actor and performer and a climax in colour is reached in the two Halls and surroundings of the stages. The two Halls hang from the shells visibly as a piece of furniture from outside, and as the inside of the shells is neutral off-white, the Halls and the Stage Tower in forms and colour will stand out like a big exotic bird.

Jørn Utzon, July 1962[1]

The two theatres were the indispensable heart of the Opera House. After feeling his way for so long, Utzon suddenly felt more certain of what it was he was searching for. His ideas, though still tentative, acquired a new sharpness.

Geometry supplied Utzon with an all-embracing instrument with which to control his forms, starting from the outside totality and extending to the smallest detail inside. It provided an intellectually satisfying means to control, and related each part much as an Euclidean theorem provides its own rewarding sense of closure for an idea. Once it was decided to base the roofs on a large generic sphere, Utzon faced the question of what to do in the halls.

Utzon had always admired the remarkable unity and variety of the simple, repetitive, cubic patterning of vernacular buildings.

Geometry also opened up for him the possibility of doing much the same using modern industrialised technologies. The folded slabs of the Opera House concourse beams and the transformational geometry of the roof ribs shared a similar geometrical approach geared to standardisation, which was not unrelated in Utzon's mind to his vernacular model.

Utzon was about to demolish one of the most cherished shibboleths of the Modern movement, which said that all buildings must be rectangular because this was what modern industrial mass-production methods demanded. He recognised his approach was challenging one of the great orthodoxies of modern architecture and it was no wonder Mies van der Rohe hated the Sydney Opera House so much.

In the Opera House, Utzon discarded the most cherished spatial orthodoxy of the twentieth century – orthogonal gridded space. As he viewed it, rectangular architecture governed by a geometrical orientation of shapes and formed by a 90-degree grid system in three dimensions was unnecessary; in its place, Utzon proposed: 'In a similar way I for instance, subdivide space by grids of converging planes fanning out from a point at even angles. This grid can again intersect with other defined shapes.'[2]

Vilhelm Lassen Jordan had been appointed to advise on acoustics for the Opera House auditoria in 1958. Since the Radiohus's completion had been delayed by the German Occupation in the Second World War, Jordan had been able to experiment with its acoustics and modify its studios until they were satisfactory.[3] Jordan learned a great amount from this. Because Jørn Utzon's and Vilhelm Lauritzen's (Radiohuset's architect) design approach to theatres and concert halls were similar, Jordan was in a position to anticipate the pitfalls that lay ahead. From experience, he knew that architects had a tendency to visualise acoustic behaviour in certain predictable and sometimes inappropriate ways.

Jordan was much more than a technician. He was able to grasp the larger picture and appreciate tactical issues while keeping abreast of the details. Jordan believed that his role was limited to providing acoustic advice and testing the architect's designs. When Utzon demanded more from his acoustic consultant, Jordan refused. His role was to provide acoustic advice. If Utzon sought creative architectural solutions to acoustic matters, he would have to find them in his own office. Jordan did suggest ways to improve Utzon's proposals, though: he constructed models based on Utzon's designs and tested their acoustic behaviour and made recommendations. However, he adamantly refused to play the part of designer, believing that this was properly the role of the architect.

Every room volume and shape has its own unique acoustic properties. Jordan based his ideas on how sound behaved in enclosed spaces, not on visual appearances or sculptural effect, but on science – by measuring it. Utzon thought in visual terms. It was a difficult habit to break. Utzon's challenge was to integrate the visual form with acoustic behaviour.

Like Lauritzen, Utzon started with the ancient Greek theatre, which, as Jordan remarked, though prevalent among Danish architects trained in the 1930s and 1940s, was fundamentally wrong. For example, Lauritzen's 1934 concept of the concert hall in Radiohuset was based on the ancient Greek theatre. The classical symphony concert hall was a comparatively recent development in Europe, with a different history entirely unconnected with Greek theatre. The symphony orchestra developed from the smaller ensembles of the eighteenth century; consequently, the concert hall inherited its conventional flat walls and flat ceiling from the smaller recital hall. Flat side walls were essential because they guaranteed that there would be sufficient side reflections to supplement the direct sound from the orchestra. The sloping profile of the Sydney Opera House's roofs prevented Jordan from achieving the large vertical lateral walls he needed – but without vertical side walls it was impossible to reflect sufficient sound from each side back into the audience. This led to a conflict between the acoustic requirements and the architectural design. Utzon's desire to reproduce the archaic Greek amphitheatre spatially exacerbated the acoustic conflict between the requirements of a modern concert hall for musical performances and a theatre for speech. The multi-purpose requirement added further to the confusion.

Radiohuset's concert hall is worth studying in terms of its similarity to Utzon's initial halls in the Sydney Opera House. It has a 6 cm thick acoustic ceiling suspended from a slightly thicker outside concrete roof shell.[4] The outside roof was structural and did not have any acoustic significance. The acoustic demands inside were handled by a thin, corrugated concrete ceiling covered with wood strips suspended from the soffit of the outer roof. The function of the inner ceiling was to disperse the sound within the concert studio. From model experiments, a ceiling with large corrugations was selected, which unfortunately looked far too heavy. To lighten its appearance, Lauritzen introduced smaller corrugations.

Utzon's competition scheme for the Opera House was surprisingly similar in its essentials, except that Utzon substituted inclined panels for Lauritzen's finely articulated corrugated shell. In both interiors, the alignment of the reflecting surfaces was perpendicular to the hall axis and so acted as a brake on the highly directional, trumpet hall shape.

In 1960, Utzon introduced radial trusses over the Minor Hall to emphasise the radial fan shape. The aim was to direct the audience's attention towards the stage, but it produced undesirable acoustic consequences. Because it was based chiefly on visual rather than acoustic considerations, it had a tendency to channel sound away from the orchestra too rapidly and to reduce side reflections to the audience to a minimum. If adopted, it is very probable that instrumentalists would have been unable to hear themselves playing. It was for this reason that the corrugations in Radiohuset's concert hall were arranged across the auditorium, instead of radially.

The competition drawings showed the two halls as rectangular spaces with their sides tilted gently in. In section, they resembled the classic shoe-box concert hall, while in plan they repeated the ancient fan-shaped amphitheatre. Ignoring Jordan's critical comments, in May 1959 Utzon repeated his first 'stepped cloud' design.[5] Jordan considered that the original convertible scheme of one large enclosure, designed to operate either as an opera theatre with the audience in front of a proscenium, or as a concert hall with the audience seating extended to occupy the whole of the stage floor and served by a mechanically operated ceiling screen which closed off the fly tower, was excellent.[6] Later, after it was abandoned, he expressed regret that it had never materialised.

The acoustic research for the Opera House was breaking new ground. For the first time, model tests were used on an extensive basis for acoustic research into the main halls. This experimental work advanced model-testing procedures, which were then still in their infancy.[7]

The early, rectangular hall cross-section conflicted with the shell profile. The challenge was to harmonise the two, to ensure the acoustics of the auditoria shells did not compete with the structural and sculptural needs of the outer envelope. Work did not begin on this until 1959. Prior to that, the auditoria walls were treated as integral with the common Opera House podium structure.

In January 1960, Utzon proposed to suspend a concave ceiling from the roof shells. His motivation was largely aesthetic, in keeping with his idea of the interior shells as clouds. Simultaneously he endeavoured to detach the ceiling from the podium so it appeared to float. This would reinforce the impression of the ceilings as a kind of light umbrella that breaks free of gravity. At the time of Ashworth's visit to Hellebæk in September 1960, Utzon was exploring the use of acoustic reflecting surfaces fixed to radial trusses spanning from the stage opening to the rear of the hall. By February 1962, the concave hall profile had been greatly refined, but it still lacked any acoustic validation. Utzon went so far as to have a plaster of Paris model of the radial segmental form made. It is obvious that he was as much concerned with the ceiling's sculptural qualities as he was with acoustics.

Around June 1960, the political situation in New South Wales deteriorated following press criticism of Utzon's design of the stage areas.[8] On Saturday 30 June, a *Sydney Morning Herald* journalist contacted Utzon at his Fordamsvej office to obtain answers to a number of the criticisms.[9] The atmosphere in the office was very good and work was progressing well. When asked for their comments, Utzon's staff confirmed that he was totally preoccupied with and could talk of nothing else but the Opera House. The source of the initial attack on 6 June was Martin Carr, the stage director of Covent Garden, whose ramshackle machinery Utzon had already inspected. He had directed his remarks at the adequacy of the stage area; since then, other matters had been raised.

According to these claims, the original scheme was unworkable for the size of audiences it was specifically required to accommodate. Additionally, the seating had been reduced to 1700; the stage lacked side wings; double the usual number of stagehands would be needed to operate the stage machinery and it would be costly. Added to this, the workshops and storage facilities were inadequate; the original roof silhouette had been changed and was now higher; and besides which, stripes were being included into the tile pattern for the roof. Whatever he may have felt privately, Utzon responded calmly to this long litany of complaints.

The criticisms from Carr were easily disposed of.[10] Utzon pointed out that the main Opera House stage was wider and deeper than the Berlin Opera House. In fact, the only point where it was not superior was the height of the grid iron, which was 1.2 m lower than Berlin's 23.8 m. Reacting to a suggestion that it would not be possible to stage grand opera, Utzon explained that Professor Unruh had prepared trial schemes for staging *Tosca* and *Aida*, both of which made great demands, and he was fully satisfied the stage would cope.

Turning to the second criticism, Utzon noted that it was never intended to provide for an opera audience larger than about 1700; the plans always envisaged a multi-purpose hall for concerts and opera, and entertainments such as pageants and mass assemblies. He wanted to assure everyone the Major Hall would seat at least 1700 for opera and about 2900 for concerts, adding that any more than 1700 for opera would be too many. Utzon then produced eight seating-plan scenarios from the *Yellow Book*, one with the orchestra near the back wall of the stage and the audience in the open auditorium in front for concerts, and another with the audience in the 'opera auditorium' and a level area in front of the stage for opera. For concerts, conferences and theatre-in-the-round, the rear of the stage could be tiered placing some of the audience behind the performance area. This would be achieved by raising or lowering sections of the stage with the lifts. He made a very convincing case.

Turning to the criticism of the stage machinery, Utzon noted that on a limited site, with space at a premium, stage machinery was crucial:

> *In Sydney they [the sets] will be built below stage and brought up by elevators. Our system will give singers a stage which is not too big, and which is not a storage room for lots of things which have no connection with the performance.*

Utzon was confident that not only would it work well but there were additional advantages, 'It will make the acoustics of the stage easier to control.' Up to now, Utzon had no reason to doubt that the original decision had been right. By lifting the performance level 12 m, he created a huge uninterrupted work space under the stage. Few theatres could boast of such a facility. It was a brilliant solution that broke with tradition. Utzon bluntly dismissed the criticism about the size of the workshops and stage, saying that they would be adequate for large operas.

On the question of the roof, Utzon was more vulnerable. The resolution to the roofs was still more than a year away. In asserting that 'The silhouette hasn't altered' he was engaging in semantics. The roofs were higher, and they would go higher still. It would have been perilous for Utzon to have admitted that, so he shifted the blame to a misreading of the drawings.

Utzon explained that the detailed drawings made the roof shells appear steeper than they were shown by the models. In practice, the adoption of a spherical geometry in September 1961 radically altered the roof profile. Utzon was right to make the changes, which represented a great improvement in every regard. But the point was that the public was not getting the scheme which had been awarded first prize. The Australian public, having reacted with shock when it first saw the Opera House roofs published, now insisted that any change would represent a betrayal. Any change was akin to cheating. Such an attitude ignored the prevailing experience that most building designs undergo substantial alterations before they are realised, and these are mostly for the better. Utzon in his reply spoke as an artist: 'It is my design. Am I going to destroy it? What we have done is to transfer the design idea into defined geometry.'

Getting to the stripes, Utzon grinned: 'I think they will look better that way.' It was that simple. The interview concluded, Utzon beamed with confidence.

During the third week of August 1962, Ove Arup and Jack Zunz travelled to Sydney via Hawaii, and Jørn Utzon joined them there. The three dined together to discuss the best way to present their case at a forthcoming meeting with the new sub-committee of Cabinet set up to deal with the Opera House. They would have to confront the Premier, R.J. Heffron, Norman Ryan, the Minister for Public Works, and Pat Hills, Minister for Planning.[11] Their chief aim was to reassure the client. During the discussions that night, it was decided that Jack Zunz and Jørn Utzon would do most of the talking because Arup was very ill with a severe cold. They decided to keep him in reserve.

Ove Arup had presented the then latest estimate of A£12.25 million (A$24.5 million) to the 6 April meeting of the SOHEC. This included A£1.4 million (A$2.8 million) for external works, and A£1.2 million (A$2.4 million) for professional fees, allowing

A£9.65 million (A$19.3 million) for the building.[12] The New South Wales Government chose 24 August for the release of its press statement giving the estimated cost of A£12.5 million (A$25 million). For the time being, it withheld an even more recent estimate by Utzon of A£13.75 million (A$27.5 million), containing an increase on the earlier estimate of a further A$3 million. The August estimate was a substantial jump and placed more political pressure on the Government since it exceeded the 10 per cent differential provided by the Act. It was inevitable that, sooner or later, the Government would be forced to seek parliamentary approval for an increase.

At the Cabinet sub-committee meeting, Premier Heffron, a decent considerate man, thanked Utzon's party for coming so far at such short notice, expressed his anxiety over the Opera House and asked for their comments on several points. Before either Utzon or Zunz could speak, Ove Arup launched into a vigorous defence: 'Well, I'd better deal with this,' he announced, after which he talked non-stop for 45 minutes.

Ove Arup rarely ever finished a sentence. Although from one sentence to the next he made little sense, his word pictures were brilliant when viewed from a distance. Unless you were prepared, though, Arup was baffling. First to succumb were the shorthand recorders, their pencils moved slower and slower as they fell behind, until finally, after 15 minutes, they stopped taking notes altogether. Ove Arup's verbal blitzkrieg non-plussed the sub-committee. When, at last he ceased, a deep silence enveloped the room – no one was brave enough to ask a question out of fear he would start again. Ove Arup had mentally exhausted the Cabinet.

All the Government wanted was a second engineering opinion. Insofar as the Cabinet had approved the contract with M.R. Hornibrook (NSW) for Stage II the previous day, there could be no turning back; nonetheless, it wanted independent confirmation of Arup's design principles for the roof structure. Yves Guion, a French structural consultant and an expert on prestressed concrete design, was contacted and went over the

Arup calculations before writing a letter to the New South Wales Government in which he confirmed everything.[13]

On Utzon's visit to Berlin in June 1962 for discussions with Professor Unruh, he had met Professors Werner Gabler and Cremer. Gabler was an architect who specialised in acoustic design. Cremer, who had gained prominence from his acoustic work on the new Berlin Philharmonic Hall designed by the great German Expressionist planner and architect, Hans Scharoun, was a professor at the Institute of Technical Acoustics. Utzon, having reached an impasse with Jordan, instead of terminating his services replaced him with Gabler and Cremer, but explained that he did this only because he required a second opinion. Henceforth, Gabler and Cremer would do similar work to Jordan. Utzon decided this was necessary because Jordan had given up. He was disheartened and perhaps could no longer see a way forward.[14] Utzon accused him privately of being a 'lazy fellow', but this does not seem very likely. The problem was much more deep-seated, that Jordan had set a limit to his acoustic consulting responsibilities and resolutely refused to design the halls for Utzon.

In Berlin, Utzon discussed the cost of model testing with Cremer and Gabler and explained how the new arrangement with Jordan would operate.[15] At the end of August, Gabler wrote to Utzon with his objections to the concave Minor Hall acoustic shell, which he thought might concentrate the sound and lead to echoes. To avoid this, he sketched an alternative with convex instead of concave reflecting surfaces and included a series of profiles. Utzon promptly replaced the concave ceiling scheme with a convex surface, but retained the overall radial theme.[16] Prior to this, the interiors of the two halls had been treated differently; now Utzon applied the same geometrical approach to both.

Having established the right volume for the two halls, the next stage was to define the acoustic profile.[17] Dropping freely curved profiles, Utzon introduced a system of circles he called a 'mother cylinder', whose radii increased in set increments. Rolling the mother cylinder across the radial sections generated a series of convex profiles. When these radial slices were placed next to each other, they formed a symmetrical ceiling shell. The revised convex sections were almost identical to those recommended profiles contained in Gabler's letter to Jon Lundberg on 17 August 1962, and were produced by Lundberg ten days later.[18] The newly configured ceiling of the Minor Hall used cylindrical surfaces with radii increasing at 90 cm intervals, to coincide with the depth of the ceiling ribs. Utzon referred to a breaking wave to explain the rolling concave sections. With this changed, and they became convex for acoustic reasons, the wave was flipped upside down and the metaphor made little sense.

This convex geometry was applied in the Minor Hall in the October 1962 drawings by Utzon's Turkish assistant, Oktay Nayman. The hall now acquired a funnel-shaped volume that radiated out from the stage. In none of the drawings, however, was the perplexing question of how to support the acoustic shell ever tackled. This was critical to the engineers because it could lead to the imposition of unacceptably high loads on the shells and the podium. In the first attempt at a ceiling structural scheme, in October 1962, the curved plywood reflector panels were carried by 90 cm-deep, radial aluminium trusses. The curvature of the 5–18 m panels was limited to four radii, with the trusses suspended from the concrete roof ribs at intermediate points. Back in London, it was incorrectly assumed that the trusses spanned all the way from the front of the theatre to the back. Poul Beckmann, the engineer responsible at Arups, subsequently recommended the aluminium trusses should replaced by plywood box beams, and a weight limit for the acoustic sandwich to be set at 90–100 kg per m^2.[19] Since the side shell arches, or 'octopus arches', were much stronger than the roof ribs, it was decided to suspend the ceiling ribs from them instead of the roof ribs. As a precaution, 'Utzon holes' were cast in the roof ribs as they were fabricated, to attach hangers for suspending the ceiling along the radials.

Utzon's ceiling diagrams were not structural drawings; they merely described the acoustic reflecting geometry calculated to best distribute the sound uniformly to the audience. The ceilings would consist of layers: an inner shell to reflect the sound, and a much heavier outer shell to isolate the interior from unwanted external noise. Each layer was assigned a function. The radial beams were the structure that carried both layers.

It took another two months to develop the circular geometry of the auditorium ceilings. In early December 1962, the reflecting surfaces in the Minor Hall were further simplified by giving them the same radius throughout. This standardised the geometry in the same fashion Utzon had earlier standardised the concrete roof elements.[20] The precise profile of each rib was defined by moving a standard cylinder acting as a rolling wave to define a series of equal radius arcs. All this took Utzon about four years.

The Major Hall had to be suitable for opera and concerts, which meant different reverberation times and different hall volumes in each case. The multi-purpose hall was essentially an acoustical compromise. This is what made it so difficult. The alternative to it was a convertible hall which would be physically modified to match the theatrical or musical performance requirements. The adoption of the multi-purpose auditorium approach ensured that it would be impossible to provide both 1.6- and 2.1-second reverberation times and thus to satisfy the respective acoustic criteria for opera and concert. Vilhelm Jordan had designed multi-purpose halls in Denmark and Iceland in the 1950s, before Utzon hired him, and would have known this, although the Sydney Opera House was far more complex than these earlier halls.[21]

A multi-purpose hall must be designed for opera – which requires a fixed proscenium opening and stage – but can be adapted for concerts by closing off the proscenium opening with demountable panels and forming a platform for the orchestra out in front of the stage. The audience number remains basically unchanged for both opera and concerts. Since the two arts need different reverberation times, if a multi-purpose hall is designed to suit opera it will not be good for concerts and vice versa. This was the great, seemingly insoluble, problem confronting Utzon.

A convertible hall begins from the opposite premise to the multi-purpose hall; it is designed basically for concerts and is converted to opera by moving the back wall of the stage forward towards the audience to establish a proscenium opening and stage. The audience number is reduced, and so is the reverberation time because it subtracts the volume of the stage from that of the hall. In the concert mode, additional seats are created by utilising the area at the front of the stage and the orchestra pit. This significantly increases the hall volume, the wall and ceiling area and hence the sound absorption and the seating capacity. In direct consequence of these changes, the reverberation time can also be increased.

The solution to the Major Hall lay in approaching it as a convertible hall – the multi-purpose hall was never a workable solution. Utzon's original scheme proposed a rudimentary form of convertible hall, but he was prevented from developing the concept further by his client. In 1963, Utzon attempted to return to the convertible hall but, just when it looked like he was succeeding Sir Bernard Heinze, convenor of the music and drama advisory panel, who had just come back from Berlin, rejected Hans Scharoun's revolutionary Berlin hall model and stopped this promising line of development.[22]

Utzon wrote of the change: 'I accepted this blindly because of my respect for my Client and his demands, although I immediately found my Consultants against me. Nobody wanted to collaborate on this, neither the structural engineers nor the acoustical specialists.'[23]

Jordan had begun by listing the hall uses according to their priority; then he proceeded to design the space to suit each use, with the aim of achieving a superior solution for the most important, while continuing to pay regard to the acoustic requirements of the lesser functions in order of priority. The Sydney competition programme was quite specific: concerts were the first priority, followed by grand opera.

Initially, the reverberation time for the Major Hall was modified by subtracting the volume of the stage tower from the main auditorium during concerts by isolating the upper part of the tower using movable panels to close it off and placing seats on the large opera stage. This was basically the multi-purpose hall approach which, in view of the acoustic limitations already enumerated, was doomed from the outset. In the early plans, about 1000 extra, movable seats were to be provided in this manner. In the *Red Book* (March 1958), the hall was shown with either the orchestra in the middle and the audience on each side, or the orchestra pushed to the back of the stage with the audience seated in a single block.[24] The audience seated directly opposite the orchestra robbed the sound quality of music reaching the fixed seats behind.

The earlier design of the Major Hall ceiling was changed by stepping the ceiling cross-profile in the middle so it matched the curved underside of the roof more closely. At the time of Ashworth's visit to Hellebæk in September 1960, the Major Hall scheme still resisted solution. Opera auditoria have a stage tower to physically isolate the stage from the audience in the event of a fire, to enable a large iron curtain to be lowered and the smoke removed so the audience is not affected. In the early schemes the fire curtain was made in three pieces like an accordion. As this proved to be expensive, it was replaced by a single curtain and a lower proscenium opening of 13.7 m. The large fire curtain and low proscenium caused a 'coupled room' effect, splitting the auditorium into two distinct acoustic volumes, each with its own reverberation time.

During the final week of August 1960, shortly before Ashworth arrived in Hellebæk, Utzon suddenly abandoned the first ceiling design and replaced it with a radically new one which Yuzo Mikami had begun to develop in February. The new ceiling consisted of numerous folded plywood-leaves which reminded Utzon of the leaves in the nearby beech forest. The triangular plywood pieces or 'leaves' forming the shallow crystalline cupola (it resembled a large tent suspended inside the roof), were angled to direct sound back to the audience. Their appearance strongly recalled the small *muqarnas* or scales of the classic Islamic honeycomb or stalactite vault. A number of models were made to illustrate the flexibility of this scheme and to demonstrate how well it fitted under the shells.

Yuzo Mikami was a young Japanese architect who worked for Utzon. Before he joined Utzon, in July 1958, he was employed by Kunio Maekawa on the Japanese Pavilion at the Brussels World Expo. In their discussions, Utzon and Mikami agreed the two principal halls should be entirely different inside. To Mikami, the two halls were like two similar-looking birds' eggs: they might appear the same on the outside, but the chicks hatched from them would be quite dissimilar. Utzon produced two small sketches, one of each hall: for the Minor Hall he drew a wave breaking to convey the rolling fluid power of the sea, as a metaphor for the evolution of its form; he showed the Major Hall as a dense canopy of beech forest foliage.[25] These two small sketches, which lacked any indication of construction or structure, were Utzon's instructions to Mikami.

To develop the forest idea, Mikami took short lengths of balsa wood, glued them into triangles and fitted them neatly under the model profile of the roof shells to maximise the auditorium volume. Photographed against the sky his tiny model, which he then used to make his drawings of the ceiling, vaguely recalled a beech forest roof. Ashworth was enormously taken by this unique 'suspended tent-like ceiling' for the Major Hall.

The Major Hall adopted the same radial arrangement as the Minor Hall, but was further subdivided into trapezoidal areas by expanding circles and diagonals to produce an irregular cupola comprised of flat, triangular panels. This was supported around the edge by elongated, triangular, vertical panels that continued the ceiling motif. Utzon worked on this scheme for three years until September 1963. Although Gabler and Cremer, the two acoustic consultants from Berlin, were less certain about the seating plan, both regarded the crystalline ceiling very highly and considered that it would provide a superior acoustic solution.

In October 1961, Utzon had agreed to a second seating

scheme for concerts, with the orchestra moved forward to the middle of the auditorium; the audience would be distributed around the musicians on two sides and behind them. The new seating plan, which overcame the problem of sound quality loss when the orchestra was placed at the back of the stage, was developed in considerable detail with the usual 1:10 models.[26]

On seeing an early version of the crystalline ceiling in March 1961, Vilhelm Jordan responded that the volume was too great and the side panels would not give enough side reflections. He also considered the triangular panels should be flatter. The main objection to the scheme from Utzon's viewpoint was the large number of joints between the panels. These carried an increased risk of sound leakage from outside if the acoustic seals failed, a risk which increased in proportion to the number of joints. The ceiling was to be supported on a framework of circular steel pipes from which the plywood panels were screw-fixed and the framework was to be suspended from the roof. This crystalline ceiling scheme is illustrated in the *Yellow Book* of 1962, and continued to be refined up until Utzon's departure for Australia in December 1962.

Later ceiling designs were more notable for their aesthetic refinement and increasing abstraction. Utzon approached the sculptural shaping of the ceiling in musical terms. In October 1962, the side walls for the Major Hall disappeared entirely, and the maze-like triangular plywood scales rose independently above the seats like a cloud separating itself from the sea.

Utzon endeavoured to transcend the immediate functional factors in his quest for a synthesis of the expressive, acoustic and structural aspects of the ceiling problem. His sketches sought to elevate the aesthetic over all else. Before the music starts, Utzon prepares his audience by seating it in a fantastic sculptured bowl. His image is the exotic plumage of a tropical bird of paradise. The crystalline cloud-ceiling drifts across above the audience like musical notes cast in the form of a cave of beech wood. The ceiling is classical, pure, geometric, symmetrical. Utzon liked to compare the internal auditorium shell to the soundbox of a violin and evidently believed there was a valid parallel between what he was doing and the task of the violin maker who determines the instrument's dimensions, proportions and curves.[27] To construct a violin is a job requiring a supreme magician of the void to shape the enclosing space of the violin so that it is filled with the finest sounds that the human ear can ever contemplate.[28] It is a nice thought, but an auditorium is much more than an enlarged resonating soundbox; it must hold an audience who will receive the sounds coming from the instruments. Its shape, therefore, must be such that it throws the sounds to them all equally without any loss of richness.

In the few months remaining before Utzon was due to leave Denmark — for he planned to move to Sydney at the end of December — his office worked feverishly to develop a new ceiling proposal based on curved radiating ribs that would need less support. Instead of suspending the ceiling from the shell ribs, Utzon now tried suspending the plywood panels between radial ribs in the same manner as the Minor Hall. The profile of each rib was determined by modelling the diffusion of sound from a source at the centre of the auditorium. In a December sketch, the ceiling plunged downwards immediately above the sound source then rose on either side to form two unequal domes, one above the stage area, and another above the auditorium seating ramp. The twin volume had a neck one-third of the way back, under which the seating was arranged both in front of and behind the orchestra. This particular scheme marked the limit of development Utzon reached prior to his departure for Australia.

Utzon had contemplated migrating to Australia in 1957. Now, with Stage I well advanced, and the roof contract for Stage II signed, the pressure increased on Utzon to establish a permanent architectural presence in Sydney. It would be another three years, perhaps longer, before the job would be ready for Stage III, the interiors, but these would require Utzon to spend much more time in Australia than previously. It seemed sensible, therefore, for him to relocate his office in Sydney. At Bennelong Point he could watch the building progress on a daily basis.

Utzon miscalculated and failed to realise how remote Australia was from London, from Europe, and the world. By closing his office at Hellebæk and starting anew in Sydney, Utzon distanced himself from his most important ally, Ove Arup, with whom he enjoyed a strong personal and professional attachment. Even when Arup was not immediately involved, his close proximity exercised an important restraining influence on his associates. Relocating the office to Sydney diminished Arup's influence.

By 1963, Ove Arup had become tired of the limitations placed on him as a consultant and wanted more time to spend on his own design work. The move to Sydney by Utzon coincided with Arup's concentration on his Kingsgate Footbridge project at Durham, which gave him the sort of creative opportunity he craved. As the Kingsgate bridge developed, Arup progressively disengaged himself from the day-to-day activities of the consultancy. And with it, his direct contribution to the Opera House also decreased. Utzon was slow to read the signs.

In Australia, Utzon had to deal with associates from Arups' Sydney office. To further complicate matters, Utzon's acoustical, mechanical and electrical consultants were all located in either Denmark or Berlin. The move to Sydney produced a host of liaison problems with his European consultants. In the mid-1960s, Australia was far less accessible than it is today.

But the air in Hellebæk buzzed with excitement and anticipation in late 1962. First Utzon had to shut down the office and arrange for his staff to transfer to Sydney. By mid-December, most of the details were settled. Utzon and his family would leave Europe on 26 December and planned to spend three months on the trip in the United States and Tahiti before arriving in Australia on 4 March. Much of December was occupied with packing and preparations for the move.[29] Utzon wrote to Cremer in Berlin on 20 December to say he was moving to Sydney and he had a little extra work to do on the drawings with the structural engineers, but promised to come back in October 1963.

Utzon arrived in London on Boxing Day. While there, he purchased a Mk 10 Jaguar saloon and arranged for it to be shipped to Sydney. The Mk 10 had been introduced that year, so it was the latest word in luxury motoring. However, in Australia people overcharged him when they saw the car. After a year, he sold it and bought a cuttlefish-shaped Citroën, the favourite of architects in the 1960s. Because the Citroën was not an English make, it hovered in an unknown territory in terms of status; with its idiosyncratic engineering it suggested individuality and its French flair was distinctive although not exactly snobby.

When the Ove Arup office got wind that Utzon was in London, Jack Zunz and Yuzo Mikami hired a room at the circular Aerial Hotel at Heathrow Airport where he was staying. Accompanied by Ove Arup, Michael Lewis, the future site manager on Bennelong Point, and Joe Huan, a bright young Chinese engineer, they travelled out to Heathrow for a conference with Utzon before he left. It was bitterly cold and snowing outside. In keeping with British tradition, the heating pipes froze and everything else in the hotel ceased to work.

The meeting, which began mid-afternoon at 3.20 p.m., got off to a good start in a friendly and co-operative atmosphere. The Arups engineers wanted Utzon to instruct them on how he wished them to solve the remaining problems of the roof vaults and tile lids. It was critical to work on the pattern and spacing of tile lids for the roofs, otherwise the work might be delayed.

By evening, Ove Arup began to complain about his cold feet. It was almost as cold inside the hotel as it was outside and Ove Arup, who was 67 and far from well, retreated to the bathroom, rolled up his trousers, filled the bath with hot water, then proceeded to sit on the edge dangling his feet in the water. Every so often Arup would toss a remark in their direction from his refuge in the bathroom. Arup's Danish stoicism and droll demeanour, struck everyone as extremely comic.[30] The meeting dragged on until 11 p.m. They stopped for dinner, but well before this Ove Arup had suffered enough and left.

The Arups group was concerned about keeping the job progressing, and were anxious because they were caught between the architect and the contractor. On one side, they were involved in arbitration in Australia over the Stage I claims and, on the other, they were coming under increasing pressure to start Stage II work on the roof. By the end of 1962, Arups had more than 50 staff employed on the project. At this critical juncture Utzon decided to take a three-month vacation, during which he would be cut off from contacting everyone, including his engineers.

Jack Zunz later dated the beginning of the decline in the relationship between Utzon and Ove Arup from this time.[31] This is a little unfair, though not entirely so, because Ove Arup & Partners' site supervisor, Michael Lewis – who was almost as important to the project as Utzon – did not reach Sydney until 5 April, a month after Utzon. Lewis had been seriously injured in an accident with a bus in Tel Aviv on his way to Sydney, which put him in hospital for six weeks with a broken leg.[32] When he did eventually reach Sydney, he was still on crutches. Utzon understood very clearly that Michael Lewis had been selected as Jack Zunz's deputy in Sydney because Zunz did not trust Utzon as the architect. Utzon saw the appointment as an essentially hostile decision and a negative comment on his abilities and his office.

An antipathy had already emerged in 1962 between Lewis and Utzon. Povl Ahm in Arups would have been the better choice as Sydney site supervisor. Ahm was more sympathetic to Utzon's architectural approach, he had worked on the job and he understood the structural background much better than Lewis, who was a newcomer to the project. But Ahm was not a close associate of Jack Zunz and this factor, not engineering expertise, was what mattered most. Zunz wanted someone in Sydney he could trust implicitly to look out for his interests. The fact that Utzon and Lewis did not get on was secondary.

The Heathrow meeting ended with the current design problems resolved, many down to the details, but with some only in principle. Ove Arup & Partners asked Utzon for his authorisation to make minor design decisions on their own, to permit the production of working drawings to proceed while he was absent, and this was granted. When the long and exhausting meeting finally ended, both Utzon and the engineers were contented and parted with warm handshakes all around.

This meeting came at the end of a productive collaboration over more than five years. There were no evident signs of bitterness or discord during the Boxing Day conference – quite the opposite.[33] If there were any dark clouds, they did not show themselves. But once Utzon left for Australia, he was compelled to deal with the new Arups site group led by Michael Lewis. Prior to this, Utzon's friendship with Arup, and their mutual respect for one another, was strong enough to see them through each crisis. This now changed. The personal contact with Ove Arup, which in previous years had been so crucial to success, was allowed to lapse.

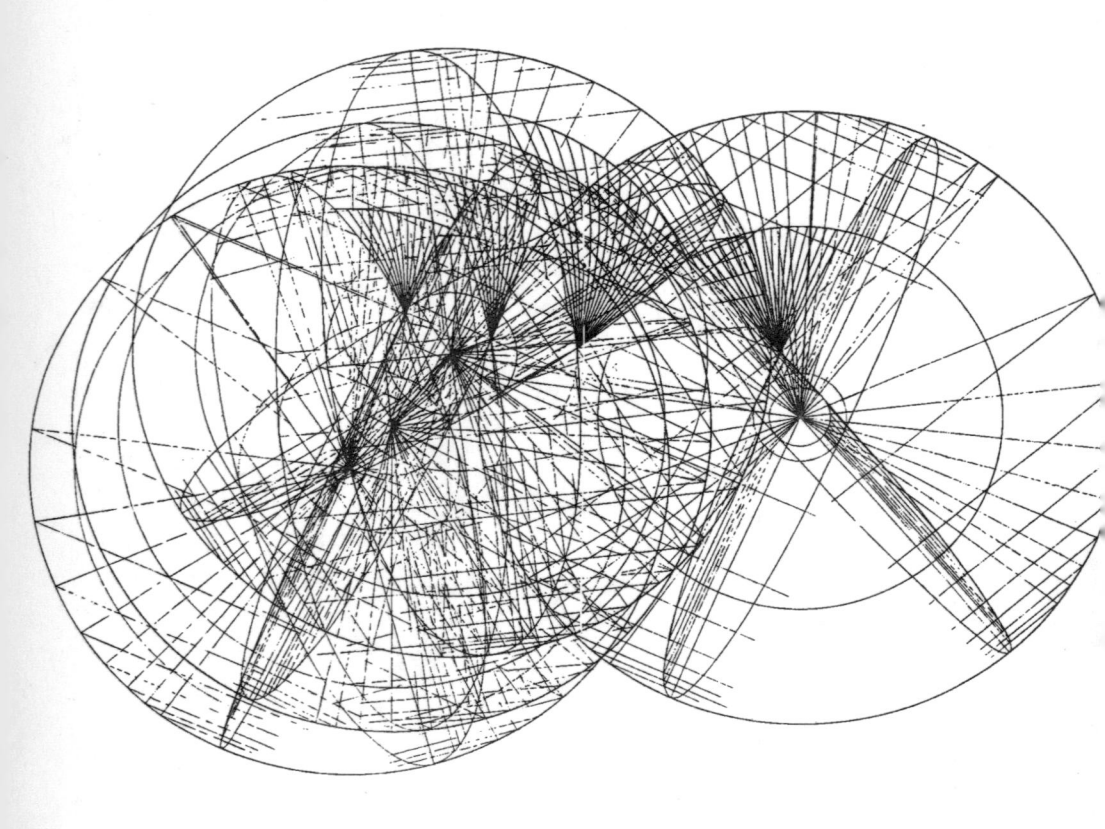

It took months to find the precise profile and locate the specific coordinates for each triangle, which defined each 'shell' in the Opera House roof. Derivation of the shells of the Major Hall from a sphere (Concert Hall).

12

Maturing the Vision
Sydney, 1963–1964

On his arrival in Sydney on 4 March 1963, Utzon was immediately thrown into the hurly-burly of a royal visit. While he was halfway from Papeete on a French Transport Aerienne flight, the aircraft received a radio message inviting him to lunch on the royal yacht *Britannia*.

On Sunday 3 March, the Queen and the Duke of Edinburgh had wandered away from Government House and spent a windy, fascinating half-hour clambering over the partly built concrete platform on Bennelong Point.[1] When Her Majesty was informed that Utzon and his family were due to arrive in Sydney the following day, the Queen insisted he be invited to the reception on board the *Britannia*. Her show of interest in Utzon so impressed Sydney's politicians that, for the first year, by a curious sort of magic, they left him alone.

Utzon suddenly descended on Sydney trailing clouds of glory. The royal invitation climaxed a wonderful week on Tahiti, at the end of a month-long visit to America. The family was excited and more than a little apprehensive about Australia. Landing at 11 a.m., with no time to change into fresh clothes, Lis and Jørn were dragged off the aircraft, bustled into a waiting car and rushed directly to the royal yacht. The luncheon invitation came as a huge surprise to Utzon; it remained a memory he cherished the rest of his life.[2]

In the wet, Sydney looked miserable and rain-splattered. The industrial route from the airport past factories accentuated its drabness. On the hasty drive to Circular Quay, from the rain-smeared car window, the family peered out in wonder at thick-set men with gargantuan beer bellies in black singlets clutching large frothy amber schooners who adorned the outside walls of shiny yellow and brown tiled pub verandas in a vernacular imitation of classical caryatids.[3] It was the Utzon children's first glimpse of Australia. Jørn Utzon was not daunted; he preferred to look beyond the brazen ugliness of the roadside. Sydney might not impress at this level, but it did have an undeniable raw energy and willingness to try new things that convinced him it would all work out somehow. He was an optimist.

In the space of a day, Lis and Jørn were torn from the Gauguin green hills and red-roofed, decrepit wooden buildings lining the Papeete waterfront and plunged into the formality of a royal visit.[4] Lis arrived bare-legged and wearing a cheap straw beach hat; however, no one appeared to notice the absence of stockings as her legs were so brown from the Tahitian sun. Lis's naturalness made whatever she wore appear stylish.

Arriving at the quay beside the *Britannia*, Utzon and Lis stood at the end of a line of Australians waiting to go aboard. By pure chance, they found themselves next to Patrick White who chatted amiably. The Utzons were the odd couple out – total strangers. Around them were civil servants, business tycoons such as the machinery manufacturer James Kirby, Edward Hallstrom, maker of Silent Knight refrigerators, Murray Rose, the Olympic swimmer, several admirals, generals and chief justices.

Doubtless the invitation was meant as a form of recognition springing from the Queen's curiosity. As it transpired, however, it was a very lonely honour she bestowed on the Utzons. Her Majesty descended to the saloon from an upper deck. The first thing Utzon noticed were her little toe peepers, next an ankle, then a calf and thigh, followed by her shoulders, until, at the very last moment, her head popped out from beneath the stair soffit. Her entry looked more comic than dignified and Utzon thought, if ever he had the opportunity, he would like to re-design the royal yacht so the Queen would be seen in her entirety from the first, not bit by bit like a print-out emerging from a telex machine.

Utzon was seated directly opposite Elizabeth II, with just a large vase of flowers in the middle of the table to separate them. During lunch, glancing under the spray of blooms blocking his line of vision, Utzon caught a glimpse of a tiny hand as it quickly reached out and took a roll. It was small and without character – the soft hand of privilege unmarked by labour.

On their own after eating, Utzon and Lis drifted back to Patrick White. Years later, White recalled their meeting. White was nettled by so much artificiality at the lunch. Marooned in a lake of social pretentiousness, Utzon's natural unaffectedness caught White's interest. Later, he recalled Utzon was a:

> *tall man as handsome as they come, but handicapped by the English he spoke, which was boneless, and to me unintelligible as his native Danish. At least I enjoyed talking to Utzon, and I think we both enjoyed standing together uneasily at one end of the saloon.*[5]

That in itself was surprising – if Utzon could charm White, he could charm any curmudgeon. White did not make friends readily; his reaction to Utzon's diction, whatever 'boneless' might refer to, seems a trifle disparaging, not to mention unfair, under the circumstances.[6]

Utzon was an inspired conversationalist and spoke reasonably good English. White lacked Utzon's generous disposition and usually came armed with a quiver of verbal darts to hurl at his enemies. He seems to have been equally hasty in his judgement of Lis Utzon, whom he dismissed as The Little Mermaid, remarking that she was, 'that plain, dank-haired mermaid kind one sees from Denmark, very pleasant. As her English is a bit vague, she smiles.'[7] White underestimated Lis, who was not at all the insubstantial creature he took her for.

Shortly after this, Utzon showed White over the partly finished Opera House. For once White was not morose: 'It has made me feel glad I am alive in Australia to-day. At last we are going to have something worth having.' Climbing up and down so many steps reminded White of the ancient Greek cities Phaestos, Mycenae and Tiryns.[8]

Jack Zunz, the Ove Arup partner in charge of the roof, was not impressed by Utzon's sudden descent from the heavens: 'And lo and behold, God [Utzon] appears from Heaven. He flies into Sydney from Tahiti. And his plane lands at nine or ten o'clock and then of course he's wheeled into lunch with the Queen …' Utzon's visit to the building site after the reception and his complaints about a number of matters further irked Zunz. Zunz attributed the breakdown in the relationship between Utzon and Arup & Partners as due to his failure to communicate during the trip.[9] He conveniently overlooked the late arrival in Sydney of Michael Lewis, his site engineer, a month after Utzon. No doubt Zunz had his own reasons to shift the blame, rather than point to the actual source of the rift. At this time, Utzon might also have acted with more consideration.

Before he moved to Australia permanently, Utzon had purchased a large block of land at Bayview Heights on Pittwater, on 20 February 1961. He had to borrow the money, but by 16 August 1962 he had discharged the mortgage.[10] This established a pattern for buying land. The site might just have appealed to him, but he was also an excellent judge of real estate. His purchase was complicated by his decision to subdivide and purchase an adjoining lot so he could surround his future house with a thick green belt to insulate it from neighbouring properties.[11] In the end, Utzon acquired a total consolidated site of about 2.43 ha. Bayview's unspoilt natural beauty and extensive water views appealed to Utzon's taste and the site was large enough for neighbours not to intrude.

Bayview, with its magnificent millionaire's panorama of Pittwater and the Pacific Ocean, is typical Sydney sandstone country. Like Hellebæk it is near the sea and removed from the city, but it was not so far as to be inconvenient and, above all, Utzon's property was spectacularly beautiful.

Utzon bought the Bayview property two years before he came to Sydney. While he went about setting up the Bennelong

Point office, and tried to hurry completion of the office extension there, Lis looked for a house near their Bayview land. She chose a large, outspread bungalow at 19 Alexandra Crescent, Bayview. It stood at the top of Fermoy Avenue, back up the hill facing Pittwater. It was very close to their land. In the middle of the front yard cutting the view of Pittwater in two stood several tall palms. Kim, the Utzons' youngest child, then six years old, was enrolled at Loquat Valley School, an Anglican preparatory school, which was quite close. The two older children, Jan and Lin, were sent to Narrabeen High School.

Australia now became home for the Utzons. The northern beaches area of Sydney was considerably more isolated in the 1960s; it took pride in its special character centred on the beach, surfing and sailing. Jan and Lin fitted in easily and quickly threw themselves into the Australian way of life. Utzon bought himself a 1 tonne 9 m Diamond class *Yachting World* keelboat sailing boat, which he sailed on Wednesdays and weekends. At weekends the family would go on day hikes over Barrenjoey Head and Lion Island at the mouth of the Hawkesbury estuary.[12]

The one thing the Utzons were not prepared for was the unrelenting press scrutiny. By nature, Utzon was an intensely private person; it embarrassed and unsettled him to find himself given instant celebrity status and to be continually watched, with his every word made the subject of public comment.

The Australian bush fascinated Utzon and offered refuge from the constant scrutiny:

> *I would like our house [at Bayview] to be incorporated in the bush just as though it were a boat floating in the sea. You don't build a wall around a boat to hold back the water, and in the same way, I wouldn't like to see the virgin bush pushed back and held back around our house ... The way I see it, the trees — and the shrubs — should flow in and around the house. That means building a courtyard, or a big terrace at least. Perhaps living-units around a big natural area.*[13]

Australian architects had already found the bush, but their work was often a relentless parody of overseas models and invariably looked stale and second-hand when compared to the Wright or Walter Gropius originals in America. Few Australian architects appeared to accept that Wright's prairie houses were a response to the flat plains of America and which had little in common with the hot, steep, sandstone ridges of Sydney's northern suburbs.

Utzon's image of a house skimming the earth, and the bush washing in and out of it like the sea, repeated his idea of the house as a boat and the roof moving in sympathy with the undulating rhythm of the surf.[14] Before the month was out on his arrival, Utzon had made preliminary sketches for the house and was storing up ideas in his mind. The roof should be wave-like, foam leaping and boiling as it is thrown from a crashing breaker. The structure would incorporate 15 m clear-span plywood U-beams resting on the outside walls. The U-beam roof resembled surfboats laid side by side and lashed together in a raft, with the plywood beams stepping up and down depending on the space below. The gaps between the U-beams would be sealed by an aluminium capping.

The beams could be arranged in a flat ceiling or rise in steps. Where light was needed, gaps could be left between beams and covered by sloped sheets of transparent Plexiglas folded over two neighbouring beams.

Utzon was not sure of his aims. The early designs repeated the Fredensborg terraced houses' containment within a simple rectangular boundary. As with Fredensborg, the floor would be raised on a terrace above the ground. The basic structural idea of two side walls, on the east and west across the contours, carrying the plywood-beam roof to create an uninterrupted space is quite simple. The main floor formed a large terrace broken into smaller areas by steps and transverse planters. The main living area and kitchen, on the sunny north side, faced the view and Pittwater.[15] The approach is from above, via an entry court covered by U-beams. The house is reduced to two main elements – a platform and a roof.

Utzon planned to remove the ground and rock to create a platform, and then carry his raft of plywood beams over it. The roof above the floor platform would rest on the two outside walls at either end. These provided the only support. Utzon gave a great deal of thought to the design of the beams. In August 1963, he lodged a patent application, accompanied by a provisional specification, for the plywood roof elements.[16] The patent sprang directly from the house at Bayview, but Utzon was also considering using similar beams in the Opera House ceilings. The Bayview house was an experiment in the application of this roof-beam prototype. If it proved a success, and the beams were strong enough, the next stage would be to use similar beams for the acoustic shells inside the Opera House's two principal auditoria. Utzon made a habit of patenting his inventions. Earlier, on 25 March 1960, he had taken out a furniture patent in Denmark.[17] It is most unusual for an architect to go to the trouble to patent a design in this way. In Utzon's case, it probably arose from his work on furniture where patents are more normal and can prove extremely profitable in the long term if the idea has some merit. Alternatively, it may have been something he picked up from his father. The importance of Utzon's Australian roofing patent lies in what it reveals about his industrial approach, and because it demonstrates that Utzon intended to tackle the Opera House interiors using his house as a test bed for the new construction components.

This is typical of Utzon's thinking. He starts with a broad premise then proceeds to develop a large-scale building system using it. In the Bayview house, this entailed first inventing a system of plywood U-beams, patenting them, then working out how to apply the patent to a range of other applications. He solves a problem once, produces a standard element, then seeks to use it in individual cases. Utzon worked the same way as an industrial designer.[18] In this he was almost unique in Australia at this time; most other architects were content to treat each problem in isolation.

Utzon's plywood U-beams eliminated rafters, battens, steel decks, fascias, gutters and plaster ceilings and, to an extent, insulation. The beam was a complete roof by itself. The metal outer lining, along with the soffit finish for the U-beams, were integral and were applied as part of the manufacturing process in the factory so they would be unaffected by the weather.

Utzon intended to keep all the trees around his Bayview

house so it would be immersed in nature, much the same as his Hellebæk house. His boat concept emphasised the insubstantiality of the European presence in Australia, and it exposed the uprooted, alien quality of European Australian culture which exists somewhere between nostalgic longing for the home country and a desire to be part of a new society. If the European encounter was mostly physical at the beginning, it also possessed a spiritual side to it. The new European forms never quite relinquished their feeling of separateness. The ship as symbol expresses this uneasy accommodation with native Australia by pushing the notion of a cultural invasion to the foreground.[19]

Utzon's image of his dwelling, detached and drifting on the tide, is a very powerful one because it highlights the lack of deep roots in white identity which lightly skims across an ageless earth, while longing to immerse itself in the bush. The Opera House is a further version of the metaphor: it is stable within itself, and although yoked to the Point, it drifts luminously in the unconscious.

The move to Sydney and closure of the Hellebæk office interrupted work on the Opera House. A temporary crisis had developed in August 1961 over the payment of Utzon's fee. This forced Utzon to give notice to three of his most senior and highest-paid assistants, Knud Lautrup-Larsen, Hartvig-Petersen and Poul Schouboe. Although the matter was promptly sorted out, the three had by then found new positions. When Utzon asked them to stay they had to refuse, since to do otherwise would have meant breaking an undertaking to their new employers. Additionally, because they had families, the proposed move to Sydney would have severely disrupted their children's schooling. Utzon maintained a permanent staff of around seven or eight architects in his Hellebæk office.[20] Consequently, the loss of three key personnel represented a severe blow at this critical time.

Knud Lautrup-Larsen had joined the office in 1959, and for a time was Utzon's right-hand man; Aage Hartvig-Petersen was the third to arrive after Lautrup-Larsen; and Poul Schouboe took care of the Kingo housing and the stage machinery contract. Fortunately, Jon Lundberg from Norway, Mogens Prip-Buus, Jacob Kielland-Brandt, both of whom were Danes, and Raymond Brownell from Tasmania, all agreed to follow Utzon to Australia where they were to form the nucleus of Utzon's new Australian practice.[21]

All the drawings and files of correspondence had to be transferred to Sydney. Utzon began to recruit upwards of five new Australian staff in addition to his European staff, together with a number of senior architects qualified as managers and job supervisors.

Following his practice in Denmark, Utzon hired many different nationalities.[22] He enjoyed the stimulus of working with a wide cross-section of people from diverse backgrounds. To a degree, this compensated for the limited pool of architects in Australia. Utzon's local architectural assistants were mostly trained in schools of architecture which followed an outmoded pre-Modern British architectural curriculum presented by lecturers recruited from England, few of whom were acquainted with Modernism. Plucked from relative obscurity in England, they were instantly translated to professorial rank by a process of academic colonisation. With the exception of Robert Maclurcan, Utzon's Australian staff comprised mostly students and recent graduates. Utzon's method of hiring staff was extremely casual: some merely wandered down Macquarie Street on the off-chance of a job, others heard by word-of-mouth at the bar of 'The Newcastle' pub on lower George Street. Leif Christensen was promised a job in Denmark, but found when he reached Australia that Utzon had forgotten about him in the meantime.

New graduates offered some advantages. As well as being cheap to employ, they were more receptive and flexible, and they responded positively to new ideas and challenges. Enthusiasm could not replace extensive professional experience, however. Utzon may have been right to hire as he did, but it is difficult to avoid the conclusion that at Hellebæk his office was much more competent and better equipped to tackle the daunting design tasks the Opera House set him than the Sydney office. In the succession of crises that developed later, the immaturity and unworldiness of Utzon's young staff was a liability. In Sydney, Utzon suffered most from a lack of sound professional advice. Over the three years after 1962, many of his best senior assistants left through lack of work and because of illness.

Utzon set the pace and advances depended entirely on his progress. And since he made the important decisions and supervised the details personally, he needed sympathetic draughtsmen to interpret the ideas he expressed in principle. A young staff offered less resistance than if Utzon had retained his experienced senior core of people when he moved to Sydney. He also needed good administrators to carry out the daily administration, so he could be free to concentrate on the design. Out of the entire Bennelong Point staff, only Prip-Buus, Jon Lundberg and Kielland-Brandt had been acquainted with the project since its inception, and of their number only Prip-Buus lasted beyond mid-1965. The problem was one of continuity.

Utzon's arrival in Sydney coincided with the start of Stage II, constructing the roof. His Danish staff reached Sydney from January 1963 on. Their office was a shed on the far east side of Bennelong Point. Any other architect would have chosen a more salubrious location in the city, but Utzon wanted to be close to his building. There were a number of advantages: he could talk to his engineer at any time; the proximity meant he was immediately aware of any development on the site; and it provided the cheapest rental on Macquarie Street.

Like all work-site offices, Bennelong Point was permanently dusty, noisy and busy with people coming and going. Dirt and grime found its way into the typewriters, drawers, correspondence files, office equipment and cabinets of drawings, while the constant yammering of jackhammers tore through the paper-thin timber walls. Making up for the discomfort, Utzon could gaze at his masterpiece growing as it slowly rose above the platform.

To provide enough room to work, Utzon added four extra bays at the east end of Ove Arup's site office. Here he would be farthest away from the construction, in splendid isolation below the Botanic Gardens. He enjoyed a panoramic view of Sydney Harbour. From morning to nightfall, an unceasing parade of cargo ships, oil tankers, lighters, destroyers, submarines, aircraft carriers and sailing boats threaded its way past his window. His office was at the far end, separated from the drawing office by a reception area and the secretary's room. The drawing office on the other side of reception formed a buffer between Utzon and the Arups office.

Utzon, on his way to Australia, had missed the first skirmish between the Government and the Opposition over the burgeoning cost of the Opera House. The Government handled it extremely badly. In order to make a start on Stage II, the Labor Government decided to amend the *Opera House Act, 1960* in anticipation of the increased expenditure which it now saw was inevitable. Rather than use the most up-to-date figure, the year-old estimate of A£12.5 million was chosen instead. The Opposition was not fooled.

On 20 February, R.N. Ryan presented the amended *Opera House Act, 1960*, which lifted the approved cost from A£4.88 million to A£12.5 million (A$25 million). Immediately Robert Askin accused the Government of 'grossly misleading' the Opposition and bungling the Opera House project.[23] Askin saw through Ryan's naive attempt to conceal the actual figure. Even as Ryan spoke, the A£12.5 million estimate was six months out-of-date. As recently as August 1962 the Minister had received an estimate of A£13.75 million (A$27.5 million).

Noting the Government's embarrassment, Askin threw more salt by suggesting that it would not get much change from A£16 million (A$32 million). The Labor Government did not trust public opinion enough to reveal the true cost for fear of an ensuing electoral backlash.[24] The Opposition, at this early stage, was unwilling to launch a frontal assault on the Government by openly attacking the Opera House, because it did not wish to incur the charge of cultural chauvinism. Instead, Askin used the Opera House to attack the Government by singling out its escalating cost. It was obvious to all that Askin was being hypocritical: how could he claim to support the Opera House while opposing money being spent on it, especially since that money was raised by a lottery?

Askin had been elected Leader of the Opposition parties in July 1959, after the demise of Morton. His first attempt to win Government, at the state poll in March 1962, failed; if he lost a second time, in 1965, there was hardly any doubt the Liberal Party would replace him as its leader. Askin was desperate, he needed an election victory: the Opera House provided the issue, if he pressed it hard, it might just give him the margin of advantage he required to sit on the treasury benches. The Government's release of an outdated estimate was a tactical mistake that was soon exposed. The Government was making it easy for Bob Askin, and very soon would lose its nerve.

After Cahill, State Labor leaders lacked his commitment and vision regarding the Opera House. Because they did not believe in the project and felt saddled with it they managed the issue badly. They viewed it as a dangerous political liability.

Once the Royal visit was out of the way, the Opposition attacked with unrestrained gusto in the second reading debate of 7 March. The Government continued its defence of the A£12.5 million estimate in the full knowledge that it was out-of-date. A month later, in April, Rider Hunt, the quantity surveyors, presented its latest estimate of A£13,993,000 (A$27.99 million), A£1,493,000 (A$2.99 million) greater than the amended figure.[25] Each time the Minister, Norman Ryan, asked for a fresh estimate, Rider Hunt bounded back with an even larger figure.

Ryan rashly told Parliament, '… the Government is confident on the advice of the consultants, that the opera house can be built within the amount of expenditure authorised by the proposed amendment.' Hoping this was the end of the matter, Ryan tossed his estimate at Parliament and cited as example to the House that the Lincoln Center in New York had cost US$142 million, on the off-chance they would see the moral that things could be much worse!

During the second reading debate, Askin reassured the Government of the Opposition's support for the Opera House and renewed his attack on costs. Askin even prided himself on forcing the Government to admit its A£12.5 million costing was unreliable. An indignant Askin accused the Government of tricking the Opposition:

> *Speaking in the purely political sense, we members of this House have been the victims of a gigantic confidence trick. We were led to believe that on a certain basis the opera house would cost a certain sum of money, whereas from the outset it has cost three times as much.*[26]

He concluded ominously, 'It seems to me that we are not out of it yet.' The Country Party pointedly hoped he was right.

The political debate was only slightly less noisy than the actual explosions from Bennelong Point. Despite the engineers' attempts to mask the sound of the platform base's reinforced columns being blasted by setting off the dynamite charges during the early morning rush hour on the Harbour Bridge, the news quickly reached the press. Before work could start on the construction of the roofs for Stage II, the columns of the base had to be strengthened. This was necessary because Utzon insisted on a heavier than expected precast vault construction for the roofs. At an early stage, before the roof had even been designed, Ove Arup had arbitrarily allowed an overall imposed load equivalent to a 60 cm thick slab of concrete, equal to about 450 kg per m². However, the new roof was much heavier and the columns supporting it had to be strengthened to bear the increased loads. The demolition work by G. Bayutti was carried out over four months beginning on 1 May, at a cost of A£17,000 (A$34,000), and further delayed the commencement of Stage II.

Ironically, at the time of Askin's attack the Opera House account enjoyed a surplus of A£3.7 million (A$7.4 million); a year later, this had increased to A£4.68 million (A$9.76 million) – the lotteries were proving successful. The fact of the matter was that the Opera House finances were not in trouble, much less a scandal. The political debate was about perceptions, not facts. The construction of the Opera House made no difference to public expenditure on housing, schools or hospitals, because it was not paid from out of tax revenue. There was no financial nexus. The Government's mistake was to behave as though some such connection did exist.

In the months after his arrival in 1963 Utzon was preoccupied finalising the details of Stage II. This involved the erection of the shells and the external tiling by M.R. Hornibrook (NSW) Pty Ltd, which commenced in January 1963, and in general preparing for Stage III, which optimistically was at least two to three years off, depending on how quickly work on the roofs could be completed.

Michael Lewis was appointed to supervise Stage II and when he finished that to supervise Stage III engineering for the interiors. In addition, he had to establish a new Ove Arup office in Australia as he had done in South Africa.[27]

It was understandable that there should be some degree of confusion following the move and Lewis's late arrival. When tile lid layout drawings reached Utzon in July 1963, he insisted on re-tracing the entire set of 350 drawings, but then failed to make use of them. They disappeared soon after they were finished. Yuzo Mikami, a former assistant of Utzon's who transferred to Arup & Partners' London office where he worked directly under Ove Arup, supervised the preparation of the tile lid drawings for Arups, a task requiring the labour of five assistants over many months. Later, Utzon admitted half-jokingly to Mikami he was glad he didn't have to pay for the work.

The tile lid drawings were properly Utzon's responsibility. However, the exact calculation of sizes involved so much mathematics, the Arups office decided to carry it out instead. If the engineers expected Utzon to be grateful, they were badly mistaken. Utzon was chagrined because their action made it appear that Arups were doing the architecture as well as all the engineering. Perhaps this was too near the truth for comfort.

Utzon's problems with Michael Lewis began very early. Hardly had he settled in when there was a blow-up between the two. Utzon caught Lewis casually wandering through the drawing office looking at drawings on the boards. Mogens Prip-Buus resembled the emaciated knight in Bergman's *Seventh Seal* in appearance. He had an explosive temper and he worshipped Utzon. Lewis's unannounced invasion of the office triggered Prip-Buus's anger, he seized a roof tile and smashed it down on a desk causing a tremendous crash and shattering the tile.

This immoderate outburst was out of all proportion to the provocation.

Soon after the incident, Utzon ordered the door opening in the fire wall between his and Arups' adjoining office to be permanently sealed to prevent a repetition. This occurred in mid-1963 while Utzon was beginning to settle down to work in Sydney. Even before work had started in earnest, his relationship with his chief engineer plummeted to the point where he refused to allow Lewis into his drawing office without advance notice. It would seem that following this incident Utzon concluded Lewis was a spy. Instead of taking his misgivings directly to Ove Arup, Utzon waited nearly three years to bring it to a head. It was typically Danish of Utzon to avoid a direct confrontation.

Work speeded up in the first year as Utzon tackled many fronts simultaneously. This encompassed starting the glass walls, later supervising the tile contract, developing the paving and cladding for the base, finalising the Minor Hall acoustics and seating layout, investigating the use of plywood in the halls and glass-wall mullions, and co-ordinating with Arups on Stage II as it progressed. The white roof tiles are a story all by themselves.

Before Utzon could start the final Stage III work on the interiors, Stage II had to be built and the contractor be off the site, and that would require a minimum of about three years. By insisting that Stage III go to public tender, the Government further delayed its commencement by at least six months while the Stage II contract with Hornibrook was wound up.

Anticipating this, in August 1963 Utzon had recommended to the chairman of the Opera House Technical Panel that Hornibrook should be appointed to manage Stage III. This would avoid the delay which was inevitable if another contractor was selected for the third-stage interior work, because of the impossibility of having two main contractors at work simultaneously on the site.[28] Utzon also remarked that Stage III was little more than a collection of vital subcontracts, and he regarded the builder as, in essence, co-ordinating the site works. He therefore requested that M.R. Hornibrook should remain on site as the main contractor to supervise Stage III. Utzon's plan offered a practical and sensible way to speed up the completion of the job.

For some unexplained reason, the Minister and his Director of Works rejected this suggestion. One can only speculate on their reasons, since the decision was later reversed.

In any case, the working drawings for Stage III were not required before the end of Stage II, in three to four years.[29] Utzon paced himself according to the timetable set by the three stages. The design of the main halls posed the biggest obstacle to completing Stage III. Utzon approached his task in much the same way an industrial designer would, by working closely with manufacturers to familiarise himself at first hand with what they were capable of and what were their limitations. Industrial designers have traditionally worked in factories to study the processes used to make the products which they design. This is founded on the belief that an industrial designer should collaborate directly with industry. It started with the Bauhaus in the early 1920s, and was taken a stage further in America by Henry Dreyfuss when he redesigned the telephone for Bell Telephone Laboratories in 1929, and Bel Geddes's new stove for Standard Gas.

Utzon kept a photograph of the hundreds of components inside a telephone handset, with the caption 'Put them [the individual components] together and dial anywhere' in his office to remind himself of a fundamental principle which he hoped to apply in the glass wall and hall ceiling elements.[30] As separate components they were useless, but assembled properly they could be used to communicate anywhere around the globe. To Utzon, the message was clear: the architect designs systems. To develop the plywood mullion elements for the glass walls and the auditoria shells he needed to work closely with a plywood manufacturer in his factory. The architectural elements of the glass walls and the auditorium shells were much larger than the components in a telephone, but in principle Utzon planned to manufacture them the same way. The main difference – and it was an important one – was that they would be assembled on the building site. When the various components were ready, they would all be brought to the building and assembled. This would guarantee better quality and a more uniform result and it would be far quicker.

Like Henry Dreyfuss at Bell, Utzon needed to find an industrialist with the requisite manufacturing expertise. The person he found was Ralph Symonds, who specialised in manufacturing plywood.

Ralph Symonds was the type of person who appealed to Utzon. He had begun as a furniture maker, but when this bored him he started inventing things. In 1923, Symonds built a surf hydroplane and powered it with a cast-off motor from Bert Hinkler's Avro aircraft. Symonds had anticipated the jet-ski by half a century. Skimming over the water, his craft bounced from wave to wave in the surf at Bondi defying dire predictions it would be swamped or battered into small pieces by the rollers. Brilliant and eccentric, Symonds's unconventional ideas were invariably based on logic; however, it was a special kind of logic that others often did not share or understand at first. Symonds was the most energetic and interesting person Utzon had so far met in Australia.

Plywood was regarded as a cheap panel cladding. Symonds fought to improve its standing and have it accepted as a structural material. In May 1958, in an attempt to interest Ralph Symonds in providing rigid plastic-finished plywood for formwork, Utzon asked Erik Kolle to make available to Symonds a model of Arups' folded slabs for the concourse.[31] Symonds and Utzon both thought plywood should be exploited for its structural strength. Utzon hoped the acoustic shells could be self-supporting and structural as well as fulfil their acoustic function. Instead of keeping the structure and acoustics separate, Utzon wanted to integrate the two aspects. This would make the construction more efficient, lighter and cheaper. In turn, nothing would be extraneous or tacked on to the main acoustic shell. Structure, material, acoustics, the decorative finish, were integral. Ralph Symonds instinctively understood what Utzon wanted because they thought along parallel lines.

Utzon felt confident about the strength properties of plywood because the 9 m Diamond keelboat he sailed regularly on Pittwater was built of plywood and it not only endured a pounding from the sea, but proved to be surprisingly strong and light, the same qualities he was looking for in his Opera House ceilings.

Utzon developed his approach around Ralph Symonds's technological capabilities, namely, his capacity to manufacture large 15 m x 2.7 m sheets when the industry standard was still 2.4 m x 1.2 m. Symonds could hot-bond thin metal sheets of lead, aluminium, stainless steel or bronze – either as a sandwich, in the case of lead, or as an outer facing for superior weathering – to the plywood substrate. The U-beam roof Utzon patented depended on Symonds's plywood technology. It was impossible to form the beam profile or create the long spans otherwise, or bond aluminium on the outside surface of the upper channel member to waterproof the roof.

Utzon's auditorium interiors were predicated on the use of Symonds's plywood and manufacturing technology. In September 1964, Utzon endeavoured to explain this to Mr Ryan, the Minister for Public Works in the Heffron Labor Government: 'The answer [Utzon explained] was found in curved plywood sheets suspended between laminated plywood girders.'[32] He listed as the advantages the large size of the sheets, which reduced the number of joints between them, and the decreased chance of outside sound leaking into the auditorium. The large sheets were better for longer wavelengths up to 12 m. Utzon emphasised that, 'The laminated plywood beams can be made of sufficient structural strength combined with light weight to enable me to leave them suspended from the ceiling only, thereby giving complete freedom to follow the ideal acoustical shape.' The strength of the units could be improved by hot-bonding aluminium reinforcing into the plywood where they were subject to higher stresses, and this process was only possible at the Ralph Symonds factory. Utzon continued,

> *the co-operation with Ralph Symonds together with the fact that the design is based on their know-how and the machinery in their factory, makes it possible to reduce the number of components to a minimum, and allows for the simplest possible solution and thereby the cheapest manufacture.*[33]

On his March 1962 visit, Utzon had inspected Ralph Symonds's development work on wall panels, toilet cubicles and cloakrooms at his Homebush factory.[34] In April he inspected a completed mock-up of a toilet cubicle and began discussions about the production schedule. The toilet cubicle was remarkable. Utzon thought like a sculptor and his idea for the toilets was wonderful. These would be made from a single continuous plywood sheet wrapped in a U, with one side shorter. Closing the open end was a marvellous S-silhouette door. In place of the traditional horse stable, Utzon transformed his toilet cubicles into a series of Baroque balcony fronts with his S-shaped doors. But the best part was the way they opened and shut in rhythmic succession like a piece of Dada-inspired sculpture.

The first task Utzon set himself in 1963 was to settle all the outstanding problems and resolve the Minor Hall.

The first hall sections to emerge in Sydney followed closely the sections produced at the end of 1962. There are only a few minor changes and adjustments to the tilt of the side and rear walls to deflect sound upwards more.[35] In Sydney, with Ralph Symonds not far away, Utzon was able to develop his plans to use plywood in the interiors in greater detail. As a first step in this direction, he retained Mr Peter Miller from Milston & Ferris, a Sydney firm of consulting engineers, to investigate some of the more intractable technical problems.

Utzon attempted to synthesise an optimum reflective profile for sound, and at the same time find a geometrical foundation in principle which could be used to subdivide the forms to enable them to be easily mass-produced at Ralph Symonds's factory. By early September 1963, Oktay Nayman in Utzon's Bennelong Point office had produced the first large plans and section of the Minor Hall at 1:50 (½ in scale).[36] The Minor Hall shell is divided into 34 90 cm deep radial beams bridging from the stage tower to the rear wall. The theatre in section is relatively high, rising to a peak a third of the way back from the stage, after which it flattened, thereby improving the sound reflections to the stall seating.

By December 1963, Utzon had reached a stalemate on the Major Hall and was becoming increasingly desperate. He now did something he should have done much earlier – ask for help. It came in the person of Joachim Nutsch, Professor Cremer's assistant in Berlin, whom Cremer permitted to come to Sydney to work on the acoustic problem in the office with Utzon's staff. Only Utzon's pride and professional insecurity had prevented him from asking sooner – he always had to find the solution himself. Had Utzon requested help earlier, years of delay and frustration might have been avoided. Utzon was extremely jealous of ideas and this sometimes caused problems with his staff when they took his ideas. On top of this, Utzon sometimes avoided a problem if it was too difficult – hoping, perhaps, that it would resolve itself.

Mr Nutsch arrived in Sydney on 10 April 1964 and stayed until 19 May. The visit proved to be extremely productive and supplied exactly the right stimulus the office needed. By the time Nutsch left Sydney the Minor Hall was, in Nutsch's words, 'acoustically functional'. The Major Hall, however, remained problematical.[37] The visit produced a tangible spurt in the development of the Minor Hall drawings. Oktay Nayman produced a complete set of preliminary working drawings between July and August the same year of the entire ceiling structure and seating layout. Utzon normally worked separately and took his hall schemes to the acoustics experts, Gabler and Cremer, who would pass comments. It was a slow, exhausting process, at the end of which – once they were all in agreement – they would take the next step which was to build a model and test it. The process was based on trial and error. Utzon strove with each new ceiling profile to optimise the ceiling shape so it balanced the requirements of even first reflections over the seating at the same time that it gave the required volume per seat and the correct 1.5 second reverberation time.

There was no established method Utzon could follow to do this, only a rough set of rules, and even the acoustic model-testing techniques employed by Cremer were relatively unrefined. No one could be certain of the result. Utzon's problems were compounded by his distance from his acousticians in Berlin. Acoustic design in the 1960s was still a black art: all Utzon could do was seek advice and continue to refine his ceiling shapes, and hope that at the end of this tedious process he might stumble on the perfect solution. Utzon tackled the Minor Hall before the

Major Hall because it was the easier of the two.

By August 1964, Utzon had found a suitable shape for the Minor Hall and begun his examination of related technical matters. He was now in a position to begin the construction of the full-sized plywood mock-ups. These were essential if the scheme was to be thoroughly investigated and modifications made to it prior to the final working drawings.[38] Under the circumstances, since the work was experimental, this was a sensible and responsible thing to do. The Labor Minister for Public Works, Norman Ryan, under attack by the Opposition, refused to sanction the plywood mock-ups. This abruptly brought all further progress to a halt. The Public Works Department refused to consider Utzon's request for mock-ups because it argued this would jeopardise the principle of competitive public tenders for the plywood. This demonstrated, yet again, the shortcomings of the Director of Public Works in the field of practical building administration. To cover its failure to make a decision, Utzon was instructed to write another report. Even after he made a small model explaining the erection sequence for the hanging ribs, Public Works still refused to budge.

The delays produced a spate of resignations at Bennelong Point in November 1964, when architectural staff found themselves without proper work to go on with.[39] Ryan, under the pressure of an election due in 1965, simply added to the problems Utzon faced.

Tests of the 1:10 scale Minor Hall model in Berlin, based on the August drawings, proved – subject to a few minor changes – to be nearly ideal acoustically. Now all that was needed was to work out the Minor Hall's construction, however further progress was blocked by political indecision. Utzon's first application to Mr Ryan to proceed with the mock-ups was in September 1964. The crisis over this issue went back to 1964, not 1965 when there was a change from Labor to a Coalition Government.

After this, the further development of the Minor Hall entailed the working out of the ceiling geometry, then construction and assembly of the prefabricated plywood components. The suspended plywood reflectors for the ceiling were to be mounted between radial beams set at 2.5 degree arcs of rotation. The radii of the circular curved plywood was standardised to facilitate their fabrication. Utzon had a wood model of the auditorium and stage tower made. This was characterised by a tent-like series of draped wedges that stepped on either side up to the middle directly in front of the stage opening. Behind the stage tower, holding up the radial beams, the stage area was closed off from the main body of the theatre and the iron curtain by a stepped structure in two planes.

Utzon called the Minor Hall ceiling his 'big jigsaw puzzle in space' but he knew how he would put it together. Disassembled into its various plywood components, a model he had built comprised 11 ready-made, curved box units. The intention was to manufacture and apply the finishes to the plywood beams in Symonds's waterside factory at Homebush, float them down Sydney Harbour on barges to the Opera House site and then lift them up into the auditorium. It would be a straightforward operation, far simpler than, say, the Harbour Tunnel which was constructed of eight huge 200 ton precast concrete tunnel units.

From early 1963, the Major Hall had languished in the too-hard basket. Sir Bernard Heinze visited Berlin on 24–25 August 1963, before the Berlin Philharmonic Hall opened at Tiergarten.[40] Heinze was eager to investigate the Major Hall seating arrangement with part of the audience seating behind the orchestra. Heinze, who was the Director of the NSW Conservatorium of Music and convenor of the music and drama advisory panel, had had a very chequered career on the conductor's dais and knew little about acoustics. He had a reputation for losing his place in the middle of a score while conducting and he was petrified that, with a section of the audience facing him, he would be laughed at. This could explain his rejection of the Berlin hall model for Sydney.

The new Berlin Philharmonic concert hall was almost completed when Heinze visited it with Werner Gabler. He would have noted the seating arranged on all sides around the orchestra. Heinze totally rejected the Berlin Philharmonic's seating scheme.[41] A week later, Werner Gabler wrote to Utzon to warn him that Bernard Heinze belonged to a class of conductors who basically could not accept any audience behind the musicians.[42] Gabler did his best to impress upon Heinze that it would be irresponsible to move the orchestra any further past the stage tower because of the increased risk of unfavourable acoustic conditions caused by the low height of the proscenium opening, but Bernard Heinze remained adamant.

Returning from Berlin, Heinze made his dissatisfaction known.[43] In hindsight, the committee and Utzon should have ignored Heinze – he no longer conducted and would never have to use the Concert Hall. The situation highlighted Utzon's dilemma – who exactly was his client? He could hardly be blamed for thinking he had at least two clients – the Minister for Public Works and the Executive Committee – and perhaps more, all with different agendas. Any decision to push the orchestra to the back of the stage put at risk all the promising work Utzon had completed and set the acoustics development back years. It was madness to alter the plans at such a late stage and destroy so much valuable work, especially since it was based on the whim of a second-rate conductor whose career was over – but that is just what happened. At Sir Charles Moses's insistence,[44] the Sydney Opera House Committee instructed Utzon that the entire 2800 seats in the Major Hall were to be placed in front of the orchestra.

Since free sound from a point source spreads outwards in all directions in an expanding spherical bubble of energy, its intensity decreases inversely as the square of its radius.[45] In other words, sound intensity decreases extremely rapidly with distance from the source. The designer of the Berlin Philharmonic Hall, Hans Scharoun, believed that from the earliest times, whenever music was performed people gathered around in a circle. Even allowing for reflections from the walls and ceiling in an enclosed room, it was still better for an audience to be as close as possible to the stage. Hans Scharoun predicated his design on having none of the 2218 seats farther than 32 m from the podium. In his Berlin hall, he placed the audience in groups on separate sloping terraces on all sides of the orchestra, similar to the vineyard terraces along the Rhine valley. The theory was to bring the audience as close as possible to the sound of the orchestra. By forcing Utzon to push the Opera House audience to the far end of a long relatively narrow hall, Sir Bernard Heinze condemned the rear half of the audience to an inferior acoustic.

Utzon's hall was not purely a concert hall within one large space, it was a multi-purpose auditorium divided into two spaces by the proscenium arch of the opera stage opening. The audience behind this opening received a completely different acoustic. It took until October 1963 for Utzon to find an answer. The new schemes made matters much worse and represented a serious regression — and, understandably, the two Berlin acoustics consultants, Gabler and Cremer, refused to have any part in it. To seat all 2800 on one side of the orchestra, Utzon compressed the existing three tiers of seats together so they overlapped. This buried the cross aisles, which were covered by the deep balconies. In a further adjustment, Utzon raised the rear of the hall, which shortened the rear ceiling skirt. The hall was a disaster but, like many disasters, it contained important consequences for the future.

Utzon now turned to Minor Hall for inspiration. The Minor Hall satisfied the combined criteria of prefabrication and acoustics, and did it better than the earlier, triangular-faceted Major Hall ceiling. There was no reason for the two ceilings to be radically different. Utzon thought, why not employ the same geometry in both? In January 1964 Cremer suggested replacing the former three tiers by a main seating ramp and balconies on both sides which worked their way around the back in the form a wide U. This had the advantage that it provided early reflections off the balcony in the middle of the hall. The new arrangement of Weinberg-style vineyard terraces began to resemble the Berlin Philharmonic seating. The main difference was the extent to which the seating terraces were pushed to one end. Along with the new seating plan, Lundberg produced a new ceiling, following the diagram he made in December the previous year of reverberation-time limit curves. In order to arrive at it, Lundberg calculated the volume each tier of seating required and drew a circular envelope above it to assess the height that he would need for the ceiling. This was then translated in July 1964 to a new section, substituting straight for cylindrical profiles, based on a profile obtained from the earlier diagram.

Like a Busby Berkeley chorus line in reverse, as the ceiling spread outwards away from the central axis and stepped up, the profile of each successive wedge of the new Lundberg ceiling shortened and was lower. By the end of July 1964, Utzon was sufficiently confident to ask to visit Professor Cremer in Berlin for discussions on the new scheme at the end of August.

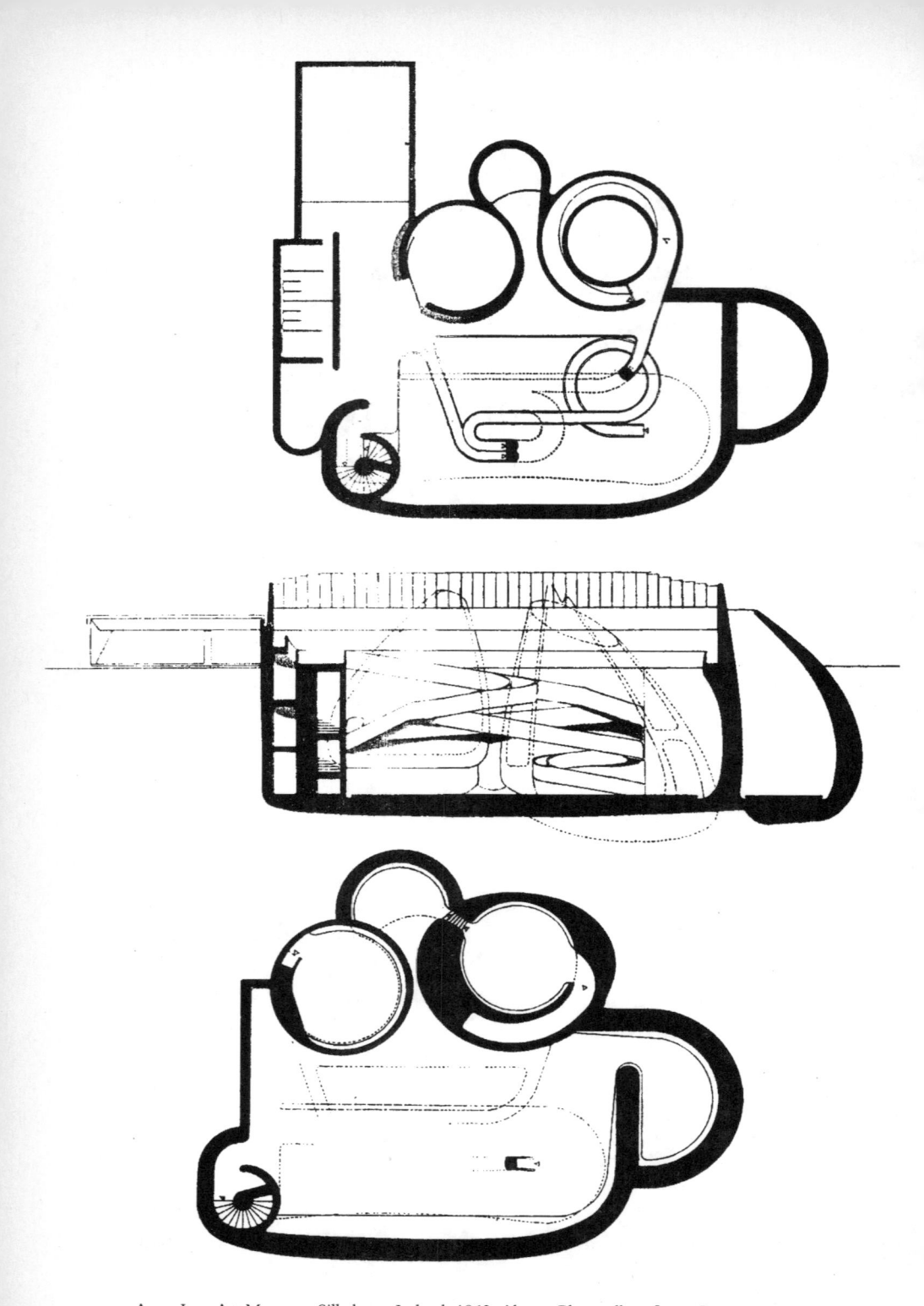

Asger Jorn Art Museum, Silkeborg, Jutland, 1963. Above: Plan, gallery floor; Centre: Cross-section; Below: Floor level.

13

A Hammer Blow
Sydney, 1964

After living in France for 13 years, Utzon's older brother died suddenly. Now both Jørn's brothers were dead and only his father remained. Utzon was shocked by Leif's illness into a realisation of the fragility of life and the utter finality of death. Compounding the loss, which he felt deeply, Utzon found himself stranded in far-away Australia. He rushed to Europe and stayed for about six weeks.[1]

Leif Utzon was just 48 at the time. He left behind Annie, his wife, and three young daughters. His death revived memories in Utzon of his mother's passing. Leif had been like a lucky talisman which Jørn had mislaid, and that made what had happened all the more poignant.

It made him think more about his own family. As children, Lin Utzon recalled, they saw very little of their father, because he was so busy and preoccupied. The public was given a very different picture of a dashing, suntanned, smiling, confident Jørn Utzon. In public, Utzon kept his worries carefully tucked away out of sight. Important as the Opera House was, it was not the most significant thing on his mind in April 1964. He was more worried at the time about Leif.[2] Utzon's first concern has always been people. It is indicative of his profound humanity and his sense of proportion, that he placed the well-being of others ahead of architecture and his career.

Jørn and Leif were close – they had shared so much growing up. Even when Leif was living in Paris, he and his family continued to provide a second, if remote, anchor in Jørn Utzon's existence. Their importance can be gauged from photographs of the two Utzon families on the terrace of Jørn's Hellebæk house in the summer of 1960. The families form a single group with two brothers, two wives and two sets of three children. They could almost be one family, so calm and relaxed are they together, sitting in the velvety sunshine. There is a unity, a oneness, but on closer inspection, it yields many differences. They are held together by the affection of two brothers as they recline on the yellow brick terrace in front of the open sliding door: Jørn and Leif at the back; the two wives in front of them; Jan, Utzon's oldest boy, his arms folded, smiles at the camera; Annie, beside him, pitches her knee to the right, half-smiles, fixedly looks ahead; Lin, in front of Lis, is distracted by one of the girls who tickles her; and Lis, with Jørn's arm tenderly draped over her shoulder, is so filled with happiness she beams. They all appear so happy and close to one another.

After Leif's affairs were settled, Annie and the three girls went back to Denmark. Utzon helped them with the move and settling in. Leif's death marked a reversal of Utzon's fortunes as, quite by accident, it also coincided with a change of leadership in the New South Wales Government and with it a rapid deterioration in Utzon's relations with his client. A new crisis was brewing over the substantial cost increase of the latest estimate, due largely to Stage II.

From now on, Utzon became more wary of life. Perhaps as an overreaction, he carefully avoided exposing himself to risks. The death of his brother sharpened his awareness of his mortality. He watched what he ate and if he noticed he was becoming too stressed, he took a holiday. His behaviour bordered on the obsessive, but it was also sensible. If it happened to Leif, it could easily happen to him. Their situations were similar: Leif was overworked in Paris, and eventually it killed him. At the very least, overwork contributed to his early death. Utzon had had a glimpse of Ibsen's white horses of Rosmersholm as they passed by in daylight and it frightened him.[3]

Leif's death affected Utzon in other ways, some direct, some less obvious. On his return from Europe in September that year, Utzon moved the design section of his office into Goddard's boatshed at 118 Iluka Road, Palm Beach. This was at the rear of the general provision store on Snapperman Beach, on the west side of the Palm Beach peninsula. The boatshed looked northeast across the Hawkesbury entrance. It had been built around 1927, and vacated in 1960 when the Port Jackson & Manly Steamship Company bought out Palm Beach Marina and moved. Utzon took over the ground floor of the two-storey structure.

The waterside location with its slipway and jetty was the Australian equivalent of his grandmother's house on Øresund. Utzon moved his senior collaborators to Snapperman Beach, leaving only a token skeleton staff of juniors to carry on at Bennelong Point. With Utzon spending most of his time at Palm Beach, the importance of the Bennelong Point office declined and, not unexpectedly, work there slowed considerably. The change may have insulated Utzon, isolating him from the pressure-cooker atmosphere on the building site, but it also curtailed his involvement in the daily round of decision-making. As a further precaution to ease the stress, Utzon cut himself off completely by doing without a telephone. With no telephone to interrupt him, he could focus completely on design. Palm Beach restored the calmness he had previously known in his beech forest at Hellebæk.

Goddard's boatshed split his office in two: one did work on the Opera House, the other, work on competitions and for other clients. The subdivision was necessary for ethical reasons to avoid accusations that his Opera House staff was carrying out outside commissions and neglecting the most important project. In reality, the demarcation was more blurred; a considerable portion of the Opera House design operation after October 1964 was transferred to Palm Beach, giving rise to the perception that Bennelong Point had been downgraded and had a lesser role. Feeling left out and less valued, many of the remaining staff at Bennelong Point began to consider leaving.

Before Utzon left for Europe, the family had moved from Alexandra Crescent, Bayview, to 65 Pacific Road, Palm Beach. The new house had a splendid view directly north towards Barrenjoey Head. Once the office settled into the boatshed, Utzon fell into the comfortable daily pattern of driving the few kilometres downhill to Snapperman Beach. Not far away was a restaurant on Barrenjoey Road which served lunch. If the day was pleasant, Utzon could break for a couple of hours and go for a sail each Wednesday on Pittwater.

The Snapperman Beach office move sent exactly the wrong signal at that moment. Whether or not he realised it, Utzon had relinquished the field to Michael Lewis. He may have succeeded at placing himself beyond Michael Lewis's scrutiny, but in the process he handed Lewis an immense advantage in his dealings with the client.

One of the great mysteries is how Utzon managed to find the time to work on other projects besides the Opera House. In 1963–4 Utzon was invited to design a project for Silkeborg and also won an important competition for Zürich. Both demonstrated his growing fascination with curves as a confident extension of his architectural vocabulary based on the Opera House. The first of these projects was the Silkeborg Kunstmuseum, or art museum. Asger Jorn, one of Denmark's most famous artists and a founder of the Cobra group in 1948, lived for much of his life in Paris. He decided to establish a museum to house his work and invited Utzon to design a suitable structure. Born at Silkeborg in 1914, Asger Jorn was only four years Utzon's senior.

The Silkeborg region, one of the most beautiful in Denmark, is much favoured by the wealthy set. Its attractive, undulating topography is exceptional, being the result of the retreat of successive ice sheets which have left behind deep deposits of gravel. Lake Langso and a deer park add to Silkeborg's appeal.

The design buried the museum in the earth, to make it less intrusive to the landscape. This also provided Utzon with an excuse to introduce curved subterranean shapes, sculpted and hollowed out like giant pots buried in the ground. At Silkeborg, Utzon's temptation to dig into and explore the subterranean gravel deposits left by the retreating ice sheets was understandable. The Asger Jorn museum design has a secretive, voluptuous quality, its main spaces excavated below ground level and only accessible from the top. The internal circulation, using crisscrossing walkways bridging the vertical gallery spaces, enhanced the dynamic interplay and added greatly to the endless quality of these spaces. In this way, the museum acquired an unfinished restless turbulence similar to an Asger Jorn canvas.

Explaining its origin, Utzon said:

> *Through my work with curved shapes in the opera house I have been inspired to go further into free architectural forms, but at the same time to control the geometry which makes it possible to erect the building out of mass-produced components. I am fully aware of the danger of using curved forms in contrast to the relative security of basing architecture on rectangular forms, but the curved form world offers something which one will never find in rectangular architecture. The ships' hulls, the caves and the sculptures prove it.*[4]

Silkeborg was the first cave-like gallery below ground by Utzon in which the spaces were fused together as a series of interlocking voids. This unrealised 1963 project became famous in Danish architecture. The greater part, up to three storeys, was buried under the ground to minimise its disturbance of the tranquil landscape around it and on account of its proximity to the town. It was based on large round pottery shapes that overlapped and merged within an outer wall, which was a mixture of curved and straight lines. At ground level, the lips of the chambers were sliced at odd angles and the open mouths covered by sloping skylights with adjustable louvres that controlled the light in the gallery spaces.

There were similarities with New York's famous Guggenheim Museum, with its great corkscrewing spiral ramp which plummets downwards in one giddy headlong rush. Utzon's museum was freer and less rigid in its geometry compared to Wright's. Whereas Wright's spiral and dome are masculine, Utzon's museum, notably the interior, was invested with an encompassing and warmly protective, feminine roundness. It had a primitive, gritty, back-to-the-womb, lactescent character. Not even the highly abstract shapes could conceal the blatant feminine character of its forms, which suggested a return to the symbolism of the ancient earth mother figure.

In no other design has Utzon managed so successfully to encapsulate the overriding Danish psychological tendency to retreat inwards, to internalise, while simultaneously imbuing his forms with a mysterious primitiveness. The museum had the same cosy reassuring order as Danish architecture in general, in which the inside is so thoroughly seductive in its perfection it becomes a replacement for the outside.

The Silkeborg museum ventured well beyond the round shapes of the Opera House roofs to a more primitive level. It was opposed above ground by rectangular beams at the access to the museum, which implied a contrary, masculine character. By comparison, the roofs of Sydney's Opera House have a hard, remote, chillingly Euclidean purity which was absent from the hollowed-out interiors at Silkeborg. Its shapes were more profoundly organic, less precise in their geometry, less defined, but they exert an even greater emotional pull.

The weight of the feminine and the masculine in Utzon's work varies, and perhaps was symptomatic of an internal balancing act within him and a reflection of his own attempt to integrate the two. In much of his work they are distinct, the separation is clear and without confusion, leaving no room for ambiguity or a relaxation of the boundaries between. Very occasionally, as in Silkeborg, the feminine, although secreted away out of sight, clearly does predominate, yet at other times, it is the masculine which dominates. The masculine was secondary in the Silkeborg art museum – treated almost as an afterthought. In spite of its immediate visibility, the masculine was a subordinate, contrasting aspect of the feminine. It strikes us as almost superfluous; nevertheless, it acted as a necessary counterweight to the extraordinary primacy given to the voluptuously enfolding interior space. Utzon simultaneously capitulates to the feminine then denies it by hiding it underground. The masculine recovered its importance a year later in the 1964 Zürich Theatre, where the leading mode was conveyed by a forceful rectangularity.

Entry to the Silkeborg art museum was indirect, through the south-west corner under a section of folded concrete beams which were used in the roof and wall. The visitor arrived in the main reception area first; on its left was a kitchen and cafeteria; to its right was a glass wall, through which the skylights over the slanted rims of the buried gallery chambers could be seen projecting from the ground, rising like breaching whales from the lawn. The roof of the reception area was formed of concrete beams staggered in groups, each beam separated by a narrow glazed gap to admit natural light. These beams were bent at right angles at their ends and carried down to the ground. The continuity of the beams was accentuated by these repeated strips of light which ran vertically and across the space.

Despite its sculptural force, the scheme was rejected. Asger Jorn died in 1973, the site was changed, and in 1982, after much dithering, a new architect, Niels Frithiof Truelsen, was invited to design a conventional, rectangular and extremely unimaginative building, a single-storeyed scheme consisting of two intersecting wings that was vaguely based on Constantin Brancusi's studio in Paris. The Silkeborg Kunstmuseum remains one of Utzon's most unsullied sculptural essays, and one of his strongest. Perhaps if it had been built its appeal would be less. Almost entirely sculptural in conception – which perhaps caused its rejection – as architecture, it impresses itself on us and gains our attention in the same forceful way that Frank Lloyd Wright's Guggenheim does. In such situations, it is impossible not to admire the architecture ahead of the art itself. No doubt Asger Jorn's work, with its strong rich coloration, would not only have withstood the competition of being placed in something so powerful, but would have gained immensely from the textural freedom and free forms Utzon planned.

Utzon's approach fused painting and architecture. He was influenced at Silkeborg by China and the extraordinary presence of Buddhist art in cave galleries. In the West, there is less emphasis on the sacral aspect of art and more attention is paid to the presentation and viewing of a work. Just as in his housing from Morocco, Utzon was torn between two sets of values and oscillates between the twin poles of the sacral and the materialistic treatment of art.

The Zürich Theatre competition took up more time and was far more important than the aborted Silkeborg art museum, especially after 1966. At Zürich, Utzon was called on to deal with a given context in an existing city. In terms of continuity, there is a sequential connection between it and Sydney in 1960, and Kuwait ten years on. Because of its obscure and convoluted history, Zürich is often forgotten. It should not be ignored because it was not built, as it remains a seminal work that links a previous great work with other significant works in the future.

The Zürich competition was drawn up in July 1963 with submissions due on 28 February 1964, giving the competitors a little more than six months to prepare their designs. The competition was limited to Swiss architects, plus five others selected from outside. Utzon competed against J.B. Bakema of Rotterdam, Hans Scharoun of Berlin and Heikki Siren from Helsinki, from this outside group of competitors, and 92 Swiss architects.[5] Max Frisch and the theatre's director, Kurt Hirschfeld, were members of a jury which also included Professor Sven Markelius from Stockholm. Utzon was in distinguished company.

The result was announced on 27 May 1964. Utzon won first prize, carrying prize money totalling Swiss Fr 30,000 (A£3063 or A$6126).[6]

Utzon's scheme was unlike the majority, which consisted of isolated buildings. His building dissolved into a carpet of rising interconnected terraces under a series of roofs formed of horizontal beams. The nearest comparison is the main staircase and platform of the Opera House. The theatre complex's roof consisted of folded beams similar to the Ove Arups beams under the Opera House concourse, but slightly wider and more open across the top. There are also comparisons with his Bayview roof scheme. Even allowing for the differences, the parallels between the roof of the proposed new Zürich theatre and the main stair of the Opera House platform were strikingly obvious.

Around mid-1964, Utzon entered the competition for the National Opera in Madrid, which was organised by the Juan March Foundation.[7] It was one of his least successful designs and did not receive even a commendation. The design contained a heterogeneous collection of competing ideas. It is hard to believe that the designs for the Madrid Opera and the new Zürich Theatre were by the same person, they are so unlike. This may be explained by the fact that Utzon was assisted by Prip-Buus on Zürich, and by Lundberg on Madrid.

In Madrid, Utzon placed a canopy of concrete beams – which look the same as those used in the Zürich design – parallel to the street. Behind them, he created two undulating wave roofs in a flattened 'S' profile so they spread horizontally to cover the public foyers. After this came the main hall, with a tent roof suspended from a huge guyed mast, which resembled a large maypole planted hastily in the middle. At the rear, beyond the mast, was the stage tower resembling an Egyptian mastaba from *Aida*. The design was extremely confused, there were too many disparate ideas pulling in different directions. The submission was unrepresentative; not even the beautifully executed model Utzon freighted to Madrid could disguise how desperate it was.

News of Utzon's Zürich competition win reached the office in Sydney by telegram in late May 1964.[8] When it was made public, Utzon mentioned in an off-hand way that he and his colleagues worked on the plans 'just for fun as a hobby' for six months in their spare time. The celebration was short-lived. Within weeks of J.B. Renshaw taking over from Heffron as NSW Premier on 30 April, the Opposition, led by R.W. Askin, resumed its campaign attacking rising Opera House costs. All pretence at bi-partisanship had disappeared.

The mood suddenly changed in Australia once it became clear troops were going to be sent to fight in the Vietnam War. People became increasingly divided over communism in Asia. Askin's renewed attacks on the Opera House now became more strident and uncompromising as the middle ground of Australian politics slipped away and people were forced to commit themselves, either to oppose or to support Australia's involvement.

On 4 May, Askin claimed that the final figure for the Opera House was more like A£18 million (A$36 million),[9] and on 18 June the Government made public Utzon's latest estimate of A£17.4 million (A$34.8 million) – equivalent to A$289 million today.[10] In a year, armed with more detailed information on the roof, the estimate had leapt from A£12.5 million (A$25 million) to A£17.4 million (A$34.8 million), an increase of A£4.9 million (A$9.8 million).[11] In an attempt to avoid further embarrassment, the Government instructed Utzon not to say anything to the press that would give away the true financial position.[12] Throwing more fuel on the fire, Walter Bunning, a long-standing and bitter opponent of Utzon's Opera House scheme, chose this moment to categorise it as 'one of the biggest bungles in our history'.[13] To further inflame the crisis, Bunning called on the Government to establish a Royal Commission of Inquiry into the project. The Country Party Deputy Leader, Mr W.A. Chafey from Tamworth, entered the fray suggesting, as a less expensive alternative, that a Parliamentary Select Committee be set up to look into the cost estimates in detail.

The Opposition routed the Government in the June 1964 debate on the cost of the Opera House. With public support wavering and the Government shaken and in disarray, Askin moved in to drive home his attack. 'The total cost,' Askin brightly predicted, 'will now be more than A£20 million, without doubt.' In the next breath, he blamed the Government for 'this shocking financial mess,' which he ventured was caused by '... mismanagement, deceit, Communist inspired strikes, and shameful waste of public funds by a Government no longer fitted to be entrusted with the State's affairs.'[14] Askin could see that he had unsettled the Renshaw Government. Taking stock, Labor concluded its survival was threatened. Until the upcoming 1965 election was out of the way, the Government concluded that it must do everything in its power to get the cost of the Opera House off the front page and neutralise it as an election issue. To achieve this it froze all decisions involving further expenditures which could be used as ammunition by the parliamentary

Opposition. Clearly the Opera House was a hyper-sensitive issue.

The Government stood its ground. It had little choice, and remained apprehensive and uncertain what to do next. Labor had inherited the Opera House from Joe Cahill and it was still reluctant to abandon his legacy, but after five testing years, the Government's resolution was crumbling. As many as 20 members in the parliamentary Caucus opposed the Opera House and supported calling an inquiry.[15] The Opera House could destroy the Government and was costing it vital votes. Renshaw faced a dangerous situation; it was his job to hold the party together. Askin had the advantage, Renshaw knew it and was placed on the defensive.

The Government reaction to each Askin attack followed the same pattern: as the pressure mounted, Cabinet went into a defensive huddle and interrogated Utzon. These question sessions only applied further pressure on Utzon and reinforced the picture the Opposition was trying to paint: to lay the blame on Utzon, as he alone was responsible for what happened on Bennelong Point. Sometimes, to vary its attack, the Opposition criticised the Executive Committee as muddled and ineffectual.

In March 1964, there had been a noticeable cooling in the relations between Utzon and the Labor Government. A number of events signalled this deterioration: on 5 March, the Minister for Works appointed a South African supervising architect from his department, Mr William W. Wood, to liaise with Utzon. In reality, Wood was the Minister's watchdog and reported directly to him on progress.[16] The choice could not have been more unfortunate. Wood, in his late fifties, had never shown interest in design before his arrival in Australia in 1962. His new job did not change that, nor did he strive to acquaint himself with Utzon's architectural thinking. Wood's appointment was a clear sign that the Government had lost confidence in Utzon. It was also an indication of the extent of R.A.P. Johnson's ignorance in architectural matters. Johnson, the Director of the Public Works Department that initially advised Hughes, and his replacement as director in 1965, J.C. Humphrey (Johnson's bother-in-law), were both lawyers. Neither was qualified in architecture or engineering.

More of a clown than a diplomat, Wood typified the way that the Department of Public Works was prepared to harry Utzon in order to take over the Opera House for itself. The true objective had little to do with either efficiency or cost control, and everything to do with taking the project away from Utzon.

The Public Works Department was customarily thought of as dully competent. Dull it may have been, but to say it was competent was wide of the mark at the upper level of decision-making and policy. It shone architecturally in the early 1960s but, with its large day labour force, it was neither notably competent nor an especially effective project manager. This was evidenced by its record of long delays and agonisingly slow progress in completing major harbour and dam projects. In 1965, the Government Architect, E.H. Farmer, basked in the reflected glory from the high design standards and numerous architectural awards won by his department. This had little to do with him personally. What happened was that Farmer, unlike his predecessor, Cobden Parkes, did not intentionally stifle new design ideas. Far from being outstanding, Farmer in fact was more interested in conservation and heritage matters and nineteenth-century architecture.

While Utzon was overseas in April, the Public Works Department initiated negotiations to lower his fee. This breached the RAIA's standard fee schedule and exposed the Government's bad faith in attempting to terminate the agreement. Utzon was being asked to cut his fees to below the scheduled rate. Considering the degree of complexity of the Opera House and the extensive co-ordination of the large number of specialist consultants, far from being overpaid, in reality Utzon was probably substantially underpaid. The fee question now became a matter of public debate, 'Was he being paid too much?' This made little difference to the final cost of the Opera House, and it was certainly not something that journalists were in a position to comment on. Just how this was supposed to advantage the project was never explained, but the Renshaw Cabinet was keen to be seen to do something, anything at all, about costs.

On 19 July, newspapers disclosed that Utzon had been paid fees of A£389,000 (A$778,000).[17] They neglected to mention what Utzon did to earn this amount, nor did they bother to detail his professional expenses. The articles made no attempt to say what a reasonable fee might be since they had no idea, but journalists were quick to suggest that Utzon had made exorbitant profits from the work. The one thing Australian journalism excelled at in the 1960s was trafficking in scurrilous innuendo. On this occasion, they implied that he had a vested interest in ensuring the job cost rose, because he would be paid more as a result. Pay him less, and the job would be finished sooner and cost less, so ran the media's reasoning. The blatant aim of this was to apply further pressure to an already groggy State Labor Government. With Sydney's conservative press barons now backing Askin, Utzon was caught in the middle of the campaign to unseat the Labor Party.

Suffering from severe election jitters, the Government desperately needed a scapegoat to pin the blame on. Utzon was the obvious choice. The situation now reached crisis point. Even after Utzon submitted a report on 9 July pointing out the unpalatable fact that it was impossible to make further economies to reduce the A£17.4 million estimate without sacrificing quality and aesthetic appeal, the Government refused to believe him.[18] On the morning of 23 July, Utzon faced renewed questioning by the newly installed Premier, Jack Renshaw, backed by a Cabinet sub-committee consisting of the Deputy Premier, the Minister for Local Government, Mr P.D. Hills, the Minister for Public Works, Mr P.N. Ryan and the Minister for Lands, Mr K.C. Compton. The grilling lasted well over one-and-a-half hours.[19] Renshaw insisted Utzon give him an absolute undertaking there would be no future cost increases. This was politically understandable but simply impossible for Utzon, or anyone, to give. Utzon was deeply shocked and bluntly asked the Premier whether Renshaw considered him incapable.

Utzon remained calm and pointed out to Renshaw his disappointment in the treatment the latest estimate had received – neither the total figure of A£17.4 million (A$34.8 million), nor the completion date were ever intended for publication.[20] Utzon then asked to be allowed to table the explanatory appendices along with the estimate, but was curtly told by Premier Renshaw that he did not wish to see the figures. Mr Renshaw, Mr Hills and Mr Ryan spoke as one when they said Utzon must accept that the Minister for Public Works was the client without evidently recognising that, as Premier, Renshaw was automatically the President of the Opera House Trust.

Confronting the committee, Utzon asked whether the Opera House Trust, whom he had served for seven-and-a-half years, would no longer instruct him as the client. Were his conditions the same as before? If not, what were the new arrangements? Was the Minister taking charge completely? Renshaw, clearly flummoxed, refused to answer. His instruction to Utzon amounted to nothing more than a hollow political platitude directed at bolstering sagging party morale and avoiding the very real question of how far ministerial authority should extend. Renshaw repeated for the second time his instruction to Utzon: Utzon should understand that the Trust would continue to do its job the same as always, however Mr Ryan was to be considered the constructing authority. It was a case of saying 'Yes Minister' and reading between the lines.

Renshaw failed to recognise the impossible position he placed Utzon in by insisting he serve two masters. Afterwards, Utzon wrote to Mr Ryan, drawing to his attention that he had always worked for the Opera House Committee and that it was the practice in Europe for buildings such as the Opera House to be carried out by the Minister in accordance with a programme and design approved by a body representing the users. It would help him if Ryan, as the relevant minister, would work with the committee.[21] At the end of the meeting on 23 July, Ryan summarised the conclusions for everyone: 'The situation is much the same as it was.' Nothing had changed. After the meeting, on 26 July, State Cabinet papered over the damage by announcing that it was now satisfied there was a reasonable chance the Opera House's cost could be confined to the A£17.4 million estimate provided by Mr Utzon. The Opposition was delighted to see the Labor hares panicked by its grass fire.

Renshaw had behaved ineptly. Utzon had earlier antagonised Pat Hills, the Local Government Minister, by submitting a proposal for the carpark and by his suggestions for redesigning the surroundings of the Opera House.[22] His proposal was enlightened and visionary for the time, but Pat Hills was one of the Labor Party's dimmer headkickers. Besides proposing a trade centre behind Circular Quay, Utzon suggested a system of elevated pedestrian ways threaded through the downtown to Town Hall. It was a wonderful idea. His primary concern was the treatment of the waterfront adjoining Bennelong Point so that it would harmonise with the Opera House, but he also wanted to maximise the Opera House's impact as the cultural and festive focus of the city. In addition, Utzon suggested a raised plaza should be built between the Cahill Expressway and the ferry wharves, to give promenaders a clear view of the harbour. His ideas anticipated, by 30 years, very similar proposals in 1994.

They were too much for Mr Hills, who wagged a stubby forefinger at Utzon and shouted to him to keep his nose out of other people's business.[23] Utzon's Quay proposal angered the Government because it caused further criticism and drew attention to the Government's failure to provide a carpark. The carpark issue could only add to the growing chorus of complaints about runaway costs. Utzon was just doing his job, but he failed to heed the Government's sensitivity with an election so near.

Utzon was disconcerted and bewildered by the intensity of the political response. Renshaw's mistrust and open antagonism in his repeated questions profoundly shook Utzon. Interviewed by a sympathetic Gavin Souter, Utzon complained,

> *I am not an actor who is used to working in the limelight all the time, and this can be distracting. It would be well if we could cover the whole site with canvas and reveal the product when it is finished. But you cannot ask for that.*[24]

The entire city was fascinated by the project, as week by week freshly cast hollow concrete segments were lifted by tower crane and slowly lowered into place in each rib. The first rib element was placed in position in November 1963. By June 1964 the casting yard was in full swing, the first supporting octopus segment was complete, and the roof was beginning to take shape over the stage and foyer of the Major Hall.

Everyone had an opinion about the Opera House. The previous year, two gun shots were fired at Bennelong Point from the opposite side of the Harbour, which narrowly missed Mr Ian Mckenzie, a resident engineer in Arups' site office.[25] Utzon received a death threat. Taxi drivers became instant architectural critics. Politicians were not going to miss out on the fun. In the end Utzon handled the cost issue the only way he knew how to, by telling the truth – or, at least, by trying not to conceal it.

A trip to Europe presented Utzon with a welcome escape from the pressure cooker of New South Wales's politics. He planned to be away for three weeks from 11 August 1964. The first week was spent at Zürich discussing his competition design, meeting city officials, and initiating negotiations over the new theatre. On the 18th, he set off for Berlin for a meeting with his acoustics experts, Professors Cremer and Gabler.[26]

Afterwards, he visited Denmark to tie up some of the loose ends left by his brother's death. The trip came at a critical time. Utzon desperately needed a breakthrough; time was running out for him to come up with a solution for the main halls so the detailed design development could begin before the elections in May 1965. While he must have sensed the increasing strain in the NSW Government, he still wanted perfection, and perfection did not follow any political timetable.

Utzon arrived in Berlin too early, since neither of the two one-tenth scale acoustic models were ready. All he could do was check that Cremer and Gabler were working from the most recent plans and agree to a number of minor changes which they suggested. He was under considerable pressure. Four months later, in an uncharacteristic blunt missive, Utzon advised Gabler: 'I am deeply worried over the situation as it has developed in relation to the obligations to my client.'[27]

Jordan, working alone at Gevninge, was more advanced, but even his elaborate one-tenth scale model of the Major Hall would not be available for testing until early January 1965 and even then he did not obtain any usable results from his measurements until 3 February 1965. Based on these preliminary results, Jordan did his best to reassure Utzon, '… they show signs that the musical quality in the concert hall may be expected to be good over the major part of the auditorium'. He ended with the caution, 'Some areas show minor deficiencies which however should not be allowed to remain …'[28]

Due to a mix-up, Werner Gabler had fallen behind. At the end of December 1964, Gabler still had not been commissioned, and so he could not order the modelmaker to proceed. A second one tenth-scale model was completed in Berlin at Professor Cremer's Institute, which yielded promising results but required further modifications. These changes were agreed to by Utzon on his next visit, in late April 1965.[29]

The two ceilings now looked similar. Utzon fondly referred to the new ceilings as a family, like a brother and sister who share the same genetic inheritance. There was one significant difference: the suspended plywood panels forming the ceiling of the Major Hall were straight, compared to the Minor Hall, where they were curved and moulded to a standard circular section derived from a cylinder of constant radius. This ensured their economical prefabrication. Both fan-shaped ceilings were intended to be constructed in the same way, from stepped laminated plywood trusses suspended from the shell arches and supported at the back of the hall. Between each pair of radial plywood trusses the soffits were lined with sound-reflecting plywood ceiling panels reinforced by hot-bonded aluminium sheets for additional strength. The inspiration for the hall ceilings now changed direction to 'a free form hanging like a cloud in the sky'.[30] The shift in inspiration was punctuated by other technical changes, and its realisation now depended on large plywood sheets to deal with the long span and reflect the sound. Only one Australian manufacturer, Ralph Symonds, could manufacture such big sheets. As well, the company was able to hot bond aluminium and inlay 2 mm thick sheets within the plywood. In keeping with Utzon's ideas on prefabrication, the manufacture of the ceiling trusses and their decoration was to be done during their production and assembly at Symonds's Homebush factory.

Utzon scheduled his next visit to Berlin for the end of

February 1965, by which time he hoped the results of the acoustic tests would be ready. Months slipped by. The Major Hall model was not completed until the end of February 1965. Tests were rescheduled for March.[31] With only minor alterations needed after the earlier successful tests in Berlin, the Minor Hall was, to all intents, ready to be drawn up. Utzon would later claim that the third and final scheme of the Minor Hall, with gallery and balcony, was all but acoustically perfect. Models had been completed in Berlin and Copenhagen and the requisite amendments had been duly made after the August 1964 visit.

Two one-tenth scale models were built of the Major Hall, one in Copenhagen, and a second at Professor Cremer's Berlin Institute. The Berlin model showed promising results. Dr Jordan and Cremer and Gabler were then to meet and pool their results. The Berlin model was based on a hall with back gallery and side balconies with a small overhang. During opera performances the rear part of the hall would be too remote from the stage. To deal with this, Utzon investigated isolating it from the front by means of a curtain.

From September 1964 on Utzon tried everything within his power to persuade Norman Ryan, Labor's Public Works Minister, to approve the new theatre designs. In 1964 and during much of 1965, Utzon's energies were increasingly taken up with writing reports and supplying construction and cost information, to the detriment of further design advances. As part of this campaign to convince the Minister Utzon, working closely with Skipper Nielsen, wrote the *Descriptive Narrative* from January 1965. As the title makes clear, it was effectively a detailed description and specification of the building. Utzon was becoming increasingly tired of Ryan's intransigence and refusal to approve the necessary funds for the plywood mock-ups. The descriptions which he marshalled at this time to support his proposal, stimulated by Ryan's stalling of the process, become even more eloquent.

In a short statement in the *Narrative* he spelt out his conviction about the fundamental flexibility of industrial production methods:

The exteriors of the building [Opera House] stand as an expression of something basic to the concept – the idea of dividing the various parts up into equal components, which can be produced industrially and afterwards put together to form a structure of the desired form, – in other words the use of machine made components in the building industry. Man can no longer afford the time nor the ability of craftsmen to hand make our buildings. We must find the machines to make our components and devise some means to put these elements together only limited to the size and weight of our mechanical age to erect them. The architect [Utzon] therefore has researched into the maximum capabilities for economical reasons of factory production and having found the scope of minimum and maximum capacity of the machine, he works within this discipline. As he works with a machine that has no intrinsic thinking capacity, he must devise a manufacturing process for the machine.[32]

Utzon placed himself in the position of challenging a pet assumption about twentieth-century machine civilisation. He believed it was possible to break away from the rule of rectangularity and the Opera House was his proof.

Once Utzon had discovered the secret of building his curved roof vaults from factory-made precast elements, with each one slightly different from a standard mould, he set about finding ways of repeating this in other areas of the Opera House. This brought him into direct conflict with the Government, which did not comprehend his aims, and did not appreciate that this was crucial to achieving its goal of cutting the cost of the building.

In 1958, Jacques Tati, the brilliant French cinematographer, satirised the failings of Modernism in his film *Mon Oncle*. Jørn Utzon took the next step when, looking beyond Tati, he visualised a new era of machine-made buildings that were no longer alienating in the ways Tati had pointedly satirised, but instead were friendly and easy to live in. The key, he predicted, lay in adapting the variable principle of the prefabricated rib-elements of the Opera House roof to new situations.

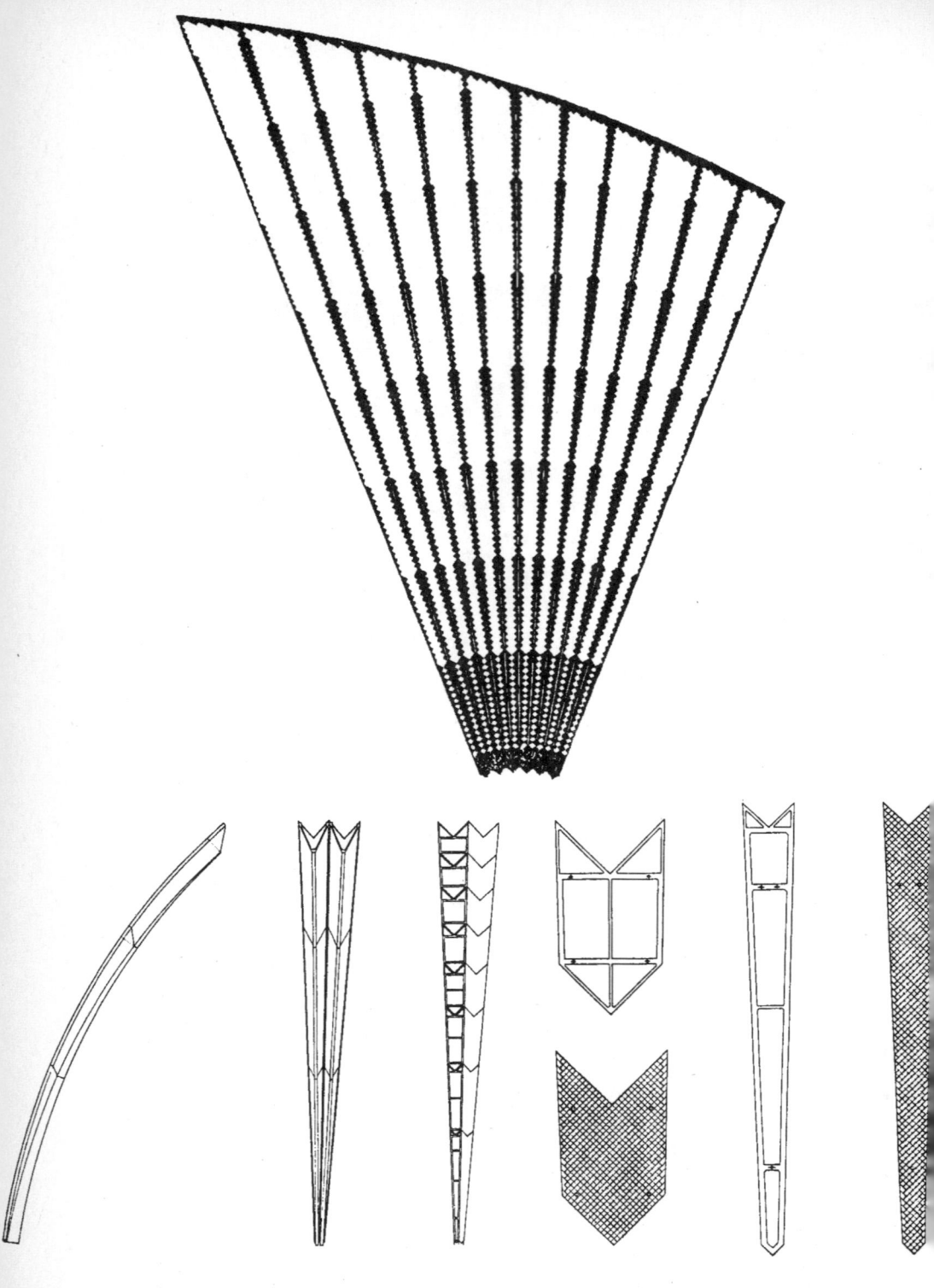

Sydney Opera House, precast spheroid lid-element. Above: Tiling on lid. Below left: Side elevation of arch rib. Below centre: Inside and outside elevation of a pair of arch ribs. Below right: Precast lid-elements.

14

A White Radiance Rising
Höganäs and Sydney, 1958–1967

Looking at a Gothic church, you never get tired, you will never be finished with it — when you pass around it or see it against the sky. It is so important that together with the sun, the light and the clouds, it makes it a living thing.

Jørn Utzon, 1965[1]

The roof tiles are one of the great glories of the Opera House that, to use Utzon's own words, 'makes it a living thing'. The expanding fish-scale chevrons of the tile plates and matt tiles that emphasise their edges were introduced to reinforce the radial pattern of concrete ribs under them. Shooting skywards, the network of joints between the matt tiles strengthens our appreciation and admiration of the roof and its structure.

In winter particularly, when the sun is lower, the blaze of light from the middle, glazed tiles dies at the edges to accentuate the difference. At certain angles, individual glazed tiles will suddenly burst with a golden radiance, and it seems the roof has been beatified by the sunlight. One instant the roof is a flat silhouette, the next it is a furnace of fiery diamonds. The cause of this remarkable phenomenon — a difference in reflectivity between the glazed and matt tiles — is so subtle that under normal daylight conditions it mostly passes unnoticed.

Utzon took special pleasure in this distinction. Rather than introduce coloured tiles around the edges to frame the tile lids, or the foot-wide black stripes he had earlier considered, he used something more subtle, which depended on the angle and intensity of the light for its effect, thereby making the viewer more conscious of what kind of day it is. Away from direct sunlight, the tiles are nearly identical. Only when they are struck by sunlight directly, and only when the sunlight glances off obliquely at a certain incident angle, does the glazed tile surface suddenly leap with a fire that startles us with its piercing brightness, as tile after tile begins to combust and turn into a miniature diamond sun, spreading and joining into a larger, swelling, hot, rising, golden radiance. It burns and burns, until it seems the sun has come down from its place in the sky and swallowed up the roof. Utzon compared the effect with the beautiful pink glow or shine effect known as 'alpenglühen', produced on snowcapped mountains when the sun is setting.

At this moment, we understand what Utzon meant by architecture that is a living thing.

Close up, the shiny glaze is almost transparent, and the intermixture in the clay body of a white coarse *chamotte* to produce a dimpled, grogged face like a wholemeal biscuit is not what we expect, but its coarseness is necessary to bounce light off in every direction. The coarseness was quite deliberate. Utzon went to considerable lengths, in fact, to avoid creating a perfect, highly glazed surface.[2] He wanted us to see what the tiles consist of, so we understand better the nature of the clay material. It was a question of truth, allowing the materials of the building to speak to us honestly about themselves. The tiles may not be very large singly, but together they teach us to respect small, seemingly very ordinary things. The tiles are a parable with a fairytale message that exalts ordinary things by showing us how they are really extraordinary if we can only discover their true nature. The tiles have their own rhetoric, rustic to be sure – countrified, rough on the surface, robust – yet inwardly, they possess magic hidden fire. They are also possibly one of the most perfect things Utzon realised in the Opera House.

In their rather special way, the 12 cm × 12 cm × 12 mm thick tiles encapsulate the essence of the Opera House and illustrate how, when a complex thing is reduced to simplicity, the result can be an extraordinary grandeur.

The tiles are a remarkable story by themselves. Their development illustrates Utzon's extremely practical approach to problems which his critics, in their rush to condemn him, frequently seek to deny. Utzon has often been represented as an impractical visionary and a dreamer. This is far from the complete story. He could be extremely practical.

The tiles were detail, but they demonstrate the importance Utzon attached to even the smallest tasks, proving that an obsession with such details and getting every part perfect, no matter how small, was crucial to the outcome. The tiles epitomise Utzon's method, and demonstrate his care and determination in the face of obstacles to achieve the exact result. He begins by understanding the manufacturing process.

The heavy tile roofs on ancient Chinese temples lasted thousands of years. Utzon visited Beijing in April 1958 and was impressed by them. When in Teheran briefly, in March 1959, he was able to observe the magnificent medieval tile-covered domes and Arabesques on the gateways. In both China and Iran, roofs were regarded as a recapitulation of the heavenly vault and as bringing heaven down to the earth.[3] The roof was a locus of the spirit. To build a roof is to invoke the divine, to build a white roof is to invite eternity.

In a century of reductionist materialism, the Opera House is notable for its return to an ancient symbolism, which explains why it is viewed as something much more than a venue for entertainment.

Utzon could have avoided many later complications by agreeing to cover the roofs with conventional, locally manufactured, glazed bathroom tiles. For various reasons which will become apparent, he rejected the obvious and the politically expedient. Utzon wanted people to walk around the building and drink it in with their eyes. The roofs were the most visible and important symbol of the building. He wanted people to admire them. Not only the material, but the pattern, the texture, everything about them, every detail, had to be comely.

The white tiles of the Opera House roof contrast it with its setting. As a Scandinavian, Utzon was accustomed to heavy, slate-grey skies. He recognised that the sun in Sydney was bright and hot. Too much sunlight might be reflected off the large areas of the roofs, and the resulting glare could present a problem to motorists and people living near the Opera House. He needed a way to break up the reflected sunlight and to avoid concentrating it in large blinding beams, the way some glass office towers do at sunset.

Laying tiles on the ground is difficult enough, but satisfactorily fixing them high on the Opera House shells was next to impossible. Adding to the difficulties, the tiles had to stay in place for 200 years or more without crazing, cracking, falling off, fading unevenly or noticeably deteriorating. Very few building materials can be counted on to last as long as that in such an exposed position. By the beginning of November 1961, Utzon felt confident he had found what he needed in Sweden,[4] at the Höganäs factory.

During 1958, Utzon had asked Höganäs for a full-scale test structure of a highly curved valley section of the roof, at the junction where the two shells meet at a support, to be constructed so he could examine the effect of the curves on the tiles. One of the major concerns was the possible effect that strains in the shell roof from the shrinkage of the concrete, creep and other differential movements caused by the extreme outer surface temperatures, might have on the tiled surface. To get a better appreciation of the problems, the tile company Höganäs commissioned Associate Professor Ove Pettersson at the Royal Institute of Technology, Stockholm, to prepare a technical report in May 1959.[5] As a result of Professor Pettersson's calculations, it was decided to use prefabricated, precast lid units fixed to the main roof structure.

Test panels were set up at Höganäs's Skromberga factory, south-east of Helsingborg, to measure the effect of weathering. By May 1963, Rudolf Olssen at Höganäs was able to reassure Utzon that the test panels were still good and these particular panels had not arched or distorted even a little compared to other test panels. Olssen makes a point of complimenting Utzon for insisting on the large-grain-size *chamotte* for the glazed tiles to reduce glare in brilliant sunlight.[6]

Utzon rapidly ascertained that none of Höganäs's regular tiles were suitable, although certain glazes and qualities in the existing tiles were of interest. The original plan was to fix the tiles to the shells by hand when the shells were complete at the third stage of the contract. Hence, the choice of the tiles and their method of fixing to the roofs were inseparable from the development of the shell roofs themselves. Every time the roof was changed, there was some effect on the tiles. The roof structure and the covering could not be considered separately. Later, when Utzon recalled his experience with the tiling of the shell surfaces in the full size mock-ups at the Höganäs factory, he would say it led directly to his desire for a geometrically perfect surface for the shell roofs. Indeed, it was the challenge of the tiles which early on forced Utzon to consider prefabricating the shells.[7]

In order to investigate the effect of colour, which was considered extremely important, Höganäs undertook a new series of experiments with tile samples ranging in colour and surface texture. Utzon left nothing to chance. Around about this time, the decision was taken to use only white glazed tiles on the main inside sections of the tile lids; this, however, left open the edges, for which a range of colours including white, black, brown and blue tiles were selected for future study.[8] A further series of laboratory and factory tests was ordered to check on manufacturing procedures and to investigate various colours, shape, surface texture options and the effect of strains in the concrete shells on the ceramic cladding. Prototype tile lids were fabricated with filled and unfilled joints between the tile lids and sent to Sydney. After two years of strenuous development, in early 1962 Höganäs was prepared to give its quotation based on a specification Utzon prepared on 25 January 1962.[9]

The method of prefabricated tile lids employed on the Opera House was adapted from a system in wide use throughout Sweden, which the Höganäs company had previously developed in response to the demand for a high-quality lightweight cladding for commercial framed buildings. Because of the long, harsh Swedish winters, it was more efficient to manufacture prefabricated clinker tile panels in factories and take them to the building site where they were quickly fixed to the building frame, than hand fixing the tiles, which was slower and less reliable.

Höganäs commenced the manufacture of prefabricated panels incorporating its tiles in 1955. Known as clinker panels, its rectangular panels consisted of a thin strong backing sheet of reinforced concrete faced with cast-in-place clinker tiles. The panels were poured face down in a horizontal form. The method used for the Opera House roof tile lids was basically the same, except that they were not perfectly flat or rectangular, but were part of a very large sphere. To fit the panels along the long curved roof ribs, radial chevron-shaped panels were substituted for the simple rectangular shape. The basic method was tried and reliable, and by 1960 there were numerous examples around Sweden of buildings clad using the Höganäs system of clinker tile panels. The only thing that was unique or unprecedented was the adaptation of this existing technology to the special case of the Opera House.

In February 1962, Rider Hunt, the Opera House quantity surveyors, received the roof tile quotations. The Höganäs tile price for the off-white tiles was A£2.2.6 (A$4.25) per square yard delivered to Sydney. This figure did not include the 27.5 per cent import duty. Höganäs's price was considerably below other prices submitted by Commonwealth Ceramics and Wunderlich of A£3.3.6 (A$6.35) and A£3.12.3 (A$7.23) per square yard respectively.[10] Even with the import duty included, it came to A£2.14.2 (A$5.42), well below its rivals. This remarkable result confirmed the value of Utzon's collaborative industrial approach of working closely with particular manufacturers. Nevertheless, Utzon still found it necessary to remind the committee: 'I have worked in close connection with the Höganäs engineers at the factory through two years, and the tile is the result of this co-operation.'[11]

To make sure all the tiles deliveries were satisfactory, Utzon arranged with a Norwegian architect, Helge Hjertholm, in December 1962 before he left Denmark, for Helge to visit the Höganäs factory periodically to check tile production.[12] Because the tile drawings were a long way off in 1962, it was not possible for Ove Arup & Partners to give Höganäs the exact quantities it required. This information was not released until July 1962.[13] Hjertholm had joined Utzon's staff at Hellebæk in

September 1958, a month before another Norwegian, Jon Lundberg, arrived, but unlike Lundberg, Hjertholm elected to remain behind when Utzon moved to Australia.

At appropriate intervals, Hjertholm slipped across the Sound to Helsingborg on the ferry and visited the Höganäs tile works. There were great quantities of snow and long periods of intense cold in the 1962–3 winter, which was especially severe that year. Øresund, the strait between Denmark and Sweden, froze and blocked shipping from moving into or out of the Baltic Sea. Delivery of the raw materials to Höganäs was affected. Also its plant at Skromberga was burnt down, disrupting the drying and cutting of the tiles. In spite of all this, the first consignment of tiles was shipped from Göthenburg (Göteborg) on the *M.S. Kennedy* in June 1963, with the remainder following in mid-August.

Höganäs did not ship its tiles in the prefabricated tile panel form. Hence, the next stage was to cast the tile panels. It was initially thought the ceramic tiles would be fixed under a separate contract during Stage III, but because Utzon and Höganäs had come up with a new method of construction for the roofs, the delivery of the tiles had to be brought forward because they were the first item to go into the forms when the panel lids were cast. Utzon's replacement of the original elliptical paraboloid by a spherical roof geometry made this far easier. Instead of 3464 main roof tile lids sizes, each slightly different from the others, the number was reduced to a mere 26 standard shapes.[14] Some tile lids were repeated over 276 times.

The tile lids converged at the podium pedestal at their base and became wider with height. Successive rib elements changed their section, becoming wider and deeper, depending on where they were located in the shell. The principle was the same as the folded slab for the concourse – which is what had inspired Ove Arup to think of the rib solution originally.

Although Utzon had agreed on the method for casting the tile lids, many problems remained. Using the Opera House podium as a factory, over one million tiles – of which there were eight different types – were cast into 4253 lids. This entailed building a concrete form with a concave spherical surface of the correct radius and fixing a grid of thin aluminium strips to it to locate where the tiles should go. The sides of the form were made of 6.4 mm steel plate and the tiles were placed face down in the mould between the aluminium strips.

One of the outstanding problems for which Höganäs did not have a solution was what should fill the grooves between the tiles during the pouring of the concrete lid-back.[15] Ordinarily, Höganäs used wet sand, but the sand adhered to the concrete. Ove Arup & Partners and the contractor were at a loss for a solution. Hearing of this, they were approached by a carpenter who offered to tell them a way if they paid him 'fifty quid'. His solution was to run heated animal glue which set on cooling along the joints. After the panels were cast, they were steam cured; the steam melted the animal glue which had a melting point of 90–95°C. The carpenter was paid his fifty quid.[16]

With the problem solved, production started in earnest. Three pre-cut layers of galvanised steel mesh were placed on top of the tiles kept apart by small asbestos cement spacers, and the cement mortar was poured to create a chevron 'ferro-cement' panel backing approximately 28 mm thick, giving the tile lid a total thickness with the tiles of 45 mm. The panels were then steam-cured overnight at a maximum temperature of 170°C, melting the animal glue from the joints.

Although some difficulty was experienced initially in fixing the tile lids to the precast rib elements, this was soon remedied. By September 1965, two months later, six elements were fixed on the shells. Utzon was pleased, and commented they 'look fantastic in the sun'.[17]

Utzon had the special gift of relating to others: people genuinely liked him and they were prepared to go to great lengths to please him. The development of the tiles was one triumph among many which testify to his capacity to excite and inspire those who collaborate with him. His positive manner produced a significant financial saving in cost, while assuring a superior outcome. It was within the powers of the NSW Government to ask the Commonwealth to exempt the tiles from import duty, but it failed to do so even though this added a further 27.5 per cent impost. Quick to complain about cost increases, the same politicians were entirely ineffectual when it came to doing something practical that might have helped. The Government was equally backward in public relations, and refused repeated calls by the Opera House executive committee to appoint a publicist to answer the lies in the press.

The success of the tiles established Utzon's basic collaborative method of working directly with industry. It was not an isolated instance, but a forerunner of his approach for Stage III. Utzon believed that the success of the project, and the best chance to reduce the final cost without threatening the highest quality, depended on his working directly with manufacturers and suppliers to draw on their extensive technical expertise and experience. Backward contractors who were not willing to invest in the development of new products for the Opera House found it easier to complain to the Minister they were being shut out. Hence politics was brought into the picture which did nothing either to improve the architecture, or produce savings.

The roofs are one of the most impressive aspects of the Opera House. Utzon added something metaphysical to them by allying them symbolically to the sky and sun.

The roofs of the Opera House evoke its era and such notable 1960s developments as the space race. Humans have long regarded the heavens with awe and longed to go there. The ancient Egyptians expressed their longing by building polished limestone-faced pyramids to serve as sky-ladders, so reflective they became blinding mirrors in the intense desert light. On 20 December 1968, Apollo 8 sped towards the moon and less than a year later, the Lunar Module from Apollo 11 bumped unceremoniously onto the dusty lunar surface on 16 July 1969. Looking back at earth from the moon, astronauts saw a small bright blue sphere wreathed in fleecy swirls of water vapour and surrounded by a thin glove of atmosphere. The spherical geometry of the Opera House vaults is a reminder of our identity as inhabitants of that lone blue-and-green planet. Its white-tiled roof vaults lift our eyes toward the sky in the same manner that the ancient pyramids, as symbols of the heavens, once did.

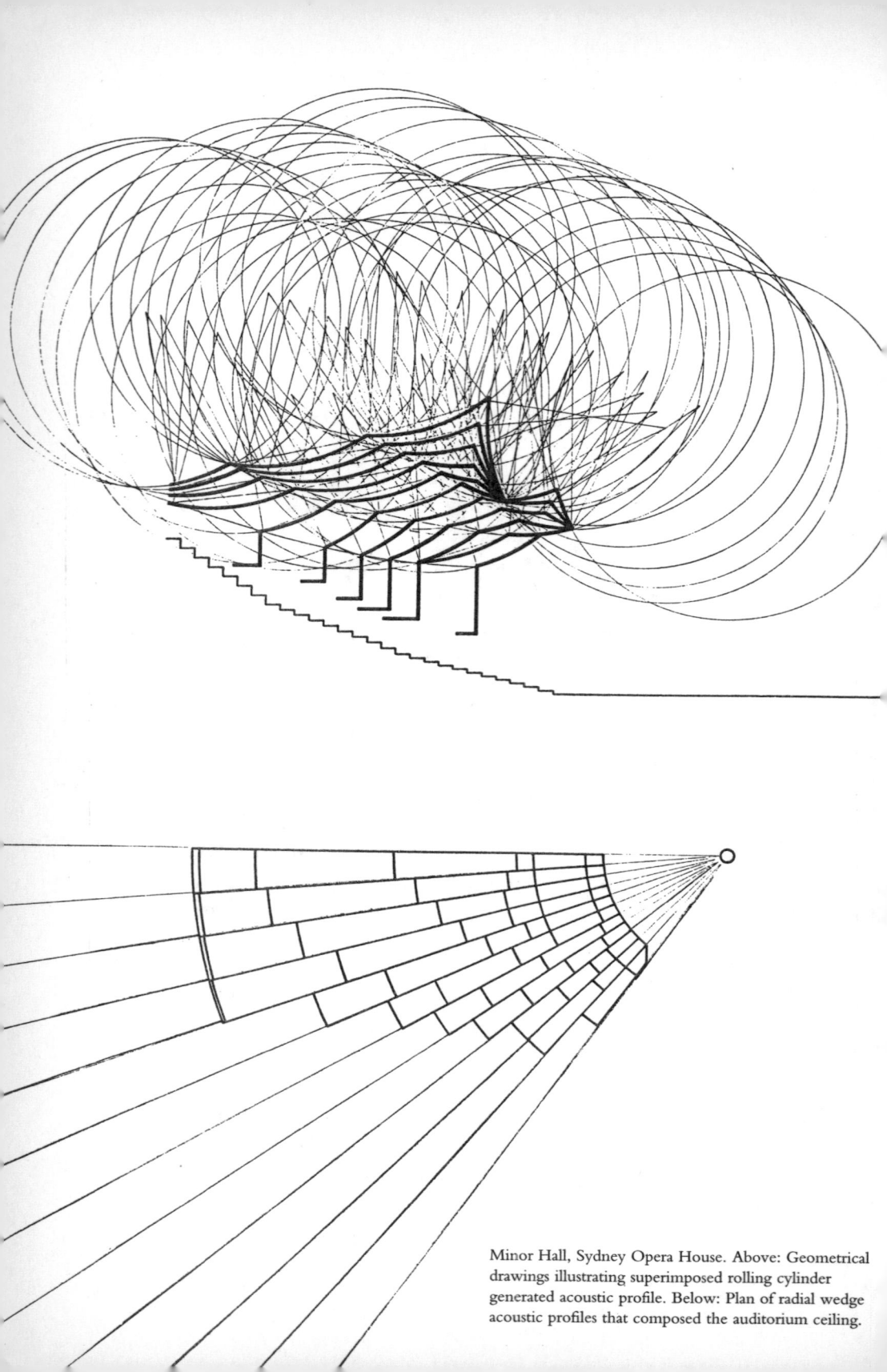

Minor Hall, Sydney Opera House. Above: Geometrical drawings illustrating superimposed rolling cylinder generated acoustic profile. Below: Plan of radial wedge acoustic profiles that composed the auditorium ceiling.

15

Ballot-box Despot
Sydney, 1965

— and if there is going to be more fuss with the new Government, God only knows how many chronological reports and narrative descriptions, they are going to ask for. I just could not bear to write another one.

Skipper Nielsen, on leaving Sydney, 6 June 1965[1]

Politics is a pendulum: first it swings this way, then in the opposite direction. On 1 May 1965 the pendulum swung to the right in the General Election and Labor lost by two seats. A new Liberal–Country Party Coalition, with R.W. Askin as leader, held the reins of government by the slim majority of 47 to Labor's 45.

The election was close — so evenly balanced it was ten days before the final figures were known.[2] After 24 years, Labor found itself out of office. The new Askin Government was not without its admirers. Joe Daniel Testa of the Chicago Mafia was so encouraged he visited Sydney for the first time in 1965.

By mid-1965, a large part of eastern and central Australia was in the grip of a great drought. In the north of New South Wales, around places such as Gunnedah, cattle were dying in the thousands. Drought provided the rural backdrop to the 1965 elections. Struggling farmers in the country looked to the Country Party for assistance as they stood by helpless and watched their crops fail and their livestock die. In the Armidale electorate, the Opera House costs issue rated well behind the provision of low interest loans for buildings for fodder storage.[3] At the Country Party campaign launch at Orange in the central west of New South Wales on 5 April, C.B. Cutler made no reference to holding an inquiry into Opera House costs.[4]

Utzon had only met Askin once, at the commencement ceremony in March 1959; he had never met the new Minister for Public Works, Davis Hughes. Far from showing any concern, Utzon welcomed the change because he mistakenly believed it might improve the situation.[5] During the eight months in the lead-up to the elections, Labor had ceased making decisions, thus halting progress. Instead of proceeding with the interiors, Utzon found himself bogged down in unproductive administration. But the atmosphere under Hughes differed little from what he had endured under Renshaw and Ryan. Hughes made a lot of noise and claimed he was doing something about curbing costs, but mostly the sound and fury of his public utterances were designed to impress his own party colleagues and placate public disquiet.[6]

Skipper Nielsen was not lying when he complained about the time he spent drafting reports. Bureaucrats use reports to delay making decisions, a fact that was immediately apparent to Utzon and his staff. The practice soon took its toll, wearing Utzon's staff down and destroying their enthusiasm. Within one month, between May and June 1965, Utzon lost three of his most senior architects: Jon Lundberg went first, followed by Skipper Nielsen in June, and then Jacob Kielland-Brandt. Kielland-Brandt was seriously ill and required an operation which Utzon recommended he should seek in Denmark. Nielsen and Lundberg were heavy losses. Nielsen – an engagingly modest and quiet Dane from Århus with impeccable English and wide practical experience – was indispensable to Utzon.

Utzon was away in Europe for six weeks during the election period. He arrived back in Sydney on 23 or 24 May to find a new government installed in Macquarie Street. No one had warned Utzon about Askin, and he somehow failed to read all the ominous danger signs. Unfazed, he actually welcomed the suggestion to set up an independent Royal Commission into the Opera House. Utzon was confident that any such inquiry would exonerate him of blame and lay to rest the baseless accusations against him.

Hughes was determined to expose the imagined corruptions of the previous Labor administration. During the elections, the Country Party had claimed that money saved on the Opera House would be diverted to build roads, hospitals and schools instead. The *Sydney Opera House Act, 1960*, made this impossible. Having talked up a scandal, Davis Hughes now set about to find one. The inquiry was an excuse to engage in cheap political muckraking.

The Government never intended holding an independent public inquiry. That was far too dangerous. Askin's Minister for Public Works decided he would conduct a secret inquiry personally. Not only did this deny Utzon an opportunity to defend himself, it allowed Hughes to make the rules. Besides minimising the political risks, it gave Hughes considerable latitude to manipulate the facts however he liked. The Davis Hughes inquiry was a sham from start to finish. It was neither impartial nor objective, and it had only one aim, to attack Labor and Utzon.

Hughes conducted his three-month inquiry from his office in the Public Works Department. Once again, the Sydney Opera House was being exploited for party-political ends. The former Minister for Works, R.N. Ryan, pointed out later: 'The Minister [D. Hughes] decided very obviously that some scapegoat had to be found to justify the earlier criticism.'[7]

At the conclusion of his private investigation of the Opera House, Hughes planned to make a devastating attack on the Labor Opposition using as his ammunition incontrovertible proof that the history of the Opera House was one of gross mismanagement by Labor in government, and that it had used devices ranging from the illegal to the improper to mislead the Parliament.[8] Hughes probably saw the speech as his political masterstroke. Since he would be making a Ministerial Statement, Hughes felt on safe ground – only one person, the

Leader of the Opposition, was permitted to speak in reply. Hughes nominated 30 August as the date for his statement. When the much sought-after evidence of wrongdoing failed to materialise after three fruitless months, the date was pushed forward to 2 November.

Davis Hughes's first serious mistake was to confuse his role as the constructing authority with the responsibilities of the client. Clause 2 (1) (c) of the *Sydney Opera House Act, 1960* designated the Minister for Public Works as the Constructing Authority and made him responsible for supervising the completion of the Opera House. It did not appoint him as the client. The *Sydney Opera House Trust Act, 1961* reconstituted the former executive committee as a trust to manage and control the Opera House. The Minister supervised the work, and the Trust made decisions about the building facilities to ensure that it would meet the needs of future users. These were two distinct functions, the Trust, not the Minister, was the client body, it represented the community interest and it made decisions to complete the project and manage and administer it afterwards. By failing to respect the client body as separate from the construction authority, under the 1960 and 1961 Acts, and by extending his powers as Minister, Hughes now usurped the role of client.

During the debate on the *Sydney Opera House Act, 1960* it was Davis Hughes in Opposition who attacked the Government for failing to establish a trust to control and manage the Opera House.[9] As a direct consequence of this criticism in April 1960, the Heffron Labor Government introduced the Trust Act the following year. The 1960 Act appointed the Minister for Public Works as the constructing authority for legislative purposes only, and made him responsible to Parliament with a technical responsibility to ensure adequate supervision. The Act did not direct the Minister to personally supervise the work, or to be involved in its day-to-day administration. He was given an umbrella responsibility to oversee and report generally. The Act did not require he take over and run the job any more than he was expected to involve himself in the hundreds of Public Works projects around the State. Ridiculous as it now seems, that is exactly what Davis Hughes decided he should do.

The weakness of the 1960 Act was its failure to define the authority of the Minister vis-à-vis the committee. Nowhere were the mandate or functions of the Executive Committee set out in relation to the Minister.[10] There was no restraint in the Act to prevent an autocratic minister from abrogating the committee and assuming the client function.

By extending to the Minister the right of supervision over the architect or engineer, the Act compromised the professional independence of Utzon and his consultants. Worried by this, Utzon tried many times to clarify his position, but to no avail.[11] In the beginning, the new Minster allowed the Trust to continue to establish user needs and performance criteria, but in March 1969, following the removal of Utzon, Hughes did away with it.[12] By sacking the Trust, Hughes deprived the Opera House of its client body and closed democratic channels for influencing its future decisions. The Minister thereafter took it upon himself to determine the community interest. The previous Labor administration worked with the Trust; Hughes sanguinely abolished the Trust because it stood in his way, thereby making himself absolute and clearing up any lingering confusion about the powers of the committee – it had none.

This was both dangerous and irresponsible and removed any check on Public Works. The Government had no way of properly establishing whether Public Works was competent, since it was now the client and service department.

The Opera House was a unique building with which Hughes's department had no experience whatsoever. The specialties of the 56-year-old Government Architect, E.H. Farmer, were hospitals and sorting out plumbing. There was nothing in his past to suggest he was even minimally qualified to handle the job Hughes pushed onto him.

It was essential Davis Hughes had someone under him to direct the project who was not in a position to argue. With its tremendous complexity and novelty, the Opera House needed the direction of someone who could work closely with others in a sympathetic yet firm manner. Davis Hughes was not that sort of person.

Utzon may have thought that he was above politics and therefore safe from political interference. With that truly Danish optimism and resolve to suppress what was going on around him, he ignored the ominous political signs emanating from the Parliament. He miscalculated badly. The Askin administration was notorious in terms of its involvement in gambling, police corruption and crime, even by New South Wales's lax ethical standards.

Robert Askin started his career as a bank clerk and part-time SP bookie. He was a colourful personality. On election night he exclaimed with evident relish: 'We're in the tart shop now, boys.' The tart shop was the government. Askin controlled the police and, via the police, a wide range of criminal activities in the state. Assisted by compliant Police Commissioners such as Norman Allan (1962–72) who took bribes from the criminals who ran the highly profitable illegal casinos at Kings Cross and his successor, Fred Hanson (1972–6), corruption was institutionalised from the top down.[13] Askin saw to it that crime did pay in New South Wales. His legacy to the state was the systemic corruption in the police and the unprecedented expansion of crime.

Between 1950 and 1975, when he retired as Premier, Askin earned A£375,180 (A$750,360). In September 1981 when he died, he left a declared estate of A$1,957,995 (worth $3.6 million today), $1.2 million more than he had earned during that time. On her death, his widow left a further declared estate of A$3,724,879.[14] A large proportion of this was unaccounted for and the Australian tax office picked up between $1.5 and $1 million in outstanding taxes. No one has yet managed to explain how Askin succeeded in accumulating such a large fortune by honest means.

The heavy fog of crime and corruption proved too much even for Sydney's flickering neon signs. A large neon advertisement over a garage at Taylor Square near the local police station said it all: the middle three letters 'SER' blacked so it read 'SYDNEY ... VICE STATION'. Throughout the Askin period, illegal casinos, brothels and SP bookmaking flourished openly while the police looked on. The Opera House offered a ready-made distraction from this mayhem and corruption.

With the election won, the Opera House's usefulness to Askin came to an end. It had served its political purpose, now the problem was what to do with it. His solution was to hand it over to his coalition partner, the Country Party, as an election prize. Hughes was of use to Askin. If Hughes stumbled, it would not be Askin's problem.

No one could have been less involved in the arts than the Premier. He was a proud philistine whose only interest in the Opera House centred on money matters. Crude and cunning in his flashy banker's suit, Askin kept his ruthless toughness concealed under an outgoing amiable personality. Confronted by anti-Vietnam War demonstrators on a drive through Sydney with the American President Lyndon Johnson in October 1966, he was heard to say: 'Drive over the bastards.'[15]

Davis Hughes got on well with Askin. The pair had entered Parliament in the same year in 1950. Hughes was more intelligent and better educated than most politicians – especially from the Country Party – but his enormous vanity had nearly caused his downfall in 1959.

With his deep-set eyes, bushy eyebrows, furrowed temples and tightly brushed back wedge of grey hair, Davis Hughes has been described as Mephistopheles in a business suit.[16] He carefully disguised his defects: when he was 30 the hair on his forehead thinned, leaving two bald patches on either side. To hide this, he brushed the remaining strands back in an unsympathetic tight 'V' wedge which contributed to his rigid and aggressive appearance. Below the forehead, deep lidded eyes added to the imperious expression and suggestion of hidden menace in his countenance. Over time, Hughes's initially alert, inquiring expression changed into a more hostile regard for the world.

Born on 24 November 1910 in Launceston, Davis Hughes's father was an engine-driver.[17] The son attended Launceston High School and repeated his final year in 1927 before he matriculated, and trained as a schoolteacher at Hobart. Davis excelled at football and tennis, and played A grade cricket.[18] On finishing teacher training in 1929, he taught at the Devonport

High School (1931–3), spent 1935 at the Friends School at Hobart, and then moved to Caulfield Grammar School. Prior to 1936, Davis Hughes studied part time for a bachelor of science degree at the University of Tasmania, which he failed to complete.

In June 1940, Davis Hughes applied for the position of temporary education officer on the civil staff of the Royal Australian Air Force. Hughes stated on his application that he had read for a Bachelor of Science degree at the Universities of Tasmania and Melbourne, after which he wrote, *'completing it in the following subjects …'*.[19] In all subsequent documents his claim to possess a Bachelor of Science degree is unqualified.[20]

Hughes, who was then aged 29, served as a navigation instructor in mathematics, and emerged from the war with the rank of Acting Squadron Leader. He seems to have been a competent teacher.

Davis Hughes evades scrutiny. One word effectively describes him: 'guile'. In June 1945, a fellow officer at Point Cook Central Flying School made the following observation about Hughes's character: '… he has a certain guile that enables him to impress one to an extent beyond the actual value of his actions and, or, words. His efforts are often designed to focus favourable light on himself and to this end he will be quite impervious to the effects, or feelings of others. Due to his ego and tendency to understate others' ability and by his actions he loses considerable prestige and status.'[21]

Davis Hughes first attempted to enter politics as the Labor candidate for Armidale. When this failed, Hughes accepted D.H. Drummond's offer to replace him as the Country Party member for Armidale when he moved from the State Legislature to the National Parliament. Hughes, who by now had risen to Deputy Headmaster at The Armidale School, resigned on his election to the State Legislative Assembly on 11 February 1950. He lost his seat in the subsequent 1953 election, but returned in 1956 and, on a second ballot, on 6 May 1958, he narrowly won the contest for Leader of the NSW Country Party.[22]

Some time before the 21 March 1959 poll, in early February, Davis Hughes vanished and did not re-emerge until 5 April, seven and a half weeks later, by which time the election was long over. Davis Hughes's disappearance coincided with a press release from the Armidale Branch of the Labor Party, charging him with falsely claiming to have the degree of Bachelor of Science from the University of Tasmania.

It is impossible to imagine any leader of a major political party disappearing for two months in the midst of a general election today. It was quite extraordinary, especially in view of the fact that his challenger, Percy Love, Mayor of Armidale, was certain to lose.

The Country Party's handling of the scandal was a farce. For weeks the *Armidale Express* faithfully poured forth a miscellany of nonsensical statements, each one contradicting the last: 4 March, 'Hughes not retiring'; 13 March, 'Hughes has Not Resigned'; 25 March, 'Hughes May Resign C.P. Leadership'; 5 April, 'Mr D. Hughes is Back on the Job'. The litany of announcements reached its peak on 15 April, 'Mr D. Hughes ... yesterday relinquished the Leadership'. Something was wrong. The question hung in the air, what was really going on? The announcements merely added further spice to Davis Hughes's inexplicable absence while they betrayed the rising hysteria within the Country Party. Not even someone as senior as Charles Cutler, who deputised as Leader during Hughes's absence, was informed of the resignation.

On 27 March, the *Armidale Express* announced Hughes's imminent discharge from a Sydney hospital – it proved premature and he left on 5 April.[23] A week later, with Hughes still in hospital, a chastened *Express* circumspectly conceded: 'Hughes not retiring'. This was followed by the revelation that he was suffering from a 'nervous disorder'.[24] Eleven days later, party officials denied for a second time that Hughes had previously resigned the leadership. If Hughes had not resigned, why go on denying it? There was a lot more to the crisis than the public was being told.

Adding to the pressure, on 11 March Mr Griffiths, the

Member for Shortland, asked the Minister for Air in the Federal Parliament, Canberra, whether the Leader of the Country Party in New South Wales had been commissioned and later promoted in the RAAF on the basis of a degree he had never received.[25] The question lay on the table of the House for two months awaiting an answer from the Minister.

Armidale was agog with speculation. The day before the election, 20 March, the faithful *Express* still refused to divulge the truth, that Mr Davis Hughes had lied about his university degree for 19 years.

On the eve of the poll, Hughes released a letter from Gloucester House, a private ward set well back from Missenden Road behind Royal Prince Alfred Hospital, thanking his campaign supporters.[26] The reason offered for his absence during the election and campaign launch was he had suffered a serious stomach complaint combined with nervous exhaustion.[27] Soon afterwards it was confirmed that he would retire and Mr C.B. Cutler, the Deputy Leader from Orange, would replace him as Leader.

The political response represented a huge over-reaction! In the 1960s, maintaining a facade of respectability was crucial, but it hardly accounts for the Country Party's hysteria. Davis Hughes was a contradiction: he was from a Welsh Baptist background, but in his later political career, self-advancement and expediency are more typical. Although he had plainly compromised himself by lying to the NSW Parliament about his university degree, the question remained whether he had committed any other improprieties. Why did he step down as leader after only 11 months?[28] Hughes relinquished the leadership on 14 April, a week before the Parliament re-convened.

At a special adjournment of Parliament on 21 April, Davis Hughes made a brief statement about his academic qualifications. He avoided any hint that he may have misled Parliament. He said, 'Though I saw them [the B.Sc. initials] in Hansard I did not take the necessary action to have them removed.' Hughes failed to explain how the initials came to be in Hansard in 1950 and why, for nine years, he took no action to correct the mistake. Under questioning, Hughes admitted it was 'a grave weakness', for which, 'I see no distinction between that and claiming the particular degree.'[29]

To forestall further accusations, Hughes admitted that a similar mistake had occurred in the records of the Royal Australian Air Force in June 1940, 19 years before. Once again, he had failed to correct the mistake. This represented an equally serious charge because it involved falsely obtaining a commission in the armed services and being promoted and benefiting financially from his deception.

Davis Hughes's evasions reveal how desperate he was. Having ceased to be Country Party Leader, Hughes no longer presented an important political target for the Labor Party. If he had not been caught out in the 1959 elections, it is unlikely he would ever have admitted to his deception. Hughes's transgression was well known in the Parliament. In a debate on 3 November 1965, in answer to charges by Hughes that the former Labor administration had misled the House over the Opera House, Mr J.B. Renshaw sharply rebuked Davis Hughes: 'You have been found out before, and you did not like it.'[30]

If the April 1959 scandal exposed the calculating opportunist within Hughes, it also helps to explain his later conduct of the Opera House matter when he became Minister for Public Works. The public exposure would have deeply humiliated him. He survived, but the wound never healed. It was Askin, more than the Country Party, who underwrote Hughes's political future. The Opera House costs issue offered Davis Hughes a second chance at glory. Many coalition MLAs genuinely believed that the Labor Government had been corrupt and incompetent. It was now up to Davis Hughes to catch the Labor Party at wrongdoing. The implacable expression on Hughes's face from photographs of the time imply that he had neither forgotten nor forgiven Labor.

Utzon did not know anything about this. His attention was focused on two important matters – finalising the acoustic design of the two main halls and discovering an immediate solution to the glass walls. It took up all of his time in 1965. The development of the halls necessitated further visits to Europe: the first was the extended trip of six weeks from April to May, to Berlin to visit Professors Gabler and Cremer, during which Utzon made a side trip to Waagner-Biro in Vienna to finalise the stage machinery; this was followed by another trip in the second half of October. Most of Utzon's time was spent at the Palm Beach boatshed with visits to the Bennelong Point site office several days each week to attend client meetings. By a coincidence, Hughes's first move against Utzon occurred when he was absent, and well before Hughes could possibly have ascertained all the relevant facts, showing that he was following a pre-determined plan.

Utzon spent the school holidays, beginning on 10 August 1965, with Lis and Kim on tiny Heron Island off Gladstone in North Queensland. Utzon's first Sydney secretary, Margaret Moorcroft, observed: 'His family meant everything to him; he wasn't wild about socialising.' Utzon didn't necessarily dislike people, nor was he unsociable, 'He was a solitary man in many ways.'[31] When Margaret Moorcroft married, Utzon very generously gave the couple a copy of the *Larousse Gastronomique* and included the humorous dedication: 'If your wife can't cook or read keep her as a pet and eat out.'

Utzon was entranced by Heron Island, by the rich luxuriance of its plants and its extraordinary bird life. Milton Moon, a potter from Adelaide, recalled meeting Utzon while waiting for the launch at Gladstone to take them to the island. Standing on the launch below the jetty was a large, handsome, fair-haired Scandinavian, who reached up to the jetty as people arrived and took their luggage and stowed it on the boat. Seeing the boat was short staffed, Utzon had hopped in and lent a hand. It was typical of his direct practical approach to life which ruled out social distinctions. He entered into everything. Moon and Utzon shared an enthusiasm for ceramics.

According to Moorcroft and others, Utzon was wonderful around children. On Heron Island he made a rabbit out of a lettuce leaf for Milton Moon's son. He was interested in shapes and playing around with materials, whether it was a lettuce leaf or the massive coral bommies that abounded with sea life. He would tread water while he stared down at the coral. When a shark appeared suddenly, Utzon darted back to the boat like a frightened seal.

Utzon befriended Joan Skibby, Margaret Moorcroft's sister, who was shy and a little overwhelmed when he persisted that instead of wading in the shallows close to the shore, it would be more fun to venture out to the reef. He showed her how to snorkel and led her down to a favourite cave swarming with sea life. She never forgot his generosity in seeking to share the beauty of the reef with her. Most of all, she remembered him saying how wonderful nature was.

The birds on Heron Island set up a tumultuous din at night. The island is a haven for sea birds, especially herons. When evening descended, Utzon took his mattress somewhere different each night and slept out under the stars to see what it was like. This way, he got to know the island. Heron Island was a perfect escape for Utzon with his love of nature, its teeming richness of life and vibrant colours.

One day, a fishing trawler arrived off the island and one of the young girls who worked at the resort was invited by the crew to go to Darwin. This upset Utzon, who pleaded with her not to go. He warned her she didn't know what she was letting herself in for. Eventually she left with the boat. Utzon was sad, 'I've told her, I've told her, I know seamen.' No matter how big or great his own troubles were, Utzon cared about others.

The vivid coral colours of the reef made an enormous impact on Utzon and influenced his plans for the interiors of the Opera House. Although these ideas were never carried out, they can be seen in the elaborate interior models he built after this holiday.

At an election night party on 1 May 1965 at Mosman, one of Sydney's smarter suburbs, Davis Hughes's daughter, Sue Burgoyne, boasted she was delighted because her father, the next Minister for Public Works, was going to sack Utzon. If true, it indicates that even before Davis Hughes was sworn in as Minister for Public Works, it was his intention to have Utzon removed.

A great story was built up around costs and Utzon's absences during 1965 made him an obvious target. Throughout 1965, Hughes played cat and mouse with Utzon. The *Sydney Opera House Act, 1960* gave Hughes total control, however, it did not set up any specific mechanism for reining in Utzon. While he searched for one, Hughes kept a careful watch on Utzon. As the year wore on, and the pain and worry gained a deeper hold in Utzon's psyche, maintaining the pretence of normality became harder, until by October the tension was unbearable.

At their first meeting, Hughes lectured the Executive Committee on how he would end wasteful expenditure. The committee was left in no doubt about his intentions. Sir Charles Moses recalled that when Hughes spoke to Utzon shortly afterwards, '… the Minister was so rude to Utzon, that Utzon thought it was funny. The next time they met, which wasn't long afterwards, and he [Davis Hughes] was very rude again, this time Utzon didn't think it so funny.'[32] Despite repeated invitations, Davis Hughes refused to visit Utzon's drawing office. The Minister never talked to Utzon's staff and never showed a genuine interest in what they were doing. Hughes rejected every Utzon overture. In total, Hughes stopped in on Utzon's site office possibly twice in ten months – this shows the true extent of his interest in Utzon's work and the progress he was making.[33]

Utzon responded to the increased political tension by throwing himself into his work. By early June, construction of the main south roof vaults over the stage areas of the Major and Minor Halls was well advanced and was attracting considerable public attention and comment.[34] This spurred Utzon on. Submitting his acoustic report following his Berlin visit in May, Utzon stated that the tests on the Minor Hall had been successful, and that he was presently working with Ralph Symonds on one-tenth scale model experiments to confirm the erection method. Evidently buoyed by his progress, he announced that two one-tenth scale models had been built separately in Berlin and Copenhagen for the third scheme of the Major Hall (1964–5) with side galleries and a rear balcony, which was, 'almost perfect acoustically, it was structurally sound and perfect'. He promised new models would be built in the two laboratories for the final scheme.

In a reference to the 1200-seat Minor Hall drama theatre, Utzon explained how important it was to take the live theatre experience into account:

> *It is very important for the actors to feel the audience's attention, and this unbroken amphitheatre that faces the actors from the other side of the orchestra pit lends itself to give the actor an easy command over the spectators. There are no separating aisles in the middle which divide the audience into two halves, and the increasing steepness of the auditorium makes the right bowl form. As one famous actor stressed, 'We want to see faces and only faces from the stage.'*[35]

In his consideration of the Major Hall with its stepped walls and ceiling, Utzon attempted to focus the space on the stage by directing the line of the ceiling profiles towards the stage so the audience would naturally concentrate its attention there. He eliminated the proscenium arch and, to reduce separation of the stage and auditorium volumes, he merged the stage and auditorium into one another. Professor Cremer's test results for the Minor Hall were forwarded in October. It recommended, and Utzon adopted, a curved rear wall in the Minor Hall.

One of the difficulties experienced in the Major Hall scheme at this time was the steep ceiling at the front which delayed reflections to the stalls and lower and middle seats. A further problem was due to the horizontal surfaces in the radial ceiling wedges which were too close together immediately in front of the stage for effective sound reflection. While very pleased by the Minor Hall results, Utzon still harboured reservations about the Major Hall, which he considered 'had some very ugly proportions'.

In early September, Utzon was coming under heavy pressure from Hughes and wrote to Gabler to urge him to push ahead immediately regardless of the cost because he regarded this as secondary to the result. 'Our problem,' he warned, 'is more to finish our scheme off in time as I am being pressed very hard by the client for final working drawings.'[36] There can be very little doubt that Utzon was keenly aware of the urgency of the work.

While Utzon pressed on, Hughes pursued an entirely different agenda. On 11 August, Hughes met the Public Works' liaison architect, Bill Wood, to discuss measures for controlling the project. The next day Wood wrote a confidential memo to Davis Hughes which provided him with details of four measures to control Utzon. The first and most efficacious measure Wood suggested was something he called 'check book [sic] control'. Simply and brutally, Utzon would be controlled by stopping his monthly fee payments. Wood also recommended that Hughes set a ceiling cost figure based on the current estimate; adopt the critical path analysis procedure for managing Stage III; and, lastly, he outlined a proposal developed earlier in conjunction with the contractor for '… the establishment of a Drafting Office or the letting out to sub-contract of the preparation of working drawings. Some 25 Architects, Assistant Architects … together with a senior Departmental architect, would be needed.' Wood doubted '… whether Mr Utzon has or foresees the engagement of staff adequate to meet the needs of this gigantic project.'[37]

The document confirms the inception of a conspiracy to remove Utzon. It initially involved Bill Wood, was later to include the contractor and, very likely, the local site office of Ove Arup & Partners which, if it was not directly a party, knew what was happening. The fourth recommendation broadly anticipated the later arrangement whereby the Hall Todd & Littlemore consortium replaced Utzon in March 1966.

On 25 August, Hughes forwarded a confidential minute to Cabinet based on his continuing discussions with Bill Wood. He also wrote to Utzon. Hughes's letter to Utzon was nakedly aggressive:

> *I do not believe that I have been successful in having your acceptance of some basic principles which must govern the construction of this project ... but it is a basic requirement that* I, *as client [author's emphasis], must always be kept fully informed as to what is being planned and that my approval be obtained.*[38]

Hughes did not refer to the Trust Executive Committee, which he plainly regarded as irrelevant. Not only did he trample on the Parliament but, in saying that Utzon had acted improperly in the past, Hughes impugned Utzon's professional reputation with vague and unfounded accusations. In looking at the way the crisis unfolded Hughes's tactic was to provoke Utzon into acting rashly.

The same day, 25 August, Hughes asked for and received Cabinet approval for the seven measures in his memo. In the preamble, and possibly to protect himself in the future, Hughes warned Cabinet that the adoption of the measures could lead to a confrontation with Utzon. In his advice, Wood advised Hughes not to replace Utzon as the designer because this would lead to a scandal with worldwide repercussions. Wood thought the best way was to adjust Utzon's fees and choke him into submission. Hughes ignored Wood on this earlier point. The internal correspondence points to the conclusion that it was Hughes's intention all along to force Utzon to leave the job. What he lacked was a plausible trigger.

The principal recommendation to Cabinet was not to commence work on Stage III until full working drawings were available. In (4), Hughes insisted that certain structural matters must be discussed with Utzon.[39] The final point required Utzon to agree to a reduced fee scale as might apply to a consultant starting work in 1965. Cabinet gave its agreement. On 22 October, to prepare the ground for the Minister to withhold fees from Utzon, the Public Works Department took over the authority to pay Utzon from the Department of Local Government which had done this since 1957. The instrument for choking Utzon financially was in place.

The first recommendation, if carried out, would have halted the work at the end of Stage II in February 1967 and more than likely for a year beyond that. It was impractical, time-wasting and expensive, and was never implemented.

Hughes now launched an attack on several fronts to loosen Utzon's support and further isolate him. At the same time, he set about gaining acceptance from the architectural profession of his plans because he recognised he would have to call on private architects to finish the Opera House after he succeeded in getting rid of Utzon. He therefore embroiled the New South Wales Chapter of the Royal Australian Institute of Architects in the dispute to strengthen his hand against Utzon. Hughes was not nearly so confident and unassailable as he appeared. Although he was in a strong position politically, architecturally his case was extremely weak.

The Government was assisted by the fact that it was the primary source of work for private architects. This made a huge difference. Earlier in 1965, a delegation from the RAIA, led by Ron Gilling, had urged the Government to increase the fee rate paid to consultant architects. In 1965–6, private architects were collectively paid A£1 million (A$2 million) by the Public Works Department, making it their single largest employer.[40] The RAIA was unlikely to bite the hand that fed it by opposing the Wood plan, but Hughes needed to be sure before he acted. No one saw this more plainly than P.N. Ryan, the previous Minister, when he charged that Hughes acted

> *for a political reason, and in the process the consultants [Ove Arup & Partners] and the Institute of Architects were brought in to bolster the case, the result of which was claimed to be a justification for non-continuance of Utzon as architect for the work.*[41]

Davis Hughes took a precaution before he implemented the Wood plan, to reassure himself that he would be able to find suitably skilled architects to replace Utzon's staff. For practical political considerations, the staff would have to be found from outside the public service.

On 25 and 26 August, Hughes set up two meetings with Ron Gilling, President of the NSW Chapter of the RAIA, to try to gauge the resistance he might encounter and to assess the local architectural profession's reaction. Utzon was away on holidays. On the pretext of seeking advice, Hughes sought to undermine Utzon's professional standing. This meeting was arranged on neutral ground at the stuffy Pioneers' Club in York Street away from Public Works and the RAIA. Hughes was accompanied by J.C. Humphrey, who had recently replaced Johnson as the new Director of Public Works. Because Hughes could not openly broach what he wanted to talk about to Gilling, he asked general questions about architectural ethics and client rights. Hughes then casually revealed to Ron Gilling his concern that Utzon did not have sufficient staff to complete the drawings on time. This was unwarranted because he had never investigated the matter or discussed it with Utzon.

To satisfy himself about the ability of Utzon's staff, all Hughes needed to do was call on Utzon's site office, which was just a brisk 400-metre walk away. It would have taken no more than an hour and saved everyone a lot of trouble later. It is a sad irony that while Hughes ran around painting Utzon as incompetent and failing to carry out his duties to his client, the RAIA elevated Utzon to a Fellow of the Institute. This was a great and much deserved honour and an indication of how highly his work on the Opera House was regarded by his peers.

Hughes's hidden objective might have been to sound Gilling out about the willingness of local architects to participate in his proposed bureau under the Wood plan. However, he could not tell Gilling this. Gilling slipped nimbly past Hughes's inquiry by reassuring him he was certain Utzon could find such extra staff as he might require – hardly the answer Hughes would have been seeking. Hughes must have been disappointed but he did not give up and a further meeting was arranged the following day, 26 August. This time it was also attended by R. Maclurcan, from Utzon's staff. He was present without Utzon's knowledge. During the proceedings, Hughes once more raised the topic of the adequacy of Utzon's staff. Maclurcan sensibly suggested to Hughes that he visit Utzon's office and see for himself.[42]

Utzon was naturally angered and appalled by Hughes's behaviour in his absence. Davis Hughes's inability to secure the guarantees he sought from Gilling may well have caused the cancellation of his ministerial statement that was due to be delivered four days later.[43]

⁂

Utzon's biggest battle with Davis Hughes arose from his demand for funding for the plywood mock-ups of the ceiling beams and glass-wall mullions. He wanted the Ralph Symonds company to do this work but Hughes adamantly refused to consider his request. The previous Minister, P.N. Ryan, had also refused Utzon's request for funds to develop mock-ups. Utzon faced an impasse: to be quite certain that what he proposed would work and to eliminate any possibility of a glitch later he needed to build full-size experimental mock-ups of the ceiling beams and glass-wall mullion elements.

With this out of the way, he would have been able to complete the working drawings and contract documents. Hughes utterly refused to give the necessary authorisation for the mock-ups and instead deliberately provoked Utzon. He was trying to push Utzon over the edge. Hughes was not stupid, he knew as well as Utzon exactly how essential the mock-ups were, and later had no hesitation in approving a similar request from Peter Hall.

This is a further example of Davis Hughes's obstructionism. To implement the Wood plan, Davis Hughes had to discover a reason for not paying Utzon. Refusing Utzon the A£60,000 (A$120,000) for the plywood mock-ups, Hughes had found his critical choke point. Without the mock-ups, Utzon could not produce final working drawings and Hughes would be justified in stopping payments to Utzon.

Utzon was a complete professional who went to extreme lengths to satisfy his client's wishes.[44] By contrast, Hughes had an overbearing manner and intimidated people until he got what he wanted. Because of political humbug, Hughes was a particularly poor manager. He seemed incapable of making decisions based on technical merit, and injected politics into everything.[45]

Davis Hughes was not in the least bit interested in architecture or aesthetics. When Hughes eulogised his friend and mentor D.H. Drummond, who gave him his start in politics, it was not Drummond's policies or his personal abilities and achievements, but his material monuments which Hughes considered worthy of praise: 'He probably has more monuments to his term as Minister for Education than any other man living.'[46] Drummond secured the Teachers College for Armidale in 1929, and Hughes may have wanted to rival him by planting his name on a far greater monument.

When Utzon met the newly elected Minister for Public Works in 1965, he entered Hughes's office to find the Minister sitting at his desk surrounded by easels on which had been placed drawings of the Opera House. Utzon was surprised because he imagined, like many other people, that Ministers for Public Works usually concerned themselves with housing, sewers, dams and harbour improvements. 'In my naivete I thought this was to please me,' said Utzon. Utzon was mistaken, 'Davis Hughes had decided to take over and become the man most associated with the Opera House.'[47]

Once he became Minister, Hughes quickly set about refashioning the Opera House as his building. Increasingly, Hughes defined the conflict with Utzon in terms of his proprietorship of the Opera House. As time went on, he appeared to lose interest in how much it cost, in cost control, and in completing it as soon as possible. The Opera House would be his great achievement. To ensure that this happened he had to get rid of his rival, the architect. Utzon had to be replaced by a less brilliant, less troublesome architect, who would do as told and not steal all the limelight from Hughes.

Hughes, like many politicians, could be described as having an edifice complex which he did not acknowledge even to himself. In a matter of four to five months of Hughes becoming Minister, Utzon realised this. From most normal perspectives,

Hughes's behaviour was irrational and counterproductive. Beneath the hard-boiled political exterior, Hughes wished to take over Utzon's project.

In the past, commentators on the Opera House have singled out Utzon as posing the greatest problem. What is usually ignored is the failure by Askin and Hughes to achieve their earlier political objectives, namely hastening the project's completion and containing the cost, with all the other unforeseen negative consequences their intervention entailed. It is because of their ignorant pettiness and shortsightedness that Australia missed its opportunity to have one of the great architectural marvels of the century.

Although his progress was slowed down by Hughes's refusal to sanction mock-ups, Utzon stubbornly pressed on with the plywood components. Plywood was to be used throughout the project for the corridor panels and ceiling slats; 15 m long and 76 cm wide bent plywood ceiling sections were introduced in the rehearsal rooms; and plywood was even suggested as a cladding element on the outside of the two stage towers facing onto the principal southern foyers. In the interiors of the two large theatres, plywood was chosen for the floor and seat shells, besides being used on the ceiling and walls. Furthermore, Utzon planned to support the glass walls using plywood mullions spaced at 61 cm, and protected from the weather by a hot-bonded bronze sheath externally.

Because Utzon's attitude to prefabrication was innovatory, he encouraged a wider and more flexible range of applications than was customary. By combining elements in different configurations, he also avoided the monotony inherent in repeating identical units which was the bane of modern architecture in the 1950s. Utzon published his ideas on prefabrication for the interiors in 1965 in the prestigious Milan-based magazine *Zodiac 14*. In it, he explained his solution to hiding the service pipe work and ducts above the irregularly shaped corridors in the base which his architectural assistant, Yuzo Mikami, had devised. This relied on two plywood elements, one a wide channel that leaned out from a wall, between which he inserted a horizontal paddle-pop shaped blind to obscure the service pipes below the corridor ceiling. The angle of the two elements could be adjusted to the width of the corridor in much the same way that a sitting person can adjust their leg for the height of the chair by rotating the lower leg at the knee joint and repositioning the foot. Mikami was delighted by the human leg analogy.

The mullions for the large glass walls at the open ends of the roof vaults and the low side openings presented a more challenging problem. In his search for an appropriate metaphor, Utzon was inspired by the movement of a seagull's wing as it lifts and falls in flight. Utzon illustrated the form principle with a photograph of a gull in his *Zodiac* article. The greatest hurdle now confronting Utzon was to make the plywood mullions light enough without weakening them so much they could not resist the heavy loads imposed on the glass-wall face by the wind. This resulted in numerous variations in the alignment of the glass-wall mullions. Standard 90 cm wide sheets of 12 mm armour-plate glass were to fan out from beneath the roof in irregular steps supported by glued laminated plywood mullions. The mullions were set back intentionally from the edge of the roof and inclined outwards to avoid any suggestion that they might support the roof structurally.

Utzon was right to pursue the plywood option. Plywood is light and extremely strong, it was comparatively cheap, and it provided a warm contrast within the Opera House to the cold concrete structure outside; besides which, its acoustic properties suited the auditoria. Wood is one of nature's wonder materials. Weight-for-weight, it is as strong and stiff in tension as steel. Its main disadvantage is the larger quantity of wood required compared to steel.[48]

Plywood is an improvement on natural wood because it is more reliable structurally and more uniform. The main objection to it was 'nail sickness' – this refers to the tendency for nails to pull out of plywood – and weathering problems. Since Utzon never considered using nails to hold the plywood together, this objection should never have been raised. Ralph Symonds could produce plywood with sheets of metal, bronze for outside protection, aluminium for increased strength, and 2 mm lead sheets inserted to improve the response of the plywood acoustic shell to low frequency, hot-bonded between the laminates or on the outside. All considered, plywood offered many other advantages besides its light weight. One of the great puzzles is why Michael Lewis from Ove Arup & Partners repeatedly objected to plywood long after his criticisms had been satisfactorily answered and rebutted, or why he failed to refine the plywood ceiling structure and mullions as Utzon had instructed. Ove Arups' renewal of the 'nail sickness' issue in its January 1966 report to the Minister, long after Ralph Symonds had advised Arups on 23 March 1965 that no nails would be used, raises some serious questions about its conduct.[49]

Ove Arups preferred steel because it was accustomed to designing in steel. Plywood was a new material with which it had no experience. Despite its early misgivings and objections, Arups' Sydney office did carry out loading tests on Utzon's plywood beams at the beginning of 1965. These went well and Michael Lewis sought the opinion of the Forestry Commission on the selection of a timber for the plywood veneers.

The Forestry Commission recommended coachwood and white birch over the white seraya favoured by Ralph Symonds: coachwood was significantly stronger than white seraya which was a tropical wood that Symonds imported from Borneo, however, white seraya was cheaper and Utzon needed to keep the cost down.[50] The loading tests carried out at Symonds's Homebush factory on the plywood ceiling U-beams also proved satisfactory.[51]

The strongest objection to Utzon's scheme for plywood acoustic shells was their suspension from the side-shell arches popularly known as 'octopus arches', on which the shell of the main roof vaults rested. Arups limited the maximum loading for the roof to 41 kg per m^2.[52] It is impossible to know whether this was anything more than intelligent guesswork. The roofs today seem inordinately heavy, much more than was perhaps absolutely necessary. There is little doubt they could have supported Utzon's scheme of laminated plywood rib supports for the acoustic shells inside since these would not have weighed more than 130 tonnes for the Minor Hall, and 180 tonnes for the Major Hall. Spread over the entire roof, the ceiling load represents a small fraction of the roof's load-bearing capability.

After announcing a trading loss on 26 February 1964 of A£200,000 (A$400,000) for the half-year up to December 1963, Ralph Symonds was placed in receivership. This was a severe set back to Utzon's plywood plans, but it was not the end of Symonds. On 10 July 1964, Symonds's receiver, Kenneth Humphreys, assured Utzon:

> *Since receivers have been in possession of Ralph Symonds Limited considerable improvement has been made in the efficiency of the operation and the company's output and sales continue to show substantial increases over the corresponding period of 1963 ... I confirm that the company will be pleased to further continue this research and to enter into arrangements for the fabrication, delivery and erection of the [toilet] stalls, glass wall mullions and Hall interiors.*[53]

The Symonds company then employed some 450 people. The aluminium-faced external cladding of the Australian National Maritime Museum built in 1988 at Darling Harbour in Sydney was supplied by Ralph Symonds, and there are numerous other important examples which attest to the company's long-term success.

If Davis Hughes genuinely doubted Ralph Symonds's financial stability, all he had to do was insist on a suitable guarantee, which would have been forthcoming.[54] At the very time Hughes raised his objections to Ralph Symonds, the Minister for Transport was entering into two-year contract with the company for the supply of plywood to the Department of Railways.[55] With Hughes obstructing progress by raising unnecessary obstacles, and in spite of the financial difficulties they were experiencing, Symonds continued to support Utzon by making available its testing facilities.

Hughes now proposed to pay Utzon not on the basis of whether he solved the architectural problems, but according to the number of drawings he produced. In other contexts this has led to the farcical situation of architects producing sheets of drawings for payment which are useless in terms of information. Utzon's first concern was to discover not just the best, but the perfect solution to each problem. When he reached this point, he made his drawings. Drawings are not an end in themselves, or some way of pretending to be busy. To be of any value, they must record practical design decisions for transmission to the building team. Davis Hughes was either incapable of seeing this or, perhaps more likely, refused to see it.

By 7 April 1965 Arups finished conducting its tests on the window-wall glass channel supports at the Symonds Homebush factory. As a result, the glass mullions were altered in a fundamental way to make them much stronger. Utzon imitated nature where the best strategy is to concentrate the material far from the centre – in the same way as in a plant stem. However, nature rarely puts absolutely all the material at the edge because the edge must be supported internally to prevent it from buckling.

In May 1965, Utzon completed a comparison of plywood suppliers for Stage III of the Opera House, which showed that Symonds was the only company with the production and testing facilities to meet his stringent quality standards. Shortly afterwards, on 18 May, Utzon requested that Symonds be named as the nominated supplier for the plywood elements and asked for approval to proceed.[56]

On 10 June, Utzon arrived in the Bennelong Point office and, to everyone's surprise, suddenly did a handstand and proceeded to walk across the floor upside down. Utzon was elated. The new 'hollow pipe' mullions he now proposed were the result of three months' work, which he had started after he became dissatisfied with the clumsiness of the earlier, solid, laminated mullions. Prototypes had been made of the new hollow mullions at Symonds. In two weeks the system drawings would be ready. His gymnastics in front of the office shows how important he considered the glass-wall mullions to be, and how hemmed-in and frustrated he must have felt in his dealings with Ove Arups and the Minister.

The design principles for the glass walls and the auditorium structures had been established back in November 1962 at a discussion between Poul Beckmann and Utzon at Hellebæk before Utzon came to Australia.[57] Before June 1965, the mullions had been designed as layers of identical plywood profiles glued together in an overlapping staggered section. Now Utzon switched to a hollow mullion section like a hollow yacht mast, to gain additional lightness and strength. It was planned to assemble the ceiling and mullion components at Symonds's Homebush factory and carry them by barge to Bennelong Point, to keep the amount of site work to a minimum. The ceiling scheme represented a further development of Utzon's patented plywood roof element system that had been lodged on 30 August 1963.[58]

There was still no common ground between the Minister and the Executive Committee on the plywood question. On 28 July 1965, Utzon repeated his demand for two full-sized mock-ups of the mullions and one full-sized mock-up of the complete auditorium beam in preparation for the production of the plywood items.[59] Ralph Symonds had all the drawings they needed to begin making the mock-ups. The corridor panels could be produced immediately since they had been fully studied and the units could be stored for installation later. In answer to a question on their experience in erecting plywood elements, Elias Ezra of Symonds referred to the company's previous experience in large plywood structures. At the 21 July meeting, it seemed Utzon would be given full approval. The Minister, R.A.P. Johnson and J.C. Humphrey were all present when Symonds received a tentative approval to continue with the mock-ups, on the condition that a satisfactory contract was drawn up for the supply and erection of the plywood elements. W.W. Wood advised that he was willing to consider a cost-plus arrangement, provided a final price was established on a time-and-motion study basis. In that brief moment, it seemed the way lay open for Utzon.

In August 1965, Utzon agreed to complete the Opera House by June 1969, on condition that work on the interiors should commence by January 1966.[60] Everything now hinged on resolving the outstanding plywood issue without any further delays. On 31 March 1964, the quantity of plywood required by Utzon's plans[61] was estimated at 15,688 m^2 of 16 mm plywood and 4273 m^2 of 12 mm plywood. The cost was further estimated at A£384,000 (A$768,000), which figure included the supply, delivery and erection of all the plywood components in the Opera House.[62] Even at twice the cost, it would have represented an extraordinary saving to the project.

At Ralph Symonds's request, in September 1965 Peter Miller, of Miller Milston & Ferris consulting engineers, unequivocally endorsed Utzon's thinking and sketches for the mock-ups of the auditorium ceilings:

> *There seems [to be] no reason why the whole ceiling should not be prefabricated and pre-finished. The erection procedures proposed would be relatively simple, and the tension supports proposed can be designed to accommodate considerable adjustment. Both site labour and the possibility of damage occurring during erection would be minimised.*[63]

During August and September, in the lead up to Hughes's October ministerial statement to the Parliament, Utzon's time was increasingly taken up with answering Hughes's questions and attending meetings with his departmental representatives. Early in September there was an air of expectation in the press. The media had been waiting since May, for four months, and the delay fuelled speculation about Davis Hughes's long-promised statement. News editors sensed a major revelation on the Opera House was about to break.

Press speculation intensified and the press in its impatience began to stake out Utzon and his family. First it was his office then, when he refused to talk, journalists started snooping around his Palm Beach house and approaching his neighbours for information. They even interviewed the real estate agent who handled the rental for Utzon's house.[64] Any gossip about Utzon was snapped up.

On 3 September Utzon advised the new Director of Public Works, Mr Colin Humphrey, that the architectural drawings were well advanced and invited him to inspect them. Three days later, Public Works descended on Jørn Utzon's office and three weeks after this Hughes ordered a review of the scale of fees for Utzon – by rights this should have been done by an expert and independent arbitrator, not a untrained politician.[65] On 27 September, at Hughes's office in the Public Works Department, Humphrey proposed that network analysis, which was a procedure that had been used in Australia for the first time on the North-West Cape US Naval Communications station in Western Australia, be used to organise work on the Opera House. Recognising the urgency of the situation, Utzon promised the drawings of Stage III would be ready within 12 months and despatched Bill Wheatland from his office to IBM in Melbourne on 3 November to study the applicability of Critical Path Network analysis and computers to managing the Opera House construction.[66]

Utzon was again quizzed about the number of his staff, and replied there were 16 in Sydney and three in Denmark, and he intended to hire four extra in October bringing the Sydney total to 20.[67] How Utzon chose to run his office was none of the Minister's business. Public Works was hugely over-staffed and inefficient. Utzon once more pressed the Director for authority to proceed with the plywood mock-ups which Humphrey and Johnson had agreed to on 21 July. Still no answer was forthcoming.

In October, Utzon called on Professor Cremer in his Berlin Acoustics Laboratory. The Major Hall still resisted solution. Tests on the Minor Hall had been concluded in June, four months earlier. On his return to Sydney, Utzon was accompanied by Joachim Nutsch, Cremer's assistant. Nutsch's arrival coincided with a major push to finalise the acoustics of the Major Hall by using the close collaboration between Nutsch and Utzon's Sydney staff to refine the auditorium shape. Utzon should long ago have undertaken something like this. The presence of the acoustician in the office speeded up design because Nutsch could check any change within days rather than months.

The acoustics was but one of a number of problems confronting Utzon, for he still had not found a way to provide enough seats in the Major Hall. The number of seats in June hovered around the 2600 mark.

This belated push by Utzon began to yield excellent results. Relating this to the Executive Committee, he observed, 'the building had progressed to a stage where it had developed its own style'. There were, he noticed, 'distinct feelings to be experienced both under the podium and inside the shell structures'. From everything that could be gleaned from the models and drawings, he felt confident 'the Opera House would be a marvellous building'.[68] The Committee was Utzon's only support now and he was genuinely pleased with the way the building was emerging.

Prompted by the Bondi and Oxley by-elections, Davis Hughes at last fixed 3 November for his ministerial statement. In the six months Davis Hughes had been Minister, except for appointing himself as Utzon's paymaster Hughes had not made a single decision of consequence. Even worse, his obstructionism was beginning to cause embarrassment. During the debate the Opposition in Parliament taunted Hughes again and again: 'The Minister has not indicated ... one item of approval that has been carried out under his Ministerial jurisdiction – not one major item could be announced to the public.'[69]

Hughes endeavoured to present himself as a strong man in control, but this picture disintegrated under the Labor

Opposition's onslaught. Taking a statesmanlike pose, Hughes unveiled the new cost estimate of A£25 million (A$50 million) and announced the completion date of June 1969. No sooner had he done so than he was cut off at the knees by the former Premier, Renshaw, 'There is just not one thing he [Hughes] has done ... He has simply accepted the advice of the same advisers [who advised us when we were in government], and has accepted the greatest increase that has ever been accepted.'[70] In a little more than a year, the estimate had shot up from Labor's A£17.4 million to Hughes's newly announced A£24.7 million – a huge increase of 42 per cent. This had resulted from the more accurate revised estimate for Stage II of A£5,295,000 (A$10,590,000), but politically it was extremely damaging for Hughes, who had pursued Labor for many years, taking it to task over similar cost rises. He now found himself in the same predicament. The experience left him smarting with anger.

Jack Renshaw spotlighted Hughes's ineptitude:

> What he [Davis Hughes] is really scared about is that an important section [Stage III] of the opera house still remains to be completed and he is now responsible for seeing that it is done. He has to make the decisions now. He did not inform the House of one decision that he has made for the future of this project.[71]

Renshaw's assessment was scathingly accurate. Davis Hughes was shown up before the House as a straw minister who had made no decisions and had not let any contracts.

Flustered and desperate, Hughes blurted out, 'If data were available now, Stage III could be commenced.'[72] The data was available, and had been since September 1964. The only thing preventing a start on Stage III was the Minister. It was Davis Hughes himself who directed that Stage III should not be commenced until after the Stage II contract was wound up.

Twelve years in the House, Davis Hughes was a novice compared to Renshaw. With the taunts, 'What has the Minister done? What has he decided?' ringing in his ears, for the second time in his life Hughes felt the sting of public humiliation. The only thing Hughes could say in reply, on the Opposition's handling of the Opera House project, was that it had not followed proper legal processes and had abdicated its responsibility. He failed to prove even this. Renshaw accused him in front of the House: 'You are acting like a shyster, not like a minister.'[73] Hughes had only himself to blame.

The November 1965 ministerial statement was significant, not simply because it exposed the tawdry nature of Hughes's conduct of Opera House policy, but because it decisively directed the focus away from the former Government onto Utzon, who could not defend himself.

The phoney cost crisis Askin had invented now enveloped Davis Hughes.

Life weaves its patterns with unexpected irony. Only long afterwards do we recognise a biting comment in some inadvertent connection.

In October, Libby Hall asked Lin Utzon and Joanna Collard to model Marimekko dresses in Sydney. Peter Hall and Libby (née Bryant) had visited the Utzons at Hellebæk on their honeymoon in August 1959. On her return to Australia Libby, who went to London originally to learn theatre design, imported the Printex fabric in the early 1960s and Marimekko clothes when the Finnish company began its fashion line.

At 19, Lin Utzon had only just begun her first year at East Sydney Technical College art school. Modelling the colourful abstract Marimekko outfits seemed like fun and she never thought to ask for any payment. With her beguiling Scandinavian looks, slim figure and blonde hair, posing in a brilliant orange and black floppy hat, she succeeded in making the outfits look more like a way of life than an adventure in modern styling.[74] For Libby Hall, it was a fortunate find.

Libby Hall was married to Peter Brian Hall. He was bright and chirpy, and had studied Latin, archaeology and English at Sydney University. For a short while he considered law but found it too boring and settled instead on architecture. In 1965,

Hall was a fiercely ambitious architect making his way in the design section of the Government Architects' Branch of Public Works, which he had joined in 1956, and a friend of E.H. Farmer, the Government Architect. Peter Hall always looked for hard things to do to prove himself. There was something inside him which craved a challenge, to demonstrate his superiority to those around him. Peter Hall was certain he was destined for great things.

Minor Hall ceiling, Sydney Opera House. Drawing illustrating the generating principle of the mother drum for one of the stepped surfaces in the acoustical reflector. Above: The mother cylinder from which all elements are obtained. Centre: Pieces of one acoustical reflector. Below: Contours of all the elements superimposed on the side of the drum to indicate the simplicity of the procedure.

16

A Conspiracy of Nobodies
Sydney, January–April 1966

> *The Opera House could become the world's foremost contemporary masterpiece if Utzon is given his head and if it is not spoilt by an attempt to squeeze it into the established patterns. What is required is that everybody, Public, Press and Politicians should want this to happen.*
>
> Ove Arup, 26 March 1963

The week preceding Christmas 1965, Utzon's staff held an end-of-year party at the Villa Franca restaurant in Paddington. The night was at once a vignette and a portent of the year to come. To begin with, the kitchen went on strike and the dinner did not arrive before 11 p.m. In the meantime, people drank, a few got very drunk, and one couple pretended to dance adagio as if at a wake. The night almost ended in a riot. Just as everyone was about to leave, a loud argument broke out in the kitchen. No sooner had it stopped than the chef burst from the kitchen and fled into the night up Liverpool Street pursued by the owner. The Villa Franca closed its doors the following day.

On the Saturday, 25 December, Jørn, Lis and their son Kim, who was nearly eight, left for a six-week holiday in Japan and Hawaii. Why Utzon should have chosen this moment at the height of his impasse with Davis Hughes to go away is difficult to understand. He needed a break from the tensions of the job and was struggling to get himself back to normal so the trip may have been in part a remedy. There may be no connection, but one of the very last things he did before leaving was check a report to the Tax Office and sign the accompanying papers prepared by his accountant.

The Utzons' two eldest children, Jan and Lin, had left earlier for Japan. Jan was studying architecture at the University of New South Wales under Professor Ashworth, who had recently been appointed Dean of the Architecture School. Lin Utzon had completed her first year at art school and wanted to pursue her interest in ceramics and textiles further; Japan, with its emphasis on traditional craft techniques, not only did this but supplied additional parallels to Denmark. She and Jan stayed four months in Japan, considerably longer than either of their parents, learning about traditional techniques in weaving, textile painting, lacquer work and ceramics.[1] She was particularly struck by the simple abstract stage sets and dramatic costumes of the ancient No and Kabuki theatre.

Leading up to the trip, Utzon was deeply depressed and despondent. Usually, it took three weeks of a holiday for him to return to his normal happy self, but this time it took much longer, a measure of the extent to which the problems of the previous year had worn him down. While they were staying at Nara, famous as an ancient capital and centre of early Buddhist culture in Japan, Lis Utzon, who was anxious about the state of their finances, wrote to Shirley Colless, Utzon's secretary, with a request that she make a second exact copy of the 1965 accounts up to the present for her to check when she returned.[2] Lis Utzon desperately hoped that 1966 would turn out better than 1965. Irrespective of what emerged, Lis requested Shirley Colless not to tell them until they had returned because she did not want to put Utzon's recovery at risk. In addition to being his closest confidante and minder, Lis was Utzon's business manager. She kept an eye on the accounts, hired secretaries and generally shielded him from a prying, intrusive world.

At the beginning of February, instead of flying directly to Sydney Utzon went by way of Honolulu, spending a week there, and he arrived back in Sydney on the 8th.[3] In Honolulu, Utzon had established an architectural partnership, largely based on commercial work, with Peer Abben, an old Copenhagen friend from the Royal Academy. In 1965, Utzon executed some sketches for a condominium development for Abben from Goddard's boatshed. Utzon spent the week with Abben catching up on their business, swimming and sailing. Well aware that his fame could be exploited and turned to account, Utzon endeavoured to separate the commercial side from his other architectural work.

Midway to Honolulu, Kim Utzon, who was sitting on the aisle seat with a great rucksack resting on his knees, Samurai sword over his shoulder and helmet on his head, startled a passing American. The man beamed at him in mock terror and inquired softly who he was protecting – the President, maybe? At this, Kim retorted disdainfully, 'I don't have a president, I'm Danish. We have a king!'[4] Compared to the great US, Denmark was minuscule, but it had its pride and its king, which, to Kim's way of thinking, made it vastly superior to a country that settled for a president.

Joachim Nutsch's work on the acoustics of the halls started the instant he arrived in Sydney on 28 October 1965. Faced with a new ceiling profile for the Major Hall which bore no resemblance to the Berlin model he had been working on, Nutsch started afresh. He was confronted by a series of problems, all of them serious. First, the hall volume was much too small. To achieve the necessary 7 m^3 per seat, Nutsch needed to raise the ceiling and widen the auditorium envelope.

The roof profile limited the volume because the ceiling was contained within it. In late November Nutsch found he could raise the ceiling by lifting some of the side areas so they were more strongly integrated within the main volume. By 12 December, he achieved a new ceiling profile for the Major Hall. His progress was protracted since, as Nutsch explained to Professor Cremer in Berlin: 'When [Oktay] Nayman and I finish fighting and sort ourselves out, only then the fight with Mr

Utzon begins. This means that we often have to start over again to come to an agreement between the three of us.'[5]

Everyone in Utzon's group worked with someone else. The special nature of the task dictated a co-ordinated approach because the solution to each problem had to be worked out simultaneously, in step and in the same direction as the others, and checked to see how it affected the rest. Constant discussions were imperative on the architectural, planning and structural considerations, as well as the critically important acoustics. Checking seating early in December, Joachim Nutsch counted 2738 seats in the Major Hall for the concert mode (of which 360 were under the gallery and side gallery), and 1850 seats for opera.

Nutsch summarised the acoustics situation thus: 'The problem ... is that seat numbers, floor and shell structure restrict the design of the hall to such an extent that the range of useful options can be counted on one hand.'[6] The height and shape of the roof determined everything within it. Returning from the Christmas break, on 10 January, Utzon's staff were amazed to discover while checking the existing drawings that Utzon's previous hall sections were based on an incorrect maximum allowable hall envelope supplied by his engineering consultant, Ove Arup & Partners.

The great battle of the previous two years had been to enlarge the volume of the Major Hall during concerts to obtain an acceptable reverberation time of 2.0 seconds. Discovering this mistake removed the problem.

On the Arups drawing, the prescribed outer limit of the auditorium ceiling was shown 8 ft (2.44 m) below the underside of the roof ribs. This was done to allow for the construction of the plywood auditorium shell, the assembly of the ceiling and the relative movement of the roof and the auditorium. From 22 November 1963 on, when Jon Lundberg mistook the engineer's 8 ft contour for the underside of the roof, he and Utzon had based all their work on this wrong profile. Lundberg subtracted a further 8 ft from the Arups' profile of the uppermost limit for the ceiling, which he had mistaken for the internal roof profile.[7] His error doubled the depth from 2.44 m to 4.88 m. The auditorium ceiling could now be lifted an extra 2.44 m all over, thereby adding a additional 2.4 m³ volume for each m² of floor area, and increasing the total volume of the Major Hall by 3142 m³.

The feeling of extreme embarrassment was soon replaced by one of intense relief – the end was in sight. A new profile was quickly drawn which, to Nutsch's critical gaze, no longer appeared to be a complete catastrophe.

Before agreeing to it, Utzon asked for a small wood model to be made so he could study the new shape. The new maximum ceiling limit helped Utzon deal with two problems: he could now increase the volume of the main hall without lessening sound reflections to the stalls by sharply tilting the connecting pieces of the ceiling forward towards the front and making them more vertical. This, in turn, increased the volume without radically changing the position of the main horizontal reflecting surfaces. The results were incorporated in drawing SOH 1392F, on which the new wood model was based.[8] The Major Hall ceiling which emerged at the end of the process was strikingly similar to the Minor Hall. Concentration resulted in convergence. Success was near.

By 3 February 1966, with the orchestra podium raised and fitted with chairs, 2518 seats could be fitted in the latest Major Hall scheme. Utzon was 282 seats short of the number Davis Hughes demanded but it represented a tremendous advance. There were various alternatives, none of them very palatable. When appraised of the situation, Professor Cremer advised Utzon against any further attempts at raising the number of seats:

> *Generally the reverberation time depends on the ratio of the volume to the area occupied by seats. I am convinced that your plan 1392H which I estimate very much and for which I congratulate you gives the highest volume which gives on the other hand useful reflections from the ceiling and which avoids coupled rooms.*
>
> *Any adding of further seats would acoustically overload the hall. If you increase the number of seats in a volume given it is similar to increasing of a barrel of wine by adding some water. You may fill more glasses but then everybody gets worse wine.*[9]

The 1:50 scale drawings of the new scheme were ready by 24 February and a model was completed on the 28th. On 14 February, Nutsch instructed Professor Cremer in Berlin that the model should be rebuilt for final acoustic testing. Politics now intervened to prevent that. Nevertheless, the Finecraft model of the existing Major Hall was updated to include all the latest alterations.

The Opera House can be divided into three parts much the same way that a symphony can be divided into three movements. As in any complex artistic construction, the division was not arbitrary. The platform was a symbolic extension of the earth; it expressed beginning and permanence, our corporeal earthbound natures. The roofs implied many things, such as an intermingling with the sky element, aspiration, and climbing a sky ladder to the sun. In the theatres we encounter the surprising third movement and conclusion, forms of extreme richness and refinement in their detail that are the counterparts of the intense region of our inner being. Arranging the construction in three stages reinforced its conception and division in its three parts.

The challenge to Utzon was to find a suitably climactic form. This was without doubt the most difficult task if he was to fulfil the audience's heightened expectations after the exterior. The hall interiors were the realisation of everything that had preceded them and were intended to come as a considerable surprise and delight to the audience.

Utzon's architecture is played out in a journey. From the ancient Greeks he derived the idea of people walking out from the city, ascending the great staircase, slowly threading their way around the sides of the shells before reaching the auditoria, where they descended to their seats in a reversed return movement. The unsuspecting audience was repeating an ancient ritual journey from darkness to enlightenment, from birth to death and then ultimate renewal. The procession winding around the Quay was a prelude to the rich intricacy and wholly unexpected voluptuousness of the theatres. As a work in two main voices, concrete and plywood, it had an introduction, following which the introductory themes are elaborated, leading to the final movement which re-establishes contact with them.

The theatre interiors continued to evolve as a synthesis of Baroque and Modern. They also contained a Japanese aspect, in an abstract glittering way. The hung plywood ceilings replicated a series of suspended tent shapes, which recognised a long European tradition of identifying music with tents as though their lightweight ethereal forms and sensuous curves somehow depicted the wave-like melodic forms of music.

The convex, wedge-shaped plywood ceiling beams, with their white and coral striped undersurfaces, gilded on the rising stepped sides, evoked the submarine exotic world of a Queensland coral reef. The reef colours were preserved in the coral stripes for the Major concert hall, a soft water blue for the Minor Hall theatre. The radial pattern of suspended curved shapes would have taken hold of the audience's eyes and drawn them implacably towards the stage. Utzon deliberately contrasted the outside of the theatres with the inside in his design to make us gasp with the same surprise we feel as we prise open an oyster shell and find, to our amazement, that it is soft and silkily lustrous to the touch.

Utzon waited until he was confident the interiors would be as perfect as he could possibly make them. Because he understood how important and climactic the final third stage was, Utzon hesitated. He had to be certain.

※

The mood in Utzon's office in February when he returned was upbeat. Everything was going nicely for once – the only question was how long this would last.

The erection of the highest roof was nearing completion and the last segment would be lowered into position on 5 April 1966. Sydney held its breath in anticipation. The building grew visibly day by day, segment by segment, tile lid by tile lid. As a gleaming sculpture on a huge scale, it also possessed a harmony of spherical parts which took hold of the imagination even as it drew the eye upwards into the sky.

Now work on the site was progressing well, many more people began to appreciate the splendour of the roofs. The building was huge, but because it was removed from the city and stood alone, it did not appear nearly as large as it truly was. Beneath the roof vaults it was now possible to see the structure of the concourse and bar areas.

For Utzon, the drudgery of meetings resumed. In early December 1965, Utzon had explained to his engineer his plan to use 9 ft x 50 ft sheets of plywood and asked for an opinion on their durability. The interiors were predicated on a maximum size sheet. Utzon likened the ribs to plywood boats and considered they could be easily erected using the stage machinery platforms. The electrical and mechanical services were to be incorporated into the rib elements at the manufacture stage. In this fashion the time for erection could be minimised and detailing could be more precise in its tolerances. And best of all, from Utzon's point of view, the ceiling elements could be mass-produced. Utzon had earlier investigated steel trusses in the Minor Hall in October and November 1962; at a meeting on 2 December 1965, he gave his reasons for abandoning the proposal. They included such problems as controlling the acoustic properties of the plywood panels fixed to the steel work, the added weight and increased tolerances, plus erection problems.

By 5 January 1966, while Utzon was still in Japan, some progress was made in establishing sizes for the internal vertical plywood diaphragms for the Minor Hall ceiling box-beams with a mixture of 1 in (25 mm) and ½ in (12 mm) thick plywood. On 18 January, Bill Wheatland repeated to W.W. Wood the urgency of a decision on the plywood. Ove Arup & Partners was ordered to submit, via the architect, a report about this for the Major and Minor Halls which was to be ready by 21 January. Later, Davis Hughes would cite it as a major factor in his decision to accept Utzon's withdrawal.

On 2 February, Utzon was instructed to submit the Arups plywood report to the Secretary of Public Works on 14 February, prior to the meeting with the Minister on 18 February. Utzon resisted, giving as his reasons: '... the Engineers, Messers Ove Arup & Partners have not put forward a full report on the structural aspects of my scheme ... Firstly, they have not, as agreed between me and their staff, worked on a refinement of the structure in my plywood scheme, and, secondly, the Engineer's report deals with some of the problems and overlooks others completely and so presents a false picture of the situation.'[10] He forwarded the report on the Minor Hall instead, and added the comment that at this stage it was not possible to judge the cost from the amount of material used and attached a full rebuttal of the criticisms in the report.

The important point to note about Utzon's dispute with Ove Arup & Partners' Sydney office over the plywood structures was that it was settled by 23 February. Utzon was greatly incensed by the attitude adopted by Michael Lewis, the partner-in-charge in Sydney. He no longer believed he could trust Lewis to act in the best interests of the job. Utzon now believed that Lewis considered the establishment of the Arup consultancy in Sydney had a higher priority to the Opera House. With the cutback in government infrastructure spending in 1965, Lewis's goal was threatened and the Minister's goodwill assumed a greater importance.

On 10 February, Utzon wrote to Ove Arup in London to voice his concerns and he appealed to Ove Arup to involve himself directly in the ceilings and the glass walls. Utzon began by explaining the problems:

> *I wrote to Jack Zunz once concerning this office here [in Sydney] and he said in a letter that I can only deal with this office here for the engineering work of the Sydney Opera House. This cannot be the case. I did not engage this office for the Opera House ... I engaged you personally because of the work you have done and we have been collaborating together very successfully.*
>
> *The situation is very bad, not unlike the situation when the first scheme for the shells was about to be scrapped. I have a perfect and ingenious scheme which takes care of every aspect of the problems in building the ceilings of the halls. I want that to be built and it needs your support and your brilliant engineering because your partners [referring to Michael Lewis*

> *and Dr John Nutt] here do not deal with the scheme and present an absolutely hopeless idea in a very amateurish way.*
>
> *I would also like to inform you that the behaviour of your partners here [in Sydney] is not professional. They are dealing directly with my client behind my back in spite of my telling them not to do so. This leads us all into trouble.*[11]

These were extremely serious charges. Utzon knew that Ove Arup had been 'slowly retiring' from the routine day-to-day work of his firm since December 1963. In Copenhagen, Arup reportedly said, 'I am playing around with amusing problems, building a bridge here and another there, but actually, I am slowly retiring, there are so many excellent engineers and architects in leading positions who will carry on the firm – in time they have become partners and this works excellently.'[12] From where he sat, Utzon had less reason to be satisfied with how things were going.

Utzon's letter must have come as a very nasty shock to Ove Arup. Utzon made the charges because he was desperate and could not see any other alternative. It would be wrong to dismiss his letter as unwarranted and perhaps as a sign of instability. He should have written in 1963 instead of waiting for the relationship to collapse.

Later, in 1987, Michael Lewis made a rather odd, if ingenuous, claim. Either before or after the Japan trip, according to Lewis, Utzon invited him for lunch. During their conversation, Lewis suggested to Utzon he should get somebody to produce the documents for Stage III – he even named Peddle Thorp & Walker, or some other firm of Sydney architects. Utzon responded that he must do everything himself like the other architectural greats. At this, Lewis replied acidly, 'if they're prepared to give you 50 years to build it.' Utzon is supposed to have said, 'I think I am going to resign.' Lewis cautioned him against resignation, saying, 'You never resign, because you don't solve problems by resigning.'

Although Lewis was mistaken about the date, the substance of the exchange and Utzon's proposal to resign is most likely correct. Lewis thought the lunch followed Utzon's meeting with the

Deputy Premier and Minister for Local Government, Mr P.D. Hills, which places it on 23 July 1964. Subsequently, Lewis stated that Utzon had moved to Palm Beach, which happened later, in October. Lewis was mistaken about the date of the lunch, as it most probably happened in February 1966 or late the previous year.[13] His account is most significant. It demonstrates that Lewis knew about the Wood plan to replace Utzon's office by a Government-run drawing office prior to 28 February, and that he was a party to its formulation.

Lewis may have considered he was helping Utzon by telling him this. The Government takeover may have appeared inevitable and, from his limited viewpoint, was desirable in the interests of everyone, including Utzon. Without letting Utzon in on his secret, Lewis hoped to persuade Utzon to go along with the plan. At the same time, being unsure how Utzon would take it and to protect himself, he did not betray to Utzon all that he knew about the Government's strategy. Utzon's charge that Ove Arup & Partners' Sydney office 'was dealing with my client behind my back' does seem, under the circumstances, to have been well founded.

Utzon must have been extremely desperate to even consider resigning. As Michael Lewis had said, resigning does not solve anything. If Utzon thought that Gunnar Asplund's resignation strategy would work in Sydney, he was sadly mistaken. It seems implausible also, to say the very least, that Utzon would have entrusted Lewis, whom he suspected of being a confidant of the Minister, with this most important confidence. Michael Lewis later insisted Utzon told him: 'Oh no, if I resign, they'll come back to me and that's when I'll get it exactly the way I want it to be.' To which Lewis replied, 'Well I think that's a pious hope,' and left it at that.[14] It was less than a pious hope but it was all Utzon was left with. Utzon believed unshakeably he was the only person alive capable of finishing the Opera House and the Government would reach the same conclusion ultimately.

If their positions were reversed, had it been Utzon who suggested to Michael Lewis he should sack his staff and turn the work over to a competent Sydney firm of consulting engineers, Lewis would have been outraged! The Lewis proposal was an insult. Prior to this, Lewis had reacted angrily to Utzon's request that he keep his non-Opera House work separate.

On 18 February, Michael Lewis withdrew the damaging report on the plywood scheme and five days later, on 23 February, reversed his opposition to Utzon's plans for the Minor Hall ceiling. In a comment on drawing SOH-1408, Lewis '… indicated that without further study, he was sure that scheme [shown as the third alternative] would work structurally and lessened the weight problem inherent in the sketch scheme indicated on the A's [architect's] drawing No. 1380.' At the same 23 February meeting, a lengthy discussion ensued on the prefabrication system to be used for the plywood-beam elements in the Major Hall.

The Monday before this, Bill Wheatland forwarded to the Minister for Public Works a comprehensive report justifying the plywood ceiling mock-ups in response to a request by Davis Hughes on 19 November 1965. His report detailed the manufacture and erection of three full-scale ceiling ribs by Ralph Symonds at a cost of around A£60,000 (A$120,000). He adduced a number of benefits: it would be less costly to integrate the mechanical services ducting, electrical ducts, electrical fire detectors and sprinklers in each rib, besides which, it made a higher standard of finish possible because the 'geometrical system inherent in the design of these elements [which] lends itself to decoration being applied in the factory and not on the site …'[15] Thus, by 23 February, every single objection by Hughes to the plywood ceiling proposal had been swept aside and adequately answered.

Ten months after he took over as Minister, Davis Hughes still had not made a single important decision. His actions seemed to have but one aim, to ensure Utzon would fail. Having already squandered nearly a year in his conspiracy to remove Utzon, he was ready to step up the pressure.

At this crucial moment, Utzon was beset by his own financial problems. These came to a head, and very likely were of such an overwhelming nature that, combined with Davis Hughes's continuing refusals, it became impossible for Utzon to go on working in Australia without a total revision of the terms of his engagement.

On Friday 25 February, Shirley Colless, Utzon's loyal secretary, drove to Palm Beach with the Utzon accounts. Utzon's sudden request to see the books took Colless by surprise. At Palm Beach, Utzon explained that he faced an enormous tax bill because the Commonwealth Tax Office of Australia demanded he pay tax on income for which he had already paid tax in Denmark.[16] Lis and Jørn then explained briefly what was likely to happen. If Utzon could not convince the Australian Tax Office to give him relief in the form of credits for his Danish tax, he would be forced to sell up and leave Australia. If this occurred, he would close down his Australian architectural practice immediately. So great was Utzon's tax liability that, on being shown his current assessment on 3 March, both Professor Ashworth and Stanley Haviland, representing the Executive Committee, reacted with unconcealed horror.[17]

Utzon's financial problems arose from his move to Australia in 1963. Tax was due in Denmark and Australia because, prior to 1 April 1981, no agreement existed between the two countries to avoid double taxation.[18] The maximum tax rate levied in Denmark was 70 per cent. From a secretary's pay of $6000 a year, the Danish Government took almost half, or about 48 per cent, and for high incomes such as Utzon's, the top marginal rate climbed to 65 per cent. Currently in Europe, Denmark still has the highest rate of tax.

In Australia, the maximum business rate was 49 per cent. It is quite conceivable that Utzon's combined tax bill amounted to 95 per cent, or it may even have exceeded his total net income.[19] A Public Works legal report speculated, 'If this is correct and the rate of tax in Denmark corresponds in any way to the rate of taxation on income from personal exertion in this country his combined tax rate might very well have approximated 100% or more of this income.'[20] Tax minimisation may account for Utzon's sudden trip to Japan, since travel expenses could be included to help reduce his net income liability.

This tax problem must have added greatly to his despair at a time when he was literally fighting for his architectural survival. Coming from Denmark, where even the charge of riding a bicycle while drunk made front-page news, his tax difficulties would have weighed heavily upon him and, in the context of everything else, possibly contributed to deep feelings of hopelessness.

Utzon's expenses were high and, while he certainly lived comfortably in Australia, he did not make a fortune – the reality, in fact, was quite the reverse.

Before 27 October 1965, when Public Works took over the payment of Utzon's monthly fees, Hughes had been powerless to stop the Committee from continuing to pay Utzon. After Hughes terminated this arrangement, although his fees were paid Utzon faced constant delays and ancillary payments were held up. The plan, very likely, was for the Government to slowly squeeze him. What it could not predict was how Utzon would react under such pressure.

It is unclear when Public Works first came to know about Utzon's tax problem. Possibly they guessed he was hard pressed financially. The first official inter-government notice to Public Works from the Federal Taxation Department in Canberra stating that the amount of A$91,310 (equivalent to about $665,000 in 1996 money) was owed by Utzon is dated 2 November 1967.[21] Since tax was levied on the net income, Public Works was satisfied that Utzon had an income corresponding to that amount of tax.

Jørn Utzon was extremely isolated: felt he had been betrayed by his consulting engineer who appeared to be in cahoots with the Minister and he had dismissed one of his own staff who had come under suspicion. The local architects were jealous of his commission and, on top of this, he found himself loaded with a mountainous tax bill.

If the past is any guide, Utzon would have asked himself what the greats in architecture – Le Corbusier, Mies van der Rohe, or Wright – would have done under similar circumstances. The only remotely comparable situation to his predicament was Gunnar Asplund's and Sigurd Lewerentz's crises over the Stockholm Woodland Cemetery (1917–40). After Asplund wrested the Chapel of the Resurrection commission from Lewerentz he resigned repeatedly.[22] Following each resignation he would be recalled and the client would acquiesce to Asplund's terms.

There was not the slightest suggestion the Minister for Public Works, Hughes, considered Utzon indispensable. The signs all pointed to the opposite conclusion. In Scandinavia, architects were admired and artistic integrity was deemed paramount – but it was absurd to think that an Australian politician, much less Davis Hughes, cared one way or the other.

Utzon's best, and possibly only escape, lay in the recognition by Hughes that the job was impossible to finish without him. That too seemed improbable. The design excellence of the Opera House was not Davis Hughes's primary concern. Utzon never really grasped that fact.

Well before this, when Ryan was the Minister, Mr Johnson, the Director of Public Works, had intimated to the Government Architect, E.H. Farmer, he might be called on to take charge of the Opera House from Utzon. Sometime later, Ted Farmer formulated a contingency plan to cover this eventuality. Farmer claimed later: 'It should be clearly stated that neither the Minister, Johnson or I contemplated or had in mind that Utzon should be fired ...'[23] The consortium was Farmer's idea, 'I suggested the idea of seeking the assistance of private architectural firms to form a kind of panel with myself as senior partner. At this time I felt that Utzon could be made to realise that if he came in as design architect he would lose no reputation and would gain a supporting organisation which would relieve him of the anxiety of project management so that he could concentrate on his own field.'[24] This explains where the fourth item of the Wood plan came from.

Farmer's plan was modelled on the 'Design Room', originally the brainchild of Harry Rembert who was prevented by ill health from taking up the position of Government Architect in August 1958.[25] Farmer envisaged the Opera House being finished the same way, with Utzon as one of his boys in the Design Room, but with the actual documents prepared by an outside firm of private architects. Farmer carried out all his large or specialised projects this way, and he saw no reason why the procedure should not be extended to the Sydney Opera House. What he failed to appreciate was that Jørn Utzon was not an inexperienced graduate fresh out of the University of Sydney, but an experienced architect with an international reputation who would react adversely to any suggestion of outside interference. In contrast to the Design Room, for whom construction was an inconvenient afterthought and secondary to the aesthetic intent, Utzon refused to separate the two and regarded any solution not based on process with abhorrence.

When Utzon met Davis Hughes at noon on Monday 28 February, in the Minister's office in the Chief Secretary's Building on the corner of Bridge Street, he had intended to discuss the outstanding A£51,626 (A$103,252) fee he was owed for managing the stage machinery contracts. This had been submitted to Public Works on 28 October 1965, exactly four months earlier, and he still had not received a proper answer. The arrival in Sydney of the machinery may have increased the sense of urgency in Utzon's mind on his outstanding claim.

After the customary pleasantries were over, Utzon pressed his claim to the Minister and asked to be paid and raised the subject of the plywood mock-ups which he indicated was causing a serious delay. Davis Hughes answered he could not make a decision without the joint report by the architect and the engineers, and drew Utzon's notice to the adverse January report by Ove Arup & Partners in support of his stand.

Utzon retorted that the report in question had been withdrawn by Michael Lewis. Hughes refused to accept this. When Utzon pointedly said this was incorrect and the report had been withdrawn, the Minister refused to check his facts. It was a stand off. After more inconclusive discussion, Hughes promised to give his answer to the A$103,252 claim by Friday, 4 March.

It was then that Utzon threatened to resign. No sooner had he uttered the words, than Hughes cut in with the reprimand, 'You are always threatening to quit ...' When Hughes persisted in this vein Utzon, exasperated beyond measure, leapt to his feet and cried out in a loud voice, 'Well, goodbye Mr Minister,' wheeled around and bolted for the door. Bill Wheatland, completely stunned by the speed of events, followed Utzon, sending a parting volley through the half-opened door, 'It's no good – *finito la musica.*'

The confrontation had lasted barely 15 minutes at most. Utzon and Wheatland left Hughes at his desk muttering, 'Just a minute … we must discuss this …' Looking back for the last time, Wheatland saw the Minister crouched over his desk, his face wreathed in a self-satisfied smirk. His play-acting finally had done the trick. Utzon had jumped into the precipice.

Utzon contained his anger and chose his words sparingly and with considerable care. Given Hughes's torment extending over ten months, his reaction was understandable and incommensurate compared to the goading he had endured over that time.

The world floated by in the distance like an unreal apparition. Utzon stood apart, a bystander observing himself from a distance. It was difficult to believe the events of the past half-hour had happened, and that after nine frantic years his connection with the Opera House was severed.

A motorist in a Vauxhall pulled over to the kerb and offered him a lift down Macquarie Street, but Utzon declined, saying he preferred to walk. On his return to Bennelong Point, Utzon drafted his letter of withdrawal. He wrote five drafts before he was satisfied. Shirley Colless typed the letter and delivered it by hand to the Minister's secretary. Not until after this was done did Utzon speak to his staff, to request them not to seek other employment just yet because he was expecting the Minister to ask him to return. Utzon's staff took the news calmly.

Utzon refused to listen when Bill Wheatland urged him to consult a solicitor before sending the letter.[26] Utzon's intention was clear enough – he wished to withdraw his services and that was not the same as a resignation. It was just what Asplund would have done in a similar situation. His letter read:

> *In the meeting between yourself and Mr. Wheatland and me today, you stated that you could not accept my fee claim for £51,000 for Stage Technique, which I have requested from you for the past several months and which is completely justified.*
>
> *I have been forced to set the 15th February, 1966, as the*

> *final date for receipt of this payment, and as you could not, at this date, 28th February, satisfy me on this,* you have forced me to leave the job. *[author's emphasis]*[27]

Finding himself without the support of the client, Utzon withdrew temporarily, hoping this would jolt Hughes sufficiently so he would behave reasonably. Utzon deliberately avoided all mention of resigning, that was Davis Hughes's fiction.

Most of the people close to Utzon opposed sending the letter. The Executive Committee, to a man, wanted Utzon to kowtow to the Minister. Some of them now begged him to go back to the Minister — because, whatever else happened, the Minister could not be allowed to lose face publicly in the dispute. Utzon had been called a charlatan, a money grabber, impractical dreamer and, worse, he could be blamed for everything that went wrong, but the Minister could not lose face. It was extraordinarily unjust. Davis Hughes had to be shielded regardless of his real intentions or any mistakes he might have made, even if that meant destroying Utzon.

Hughes held a press conference at Parliament House late that night. After ten months of inaction, within a few hours Hughes tossed the entire future of the Opera House into the air. Having haggled, obstructed and delayed month after month, suddenly, Davis Hughes was a model of decisiveness. The letter did not reach his office before 3 p.m., yet news of Utzon's resignation — as Hughes chose to call it — caught the evening bulletin on ABC radio at 10 p.m.[28]

Hughes's handling of the affair, the quickness of his decision, the instant round of consultations after many months of dithering, all point to the fact that he had been preparing for this eventuality for some time. Unlike the panic that surrounded his own political crisis in 1959, there was now a complete absence of hysteria. Everything was done without delay and with a minimum of fuss. For it to proceed this way so rapidly, it had to have been planned well ahead.

Hughes may well have been tipped off. Who told him? Most probably it was Wood.

Most people would have waited a day or so to ponder the

consequences. Hughes did not; he could not get Utzon's resignation to the press quickly enough. He knew if he failed to act quickly Utzon might withdraw his letter. This possibility had to be eliminated, otherwise he might lose his one chance to get rid of Utzon. Utzon could change his mind. It was absolutely crucial the news was made public immediately.

Picking up the telephone that Monday afternoon, Hughes explained to the Premier about Utzon's fees and the letter of withdrawal, which he referred to as a letter of resignation. Next he spoke to the Public Works Director Colin Humphrey, and later to Corbet Gore, the builder for Stage II, and Michael Lewis, Arups' senior site engineer.[29] Both Lewis and Gore went to Hughes's office to assure him of their support.[30] Hughes even found time to write to Cabinet.[31] The public was told only what Hughes wanted it to hear – he did not mention the plan to finish the Opera House, saying only that he would.

On the evening of the 28th Hughes announced that he did not foresee any difficulty in completing the Opera House without Utzon: 'a great deal of planning of stage three, the completion of the interior, had been done.'[32] One wonders why Hughes did not say this earlier because it directly contradicted his previous criticism of Utzon – that he was holding up Stage III.

Utzon's fate was sealed in August 1965, although it may even have been earlier. There was nothing even mildly spur-of-the-moment on Hughes's part about the events of 28 February. Hughes grasped the opportunity Utzon presented to him. No one would ever again accuse him of indecisiveness.

Utzon now lived at Palm Beach at the bottom of Ebor Road surrounded by the angophoras and banksias of Mackay Reserve. The thick bushland supplied news reporters and telephoto lensmen with a ready-made hide. They assembled outside his house around six in the morning, before Utzon left at 7.30 a.m. Using the backyard shrubs for cover, Utzon silently slipped out by the rear gate through a neighbour's garden into a waiting car. He did not come into the office that day, but went direct to a terrace at 89 Jersey Road, Paddington, where his older children were living. It was just as well – the entrance to Bennelong Point was thick with reporters.

Utzon settled himself in the darkened first-floor room of his children's terrace. Outside, a half-breeze snatched at the battered Union Jack flag on the upstairs veranda which flapped listlessly. Smiling as though the previous day had not happened, Utzon relaxed on the settee with a small white cat curled up for company beside him. Wheatland and Prip-Buus joined him and they went for a leisurely walk around the lake in nearby Centennial Park. In the bright late-summer sunshine, they discussed Utzon's options and made a list of nine points to present to the Minister. They were greeted on their return by Peer Abben, who leaned expectantly against the front gate. Abben, Utzon's Danish colleague in Honolulu, was returning to Hawaii from the Middle East.

In his reply next day, Utzon listed his nine points.[33]

Davis Hughes took Utzon's letter of withdrawal to State Cabinet on Tuesday morning and Cabinet, unified by the crisis, gave Hughes its unanimous backing to handle the matter as he saw fit. With victory in sight, Premier Askin issued a statement which said that the Government regretted what had occurred.

At 5 p.m. on Tuesday, accompanied by Prip-Buus and Wheatland, Utzon met Hughes in his Parliament House office with the Director, Humphrey, for a two-and-a-half-hour discussion. Utzon presented his conditions and blamed Arups' Sydney office for, in his opinion, undermining the client's confidence in him. Making reference to the 25 January 1966 report by Dr John Nutt on the plywood, Utzon pointed out to the Minister that the report had already been rescinded. When Hughes refused to accept this, Utzon rose and placed a copy of the Arups letter on the desk in front of him. Hughes turned away and refused to read it.

They then began the arduous process of considering Utzon's list of demands. Looking jaded and tired, Hughes rejected terms 3, 4 and 5, which would have given Utzon final approval of all details, overall control of the surroundings of the site, though not necessarily of the work itself, and an instruction directing consultants that the architect was in charge and the client agreed not to by-pass him by communicating directly with them and the contractor. There was nothing unusual in this: these were standard conditions which applied to all architects and their clients. The ultimate insult was Hughes's rejection of the RAIA's

The Utzon family house outside Ålborg, at Nørre Tranders Vej 65. This was Jørn Utzon's home from 1925 to 1937.

The dichotomy of floating roofs linked to the sky and a platform identified with the earth is exemplified by the composition of flamboyant roofs springing from Kronborg Castle.

Hammermill Wood beech forest, autumn, Hellebæk.

Utzon's first architectural work, the cabin at Ålsgårde, 1940.

The Fredensborg houses on terraces step up the grassed slope of a shared common, 1962–3.

The Fredensborg clubhouse is introduced by a pergola, steps and terrace.

Sydney Opera House, 1956–66: aerial view.

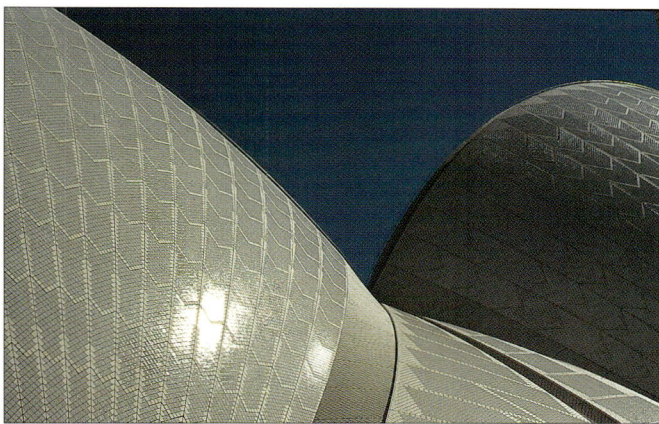

Like a ballet dancer, the rhythmic succession of the varying-sized, similar-shaped roofs in series is emotionally satisfying.

Below left: Restaurant and south foyer roofs: the structure is a folded concrete vault.

Below right: In the right light, the tiles glow with fire.

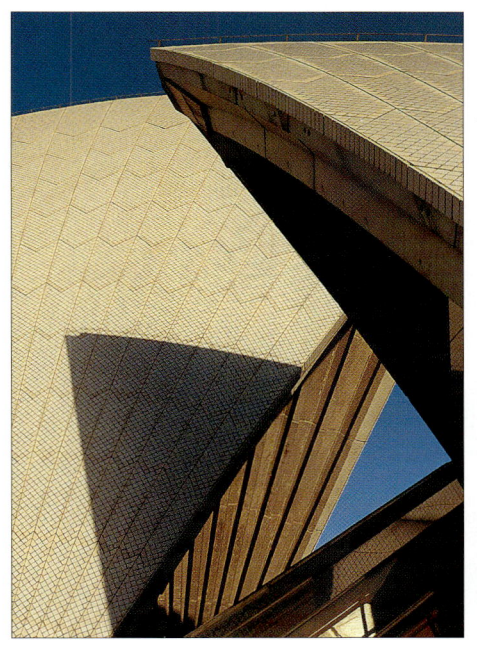

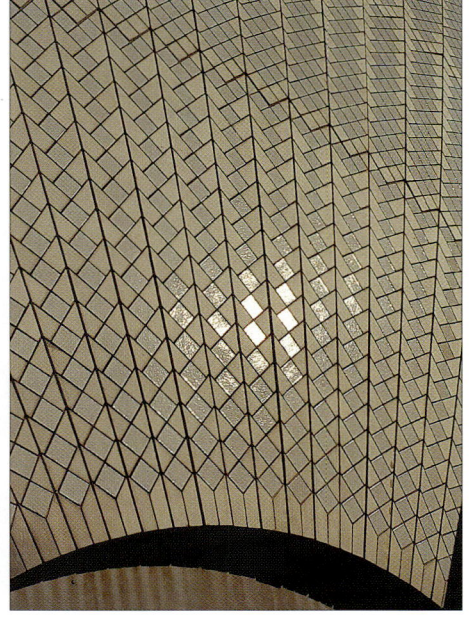

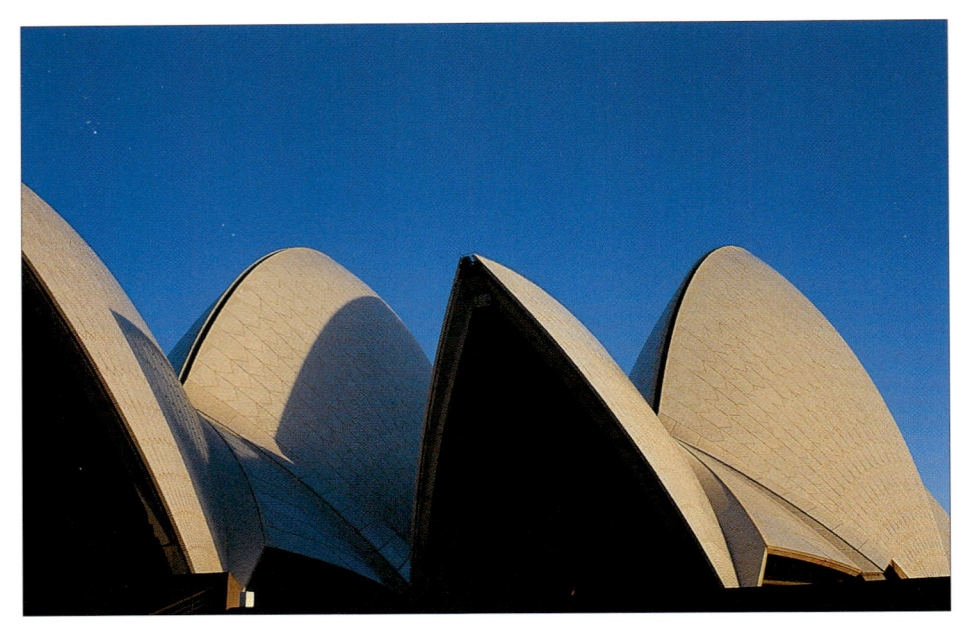

Above: South view of Sydney Opera House platform and vaults.

Left: Glass walls suspended over the second floor lounge/promenade of the Opera House concert hall.

Below: Inspired by gull's wings, the glass roof of UNO-X service station, Herning.

Opposite above: Interior of 'Can Lis', living room. Utzon's organic testament: simplicity, understatement, forms revealed by light, unity of material, allied to the vernacular. *Søren Kuhn and Arkitekens Forlag*

Opposite below: 'Can Lis', Utzon house, Mallorca, 1971–2. Like a small Minoan palace, it stands proudly on its cliff above the Mediterranean. *Søren Kuhn and Arkitekens Forlag*

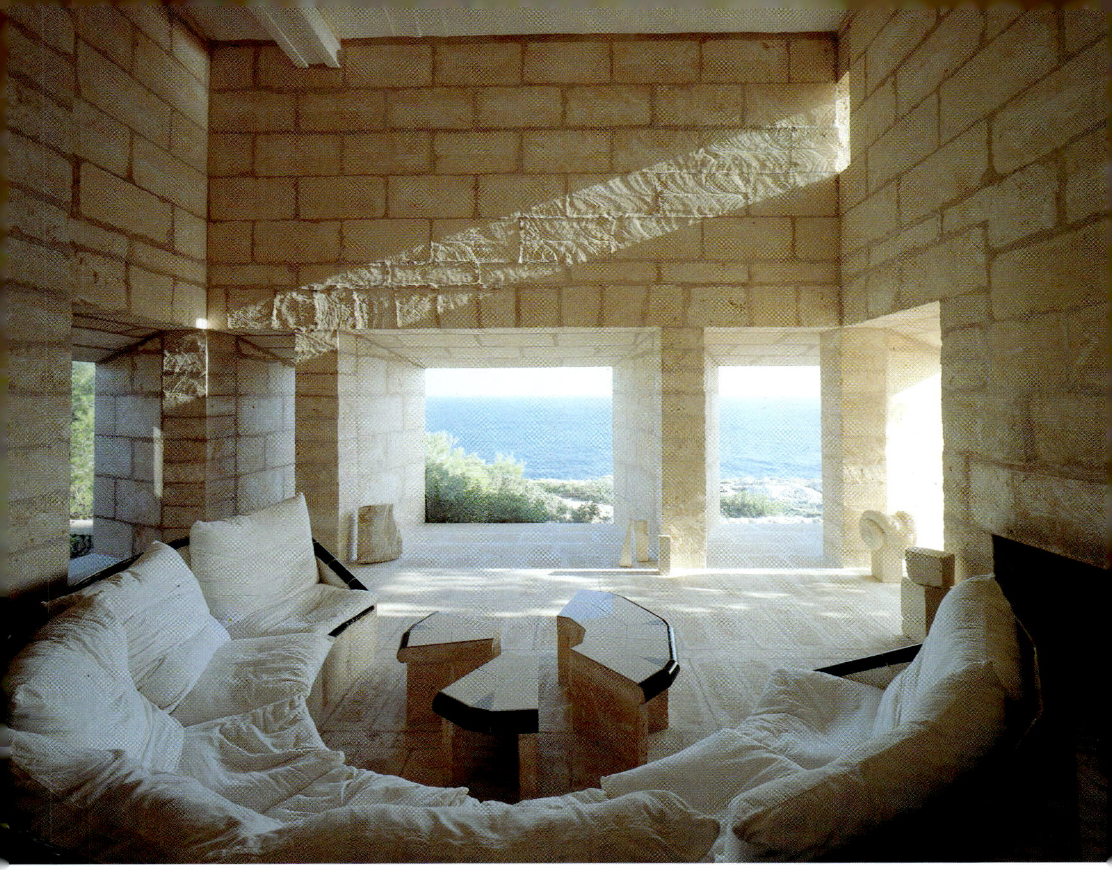

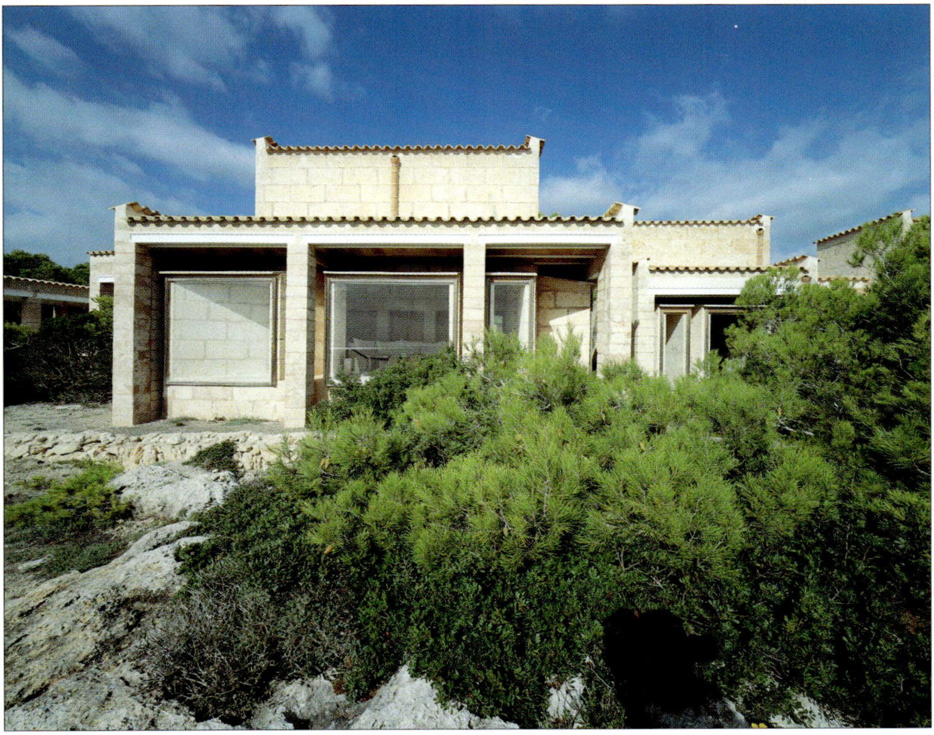

Right: Bagsværd Church, 1968–76; the north elevation and entry court are reflected in a nearby pond.

Below left: Using a kit of standard precast concrete elements, Utzon created the twentieth-century equivalent of a stepped medieval stavkirke.

Below right: Interior of Bagsværd Church: the shell ceiling curves overhead like a breaking wave to admit sunlight.

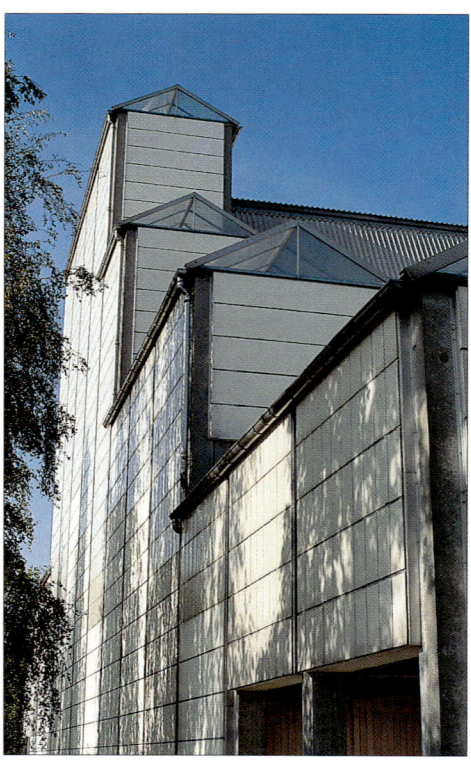

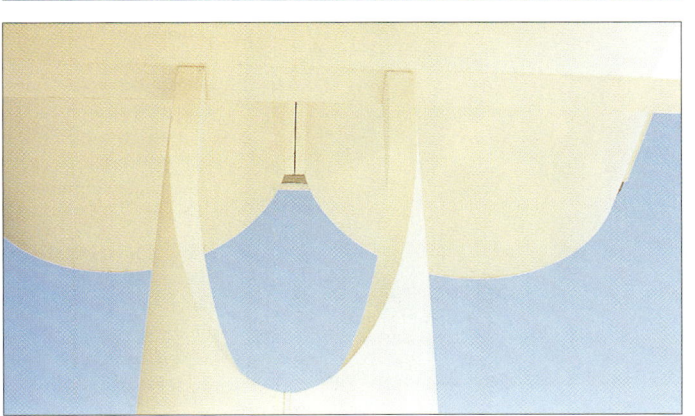

Above right: The porch canopy was modelled on the Anaiza black tent.

Above left: National Assembly Building, Kuwait, 1971–83; main south entry porch, with half-circular precast concrete roof beams overhead.

Left: Semi-circular precast columns support the north porch tent roof over Utzon's public square.

Below: Sky and roof join in a dialogue beside the Persian Gulf.

Above: The Paustian furniture showroom, Copenhagen North Harbour, 1986. The standard concrete elements were modelled on an eleventh-century Chinese code for temples using standard precut timber members.

Below: Interior of the Paustian furniture showroom: the standard column-and-brackets echo the vertical rhythms of the beech forest.

standard conditions of engagement, in particular 4 (j), not to deviate from the original design, and (m), that the employment of firms of consultants should be at the architect's discretion.[34] Hughes also demurred at Utzon's request for the Technical Advisory Panel to exercise final authority on all programme and technical matters through the Executive Committee.

It appears the last thing Hughes sought was a reconciliation. No matter how reasonable Utzon's points were, they had to be rejected. Any backdown by Hughes would politically cost him dearly.

In the strictly technical debate, Hughes appeared to be out of his depth and unable to comprehend what Utzon said. Right and wrong did not matter to Hughes, he knew that the real game was about perceptions, that in politics what counts is not facts, but giving the impression you have won.

The Minister insisted that Utzon be retained on a sub-standard professional basis. Worse still, Hughes refused outright to read Ove Arup & Partners' retraction. How could anyone negotiate with him if he adamantly refused to recognise a fact when it was presented to him in black and white? It was also becoming more apparent by the hour that Hughes lacked the acumen to grasp the issues being presented to him.

Utzon again reiterated his complaint against Bill Wood, the Department's aged South African departmental liaison architect. Utzon asked for him to be replaced by two architects who would also sit on the Technical Panel. Hughes resisted, although this involved nothing more complicated than a straightforward administrative arrangement. The ninth point, which called for a 'complete clarification of the terms of reference of all parties', totally stymied Hughes.

With Hughes sinking to his lowest ebb, Utzon was positively sparkling. Ironically, all the ninth point demanded was that the Minister establish an effective and unambiguous chain of authority, something he had himself been insisting on. The failure to define the Minister's and the Executive Committee's respective roles continued to be a source of inefficiency and confusion. To clarify this, in point six, Utzon requested that the Technical Panel should be responsible for all programme design and technical decisions. As architect, it was essential he knew who had authority over what.

The meeting ended at 7.30 p.m. Nothing had been achieved, there was no agreement on even a single point. Hughes was back to stonewalling – the only question was how long he could continue to obstruct before it became obvious to everyone. Utzon and his two friends slipped out the rear door of Parliament House into the night.

Hughes's game-playing was typical of conservative political behaviour. Lying was an essential element of the political game and was justified if it secured a desirable political end. Had not the Prime Minister, Mr Menzies, lied about the reasons for Australia's entry into the Vietnam War?[35]

The Sydney Opera House crisis has to be seen against the larger background of an increasingly virulent anti-Communist mood in politics. Vietnam split Australia and encouraged extreme views, and the Opera House soon became enmeshed in and part of the same opposition to the right. Opposition to Vietnam and opposition to Hughes went together. Davis Hughes, many people reasoned, represented the same politics of deceit.

Many people agreed with Patrick White when he said that Davis Hughes could not, or would not, understand the importance of the Opera House as one of the few truly worthwhile things to happen to Sydney in decades. For them, it symbolised a new and better Australia based on tolerance. One architecture student exclaimed, 'This isn't good enough Mr Hall – no matter how well you finish the Opera House, we, Australia, the whole of the world is being cheated. We will never see this building as it was meant to be [seen] and we will never stop feeling sorry.'[36]

The Opera House crisis united people in the arts and from many walks of life. The issue cut across class boundaries. It was a fight that encompassed decency and beauty and much more; the idea of a civilised society and the role of culture was under threat; undermined by the rising barbarism of the war. This lent a common theme to the protests as people rushed to protect freedom of expression as a main plank in a society in which art and culture were esteemed.

There was not much anyone could do. In the confusion

events moved far too quickly for that. Many people felt the wrong done to Utzon very personally. Davis Hughes's power was based on his rural New England electorate 560 kilometres north of Sydney, which was remote and parochial. The protests in Sydney may even have produced a backlash in the country and strengthened support for Hughes by turning him into a bush hero.

Askin held government by a tenuous majority of two seats. If removing Utzon strengthened his grip in the country and city, he had won – and in politics winning is the only thing that counts. At a meeting of the Armidale State Electorate Council on 19 March, a Country Party delegate felt that: '... all the talk among the cafe society by long-hairs and others about the spirit of the opera and mystique "and all this rubbish" made him rather sick. "Don't these [city] people realise that there are a lot of people fighting a war? Don't they realise there is a rather nasty drought about?" he asked. "Yet they want the Minister [Davis Hughes] to throw money about without heed just as Mr Utzon decides." The only spirit he wanted to throw about the Opera House, Mr Mair added, "was a few thousand gallons of petrol, with a match ..."'[37] The council's chairman echoed this sentiment by adding that Mr Hughes did not quite realise the degree of support he had in the country for the stand he had taken. Extreme opinions such as these did not go unchallenged. J.R. Ellis, a University of New England historian, countered by quoting Hermann Goering: 'Every time I hear the word "culture" I reach for my revolver.'[38]

In the Parliament on the Tuesday afternoon, Davis Hughes made passing reference to his plan to replace Utzon with Australians.[39] Hughes did remind Parliament that Utzon was not Australian. The Minister was impatient to end the negotiations with Utzon.

Within days of Utzon's withdrawal, Hughes began to implement his plan to install a panel of outside architects.[40] Three days later, on Thursday, Utzon's office learned that the Government Architect would take charge of the job with members of his team, including several of Sydney's leading private architects, supported by 30 or so architects.

On Wednesday afternoon, 2 March, at the suggestion of J.C.

Humphrey, Utzon met the Director and the Government Architect, to discuss the 'taking over arrangements'. Humphrey dryly announced that he was taking over and asked Utzon's co-operation to go over the details. Utzon had given notice to his staff to take effect on March 14. Humphrey intimated he expected Utzon's full co-operation and requested him to give the Government all drawings, documents, reference material and his ideas, which Farmer would need to help set up the consortium and complete the Opera House in the spirit Utzon intended. Anticipating this, Utzon ordered that all the drawings and files should be locked away to prevent the Government Architect getting access.[41]

When Humphrey stopped speaking, Utzon launched into an inspired speech about the work of the architect in which he explained his views on the architect's responsibility to his client, the public and himself. At the finish, the Government Architect looked very ill-at-ease and the rest were holding back tears.[42] Utzon's speech changed nothing. Humphrey and Farmer were public servants, they were duty bound to carry out their minister's instructions.

Whereas people were at first inclined to support the Minister, by the third day the tide was beginning to turn in Utzon's favour and a backlash was building against Hughes. The public did not trust him. After the initial shock, the public now had time to consider its verdict. Far too many questions remained: Did Hughes know what he was doing? Could he finish the Opera House properly? Would he spoil it without Utzon? Even the conservative side of politics had to admit it looked like a disaster in the making. The main question bounced and hung suspended in the air like an exploded tear-gas canister. Nothing about it made the least sense.

At around 12.30 p.m. on Thursday, a large crowd gathered outside the gates of the Opera House. The newspapers' reports said there were only 300, but the crowd was at least four times that. Students and professors from the universities, leading arts figures, architects – some of whom had been threatened with dismissal if they attended – stood around and waved placards proclaiming SAVE OUR OPERA HOUSE and GRIFFIN NOW UTZON.

Several people, including Harry Seidler, an Austrian disciple of Walter Gropius, Hal Missingham, Director of the NSW Art Gallery, and Patrick White, Australia's only Nobel laureate in literature, who came wrapped as usual in raincoat and blue beret, addressed the crowd. White, obviously captivated by the Opera House, pointed out that it was the most wonderful thing that had ever happened to unimaginative Sydney. Relishing the opportunity to bruise a few philistines, White observed, 'It is a great work of art ... I don't think others have the imagination to finish it.' Commenting on Hughes's plans, he predicted, 'All sorts of incongruous details would be stuck on by people.'[43]

At the end, the demonstration moved off in hushed silence up Macquarie Street to Parliament House where a deputation, led by Professor Denis Winston, presented a petition with 3000 signatures calling on the Premier to reinstate Utzon. That same evening Davis Hughes flew to Armidale, away from the storm.

On Friday Utzon saw the Premier, Mr Askin, at 4.30 p.m. in the Premier's Department. Entering through the heavy Victorian ante-room, he found Askin ensconced behind a huge purple inlaid desk. The little rotund Premier with the cheerful face listened to Utzon patiently as he repeated the story about Michael Lewis rescinding the ceiling report. Although he seemed friendly and receptive to Utzon's requests, Askin firmly refused to discuss any matters which he considered were the proper prerogative of Davis Hughes. Askin disarmed Utzon with the remark that Mrs Askin would not be amused if Utzon did not return! No one was quite sure whether he meant it. Utzon had met his match in charm.

In a show of concern, the Premier telephoned Hughes in Tamworth and convened a meeting early in the next week. Utzon was impressed and encouraged by Askin's attitude, not simply by his friendly spirit but because Askin promised to keep his door open. There was still hope. Before he left, Utzon agreed to say no more to the press than that the talks had been friendly and he and the Government had reduced the areas of difference.

Emerging in the dark at 6.45 p.m., Utzon left the Premier's Department by the rear yard to avoid a knot of news reporters. As he was poised to vault over a wall, Wheatland, with remarkable quickness of mind, grabbed hold of him and prevented him from plunging seven metres down onto the concrete footpath in Phillip Street. His quick thinking saved Utzon from serious injury.

In Bridge Street reporters caught up with Utzon and backed him up against a brick wall. Every avenue of escape was cut off. Surrounded, Utzon stood with his face screened by leaves, pressed in on all sides by the reporters, and attempted to explain: 'I have only one desire – to make an opera house that is good for opera, not a piece of architecture or a tourist attraction.' He said there had been many misunderstandings about acoustics, about things falling down, but he thought the Opera House should not be treated as a political football for the press to kick around. For perhaps the first time that week, Utzon saw some hope the dispute might be resolved.[44] During the meeting, perhaps on the principle that desperate men will believe anything, Askin justified Hughes's actions by saying what great pressure Hughes was under from his electorate.

The Government was jittery – it had not counted on such strong vocal support for Utzon. In a letter to Hughes on 4 March, the President of the NSW Chapter of the RAIA criticised Public Works's separate contracts with Utzon and Arups and expressed the opinion that Hughes had been badly advised. Gilling recommended that Utzon should be given full design control and stressed that an architect winning a competition should be commissioned to carry out the whole of the work under the Institute's Conditions of Engagement and Scale of Charges.[45]

Under questioning, Humphrey and Hughes misled Ron Gilling, saying that no one in Public Works had been authorised to make approaches or form a panel of architects to replace Utzon, which they knew was untrue. At 6.30 p.m. that night, while Utzon was in conference with Askin, Gilling issued a press and radio announcement categorically denying that a panel of architects had been formed to work on the Sydney Opera House. Furthermore, he noted, it was not the job of the Institute to assist in setting up such a panel.[46]

Utzon heard Gilling's statement on his return to Bennelong Point. After the horror of Monday, the fight was now turning in

Utzon's favour. By Friday, at the end of four days of intense political activity, the Government appeared to want to listen. Utzon could only tell the truth; for him the job, not his position or future, was what mattered.

In the tiny kitchen of the prefab hut on Bennelong Point which was their office, Gilling's refusal on the radio to assist in setting up an architects' panel was greeted by shouts and screams of delight. The unbearable tension of the first week suddenly dissipated and tense faces relaxed into blissful grins. Everyone had feared the Institute would cave into Public Works, but now Gilling appeared to be defending its principles. The hope for some kind of compromise was almost palpable following the Askin conference. Satisfied, Utzon told everyone to go home.

The media safari had just begun. Reporters went into a frenzy of telephoning Utzon's house at Palm Beach. Lis Utzon was polite but vague when asked about the whereabouts of her husband, saying he was in the country with a friend. Utzon spent the weekend showing Peer Abben around and ducking reporters. Lis and the children were less lucky, they were stuck with the constantly ringing telephone and answering the door. Talking about the future, Lis admitted they all enjoyed Australia and hoped to stay, but added she would not try to influence her husband's decision. That, she said, 'is his own responsibility and we will not interfere'.[47]

The crisis now entered its second week. At the suggestion of the Premier, Hughes agreed to meet Utzon at 3 p.m. on the Monday.

Though by no means universal, there was wide support for some kind of intervention to inject reality into the Opera House situation. At the same time, no one could say precisely what they meant by reality. 'Practical' and 'realistic' were debased currency, vague slogans introduced into the meaningless political rhetoric. What was a realistic price for a masterpiece – did anyone know? No one, it seemed, and least of all Davis Hughes, had the vaguest notion. Was it realistic to pay US$100 million for 18 F-111A aircraft that did not exist in 1963 when they were ordered and which, when they were finally delivered in 1973, cost more than US$320 million – three times the original estimate? Why was their case any different to the Opera House? Which purchase was more acceptable, an Opera House or 18 strike aircraft that could not even fly to Jakarta and back?

As before, Davis Hughes saw Gilling ahead of Utzon. Hughes was leaving nothing to chance. On his arrival at 11.15 a.m. on the 7th, the RAIA President was greeted by Hughes holding a copy of the draft conditions for Utzon's re-engagement.

Gilling, objecting that not enough had been done to bring Utzon back with full control, refused to discuss Hughes's terms. Word had already leaked to the press that Utzon was going to be offered the role of 'design control'. The document in Hughes's hand demoted him from architect-in-charge with direct responsibility to the client to the subordinate function of 'design architect'. Taking over from Utzon was 'a team of leading architects in private practice headed by the Government Architect to act as the executive and administrative organisation responsible to the Minister'. Ominously, the Trust was left out altogether, what its role was, or how it would function – if at all – was anyone's guess.

The Government Architect's plan to replace Utzon is dated 15 March and was drafted by Farmer's assistant, Charles Weatherburn who, in an extraordinary act of self-promotion, was named Architect-in-Charge. The document developed the earlier suggestions by Bill Wood in August 1965, which must have been in Farmer's mind if not under active discussion for some time.[48] In the preamble, Weatherburn refers to a plan to appoint a consortium of senior private architects under the control of the Government Architect.

At 3 p.m. Utzon, accompanied by two of his senior staff, Wheatland and Prip-Buus, saw Davis Hughes in his Public Works office. With the Minister were the Director, the Government Architect, Farmer, Chairman of the Trust, Haviland, and Professor Ashworth. Hughes outlined his terms and stated that he sincerely wanted Utzon back to ensure that his design was faithfully executed – however, this could only take place on the new terms.

The Minister's office was a large room in the sandstone Chief Secretary's Building. With its deep loggias behind Renaissance arcades, it was all majesty and style and gravity. When asked for a response, Utzon stepped onto the veranda so he could confer in private to consider the offer. At the end of three-quarters of an hour he returned and the discussion resumed for a further 90 minutes. The talks were now deadlocked. Remembering how much more amenable Askin had been on the Friday, Utzon dashed across Bridge Street to the Treasury Building, but Askin had already left. Hughes demanded Utzon's total capitulation and Utzon, in his desperation, looked to Askin to break the impasse. It was a forlorn hope – the last thing Askin desired after having handed Hughes the Opera House to get it out of his hair was to allow himself to be drawn back into the dispute.

Utzon succeeded in seeing Askin the next morning. The meeting changed nothing. After seeing Utzon, Askin and the Cabinet met and duly ratified Hughes's terms. At their meeting, Utzon informed Askin it would be difficult to complete the Opera House, not because there were not architects capable of doing it, but because only he could do it the way he wanted it.

Utzon rejected the terms as unworkable – the word he used was 'impossible'. Hughes refused outright to countenance Utzon's reinstatement with full control. By now it was obvious to everyone, including Utzon, just where the Askin Government was headed. Its only concern was to push ahead and see its terms implemented. Tuesday's talks merely re-confirmed Utzon's removal from the Opera House. Even the desperate appeal by the Opera House Trust's Chairman, Stan Haviland, to the Premier for an independent arbiter to be appointed to settle the differences was cursorily dismissed.[49] The negotiations were a sham from the outset, forced on Askin by the public protests. No one in the Government believed in them or took them seriously. Their only effect was to delay matters.

After a tense week of high drama, Utzon was strung out and at breaking point emotionally. Having tried Askin, he now turned to the Labor Opposition. On Wednesday afternoon he saw Ryan and Renshaw at Parliament in advance of the presentation of a petition in the House requiring Utzon's services to be retained until the completion of the Opera House. In the debate the former Minister for Public Works, Norman Ryan, roundly trounced Hughes. The debate made very little difference. In response to Ryan's accusation there no longer existed a legitimate basis for dispute between the Government and Utzon,[50] Hughes lamely replied, 'that a change is necessary to bring costs of the opera house and the programming procedures under a greater and stricter control.' Lacking any supporting detail or demonstration of how exactly all this would work, Hughes's attempt at justification convinced no one outside his party.

Utzon faced an excruciating choice. After nine years the Opera House was slipping from his grasp. At his Bennelong Point office he broke his silence. 'The final conditions put forward to me by Davis Hughes were impossible,' he commented. 'I can't accept them, I dare not go on.' He was tired and emotionally drained by the events of the week. Words tumbled out as if delivered by some inner mechanism unwinding within him.

'The main thing is the building.' Utzon was no longer thinking deliberately, his feelings plucked out the words as his agony spilled over. 'I am out of it,' he sadly announced, 'It is finito.' There was nothing more he was able to do. Utzon became overwrought and stopped. He stood there, choked, unable to talk and paused half an hour to compose himself. The whole idea of the final details, he believed, must be left with the architect. How could a politician supervise the details, he asked?

Utzon then resumed and attempted to explain: 'We have tried desperately to get confirmation and approval of our drawings, but this has not been possible because they [the Government Architect] have no staff capable of dealing with it.' That was a separate problem. While Hughes continued to oppose a settlement, no one could do anything further or act.

'We want to get the spirit and they have cut the spirit out.' Utzon saw his position very simply, 'You must have confidence, and only by having confidence can you help the architect, and that is what I ask for, confidence.' Utzon stood in a desert, his words, his hopes, the future, all swallowed up by the sand of politics.

In the wake of Wednesday's drama, Thursday 10 March descended to farce. On Wednesday night Ronald Gilling persuaded Utzon and Davis Hughes to agree to one final meeting. It was a desperate ploy, but sometimes desperate actions do result in a compromise. It was worth a try. To avoid the press, Utzon suggested they meet at a clandestine rendezvous.

The chic spy movie had burst onto the early 1960s silver screen in such films as *From Russia with Love*, *Goldfinger* and *Thunderball*, starring Sean Connery, and *The Spy Who Came In From the Cold*. Grown men, not just kids, were influenced by them; among them Ron Gilling, who probably considered he was an Australian James Bond, bringing Utzon in from the cold. In the ensuing car chase across the city through North Sydney's winding back streets, as Utzon tailed Gilling on his erratic course, every so often Gilling would thrust his arm out and wave it or point according to some meaningless code to give them directions. After half an hour, Utzon reached his destination, a sleazy motel at Lane Cove which Gilling owned in part. In Cold War fashion, by 7.30 p.m. the two teams were assembled.

There followed a game of musical chairs, at the end of which Hughes produced a rough organisational chart with Utzon's name illegibly scribbled below a hook at the far end of the top horizontal bar of the diagram like an executioner's noose. He was asked to agree to this. When Utzon asked for a fortnight to consider the proposition, Hughes winced visibly and the Director looked concerned. The timetable of their elaborate Schlieffen Plan was threatened. Hughes said he would think it over and offered to give a reply by the morning. Utzon won $10,000 to pay his staff, but the outstanding $102,000 payment from October which Hughes had promised he would decide on 4 March was rejected. For someone who openly accused others of lying, Hughes's own record for keeping his word was terrible. Weatherburn, who assisted Farmer, now insisted Utzon give his decision by Tuesday 15 March at the latest.

With this settled, everyone relaxed. Walker, secretary of the SOHEC, managed a gingerly smile, and whisky was poured all round starting with the Minister. Misjudging the mood completely, Farmer, the Government Architect – in what he no doubt thought was a gesture of reconciliation – walked up to Utzon and playfully tapped him on the chest with his pipe then added, 'I'm sure we will get on well together old boy.'[51] He was wrong: not even Utzon with his brilliant imagination could have anticipated how disastrous that would have been.

What Farmer and many others, including Gilling, wanted from Utzon was some token recognition of their worth. On his return to Parliament that night, Hughes promised to make a statement in the morning. It was Hughes's political needs in the Parliament, not anything else, which was now driving the negotiations.

Three weeks passed. Monday 14 March, opened confidently with a public rally by 1000 people at the Sydney Town Hall arranged by the Utzon-in-Charge Committee. There was wide support for the Utzon cause but it was diffuse and existed largely outside the main party organisations. Harry Seidler, a number of architecture professors, Professor F.S. Shaw, an engineer, who lauded the acoustic design, Dr Philip Parsons, a lecturer in drama, and Betty Archdale, the prominent headmistress of Abbotsleigh private school, spoke in turn and were followed by many others. None of them had any real political influence. Dr Parsons, in a speech loaded with irony, warned against accepting the great old Australian adage 'near enough is good enough' and 'she'll be right mate'. Mr Michael Nicholson, a 50-year-old sculptor, queried, 'Is this Australia? Land of the free? Now occupied by hordes, Bound to inaction and the telly,' before announcing that he would begin a hunger strike.

The next day, Utzon sent the Minister his reply: 'such a proposal is not only unpractical but quite unacceptable to me.'

Three days later, on Friday, the Government Architect appeared at Utzon's office surrounded by numerous reporters and spent five minutes taking over the drawings. That same day, 18 March, Utzon submitted his final claim for professional services amounting to A$1,583,636. He had previously received A$1,090,000, which left A$493,636 outstanding.[52]

While Edward Farmer was occupied with his acting on Bennelong Point, a crisis enveloped his office which challenged the Minster's credibility in a way that could not have proved more damaging. For some days, a rumour circulated among Farmer's architectural staff that they would be asked to work on the Opera House. On Thursday and Friday, 17 and 18 March, a petition to the Minister was drawn up which read in part, 'Utzon is the only Architect technically and ethically able to complete the Opera House as it should be completed,' and circulated within the Government Architect's Branch. Eighty-two architects signed it. This was more than three-quarters of the Sydney office. Fourteen of the signatories were senior architects.

The mutiny in Public Works revealed how disenchanted the architectural staff was, and what little regard and respect they had for their boss the Minister, whose political judgement and statements were totally at variance with professionally informed opinion. Their action was a decisive blow that undercut the Minister's authority and credibility.

A few even compared the similarities between the slanderous accusations made by the Sangallo clique in its 1550 plot against Michelangelo, and Hughes's disgraceful innuendoes and slanders against Utzon. Forced to defend himself, Michelangelo told the Farnese Pope, Julius III: 'I'm not and I don't intend to be obliged to discuss with your Eminence or anyone else what I ought or intend to do. Your duty is to collect the money and guard it against thieves, and you must leave the task of designing the building to me.'[53] The principle was the same: architects, not politicians, design buildings. Any other way courted disaster.

In behaving as he did the Government Architect, Ted Farmer, demonstrated how out of touch he was with his staff. Not since 1808, when Governor Bligh was deposed during the Rum Rebellion, had there been a serious mutiny such as this in the public service.

The first signature on page two of the petition was that of Peter Hall. Ted Mack, who later became a very successful mayor of North Sydney and an independent MLA and MHR in Parliament, recalled Peter Hall coming in on Friday 18 March and signing his name, while he fulminated about the horrible injustice done to Utzon, saying how important it was to keep Utzon on the job.[54]

The petition was leaked to the *Sydney Morning Herald* that afternoon and was published the next day, Saturday 19 March.[55] The Minister and Director were thunderstruck. The petition did not directly affect the Government's scheme to complete the Opera House by setting up a panel of private architects, but in the event that the plan ran into trouble it removed a fallback position, should they need to use the Government Architect's staff to finish the task. The refusal by Hughes's own architects to work on the project was a significant moral blow to his prestige, as well as a practical setback to the Government. At the same time as the petition, Farmer received word from Jack Torzillo of the Edwards, Madigan, Torzillo partnership that he was declining Farmer's invitation to head the new drawing office. Torzillo was Farmer's first choice. The Government's plan now tottered on the brink of collapse.

On Monday 21 March, at 11 a.m., the 14 senior architects who had signed the petition to Hughes were summoned to Director Humphrey's office. They were made to wait outside for an hour. As they strolled along the hallways for the meeting they were aware of PMG telephone technicians in blue coveralls with tape recorders going into the PABX room to install telephone taps. The meeting turned into a very peculiar affair – no one knew how to behave under the circumstances. In the Director's office, sitting shoulder to shoulder behind a large cedar desk with the Government Architect, who looked like death, Colin Humphrey waited solemnly. Visibly annoyed, he held up the Public Service Act and admonished the malcontents to make amends. The rebels were not given chairs or allowed to sit. Except for a complaint about their telephones being bugged, they remained silent. Farmer started to weep in front of everyone. He bitterly accused them of betraying him in the first insurrection in Public Works's history. They would never be promoted, he ranted, they were all finished.[56] At the end, they were handed a counter-statement to sign.

After intense questioning, the 14 refused to sign the Director's proffered counter-document. The meeting, which began with the Director firmly in charge, now plunged into disorder. The threats and intimidation had failed, no one cared any longer. The group returned after a lunch adjournment with a counter-statement of its own. The Director's attempt to nullify the effect of the anti-ministerial petition was sinking rapidly. The entire thing was a terrible bureaucratic miscalculation. What it achieved was a further weakening of the Director and Government Architect's position. The Minister had succeeded in diminishing his servants. What little moral authority the Director still retained was dissipated by his clumsy attempt to bully the 14 into denying their principles.

The mood in Utzon's office, which earlier had seesawed up and down as events unfolded, settled into a quiet, resigned exhaustion. At the end of the first fortnight Shirley Colless thought they all looked tired and sad:

> ... but the shattered feeling of the first fortnight, when we felt there might be some hope, has now been replaced, for me at any rate, by a certain fatalism and a great sadness. What I feel most is this sadness, that we in Sydney have had this chance in a world gone mad over the 'quick jobs' and 'that'll do, Jack' and 'what's in it for me?' to assist in the creation of something of almost incredible perfection and beauty, something which would have lived, barring a H-bomb, for centuries and boosted Sydney in a way that no number of curtain wall AMP Buildings could possibly have done ... I suppose ... in the whole of my life I have never been connected with anything so wonderful as this house — it is a dream building.[57]

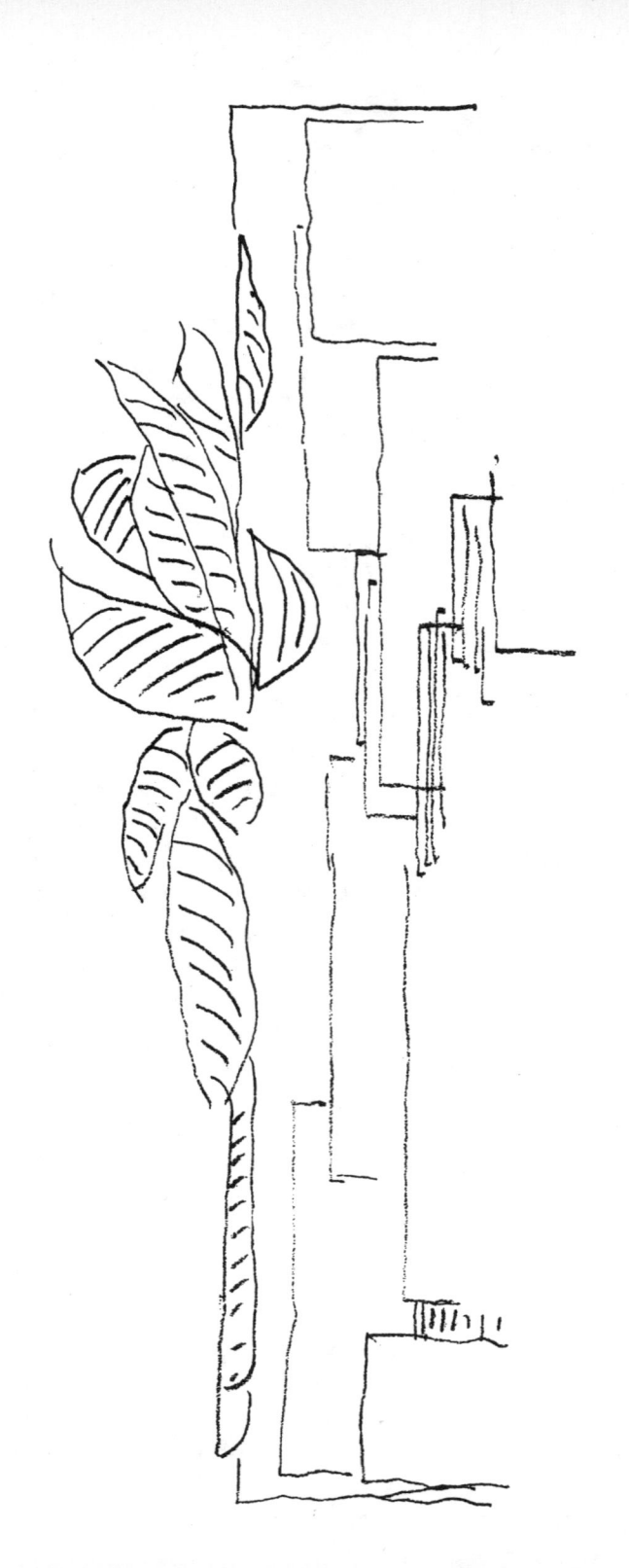

In an early sketch predating Utzon's scheme for his Bayview house, Sydney: a gigantic leaf-like roof spans the terraced floor – it can either jump across in a single large leap, or many small ones.

17

Tangles in the Web
The Opera House After Utzon, 1966–1973

I believe the sacking of Utzon was the greatest tragedy that happened in the history of the opera house ... His resignation was a loss to this country. It was also a tragedy. Now we must face not $50,000,000 but $85,000,000 as the final cost, but it is likely to go even higher. I predict now that this building will not be finished for $85,000,000 ...
P.N. Ryan, MLA, 19 March 1969[1]

A friend asked Michelangelo his opinion of someone who had imitated in marble several of the most famous antique statues and boasted that his copies were far better than the originals. Michelangelo answered:
  'No one who follows others can ever get in front of them, and those who can't do good work on their own account can hardly make good use of what others have done.'
Giorgio Vasari, 1568[2]

Early snow blanketed the Southern Alps and Sydney shivered in the dawn. That Thursday, 28 April 1966, there was an unseasonable chill in the air. In the afternoon, preparations at Sydney Airport for Qantas flight QF588, bound for Nadi, Honolulu and San Francisco, went ahead as usual. A few minutes before 5 p.m., moments before the aircraft door closed, Jørn Utzon, Lis and the three children clambered up the stair and boarded the aircraft.

Utzon slipped out of Sydney, never to return. He left behind swarms of disappointed reporters, photographers and television news teams, agape at the precision and speed of his exit. Their prize, the evening news story of the day, evaded their lenses and flew off into Hawaii's sunshine.

Fooling the press was Utzon's final triumph in Australia. Everything was carefully planned: he and his family travelled under false names and they arrived at the airport just an hour ahead of the scheduled departure time. Jumping from two cars parked on the tarmac, they joined the aircraft only minutes before it departed. The Utzons passed through the overseas terminal unnoticed, bypassing the customary pre-flight formalities. The ticket booking was done at short notice the same day to avoid it being leaked to the press. Utzon complained later that he left Australia clandestinely like a criminal, but the fact is he did so by choice.

One airport official remarked, 'Only prime ministers and dangerous prisoners usually get this VIP treatment'.[3] Utzon was neither a dangerous criminal nor a prime minister, but a relatively new category, a cultural fugitive like Eugene Goossens and the writer George Johnston. Utzon found himself at the centre of a raging artistic scandal which the media pursued for all it was worth. The unrelenting scrutiny left Utzon with no alternative and he fled.

Utzon was by nature an intensely private individual for whom all the prying into his affairs by the newspapers and interference in his family life, during the Opera House crisis, was extremely painful. Davis Hughes wanted the Opera House as his own private fiefdom to promote his political career. As has been said, his actions were designed to focus maximum attention on himself, and to this end he was quite impervious to the effects of his actions or the feelings of others. With the tax debt still hanging over him, Utzon felt he was left with no choice but to leave.

He definitely did not feel like a VIP. Quite the opposite. For some reason Utzon could not understand, the news reporters were only interested in him. He became the story and Davis Hughes was left alone. It did not make sense. All he had ever asked was to be allowed to do his job. He came to Australia to give Sydney a masterpiece. Why was he being hounded and punished? Why could they not leave his family alone? The atmosphere was different now: Kim had been involved in a playground fight at school; Lis and the children's lives were disrupted; it was impossible to go on living normally under such conditions.

Before he left, Utzon promised to come back in two years. That was his plan and he was sticking to it. He was not abandoning the Opera House, even though it looked that way, because he was convinced the Government panel would fail. In his final statements in Australia and for some time afterwards, Utzon repeated his willingness to return and finish the Opera House. When he left, he took an incomplete set of the Stage III drawings with him, leaving a second set with his solicitor, R.W. Nicholl.

Before going, Utzon talked to the Danish journalist, Bjorn Westergaard, and told him how stupid it was for a panel of architects to think that they could finish the Opera House without him.[4] If they did not alter his design, Utzon estimated it would be a year before they discovered this. Even in defeat, he remained bravely confident, 'If the Government wants the Opera House as it should be then they will ask me back to take charge.' If not? 'It will turn out a mess if I am not.'

Utzon was clearly worried. 'The architect's creation,' he averred, 'is largely in his own mind. No person can copy it.' He was certain of this. No other architect could possibly know how the interiors of the Opera House should be because only he knew and this information was locked away in his mind.

Utzon regarded his withdrawal as a temporary setback. He thought when Hughes came to his senses he would realise how indispensable Utzon was. Utzon did not doubt for a moment that Hughes would call him back. It never occurred to Utzon that this was not an option for Davis Hughes. Bringing Utzon back would be tantamount to committing political suicide. Askin would kick him out of the ministry and the Country

Party would disown him. Any retreat would finish Hughes. Utzon was naive to believe it could happen.

Utzon's structural engineer, Ove Arup, whom he had appealed to for help in February, arrived in Sydney the day before Utzon left. Even so, Arup still could not fathom why Utzon refused to return his calls. He came too late, much too late. The curtain had fallen.

Arup arrived a fortnight after Davis Hughes had announced the appointment of a panel of three Sydney architects to replace Utzon, on 19 April. The panel comprised D.S. Littlemore, Lionel Todd and Peter Hall, under the direction of the 57-year-old Government Architect, E.H. Farmer. To replace Utzon, Hughes appointed not one, but four architects! George Molnar hit the mark with his biting cartoon: 'Mr Hughes is right. We must have control of expenditure, whatever it may cost.'

Utzon's departure abruptly closed the creative phase of the Sydney Opera House and disrupted the continuity of its design development. With Utzon's link to his creation irretrievably ruptured, it was inconceivable that the Sydney Opera House would ever amount to much more than a flawed half-masterpiece. Norman Ryan was correct when he said that it was the greatest tragedy that happened to the Opera House and a great loss for Australia.

Letters of support for Utzon flooded in from around the world. Some 26 eminent architects and academics sent telegrams. Their opinions made no difference and were quickly brushed aside by the Askin Government.[5] Neither the world's leading architects nor world opinion voted at general elections.

Throughout March and April, Utzon had worked on preparing his claim for outstanding fees from the NSW Government at 18 Windsor Street, Paddington. Closing down his office entailed finishing the accounts, paying salaries, etc. By Wednesday, 6 April, the accounts were done and Utzon decided to have a last picnic at Palm Beach. He chose one of his favourite spots, a sandstone rock ledge at the south end of the beach past the rock pool. At the cliff base, the wind had sculpted a veranda deck complete with bench seat and protruding canopy.

It was a sunny day with the deep blue swell of the sea dashing against the rocks and rolling waves of coruscated water flashing in the sunlight. Loading their trays with lobster, chicken and beer, the office lazed about and soaked up the afternoon sun. It was typical of Utzon's style – keeping everything open and unpretentious, yet looking out for everyone. It was a dismal, melancholy afternoon which downplayed the tragedy of the end of Utzon's Opera House. Because Utzon's staff were so young, most in their early to mid twenties, with the oldest maybe 35, they found it difficult to absorb that this was really the end.

Utzon was in good form. He fought the crisis with humour, poking fun and joking. Laughter buoyed up everyone's spirits even on the most depressing days. Utzon loved to impersonate people such as Ron Gilling pretending he was a mad antipodean James Bond with his Beretta blazing away on a wild car chase up and down North Sydney's maze of streets instead of Nice. The farewell barbecue took place the day before the last segment of the big A2 shell was dropped into position. The coincidence lent a sense of finality, a certain closure, to the proceedings because it vindicated Utzon, even in his hour of defeat. No matter what Davis Hughes said or did, it was his roof and his building. No politician could take that away from him.

Utzon's first stop after Sydney was Honolulu for a break. After a few weeks there and talks with Peer Abben, he planned to go on to Mexico and Denmark, to start work on the final drawings for the Asger Jorn Museum at Silkeborg.

At the same time that he left Sydney, when everything appeared so negative for him, Utzon was notified he had been awarded the Bund Deutscher Arkitekten Prize and Plaque for the Sydney Opera House. Normally the prize was given to a German; in 1966, however, the German architects' association decided to make a radical departure from its established rule and award its prize to Utzon.

Coming when it did it was an especially bitter irony, but for Utzon the coincidence further enhanced the award's significance. When Utzon wrote to the Germans at the height of his confrontation with Davis Hughes to suggest they withdraw their prize, they refused to do so. This pleased him even more. The ceremony at Lübeck in West Germany was something positive to look forward to, especially in view of Germany's reputation as one of the great architectural cultures of the twentieth century.[6]

Utzon never completed another project which was dear to his heart – his Bayview Heights house. The first proposal was submitted to Warringah Council in February 1964. The fourth and final scheme only received approval on 23 December 1965, by which time it was too late. He retained the ideas from the Bayview house. The effort was not wasted entirely – the imagination after all, is portable. The Bayview house served as a dress rehearsal for his house at Porto Petro on Mallorca in 1971.

For over two years Utzon had studied a range of alternatives for the Bayview Heights house. His family was almost grown up. The two oldest children, Jan and Lin, were young adults in their early twenties. Ten years separated them from his youngest, Kim. Utzon wanted a dwelling that would allow them all to live together harmoniously, which simultaneously would provide greater autonomy for the two older children.

On 16 April 1964, Utzon had written to Warringah Council setting out his approach and explaining why he had split the dwelling into three units on the large six-acre site. The main unit would be used by Utzon, his wife and son Kim; the guest house was for his two older children who needed the greater freedom this arrangement would provide; and the studio was needed to keep the private and professional activities separate. Council disagreed; it regarded what he was proposing as constituting two dwellings and demanded that he should subdivide the site.

After three months, Utzon replied: '... from the experience of the family's life, it is a must that these three regions are separated, and from the point of view of the existing landscape, it is also preferable to have 3 smaller units.'[7]

The first scheme of three units is dated 5 March 1964, and

consisted of a main house facing north, a guest house some distance to the west, and the studio further up the hill behind the main unit. Road access was from the west: the road curled up and past the two smaller units before terminating at the rear courtyard of the main house. The courtyard in the south-eastern corner led into an elaborately terraced living area and sun deck at the front with a series of small bedrooms on one side, and the dining area below the courtyard, forming a solid exposed bastion in the north-eastern corner.

Utzon intended to test the aluminium-covered plywood U-beam patent which he developed in conjunction with Ralph Symonds by using them as a roof. The beams would rest on a double 38 cm thick skin of horizontal concrete precast wall elements, made by placing the elements one on top of the other. The assembled wall elements were held in place by vertical tie rods. Sitting on top, the plywood U-beams were waterproofed by capping the adjacent vertical blade with a half-round aluminium cover piece. The introduction of the multi-functional U-beams – which acted both as roof covering, insulation and skylights – freed up the interior by eliminating the need for internal structural supports, so the house could be developed as a series of interconnected terraces down the hillside.

Utzon took pleasure in natural features such as a lake, a little river or, in the case of Bayview, the hilltop, which became a springboard. On his visit to Frank Lloyd Wright's rambling complex Taliesin East at Spring Green, Wisconsin, in 1949, Utzon was much taken by the gentle way that Wright had subordinated his building form by placing it below the brow of the hill. Taliesin is Welsh for 'shining brow'. Similarly, Utzon wanted to maintain the green eucalypt brow above the Bayview house. To ensure this happened he placed a covenant on a large portion of the site to protect the vegetation and the natural profile of the hilltop seen from Pittwater and Mona Vale.

Like a sculpture with its stepped side walls, the Bayview house took up where Fredensborg left off. There was a significant difference. The Bayview house was less self-contained, more open; spatially, it reached out to the horizon between the dual arms of its side walls. Initially, Utzon visualised the roof as a burgeoning, leaf-like growth whose folded leaflets spread sideways to enfold the 15 m wide space. A sketch caption summarised his premise:

> *The roof can be hanging above, it can be spanning across or jumping over you in one big leap or in many small ones. The problem is to master the water-proofing, the structural requirements and the heat insulation in one mass-produced element, which in combination with itself can give various roof-forms, a nice problem to be solved.*
> *This platform, courtyard-house shows a vivid roof-grouping formed by such an element-composition.*[8]

Utzon was very aware of the sun in Australia. In the main unit and the guest house, the living areas that face towards Pittwater have sun decks at the front. In the guest house, a small swimming pool was added to the sun deck to bounce the light inside. In all three units, the landscape is held and framed at the sides. Indeed, the fronts of the units resemble a proscenium arch in the theatre. The deliberate use of the stage opening as a frame, after the example of the frame around a painting, has a limiting function. At the same time that Utzon appears to release the interior into the landscape by removing all interior supports and divisions, he introduces a frame to limit it and by this means gives it a centre, so we have a focus. Thus the front of his house becomes a kind of modified veranda, layered in depth. The house is a stage with its terraced floor ascending in steps towards the pierced front of its proscenium opening. Utzon turns life into a play by transforming the house into a stage.

The later changes to the plans were mostly directed at consolidating the site layout and reducing the complexity of the internal planning. Utzon was preoccupied with developing the roof and precast concrete wall elements and, to a considerable extent, this took precedence over everything else – to the detriment of the earlier idea of lightness and opening up the house to the bush around it.

To gain council approval, on 25 November 1964 Utzon attached the guest house to the main building, on the east side of the main entry courtyard. This was given approval in principle in December. By then, two prototype plywood U-beams had been fabricated for the Bayview house. In November, a full size U-beam was tested and approved at the Ralph Symonds factory by Peter Miller, an engineer Utzon had brought in as a consultant.

In May 1965, the much-simplified design had almost reached its final form. This saw the formerly separate house units drawn closer together into a consolidated composition divided into a living wing linked to a bedroom wing, with the studio still isolated from the rest. The three units now fanned out across the hill in an array perpendicular to the contours, so as to give each an exclusive framed view of Pittwater. The width of each unit was regulated by the standard 15 m dimension of the roof U-beams. In general, Utzon began by planning the two side walls 15 m apart, after which he placed the plywood beams on top spanning across them. This resulted in stubby boxes that were not nearly as graceful as his horizontally extended 1950 Hellebæk house.

The idea of parallel walls and the roof beams stepping up and down, together with the minimum of internal divisions, was the same as in the Melli Bank, Teheran and the later Bagsværd Church. In a third scheme, Utzon shifted the courtyard from the back around to the west, in the middle between the living area and the dining area at the back.

A few days before he left for Japan, on 17 December 1965, Utzon had lodged the final development application based on a new concrete plank wall system. It was similar to the previous scheme, except now the rear courtyard was replaced by a covered terrace and the living wing was more compact and self-contained than before. Where the living area overlooked Pittwater, Utzon broke into the strong boundary walls and opened up the ends at the front. The side walls now resembled horse blinkers and stuck out past a pair of terraces at the front, in order to trap the view across the front more strongly. It was gaol-like and introverted, the fortified severity of the side walls being reinforced rather than relieved by the stepped section. In places, gaps between the roof U-beams admitted sunlight into the enclosed, covered, terrace areas.

Utzon never fully resolved the conflict between his new plywood beams and his attempt to create a more open, unconfined exposure of the interior to the outside landscape. The proportions of the house are awkward and reflect both the standard plywood beam and the module of the new concrete plank wall system. Everything inside is subordinate to the movement from up the hill, down the terraces to the view of Pittwater. In contrast to the more subtle, Japanese way of concealing the prospect as a surprise until the last moment, Utzon is a little too obvious.

The Bayview house had little in common with Utzon's initial vision of a house riding over the waves of sandstone and the spiky heads of blackboy grasstrees like a boat. The roof, it is true, resembles a collection of boats roughly lashed together across the side walls, but the parallel ends there. Utzon started out with the idea of a light, shimmering object open to the bush around it. At the end, only the roof expressed this – the rest is weighty, tightly bound within itself, and rests heavily on the earth.

At Bayview, Utzon continued the contrasting interplay between ground-based forms and floating cloud-like roof structures. One was static and heavy denoting permanence, the other weightless and dynamic, denoting transformation.

As in the Opera House, Utzon settled for two materials, concrete and plywood. The same precast concrete planks were to be employed in the floor and the walls and, resting on the side walls, he laid the plywood U-beams side by side so they looked like a cloud ceiling. Utzon was fascinated by such natural phenomena as gaps in clouds which produced beams of sunlight that illuminate just one spot on the ground. He wanted to create a similar effect in the Bayview house by admitting an occasional beam. In his later house on Mallorca, this effect was realised by leaving a high opening that allowed a slanting beam of light to rip through the dark interior.

Peter Hall was born on 16 May 1931, at Narrabri, a small country town on the Namoi River in the north-west of New South

Wales. He was the only child of the local postal inspector. His start in life came in the form of a scholarship to Cranbrook, a fashionable private school in East Sydney. From then on, he cut himself off socially from country life. He had escaped from the bush and never went back.

At Cranbrook, Hall excelled at cricket and led the debating team. He was an all-rounder, excelling at sport and intellectually precocious. In 1949, Hall went to Wesley College at the University of Sydney, where in 1956 he graduated with double degrees in arts and architecture.

Performing, doing well, being admired for his achievements, were very important to him. His fluency as a speaker and excellent presentation skills had brought him to the notice of E.H. Farmer. By 1966, Peter Hall had established himself as a favourite of the Government Architect. While he was working with the Government Architect he completed a number of significant buildings, notably the Goldstein Hall at the University of NSW in 1964, additions to the Darlinghurst Courthouse and the Registrar General's Office in Sydney.

Peter Hall adopted the then currently fashionable English Brutalist idiom of stark board-marked off-form concrete, dark clinker bricks and stained rough-sawn hardwood. He was clever without necessarily being original. His architecture had an up-to-the-minute smartness, a jaunty, almost swaggering flair, but it stopped there. Peter Hall was in a hurry, but in spite of all his ambition, by 1966 his career was stalled. There was nowhere farther for him to go in the Department.

At this juncture he was called on to finish the Opera House in Utzon's place. Hall was nearly 35 years old. He had only ever worked in Public Works, and knew nothing about theatre acoustics or designing opera houses. He was pushed into the job. Any sensitive person would have immediately seen that what he was being asked to do was commit artistic perdition. Peter Hall never saw it — his ambition outstripped his cleverness.

Hall was unused to thinking through his decisions soberly and he agreed to work on the Opera House without fully considering what might be involved, or appreciating the future ramifications. Prior to making his 19 April decision, Hall spent a tortured week agonising over whether to take the job. In the end, it mostly came down to the proposition 'Why not?' and the final decision was very quick. He did not worry whether it was a wise decision, or consider it in detail. Peter Hall liked to be at the centre of things and feel important. The attention increased the glamour of the job offer. Ultimately, Hall was seduced by the challenge, by the thought that he was taking Utzon's place.

For a while, he hummed and hahed so much that Ted Farmer, wearied by his prevarication, said finally he must realise that taking the job and completing the Opera House would make him famous. The prospect of fame, on top of all the money, helped him decide. Farmer sensibly warned Peter Hall he could not fail.

Hall was surprisingly naive. Five hours before the announcement of his appointment he spoke to Utzon by telephone, to justify his decision and ask for Utzon's blessing or, at the very least, his tolerance. He almost seemed to be asking Utzon to excuse him for what he was about to do. This placed Utzon in an invidious position. Utzon responded with remarkable candour and honesty, 'You're a very brave man, but I don't think you can do it.' A little overwhelmed by this, Hall is reported to have said, 'I can't do it as well as you. You're cleverer than I am. That's why I'd prefer you to do it. Will you go and see the Minister again?'[9] It was a monumentally stupid thing for Hall to say.

Hall and Utzon had met before 1966 – in 1959 when Hall had called on him at Hellebæk to ask for a job. Utzon turned him down because Hall was not able to stay long enough but Peter and Libby were hospitably received in Denmark and attended a party given by Utzon. Prior to this, Hall had produced a sheet of Opera House details for Stephenson & Turner's Opera House competition submission. That was the total extent of his experience of performing arts centres. Peter Hall's appointment to replace Utzon on the Government's Architectural Panel was announced on Tuesday, 19 April, ten days before Utzon left Australia.

Behind the scenes, the plan very nearly collapsed before it was launched. The push in Public Works for a change of administration on the Opera House had come from the Director, R.A.P. Johnson. His motive is unclear: whether from a sense of public duty, or from the bureaucrat's ambition to expand the role and importance of his own department, or both. There can be little doubt that Johnson's actions far exceeded what was called for by his legislative responsibility of supervision.

Ted Farmer absolved himself by saying that he had no alternative: if he refused he would have to resign. Farmer was much too adroit to let it come to that. The great flaw in Hughes's plan was the choice of someone to replace Utzon.

Farmer violated his own selection criteria by inviting Peter Hall to take over. One of the basic stipulations was that panel members should come from private practice. Hall had joined Public Works as a trainee and had never worked in a private office in Australia. To join Hughes's panel, Hall first had to resign from the public service. This demonstrated more than anything how desperate Hughes and Farmer were.

Peter Hall rescued Farmer and Hughes from an embarrassing predicament. He was their final option, for talented, ethical architects had refused to besmirch their careers by associating themselves with Davis Hughes's scheme.[10] Farmer respected Hall as a friend, and thought he knew what to expect from him after years of working together.

Farmer was adamant that Peter Hall was the Government's choice. The Architectural Panel, he insisted needed 'a really top-line design architect' who was also a 'colourful personality'. Farmer required of such a person that he be prepared to temper his design aspirations with the realisation that their implementation had to be based on a firm practical foundation and knowledge of construction and costing.[11] In other words, he must be pliable and not seek perfection whatever it cost. Hall could be relied on to compromise. He could be trusted to do things Farmer's way. No wonder Farmer said: 'It was indeed fortunate that I was able to persuade Peter Hall to come into it with me.'

The Architectural Panel consisted of two other partners besides Hall. If Peter Hall was Farmer's choice, Lionel Todd was decidedly not. Aged 36, from Hanson, Todd & Partners, Lionel Todd was a friend of Davis Hughes and his insurance policy. Farmer knew Todd well and considered him to be a 'perfect nuisance'.[12] The Panel was getting off to a fine start. It was up to Todd to produce the contract documents. The third Panel member, David Littlemore, then aged 55, and from Rudder, Littlemore & Rudder, was charged with supervising the construction. Given the accidental make-up and disparate personalities of the Panel, it was a miracle it worked at all, much less that it ever managed to complete the job.

For a group of supposedly 'practical' architects, the Panel had many shortcomings. A fortnight before the result of the Opera House competition was released, on Saturday night 12 January 1957, there had been a tremendous bang and thunderous noise from Sydney's Kingsford-Smith Airport. Half the eastern suburbs heard it. It was made by 100 tons of steel in a large 105 m x 46 m aircraft hangar roof collapsing, which resulted in A$200,000 worth of damage.[13] David Littlemore was the supervising architect for the hangar.

If a similar accident had happened to a Jørn Utzon project, one can only imagine the fuss Davis Hughes would have made. Since it did not involve Utzon but a member of his Panel, Davis Hughes obligingly ignored the mishap.

This was but a foretaste of what the future contained. After March 1966, the Minister for Public Works conveniently reversed his previous policies on cost control, reliable estimates and completing work on time. Instead of refusing everything, as he had previously done with Utzon, Hughes gave the Architectural Panel a free rein. With his own political future at stake, the traffic lights abruptly switched from red to green.

The nine years under Labor, Hughes claimed, had been years of sheer incompetence, great confusion and a total loss of control and demonstrated the whole project was in a state of suspended animation.[14] His words now seem prophetic, considering what was about to unfold in the three years after 1966.

It was true that Utzon and Labor moved slowly, with a spend rate of A$4 to $5 million per year, but this had the advantage that it kept expenditure within the annual income from lottery receipts and was fiscally responsible.

George Orwell once wrote: 'In power politics there are no crimes, because there are no laws.' This was especially true of Davis Hughes. Hughes's employment of a double standard was most apparent in the matter of architectural fees. Jørn Utzon received a total payment of A$1,250,000 for nine years' work up to 1966.[15] In his confrontation with Utzon, Davis Hughes insisted that Utzon re-negotiate a lower fee. Davis Hughes considered this matter so important he included it in his confidential minute to Cabinet on 25 August 1965. At one point, Hughes insisted he keep a close personal watch on payments to Utzon. In Cabinet he said: 'Serious consideration must be given to raising this question of his [Utzon's] fee with the Architect with a view to providing a reduced scale, as would be arranged if a consultant were being engaged to undertake a work of the value of the present estimate.'[16]

Far from reducing the fee scale for the Architectural Panel, Davis Hughes ultimately quadrupled it. At the beginning, the Panel's fee remained much the same. On 22 April, the three new members of the Panel calculated they stood to earn $1,200,000 over four years between them, at a rate of $300,000 a year. This was twice what Utzon was paid.[17] This calculation subsequently turned out to be unduly pessimistic. On 31 December 1968, a little more than two years later, they repeated the exercise.[18] The result was most pleasing. Subtracting a salary and overheads bill estimated at $1,250,000 for the five years from 1969 to 1973, from an increased total fee of $2,750,000 the three partners now stood to earn $1,500,000 between them, giving each an annual income of $100,000 (equivalent to $630,000 in 1996). The cost of the three-member Architectural Panel came to $550,000 a year, four times what Utzon was paid on average over nine years!

The total fee amount was even more outrageous. By 30 June 1974, the Architectural Panel had been paid $4,539,029.

This amount did not include $159,910 in expenses. Under a special arrangement, architects employed by Public Works who were seconded to work for Peter Hall received an additional salary cap on top of their government pay. This generous top up from the Government added a further $1,080,837 to the architectural bill, and was in addition to the $746,365 paid to the technical site staff by Public Works. Instead of decreasing the architectural fee as he pledged, Davis Hughes actually increased it fivefold to a grand total of $6,526,141. Considering he was elected on a plank of reducing public spending and waste on the Opera House, this amounted to a truly monumental about-face.

Davis Hughes characterised the $120,000 requested by Utzon for plywood mock-ups as a 'tremendous sum of money'. When approached by Peter Hall, he agreed without demur to an Architectural Panel expenditure of $369,464, three times the Utzon amount, to be expended on models and research.

Fame, even when people seek it, can overwhelm. Fresh from a study tour of Europe, Peter Hall tried to fill his new celebrity image. Without warning, he turned himself into a living caricature of a successful, international jet-setting architect, kitted out in a sleek gaberdine suit, black eyes shaded behind dark sunglasses like Marcello Mastroianni, while he sucked on a cigar and sped across Sydney in his new Jaguar XK150 roadster. In the flick of an eyelid he had become Mr Toad of Mosman, with his five-car garage. The man behind the Casanova facade was desperately insecure.

His marriage to Libby was over. She regarded his decision to take over from Utzon as wrong and said so.

Ignoring the fact that Utzon had returned to Denmark, Davis Hughes continued to attack him. Hughes's main complaint was that there were no more than 1800 seats in the large hall and he used this as a pretext to order a redesign. When the Leader of the Opposition, J.B. Renshaw, stated that he would welcome a full public inquiry into the Opera House, Davis Hughes promptly rejected Renshaw's 6 June suggestion, saying, 'I don't think there is any need for a public inquiry'.[19]

Hughes was unable to accept that Utzon was now out of reach. With him gone, Hughes resigned himself to flogging Utzon's ghost. Why? – perhaps Utzon triggered feelings of inferiority. Although Hughes would have vigorously denied it, somewhere inside him may have lurked a desire to be creative, but since he lacked all ability in that direction, he could only take over someone else's creation.

Even from halfway around the world Utzon's bitter cry of disappointment could be heard. In an interview for Copenhagen's *Politiken*, Utzon alleged he might 'just as well have spoken to a wall' as talk to Davis Hughes. When informed that Hughes had authorised the redesign of the main hall, Utzon's pent-up chagrin ignited: 'They can tear that so-called Opera House down for all I care.'[20] He was at the end of his tether. Copenhagen was not nearly remote enough to discourage his supporters from contacting him. Each time they did, a new battle with Hughes would flare up.

At the end of 1966, the Architectural Panel submitted its review with a range of options for what should happen inside the Opera House.[21] Big changes were contemplated. In particular Ben Schlanger, a theatre architect from New York, and Peter Hall held long discussions in June and September while Hall was overseas and these strongly influenced Hall's recommendation on the main hall. The December 1966 review suggested that grand opera and ballet be confined to the Minor Hall in order to free the Major Hall exclusively for symphony concerts and musical works. This was much less simple than it sounds, because it affected all the remaining performance spaces within the Opera House and would entail a total replanning and redesign of the Major Hall.

The review ignored both the requirements of the competition in 1956, as well as the original user intent. If adopted, the Opera House would be seriously compromised by eliminating opera from the main auditorium and doing away with the 1200-seat theatre in the Minor Hall. Chiefly, it got Peter Hall off the hook acoustically and eliminated planning problems for which he could find no answers.

The Opera House provided a pretext for overseas travel and soon everyone wanted to go overseas.[22] Peter Hall and Lionel Todd went, only David Littlemore stayed behind. Given that none of them knew much, travel was probably their only way to find out.

From 20 June to early October 1966, Hall toured the United States, England, Europe and Japan. The need for these repeated overseas trips demonstrates just how ill-equipped and lacking in experience Hughes's new Panel was; to make matters worse, they were under intense pressure to catch up to Utzon. This, as the later delays demonstrate, was simply impossible.

When asked to give its opinion in March 1967, the Trust's Technical Advisory Panel roundly rejected the new proposals as most unwise. In its stead, the Trust requested that a dual-purpose hall, with an audience of 2000 and volume of 20,133 m^3 or 9.9 m^3 per person, be adopted.[23] The dual-purpose option (c) conserved the stage machinery and provided adequate facilities for opera and ballet. On 21 March, 11 days later, Davis Hughes announced the elimination of opera facilities in the Major Hall; henceforth it would be a single-purpose concert hall. Some might have called it a major victory for a minor Peter Hall.

The Minor Hall, which till then had been seen as a drama theatre seating 1200 people, was re-assigned as the opera theatre, and drama was relegated to the cramped and unsuitable space under the concert hall, which prior to this had been designated as a 300-seat experimental theatre.

With the disappearance of opera from the large hall, drama lost its importance in the Opera House. More embarrassing was the huge 8495 m^3 cavern of useless space left over beneath the stage of the Major Hall, where the stage machinery should have been. This was to be converted into a recording studio.

The outcome was a travesty of the original plan. After years of criticising Utzon for not satisfying the conditions of the competition brief, Hughes now completely abandoned a major requirement of the building programme. Hughes faced an unwelcome prospect, for Peter Hall advised him that the acoustical requirements could not be met by a multi-use hall. In a stroke, Hughes robbed the roof design of any validity. His Opera House is a perversion. Having been conceived with the intention of broadening, not narrowing, the scope of musical performances which could be offered to audiences, it now betrayed Eugene Goossens's original vision. To make matters worse, it was unnecessary. Peter Hall and his advisers had been too hasty, and the main conclusion arising from their investigation later turned out to be untrue. Jørn Utzon's Opera House was dead, but the slanders continued.

There is little doubt that Utzon could have completed his design of the Major Hall soon after the Minor Hall in 1964 on the basis of a single-purpose facility. There is no comparison in terms of difficulty between a single-purpose and a multi-purpose auditorium. The review conclusion – that a successful multi-purpose hall for concerts and grand opera was impossible – was wrong. While it probably saved Peter Hall's sanity, the price of this small victory was the emasculation of the Opera House. The public got less than half a building.

Hall was wrong because such halls have been built successfully. A hall for opera and symphonic orchestral performances requires different reverberation times, of 1.6 and 2.0 seconds respectively. Since reverberation time is determined by the physical volume of a hall – the larger a space, the longer its reverberation time – the new Architectural Panel assumed it was impossible to achieve a hall having two different reverberation times, or if not impossible, inordinately cumbersome, not to mention costly.

The dual-purpose hall was a recent 1950s phenomenon, although some had been built earlier. Inevitably, these halls were an acoustic compromise. The Sydney Opera House brief was based on one of them – the San Francisco Memorial Opera House, which was an opera house with a temporary stage shelter for concerts.

There were two fundamental possibilities: a multi-purpose hall with a compromised reverberation time which satisfied neither use optimally, and a convertible hall which could be adapted acoustically to satisfy the divergent reverberation requirements. The report failed to consider this last possibility. The review was based on insufficient and one-sided technical information and was produced in haste. As a consequence, it only considered a multi-purpose hall which, it concluded rightly, would not be functionally satisfactory. The convertible hall entailed installing a mechanism for altering the volume and sound absorption characteristics of the hall to suit each type of performance.

The ultimate and indisputable proof of the convertible-hall concept is Tokyo's Orchard Hall, completed in 1989. It is the work of Yuzo Mikami who worked for Utzon at Hellebæk and is the result of his determination to prove that the convertible-hall concept was the best and only feasible answer to the acoustic conundrum presented by the Major Hall. The Orchard Hall at Shibuya, seating 2150, has a mobile acoustic shelter on its stage in three parts which can be retracted along tracks in the floor mechanically to the back of the stage, converting the hall from concerts to opera.[24] The changeover can be accomplished in less than 24 hours. In terms of technology, nothing prevented either Jørn Utzon or Peter Hall from doing the same in 1966.

There were many unintended consequences from the decision to adopt a single-purpose hall. Because the two halls were to be used for purposes not originally intended, many additional changes had to be made. There was a downgrading of all the performing arts, especially drama, within the building as the price of a single-purpose concert hall. These produced a host of compromises and unsatisfactory, costly alterations.

One of the finest stage machinery arrangements in the world at that time, which had already been paid for, had to be scrapped. This was especially regrettable because Utzon's idea to replace the normal side stages by a large-scale vertical transportation system under the main and back stages in itself was a revolutionary idea which could have had a big influence elsewhere. The elimination of the machinery from the Major Hall stage meant that the golden opportunity to assess its merit was lost.

The stage machinery alone cost A£2,271,353 (A$4,542,706), or A£2,788,491 (A$5,576,982) when the stage lighting is included. The machinery was eventually sold as scrap metal for $1 a ton and cut up. The stage tower in the Major Hall, which had cost an additional A£1,035,070 (A$3,070,140) was dismantled and disposed of.[25] The total cost of the changes was A$9,446,140, about A$78.4 million in today's money.

This was all about expediency. But it was a classic instance of being penny-wise, pound-foolish. The cause of the dispute with Hughes over Utzon's fee of A$102,000 for supervising the design and documentation of the stage machinery was clearly documented beyond any doubt. There is a letter from Waagner-Biro Aktiengesellschaft, dated February 1964, which confirms Utzon's crucial design and documentation role in the performance of the contract.[26] Evidently Davis Hughes never consulted his own departmental files, or if he did he took no notice of them.

To some it may seem trivial and inconsequential, but the series of four main roof shells, one set each for the Major and Minor Halls, were conceived to cover and simultaneously express on the outside the four main elements of the theatres, namely the foyer, the stage tower, the auditorium and the northern lounge area. Utzon envisaged the roofs as functional sculpture. The height and sizes of the shells revealed what happened inside them. Utzon likened the relationship to a walnut: 'You look at the bulging shape of a walnut,' he said, 'and inside you see a bulging kernel. Then you understand the way it is.'[27]

Far from being arbitrary, the height and width of the shells and their arrangement reflected the internal volumes and functions. Converting the Major Hall into a single-purpose hall for concerts destroyed the *raison d'être* of the roof composition and the relationship between the Major Hall and the Minor Hall was entirely falsified.

The roofs made sense only with the theatres as Utzon designed them. For anyone who appreciates the architectural significance of the Sydney Opera House and the splendour of its composition, the May 1967 decision was an unmitigated disaster. What made it even worse was that it was not even necessary, since it was well within the capacity of the technology and acoustic expertise of the day to develop the Major Hall as a convertible hall for concerts and opera.

This was not the end of the chaos and waste. After nearly half a year's work developing concrete glass-wall mullions and completing the architectural drawings to 80 per cent stage, the Panel found that low-frequency vibrations would be transmitted to the concrete podium structure through the mullions. They were forced to abandon the concrete mullions and replace them with steel. This wasted considerable time and added a further substantial cost to the architectural fee.[28] The change to the programme was little short of disastrous and resulted in a delay of a year and a half.

Whereas in 1966, Ove Arups had rejected hanging the glass-wall mullions from the shells, in 1968 they dropped their opposition and agreed that this was feasible after all. Although nothing had changed in the roof, the loads imposed by the glass walls on the shells were now declared to be within their carrying capacity.[29]

Two years after Utzon withdrew, in 1968, the Architectural Panel was still busily writing reports.[30] The job was not going anywhere. Late that September, a completion date was established for the end of 1972, and subsequently revised to October 1973. Putting off for as long as he could any indication of when the project would be completed, Davis Hughes found that he was powerless to dictate either the completion date or the final cost.

On 18 March 1969, Mr Cutler, the Deputy Premier, introduced the *Sydney Opera House Act (Amendment) Bill* into Parliament, which lifted the maximum authorised expenditure from $50 million to $85 million without any provision for the usual 10 per cent margin.[31] This represented a major increase under Hughes's administration of an additional $35 million in three years. P.N. Ryan, during the second reading, correctly predicted that this would not be the end. He was right, the final cost shot to $100.8 million not including the organ, which was not ready until 1976, and added a further $1.2 million, bringing the final figure to $102 million.

During this debate Ryan indicated that he had recently received from Utzon drawings for a multi-purpose hall, exceedingly satisfactory for both concert and opera, with seating for 2800, which were the product of further continued work by Utzon in conjunction with Dr Cremer and Dr Gabler in Berlin. Ryan offered the plans to Hughes for evaluation and proposed, before it was too late, that in order to avoid falsifying the interior and since the bill would not do what it said, an all-party committee be appointed to examine the alternatives.[32] Amid a cry of, 'You are pathetic' from Davis Hughes, the last opportunity to save the Opera House interior slipped away.

Davis Hughes brimmed with confidence. Within less than two years he would have less reason to be. Politicians generally failed to make allowance for the impact of inflation on the cost of the Opera House. In the 14 years after 1960, the building price indices rose by 123 per cent. A $10 million project in January 1960 would have cost $22.3 million in October 1973 when the Opera House was completed. Utzon's July 1965 estimate of $48.4 million coincided with the commencement of a period of rising inflation. Soon after Askin became Premier, his Government stopped further spending and this caused a serious slump in the building industry, which then resulted in a sharp fall in the building price indices, of 11 per cent between September 1965 and May 1967.[33]

The fall was short-lived. After June 1967, the building industry entered a three-year boom of high inflation, during which building costs climbed 48 per cent. Between May 1967 and October 1973, the period of Hughes's administration, the increase totalled 80 per cent. Overall inflation had a substantial impact on the total cost of the work on the Opera House under Davis Hughes. By delaying the start of Stage III for so long, Davis Hughes caused a huge cost increase by pushing the work into a period of hyper-inflation.

Stage III should have cost $45 million, not $80 million, which it did eventually. Hughes can take the credit for a $35–40 million hike in the cost of Stage III. The three-year delay in starting Stage III, followed by panic and a rush to make up the lost time, proved extremely costly and undermined quality. It has been estimated in similar cases that the 'ransom effect' of finishing a job in a hurry can increase the cost by a factor of two. This seems about right when applied to the Opera House interiors.

If Utzon had been allowed to begin Stage III in September 1964, as he requested, the work would have gone ahead during a period of falling, not steeply rising, building prices. Hughes's shilly-shallying, the appointment of a new team and the review of the programme, at a minimum delayed the work by three and a half years. This had a decisive effect on the final cost. Without Hughes's interference, the Sydney Opera House could have opened in December 1969, the date suggested by Utzon at the July 1964 conference with Renshaw, and cost around $65 million, not $98.7 million plus.

The estimates themselves reveal this. The largest cost rises occurred under Davis Hughes and not, as claimed, under the previous Labor administration. On 3 November 1965, Hughes told Parliament immediately prior to the Bondi by-election the Opera House would cost $50 million. In a brazen political gesture, the following September, he released a false estimate of $37.5 million, a reduction of $12.5 million on the earlier 1965 figure![34] Changing the wording from a fixed absolute amount, to 'a payment towards the eventual cost of the work', he was playing with semantics. This made no appreciable difference to the cost, which continued to climb steeply.

Two years later, in September 1968, the estimate reached $85.0 million. This was the first in a series of sizeable jumps. The 1968 amount exceeded Utzon's July 1965 estimate by a whopping $35.6 million. Other increases followed, but at longer intervals. In November 1971, for instance, Hughes announced a figure of $93.0 million, adding a further $8 million. Four months later, the amount jumped to $99.5 million. The final estimate was $102 million. The total cost increase under Davis Hughes's administration came to $52.6 million. Not only had Davis Hughes failed to prevent further cost rises, he had presided over the largest cost blow-out in the history of the project. A *Sydney Morning Herald* editorial said what many must have been thinking: 'Mr Hughes' two main reasons for getting rid of Mr Utzon were to get control of costs and to stop indefinite delays. He has done neither. Many people may feel that if we are to spend $100 million on the Opera House and wait another five years – or is it ten? for its completion, we might as well have kept Mr Utzon to finish the job.'[35]

The worst aspect of it all was the failure of Hughes's much trumpeted cost-control measures. By March 1970, Rider Hunt gave a warning to Hall, Todd & Littlemore about cost control which they concealed from Hughes. Then on 13 May 1971, it was confirmed that the end of 1972 was not a realistic completion date and could not be achieved, and the $85 million budget would be topped by $5–10 million. By the end of May it was apparent that effective cost control had broken down on the project and the actual increases now far exceeded what was allowed. By October 1971 even Davis Hughes knew that his prediction in March 1969 was a sham, as he asked Cabinet for approval to commit funds beyond $85 million.[36]

Near the end, the spend rate exceeded lottery receipts. In 1972–3 it rose to $20,966,242, forcing the Public Works Minister to borrow $22 million from the General Loan Account to provide bridging finance.[37] Advances from this source totalled $9,371,454 at 30 June 1974. It was the only time that public spending programmes were in any way affected by the construction of the Opera House, and it happened not under Labor, but under a Country Party Minister. This financial crisis explains why the forecourt and approaches to the Opera House were not properly completed, why work-as-executed drawings were never made, and why Sydney had to wait until March 1993 to get its $40 million Opera House carpark. Hughes had literally run out of money.

In the nine years Utzon worked on the Opera House, $15,072,855 was spent. Stages I and II combined cost $18,168,655, a small fraction of the grand total of $98,709,085. Utzon's share of this total was just 15.5 per cent – the remaining $83.64 million was due entirely to Davis Hughes!

Few projects highlight the mismanagement of large projects by the NSW Government Architect better than the State Office Block on Phillip, Bent and Macquarie streets. The contract was signed at the end of 1962 for $11.5 million, but rose to $15.6 million, an increase of $4 million or 35 per cent, a figure that exceeded the total spending on the Opera House under Utzon.[38] Was this what Hughes meant by the efficiency of the competitive public tenders system?

Davis Hughes's failure to keep his promises was hardly surprising. What is remarkable is that anyone ever believed him. His effort to reform the administration was soon discarded when it was found not to work. Hughes did everything the wrong way: four architects were brought in to replace Utzon and Hughes greatly enlarged the bureaucracy. The reality was a doubling of the cost and a marked decline in efficiency. Charles Weatherburn, acting as both the Assistant Government Architect and the G.A.'s representative on site, soon had to be removed when he was discovered writing letters to himself in one capacity and then addressing replies to himself in the other.

By closing down Utzon's office of 15 or so dedicated young architects, Hughes substituted a larger, more expensive one in its stead along public service lines. It was less efficient, numbers beginning at 25 to 30, expanding to 65, and finally peaking at 105 draughtsmen. For the next nine years, until his retirement in 1973, E.H. Farmer spent four days out of five at Bennelong Point, which prevented him from carrying out his duties as Government Architect. This too had to be paid for. The Minister's takeover of the Opera House diverted valuable human resources away from their proper official responsibilities.

Before an incredulous Parliament, on 28 September 1966, in his best schoolmaster manner, Hughes lamely excused his failure to initiate new construction by saying Peter Hall '… has had to deal with important matters including that of increasing the area of seating and increasing the volume of the hall to increase the reverberation time, and so on.' The Government had 'assembled an architectural drawing staff of high standard and a size to meet all the present requirements of planning.'[39] With staff numbers bolstered at this time to 25, there was precious little work. By January 1969 the office had reached 51, three times the size of Utzon's 1965 office.[40]

Davis Hughes used the project to justify a number of pointless overseas Opera House junkets. Ostensibly they were to inform him about performing arts centres. In practice, the trips were glorified holidays and grand tours at taxpayers' expense which did not save a single Opera House dollar.

On 17 May 1966, 115 of Utzon's drawings were secretly handed over to Charles Weatherburn, under terms negotiated by R.J. McKay, the State Crown Solicitor, and R.W. Nicholl, acting for Utzon.[41] Contradicting Hughes's later statement, 15 were of the Major Hall and a further 15 of the Minor Hall. However, they did not provide much in the way of answers that Peter Hall and the others were looking for.[42] This is puzzling because eight of the drawings were exhibited in Philip Nobis's *Unseen Utzon* exhibition in 1995. If a final-year architecture student could reconstruct Utzon's architectural intentions from the material, how was it that the Government Architect and Peter Hall, with years of experience, failed? Utzon was paid $160,000 for these plans and the amount was later deducted from Utzon's total claim submitted on 14 April 1966 for outstanding fees.

In the 1967 writ by Nicholl & Nicholl against the Government, Utzon claimed the balance owing to him from the total of $1,599,342.20. To keep Utzon out of court and force him to accept the Government's offer, the Crown Solicitor pursued a plan to stay the action indefinitely by bringing a cross-action against Utzon for $1 million damages.[43] Later it was decided to limit this to $355,000, the amount Utzon was claiming, to discourage him. One strategy canvassed by the Crown to bring about a settlement with Utzon was to threaten to require him to disclose his financial position re his outstanding tax and embarrass him in this manner. It apparently succeeded. In February 1970, the matter was belatedly settled when Utzon agreed to a final payment of $46,000, bringing his total to $1,296,000. The stinginess of the Government's treatment of Utzon contrasts with its lavish treatment of the Panel.

It was typical of Hughes that he did not stay to the finish of the Opera House. With an eye to his own career prospects, Hughes resigned from Parliament on 17 January 1973 to take up the sinecure post of NSW Agent-General in London. The Opera House was opened by Queen Elizabeth II on October 20, nine months later. In April 1966, Peter Hall was expected to sacrifice his architectural and ethical principles to save Davis Hughes's political skin. At the end of it, Hughes showed his gratitude by skipping off to London.

On a visit to London in 1971, Davis Hughes called on Jack Zunz at Ove Arups' offices in Fitzroy Street. Zunz generously invited him to a night at the theatre.[44] The spectacular Royal Shakespeare Company production of *Much Ado About Nothing*, directed by Ronald Eyre, was exceedingly popular and Zunz had great difficulty obtaining six seats for Ove Arup, Hughes and their wives. He immediately received a message from New South Wales House that the Shakespeare was unsuitable – Zunz was left wondering whether Hughes might have been overly sensitive about the play's title in connection with what he had done to the Opera House. Instead, Davis Hughes chose the musical *Fiddler on the Roof*. One wonders what difference the change made: both were cruelly accurate, but *Fiddler* was the more telling in terms of Hughes's taste in theatre.

If Davis Hughes had not identified himself so intimately with the Opera House, he would certainly be forgotten. He sought to give himself a place in history no one could easily erase. In Armidale, the springboard of his political career, Davis Hughes is all but forgotten. He has no splendid memorial, just one street, 'Hughes Place'. It is a cul-de-sac near the

Drummond Column, memorial to his mentor David Drummond, lying directly below it on the north–south axis. In a laconic Australian way, this street is a very effective symbol: it is suburban, short, undeviating and leads nowhere. History, in its indirect way, has delivered its verdict on Davis Hughes: those who forget others are themselves likely to be forgotten.

Charmian Clift, a gifted writer who had recently returned to Sydney from Hydra, thought Hughes's sacking of Utzon was just another case of Frostratus burning down the Temple of Artemis at Ephesus, one of the wonders of the ancient world, so he could be famous and get his name in the history books.[45]

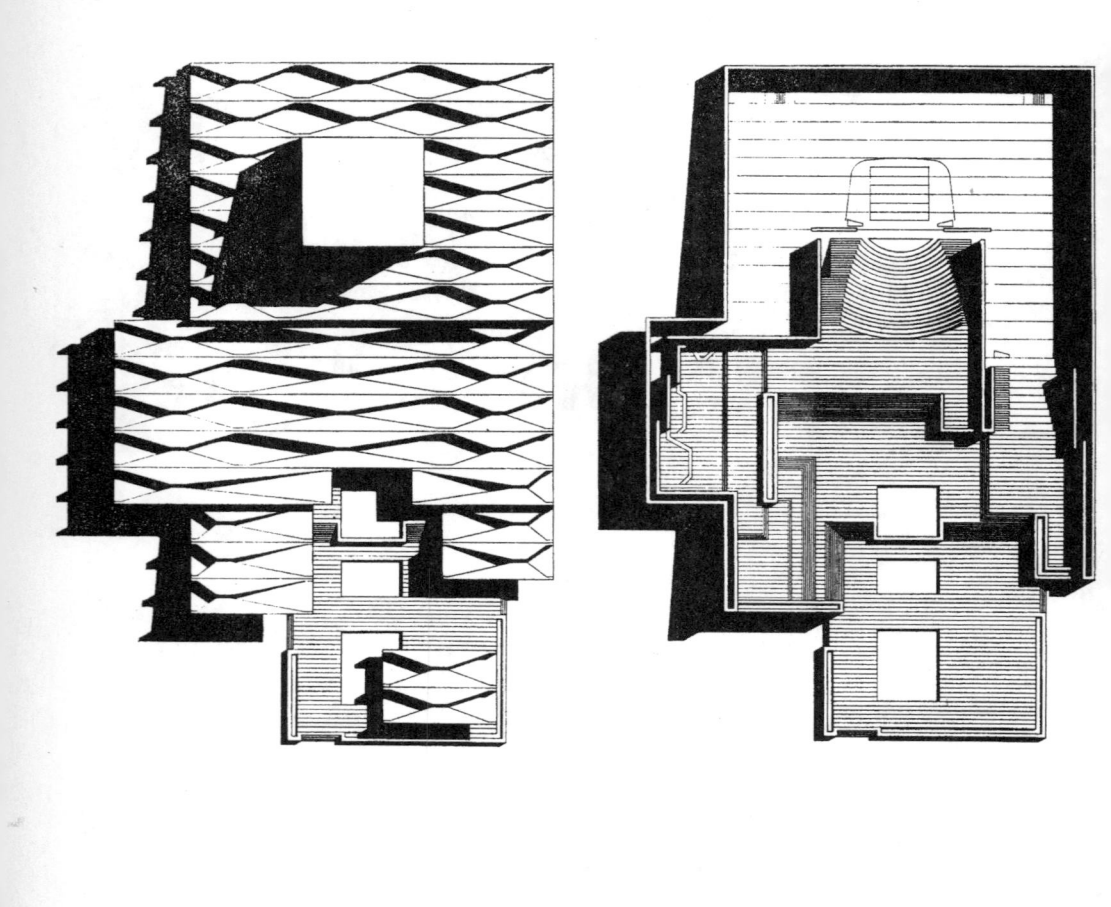

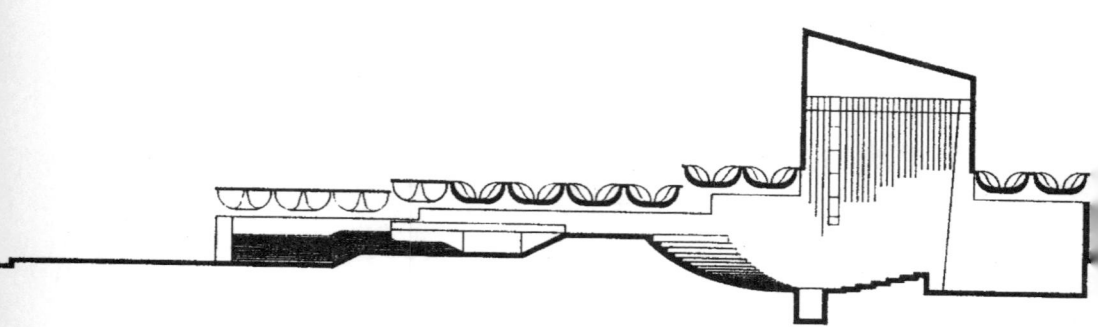

Competition scheme for New Schauspielhauses, Zürich, May 1964. Above left: Roof plan. Above right: Floor plan. Below: Longitudinal section. The project was abandoned in 1970.

18

Back in Denmark
Hellebæk, 1966–1970

Utzon sustained a devastating blow in 1966. It was impossible to return to Denmark and pretend nothing had happened. Yet that is exactly what he hoped to do. He needed to put the past behind and move on. The wraith of the Opera House did not allow this, it followed him to Denmark and damaged his reputation. Clients considered he could not be trusted to respect a budget.

Utzon only ever intended to withdraw temporarily from the Opera House and never saw his action as permanently severing his connection with the work. He was firmly convinced it was only a matter of time before Davis Hughes realised his mistake and called Utzon back on his terms. His repeated promise to complete the Opera House to his supporters in Sydney encouraged them to redouble their efforts on his behalf.

The high drama of his sudden departure made Utzon famous around the world; over the years this fame would continue to grow as the legend extended itself. The most important part of the Opera House – the interiors – still remained to be completed. The House was half finished. How could he not be caught up emotionally under the circumstances? It was only natural that people would ask him his opinion on what should happen. In turn, this meant he was never free of the Opera House.

His life was split between the unfinished work in Sydney and beginning anew in Denmark. Short as it was, the Australian interlude altered his relationship to Denmark. He had outgrown the smallness and provincial conservativeness of Denmark and it now appeared in a quite different light to before. Every now and then the telephone would ring, and an Australian voice would ask him to comment on some new pronouncement by Minister Hughes. During the first year this happened frequently, shattering his peace and ruffling his self-possession for days afterwards.

Utzon was chained to his creation. No one could have foreseen that this would happen or that the Opera House would spin its own myth, one that would take hold and continue to grow in the public imagination.

Although no one fully believed a fraction of what they heard, many were convinced Utzon was responsible for the cost increases. The world was left wondering. Was Utzon incompetent? What had really happened? Was he defeated by the intractability of the acoustics? Did he leave because he did not know how to complete it? Was he the victim of a conspiracy? Utzon's refusal to speak about these matters left the questions hanging in the air unanswered and added an extra dimension and spice to the mystery.

When Utzon talked to journalists, he was tempted to embellish, exaggerate and invent absurd incidents for his own enjoyment, and to cast doubt on the very idea of history. No matter how much he mocked history and attempted to make it look silly, people drank it up and thirsted after the myth. He never seriously attempted to give a full insider's account; people were free to believe what they wanted to believe.

Utzon was his own enemy. Instead of clearing his name by publishing a full and accurate account of events in Sydney to set the record straight, he evaded the issue. He could have restored confidence in himself by explaining the facts. But he was entangled in his inhibitions and hurt. Publishing a truthful, detailed, personal account of all that that happened in Sydney would have helped clear his name and assisted in rebuilding his career, but it meant confronting flaws within himself. He lacked the strength of character to do this. All he seems to have wanted was for the emotional pain to subside and for all to be well again.

As the building's fame around the world spread, Utzon struggled to maintain his equilibrium. Withdrawing helped. Most people would have been totally devastated by the events. He survived, but only just. That is not to say he did not pay a high price, even with Lis doing her best to shield him. For the children, it was impossible for them not to be affected to some degree.

Utzon turned to his family for solace and cocooned himself. As innocent bystanders, the two older children, Jan and Lin, fielded journalists' intrusive telephone calls, and answered unexpected knocks at the front door at all hours of the day. Fending off the news media became second nature. They quickly learned to concoct stories: Jørn was away sailing, their parents were holidaying in Spain – almost anything would suffice. Occasionally their stories were true, often they were only half-true. It did not matter. They all became adept at deflecting the world's curiosity.

In some ways, the returning Utzons were like a modern Swiss Family Robinson, shipwrecked castaways who had returned to civilisation after making a life on a remote island. They were the subject of curiosity as well as pity. Offers of support poured in from many quarters.

They now returned to their Hellebæk house and resumed their lives. The two older children had to wait until October before recommencing their studies: Jan enrolled in architecture at the Academy of Fine Arts; Lin at the School of Arts and Crafts in Copenhagen (Kunsthåndværkerskolen, 1967–70) where she studied textiles. Her intentions, though not exactly clear, were along the lines of a career in fashion.

Compared to the daily saturation coverage by the press in Sydney, the treatment in the Danish press during the crisis was restrained and tactful, but it hit a peak around March 14, when Utzon had rejected Davis Hughes's offer. There was, understandably, considerable support for Utzon in Denmark. Utzon's old professor, Steen Eiler Rasmussen, wrote a defence in *Politiken* in March,[1] along the lines that Australians did not understand Utzon. Halldor Gunnløgsson, Utzon's friend from his former student days, who was now a professor at the Royal Academy, jumped into the fray with his own defence of Utzon and was backed by Knud Lautrup-Larsen, who had previously worked for Utzon for four years.[2] Throughout March, Danish newspapers carried reports which were largely based on Australian stories. There was even a comment from Ove Arup who complained that Utzon had ignored his invitation to meet.[3]

Hard up financially, Utzon was presented with a range of choices. He was offered professorships in the United States and in Denmark by his old friend Tobias Faber in his capacity as Rector of the Royal Academy of Fine Arts. There were jobs for him at Silkeborg, Sweden, Zürich and Saudi Arabia. Rejecting Faber's offer for a second time, Utzon gave a lecture to his son Jan's design class instead. Utzon preferred to talk to students rather than play the grand professor. He was offended, and a little intimidated, by the pretensions of academia in a way Faber obviously was not.

Utzon saw his future in terms of designing, he did not see himself as a lecturer. He was a gifted speaker with his unassuming mixture of candour, personal experience, and something approaching a messianic devotion and commitment, which rubbed off on others. He talked about architecture in a spontaneous, direct way that brought it to life. His insights sprang from an emotional core deep inside him. He could not be a lecturer, a dissector of intellectual tissue, and he was not tempted to relinquish his freedom for the financial security and the weekly round of lectures and studio classes.

Soon after his return, Utzon gave a public lecture on the Sydney Opera House to his Danish colleagues which, to his disappointment, received a mixed reception – many were clearly sympathetic, but there were others who were inclined to believe the NSW Government's version. This came as a shock.

The project which most occupied Utzon on his return until 1970 was the theatre at Zürich. Although it was ultimately abandoned, and this must have come as a shattering disappointment following so soon after Sydney, it served as a bridge between the tentative experimentation in Sydney in 1960 and the more mature Kuwait National Assembly complex in 1971. Aspects of the formal geometry were carried over from Zürich and later invested in the Kuwait project. While there is a great deal about the Zürich theatre which stems from Sydney, it also contained ideas that were developed more fully later on.

A considerable amount of what Utzon learned about geometry and precast concrete in Sydney went into the Zürich theatre. He gained immensely from his long apprenticeship to the Sydney Opera House. It transformed his architecture and his thinking and showed him how he might realistically achieve the goal of integrating a new sculptural and human approach using the twentieth century's anonymous industrial building technology in an additive mode. This lent to his later work a greater flexibility and confidence.

At Zürich, Utzon was called on to deal empathetically with an old city. The site of the new theatre was an open square crisscrossed by car traffic, and was bordered by an important throughroad. It consisted of an unprepossessing patch of green, surrounded by old buildings and roads on all sides, in addition to which, plonked squarely in the middle, was a public lavatory and kiosk. To further complicate matters, a tram tunnel ran past it. It would have taken Alexander the Great to cut through Zürich's Gordian knot of motor vehicular traffic routes.

The challenge was to fit the new theatre into a static city framework consisting of a 1910 art gallery by Karl Moser below it, and a classical gymnasium immediately above it, in the midst of a historic district containing a scattering of tightly packed teaching institutions, dominated by the Cantonsschule (high school) farther up.

Hacking a path though this traffic jungle was only the beginning of Utzon's problems; as it existed, the immediate city around the theatre site lacked a proper focus – some monument or building or open space to draw the disparate urban threads together. Utzon had demonstrated in Sydney that, faced with a more difficult but essentially similar challenge, he was just what was needed. In fact, one newspaper in Zürich went out of its way to praise Utzon for his gift 'of adjusting a building's form and structure to the landscape or architectural environment for which it was meant, without betraying his conviction that a modern architect should use contemporary materials, namely concrete, steel and glass, as a formal language inspired by the material itself, and should at the same time release its unsuspected possibilities.'[4]

At the start, it all seemed to go extremely well. In July 1963, at the time of the competition, Zürich's population stood at over 400,000 people. Zürich, the largest and most German of Switzerland's cities, possessed a puritanical atmosphere that was a challenge to the artistic vision.[5] In these circumstances, the low-key neutrality of Utzon's plans may have been advantageous. Certainly, Zürich was very fortunate to have the celebrated novelist and playwright Max Frisch, who grew up there and understood the city culture, write the introductory overview for the competition. He stressed the importance of encouraging an intimate relationship between the audience and the actors as being one of the most valuable qualities of live theatre. Prior to becoming a playwright, Frisch had been an excellent architect. After Sydney it must have felt strange to Utzon, and reassuring at the same time, to be dealing with a client who understood architecture.

The programme required a drama theatre to seat 1000 with a maximum limit of 1100, and a minimum allowable space allocated to each seat of 90 cm x 55 cm. The specification of the drama function was precise and detailed, much more so than for Sydney.

It is quite easy to see why Utzon was successful in the competition. He had benefited enormously from the Sydney Opera House experience and his design is less a building than it is an environment or landscape. The roof was the part given most emphasis. It was composed of folded beams, very similar to but slightly wider and more open than the folded beams that form the main stair and concourse of the Opera House at Sydney.

The theatre space, like its early Sydney Opera House counterpart, was based on the ancient amphitheatre, but on this occasion it was an oval, egg shape which narrowed towards the stage and was widest at the back, made by scooping out and removing the auditorium volume from the base. Circular bench seats would allow the audience to see the faces on the other side. The theatre was simplified into a system of stepped terraces in the base, over which Utzon unrolled a carpet of folded concrete beams. Both the roof and wall elements were horizontal; the only non-horizontal, vertical accent was the stage tower, which Utzon kneaded into an upswept ski jump sliced diagonally to give a steeply inclined roof to shed the snow.

Utzon solved several problems at Zürich which lacked solution in Sydney. The patrons would arrive directly under the theatre, being received in a 600-vehicle carpark protected from the weather and within the theatre complex. This was an enormous advance over the Sydney Opera House which had to wait until 1993 to get its carpark. Whereas Utzon was unable to provide sufficient side and back stage areas for Sydney, he made generous provision for these areas in his Zürich scheme.

The predominant mood of the theatre model was one of restrained anonymity. The boundary between building and landscape has dissolved, its form is exposed as an upthrusting, folded, osseous formation of ribs which melt along the edges. The new theatre would be a hybrid of mountain and city: structural and monolithic after the mountains; urban and artificial to resemble the city around it.

It was probably this quality that appealed to the jury, the idea of the theatre's absorption by its surroundings. It is less an isolated object to walk around and admire, a building in the strictly conventional sense, than a constructed terrain. The freedom of the staircase form, its stepped character, is an invitation to explore further. It climbs up the hillside in a beautiful series of terraces that form 'a flat, relief-like carpet of building with a structured roof'. The terraced base is essentially a wide staircase laid out across the mountainside with the roof later drawn over it as protection. Once again, Utzon successfully linked his work to nature by injecting a primitive nuance into it. The rhythmic folds in the roof-beams shunt the building forward up the hillside. The jury's phrase, 'relief-like carpet', about sums it up.

The roof was in three sections. Each folded raft of beams presented itself as a flat, even carpet spreading out as it is unrolled to cover the base. The unity of the roof integrated the lowest and topmost sections of the site in a continuous fabric. Like flat pastry on a board which has been pinched by human fingers, there is something about it which is inviting, irresistible in its way, which tempts us to break off a piece and put it in our mouth.

The scheme of the new Zürich theatre was a larger and grander version of Utzon's Bayview house, which in turn derived from the 1958 High School at Helsingør competition. The folded beam roof and the contrasting vertical residential tower there present a striking similarity with the theatre. But whereas the school was centralised around an atrium court, at Zürich Utzon developed a linear theme of successive levels ascending from Heimplatz Square at the bottom to the stage tower structure at the top. Deferring to the city, simultaneously functional and anonymous, it is gently non-assertive and exactly right.

Rather than forcing an ostentatious monument on Zürich, Utzon offered the city a signatureless platform, which was inspired by the mountains and revisited memories of the sombre terraces of Mexico's Monte Alban. He drew the mountain down to the city: his theatre is a foot – ankle, instep and toe – an extension and a termination to the mountain. Utzon avoided anything suggestive of pretentiousness; its poetics arise from the means he employs and are expressed in terms of a modern industrial vernacular. This made it appear all the more appropriate when set against the stunning backdrop of Zürich's lake and mountain peaks. His giant's stair led up to a high altar – the stage.

The Zürich Schauspielhaus had been the main focus of German theatre in Switzerland from the 1930s to the 1960s and retained its leading position as one of the principal playhouses of Europe. Kurt Hirschfeld had arrived in 1938 and helped to shape playwrights such as Friedrich Durrenmatt and Max Frisch. In 1948 he staged the first performance of Bertolt Brecht's *Herr Pentila und sein Knecht Matti*. For a second time Utzon was hit by bad luck: Hirschfeld died unexpectedly in 1964 at the age of 62 at a crucial moment in the establishment of the project. Hirschfeld, like Cahill at the Opera House, was the key driving figure behind the new Schauspielhaus. As the theatre's artistic director and promoter, Hirschfeld could be said to be even more crucial than Cahill. History repeated itself.

Utzon had appointed Jon Lundberg, before he left the Sydney office at the end of May 1965 to go to Europe to start his own practice, to oversee the Zürich theatre project while he found his feet there. After Hirschfeld's death, there followed a succession of theatre directors with different ideas and requirements.

Working patiently, Utzon accommodated the changes demanded by successive directors as best he could while trying to deal with the changing traffic conditions around the theatre. This resulted in a series of plans, each different in detail, and satisfying the various requirements and altered traffic conditions. Early on, before the theatre project was voted on and approved, Utzon was paid a fixed sum for his design services which did not increase with the amount of work. There was no provision in his fee for the great number of changes; consequently Utzon suffered a substantial financial loss without any guarantee the project would proceed. Until it was approved, his work was strictly speculative. If the project was terminated Utzon had to bear the loss. Utzon's financial commitment grew in proportion to the number of changes, which worsened when it was decided to delay the start. In April 1969 the situation had become so bad Utzon was forced to apply for compensation for work he had already done. Because of the complex nature of the project – which involved stage machinery, installations and alignment with traffic lanes, and to ensure a realistic estimate – the drawings were required to be at a larger scale and far more accurate than was normal for an unapproved 'Abstimmungsprojekt'.

Utzon devoted five years to developing the theatre and re-arranging the plans in co-operation with Zürich's Board of Works, or Hochbauamt. The main obstacle to be overcome was the road traffic. It was supposed to be re-routed initially, taking it around the square in front of the theatre and underground with some extra traffic lanes. In 1968, a commission to consider the traffic proposal was established by the Zürich Canton Parliament. By April 1969 Utzon had finalised the last of the alterations and was ready. Utzon expressed extreme pleasure in the revised scheme which, with its various functions now working perfectly, he felt was beautiful.[6] Simultaneously, he submitted a scheme to deal with the complex traffic situation which involved widening Hottingerstrasse and Zeltweg on one side, and running them into

Seilergraben on the other via a tunnel under the new Heimplatz, a square below the new Schauspielhaus.

Under the existing traffic arrangement, road traffic crossed Heimplatz in front of the Kunsthaus from the north-east to the west. In the new plan, Utzon re-routed the tram lines and five lanes of traffic from Hottingerstrasse under the new theatre's forecourt terrace in much the same way as he separated pedestrians and motor cars under the concourse of the Sydney Opera House. Instead of using folded beams to span the roadway, the podium was to be supported on two rows of columns interspersed between the traffic lanes and the trams to provide a drop-off lane at the theatre. The forecourt above the roadway effectively bridged the traffic and connected the new theatre to the old art museum, to satisfy one of the earlier requirements. While this was undoubtedly a substantial improvement on earlier designs, it effectively isolated the new cultural centre on an island within the old quarter and ringed it with road traffic. Not everyone saw this as an advance.

The proposed road and traffic changes entailed widening some of the streets to take the increased traffic flows, the demolition of the old Schauspielhaus which dated from 1888–9 (Haus zum Pfauen, or House of the Peacock) and its replacement by a small building with a pedestrian overpass linked to the new Heimplatz. Because of its bulk and size astride a main traffic intersection, the only way the new Schauspielhaus and existing Kunsthaus could be physically integrated was by separating traffic from pedestrians by placing the latter on an elevated deck structure. This was a typical problem in many old cities in Europe with a fixed street system and increased road traffic. Zürich faced a choice between people, maintaining a civilised urbanity, or turning the city holus-bolus over to the motor car. It seemed inevitable that, if implemented, Utzon's proposal to augment multi-lane roadways would totally alienate the new square from the old quarter.

Unfortunately, Heimplatz square and Utzon's new Schauspielhaus could not be achieved without the new traffic proposal. The feasibility of the cultural centre depended on the implementation of the traffic changes – the one would not work without the other. Both had to be agreed together. A rejection of the traffic plan also meant the rejection of Utzon's project.

A pencil perspective view of Heimplatz from the Kunsthaus reveals how Utzon envisaged the integration of the theatre and the ageing art museum. Wide stairs in front mount a widened Hottingerstrasse to the theatre and connect it with the lower Kunsthaus. The low horizontal profile is capped by open, upturned, half-cylindrical, precast beam elements resting on the walls. Their side faces have been sliced into between the ends to produce a narrow beam section at the middle. Instead of a bland, semi-cylindrical section, they now have delicate, elliptical sides. Up from the entry court, the same beams are reversed and look like rows of upturned rowing sculls. This reversal of the beams differentiates the theatre and stage areas at the rear of the building from the front forecourt area. The half-round beams present a rounded silhouette. Utzon re-used an identical geometry for the precast concrete beams in Kuwait.

By February 1970 the drawings and documents were practically complete and Utzon's Swiss partners were able to calculate the project's cost. An internal row now broke out over whether to give priority to building a drama theatre or an opera house.[7] It sounded like a repeat of Sydney. Under mounting public opposition, in 1971 the traffic proposals were dropped. In 1972, the following year, the final blow fell when the Swiss Federal Government declared a temporary halt to all public building (federal, cantonal and communal) in a step towards halting inflation. This brought Utzon's plans for the New Theatre to an end. The failure of Zürich was typical. It was a time of repeated disappointments for Utzon. Nothing ever seemed to be built as a result of all his hard work.

In the Zürich theatre, Utzon set out to correct as many of the shortcomings in the Sydney Opera House as he could. Inside, in the theatre, Utzon amended the earlier competition scheme by introducing an upper balcony at the rear. The ceiling was remarkably similar in concept to the Minor Hall of Sydney's Opera House (it even had the same diagonal walls along the sides pointing towards the stage which continued upwards into the ceiling). Whereas in the earlier Zürich scheme, the stage-tower roof gently pitched upwards against the lake, it was now tilted at 30 degrees the other way so it followed the slope of the mountainside.

Utzon was still entering competitions. However, his theatre design for Wolfsburg is far less significant than Zürich. Wolfsburg is 'Volkswagen town' in Germany. In the 1965 design competition, Utzon received third place behind Hans Scharoun and Alvar Aalto.[8] Although his Wolfsburg scheme shares some similarities with Zürich, it is more heavily sculptural, if that can be imagined, and boisterously Baroque. Utzon excavated into his base platform and removed the theatre seating ramp in rounded sections, each tier of which was reached individually by stairs sunken into curved trunk-shaped channels. Except for a Baroque flourish of the flying porch roof at the front, which introduced the theatre, the main body of the building was buried into the hillside and hidden under two sets of low flat roofs.

In Denmark, most architectural projects were in the hands of government bureaucrats who were reluctant to entrust Utzon with a major commission because of his reputation for not controlling costs. Many Danish cities would have welcomed a building by him, but their officials were hesitant and afraid, and ultimately caution prevailed.

Denmark boomed in the late sixties but little of the new work found its way to Utzon. This gave him leisure to think and formulate his approach, which he labelled 'additive architecture'.[9] This idea derived from vernacular building such as he had observed in Morocco and traditional Chinese architecture. Utzon was impressed by the way so-called primitive builders repeated the same basic unit of construction with only minor variations. He reasoned that it should be possible to duplicate this using industrially produced components, and so avoid the monotony found in so much industrial building going on in the 1960s. His aim was an industrial vernacular along additive lines which he compared to adding more trees to the forest, more deer to a herd, more stones on the beach or more morsels to the Danish 'frokost' lunch board. In such a manner, by varying the components, he could satisfy a variety of functional requirements with the same basic system.

The additive approach was developed in a number of projects such as a textile school at Herning, a new town centre for Farum in a competition in 1966, the Espansiva timber component house system for the company Espansiva Byg A/S (1969), and a sports stadium for 30,000 including an indoor sports hall at Jeddah in Saudi Arabia (1969). The idea of a kit of components was also applied to furniture in his curved Utsep modular furniture system, which used a combination of straight and arced units to develop variable geometry seating options.

In 1966 Utzon submitted a plan for a new town centre on the edge of Farum, north-west of Copenhagen. The road access was restricted so Utzon based his layout on the closed bazaar, giving emphasis to the few entrances leading into it. The buildings faced onto an internal covered street system with squares moulded around a long serpentine spine armature. There were two unit types: a tall, prefabricated, upright, curved, partially domical roofed bazaar shelter formed in radial segments that produced the curved street alignment, to which were attached barrel-vaulted shop units joined like ribs on each side of the street. The shops, because they were in modules, could be of any desired depth. The idea, as well as the geometry and domical shapes, were all the result of Utzon's previous encounter with Iranian bazaars.

The bazaar has been called a synthesis of closed and open spaces. Its essence, after an initial feeling of restriction, is to lead by way of a dark passage to a brightly lit terminus.[10] In this fashion it provides a spatial parable for the journey from darkness to enlightenment, consisting of a linear succession of domes leading from one focal or nodal event within the city – namely bath houses, caravanserais, colleges, shrines and mosques – to another, from which arises a secondary system of lesser residential paths. Deprived of its rich traditional connections, Utzon's re-use of the Iranian bazaar in the context of a modern shopping centre was forced and bizarre, especially since his street did not lead anywhere and lacked the traditional blanket of housing surrounding it.

The most interesting feature of this unrealised project was its elaborate vertebrae of large, identical, precast concrete segments. Something similar occurs in the enclosed sports arena of his Jeddah Stadium design in 1969. This instance is more elaborate than Farum. In keeping with Utzon's idea of an organic architecture capable of growth and change, he employed a suite of five standard units which constituted the architectural idea in much the way a musical idea is based on a recognisable melody. The composition was anchored to a 30,000-seat stadium which could be extended by the addition of further units in three stages.

The access roads constituted the backbone to it all. Here, as he had done many times before, Utzon adopted the tree metaphor, with the trunk and branches spreading out and serving the various parts. Since it was made up of the same five basic units, it compares to Arab architecture, which also is extremely geometric and repetitive. Because Jeddah is a hot region, shade was essential. The stadium grandstand consisted of three seating tiers under a roof which was folded into an elegant multi-faceted canopy to emphasise the strong contrast of sunlight and shade.

Utzon's most impressive achievement in this unrealised scheme is the clever way he integrated climatic, structural and industrial factors in a flexible structure in perfect harmony with traditional Arabic architectural principles.

The Espansiva system house in 1969 was initiated by a group of Danish timber merchants from the Timber Association who founded the Espansiva Byg A/S limited company for this specific purpose.

Denmark is a brick country, similar to Holland. Very little stone suitable for building purposes is available and Denmark imports most of its timber. The proposal to do away with bricks was more than radical – it bordered on the subversive. Bricklayers are the bane of the building industry everywhere. They have the power to halt most projects if they so choose. This has allowed them to dictate their terms to the building industry in many countries besides Denmark, thereby making brick and masonry work expensive and holding up jobs. A building system which eliminated bricks would theoretically be immune to such blackmail. This consideration, if not uppermost, played an important role in the timber merchants' thinking about the new Espansiva timber component house.

In April 1969, as a trial, Utzon erected a prototype house at 64 Bøssemagergade in the old section of Hellebæk near his father's cottage. The construction was similar to previous experiments with precast concrete modular units: on this occasion, the heavy, laminated, glued, wood frame in large sections, which replaced the heavy concrete members, rested on top of concrete pipe footings along with a floor decking of lightweight concrete planks. Once the structural units were in position, the outside could be enclosed using a selection of wall panels bolted to corner posts. The pitched roof was aluminium on the outside fixed to a base of stressed-skin plywood insulated with Rockwool. With this basic four-post frame unit, Utzon was able to produce a wide variety of different configurations.

The prototype house looked very Japanese, with its bare white outer walls and a mixture of brick, lightweight concrete and wooden cladding under wavy roof tiles. There the comparison stopped. Traditional Japanese domestic architecture is extremely frugal and minimal. Utzon's Espansiva system house was overdesigned, with almost twice the number of timber posts and roof rafters it needed structurally. The intention was to offer it for single-storey application in one-family houses, schools and motels, but the timber section sizes were many times too large. Although good in theory, in practice the additive principle multiplied the structural redundancy of what was already an over-sized structure. After a triangular, plywood plate bracing was added between the column and rafter, it looked clumsy and heavy-handed. This being Denmark, the glazing between the timber frames was largely confined to the internal courtyard. On the positive side, the room arrangement around an internal atrium court excluded the sights and sounds from the nearby street and added to its privacy.

Thirty of the houses were built in Norway, six or so in Denmark, including the Hana Hedin house at Birkehøj, together with some units at Jutland. The Espansiva system was sunk by the banks who would not advance finance for what appeared to them to be unfinished houses. Without a source of finance the experiment collapsed and the Espansiva company went out of business.

It was not a total loss as Utzon converted the trial house at Gammel Hellebæk into a very spacious and pleasant drawing office for himself.

Lin Utzon met Alex Popov the year before she left Australia. Popov's term as editor of *Tharunka* (the University of New South Wales's student magazine) ended in 1964 when he handed it over to Richard Neville. Lin was introduced to him at his graduation party in April 1965 while she was in her first year at art school. He had completed his arts degree the year before. After the Utzon family left Australia in April to return to Denmark, Popov waited till September 1966 before hurrying after Lin, stopping briefly at Holland Park in London to call on Neville before resuming his headlong rush towards Copenhagen.[11] For several years, Popov commuted across the North Sea by ferry between London where he was working and Copenhagen. In 1969, he moved to Copenhagen permanently. A week after Lin's twenty-third birthday, on 31 May 1969, she and Alex Popov were married.

The wedding was important to Jørn Utzon. Lin was the most artistically gifted of the three children. In Hawaii when the Sydney Opera House was opened, Jørn proudly proclaimed Alex Popov as one of his happiest legacies from Australia. By then Lin had borne a son, the first of two grandchildren.[12] In 1969, having reached the end of her textile studies at the Kunsthåndværksrskolen, Lin embarked on two years of cutting and costume design at Margretheskolen in Copenhagen. While she did this, Alex Popov began his architectural studies at the Royal Academy which he completed in 1972.

Popov had relatively little contact with Utzon's architectural practice at the beginning. Later, after he completed his master's degree in architecture and by the mid-seventies, there was a noticeably closer involvement. Popov gained considerably from his proximity to Utzon in terms of such ideas as an anonymous industrialised vernacular and additive form. His house for Lin on Mallorca attests to the depth of Utzon's influence and the obvious debts and similarity of his approach.

The failure of the Zürich Schauspielhaus project to go ahead numbed Utzon and then brought on a serious plunge into depression. No matter how terrible the news, Utzon never allowed others around him to see the depth of his inner despair. Shortly after the Zürich decision to cancel the new theatre reached Hellebæk, Alex Popov and Lin dined with Utzon and Lis. During the evening Utzon was subdued and said little until finally Alex Popov asked him about Zürich. Utzon could no longer avoid the topic and was forced into announcing that the job had been terminated.

Zürich had offered Utzon hope after the disappointment of Sydney but it too fell a victim to politics. Five years after the Sydney tragedy, this delivered a double blow. Compared to the rough-house politics of Davis Hughes in Sydney, Zürich was a relatively sterile, surgical amputation. For years Utzon had carried on the pretence of normality; now, enveloped by a grey fog, the brittle facade he had maintained so painstakingly collapsed. Utzon sank into immobility and helpless despair. For several days, Alex Popov drove around the countryside with Utzon stretched out on the back seat, traumatised and barely aware of his surroundings.

Depression affects many people and is many times worse in creative individuals. Utzon, being such a perfectionist, was particularly prone to it and suffered periodic episodes of 'talking black'. Accompanying such episodes he was also afflicted by terrifying blackouts which temporarily erased his memory. Utzon's depressive collapse was most acute after Zürich.

Sometime after his return, most likely in 1968 or perhaps later, Utzon removed the large models of the Opera House interiors from the Hellebæk factory, took them down to the beach at Ålsgårde and threw them in a pile. In Denmark, people celebrate the summer solstice with bonfires, sometimes throwing dolls into them as a re-creation of witch-burning from an earlier era. Utzon set fire to his bonfire of models and expunged the Opera House from his life.[13]

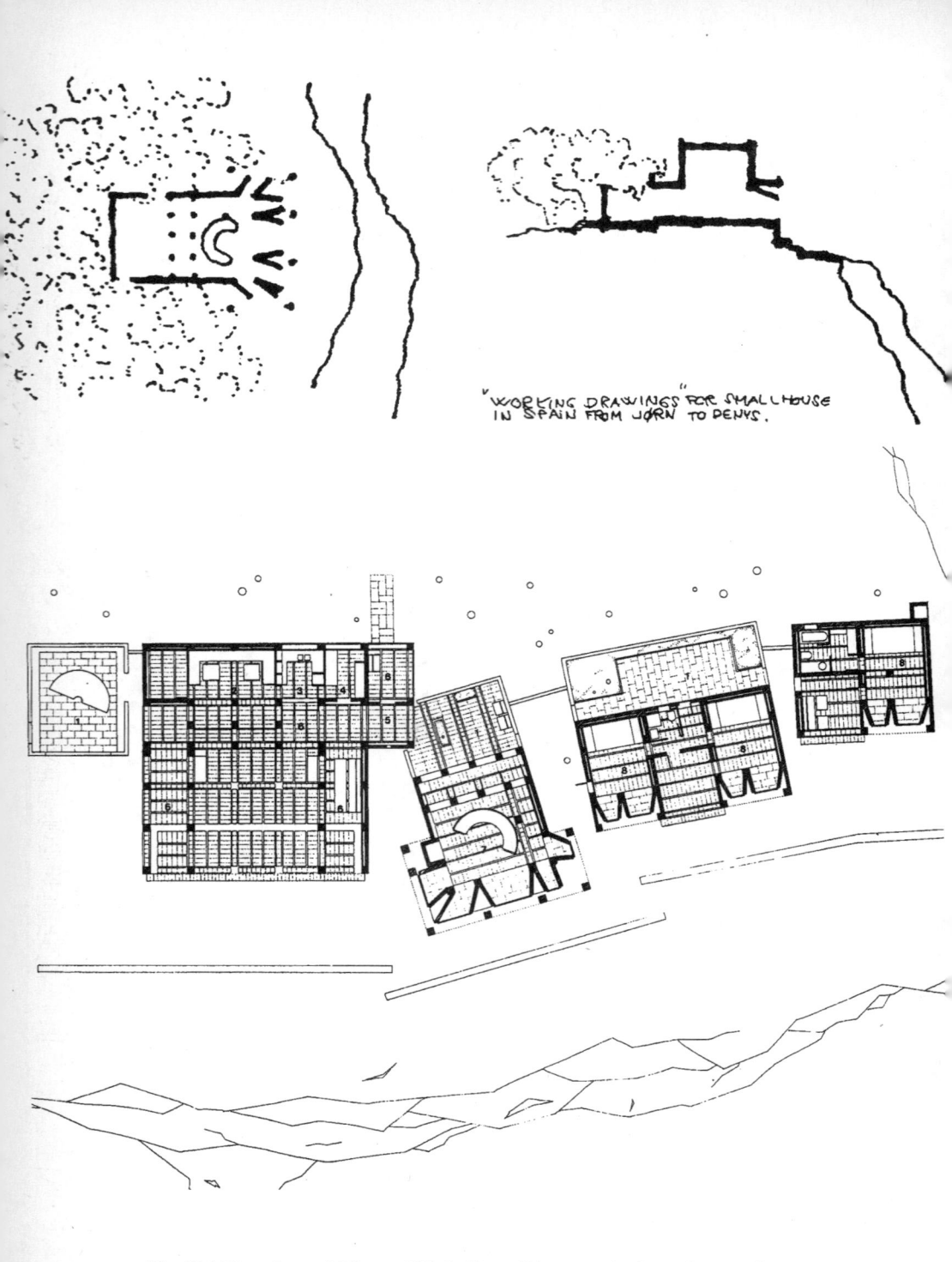

"WORKING DRAWINGS" FOR SMALL HOUSE IN SPAIN FROM JØRN TO DENYS.

'Can Lis', Utzon house, Mallorca, 1971-2. Above: Diagrammatic plan and section demonstrate the relationship of interior to the cliff and Mediterranean. Below: Plan consisting of four pavilions (left to right): dining and kitchen pavilion facing open court with side entry from street; the living/sitting room forms a sculptural cockpit that looks out through deep-set window enclosures which frame the sea view; two separate bedroom pavilions with bath and toilets.

19

Laying Low
Denmark, Hawaii, Mallorca, 1971–1972

The sea spreads far below; its blue whale's back
Forcing no limits on us;
Beyond rain-laden ranks of olive trees
And rising, sail in convoy through clear sky.

Robert Graves, 'The Crab-tree'[1]

Instead of paying Utzon the architectural fees it owed him, the New South Wales Government threatened him with a counter-suit which would have tied him up in court for a considerable time and required his presence in Australia. Neither party wanted this. To avoid going to court, on 23 June 1970 Utzon accepted a substantially reduced settlement of A$46,000. Davis Hughes, as the Minister for Public Works, was spared the humiliation of having damaging revelations about his maladministration of the project aired in public.

Utzon's father Aage had been ill for some time. He rarely complained, and stoically believed in maintaining a positive outlook, leavened with good humour and the occasional joke. Once his eyesight failed Aage lost his independence, which went strongly against his grain. In 1970, Utzon embarked on a project to design an unorthodox two-tonne yacht for his own use. He consulted his father on the hull shape. By then, Aage's sight had deteriorated so much that he could not see the model properly and was forced to run his hands over the model to assess its shape, before he gave his approval and said how enthusiastic he was.

Subconsciously, Jørn Utzon may have wanted his sailing boat for his family. Ships were an important component of the Utzon identity. The new yacht had something in common with the Bayview house, it was more a sea-house for the family than a fast racing hull, with its weird split hull and third hull sandwiched in between, that fused into a pointed bow. Utzon named it 'Tri-Tail' on account of this.

Aage Utzon was famed for his double-ender yachts. His son now outdid him with a triple-ender. The hull design was peculiar to say the least. Its beam to wetted length ratio was 3.4, compared to 11, the ratio generally considered optimum for speed through water. Instead of reducing the beam and making the hull slimmer, Utzon widened it by folding two outer hulls backwards from the bow around a shorter third hull in the centre. It looked like a compressed trimaran that had been pinched at the bow. Instead of one normal, blunt stern, Utzon's yacht had two pointed sterns fused at the deck that came together at the bow like Siamese twins.

Beneath the water line, Utzon's triple-melded hull resembled a swan with its legs trailing. Possibly Utzon hoped his hybrid would possess the stability of a trimaran, combined with the manoeuvrability of a monohull. In the event it was stable but very slow. To prove his unorthodox hull shape, Utzon conducted a great number of large model tests in the tank at Helsingør.

His yacht's dimensions were relatively modest. It had a displacement of 1900 kg (two tonnes) and measured 10.5 m, with a 3.05 m beam and 1.85 m draught, and carried 50 m^2 (538 ft^2) of sail.[2] The Al-boat company at Helsingør built the aluminium hull, which was ready in June 1971. In the water, Utzon discovered the mast was wrongly positioned and it was moved and the ballast adjusted. Not before the summer of 1972 did Utzon venture to sail north out of the Sound and on up the west coast of Sweden.

Utzon's triple-ender was a better symbol than it was a sail boat. It was certainly no wave-piercer and proved sluggish and slow to respond to the helm. To compensate for its lack of performance and manoeuvrability, it had a capacious interior and was stable in storms. Other than that, Utzon had produced something that was a cross between a house-boat and a sailing boat. It was slow and comfortable, a cruise boat with sails. In the normally curious yachting world, its appearance was greeted with silence.

Utzon's triple-ender performed more like an ugly duckling than a graceful swan. It proved such an expensive failure, and was so costly to build, it bankrupted its builder, the Al-boat company.

Aage Utzon did not live long enough to see his son's new yacht. He died on 14 November 1970, seven months before it was finished. In Nordic myth, besides their connection with death, boats are also symbols of the departed hero's journey into the spirit world, so it was perhaps more than coincidental that Jørn Utzon began his own yacht around the time his father died. Aage Utzon was buried in the Hellebæk churchyard unostentatiously under a large plain flat stone slab bearing the name UTZON in capital letters.

In December 1969 Utzon had entered the competition for a National Museum devoted to landscape studies at the ruins of the famous castle of Hammershus, on the island of Bornholm in the Baltic. Hammershus was built by the Archbishop of Lund, in Sweden, in the 1250s, on a cliff top below the northernmost tip of Bornholm. It is one of the largest castles in northern Europe, in a region famous for its wilderness. The museum site was to the east of castle, back from the rugged coast and protected by a deep ravine.

The centre was to have an exhibition hall, restaurant, cafeteria and toilets, along with the usual tourist facilities. Utzon's solution was elegant and simple. The steepness of the ravine limited access for visitors on foot. To deal with the access problem, Utzon devised a series of interconnected, elevated bridges to link the three main pavilions. These were expressed as simple metal-clad sheds with sloping skillion roofs, and their floors raised on slim steel stilts, so they overlooked the thick wood below them. After all his effort, the project was cancelled. Utzon was so enraged he refused to pick up his drawings.[3]

In the early 1970s, Utzon operated from three locations: Hellebæk, Hawaii and Mallorca. In the years after 1966, while the Opera House was being completed, he dropped below the public horizon and, to all intents, it looked as though he was seeking public invisibility. Two major events, the Zürich debacle and his father's death, coming after the numerous uncompleted projects and unfulfilled hopes, heightened the sense of disappointment at this time.

Utzon worked his way through the crisis. When fortune appeared to desert him, he turned to new challenges and new horizons to occupy himself. The Kuwait National Assembly Complex, which he designed in 1971, was such a challenge; his house on Mallorca was another. Both occurred at around the same time. Coinciding with the start of work on the new house near Porto Petro on Mallorca, Jørn and Lis left Denmark to settle there permanently. Later, in September 1971, Utzon escaped to the Pacific to Hawaii where he had a part-time job teaching at the Manoa campus of the University of Hawaii starting in the fall semester. Utzon had become acquainted with Hawaii in the 1960s, often breaking his journey there on his frequent flights to Australia. It is normal for an architect's career to have ups and downs. Work is as unreliable for architects as it is for actors; one moment there is nothing, the next he or she is being swamped. Hawaii was an interlude that helped fill in the blanks and bought Utzon time to think.

Bruce Heatherington, a Canadian, was responsible for inviting Utzon to Hawaii. The architecture school was small with only 50 students. During his stay, Utzon ran a design studio and taught a class in climatology in which he related building form to climate. With such small studios, his teaching responsibilities were light. In public, he explained his presence in Hawaii as arising from the need to study the effect of hot climates for Kuwait. Hawaii, he said, provided an ideal location to do this. The proposition that Honolulu, with its lush volcanic setting, contained any lessons for Kuwait City, sited on the margins of the Arabian desert, is so implausible it is surprising no one challenged him.

Utzon also gave a single public lecture on the Opera House and showed his slides of its construction. He was still very sensitive and the wounds remained perilously close to the surface. He appeared to be laying low in Hawaii and, probably because of the Opera House, may have wanted to escape further attention.

In Hawaii he spent time with his old friend Peer Abben, with whom he had a loose partnership arrangement. Utzon purchased a tract house on the north-eastern, windward side of Oahu away from Honolulu, at Kailua. He seemed to be resting, taking life easy. His days were spent quietly enjoying the warmth, the sun and the beach.

The law gives Danish citizens the option of not paying tax if they live for one day more than half a year – 183 days – outside Denmark. What better place was there for Utzon to qualify than Hawaii, where the sunshine was stronger than the tax burden?

Professor Leighton Liu shared an office with Utzon at the School of Architecture. He was very impressed by Utzon as a person and recalls from their brief association that his humanity and generosity of spirit were the things that struck others more than his stature as an architect. To Liu, 'He was a very elegant gentleman.' Utzon spent his time relaxing quietly in Hawaii, swimming, going on walks and shopping. While there, he did not design anything that was notably important.

Both Utzon's sons studied architecture. Jan Utzon, being the eldest, assisted his father at first from 1970 on. After Kim Utzon qualified in 1981 and became active, Utzon and Associates was established later. Now that he had two sons attending to the day-to-day responsibilities of the practice, Utzon could afford to spend more time away and suit himself without disrupting projects.

No country, least of all Denmark, can stand apart from the world. Because it is so small and lacks energy resources, Denmark is especially vulnerable. Utzon was in Hawaii when the six-day Arab–Israeli war broke in October 1973. No sooner had it started than it was over. The news pictures testified to the deadly swiftness of the conflict, with the shattered lines of boiled Russian tanks, the scattered remains of Egyptian armoured columns, and gutted MiG fighter aircraft destroyed on the ground by rocket fire. Expressing Arab indignation, OPEC retaliated and world oil prices quadrupled. To deal with the crisis, the Government in Denmark halted building activities which immediately caused widespread unemployment among Danish architects. The oil-shock affected everyone; the world economy was in chaos, and no one knew when petroleum production by OPEC would return to pre-war levels. The situation was unstable.

Utzon, like millions of other people, was affected. For Utzon, just as for many other architects, it represented a dire calamity and the end of his domestic practice. In other parts of the world, such as Kuwait, the oil-shock meant increased income, for even with its exports cut Kuwait's earnings from petroleum soared. Kuwait's problems were more political in nature. Utzon decided to ride out the uncertainties in Mallorca.

The English poet and novelist, Robert Graves, had moved to Mallorca in 1929, and established himself in a large plain stone villa at Deyà on the north coast. Except for the war years, when he moved back to England, Graves remained there till his death in 1985. When Utzon arrived in 1971, there was a sizeable expatriate English and Scandinavian community already basking in the warm, rejuvenating sunshine and 20 per cent income tax rate.

During the Sydney Opera House days, Utzon and Lis had spent a pleasant vacation on the Balearic Islands. Well back from the sea, the countryside was hard and spiky, its bones sticking through a decrepit cardigan of low pine, myrtle and cactus, produced by the light winter rains and left to struggle on through the summer heat. One day, while they were exploring the Mallorquin countryside along the south coast, Jørn turned to Lis and asked whether she would like to own the mountain in front of them. Because the land was unsuitable for farming, the local farmers were eager to sell. Word spread, and Utzon was inundated with offers.[4] Utzon ultimately purchased land parcels on the cliffs south of Porto Petro for his first house, 'Can Lis', at around the same time that he bought his mountain.[5]

Mallorca has a rich vernacular architecture and an involved history of invasions by the Phoenicians, Carthaginians, Romans and Arabs. Its three-century Arab legacy, from the tenth century to the reconquest by Spain, left it with an abundance of Arab baths, castles, a tradition of rectangular courtyards, arched entrances, plain facades and distinctive glazed *tribuna* balconies. The combination of Mediterranean and Arab influences, and

Mallorca's nearness to Spain and Europe, proved irresistible for the Utzons.

Utzon chose the coast near Porto Petro, 70 kilometres southeast of the capital Palma, for his house – the opposite coast to Robert Graves. Utzon was 53. The house is perched on top of a cliff looking towards Africa. The area was known as Colonia del Silencio – the colony of silence – which must itself have exerted a strong appeal on Utzon. A more romantic location could hardly be imagined. It was well off the charter-flying tourist itinerary and secluded from the world.

Utzon's house sits on the top of a cliff 20 metres above the sea, drenched by salt spray. The rugged south coast forms a natural fortress of crescent-shaped battlements that tumble unsteadily into the sea, their continuity broken every now and then by a tiny cove embrasure or sandy beach. It is cold and damp enough in winter to require an open fire.[6] The site forms a narrow strip along the edge hardly more than 30 metres deep, pressed between a road at the rear and the cliff edge. The cliff is not sheer, but drops by stages into the sea in a series of large, undercut, terraced ledges.

Utzon completed 'Can Lis' in 1972. It is a genuine masterpiece, as perfect as Utzon could make it. Unlike Sydney, Utzon was at last able to do exactly as he pleased in his Mallorquin house. The Opera House never fulfilled Utzon's aesthetic ambitions for it.

'Can Lis', with its overpowering simplicity, spills out in many different directions. It is both a frame and receptor of the horizon and a village in miniature straddling the cliff top, a place of silence and tranquillity reaching out to the universe. It does many things with the light: altering its effects, filtering, reflecting, slicing it into single beams to catch each aspect of the day. On the outside walls Utzon mounted large, rectangular, splayed, stone frames. These resemble Le Corbusier's deep-set windows in his Ronchamp Chapel near Belfort in France but, in a departure from Le Corbusier, Utzon placed them on the outside projecting forward of his facade. In the late afternoon, a blade of golden light slices through a vertical slit from high up in the main living room, and slowly moves across the stone floor.

The materials are the same as the local Mallorquin buildings. Porous limestone was brought from a local quarry between Campos and Santanyí 15 kilometres away. Utzon employed a local builder from Santanyí, Jaime Vidal, who understood traditional methods. The soft yellow tufaceous stone was sawn into blocks using a circular saw which left its mark on the stone. For horizontal support over the openings, standard precast concrete beams were built into the stonework. Under the roof, the same beams carry 60 cm, curved, Catalan, arched, terracotta tiles, on which the concrete roof was poured and flat-tiled. Double beams were provided under the parapets which were then capped with Roman pan-tiles.

The house was built from the same local sandstone in 20 cm x 40 cm blocks, 10 cm or 20 cm thick, laid up with a cavity. The attractive sandy yellow stone is used throughout, in the floors, walls, and deep window embrasures – even the furniture, benches, tables are made of stone. For a house built by hand and using traditional Mallorquin methods, it seems ironical that it should represent the fulfilment of Utzon's ideas about using a simple kit of parts. If, instead of precast concrete, he uses a rectangular block of stone for his basic unit, the principle is the same – one material, one process, a few standard elements.

'Can Lis', like the Opera House in Sydney, occupies a border between land and sea. It is married to the horizon. 'Can Lis' runs along its rough stretch of cliff top, a group of oddly angled, separate pavilions whose windows draw us forwards towards the sea and on to the airy distances beyond. Its stillness recalls the calming peace of a temple and invites us to sit in silence and meditate, drawing in nature around us. The intense quietness of the space focuses on the immediate world of our senses.

It is impossible to ignore the horizon at the edge of the sea. It dazzles the eye, pulling it back again and again. It is an ever-present accompaniment to existence in this house, wherever you turn it is there, a faint, blue, misty, arching line gently running across your vision, calming and distancing everything, plunging life into infinity. Light pours through each window embrasure like honey. 'Can Lis' strips away the clutter of daily living leaving only what is essential. It is basic, primitive, somehow fundamental in its reaching out into nature. The very name of the locality, Colonia del Silencio, which suggests an earnest desire to retreat in silence from the world, appealed to Utzon.

The disappointments of the past, the failure to realise the Bayview house, the accumulated store of ideas, were all invested in this wonderful Mallorquin house as a concentrated experience. Nothing else by Utzon is as personal, so bound up with his daily rituals and joys, so austere yet so rich in details, so underplayed yet so easy and apparently effortless. It is as universal as Mies van der Rohe's Barcelona Pavilion was in 1929, but it has a message from a new age Mies could never appreciate. At the beginning of the twentieth century, architects imagined an industrial utopia was about to unfold; Utzon has moved on from there, he has gone back into the past to an earlier age, to rediscover a universal deeply ingrained sense of dwelling anchored in the earth that once again renews our awareness of the earth and sky.

The Mallorquin house is Utzon's counter-theorem to the Barcelona Pavilion. Mies's pavilion could just as easily have been realised in Berlin or Buenos Aires as Barcelona – the location made very little difference to the result. The Barcelona Pavilion chopped space into smaller pieces, pressed it between the horizontal plates of the roof and floor, and shunted it back and forth against vertical wall planes. The interior re-packaged cosmic immensity in a smaller, intimate version that flowed back and forth in an open, interconnected series of fluid volumes. From the opposite direction, Utzon built his forms by adding similar units, the same as a Moroccan village or a wasps' nest is built from an aggregation of parts. Mies begins with the cosmos and reduces it to an abstract Euclidean model at the human scale; Utzon begins with a room which is already human in its scale, and adds on to it, extending it atomically into the universe. Mies's pavilion belongs to the Western tradition of rational Euclidean abstraction, Utzon's retreat on Mallorca is contingent and palpably physical in its appeal to the senses. Mies divided the universal into small abstract units; Utzon begins with concrete, human-sized units, then builds by addition until his structures spill out into the universal.

Utzon based his Mallorquin house on a heap of sugar cubes.

One day he arrived early in the morning at the small fishing harbour of Cala Figuera to look at the site. The following day, sitting at a café, with the image of the cliff top still vividly in his mind, Utzon spread out a packet of sugar cubes on the table in front of him and arranged them into a model of the house.[7] The fact that it is made from large blocks of yellow limestone, not sugar cubes, is inconsequential, the individual sugar-cube shapes are readily recognised in the shapes of the four pavilions.

More than anything else, 'Can Lis' resembles the ruined Minoan Palace at Knossos on Crete. It is of course incomparably smaller, more of a mini-palace, and somewhat reminiscent of a temple by the sea. The rooms and courtyards form a labyrinth that has precisely the same irregular chaotic feeling as on Hydra and Mykonos and other islands in the Greek Cyclades. The four pavilions are crushed together so completely, and at such oddly fortuitous angles, they have fused together, but not so tightly as to destroy each sugar-cube shape. One room leads into the next, and on to the chamber beyond that, and so on; wandering through it you stumble across unexpected views, glimpses of secret corners, small scraps of landscape jump out, framed or released in a spontaneous exchange with the outside. The whole of it is so fragmented in its parts it appears to be much larger than it really is. In this regard, 'Can Lis' is exactly like a Mediterranean village. It was meant to be that way – an anonymous group of stone blocks, walls, colonnades, windows, terraces and plants.

The four pavilions stretch out along the cliff in line, the kitchen and dining area in the westernmost pavilion, which extends forward towards the cliff edge in two colonnades at the sides of an atrium; after it is the living room, which has a courtyard at its rear. Beyond, the third pavilion lunges sideways, partly overlapping the preceding pavilion; this has two bedrooms and bathroom which share a covered outdoor court at the front. At the very end, the last pavilion consists of a single bedroom, bathroom and covered court, and swivels back onto the original alignment. At the opposite end, next to the kitchen, Utzon built a free-standing court with half-circular openings in the tops of the low walls to view the sea and the sunset, and a semi-circular table covered in deep blue tiles for outdoor meals at the back.

On an island as small as Mallorca, surrounded by the Mediterranean on every side, the horizon is omnipresent. It dominates the edge, casting its spell over everything. Robert Graves responded to the enchantment of the sea's entrapment in the poem 'Horizon':

> *On a clear day how thin the horizon*
> *Drawn between sea and sky*
> *Between sea-love and sky-love;*
> *And after sunset how debatable*
> *Even for an honest eye.*[8]

The large goggle-shaped windows on the outside of the house are arranged individually and point in different directions to catch the sunlight one after the other. From early in the morning to sunset, each in turn is filled with golden light, then empties gradually until it surrenders to the darkness. The procession of daylight across the living room shifts hour by hour during the day, following the path of the sun.

The house is constructed simply, the walls and columns support beams which carry the terracotta roof vault. Because the local limestone was porous and water-absorbent, Utzon constructed the external walls of two stone skins and left a cavity between to keep the interior dry. Along the sea front, each window opening has a large, splayed, rectangular, stone embrasure, 80 cm or so deep, so large a person can stand inside them. These box-like window frames are like medieval castle windows or giant amphora turned on their sides with their bottoms knocked out. They point in different directions and the glass is fixed on the outside edge to make it invisible from inside the room. This unusual detail of the glazing is extremely successful – so successful the windows appear to be unglazed and open to the air, like an ancient Greek palace.

Utzon broke up what was a sweeping panorama of the Mediterranean into separate vignettes. Each triptych is snipped into longer and shorter lengths, with gaps in between them that separate each vista, and sections of scenery are left out. Instead of a single sweeping view, the outlook is reduced to a tantalising series of pictures whose incompleteness challenges the imagination in the way a movie sometimes plays with reality, letting us see some things, hiding others.

The terracotta vaults resting on precast concrete beams covered by concrete and flat tiles resemble the Bayview house in the way they divide the room into bays; however, instead of plywood U-beams, Utzon substituted the Mallorquin equivalent – precast beams in a terracotta vault. This demonstrates both the persistence and adaptability of certain Utzon ideas. His primary concern is to keep the unity of his construction – technology is subservient. In whatever he does, his first objective is to maintain and reinforce the monolithic effect so the result seems to be quarried out of the solid rock, like a cave.

Beautiful blue, white and brown tiles create a focus in the spaces, their lustrous richness providing a sensuous opposition to the hard plainness of the walls with their saw marks. The tiles add an exotic Moorish counterpoint and make a subtle allusion to Antonio Gaudi's work in Barcelona. Because the name of the street is Cala media luna, Utzon featured a crescent moon opening at the entrance. Walking from the street into the covered porch, you are greeted by a square of white tiles edged at the bottom by a series of triangular-shaped blue inserts, in the middle of which is a crescent moon opening through which some pine trees and the sea can be glimpsed on the other side.

At the rear of the living room is a low semi-circular stone bench, the back and seat of which has been faced with white tiles, and edged by half-round blue tiles. Comfortable linen cushions soften the tiles. In the middle is a low table made with flat slabs of stone placed upright on their edges and used for supports, with horizontal pieces of stone laid out across them on top. The table forms an incomplete polygon divided into three wedges, in diminishing sizes. The gaps between can be used as a leg space to stretch out in. At the table's corners, practical grey tile triangles fill the gaps between the white tiles. Like everything else in the house, the seat and table form a beautiful sculpture. It is perfectly in keeping with the cubic simplicity of the room.

The shape, a semi-circle, adds to the pleasure of being with friends since it draws everyone a little closer and brings a renewed sense of intimacy to the circle. People look across at each other, watch each other's expressions, much the way Utzon intended in his theatre designs. The seating circle is a small theatre both in its shape and the way it intensifies and enhances the social experience.

Architecture's poetry arises from simple small things, from the direct honest expression of the materials, from the way Utzon carefully reveals and explains the construction to us, to the way the daylight is subtly transformed hour by hour throughout each day. In a high corner of the living room left of the fireplace, Utzon left a narrow vertical aperture. This was probably something that occurred to him in the midst of building. The rough way the blocks have been cut has the appearance of an unplanned afterthought. Open to the south-west, it attracts the dying afternoon sun, an early reminder the day is coming to an end. The light from this slit creeps up the wall slowly, shortening as it does, sweeping across the grooved saw marks on the stone face like a prison searchlight, before expiring suddenly into darkness.

'Can Lis' on Mallorca is arguably Utzon's greatest work. Manuel Cabellos, a local Mallorquin architect, said of it, 'Utzon understands the spirit of the Mediterranean, the light, the landscape, the sea and local materials, even more so than our native architects.' It is an opinion worth pondering.

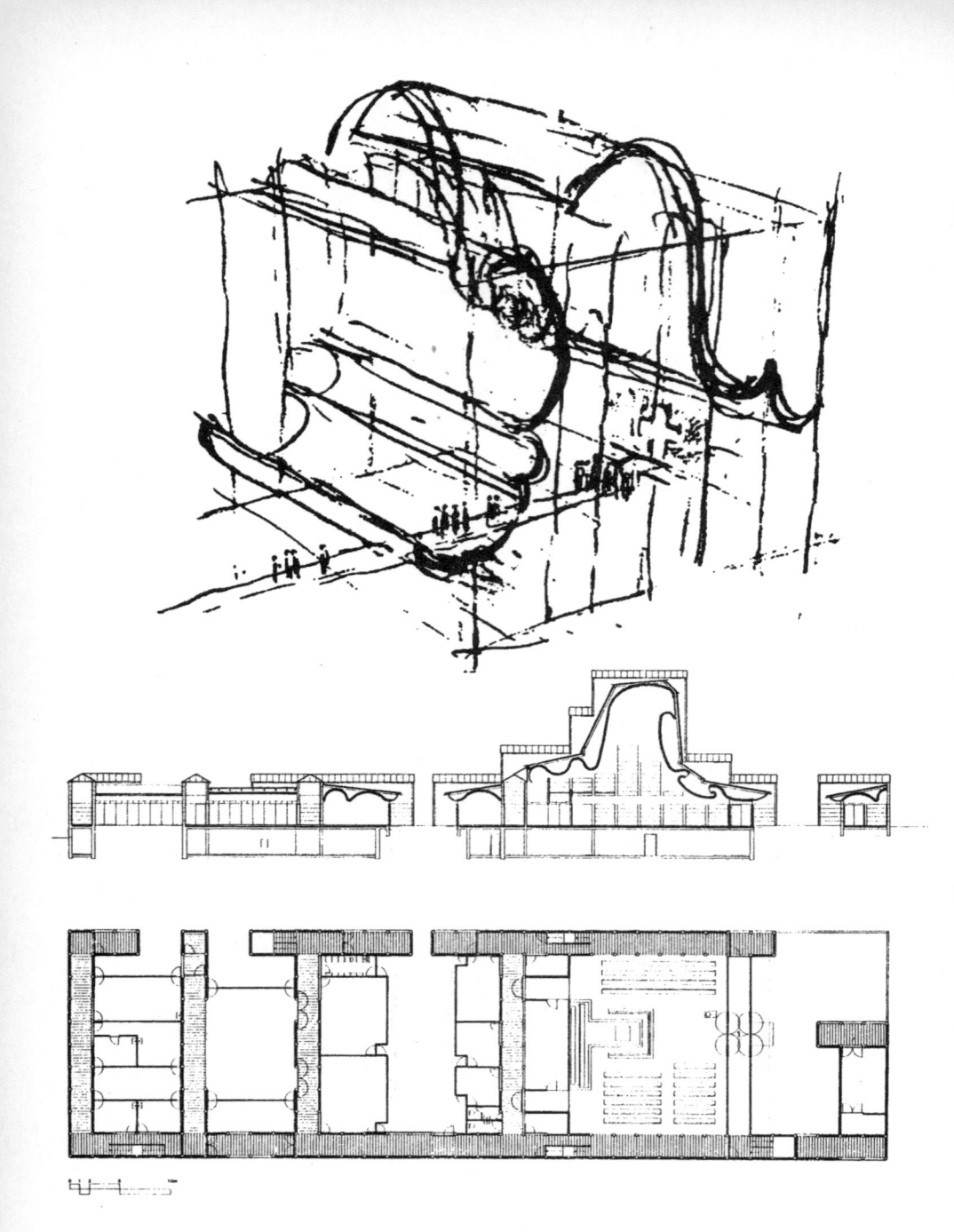

Bagsværd Church, North Zealand, 1973-6. Above: Sketch: the curving vaults ascend high above the altar in the form of a breaking wave which admits light into the church. Centre: Entry: proceeds via a courtyard on the north, ancillary parish hall, meeting rooms and such like are on the south. Below: Plan.

20

Flowers of Light
Mallorca, 1973–1976

A little after 2.45 p.m. on Saturday 20 October 1973, Queen Elizabeth II officially opened the Opera House. The spectacle was witnessed by 15,000 guests who crowded onto the steps and forecourt in front of the royal dais. Her Majesty was unsettled by a strong north-westerly wind, gusting at 45 knots, which swept the site, forcing her to clutch her hat tightly.

Queen Elizabeth noted that the Opera House had captured the imagination of the world and expressed her opinion: 'controversy of the most extreme kind attended the building of the pyramids, yet they stand today – 4000 years later – acknowledged as one of the wonders of the world. I believe this will be so for the Sydney Opera House.' Moments later, from high on the ridge of the nearest shell, a didgeridoo commenced its monotonous droning beat and the tiny figure of Aboriginal actor Ben Blakeney, sharply silhouetted against the sky, loudly proclaimed: 'I am Bennelong. Two hundred years ago fires burned on this point, the fires of my people …'

At the signal 'Anchors away', a fanfare of trumpets blared forth to herald the flypast of three flights of F-111s in tight V-formation, with their wings extended, which looked like giant menacing Bogong moths as they slowly clawed their way across the sky leaving thick black smoke trails behind. Known as 'the flying Opera House', the final cost of buying the F-111s substantially exceeded that of the Opera House, an irony lost in the excitement of the moment.

Half an hour later, after making a short tour of the building, the Queen walked to the northern broadwalk to launch the harbour carnival. Watched from many hundreds of small craft and yachts thronging the waters around it, bright pink, 120 m long streamers were unfurled from the northern end of the Opera House in a gesture symbolising the launch of 'a great ship of sail' and 60,000 hydrogen-filled balloons, imprisoned under nets in two barges on either side of the point, leapt into the air and filled the sky overhead with giant clouds of rising confetti, which were quickly carried off by the wind.

The Premier, Sir Robert Askin, made the most of the occasion. Like natural parents who have been forced to give up their child for adoption, the NSW Labor Party Opposition stood by helpless, while the Liberal and Country Party fussed over and made much of the newly born, beaming over it before a world audience and keeping up the pretence they were its natural parents. With Her Majesty the Queen officiating, the ceremony legitimised the substitution. A new Labor administration led by Gough Whitlam had been elected to office in Canberra less than a year before, in December, and Askin was anxious to dampen the assertive independence of Labor's 'new nationalism' with a banal display of loyalty to the sovereign.

There was one notable absence – Jørn Utzon. He spent the spring semester teaching in Hawaii, but shortly before the opening ceremony he left for South-East Asia, thereby making it impossible for the media to contact him. At the end of this he returned to Denmark and by mid-October was back in Mallorca. In an interview in April in Hawaii, on being asked whether he would like to attend, Utzon had replied 'We'd like to very much, of course. But so far, we haven't had an invitation – even though a Sydney evening paper told us we had.'[1] Later, after he received an invitation, Utzon declined, giving as his reason the excuse that his presence would cause embarrassment and re-open the controversy. Utzon stated that he did not want to stir up any bitterness and observed that there had been far too much criticism already. In fact, it was too much criticism that caused the trouble in the first place. In his opinion, Australians ought to be more gentle in their criticism. To criticise is to run the risk of 'destroying their own talent and achievements, or losing their talent to other countries. Artists thrive on encouragement, not criticism.'

At this, Mrs Utzon interjected: 'After all, you don't drag out a young plant by the roots and tell it, "you're not growing fast enough".' Utzon concluded, 'The main thing is that the Opera House will be a great stimulus to Australian culture.'

Five years later, Utzon explained that he had declined the invitation to the opening not for any negative reasons but because he considered it was the most diplomatic thing he could do under the circumstances.[2] He described how an enormous number of newspaper journalists had pursued him asking for the 'true story' of the Opera House and his 'bitter recriminations'. Knowing that there was no way to avoid the press if he came to Sydney, especially since he would be in the company of people such as Davis Hughes, whom he knew would be attending, this would increase the chances of a resurrection of the controversy. In Utzon's judgement, the publicity could have easily overshadowed the celebrations and embarrassed the guests who had nothing to do with the matter. By not coming he prevented this happening.

Utzon asked why, since Sydney people like the Opera House, they didn't ask him to design something else for them. Reflecting on his time in Sydney, Utzon said he considered the eight years he had spent working on the project among the happiest and most productive of his life. Looking back to the time at Palm Beach, he recalled how terribly upset Lis was when they left their house there. To make up for the disappointment, 'I built her another one as close as I could get to the style and environment in Spain ['Can Lis' on Mallorca]. It's a holiday house.'[3]

Utzon's isolation was due to other factors more than a direct antipathy to the press. When it suits him and he feels it is in his interest, he will talk very amiably with journalists. Nevertheless, his condition goes well beyond what may be diagnosed as extreme shyness or hyper-sensitivity, and amounts to real social phobia. In hiding himself away and refusing to speak to people, he passively stimulates rather than dampens curiosity about him.

Denmark was severely affected by the 1973 oil crisis following the six-day Arab–Israeli war. With public building projects halted Utzon arranged his life in a triangle, dividing his time between Mallorca, Hawaii and Styrsö on the coast of Sweden south-west of Göteborg, where he found a suitably isolated skægarden (primitive vacation house) for the summer.[4] The west coast, during the summer season, attracts many visitors, especially to Bohuslan (Bohus County) with its small fishing villages, rugged coast, long fjords and numerous small islands. A skægarden there is highly prized and extremely expensive to buy. The artist Carl Wilhelmson, attracted by its rugged, weather-beaten fisherfolk and picturesque villages, painted it early this century. For Utzon, it provided a hideaway and sailing ground.

Back in 1967–68, not long after he had returned to Denmark from Australia, Utzon was invited to design a school complex on the eastern outskirts of Herning comprising several colleges, including export and textile design, with which the school would share subjects, teachers and buildings.

Because the school's future had yet to be decided, Utzon considered it prudent to explore a variety of possible development scenarios and arrange the college buildings using smaller units which he could combine very freely.[5] This was a further application of the additive principle. Thinking about the problem, Utzon concluded that it was desirable to have a free choice of height, size and lighting for each room type, depending on and related to their use, but based on a single, overriding common denominator of a horizontal frame, which would serve as a structural base for the roof, at door height level. The individual, hat-like roofs rested on identical height posts at the corners of each room. The common door height frame became in effect a surrogate platform, on which, in the same manner as the base of the Opera House in Sydney, the different roof shapes – varying from low, half-barrel vaulted skylights to tall, upswept, concave skylights – were mounted. The roof could be developed in any direction to satisfy the volumetric and daylight requirements. Below the roof plane, Utzon placed columns at the corners of each room, leaving a substantial gap between them, to form internal corridors and allow access to the interior. Since the roof loads were borne by the four corner columns, each room was enclosed by non-bearing elements.

The cellular additive principle might be applied to a single house, to a group of buildings such as a school, and even a town; from the very small, to a very large, it accommodated continuous outward expansion and growth.

Herning is in a flat and uninteresting moorland in central Jutland west of Århus. By the 1970s, its textile industry was in decline, threatened by cheap overseas producers, and consequently production, but not design and marketing, was moved offshore. Therefore Utzon's textile design school was never built, at least not in the form Utzon envisaged. The only lasting result of the prototype for the additive school-construction system was the completion in 1970 of one small node known as the Experimental house or Utzon museum (Utzon Huset).

Aage Damgaard is an eccentric character whose favourite hobby was riding bulls. His other interest was encouraging and supporting public art in Herning. He was an excellent and discerning judge of art and architecture, thus his 1965 Angli shirt factory was designed by the firm of C.F. Møller and was remarkable because of its unusual, hollow, circular plan resembling a fat, curled leech.

One of Damgaard's early important decisions was to place a small surcharge on the shirts manufactured at his Angli factory of 1 p, the money from which was judiciously invested in works by artists such as Robert Jacobsen, Sven Dalsgaard, Carl Henning-Pedersen and many others. Their artwork was donated to Herning council for display at sites around the city. In a second initiative, Damgaard invited artists to set up studios in his factory with the idea of improving the quality of design through their direct involvement and to encourage a cross-fertilisation between art and production. The idea may have derived from Marimekko in Finland, who did something rather like this much earlier than Damgaard, or it may possibly have been his own idea. He was extremely generous and permitted the artists great freedom, with the result that when the Angli factory was converted to the Herning Art Museum in 1977, along with his own art collection, the artist's work rooms were preserved in the new museum.

Utzon's tiny experiment sits by itself in farmland on the south side of the main access road running past the Herning Kunstmuseum. A windbreak partially screens the exhibition centre on the east side, otherwise it is relatively isolated from the main section of the art park and on its own. Its silhouette from a distance is determined by its roof, really a series of distinct individual roofs since each room within it has a separate roof unlike its neighbour. The predominance of the roofs is emphasised by the outline of the main roof in the shape of an upswept funnel, with a sharply chiselled top to trap the northern light. It is more than double the height of the other roofs, which all stand on the same continuous base. This funnel roof draws the sky down into itself past tilted louvres through the sloping-top skylight and into the metal-sheathed roof, filling the square, upswept void with a soft radiance.

Normally, the house is entered through a tiny courtyard, quite empty except for a bare tree; this leads into a hall, and around the hall are grouped the three exhibition spaces, plus a kitchen and store. At the room corners, at right angles, large triangular pairs of plywood plates stiffen and brace the top of the columns and prevent any sideways distortion or movement of the frame. Because they are repeated they can be seen in each neighbouring space, which establishes a pleasing rhythm and reiteration of the triangular motif throughout the complex.

The generous roof volumes release the exhibition spaces vertically and allow them to float upwards. Without them the interior would feel unduly low and restrictive, if not claustrophobic. From inside, it is possible to see out through low horizontal strip windows, but on looking up the rooms expand and become enlarged by large skylights which draw in the sky and permit framed views of the variously arched profiles of the neighbouring metal-clad roof vaults.

This accentuation of the upper volumes above each room alleviates the sensation of smallness inside. Nowhere is this more so than in the first of the exhibition spaces. Here the room surges upwards, narrowing as it does into an inclined skylight which is protected on the outside by fixed aluminium louvres. Through this, daylight washes softly down, bathing the tall, convex, internal roof surfaces with a gentle chiaroscuro of light and shadow.

Part of the success of the Utzon Huset is its functional ambiguity which allows it to serve a variety of purposes. In 1985, for instance, one of its rooms was used as the venue for a piano recital by Teddy Teirup broadcast on local television.[6]

Although there are windows, these are placed low down in the wall so that students working at their desks could see outside, but generally the building turns in on itself and rejects its surroundings. The roof volumes further emphasise the interior orientation and the feeling of isolation from the outside, which is extremely typical of Utzon. The roofs, as mentioned earlier, consist of an assortment of small to large half-barrel vaulted skylights, staggered to create a play of overlapping and opposed profiles that register the room volumes of what are presently the three exhibition spaces. At the east corner, they come to a climax and are dominated by the largest roof.

As an additional barrier to the outside, a low hedge has been planted around the complex to establish a last defensive perimeter and seal it off from the surrounding ploughed farmland. The Herning Utzon Huset was a trial run for something larger and more important. It is quite significant because, although it is a small experiment in overhead lighting, it was a rehearsal for the Bagsværd Church's roof lights and exploration of an enlarged climactic roof which releases the contained horizontal forces of the space upwards in a powerful symbolic drive.

Of Utzon's mature works, Bagsværd Church must be considered one of his most successful and important. Inasmuch as Lin Utzon, his daughter, was responsible for the design of the textile furnishings, this makes it doubly significant since, in addition to its purely formal achievement, it is also a record of Utzon's closeness to his children. Bagsværd is a high point in the middle years from 1974 to 1976, representing as it does a rare success for Utzon – a project that was not abandoned or mutilated by the client, or unduly interfered with.

Some 20 km north-west of Copenhagen, Bagsværd is fairly typical of the well-ordered but uniformly unexciting new dormitory sub-centres which arose on Copenhagen's fringes in the 1960s under the 'green finger' plan to expand the city radially with urban spines penetrating into the countryside. Besides Vilhelm Lauritzen's admirable old Gladsaxe Town Hall from 1938, Bagsværd's only other outstanding feature is the giant pharmaceutical supplier, the Novo Nordisk company, famed as a producer of insulin and other diabetic products, which established its headquarters there in the early 1960s.

The village of Bagsværd was incorporated into the nearby Gladsaxe parish when the original Bagsværd Church was pulled down to provide bricks for the restoration of the old bishop's palace in 1537, thereby beginning Bagsværd's tributary relationship to Copenhagen. A new church was proposed in 1913, but the outbreak of the Great War and later the strained economic conditions of the inter-war years delayed its start. In 1948, a church committee was set up and a subscription raised, after which Bagsværd became a separate parish. Not until 1964, a further 18 years, was a site found on the Bakkegards land, north of the main town centre, and next to the main road.

Jørn Utzon was invited in 1968 to produce sketch plans for the new church and these were later unanimously approved. Since the Lutheran church in Denmark is state funded, Utzon had to submit his sketches to the Ministry of Ecclesiastical Affairs for their detailed consideration and for approval to proceed. When the costs exceeded the budgeted funds, his scheme was adapted and reduced in size. Final construction was delayed until April 1973, awaiting Ministry approval, which was only given after the

Borough of Gladsaxe volunteered to contribute Kr 1 million.

Centuries of tradition have produced a recognisable church style in Denmark with certain formal mannerisms and time-worn traditions. Utzon ignored many of these conventions in Bagsværd Church. The building as completed does not look even remotely like a church on the outside — it might pass for an iron foundry or factory perhaps. Missing are the pointed arches, buttresses, ribbed vaults, stained-glass windows, towers, pinnacles or spires, any of the many expected detailed cues which betray an ecclesiastical function. Instead of updating the Gothic, Utzon travelled back to the remote era of the early *stavkirke*, or stave church, when pagan and Christian were mixed, and Christianity was struggling to establish itself on the wild frontier lands of Scandinavia.

Utzon's Bagsværd Church is essentially a modern interpretation of the ancient *stavkirke* executed in precast concrete instead of pinewood. It obeys the same formal inflections, has a similar double-walled structure outside with a stepped profile rising to a climax, and employs the same material throughout — pine boards and shingles and vertical staves in the earlier original, and concrete frame and precast concrete planks in Utzon's.[7] The *stavkirke*, which literally means a pole, pillar or staff church, got its name because the roof was supported by wooden columns. In English, it was termed a mast church in recognition of the height of the columns. Bagsværd is a concrete pole church, but unlike the *stavkirke* it lacks the warmth of the pine, so Utzon shrouded the cold concrete and pews in a thin, translucent film of white paint. He also shifted the expression away from darkness and moved it towards hope, away from superstition to a belief in human perfectibility. Instead of the *stavkirke*'s rain-slicked shiny black pitch-painted or honey pine shingles flashing in the forest gloom, and a mysterious dark interior reaching up ever so high, Utzon enveloped the interior surfaces and contents in a white fog to symbolise purity and calm in the face of eternity. This simultaneously draws light down into it and sends the human spirit soaring.

The majority of surviving stave churches are in Norway, but there is an even older Danish tradition which Utzon may have inadvertently alluded to. Utzon's sources are often deeply

Danish, without him consciously recognising this. The site of Heorot, the best of buildings and the ancient ring-Danes' great mead-hall mentioned in the poem *Beowulf*, was but a short distance from Bagsværd. It was described as being the greatest of hall buildings, 'the hall rose up high, lofty and wide-gabled'.[8]

The ship and the royal hall were important symbols of the old Danes. Utzon's Bagsværd Church mixes them both in its self-contained ship like 20 m x 68 m rectangular shell and lofty noble profile of a royal hall.[9]

Utzon had not designed a church before and was unacquainted with the standard ecclesiastical requirements. He confessed as much by asking 'How does one build a holy interior?' To which, after stopping him, the Reverend Bernard Willer replied: 'You do not build a holy interior. A holy interior is a place that is consecrated. It may be under a tree, or anywhere. In no way attempt to create a holy place.'

What Utzon was being asked to provide was a protected place of assembly where religious services could be held. Søren Kierkegaard's sharp rebuke in 1854 has been taken very seriously by the Danish Church, especially his demand for 'order in the accounts', or, more simply, honesty and following a more down-to-earth and practical approach.[10] Utzon's honest expression of materials and refusal to compromise the austerity of the church's exterior is allied with his conception of the church as a 'gadget for holding a service', which echoed the famous words of the French Modernist Le Corbusier that, 'We must look upon the house as a machine for living in or as a tool'.[11] This reflected a similar determination and preference for unaffected honesty which Søren Kierkegaard, were he able to, would warmly have approved.

Utzon's decision to use only one material in the interior bears comparison with P.V. Jensen Klint's Grundtvig Church. This was a medieval country church translated to a metropolitan scale and built of yellow bricks which are used for the floor, walls and vaults, both inside and outside. Utzon also limited himself to one material, concrete, which he used for the structure, floor planks and wall panels. Even the timber doors have been painted white to give the impression of the unity of material.

One of Utzon's least recognised abilities is his capacity to take something old and give it a new interpretation. Religious architecture has always struggled to find ways to make real the idea of an other world of the spirit beyond the material world we see about us. Mosaics, frescoes, geometry and mathematics, standing as symbols for the ineffable and God, have all been used to this end at one time or another. Utzon chose a form from his period by incorporating a shell concrete ceiling. In much the same way that he did in Sydney, he adopted the principle of the rolling cylinder, or 'mother cylinder', as he sometimes called it, to take charge of the formation and geometry of the shells. The section drawing through the church describes a wave breaking. The shells lift as they travel north and rise to a crest, reaching a climax immediately before they curl and break, and crash down onto the beach. As an introduction to the inside wave ceiling, Utzon formed a small enclosed court which serves as a metaphorical beach or cove, and entry atrium to the church. Entering the church, the worshipper emulates a surfer walking into a wave across the wet sand into the shallows.

Beginning with the small shells above the candidates' room and offices on the south side of the church, the ceiling profile lifts progressively and grows in amplitude, rising clear above the sacristy before it commences its final overarching ascent and breaks open on the north. Utzon introduced circles of differing radii joined together to produce a continuous tent membrane of concrete which gives the ceiling the same fluid movement as the surf. To explain the interior, Utzon said, 'I am inspired by the clouds and have created a space that fades upwards.'[12] Later, he added:

> *I used to lie on the beach at Hawaii at night. Because of the Trade Winds all the clouds are alike. They're like balls of cotton wool drifting slowly by. Just drifting. The Trade Winds blow differently to our [Danish] winds. It's like a very strong force that you can almost lean against. As I lay there, I thought, 'What a lovely place for a church service.' And the beach is actually used for weddings. But those clouds above and the light in between and then the beach gave me*

the idea for the ceiling [Bagsværd]. I used a modern method of spraying the concrete on gently rolling cylinders.[13]

Utzon's metaphoric inclusion of clouds in the ceiling not only exploits the dual symbolic association with the 'Upper Waters' from antiquity, drawing on its meaning as an intermediate zone between the formal and the non-formal, it also revives a previously venerated connection of church ceilings as 'heavens'. Ceiling frescoes of clouds with cherubs and the Holy Family were very common in seventeenth-century Italian Baroque church architecture; however, the association of clouds with spirit and spiritual ideas extends back even farther, to the Old Testament. Thus in Exodus, '… the cloud covered the tent of meeting, and the glory of the LORD filled the tabernacle.'[14] The cloud above the tabernacle guided the Israelites through the wilderness, where it settled down, they camped, and where it went, they followed.

The use of the cloud metaphor in the Bagsværd Church ceiling, which Utzon restated as a climactic wave breaking into flowers of light whose petals softly shower down on the worshippers, penetrates deep into ancient Judaic symbolism, with the idea of God manifesting his presence in a cloud. The shell cloud-vault of concrete could be said to be a sign of God's presence at the place of meeting. In a space, which Utzon has described as fading upwards, the movement is from below, up into the light.

Utzon clouds are really large folded concrete vaults sprayed onto wire mesh with a gun to give a finished thickness of 80–100 mm (3–4 in). The basic structure consists of two long side walls spanned by beams which form the ceiling and are expressed as thin folded concrete shells. The idea is basically no different from his earlier Melli Bank and Bayview house schemes. The maximum span of the ceiling is 17.35 m (57 ft). Rough boards were used for shuttering and their imprint can be seen clearly on the underside of the finished shells. These have a layer of asphalt on top for a barrier against damp and a further 200 mm layer of insulation on top of that. Rafters were fixed on the shells to support the aluminium outside roof and its wood frame. Normal expectations are thus contradicted, since it is the lightweight cloud ceiling which provides the structural support for the roof, not the other way around.

Two 2.45 m wide concrete frames were placed one on top of the other and cast together to form the double wall on either side of the church interior to support the ends of the shell structures. Once again, the observer is struck by the similarity with the double-walled frame of the *stavkirke*, which in Utzon's example acts in a similar fashion to a carpenter's horse, as an internal concrete buttress to prevent the shell structures from falling over sideways. White concrete in 120 mm (5 in) thick slabs was mounted outside the walls and covered with white tiles. These panels obscure the interior section behind the stepped wall profile, which subtly hints at what is going on internally without actually revealing much.

The tiles on the outside are used in a similar fashion to Sydney. Matt as well as glazed tiles have been applied to the rectangular panels of the long stepped side walls. At sunset, when the sun is low, the glazed tiles around the edges of the panels suddenly blaze with a golden light and glitter like jewels on fire in the dying light. Like ancient Heorot's steep roof shining with gold, at the end of day the lofty gables of Bagsværd glitter with flashes of gold.

The simple structural scheme of two side walls spanned by folded shells is in conflict with the longitudinal orientation of the space, and it tends to pull everything sideways towards the organ on the right-hand wall instead of allowing the eyes to rest calmly on the altar and pulpit in front. The intention was to produce a space in which worshippers could participate and feel included. While the transverse folded shells provide an appropriately dramatic introduction and climax to the church's interior after people have entered from the north courtyard side – pressing down at the door threshold, only to spring up soon afterwards – the enforced sideways displacement from left to right, after people are seated, is an unwelcome distraction.

The church accommodates extra functions in the southern end, such as confirmation rooms, a meeting hall and youth centre, arranged in a ladder of alternating corridors and courtyards and offices parallel with and in step with the ceiling cross-vaults.

On the east side, adjacent to the busy main road, Utzon isolated the offices to exclude noise and dirt by providing a long corridor from the church interior behind a windowless wall which is lit from above by a daisy-chain of light from a continuous double-pitched and glazed skylight that rises in three steps to the church ridge. On the opposite, west, side along Taxvej, he breaks into the same outer wall to open up the interior courts to the outside.

In keeping with his idea of a kit of parts, Utzon introduced pseudo-industrial elements for the altar, pulpit and font. It may look the same as Charles Eames's selection of standard industrial catalogue components, but it is not. The hollow double-walled elements are not standard off-the-shelf components but were specially made of prefabricated, burnished white concrete and have overhanging slab tops curved underneath to echo the convex shapes of the ceiling. The ceiling shells and all the concrete walls inside have been whitewashed with lime mixed with white cement. Behind the altar, separating the church interior from the vestry immediately behind it, Utzon erected a screen wall in thin Flensborg bricks placed edgewise in a triangulated pattern and painted white. This is disturbing because the increment of change from the larger shell forms to a busy optical pattern in the triangulated brick screen is too great.

Alvar Aalto's furniture can be found in many locations and fits in well. The heavy, knotless, pine, custom-designed pews are neither sympathetic nor incongruous, they come somewhere in between, and lack the delicate treatment of the concrete frame and the soft melting harmony of the limited colours. This is partially corrected by finishing the furniture with a translucent white solution to harmonise it with the rest of the white interior.

Bagsværd Church is the only public building completed by Utzon since Sydney over which he has exercised complete control. There is another sentimental reason why it stands out. Utzon's family plays a central role in his life. Just as Aage, his father, helped him, he has done the same for his children. Bagsværd is the result of his collaboration with Lin Utzon who was assigned the task of designing the altar-cloth and three banners known as antependiums, together with the desk cloth on the altar and the carpet.

Utzon's idea of letting Lin do the textile furnishings is in the main successful. She chose a common motif of crosses and flower petals in the four colours of the ecclesiastical year – white, green, violet and red.

This was an early work by Lin and there are indications of hesitancy and lack of sureness, even of caution. For whatever reason, the textiles suffer from indecision. They neither add colour in a bold way, nor maintain the softened palette and delicacy of the architecture, but fall in between. One need only recall the boldness of Matisse's cutouts or vestments for the chapel at Vence in France to recognise this. It may have been asking too much at the time. Because she has not been able to find quite the right line between boldness and delicacy, the vestments have ended up as a mere decoration and do not contribute as they should to the mood of quiet simplicity throughout the church.

Setting this aside, the overall success of Lin's Bagsværd textiles resulted in an invitation to develop a new range for Royal Copenhagen Porcelain in 1980 which produced a superbly elegant dinner service executed using torn transfer sheets of pure porcelain colour in deep blue and silver. A year later, Lin was contacted by Romaldo Giurgola (the designer of Australia's new Parliament House in Canberra), from New York, who had seen her work for Royal Copenhagen Porcelain, to ask her to make a large decorative porcelain mural for a hallway at the Volvo headquarters building in Göteborg. This subsequently led to further commissions at San Jose, California, in 1986 and at other sites in the USA. Jørn Utzon's idea to help his daughter really worked, but only because he was right about her being very talented.[15]

Utzon's Bagsværd Church was inaugurated on 15 August 1976. The shells react well to music and voices. During an evening concert someone remarked, 'It is so beautiful it hurts'. In Denmark, professional organists are employed by churches and this results in a consistently high standard of performance. Consequently, acoustics are important. The varied shapes in the ceiling shells give Bagsværd Church perfect acoustics.[16]

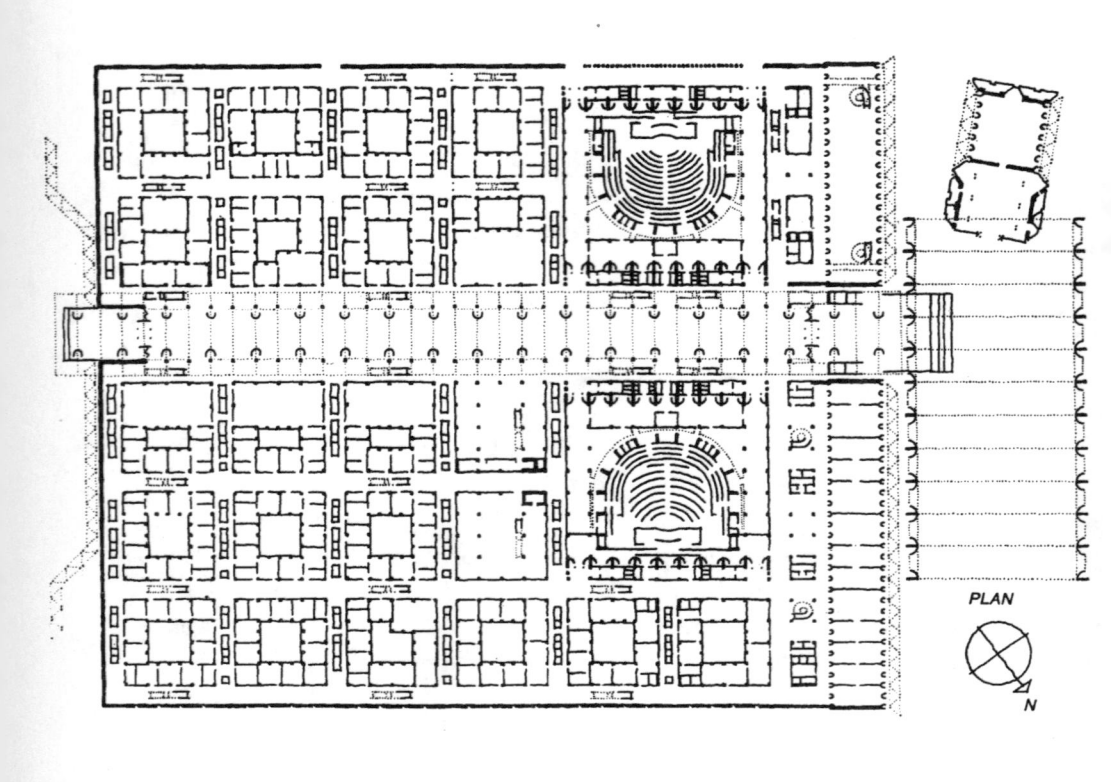

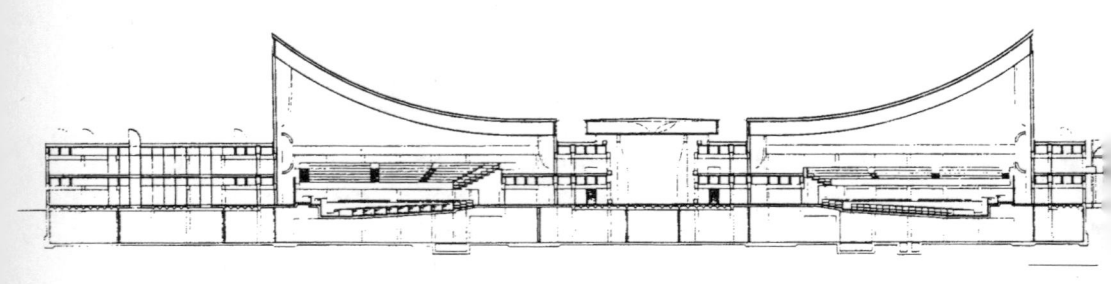

National Assembly, Kuwait, 1971-83. Above: Preliminary plan, later the mosque, main entrance and southern conference hall were eliminated destroying the symmetry. Below: Cross-section through conference and assembly hall.

21

'It isn't necessary'
Mallorca, 1977–1983

Early Tuesday morning, 27 February 1991, Coalition forces led by a Kuwaiti armoured column swept into Kuwait City.[1] The seven-month occupation by Iraq was over. People rushed into the streets in their thousands in a frenzy of celebration. The clean-up began.

Thick clouds of smoke rolled in without interruption from the north from the large burning oilfield of Ar Rawsatayan, and a bank of dense fog engulfed the Persian Gulf city. Only just visible through the smoke haze, the sun was reduced to a faint disc that emitted no light. Out of the total of Kuwait's 1196 oil wells, at least 732 were blown by the hastily departing Iraqis and converted into monstrous Roman candles spewing flame and thick sulphur-laden black smoke plumes that turned day into night.[2] It was a picture of Hell as only Dante could have conceived it.

West from the old city, along the waterfront, on Arabian Gulf Street, the hard-pressed departing Iraqi troops had been particularly thorough. In the remaining hours before the Republican Guard pulled out, Iraqi troops set ablaze the historic Sief Palace where Cabinet met, the great National Museum, the Salam Palace, a guest house for visiting dignitaries and, as a climax to the destruction, Jørn Utzon's National Assembly Building complex.

Six hotels and the Emir's executive offices were left burning.[3] For some inexplicable reason, the city's banks and the stock exchange were spared.

Flame spurted through the National Assembly's concrete grillework and wall openings in roaring super-heated jets whose searing fingers tore at and scorched the outside walls. The wide internal street which divided the complex in two was transformed into a huge horizontal chimney sucking air in at one end through the smashed entrance and belching out a mixture of fiery debris, ash and dense smoke at the other. The largest and most prestigious public building completed by Utzon since the Sydney Opera House was quickly reduced to a smoking, charred ruin.

Later that same year in July, at the instigation of the Americans, the work of restoring and rebuilding the National Assembly building was hastily commenced with the aim of making it ready in time to receive the newly elected Majlis parliament on 20 October 1992, 16 months later. If inflation is discounted, the cost of rebuilding was 19.4 million Kuwait dinars (US$72 million), an amount equal to three-quarters the original building cost.[4] The interior was substantially altered during the restoration. This Middle Eastern Emir's vision of palatial splendour is like a vapid costly re-creation of J.R.'s ranch 'Southfork' in the *Dallas* television series. It hardly needs to be said that the new interior is entirely at odds with the original created by Utzon in 1983, in which restraint, not showiness, governed everything.[5]

Kuwait is very political but its politics are in the main oil politics – who controls the oil revenue, how it is re-invested and who profits. To broaden his popular appeal when Kuwait became independent in 1961, Sheikh Abdullah III promised a constitution and a parliament. By the end of 1962 he had realised both of his promises. The parliament was a luxury the Emir would have preferred to be without. There are times when a concession is in order. What he sought was the outward appearance of democracy, not actual democracy, and to achieve his aim he limited the franchise to only those male citizens who could prove that their ancestors lived within the walls of the old city before 1920. This represented only 65,000 people out of a total of 800,000, or less than eight per cent of the population.[6]

The Sabah family has ruled Kuwait since 1756. Even under such a flawed system, Kuwait was still the most democratic of the Gulf states. In practice, Sheikh Abdullah III Al Sabah (1950–65) and his successors control the electoral system. The parliament was established after a period of criticism of their rule. Even so, the parliament did not pose much of a threat since, if it proved too troublesome, the Emir could order its dissolution.

The new Parliamentary Assembly complex has its origin in the 1968 Master Plan by the British planner, Sir Colin Buchanan, perhaps best known for his work on traffic in cities.[7] One of the largest and most difficult problems confronting Kuwait City was its heavy reliance on the motor vehicle which made it imperative to deal in some way with the negative impact on the rapidly expanding city that building new giant expressways produced – expressways which could isolate traditional communities and cut the city off from the sea coast.

Buchanan produced four plans at different scales. There was one missing ingredient which Colin Buchanan needed to put flesh on his planning skeletons – architects to draw up concrete proposals. Dr Omar Azzam, an Egyptian and the United Nations representative on Middle Eastern planning affairs, was approached for advice. He had worked in Kuwait in 1967 and was responsible for Professor Franco Albini in Milan and Sir Leslie Martin from Cambridge being involved at that time. The new advisers shifted the emphasis substantially towards architecture, which was now taken very much more seriously.

The selection of Sir Leslie Martin was extremely fortunate for Utzon. One of the judges in the earlier Opera House jury, Martin's enthusiasm for Utzon's work was undiminished and as chief writer and adviser on the panel to the Master Planning Committee, he played a leading role and was influential in its decisions. Dr Azzam visited Martin at Great Shelford near Cambridge. The result of their encounter had important consequences for Kuwait City and for Jørn Utzon. At Martin's suggestion, the Master Planning Committee undertook a series of imaginative architectural experiments that threw open Kuwait's door to the world's most exciting and creative architectural talents.

Four firms of architects were initially invited to prepare plans of the city over nine months. The four were Georges Candilis, Alexis Josic and Shadrock Woods (Paris), Reima Pietilä (Helsinki), Peter Smithson (London) and Ludovico Belgiojose and Enrico Peressutti of the BBPR Partnership (Milan).[8] Smithson, who was awarded the Ministry of Public Works project, was later rejected because his fees were too high.

Under the direction and chairmanship of Sheikh Jaber al Ahmed Al Sabah, the Prime Minister and Emir of Kuwait after 1970, the Master Planning Committee embarked on a remarkable experiment in architectural patronage which resulted in two world-class buildings: Reima Pietilä's delightful, bright, multicoloured tiled Ministry of Foreign Affairs, and without question the best of the two, Jørn Utzon's truly remarkable National Assembly Building.

Commencing on the east, and running west along Arabian Gulf Street, sites were allocated starting with the National Museum, followed by the National Theatre, then the National Library. Ultimately the National Assembly Building was given the site reserved for the National Library – where it presently stands and should rightly be.[9]

At first, a multi-use Conference Centre was included in the parliamentary complex. In the initial and all schemes prior to November 1973, Utzon used the Conference Centre as a counterweight to the Parliamentary Assembly Hall. The Conference Centre was necessary to maintain the visual symmetry of the composition.

The current National Assembly Building, at 56,250 m^2, is less than two-thirds the 88,258 m^2 (605,490 to 950,000 ft^2) size of the Sydney Opera House.[10] One-third of it is occupied by a basement carpark. Expressed another way, the Opera House is one and a half times bigger than it in size. As with the Opera House, the parliament is divided in two by an internal street. This time, however, the halls were incorporated within the main body of the building and only break through the rooftop as suspended canopies which serve externally as symbols of its primary democratic function.

Whereas the base of the Opera House was cast in situ, the Kuwait parliament was assembled from precast concrete elements along much the same lines as the roof vaults of the Opera House. There are further similarities: both the Kuwaiti parliament and the Opera House are near the sea. Although the parliament's surroundings may not be as attractive as Bennelong Point, as it lacks an enveloping harbour as a necklace around it, Utzon's parliament is tremendously enhanced by its proximity to the Persian Gulf. The location was significant for historical reasons because it provided a reminder of the maritime traditions of Kuwaitis as traders and mariners.

Utzon likened the parliament building plan to a tree spread out on the ground with its roots closest to the sea, and its crown pointing towards the desert.[11] The trunk represents the central street and the main circulation; from the trunk, courtyard offices cluster like leaves hanging from the spreading branches. To the right side of the base, in place of the tap-root, Utzon located the mosque, outside the office grid. The gridiron arrangement of corridors and rooms was reminiscent of Bagsværd Church. The basic hollow-square office module was grouped around an internal courtyard. It was Utzon's contemporary version of the traditional Arab house inside the old walled city.

Utzon was fascinated by traditional Arab responses to climate in the souk, which is where he discovered his model for the central street through the parliament and the courtyard cores of the office modules. From the desert, the draped tent-roof over the assembly spaces added a further striking non-urban source to the ensemble. In his quest for indigenous motifs, Utzon even based the cylindrical columns that hold up the parliament's roofs on the local date palm trees. Palm trunks were formerly employed as beam supports under the roofs of traditional Kuwaiti houses. The parliament's palm columns are pinched at the top in exactly the same way as a palm trunk is below the fronds. There was nothing especially new about the idea, the ancient Egyptians carved decorative column capitals based on papyrus, lotus, and palm motifs 4000 years before Utzon!

Arab towns are wildly chaotic. 'Kuwait', which means 'Little Fort', retained its old wall until 1950 when most of the old city disappeared in a flood; what was not destroyed by the flood has been quickly torn down since. Very little now survives except for the vestigial mosques which were spared and stand as ghostly reminders of once-vibrant neighbourhood communities. Within the wall, which was an important part of city's identity, the houses packed together tightly in an interlocking crystalline jumble of cubes whose boundaries were marked by pointed crenellations. Starting out as narrow, shadow-filled labyrinthine lanes, the spaces between the house cubes fed like tiny rivulets into the wider stream of the souks, before flowing on and joining even larger squares around the mosques.

Utzon wished to recapture the same closeness and dense proximity of Arab town life. The secluded office cells and narrow alleys of the parliament are divided into two town districts by the souk-like street in the middle. There is an important, even crucial, contrast: whereas the Arab town was irregular, everything in the parliament is strictly rectangular, plumb and correct. Even though he was inspired by mud-brick Arab houses, in his parliament Utzon had to compromise with modern technique, since his building is made with precast elements, not hand smoothed mud. The rectangular office module cubes are square and true, lined up in formal regiments on both sides of the equally formal covered street. In theory, Utzon encouraged a certain amount of flexibility in the office modules, but in practice these have the same identical room divisions around each courtyard. The stairs, toilets and other services are accommodated in the corridors between the hollow office squares.

Utzon's 1970 competition scheme was extremely elegant, with its incorporation of his additive-form principle it permitted him a degree of spontaneity that was entirely in keeping with the Islamic spirit.[12]

At one of the early meetings with Sheikh Jaber al Ahmed Al Sabah after Utzon had won the limited competition, the Prime

Minister picked up a Coca-Cola bottle and placed it firmly beside the Assembly Building and announced, 'Let's make an American skyscraper.'[13] Utzon stiffened in horror; he did not know what to say, and he did not dare contradict the Prime Minister in front of his advisers. For an instant he stood rigid, biting his tongue. Sheikh Jaber's suggestion was made on the spur of the moment. After a silence, Utzon smiled at the Prime Minister before reaching across the table and picking up the bottle which he gently removed to the edge some distance from the parliament building.

'I think not!' Utzon said firmly. That was the end of the matter. The skyscraper was never mentioned again. The threat was removed. Many more threats would arise in the future.

To Utzon, a skyscraper implied the elected representatives travelling up and down from their offices to the parliamentary chamber in a lift, instead of walking as was their style in the past. In his view, it was contrary to the Arabian, horizontal way of living. More importantly, it destroyed the symmetrical composition of his two roofs balanced equally on either side of the internal street.

In his competition scheme, at either end of the central internal street, in lieu of a traditional fort's two gates, Utzon substituted two entrances. The Kuwaitis are descended from the Anaiza Bedouin, who migrated to the coast during a drought in 1710. Their traditional dwelling was the black tent of goat's hair, an example of which has been erected beside the gutted National Museum.

The coarse tent cloth is comparatively heavy, making it impossible to stretch it out flat; it therefore hangs naturally forming deep valleys between the pole supports. Noting this, Utzon repeated the tent's gentle folds in his concrete suspended roofs, to recall the black tent.

The Conference Centre west of the internal street balanced the parliament's Assembly Hall on the opposite east, side. At the front, between the parliament and the Gulf, he placed a third, similar, but even larger hanging roof, which was left open without any side enclosure so it shaded the public square. At one end of this, partly covered by the roof, he located the parliament's mosque.

Utzon initially started with three rows of eight office modules on both sides of the central street which gave him a perfectly symmetrical composition, except for the one isolated dissenting accent of the mosque.

The three hanging pseudo-tent roofs symbolised the three important functions of the parliament. The Conference Centre and the National Assembly Hall roofs sloped inward towards each other; across the front to embrace the Gulf, turned at right angles, the third, larger, roof formed a giant porch. Viewed from above, the parliament has the same symmetry as a human face, with a nose representing the street in the middle, two eyes balanced on either side and a firm chin below the mouth.

It took three years to finalise the design and incorporate all the revisions in the *Blue Book* document of November 1973.[14] The *Blue Book*, which was the Kuwaiti equivalent of the *Red Book* for the Sydney Opera House, contained a final series of plans, sections and elevations, supported by engineering details of the precast concrete elements. By the time Utzon was interviewed at the Halekulani Hotel in Hawaii in April 1973, the Kuwait parliament had replaced the Opera House as his creative focus.[15] Talking in Hawaii, Utzon boasted that the Kuwait parliament was twice as big as the Sydney Opera House. This was an exaggeration, but one that nevertheless demonstrated how important it had become to him.

Not long afterwards, the project cost was found to be excessive and Utzon was required to reduce his scheme by 30 per cent.[16] He achieved this by shortening it from six to four modules. The main entry was moved from its earlier north-west location next to the public shaded square facing the Gulf, to the opposite, south-east side. This reversed the building's orientation and so rendered the large entry porch canopy superfluous because it no longer acted as a shelter for the main entrance to the parliament. The existing position of the public square at the rear was plainly ridiculous. A further result of moving the entrance was that the Assembly Hall auditorium, which had previously been close to the main entrance, now stood at the far end of the street.

Representatives of the parliament now queried the necessity of a conference centre. After due consideration, they decided to eliminate the conference facility entirely because it would interfere with the legislative work of the assembly.[17] A large conference facility was later built at Burgan, south of the airport, instead and the area freed by its removal was re-allocated to the audit and control bureau, and additional small meeting rooms added. Instead of placing the mosque outside, as Utzon advocated, it was moved inside the parliament building where it would be more accessible and convenient. The disbandment of the Conference Centre more than compensated for the large reduction in the total building area.

These substantial changes completely undermined Utzon's original aesthetic intent and overturned the functional rationale of his plan. His intention all along was to design a flexible plan, however these changes and later ones between 1973 and 1978 destroyed the architectural composition and its symmetry. The relocated entrance undermined the porch roof as an effective symbol of participatory democracy. What had been the chief external symbol became a faux-climax: instead of its intended use as a public forum, the square became an expensive VIP carpark. By falsifying the boldest and most sculpturally exciting part of the parliament, the linkage to the Gulf was also destroyed as well. The elimination of the reflecting pool around the mosque and the square which was part of the same symbolism further degraded Utzon's plan.

Utzon's parliament has survived, but at a considerable cost aesthetically. That it did survive at all testifies to the strength of Utzon's concept. In the interim, the building also lost much of its functional clarity and its symbolism was subverted. So much of the strength of Utzon's architecture is concentrated in the building's bones, in the beautiful articulation of its skeleton, that it has survived, and survived impressively. The fundamentals proved more robust and enduring than any of the changes.

The sensuously formed and crisp, intriguing discipline of its circle-inspired geometry resulted in a supreme work of sculpture, which, although its planning was severely compromised, still makes a profound impact. In Denmark, Utzon sought ways to introduce light into his buildings; in Kuwait, he discovered new ways to shade the interiors and turn them into sources of delight and coolness.

The delay to the parliament project at this time cannot be explained by financial problems – indeed, Kuwait in the years after 1973 had never been so prosperous. After the October Yom Kippur war, Kuwait hosted a meeting of the Organization of Arab Oil Exporting Countries (OAPEC), which decided on an oil boycott of Israel's supporters. Even with Kuwait's production slashed to around two-thirds the 1973 level of 3 million barrels per day, the steep increase in petroleum prices more than made up for this and resulted in annual oil revenue soaring to US$7200 million, which left Kuwait with excess funds of US$4300 million for investment abroad.[18] The Emir, Sabah III, now ran into political opposition in the existing Assembly and this caused him to have second thoughts. The conflict came to a head in August 1976, and the Emir suspended the fourth National Assembly, then ordered its indefinite suspension. The parliament remained in abeyance until Sabah III's death on 31 December 1977.

The delay in the plans for the new parliament building encouraged further criticism and revisions, in particular, objections were raised to the large shade roof and the public square. Were they absolutely necessary? Kuwaiti politicians conduct their business indoors. The *diwan*, or reception hall, offers a comfortable and dignified place to hold discussions, the ruling elite did not require a square, that could only be in the interests of an underclass rabble. Squares and piazzas were a Western idea.

The big outside roof terminated the internal street in front of the Gulf. Utzon thought of the big square as a place where ordinary Kuwaitis could meet their leaders under the same roof. The heat created a requirement for shade and exposure to the breeze: 'The big open hall, the covered square seems born out of the meeting between ocean and building complex just as the surf is born out of the interaction between sea and beach.'[19] Utzon placed his building in the zone between the desert and the Gulf. Again, Utzon chose the surf to act as a symbolic transition in his endeavour to ensure his building became 'an indispensable part of the landscape', and promoted 'a feeling that it has always been there'. For Utzon, it is neither one thing nor the other, neither beach nor the sea, but a little of both – a sneeze in infinity.

It was a grand idea – much too grand, and far too explicitly democratic to be accepted at the top in Kuwait.

As a democratic symbol, the parliament's white tent symbolised the Bedouin heritage of the Anaiza. Its physical shade implied a further protection of the people. In support of his argument, Utzon recalled the old Arabic saying, 'When a great leader dies, his shade disappears.'[20] Utzon's roof was a symbol of the leadership, its shade was an assurance of their preservation. He was far too optimistic and in advance of his clients, and showed a degree of naivete in respect to the political realities inside Kuwait.

The controversy over the canopy became deadlocked. To overcome the impasse, Utzon arranged to have a meeting with the Speaker of the House whom he regarded as the real client. The Speaker in the Assembly, unlike the Emir, supported democracy. Kuwaitis habitually regard Europeans working for them as highly paid servants. So far as Kuwait's leadership was concerned, Europeans were unimportant. After numerous attempts, Utzon finally succeeded in arranging a meeting with the Speaker of the National Assembly. When Utzon approached the Speaker, he was in a group in a large room all dressed, as Utzon describes it, in white night shirts. The Speaker was a tall imposing man. After being introduced, Utzon stated he wished to have the big roof.

'It's not necessary,' came the immediate reply.

Moving forward, Utzon reached out and took the Speaker's hand and raised it, then said, 'We simply must have it,' at which he let go of the Speaker's hand.

Two weeks later the canopy roof was approved.[21] It was a significant win for Utzon. Without the canopy, the building would have lost all connection with the sea. Because of the decision, the sea and the breeze now became a part of the building. What caused the Speaker to change his mind? Utzon had touched him.

Utzon was inspired to a high degree by the vernacular and landscape. The selection of the colour for the outside precast concrete in Kuwait is a case in point. To find the colour, Utzon asked to be driven around the city. This went on for quite some time until suddenly Utzon leaned forward eagerly in his seat and asked the driver to stop. He got out and picked up a stone from the road. Holding it in the air, he exclaimed 'This is the colour,' gesturing at the off-white broken stone from the road.[22]

Not everything Utzon says can be trusted. The selection of the precast-concrete contractor is one such story. At his hotel, Utzon got into conversation with a man working there whom he discovered to his surprise was extremely wealthy. Utzon explained that he was building the new parliament out of precast concrete and that there was no factory in Kuwait to produce the precast elements. Precast concrete would make a very profitable business, Utzon suggested to the Kuwaiti. At his suggestion, the man invested in a new precast concrete factory and this was how the precast units came to be made for the parliament. It might almost be a story from *The Thousand and One Nights*.

Utzon's fanciful account is not only highly improbable, it is totally at variance with the facts. Kuwaitis, particularly wealthy Kuwaitis, do not wait on tables in hotels serving tourists to while away their leisure hours!

The true account is utterly different.[23] When the Ministry for Public Works let the initial contract, the tender was won by a Korean company. The Koreans then contacted Max Walk, a German engineering consultant in Zürich, to assist them. The Kuwait Prefabricated Building Company (KPBC) was very upset that it had lost and applied political pressure, with the result that a second tender was called and, to no one's great surprise, KPBC was successful this time and carried out the precast work.

The precast concrete work was beset by problems. At the beginning, the rejection rate was extremely high – 3500 units all told were rejected – because Utzon insisted no repairs should be carried out on defective elements. To overcome the high incidence of chipped or damaged corners and edges, chamfered edges were introduced and the specification was changed. Utzon insisted that the off-white colour should be integral, however in practice it was much easier to paint the precast units afterwards. This was exactly the same battle Utzon and Skipper Nielsen had waged and lost on the Sydney Opera House concrete. Kuwait was a compromise. To direct the high pressure management of the project, KPBC appointed a number of British engineers from Bovis who were instrumental in seeing the parliament through to completion.

Work did not start on the National Assembly site until July 1978.[24] Well before this, further substantial changes were introduced. Egyptians are highly respected in Kuwait as people of some intellectual sophistication. When problems arose with the parliament in the past, it was the practice to consult Dr Omar Azzam for his suggestions. On one occasion, unfortunately, he revised the entire parliamentary layout with the result that the final building is no longer Utzon's but Utzon's original scheme as modified by Azzam.

The changes continued. In the Assembly auditorium, the client rejected Utzon's idea of allowing natural daylight and requested cathedral windows instead.

History was about to repeat itself. By 1979, Utzon could stand it no longer and withdrew from any direct involvement in the National Assembly Building project. This time his withdrawal was not total. Jan Utzon maintained contact with visits to the site during construction and reported back to him on any changes. Utzon continued to be involved, but only distantly. Jan had been there from the start, so he was well versed in the project's history and could therefore continue to be Utzon's eyes without interrupting the work.

By pulling out at the beginning of construction, Utzon undermined his own credibility and introduced a sour note. Inevitably, there was a falling off in the quality because of his decision.

The large canopy, instead of being made of precast elements the same way as the vault ribs of the Opera House, was created in three in situ semi-circular cast sections for purely pragmatic reasons.

The roots of democracy in Kuwait are shallow. For example, when Sheikh Jaber III's involvement in the 1980 collapse of Kuwait's unofficial stock exchange was exposed, implicating the ruling family in the scandal, the Sheikh abruptly dismissed the

National Assembly on 3 July 1986. Despite widespread agitation, the parliament stayed closed until Saddam Hussein's army rolled into Kuwait on 2 August 1990.

There is nothing permanent about parliamentary democracy in Kuwait, it can be terminated at any time if it becomes too much of a nuisance. The surprising thing, in the circumstances, is that Utzon's Kuwait parliament turned out as well as it did, that after so many compromises, alterations and deletions it was not ruined completely. Any other building certainly would have been.

Today, the National Assembly sits like a fortress in hostile territory surrounded by a metre-and-a-half high concrete tank barrier, with security strongpoints at intervals manned by sullen troops in mottled tawny desert fatigues standing stiffly beside their machine guns. The building perceptibly withdraws behind a false arcade of pointed niches, which is a purely decorative addition and looks it.

The current interior is not by Utzon. In the 1990s renovations by HOK, the teak boarding which Utzon used throughout the interior was not replaced because it was not considered ostentatious enough and elaborate chandeliers were imported from Italy. There were further changes: the air-conditioning ducts which Utzon had deliberately exposed in the Assembly Hall were covered over and disguised by *mushrabiyya* screens.

On completion, the client decided that Utzon's building looked unfinished. Utzon had envisaged that 'The building can grow sideways away from the Central Street, and its outer boundaries will change as time goes by. These changing outer boundaries of the system are closely related to the ever-growing Arab or Islam bazaar.'[25] The proposed organic irregularity and intentional incompleteness can be likened to the growth principle in ice crystals which form the endless patterns of snowflakes. Utzon even added external buttresses similar to buttresses on an Arab fort. These, together with everything like them, were thrown out. False arches and panel elements were added to give the outside of the building a more finished look. Utzon had sought to imitate the Middle East and its values, only to discover his clients really wanted something akin to a modern Versailles.

Deprived of its matching pair of Conference Centre and the National Assembly auditorium roofs, the building now appears unbalanced and unsatisfactory, like a face with only one eye, the beautiful symmetry permanently scarred. The absence of axial balance, when everything about the architectural composition implies symmetry, leads to a certain lopsided awkwardness and negation of our expectations. Ignoring this for a moment, the current building does possess an integrity and a simple nobility, a sensuous range of shapes and an intriguing elegance in its geometry which is unexpected and fresh. It wins us over, like Utzon as a person, by the sheer strength of its convictions. It is irresistible in its way: it insists on engaging us and holding our interest. That, in the end, makes it quite a marvellous thing.

The parliament is at its best in the late afternoon, with the descending sun brightening the waters of the Gulf. In the case of the Sydney Opera House, its best time is the quiet of dawn.

At the end of the day, before the sun sinks behind the refinery on Bubiyan Island and gilds the waters of the Gulf with red fire, the parliament appears to stir, to blink and furtively eye the horizon from under its broad upturned sombrero, half-blinded by the powerful, slanting light. The broad porch is huge, the dimensions alone (it is 82.5 m long and almost 34 m deep) fail to suggest its real size. Because the parliament building tilts west of north, in late afternoon the sunlight slices in under the roof and sprays the white folds of concrete with gold dust, brushing lightly across the exposed ridges and drowning the valleys between in deep shadow.

Across the front, the outer mantle of the tops of the semi-circular section columns have been cut at an angle to expose the central upright supporting the roof at points between the roof beams. Where one would expect the columns to be thick, the concrete is as slender as a reed. The opposition between the upturned swelling roof beams and their supports, the narrow, blade-like column heads crowned by florescent roof-buds, is as unexpected as it is dramatic.

The close spacing of the columns and the horizontal beam braces have converted the western face into a huge solar screen that protects the parliament behind it. In the intense afternoon light, the rounded roof beams and the columns seem extremely voluptuous. The roof is an acknowledgement of the sea. It has a similar character to the hand-smoothed walls, the flowing secretive tunnels and dark inner chambers of Arab earth buildings, a sensual feminine quality that forces its way to the surface in spite of being repressed.

The parliament is a magnificent sculpture resting on the edge of the desert facing the sea – sculpture wrought on the same grand scale as the landscape around it. It is reminiscent of ancient Egypt and the great temples at Karnak, with its axial connection to the Gulf and its precise, formal, almost sacred geometry. In a similar fashion, it also has a powerful, lyrical, secretive, even mysterious quality. One can only try to imagine what it might have been like with its reflecting pools and the mosque in front. It would have looked even more splendid and elegant with its mirrors of water, and even more in harmony with the nearby sea. As it stands today, it expresses a quite significant message about democracy in Kuwait – that it too really is dispensable.

The porch expands to the outside like a giant tent opening itself. Albeit, a monumental tent. Without any walls to hold the space in, the interior stretches out to the sea and the sky. It is prevented from being uprooted completely and blowing away into the desert by the parliament, at its back, which stands there as a brooding, silent presence. The roof's white, concrete, arching folds are pinned to the blue sky by the row of white stiletto-like columns across the front. The power of the forms arises from their rich ambiguity and visual suggestiveness. They bring to mind curved and cut bamboo, or a lily bloom exploding atop its stem, beside the obvious palm-trunk metaphor.

The feeling is one of freedom, a kind of loose openness, the space drifts without an anchor. In his sea-fort parliament, with its white Bedouin tent on the edge of the Persian Gulf, Utzon explored the nomad's unique territory. The result is one of the most eerily memorable buildings of the twentieth century, a tendentious symbol of democracy which overshoots the mundane world of day-to-day politics.

Utzon's internal street is as important as the sea porch. Inspired by the traditional Arab souk, it forces its way into the building and divides it in two. The 130 m (427 ft) long by 10 m (33 ft) wide channel of the central street is a Suez Canal through the parliament, ending on the north-west side under the outside canopy. The standard, semi-round, open columns were used to support the roof, which itself is made from the same half-round drum-shaped precast beam elements Utzon developed for the Zürich Theatre. Along the sides, the beam roof elements rest on two narrow longitudinal beams. This is raised above the adjoining roof and creates light slits in between the parliament's roof, not unlike the great hypostyle hall of Karnak in Egypt.[26] This explanation fits the parliament much better than Utzon's acknowledgement of the souk. Possibly it draws on both. In reality, Utzon's concept of a central passageway forming the core of the building is closer to ancient Egypt. The outstanding Danish art historian, Lisbet Balslev-Jørgensen, recently wrote, 'Utzon's houses on Mallorca show his goal in life is to build a house with the same knowledge as a traditional craftsman. The experience of hundreds of years added to the knowledge of today.' It is hard to imagine a clearer statement of what Utzon was aiming at in his parliament.[27]

From the Central Hall, at right angles, smaller separate corridors connected the offices. Near its end, on the right, was the National Assembly auditorium. Under the second floating roof, and rising through the two upper levels of the parliament, it was restored following the Iraqi invasion and extra lighting for television was included in continuous suspended fittings below the ceiling between the convex roof beams. Remedial acoustic measures were introduced to solve the problem of dead spots in the front corners.

As a space, the Assembly chamber is less impressive than the outside porch, in part because it is much more conventional. Utzon would appear to have given up at this point. The technical demands of acoustics, lighting and air conditioning proved too much and added little in the way of further character.

Utzon framed the original Speaker's dais with a backdrop of panelled teak. This has been removed. The half-circular

Assembly chamber holds 120 representatives in five rows of brown leather seats. Behind these seats there are another 222 seats for VIPs and reporters. The horseshoe gallery on the first floor level has seats for a further audience of 732. At the front, the gap between the main parliament and suspended Assembly roof has been closed in by a curtain of glass, in V-shaped panels, to admit daylight.

The mosque is tucked away in a corner. It is unlike anything else in the parliament, with its exquisite traditional tile work by Moroccan craftsmen who were brought to Kuwait especially. Above the dado, its plain ceiling undulates in wavy-curly steps as it rises above the *qibla* and joins a standard half-barrel vault directly opposite the *mihrab*. The mosque was completed without Utzon.

Climate and technique are issues that continually refresh architecture. Utzon has generally distrusted style as a starting point and instead has displayed a much greater devotion to technique and climate as the foundation for making his forms. This accounts for his adoption of the courtyard as the nucleus of the rectangular office modules. His courtyards serve as light wells and ventilate the basement. In the parliament building at present, each courtyard has its own, different garden.

In dealing with the intense sunlight, Utzon developed overhead sunlight breakers of precast concrete as a modern version of the traditional Islamic window grille. His sun-breaker blades have arched diaphragms to separate the pairs of blades and span the courtyard openings in the roof in rows so they can intercept the overhead sunlight. They are both functional as well as beautiful, letting in the sky and catching any breeze. Best of all, they cast ever-changing patterns of light through the course of each day.

The Kuwait parliament is Utzon's answer to his critics after the Opera House. It showed beyond any doubt he was capable of working at a large scale and could succeed under the most trying conditions. The changes to the parliament were caused by politics, not any failing on Utzon's part. If there is a flaw in Utzon, it is his brittle personality and inflexibility. On occasions, he seems too impatient about getting his own way and too sensitive to criticism – which led this time to a repetition of his withdrawal, for a second time from a major project.

Despite its vulgar, pretentious interiors, the Kuwait National Assembly building must be counted an extraordinary achievement, one that reaffirmed Utzon's ideas on additive architecture implemented with large precast concrete elements.

As a small country in terms of actual land area poised on the edge of the desert beside the Persian Gulf, Kuwait is a combination of things. Geography forced its people to spill over into the Gulf. Utzon has succeeded in expressing that historical reality. The building says much about the desert-and-sea quality of Kuwaiti life; it renews the ancient threads of Arab tradition, from the Bedouin tent to the Arab house and the souk. On a different plane, Utzon re-formulated the Western ideal of democracy using familiar Arabic idiomatic expressions borrowed from the local vernacular to generate a broader, more universal meaning.

Utzon has an outrageous sense of humour. If he insists on playing a clown, it is for his own amusement and the amusement of his friends. Humour is out of place in architecture. Architectural jokes last long after the audience has stopped laughing. Funny buildings can be hilarious, but the humour quickly wears thin and when it does, the building can be terribly irritating. Even wonderful jokes pall in time. It was fortunate that few people recognise the joke in Utzon's UNO-X petrol station at Herning in Jutland, because it was a very private joke. Without repeating the Opera House, the glass canopy of the Herning petrol station looks just the same as the Opera House's glass walls should have looked.

Vitia Lysgaard and Johannes Jensen founded Tankskibsrederiet Herning A/S in 1963.[28] It started by chartering coastal tankers in northern European waters and in the mid-1980s it moved into local distribution of its refined products. The Herning petrol station was the forerunner of a chain of service stations planned for Jutland. This may account for its extraordinary splendour.

Peter Hall, who took over design of the Sydney Opera House in 1966, abandoned Utzon's plywood scheme for the glass wall mullions. Utzon has had the last laugh. The glass canopy over the bowser pumps in the Herning UNO-X petrol station is a smaller, horizontal realisation of the rejected Opera House glass walls. Utzon made a very important point retrospectively to show how wrong Peter Hall was. What he has demonstrated is how superior his original proposal is compared to Peter Hall's Modernist cliché in Sydney today. Complete transparency is a bore. Seeing everything at once removes the suspense and leaves little for the imagination to work on. Peter Hall was a full frontal man; his transparent glass walls look the same from every direction and hide nothing.

The UNO-X service station is set back off the road – not that anyone would be likely to miss it. The first and most noticeable thing about it is the canopy over the petrol pumps. From directly in front the glass roof is invisible, a mere series of tilted mullions that heave up and down in a wave-like motion that subsides on the departure side. Viewed sideways, the mullions thicken and the visible area of glass decreases until a point is reached when, driving up to the pumps, the canopy becomes a solid structure of rhythmically inclined beams hinged at the top and turned down onto a triangular-shaped concrete-beam edge support.

Walking or driving under the canopy is an unforgettable experience; the mullions appear to move and produce a sensation analogous to a multiple time-exposure photograph. No single idea dominates; it seems to evoke a range of associations. The immediate feeling is of being trapped inside a wave while the surf rolls on past. In a kind of latent Futurism, the bent planes of glass evoke the flapping up and down movement of gulls' wings and carry the suggestion of speed and movement. The most wonderful aspect of it all is its transformation of sunlight. Depending on the sun's position, the light is sliced into striated bands of light and shadow by the narrow pine mullion blades. The Opera House glass walls would have produced exactly the same magical effect. From Kirribilli, to the north, the glass walls would have been transparent, but from all other angles and especially from the sides the glass would have been increasingly shaded by the deep plywood mullions. The early morning and later afternoon sunlight would have been excluded. Utzon's plywood mullions were not simply structures for hanging the glass, but provided sun control and would have contributed to the spectacle of light and shadow during the day. Inside in the northern terraces the shadow effect would have been stunning.

The petrol-station canopy makes us appreciate the rich effects of sunlight, how it can suddenly transform the tawdry and invest the things about us with unexpected vitality. Beneath the canopy the rising and falling mullions, each inclined at a slightly different angle, intercept the sunlight and cast shadows on their neighbours. From underneath, they present splendidly varied patterns of light and shadow, which express motion and are syncopated, like driving in a motor car and watching everything flashing past. Utzon did this with a few timber beams and the sun.

A second joke is tucked away inside. Like many petrol stations, the UNO-X station contains a drive-through carwash. This one is unlike any other. Besides the rotary brushes and water sprays, Utzon constructed a small version of the large *diwan* or reception hall in the Kuwait National Assembly building. It has the same round columns, the same long shape, except of course it is much smaller. After all the political interference in his architecture, the arbitrary changes of programme, Utzon could still see the funny side and this was his final comment on the absurdity and smallness of politics. He has converted the solemn space where the legislators sit and cut deals and has turned it into a carwash. Possibly he was thinking how nice it would be to launder all politicians, who knows? A drive-through to regularly wash politicians clean is something no country should be without.

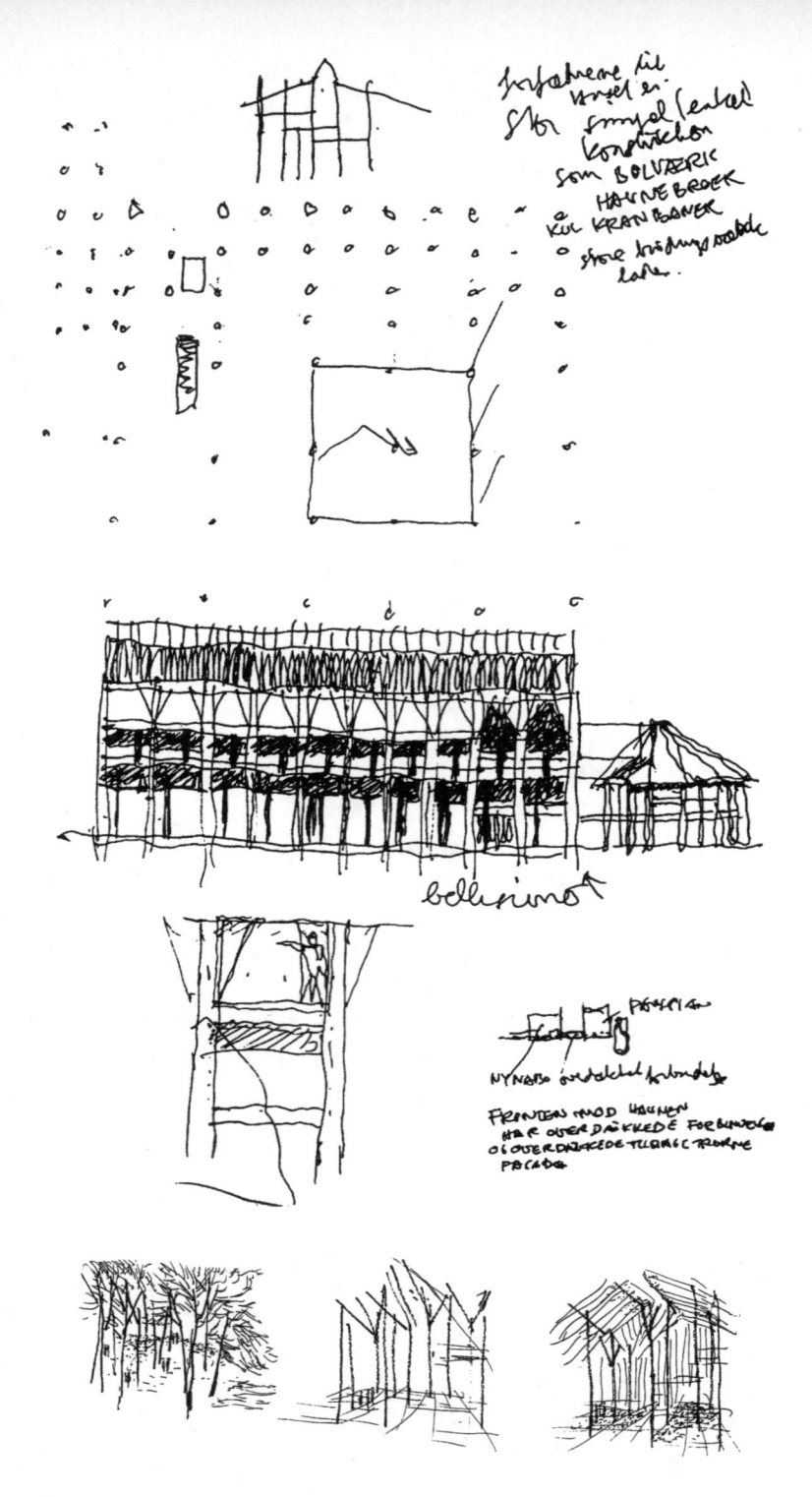

Paustian Furniture Showroom, Copenhagen Harbour, 1986. Sketches: a simple columned hall of prefabricated concrete columns and beams recalls the magnificence of the beech forest.

22

Solitude
Mallorca, 1984–

There is, one knows not what sweet mystery about this sea, whose gently awful stirrings seem to speak of some hidden soul beneath ... the waves should rise and fall, and ebb and flow unceasingly; for here, millions of mixed shades and shadows, drowned dreams, somnambulisms, reveries; all that we call lives and souls, lie dreaming, dreaming ...
Moby-Dick, Herman Melville, 1851[1]

The sea is a universal magnet. Jørn Utzon is a sea addict, one who in answer to its siren call, planted his mast-head lookout atop a high Mallorquin cliff to keep a sea watch over the sparkling Mediterranean. Before the endlessly unrolling manuscript of the sea, the sky scribbles on wave upon wave, eternity, eternity, eternity, in as many shades of grey.

Utzon was 66 and in sound health when the National Assembly complex was finished. There was no reason for him to stop working. In appearance, he had changed little since he worked in Sydney; his hair had receded and noticeably thinned, and his once erect carriage was more stooped, but otherwise he was surprisingly unmarked by the years. Time treated Utzon kindly, he looked preternaturally youthful, tanned and fit for his age, almost as handsome and distinguished as ever. He most definitely did not present, even remotely, the image of a broken man some might have pictured. Utzon took good care of himself.

There was very little ailing him physically. He suffered from a circulation problem in his legs which was painful and a nuisance at times, but he was, after all, very tall. Each day he swam, sailed as the opportunity presented itself, exercised and watched his diet. Ill health was not the reason Utzon retired – for him architecture was important, but he had no intention of allowing it to crowd out his life to the exclusion of all else. Rather, he wished to enjoy his remaining years to the full.

In 1984, Utzon said he was too ill to go to Queensland and sent Jan instead to represent him on the Duck Island Resort project on the Great Barrier Reef north of Rockhampton. The development had been floated by Sir Francis Hasset, a retired Chief of General Staff (1973–5), using his family company, Turtle Cay Resort. The resort designer, Desmond Muirhead, who had seen the Kuwait National Assembly and been greatly impressed by it, strongly recommended Utzon's participation.[2] In Sydney, in front of the Opera House, Jan was quoted saying, '… I've always wanted to come back.'

It was not certain whether Utzon was really ill or, as happened in 1973 in Kuwait City, he preferred to give Jan the opportunity. The developer saw an advantage in stamping the Utzon name on his project and Jan's presence did that almost as well as Utzon himself, and with less inconvenience. This established a pattern as increasingly Jan filled in as a surrogate for his famous father. Jan Utzon's youthful enthusiasm and brimming self-confidence on such missions knew no bounds. He brashly compared the island resort's mix of Polynesian grass huts along Australian homestead lines – the outback meets Tahiti – to a Beethoven symphony, when a more accurate comparison would have equated it with the movie version of the *Thorn Birds*.

Utzon was a survivor through and through. Too many of his friends had fallen in the thick of battle for him to wish to follow in their footsteps. The example of his friend, Johan Otto von Spreckelsen, famed for his spare geometrically pure churches, who became a victim of the Byzantine political manoeuvring surrounding the completion of his superb Grande Arche de la Defense in Paris for the French Bicentennial in 1989, in particular haunted him. Otto von Spreckelsen may have reminded him of his brother Leif, who had also died of a heart attack in Paris 25 years earlier. For whatever reason, architecture was beginning to seem like a very dangerous occupation. No matter how he viewed it, nothing — not the rewards, the money, the creative highs or the prestige — could possibly compensate for the premature termination of a life such as Spreckelsen's or his own, if that was the ultimate price to be paid for achieving architectural excellence. As if to underline this conclusion, von Spreckelsen was 11 years younger than Utzon at the time he died.

Utzon withdrew by degrees, imperceptibly shuffling sideways from the centre of events and towards the outside. For ten years or so he continued to be involved at the early conceptual stages of projects, while leaving the heavy practice duties to his sons. His main contribution consisted of doing the early picturesque sketches, dash and scrabble doodles, talking to clients in the preliminary stages and later in promoting projects. Utzon effectively became a senior consultant to Utzon and Associates, operated jointly by his two sons Jan and Kim. They produced the drawings and specifications, and saw to the contracts and administration.

There was trouble on an entirely different family front. By 1980, cracks had begun to appear in Lin Utzon's marriage to Alex Popov, which till then had been a great source of pride to Utzon. Like many fathers, Utzon was especially close to his daughter, and Lin was the most artistically gifted of the three children. After his graduation from the Royal Academy, Popov taught in the design studio classes there and proved very popular with the students, but this closeness also exposed him to temptation. Emotionally as well as physically Lin resembled her father. She was quite vulnerable and easily hurt and kept her feelings buried. She was also extremely loyal, but eventually they separated. It was a very painful moment for Lin, it also deeply wounded Utzon and her mother. Utzon, who had been quite proud of Popov and his achievements till then, now felt betrayed by him even more than Lin.

Subsequently, Lin married Steph Beaumont, an Afro-American from Miami. Beaumont, who knew he was chronically ill before he married Lin, only told her of this afterwards. Instead of walking out, Lin endured the strain of his illness and once again demonstrated her loyalty to others by staying with him until he died in August 1993. Tragedy and self-denial were piled on top of her earlier unhappiness. The circumstances were entirely different, for Beaumont had initially concealed his illness to demonstrate how much he wanted her to remain a part of his life, and was less of a betrayal therefore. However, this made little difference in the end and only intensified her sadness by adding to the feelings of loss and wasted potential.

Utzon and Lis felt great concern for Lin's unhappiness. They were powerless and could only hope for a change of fortune. Lin, for her part, coped much the same way as her father did in similar circumstances, drawing comfort from the ancient pernicious myth that suffering strengthens the artistic soul. Life did not disappoint her. Lin stayed with Beaumont to the bitter end and, on top of caring for him, even managed to effect a reconciliation between Beaumont and his mother before he died.

The one development that irritated Utzon's critics and opponents in Australia was the growing international recognition he received for his work on the Sydney Opera House. Personally, Utzon was singularly unimpressed by medals and awards, even when people made a point of recognising his earlier contribution.

The hollow, grandiloquent gesture by the Royal Australian Institute of Architects, which awarded its 1973 Gold Medal to him, was a perfect illustration. It blithely ignored the NSW RAIA Chapter's grovelling and failure to protect Utzon properly against Davis Hughes's attack on professional standards and the fee scale. The timing of the award, which coincided with Peter Hall's triumphant completion of the Opera House the same year, added a further scene to this Australian comedy of errors. Perhaps the RAIA was sincere, if ill-advised, but no amount of medals could possible assuage the insult or repair the past damage to Utzon caused by its failure to defend him in 1966. There was no getting around that. If the medal was meant as a sign of contrition, some kind of a reparation, a gesture of kindness, it came much too late to have any real meaning. Utzon accepted the award, then stayed away from the award ceremony to avoid the poisoned odour of hypocrisy. He has received many awards since, but none with the same prestige or personal significance to him as a Scandinavian as the 1982 Alvar Aalto Medal from Finland.

Much more than medals, Utzon longed for work opportunities. Speaking at the ceremony for the Royal Institute of British Architects' Queen's Gold Medal for Architecture, Utzon commented dryly, 'If you like an architect's work you give him something to build, not a medal. You don't ask Rostropovich down to give a medal, you ask him to play and then give him a medal.'[3]

The RIBA Gold Medal was accompanied by an honorarium for £10,000 (A$20,000) which was mailed directly to Utzon at his Mallorca address. In his customary manner, Utzon picked up the bundle of letters and winnowed out the ones that caught his interest, then threw what remained of the postal chaff, including the cheque, in the garbage. In London on 29 June 1978 he was asked had he received his cheque. Utzon was dumbfounded. The second time the British Institute handed the replacement cheque to Utzon personally.

Sir Denys Lasdun, the architect of the National Theatre on London's Southbank, praised Utzon, describing him as being 'a great significant architect, one [of those] who, with his unique interpretation of, and insight into architecture, speak through their buildings.'[4] In his tribute, Norman Foster, most famous for his remarkable Hong Kong & Shanghai Bank, and who had visited Utzon's Hellebæk house as a student, added, 'I was moved by the simplicity, joy and strange combination of rationalism, discipline, systems thinking and total poetry in terms of landscape … in simple terms, almost an anonymous architecture, no clichés, but an incredible integrity and honesty.'[5]

Ole Paustian was a client who shared Utzon's devotion to simplicity. The Paustian showroom, which opened in 1986, represented a culmination of sorts for Utzon.

Paustian began his career importing and selling furniture, and besides having a shrewd business sense he also possessed a well-developed sense of humour. In their culture, the Danes have retained a strong sympathy for the poor. At a party celebrating the opening of his furniture showroom and store at North Harbour, Ole Paustian found himself seated next to a gatecrasher who had wandered in from the pier. When the time came to leave, the man grandly began helping himself to the remaining bottles of wine on the table. Thus occupied, he noisily berated the showroom's owner with choice epithets such as smuck, arsehole and grinding capitalist. Unaware who Paustian was, the gatecrasher was surprised when the man sitting next to him reached across the table and started loading extra bottles into the baggy pockets of his stained greatcoat. This was typical of Paustian, and shows his humour, generosity and lack of pretence. Any other person would have rescued the wine or ejected the hobo but Ole Paustian did nothing of the sort.

Ole Paustian started by selling Alvar Aalto furniture from Artek in Finland. Artek's furniture range was very simple and natural and should have been cheap to buy, since it was originally intended to be bought by the ordinary working man.

Apparently, no one likes to be seen to buy cheap. In the world of furniture, quality is equated with a gargantuan price tag. Once Ole Paustian digested this fact, he was on his way. These days, Artek furniture is expensive and smart and well beyond the reach of the average person for whom Aalto intended it.

In May 1987 Ole Paustian located the new Paustian showroom opposite the huge Svanmøllen power station which, sentinel-like, watches over Copenhagen's North Harbour. Tucked tightly amongst the congeries of warehouses, dockside cranes, trucks, railway tracks and containers, the pier is a messy vital place, always untidy and changing. It requires a very robust building to withstand such visual cacophony.

The Paustian building has a similar industrial character to the wharf structures surrounding it, but this is misleading in as much as there is far more to it than is immediately apparent. It is Chinese, but Chinese in a way that needs some explanation, a kind of updated Chinese temple if you will, that makes use of standard components. It also repeated one of Utzon's favourite ideas – the beech forest metaphor – which was at least 40 years old since it had first surfaced when Utzon and Tobias Faber were working on the Crystal Palace competition.

The beech is part of the Danes' national ethos and is mentioned in the opening lines of their national anthem:

> *There is a lovely land*
> *With spreading, shady beeches*[6]

The writer Karen Blixen (who wrote under the pseudonym Isak Dinesen), best known for her 1937 novel *Out of Africa* and the short story *Babette's Feast*, is buried under an old beech tree at Rungsted, such is the depth of its significance to Danes. Utzon has repeated the analogy with the beech forest many times in his architecture. This poses the interesting question – what does it actually signify. At an elementary level, Utzon applies it to any extended space with columns. The question remains whether it has a further more specialised meaning, or is just something which we should avoid reading too much into. The spreading beeches form a canopy or roof over the ground so, in that sense, the beech forest offers an explicit analogy of natural shelter, but one which it is hard to develop in depth, much beyond demonstrating Utzon's heavy reliance on nature for his inspiration. Or it might simply be a case of gilding the lily with a nice story?

The Paustian showroom has an industrial character and employs standard precast concrete elements, columns, roof joists, T-floor beams, standard handrail sections, etc., in much the same way that a plastic Christmas tree is assembled from clip-together pieces. It is a prefabricated industrial shed with a high open interior, under a simple double-pitched roof with a long skylight straddling the ridge for daylight, supported by square section concrete columns. There is nothing remotely unusual about any of this. Where it is different is the manner in which Utzon has assembled the standard industrial parts.

Not everyone who walks into the Paustian showroom will instantly be reminded of a beech forest. The connection between the concrete roof and a dappled green beech canopy is at best tenuous; even the triangular brackets on top of the columns which are intended as branches are not easily recognised as such. The reiteration of the beech forest demonstrates Utzon's romanticism, his need to inject poetry into industrial forms to soften them so that they are more appealing. No one would guess, without being told beforehand, because the analogy only exists in Utzon's imagination.

The Paustian showroom is part of a series that evolved from Utzon's proposal for a new enclosed swimming hall to replace Vilhelm Dalerup's delightful timber lake pavilion beside Gyldenløvesgade, at the end of Lake Peblinge, west of Copenhagen city centre, in June 1979. The proposed centre was to have a modern enclosed swimming pool and Utzon's scheme, like the later Paustian showroom, had a peaked skylight instead of a ridge capping its pitched roof. In the earlier Lake scheme, the beech-forest analogy is more evident in the wide roof which was supported at intermediate points by four sets of branches springing from each crude column-tree. The Paustian showroom and the Museum of Modern Art scheme which followed it took the branching motif at the head of the columns further and abstracted it to the point that it lost any direct structural meaning and advantage and became a kind of structurally inspired decoration instead.

The beech motif in the columns of the Peblinge Sø indoor swimming pool is at best obscure. Utzon arranged the columns back from the facade, close together at the front, but towards the rear every second column aisle is omitted. It feels lighter and more open here, a distinction which Utzon likened to the natural growth of the forest edge which is more dense than the interior.

Utzon is never obvious. The roof of the showroom may appear at first glance to be a single saddle-back roof, but in fact it is two, not one, unequal sloping lean-to roofs, juxtaposed and connected by a skylight bridging the gap between them. Spatially, as well as structurally, it is two roofs. On the upper levels, the columns are linked by a continuous exhibition deck around an atrium.

The inspiration is subtly Chinese. For at least a thousand

years, and probably much longer, buildings in China were made according to a standard formula which was applied regardless of the size and weight of the temple roof. The roof was supported by wood columns and elaborate sets of blocks and corbelled bracket arms. During the Sung Dynasty, in 1091 AD this formula was simplified to a series of standards set out in a guide titled the *Ying-tsao fa-shih*.[7] Utzon borrowed the Chinese conception of a standardised wood frame and applied it to precast concrete. His column brackets are an updated version of the very elaborate Chinese temple bracket array. Within the showroom, the triangular brackets have been aligned in the same direction as the cross-beams they support, but under the eaves they are turned sideways in exactly the same manner as a Chinese temple.

In his twentieth-century version, Utzon has even repeated the temple stylobate or base. Like the temple it is modelled on, the showroom resembles a large piece of knock-together furniture assembled from ready-made elements. In view of the building's purpose as a furniture showroom, this treatment of architecture as a piece of furniture seems especially appropriate.

The tolerance gaps between parts of the structure are exposed and the stair and balcony railings are capped by deep blue ceramic tiles. These tiles pick out and emphasise special features Utzon wishes us to notice. The restaurant is in a detached two-storeyed staggered block.[8] This rather squat cube has small square windows punched in it. Lin Utzon contributed the triangle-patterned ceramic tiles on the white walls in the reception area and kitchen.

The Museum of Modern Art (*Danske Museum for Moderne Kunst*) scheme in April 1988 took the Paustian showroom model to the next stage. Unmistakably Utzon, it was a proposal developed for Erik and Margit Brandt's Tulstruplund estate near Fredensborg. In a typically Danish farmland setting, it incorporated an existing main building with an avenue of trees leading up to it, and a small lake on one side, with a large barn on the other. The building was to be far more than a museum, the general idea being that it could be used for plays and music performances with the galleries on either side of the central ramp providing seating for audiences.

The museum would sit on the edge of the lake in the southern portion of the Tulstruplund estate and was to be in two sections: an internal terraced floor on the ground level comprised the main exhibition areas; below it were rooms reserved for watercolours and additional exhibitions not unrelated to the main hall; over the whole, Utzon mounted a plain, barn-like, outer white shell. The roof was pitched to the north in a great sweep of roof which, as it neared the rear, collided with a smaller, lower, oppositely-pitched roof. At this junction Utzon introduced a transverse skylight to admit north light.

The Tulstruplund arrangement was yet a further variation of the platform idea. On this occasion the platform, represented by the terraced exhibition floor, was to be set into the ground so it would be invisible from the outside. For contrast, Utzon introduced Aalto-like serpentine walls that would interweave around and between the internal columns, dividing and enlivening the main exhibition level.

The long bare walls at the sides were stiffened vertically by sloping buttresses on the outside. These were thick at the base and tapered as they rose. Large beams held up by four rows of round columns, crowned by half-round brackets for extra rigidity, spanned between the side walls. Although the structure was to be of concrete, the expression clearly derived from timber construction, the same as the Paustian showroom.

Inside, the 32 bracketed columns would rise in an ascending harmonic scale which, except for the ceiling sloping upwards, is identical in effect to the Great Cordova mosque. Both maximise the hypnotic impact of the gridded space and the repeated, identical, column capital motif. At Tulstruplund Museum of Art, Utzon introduced a further variation to the Cordova mosque – the sloped ceiling which causes the columns to step up one behind the other from front to back, row after row, according to their distance from the lake front, which adds considerably to the visual effect.

In order to link the interior to the landscape, Utzon provided a large, uninterrupted glass wall on the low southern face beside the lake. Utzon's scheme was never realised. While it was clearly related to the earlier Paustian furniture centre, the idea of a columned hall under a single-pitched roof represents an unexpected, yet important, next stage in Utzon's refinement of the idea and advanced its spatial sophistication.

Utzon turned 70 in 1988. He was by now established as a national legend – a development he personally abhorred. This happened despite the fact that he had completed pitifully few buildings since his return to Denmark in 1966. In a perverse way, his legendary status was out of all proportion to the number of his works, it grew inversely to their number. Their scarcity seemingly enhanced rather than diminished his standing. He was a person wrapped in myth and conjecture. Many Danes had heard about the Sydney Opera House, but few knew the story in all its convoluted detail. Utzon's fame largely rested on that single, ambiguous achievement. All he really wanted was peace, the chance to make a decent living from his architecture, but with each passing year he became more a captive of his own legend, which existed and enlarged itself quite independently of him.

To celebrate his birthday, the Copenhagen dailies *Politiken* and *Berlingske tidende* each published full-page interviews accompanied by summaries of his career.[9] They were well illustrated, but they avoided offering a considered critical assessment of his achievements and position within Danish architecture. In a country where the culture tends to the same pleasant flatness as the landscape, Utzon stood out as a formidable mist-shrouded peak. This may have terrified commentators unused to such heights or possibly, behaving with inimitable Danish tact, they judged such an assessment to be premature. Whatever the excuse, the Danish public was left with the firm impression that here was a very nice and decent man. Whether or not he was a great architect was left hanging in the air.

The editor of Denmark's *Arkitekten* magazine, Kim Dirkinck-Holmfeld, had no such doubts in his assessment of Utzon. In an unusually effusive essay in 1993, five years later, Dirkinck-Holmfeld singled Utzon out as without rival and stated without reservation that he was the most outstanding architect Denmark had produced in a century. In Dirkinck-Holmfeld's estimation, Utzon was part of the stream of Modern architecture emanating from such notable functionalist exemplars as Le Corbusier, Mies van der Rohe and Alvar Aalto.[10] A number of exhibitions of Utzon's work were held, one at the Århus School of Architecture in April 1988, to coincide with a series of lectures there by Utzon. A later exhibition, mounted at Lund in 1994 by the Skissernas Museum appeared to support Dirkinck-Holmfeld's contention.[11] The Århus exhibition by a group of 14 students, consisting of large models and photographs, was later sent to the Pompidou Centre in Paris as an official Danish exhibit.[12]

Utzon did everything he possibly could to help his children, directly and indirectly, in their professional careers. His name alone was invaluable. Increasingly, Utzon acted as a spokesperson and advocate for projects associated with the Utzon name, but they were frequently inferior to and lacked the flair and vision of his earlier projects. Many architectural observers started to question the extent of his contribution. The works themselves seriously damaged his reputation. In some instances, it was quite apparent that Utzon's connection and involvement in the proposals was at best quite minor. There was no question that Jan and Kim were not competent – they were – but just as clearly, it was becoming obvious to everyone they were either naive or were being used by unscrupulous developers who took advantage of the Utzon name to promote their own development goals. This resulted in such embarrassing fiascos as the Star-tower above Århus in Jutland, which justifiably provoked tremendous community concern, ridicule and anger. Mistakes such as this did little to enhance Utzon's reputation and name, especially since Utzon himself gave every impression of supporting the projects. The extremely silly Madrid Opera scheme in 1964 had demonstrated he was capable of making serious errors of taste, and now, in the second half of the 1980s, motivated by paternal sentiment, he waded into far murkier waters.

Utzon was certainly not forgotten. The Danes continued to be fascinated by him and this resulted in a number of major opportunities for Utzon Associates, such as the Kr 125 million proposal for Langelinie Pier, and a second, even larger, project for Kr 1500 million: the Kalkbrænderi Quay site adjacent to the Svanmøllen power station in North Copenhagen. In terms of their size and budgets, both these projects represented major undertakings for Utzon and, in the latter instance, it was much bigger than anything he had yet attempted. They need to be seen against the background of a world trend in urban redevelopment to reclaim run-down waterfront areas and obsolete industrial land for public use and access, in order to recover these areas and reconnect cities with their historic water frontages and renew them. The UK division of Islef, for instance, was responsible for the Greenland Passage housing in London's Docklands.

The Paustian showroom was a modest start that opened up further lucrative opportunities for Utzon Associates, namely, the entire redevelopment of the southern section of the Kalkbrænderi Harbour foreshore from the Svanmøllen power station around to the Paustian showroom. The thinking was nothing if not ambitious and verged on the grandiose with the builder, Christian Islef, providing 90,000 m^2 of new floor space for an investment of Kr 1500 million (A$300 million).[13] Utzon Associates was employed to make the preliminary scheme. In practice, this meant Jan and Kim with Jan, as the eldest, in charge.

Langelinie Pier was a considerably smaller project, although still very substantial, and had the entrepreneurial company Hoffmann & Sonner as its developer. At the beginning, late in 1985, it was proposed to provide a 500-room hotel and congress centre strung out the full 914 m length of the pier, which dated from the nineteenth century and, until recently was an important part of the city's free port. Alienating public land and handing it over for commercial use was bound to meet with stiff opposition. The Utzon name was an insurance against repeating the London Docklands' catastrophe in Copenhagen, but it placed Utzon in the invidious position of a Trojan horse. Ultimately he had little say in the outcome, nor could he prevent it from becoming a catastrophe; but regardless of this, the project was associated with his name all the same.

The Utzon Associates' Langelinie scheme placed considerable emphasis on the creation of a walking street similar to Copenhagen's famous Strøget. There was, however, a very important difference: Utzon's walking street would not be on ground level, as Strøget is, but would be elevated 4 m above the Quay, to leave the ground clear for vehicles and service access. In the four floors above it were facilities for the general public, hotel rooms, shops and more shops, in a series of low connected blocks. In front, linked by bridges, were five free-standing pavilions lower in height with bars, restaurants and the like. Near the pier end, on the far side of an open square which acted as a forecourt, was a large conference centre. Opposite it, was a distinctive, 60 m or so high tower whose top terminated in two shapely horns, for easy recognition, to provide an iconic distinguishing landmark for the project.

In a level country such as Denmark, especially Copenhagen, with its impressive uniform skyline that is most unusual today, in a world where the centres of cities are filled with competing Manhattan towers, a tall tower or dome stands out and soon becomes a landmark. Jørn Utzon introduced the Langelinie tower to perpetuate the same theme of the city's other towers and spires and extend it to the harbour. Compared even to the Kuwait parliament, it was a very large project. On the main south elevation, the Utzons imposed a strictly regulated uniform warehouse facade of heavy, identical, segmental-arched openings and piers, in counterpoint with the more exuberant free-standing pavilions.

The project was estimated to cost around Kr 125 million (A$25 million) in September 1985.[14] At this point, it was shelved by the conservative City Council for several years while the Council explored an alternative proposal by Henning Larsen, Bent Severin and Arne Meldgaard.[15] Interest revived briefly in early 1988, accompanied by a flurry of publicity, then it sank again, this time permanently.[16]

The 90,000 m^2 Kalkbrænderi southern basin proposal was many times bigger again than Langelinie. In outline, it was driven by the very attractive idea of housing 3000 people in a variety of building types containing mixed uses, including shops, a supermarket, offices at the harbour edge, an extremely large marina, a museum pavilion and a restaurant pagoda over water.[17] In addition, there would be parking for 650 vehicles at ground level, and seven to eight storeys of housing. The development would create a 25 m high wall around the basin, from Svanmøllen power station to the Paustian showroom on the opposite side, all facing inward with the main northern railway line to Helsingør at the back. The new development would have formed an insular harbourside block detached from Copenhagen.

Utzon's connection with the scheme is a puzzle. Architecturally it was undistinguished and any reasonably competent commercial architect could have produced it just as easily. Beyond his name, there was little to connect it with him, certainly in terms of the actual design quality. It was typical of the many flash-in-the-pan projects from the time, with their expensive models. The long blocks of seven- to eight-storeyed housing presented a depressing and daunting visual barrier to the outside. Not even the playful Indian- and Nepalese-inspired floating pagodas and temples were able to relieve a heavy feeling of incarceration.[18]

Utzon really does not appear to have been deeply involved. He was photographed standing smiling beside Kim Utzon and Islef's Director, Tom Petersen, but beyond the promotional publicity his participation appears to have been slight. Once again, he was being a good father and supporting his sons. As architecture, it was not exactly awful − if the overdevelopment factor was ignored. The public is very sophisticated and not easily fooled today and expects much more than Utzon was offering. His two schemes for Copenhagen's waterfront were disappointing, the latter more so than Langelinie, and this hurt Utzon. They were nothing like his earlier work. It was now becoming obvious to many observers that Utzon was not deeply involved or committed in a design sense. If this proved to be correct, it raised the question only he could answer − why he was prepared to allow his name to be cheapened in this way?

The Utzons continued to work on the Svanmøllen project for a number of years until 1991, when Jørn Utzon proposed that it should be completed in readiness for 1996, when Copenhagen would be the cultural capital city of Europe. With Ole Paustian's support, Utzon and Kim Utzon undertook a number of important changes in the interim, including an enclosed multi-storeyed glazed atrium shopping centre, a large indoor swimming hall and assembly house. The claim that the giant curved shapes were a fantastic construction in the caption under an internal perspective was pure unbridled hype, which further emphasised the absence of originality and detailed sensitive thought.[19]

The project that harmed the Utzon name even more than Svanmøllen was Jan and Kim Utzon's proposal to build a 155 m (510 ft) high 'Star-tower' overlooking Århus. Situated midway down the Jutland peninsula on its east coast, and with a population of 200,000, Århus is an important tertiary education centre, port and major ferry connection. It also has a lively and well-preserved old town adjacent to the port.

Århus, which received its charter in 1441, has an extremely good record when it comes to preserving its superb architectural heritage. The community had sensibly resisted the temptation of following Ålborg's example of turning its old city into an entertainment district given over to night clubs.

Utzon was mixed up in the project, but exactly how much is hard to determine. Somehow, he failed to see the proposed tower was a modern Colossus, standing erect and phallic on the ridge above a new Scandinavian Rhodes. The square Star-tower, with its steep, pyramid-shaped, transparent peaked hat, was to be placed just beyond the ring road where it is cut by Nørrebrogade, the main traffic artery leading directly from the harbour, and diagonally opposite C.F. Møller's internationally admired Århus University campus, a source of endless pride.

Utzon may have believed that it would benefit Århus in some way to have the new landmark. Its height of 150 m ensured it would be seen from 30 kilometres away, and out on the Store Bælt.

The proposed tower caused great offence, not only in the general Århus community, but for once the University was agitated as well to a degree not seen for many years. The Utzon tower would dwarf everything in its vicinity, including the nearby 56 m high book tower of the State Library, one of Århus's tallest structures. The extravagant inappropriateness of Utzon's Kr 700 million (A$140 million) Star-centre, with its enclosed square, boutique shops and hotel, drew an understandably angry response from almost every quarter.[20] It was badly out of scale with its surroundings. Standing on its inadequate diminutive pedestal of two-storeyed shops, it was ill-proportioned and gross.

Discussion and protests raged for three years from early 1990 to 1993. In the past, campanili or bell-towers were symbols of power. The Star-tower's raw power statement provoked the strongest reaction. Utzon was naive not to anticipate this. A clearly outraged Professor Gunnar Thorlund Jepsen had this to say: 'We all know that some have a vulgar taste and a complete lack of understanding of the whole picture. They think that size and pomposity is the only thing that counts. Hitler, Stalin and Mussolini were such types. But who would have thought that the city planner and Lord Mayor of Århus cannot get their towers large enough or vulgar enough either.'[21] If the proposal had been by Albert Speer, Hitler's architect, no one would have been in the least bit surprised, but it seemed inconceivable coming from an Utzon. But, as Professor Jepsen was quick to add, the tower was designed by the sons and not the father.

In his defence, Utzon countered that he was thinking about the landscape. Even here he stumbled, only later to retreat, replying lamely to a great barrage of criticism and relying on Jan Utzon to act as his spokesperson, that he was sick of all the carping. Utzon was in no mood to fight – he had allowed his name to be exploited and compromised over what was plainly a vulgar commercial deal. Now he suffered the consequences. In a less inhibited society, the criticism would have been a great deal rougher; even so it proved too much.

Not one of these commercial schemes in the late 1980s and early 1990s came to fruition. They wasted Utzon's time and damaged his reputation.

Ironically, while Utzon was so engaged assisting entrepreneurs, he was about to be reminded that one man's paradise is another man's development opportunity. Working with developers was one thing, but living alongside the results was quite another matter. In its unending search for an unspoilt corner of the planet to ravish, Club Med planted a new 484-room village at Porto Petro close by Utzon's 1972 'Can Lis' house. The peace of Colonia del Silencio was shattered by the non-stop smack of tennis balls on the resort's 16 courts; frenetic rock music all day long; the crack of golf balls ricocheting off pine trunks; and occasional shrill screams late at night. After 20 years on his cliff top, it was time for Utzon to move on.

Utzon had acquired a second site inland over 30 years earlier, in the mid-1960s, at the same time as 'Can Lis' and while he was still living in Sydney. The land was set well back from the sea, overlooked by the battered ramparts of the fourteenth-century Castell de Santuari, one of four ruined castles abandoned by the Moors. Utzon's site was in the rugged foothills of the Sierra del Levante range which runs back from and parallel to the south coast. The move meant an escape from the high humidity on the coast and 'Can Lis', the old house, was turned over to the Utzon children for their holidays.

The countryside is straight out of a Hollywood Western, so dry and hard and boulder-strewn is it under its thick prickly jacket of holm-oak, pine, myrtle, cactus and agaves. A winding, stony road leads through the hills, until very unexpectedly, out of nowhere, 'Can Feliz' pops up in the distance on a shoulder beneath a jutting spur, drowned in the lengthening afternoon shadows. Far off, the sea is a faint smudge of blue.

Utzon likes to immerse himself in the landscape: 'When I first arrive, I go for a walk around the site and the site tells me what to do.' He seems to imply that the site, almost by itself, creates the building form for him. This understates his own contribution, and downplays his capacity to read and interpret what is already there. When he designs a house, Utzon draws on aspects of the environment, on connections, a relationship that is continuous … interflowing.

The landscape surrounding 'Can Feliz' is hard and waxy. Possibly this caused him to set boundaries and fix a line around the house, between it and the landscape, which he has expressed with terraces. 'You feel you are on board a ship where you can concentrate on sprucing up small areas ... It's like a ship on the high seas ... those horizontal planes and walls make a very fine contrast with the undulating landscape.'

His two Mallorquin houses are very different. One on its cliff top, the other isolated on the instep of a mountain, spilling its interior forth over the terrace edge towards the sea. 'Can Lis' was a house of walls and pierced openings. Its successor is predominantly a house of columns. They are both made with the same materials and the same traditional technique. The source of their difference comes from where they are.

The columned hall is more ancient than Xerxes. Utzon likened it to a forest and the light penetrating between the paired columns at the front to the furtive shafts of sunlight between forest tree trunks. Utzon transported the beech forest to Mallorca. In the middle of 'Can Feliz' the dining room and the kitchen at the back are both protected by a veranda. This produces a wonderful, subdued, reflected light which is one of the reasons for having a veranda in the first instance, since it was an Arab innovation developed partly for this reason. The Hindi term for veranda, *baramda*, means 'come forth', which exactly fits Utzon's veranda.

Plants are a record of site conditions. A house, much like a seedling, should be adapted to the same factors of drainage, sunlight and wind, to mention only a few. Utzon considered these aspects and calibrated his design so it intertwines with the hillside. This involved much more than simply drawing plans.

The design grew gradually over time: '... I have often thought about where one could build here – It would be too brutal to place the house at the top of the site, and wrong to place it down along the road. Again and again I sat on this mountainside, in different places until one day I found the right spot. A place from which the landscape seemed most powerful. Strangely enough, it was where the house could be integrated with the mountainside in the most beautiful, harmonious way ... Then I began to think that this is how a stream trickles through the landscape – just like a poem.'[22]

Although the two houses are built using the same methods and of similar 40 cm x 40 cm and 40 cm x 20 cm stone blocks, a house on a cliff must be different to one on a mountain. The mountain house has a yellow-tiled roof, unlike the earlier cliff house. The latter house stretches out along the cliff top like a series of interconnected railway carriages that twist and turn at intervals. Its rooms fan outwards in various directions to capture the sea and in response to its extreme sea exposure.

The mountain house, likewise, offers a description of its landscape in the form of a visual onomatopoeia. Its shape is reminiscent of a comfortable old armchair that enfolds and holds the body. The spurs at the sides form the armrests, the mountain its back, and the sloping ground in between the two portals of the spurs acts as a cushioned seat on which the Utzon house rests. The plan is a summary of the setting: the spurs have been translated into the living room at one end and the master bedroom at the other, the columned porch or veranda containing the kitchen and dining area becoming the seat.

Because the cliff top was flat, the roof of 'Can Lis' was flat as well. The pitched tile roof of 'Can Feliz' echoes the mountain and even falls in the same direction.

Mountains are places of concentration, in contrast to cliffs which mark lines of cleavage. Both houses were inspired by their respective sites – from the macro to the micro, from the mountain or cliff, so it is with each, both are subtly inferred topographic statements.

'Can Feliz' stands alone on the mountainside. Because it has no immediate neighbours, it reminded Utzon of a Japanese temple. He built it in stages, beginning with the foundations, stopping for a while to consider, then fixing the height of the roof. In this manner, Utzon was able to introduce changes, modify parts he was unhappy with, take in or let out spaces, adjust walls and window openings, in the way a seamstress works on a garment, increasing or letting out a tuck until it fits perfectly. The proportions are the result of trial and error, not some arcane mathematical formula. Utzon experienced each space, and sat in it to see how it felt.

Jan and Kim Utzon assisted him by producing the drawings and building models beforehand. But the house is really the result of Utzon's direct way of working with no set completion date and with the freedom to change anything by talking to the masons as it proceeded. Kim set out the floor plan on the ground with stones heaped into small dolmens to indicate the column locations. At intervals, Lis and Jørn would sit in one spot and look around this way and that. At each step, as the parts were built, they would discover something new and this would lead to changes.

When the builder arrived with the drawings, Utzon walked around placing stones at the corners. After a while, the custom developed that when some part had to be torn down or altered, or both, the masons would arrive in the morning to find six bottles of wine stacked neatly beside the offending section of the work.[23] The wine was an instruction and an apology which said, 'I'm sorry, but it all has to be redone.'

Today clients are in a hurry. It is impossible to anticipate every visual frame, the precise arrangement of each room, each window, path and terrace. These are best worked out on the site. Thus architects have long imitated the practices of the sculptor in this regard, by walking around and looking at the work from every direction, noting the light, etc.

The 'Can Feliz' cross-section is not a lot different from the Paustian showroom and the Museum of Modern Art. Besides its low-pitched saddle roof, the distinctive way the gables are stepped and capped by Roman pantiles recalls the Fredensborg housing.

The 1994 house is more conventional than 'Can Lis', although it repeats the same vernacular vocabulary. If they are very similar, the similarity ceases beyond a certain point because they are at very different locations. The setting and the magic are peculiar to each.

Of the two houses, 'Can Lis' is unmistakably the authentic Utzon masterpiece. 'Can Feliz' is large and barn-like and although more polished in its execution, a fastidiousness has crept in to it. The details, for all their simplicity and lack of pretension, have become clichéd and caricature the Mallorquin vernacular. This is always a danger when something is repeated.

The new house is less imprisoning than the first. At 400–500 m² 'Can Feliz' is a small palace. A precious quality has been lost in the intervening years since 1971 – the sense of intimacy. The east living room has the same stone picture frames on the outside as the cliff house, but they do not point anywhere in particular. They have lost their former meaning, which has been replaced by a mood of nostalgia for the previous house. The deep splayed reveals of the frames are simplified as paired columns, so the construction is not even the same. One is reminded of non-functioning naval guns welded to their gun carriages and left pointing aimlessly in no specific direction.

Utzon's nomadism has affected the furnishings. Very little is fixed, so much so the house even seems a little like a stone tent inside – perhaps an acknowledgement of the great Kuwait canopy. The increased openness and the mobility of the interior objects belong more to tent cultures than European ones. To avoid detracting from the plain handsomeness of the stonework, Utzon banished pictures from the walls and has designated the windows his pictures instead. The lightweight cane furniture scattered around seems very ephemeral by contrast with the structure and the monumentality of the house. The largeness of the house inside is amplified by its extreme bareness.

The outside is more confident and relaxed, more playful even. The pantile copings slither and wriggle snake-and-ladder fashion, step by step, up the gable to the ridge. However, something is absent in 'Can Feliz'. Utzon was 23 years older, but it is more than a matter of the years, the circumstances were different to 1971. In 1991, Utzon was no longer under the same pressure to prove himself to the world. 'Can Feliz' is remarkable in its quiet way, but 'Can Lis' has the edge. Each belongs to a separate and distinct phase in Utzon's life.

A lifelong admirer and friend of Utzon, the Danish historian and academic, Tobias Faber, observed recently, 'Here in his own house he [Utzon] appears somewhat shy and extremely modest.'[24] These qualities of extreme shyness, abnormal modesty and forever, gracious charm, are a good summary of Utzon from someone who knows him well. In choosing the name 'Feliz', which means 'happy' and 'fortunate', for his new house, Utzon clearly indicated his ambition for the future.

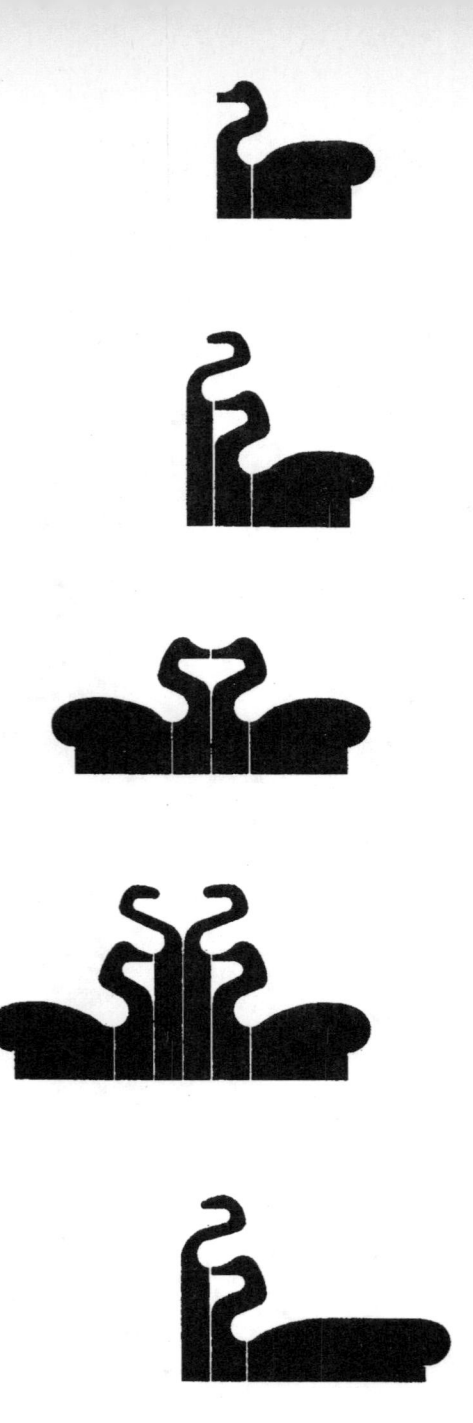

Utsep furniture, 1968, illustrates Utzon's additive principle by juxtaposing swan-shaped modules to achieve more complex configurations.

Reflections

The new house on Mallorca was a great source of joy to both Lis and Jørn Utzon. Tobias Faber has commented, 'One of the reasons that the new house is so moving is due to the Utzons' intense joy in living here and exploiting all the other qualities of the house and place.'[1] As a dwelling, it was remarkable for its lack of ostentation. Its joys are simple joys — looking at the sea in the morning, watching clouds float past and studying the intricate travelling arabesques of shadow and light cast across the golden stone walls by the sun.

Little of anything in the house is fixed. To live there is to live in a Bedouin tent in the desert caught in an unvarying daily cycle, where all the material objects have assigned positions yet are impermanent. The house is full of such conundrums that constantly delight and make each day one of discovery and invention.

The Utzons' children visit them regularly and stay at the coast house.

Living is never easy. Ill-health is but one of a number of obstacles. Lis Utzon, always bright and helpful, and Utzon's stalwart support, has suffered episodes of illness that left Utzon bewildered and apprehensive in their aftermath. Suddenly deprived of her vigilant protection, his world, which he has shared with Lis for almost half a century, was strangely bereft and chaotic.

Denmark is well known for its strong tradition of story telling. Utzon shares that native gift. He has a tendency to drift from the real into fantasy without quite being aware he has crossed the boundary. Perhaps it is the extreme conservatism of Danish life, its very ordinariness, that forces some Danes into a separate dream world. Utzon delights in telling tall tales. This can be very charming, but it is fraught with danger professionally. The architect must have his feet firmly on the ground, even if his head drifts upwards into dreams.

The pressure of being an artist encouraged Utzon to cultivate vagueness, references to nature that are not always explicit or thought through, which sound profound but often lack any genuine meaning and provide a kind of cape that embellishes his reputation. How much of this is real, how much is assumed, is hard to tell after so many years; it is so embedded in his way of thinking and presenting his ideas. Utzon is not a philosopher, even if he is attracted to making philosophical comments linking his architecture to nature. In the past he has been anything but careful in acknowledging the actual sources of some of his ideas.

Utzon has made many mistakes. He did not handle the confrontation with Davis Hughes sensibly and became so desperate that it led him into surrendering and handing over to others his greatest asset – his right to complete the work he had originated. It was a mistake of the first order, which he dearly paid for.

On the Sydney Opera House, there have been suggestions from time to time that the interiors should be reinstated as Utzon had planned them. It is important to realise in this context that however tempting it is to want to go back and correct history, this is usually not possible. This appears to be the case in this instance. Sydney lost its chance to complete one of the most remarkable buildings of this century when it allowed Davis Hughes and the Askin Government to have its way on the matter. There really is no going back and reversing what happened in 1966. The interior drawings for the main halls were never finished, and the necessary plywood prototypes for the ceilings and the glass walls were not built and tested.

Utzon's attitude on this matter is unambiguous.[2] In response to recent Australian appeals for his help in April 1997, he replied that the idea of rebuilding the Sydney Opera House was impossible for a variety of reasons, including the risk to the structure. In his opinion, no one who was knowledgeable about the Opera House would take the responsibility of recommending to the New South Wales Government that it would make economic sense or be technically possible to tear down and rebuild.

The main hall could very likely be made to work as a convertible hall for opera and symphony concerts as Yuzo Mikami, Utzon's Japanese assistant, has demonstrated so convincingly in his Orchard Hall in Tokyo, but that is not what is being suggested. The multi-purpose hall, as conventionally proposed, is a non-starter functionally and acoustically. But in any case, Utzon has absolutely forbidden anyone to work on his drawings for the interiors and the glass walls, whether his staff from that time or anyone else, ruling that, 'It is not feasible!'[3]

One aspect that is rarely discussed is Utzon's exposure to depression and the effect this has had not only on his life in general, but on his work in particular. Utzon has shown remarkable restraint, a lack of acrimony or bitterness to others and an extremely generous nature. He seems too perfect in this regard, too nice, too charming, for it to be the whole truth. Chronic depression may be the obverse face to all that charm. Is there a dark side, something he has kept hidden from us, which he feels he has to hide? It is an important question for which one can offer, at best, only a very incomplete, unsatisfactory answer.

Utzon's pursuit of solitude, his reclusive life spent close to nature, suggests he finds in nature a balm to an inner hurt or disturbance, an escape, a place where he feels he is not being watched and judged. It is known that Utzon is subject to dark moods and fits of 'talking black' where he is gripped by depression. It seems to have affected his life and limited his capacity to work with other people. Utzon alone knows the true extent of this dungeon, but in assessing his behaviour the frequent need for holidays during a crisis — such as happened at the end of 1965, when he absented himself from Sydney at the height of the crisis when it was entirely inappropriate – indicates a very real problem and dilemma for Utzon in controlling his depression.

Utzon is untypical of Denmark in being so universal, both in his reaching out to the world for his sources and wanting to travel and see so much. For centuries the kingdom of Denmark has been shrinking, leading Danes to the idea that they should focus on the development of their culture through introspection rather than looking outwards. Utzon has defied this pattern, preferring to open up his vision and expand upon Danish themes, allying them with ideas and possibilities from a tremendous range of geographical and historical settings. Nevertheless, traces of his Danish heritage are unmistakable. Utzon has enlarged the reach of Danish architecture, introduced new sources of inspiration and released it into a wider world frame.

Denmark has its own uniquely quiet and understated character. The Icelander, Olaf Olafsson, possibly because he is an outsider, was provoked by the flatness of Denmark: 'When I looked out through the window at the endless flatness of Denmark, I could not help missing the mountains in the vicinity of Reykjavik – Esja, Skardsheidi, even the Oskjuhlid hill. But here – not a rolling foothill in the summer mist, nowhere a mountain in the clear daylight of winter. Flatness, nothing but flatness, as far as the eye could see.'[4]

Now that Utzon is 80 years old, there is a demand to squeeze yet another building from him while this is still possible. It may be guilt for past neglect, or a desire to honour him. Scattered about Denmark are places where nature has crafted something unique and wondrous. They possess their own rather unique appeal. Utzon has admirers in Denmark who have selected places such as Skagen and the islands off Bornholm and Samsø, and have honoured him by asking him to design something there with his son Kim.

At the very tip of Jutland, surrounded by water, where Skagen extends a shallow finger of sand and pebbles cautiously into the sea, Utzon has found a new challenge. Overhead, the sky is filled with a purity of light, reinforced by reflections from the surrounding sea. The daylight has a piercing pervasive brightness and sharp intensity which captivated artists from the 1880s on. It is like no other place in Denmark, its special status being based on the intensity of the light on the landscape. The Skagen school of painting is said to constitute the very essence of Danish art. Not even Samsø's Stavns fjord or Bornholm compares with Skagen.

The road north stops at Grenen. The proposed new Skagen Odde Centre is situated on the northernmost rampart of Denmark. Old Skagen, which had once been larger than Copenhagen, was buried under invading sands in the nineteenth century, leaving only the top of a church spire exposed.

The Skagen Point Centre which was planned for completion in the summer of 1998, has two roles: one, dedicated to science, looks into the geo-physical past, the formation of the landscape and development after the last ice age; the other, artistic, is turned over to the works of the Skagen artists.

The main theme of the project is long, extended horizontal walls to emphasise the lightly undulating dunescape around it. Skylights sticking up past the walls indicate that there is something inside, and entice visitors by piquing their curiosity. The interior within the walls is sheltered, protected and intimate, constructed after the characteristic manner of the West Jutland farmstead, with four wings around an enclosed courtyard. The courtyard forms the calm heart of the Centre. Behind the walls the column-supported roofs of the entry yard insulate the complex against the climate. By turning left or right, the visitor enters the scientific or art museum side, both of which are interrupted by views out into planted courtyards.

Utzon summarised his aim as, 'building something for the silence; the scarce commodity of our time; something that differs from Disneyland, Legoland, etc. Man has always searched for the purity of nature and built in nature so as to experience the universe and explore one's own mind.' Utzon urged, 'We must build places for calm and contemplation. To me, nature is a source of endless [spiritual and creative] inspiration.'[5]

In the Samsø Island project, called 'swift torrents', Utzon

turned to the idea of the twelfth-century round church that faced out in all directions, such as the Østerlars Church on the island of Bornholm. The Centre would contain large and small rooms for lectures, meetings, music and exhibitions, with a large hall surrounded by arcades at the northern end of the courtyard. There would also be a cube space 14 m high, with skylights to let the sunlight slip inside, and large, niche-shaped recessed windows to the north, having a view to Marup Vig and the North Sea. The other display and meeting room would face Stavns Fjord to the north-east.

Utzon's scheme has planted it high on the ridge, turning and looking in different directions, with not one room square. Once again, the visitor would be greeted first by an entry courtyard and from there step into the inner courtyard surrounded by a gallery which connects to the room spaces. On this journey he or she would experience the landscape unfold along the way. Utzon claimed each phase would be like a poem read aloud in which the rooms are like the verses, each different, yet all a harmonious part of the whole.

These last two projects refine themes that were present in Utzon's work from the beginning, themes he has pursued all his life, and which stress the need for an architecture that is allied to nature. It is the same feeling he got from the sea. Indeed, the sea explains how Utzon approaches nature in general: it acts as a catalyst, something he can turn to when he feels a need for calm and contemplation, which at the same time enriches and opens up fresh avenues and possibilities.

Appendices

Appendix A

Sydney Opera House: architectural and secretarial staff

Based on the Index of Sydney Opera House Plans supplied to Nicholl & Nicholl, solicitors, in March 1966. Key: (H) Hellebæk office; (BP) Bennelong Point, Sydney, office.

Architects

BREDEN, Ian (Australia) April 1965–February 1966 (BP)
BUHRICH, Clive (Australia) July 1965–February 1966 (BP)
BROWNELL, Raymond Preston (Australia) May 1961–November 1964 (H, BP)
BUZZOLINI, Sergio (Switzerland) September 1964 (BP)
CAMPAGNONI, Peter (Australia) October 1965–February 1966 (BP)
D'ARCY, Frank Joseph (Australia) June 1963–October 1964 (BP)
DEVINE, Ron H. (Australia) November 1965–February 1966 (BP)
FISCHEL, Erik (Switzerland) April 1965–February 1966 (BP)
GREENBURG, Alan (South Africa) September–November 1962 (H)
HARTVIG-PETERSEN, Aage (Denmark) January 1959–November 1961 (H)
HJERTHOLM, Helge (Norway) 1958, March 1960–February 1962 (H)
HOPKINS, Paul (Australia) January 1965–February 1966 (BP)
HOYER, Jan Gudmand (Denmark) no date (H)
IRMING, Mogens (Denmark) October 1962 (H)
JACOB, Charles Hall (USA) September 1960 (H)
JARVIS, Osmond Raymond (Australia) August–December 1960 (H)
KIELLAND-BRANDT, Jacob (Denmark) October 1959–July 1965 (H, BP)
LA COUR, Charlotte (France) 1958–March 1959 (H)
LAUTRUP-LARSEN, Knud (Denmark) May 1959–November 1961 (H)
LUNDBERG, Jon (Norway) November 1960–June 1965 (H, BP)
MACLURCAN, Robert Geoffrey (Australia) p/t 1964–1965 (BP)
MIKAMI, Yuzo (Japan) January 1959–February 1961 (H)
MONEO, Jose Rafael (Spain) November 1961–April 1962 (H)
MYERS, Peter (Australia) January 1965–February 1966 (BP)
NAYMAN, Oktay (Turkey) May 1962–February 1966 (BP)
NIELSEN, Olaf Skipper (Denmark) March 1959 (H), November 1960–June 1965 (BP)
PRIP-BUUS, Mogens (Denmark) May 1959–February 1966 (H, BP)
SCHOUBOE, Poul (Denmark) July 1961–September 1962 (H)
SIMPSON, Paul (Australia) no date (BP)
TAKEYAMA, Minoru (Japan) August–November 1962 (H)
THOMAS, James Robert (UK) March–October 1960 (H)
TOMASZEWSKI, Michael Krzyszlof (Australia) August 1965–February 1966 (BP)
VODDER, Knud (Denmark) March 1960–April 1961 (H)
WESTMAN, Leslie (Australia) July–October 1965 (BP)

WILSON, Mary (Australia) no date (BP)
WHEATLAND, William Charles (Australia) May 1963–February 1966 (BP)

Secretaries

ATKIN, Elsa (Australia) 1965–1966 (BP)
COLLESS, Shirley (Australia) February 1965–April 1966 (BP, Paddington)
CORYDON, Gerda (Denmark) 1959–1960 (H)
MOORCROFT, Margaret (Australia) 1963–1964 (BP)
NIELSEN, Jean (Denmark) 1957–1959 (H)
WEISS, Wendy (Australia) 1965 (BP)

Appendix B

Works and projects 1944–1998

(italic projects were built)

1939	*Small dwelling, grandmother, Martha Olsen property, Ålsgårde,* completed 1940.
1944	Bellahøj (competition), 3rd prize, multi-storey housing in Copenhagen (with Tobias Faber).
	Ålborghallen (competition), honourable mention.
	Royal Academy Gold Medal: subject an academy of music with concert hall.
1945	Project for a crematorium.
	Water tower and sea mark, island of Bornholm.
1946	Utzon starts his own office with various factory buildings for fish-products and a chemical factory.
	Falköping, Sweden (competition), 4th prize, community centre, theatre.
	Borås Bebyggelsesplan, Sweden (competition), with Tobias Faber, honourable mention.
	Architectural Association's one-family houses and town planning (competition), 1st and 2nd prizes.
	Næstved Idræsarlaeg, Denmark (competition), 3rd prize, sports centre.
	Hobro Pavilion, Denmark (competition), 4th place, restaurant and community centre.
	Design for the Crystal Palace competition, London, with Tobias Faber and Mogens Irming.
1947	Århus Idrætsanlag, Denmark (competition), mention, sports centre.
	Housing development, Morocco (project).
	Paper factory, Morocco (project).
	Central Railway Station, Oslo (project with Arne Korsmo).
1947–8	'Vika' town planning for Oslo Centre, Norway. Office buildings with Arne Korsmo.
1948	School of Commerce, Göteborg, Sweden, with Arne Korsmo.
	Housing competition for Borås in Sweden.
	Planning of cement factory and factory for prefabricated elements, Morocco.
1950	*Chemical factory, Copenhagen.*
1951	Utzon house, Morocco – design only.
	February first scheme for Utzon house, Hellebæk.
	September second scheme for Utzon house, Hellebæk.
1952	April *Utzon house, Hellebæk, North Zealand,* completed.

Development plan for the Skoyen–Oppsal area, Oslo, Norway, with Arne Korsmo.
1952–3 **House, near Lake Furesø, Holte.**
1953 **Villa Arnung, Nærum.**
House, Præstevanget 15, Hillerød.
Skaanske low-cost housing competition for 'Scania house types', a new type of family housing in Skane in collaboration with Ib Molgelvang, 1st prize.
Langelinie Pavilion, Copenhagen (competition), 4th prize, restaurant and yacht club facilities.
Skanse gardhouse.
1954 Open inter-Scandinavian competition for one family-housing + town planning, Scanian types of house, 1st prize.
Villa 1, Rungsted.
Villa 2, Rungsted (family house).
Marieburg, Stockholm (competition), 1st prize, administration centre + 1000 flats.
Invited competition, Lund, Sweden, housing – 60 one-family houses, 1st prize.
1954–60 Elineburg Housing Estate, Denmark (competition), 2nd and 4th places in first stage, 1st prize final stage.
1955 January – **21 rowhouses, 21–59 Østervag, Skjern,** south-west Jutland, collaboration with Bent Alstrup.
Villa Frank, Vedbæk, north-east Zealand, with Bent Alstrup.
Villa Lillesø, Furesø.
1956 **Villa Dalsgard, Holte, North Zealand.**
June–April 1966 **Sydney Opera House** (competition), 1st prize, Utzon collaborates with Erik Andersson, Utzon the dominant designer.
1957–60 **Kingohusene Housing Estate,** near Helsingør, Denmark, 63 Kingo-houses.
1958 Danish Labour Party Education Centre, Copenhagen (competition), 1st prize.
Melli Bank, Teheran, Iran. Built by Kampsax A/S.
Workers' high school, Højstrop, Denmark (project).
High school, Hellebæk, Copenhagen (project).
Labour Organisation College at Helsingør (competition), 1st prize.
1959 Birkehøj, project for a small town in North Zealand, Denmark.
April Town plan of Frederiksburg, Denmark (competition), 1st prize.
1960 Pavilion complex, World's Fair, International Exhibition Centre in Copenhagen (project).
National Museum, Copenhagen (competition project).
Elvira, Spain (competition), for a Mediterranean town.
Eliveberge housing, Sweden, scheme for a shopping centre.
1962–3 **Danish Co-operative Building Company Housing Development, Fredensborg, Denmark.**
1963 Asger Jorn Art Museum, Silkeborg, Jutland (project), (drawn by Oktay Nayman).
May First sketches of the Bayview house at Kara Crescent, Bayview.
1964 February Scheme 1, Utzon house, Kara Crescent, Bayview.
April Shopping centre at Mona Vale, 12–14 Waratah Street, Mona Vale.
May Results of Zürich competition announced 27 May, 1st prize (drawn by Mogens Prip-Buus).

	June Scheme 2, Utzon house, Kara Crescent, Bayview. August National Opera, Madrid, international competition organised by the Juan March Foundation. September Redevelopment scheme for Sydney Cove area.
1965	University Art Museum, Berkeley, California (competition). December Final approval, Utzon house, Kara Crescent, Bayview, 23 December 1965.
1966	School at Herning (project). Theatre for Wolfsburg, Germany (competition), 3rd prize. Farum town centre, Denmark: commercial and town plan. **Povl Ahm house, Harpenden, Hertfordshire, UK.**
1967	Centre for higher education and *skning* in Odense, Funnen, Jørn Utzon and Peer Abben.
1968–76	**Bagsværd Church, Bagsværd.**
1969	School centre with technical college, Herning, Denmark (project). April **Espansiva Byg A/S Timber Component House System** (project) for Timber Association. 30 built in Norway, 6 or so in Denmark including Hana Hedin house at Birkehøj and units at Jutland. Utzon built a pilot structure at 64 Bøssemagergade, old Hellebæk DK 3150, which he used as his drawing office. Jeddah sports layout and stadium for National Sports Centre, Saudi Arabia (project). December National Museum for study of landscape. Competition requires visitor centre, restaurant and cafeteria, carparking.
1971–2	**'Can Lis', Jørn Utzon house,** sandstone house at Cala media luna.
1971	June **10.5 m long aluminium yacht with fused twin hulls.**
1971–83	**Kuwait National Assembly Complex, Kuwait City, Kuwait.** Construction 1979–83. Designed in 1971, scheme revised November 1973.
1979	February Danish Heart Foundation Training Centre at Skagen, North Jutland. June Sopavilionen (swimming hall), baths and restaurant on Peblinge Sø (Lake Peblinge), Copenhagen.
1985	September Hotel and congress centre on Langelinie, Copenhagen (914 m long x 82 m wide). Kr 125 million project proposed by Jørn Utzon with entrepreneur H. Hoffmann & Sonnen A/S.
1986	September **Paustian furniture showroom, Copenhagen free harbour,** by Utzon Associates with sons Jan and Kim. 2000 m^2, completed May 1987, receives Betonelement-Prisen, 1987. Entrepreneur H. Hoffmann & Sonnen A/S.
1988	April Danish Museum for Modern Art, Fredensborg, project by Jørn with Jan Utzon. 3000 m^2, promoted by Erik & Margit Brandt. April Utzon and Chr. Islef proposal for Kr 1.5 billion redevelopment of south basin of Kalkbrænderi from Svanemøllen power station around to Paustian Centre discussed with Mayor Egon Weidekamp, in collaboration with Jan and Kim. June Hotel at Kalundborg, west Zealand, Denmark, project by Jørn Utzon.
1989	July **Esbjerg Concert Hall for Esbjerg, Jutland,** to accommodate 1100 and to cost Kr 100 million (A$20 million) promoted by Musikhus A/S, director, Reidar Faurbye. Completion for 1994, delayed. Jørn + Jan Utzon. July Bornholm (2 projects): Naturama science museum project at

	Gudhjim; history museum with shops and restaurant at Hammerhavn.
1990	February Controversial project for 155 m skyscraper on hill top at Århus and boutique complex to cost Kr 700 million, provide 36,000 m^2 space. Rejected as unsuitable.
1991–4	**'Can Feliz' Utzon's second house on Mallorca,** completed in 1995 (1992–5) in Sierra del Levante mountains behind Alqueria del Blanca, south-eastern Mallorca.
1995	October 2 projects: 'Swift torrents' museum proposal on ridge of Samsø Island overlooking Stavn Fjord combining science and art facilities; Skagen Odde Centre, Grenen, North Jutland, in collaboration with Kim Utzon, art and natural history museum. For completion mid-1998, delayed.

Furniture

1947–8	Cabinetmaker's competition, 2nd prize, furniture. Cabinetmaker's competition, 1st and 2nd prizes, glass.
1950	Museum of Modern Art, New York: prize design for modern furniture, chair by Arne Korsmo and Jørn Utzon. **Pendent lamp U 4860,** Kr 38; diameter 19 cm, for Kemp & Lauritzen, Denmark.
1958	**Jørn Utzon furniture system developed for the workers' college at Helsingør.** Development delayed until Utzon returned to Denmark in 1966, taken up by Fritz Hansens Eft. December 6 Dansk Patent Nr. 90550, Polstringselement lodged, granted 6 March 1961. Stool seat back attachment.
1960	March Dansk Patent Nr. 93100, Mobel, navnlig stol eller bord, med sarg or ben. Granted 18 June 1962. Svensk Patent Nr 93842, USA Patent Nr 2435064.
1968	April **Sydney Opera House furniture** by Utzon exhibited at Danish Week in Britain at Oscar Woollens, London. Marketed by Fritz Hansens Eft.
1969	May Danish Furniture Show 1969, Bella Center, Copenhagen, 13–18 May.
1970	**Jørn Utzon chair for Fritz Hansen A/S, Allerød, Denmark.** Mobilia, 178–179, May–June 1970.

Appendix C

Awards and prizes

1945	Gold Medal (Minor) Royal Academy of Fine Arts, Copenhagen.
1947	Bissen Prize.
1949	Zacharia Jacobsen Award.
1957	Eckersberg Medal (est. 1883), bronze medal designed by Harald Cowarden in memory of C.V. Eckersberg, Copenhagen.
1966	Honour Plaque, Bund Deutscher Arkitekten (Germany Architectural Association) Lübeck, W. Germany. Ceremony 7 June.
1967	C.F. Hansen Medal, Royal Academy of Fine Arts, Copenhagen.
1970	Mobel Prize (Danish Furniture Prize for 8108 chair), Copenhagen. Honorary Fellow, recognition by American Institute of Architects (AIA).
1973	Gold Medal, Royal Australian Institute of Architects, Australia (RAIA).

1978	*Gold Medal*, Royal Institute of British Architects, London, UK (RIBA). £10,000 (A$24,295). Ceremony on 20 June. *Thorvaldsen Medal*.
1979	*Lakerol Prize*.
1981	*Architecture Prize*, Danske Arkitekters Landsforbund (est. 1981). Kr 75,000 (A$16,008) presented by Soren Nielsen. Ceremony on 23 November.
1982	*Alvar Aalto Medal*, Helsinki, Finland. August.
1986	*Niels Prize*, Denmark. Kr 100,000 (A$21,343).
1987	*Fritz Schumacher Prize* (est. 1949) Technical University of Hanover, W. Germany, DM 30,000 (A$24,365).
1992	*Wolf Prize* shared with Frank O. Gehry and Sir Denys Lasdun, Jerusalem, Israel, US$100,000 divided equally among co-recipients. US$33,333 (A$48,962). May.
1998	*Sonning Prize,* presented to JU by Kjeld Møllgård, Rector of the University of Copenhagen in the Great Hall on 17 April. Worth Kr 500,000 (A$111,000). Previous recipients include: Albert Schweitzer, Bertrand Russell, Niels Bohr, Alvar Aalto, Sir Laurence Olivier, Haldor Laxness, Karl Popper, Ingmar Bergman, Gunter Grass. Utzon was the first Dane to receive the prize since Niels Bohr in 1961.

Abbreviations

Individuals

AU	Aage Oberg Utzon
CM	Sir Charles Moses, Managing Director, Australian Broadcasting Commission
DH	Davis Hughes, Coalition Minister for Public Works, New South Wales
HA	Henry Ingham Ashworth, 1907–91
JN	Joachim Nutsch, acoustical assistant to Professor Cremer (LC)
JU	Jørn Oberg Utzon
JZ	Sir Jack Zunz, Ove Arup & Partners
LC	Lothar Cremer, Dr Ing Professor of Acoustics, Berlin
LM	Sir Leslie Martin
LU	Lene Utzon
NR	Philip Norman Ryan, Labor Minister for Public Works, New South Wales
OA	Ove Arup, founding director of OA & P
SC	Shirley Colless, JU's personal secretary in Sydney
TF	Tobias Faber, former Professor in Architecture, Royal Academy of Fine Arts, Copenhagen
VJ	Vilhelm Lassen Jordan, Danish acoustician
WG	Werner Gabler, architectural acoustician, Berlin
WW	William Wheatland, JU's Sydney office manager

Institutions

ABC	Australian Broadcasting Commission
ALHM	Ålborg Local History Museum
ANL	Australian National Library, Canberra, ACT
AONSW	Archives Office of New South Wales
DWLPA	Dennis Wolanski Library of the Performing Arts, Sydney Opera House

HKTf Helsingør Kommune, Teknisk forvaltning, Denmark
HTL   Hall, Todd & Littlemore, architects' panel which replaced Utzon in Sydney after 1966
IUA   International Union of Architects
M & DP Music and Drama Panel of Sydney Opera House Executive Committee
ML   Mitchell Library, State Library of New South Wales
OAP   Ove Arup & Partners, Consulting Engineers, London
OHC   Opera House Committee
OHT   Opera House Trust
Ra   Rigsarkivet, Copenhagen, Denmark
RAIA Royal Australian Institute of Architects
SOH   Sydney Opera House
SOHEC Sydney Opera House Executive Committee
TP   Technical Panel of SOHEC

Publications

A   *Australian*
AEx   *Armidale Express*, Armidale
AJ   *Architects' Journal*, London
BT   *Berlingske Tidende*, Copenhagen
CAPD   *Commonwealth of Australia Parliamentary Debates*, Canberra, ACT
GW   *Good Weekend* magazine, *Sydney Morning Herald*
LA   *Living Architecture*, Copenhagen
LI   *Life International* magazine, New York
NSWPD   *New South Wales Parliamentary Debates*, 3rd Series
P   *Politiken*, Copenhagen
RAGNSW *Report of the Auditor General of New South Wales*
S-H   *Sun-Herald*, Sydney
SMH   *Sydney Morning Herald*, Sydney
TBPNSW *New South Wales Treasury Budget Papers*, for NSW Government
WD   *Woman's Day*, magazine, Sydney
Z   *Zodiac*, Milan

Bibliography

Aalborg Vaerft Gennem 75 Ar, Aalborg Local History Museum, Aalborg.
Aarre, Bent & Ebert, Jan, *Bogen om Spidgatteren*, Sejl og Forlag, Copenhagen, no date.
Ahlberg, Hakon, *Gunnar Asplund, Arkitekt, 1885–1940*, AB Tidskriften Byggmastaren, Stockholm, 1943.
Ahlin, Janne, *Sigurd Lewerentz, architect*, MIT Press, London, 1987.
Aitkin, Don, *The Colonel: A political biography of Sir Michael Bruxner*, ANU Press, Canberra, 1969.
— *The Country Party in New South Wales*, ANU Press, Canberra, 1972.
Asplund, Gunnar et al., *acceptera*, Bokforlag Saktiebolaget Tiden, Stockholm, 1931.
Anker, Peter, *The Art of Scandinavia*, 2 vols, Paul Hamlyn, London, 1970.
Balslev, Lisbet Jørgensen et al. *Vilhelm Lauritzen: A modern architect*, trans. Martha Gaber Abrahamsen, Bergiafonden Aristo, 1994.
Beauvert, Thierry, *Opera Houses of the World*, trans. Daniel Wheeler, Thames & Hudson, London, 1996.
Betser, Arthur, *The Proper Yacht*, Adlard Coles Ltd, London, 1966.
Bettelheim, Bruno, *The Uses of Enchantment: The meaning and importance of fairy tales*, Thames & Hudson, London, 1976.
Blaser, Werner, *Courtyard House in China: Tradition and Present*, second ed., Basel, 1995.
Bolton, Geoffrey, *The Oxford History of Australia: vol. 5, 1942–1988*, Oxford University Press, Melbourne, 1990.
Brawn, Michael, *Arup Associates: The biography of an architectural practice*, Lund Humphries, London, 1983.
Chang, Amos Ih Tiao, *The Existence of Intangible Content in Architectonic Form based upon the practicality of Laotzu's Philosophy*, Princeton University Press, Princeton, NJ, 1956.
Caldenby, Claes and Hultin, Olof (eds), *Asplund*, Rizzoli, Stockholm & New York, 1985.
Dannat, Trevor, *Architects' Year Book 6*, Elek Books, London.
Davidsen, Lene and Kirkfeldt, Susanne S., *Jørn Utzon. Arkitektskolen Oplag No. 3*, Aarhus, June 1988.
Det Gamle og Nyere Kolding, P. Eliassens Koldingbog, Anden Del, Kolding, 1975.
Drew, Philip, *Sydney Opera House*, Phaidon, London, 1995.
— *Third Generation: The changing meaning of architecture*, Pall Mall, London, 1973.
Ebert, Jan, *Danske lystbade, vol. 1: 1866–1940*, Cervius, Copenhagen.
— *Danske lystbade, vol. 2: 1940–1986*, Cervius, Copenhagen.
Ellis Davidson, H.R., *Viking & Norse Mythology*, Library of the World's Myths and Legends, Chancellor, London, 1982.
Faber, Tobias, *Danish Architecture*, Det Danske Selskab, Copenhagen, 1978.
— *Jørn Utzon:Houses in Fredensborg*, Ernst & Sohn, Berlin, 1991.
— *Kina – Danmark – arkitektonisk set*, Kunstakademiets Arkitektskole, Copenhagen, Nytaar 1986.
Fisker, Kay, *Development of Scandinavian Architecture during the past fifty years*, unpublished ms, 1951, Samlingen af Arkitekturtegningen Kunstakademiets Bibliotek, Copenhagen.

— *Contemporary Danish Architecture*, unpublished lectures presented to Association du Artisans d'Art, April 1958, Paris.
Frampton, Kenneth, *Studies in Tectonic Culture: The poetics of construction in nineteenth and twentieth century architecture,*. MIT Press, Cambridge, Mass., 1996.
Frey, Albert, *In Search of a Living Architecture*, Architectural Book Publishing Co. Inc., New York, 1939.
Fromonot, Françoise, *Jørn Utzon: The Sydney Opera House,* Electra/Gingko, Milan, 1998.
Gardiner, Stephen, *Kuwait: The making of a city*, Longmans, London, 1983.
Gillmer, Thomas C., *A History of Working Watercraft of the Western World*, second ed., International Marine, Camden, Maine, 1994.
Gillsater, Sven, *Wings over the Kattegatt – a Swedish coastline*, Spektra, Halmstad, Sweden, 1977.
Goldsmith, Margaret E., *The Mode and Meaning of Beowulf*, Althone Press, London, 1970.
Griffiths, Tony, *Scandinavia*, Wakefield Press, Adelaide, South Australia, 1993.
Guide to Danish Architecture, 2 vols. Arkitektens Forlag, Copenhagen, 1995.
Guide to Modern Danish Architecture, Arkitektens Forlag, Copenhagen, 1969.
Haan, Hilde de and Haagsma, Ids, *Architects in Competition – International Architectural Competitions of the Last 200 years*, Thames & Hudson, London, 1988.
Hickie, David, *The Prince and the Premier*, Angus & Robertson, Sydney, 1985.
Hiro, Dilip, *Desert Shield to Desert Storm*, Paladin, London, 1992.
Hubble, Ava, *The Strange Case of Eugene Goossens and Other Tales from the Opera House*, Collins, Australia, 1988.
Høeg, Peter, *The History of Danish Dreams*, trans. Barbara Haveland, Harvill Press, London, 1995.
Højrup, Ole, *Landbokvinden: Rok og Kaerne, Grovbrodog Vadmel*, G.E.C. Gadsforlag, Copenhagen, 1964.
Izenour, George C., *Theatre Design*, second ed., Yale University Press, London, 1996.
— *Theatre Technology*, second ed., Yale University Press, London, 1996.
Jacobsen, Helge Seidlin, *An Outline History of Denmark,* Host & Son, Copenhagen, 1986.
Joedicke, Jurgen, *Shell Architecture,* Reinhold Publishing, New York, 1963.
Jordan, Vilhelm Lassen, *Acoustical Design in Concert Halls and Theatres: A personal account,* Applied Science Publishers, London, 1980.
Jørn Utzon – Udvalgate Arbejder 1942–1988, Skissernas Museum, Lund, Sweden, 1994.
Kaldor, Andras, *Opera Houses of Europe,* Antique Collectors' Club, Woodbridge, Suffolk, 1996.
Kirkham, Pat, *Charles and Ray Eames: Designers of the twentieth century*, MIT Press, Cambridge, Mass., 1995.
Knight, Stephen, *Corpse at the Opera House,* Allen & Unwin, Sydney, 1993.
Kruuse, Jens and Kjær, Kristian, *Danmark i Digtning og Kunst*, Thaning & Apel, København, 1967.
Kuhner, Robert A., *Eero Saarinen: His life and work*, Council of Planning Librarians, New York, 1975.
Laursen, Andreas, *Danske fiskerbaade – gennem 100 aar*, Host & Sons, København, 1972.
Lund, Nils-Ole, *Nordsk Arkitektur,* Arkitektens Forlag, 1991.
Marshall, John R., *Social Phobia: From shyness to stage fright*, Basic Books, New York, 1994.

McCoy, Esther, *Art and Architecture Case Study Houses*.
Menuhin, Yehudi, *The Violin*, Flammarion, Paris & New York, 1996.
Messent, David, *Opera House: Act one*, self-published, Sydney, 1997.
Modern Norsk Arkitektur, A5, no. 1–2, Redigeres af Arkitektstuderende i de Norsk Lande, Oslo, 1956.
Mollat du Jourdin, Michel, *Europe and the Sea*, Blackwell, London, 1993.
Moss, Robert, 'Spidsgatters: The strength and grace of double-enders,' *Wooden Boat* (USA), no. 7, September/October, 1987, pp. 50–5.
— 'Scandinavian Jewels', *Classic Boat* (UK), no. 64, October 1993, pp. 60–5.
Murphy, Mary, *Challenges of Change: The Lend Lease story*, Pot Still Press, Sydney, 1984.
Murray, Robert, *The Split: Australian Labor in the Fifties*, Hale & Iremonger, Sydney, 1984.
Neville, Richard, *Hippie Hippie Shake: The dreams, the trips, the trials, the love-ins, the screw-ups, the sixties*, William Heinemann Australia, 1995.
Norberg-Schulz, Christian, *Arne Korsmo*, Universitetforlaget, Arkitekthogdkolen Oslo, Oslo, 1986.
— *Church at Bagsværd, near Copenhagen, Denmark. 1973–76*, Global Architecture 61, series ed. Y. Futagawa, Tokyo, 1981.
— *Modern Norwegian Architecture*, Norwegian University Press, Oslo, 1986.
— *Nightlands, Nordic Building*, trans. Thomas McQuillan, MIT Press, London, 1996.
Olafsson, Olaf, *Absolution*, Phoenix House, London, 1994.
Olufsen, Einar, *Hvide Sjl: Lystfartojernes Udvikling fra Vikingetid til Vore dage*, Gjellerup, 1964.
Ove Arup, 1895–1988, The Institute of Engineers (UK), London, 1988.
Ove Arup & Partners, *Selection of Working Drawings for Roof Structure – Sydney Opera House*, Selected by Yuzo Mikami for OA & P, London.
Ove Arup & Partners 1946–1986, Academy Editions, St Martins Press, London, 1986.
Paulsson, T., *Scandinavian Architecture*, London, 1957.
Peters, Dick, *Operation Concrete Butterfly*, Angus & Robertson, Sydney, 1973.
Rasmussen, Steen Eiler, *Byer og Bygninger II. I Tegninger og Ord*. Fonden Til Udg i velse af Arkitekturvaeker Arkitektskolen i Århus, November 1991.
Reading, Geoffrey, *High Climbers: Askin and others*, John Ferguson, Sydney, 1989.
Rice, Peter, *An Engineer Imagines*, Ellipsis, London, 1993.
Robertson, Donald, *Pre-Columbian Architecture*, George Braziller, New York, 1963.
Rosa, Joseph, *Albert Frey, Architect*, Rizzoli, New York, 1990.
Rosen, Carole, *The Goossens: A musical century*, Andre Deutsch, London, 1993.
Sametz, Phillip, *Play On: 60 years of music-making with the Sydney Symphony Orchestra*, ABC, Sydney, 1992.
Schama, Simon, *Landscape and Memory*, Fontana, London, 1996.
Schildt, Goran, *Alvar Aalto*: vol. 1, *The Early Years*, 1984; vol. 2, *The Decisive Years*, 1986; vol. 3, *The Mature Years*, Rizzoli, New York, 1989.
Shapcott, Thomas, *Mona's Gift*, Penguin, Ringwood, Vic., 1993.
Stierlin, Henri, *Ancient Mexico*, Living Architecture, Macdonald, London, 1968.
— *Mayan*, Architecture of the World Series, Benedikt Taschen, Lausanne, 1963.
Swanston, Michael (ed.), *Beowulf*, Manchester University Press, Manchester, 1978.
Training Units, vol. 8, in *Units of the Royal Australian Air Force: A concise history*. Australian Government Publishing Service, Canberra, 1995.

Utzon, C. Chr. Lausen, *Familien Utzon: En Stamtavle over Slaegten*, Konrad Jørgensens Bogtrykkeri, Kolding, 1907.
Utzon, Jan, *Three Generations*, Anders Nyborg, Rungsted Kyst, Denmark, 1988.
Utzon, Jørn, *The Sydney Opera House*, Arsskrift, 1967, Udg af Kunstakademiets, København, 1967.
Webber, G.P., *E.H. Rembert: The life and work of the Sydney architect 1902–1966*, University of Sydney, Sydney, 1982.
Weston, Richard, *Alvar Aalto*, Phaidon, London, 1995.
Wrede, S., *The Architecture of Erik Gunnar Asplund*, Cambridge, Mass., 1980.

Acknowledgements

A biography is a mosaic, a compilation of fragments that arrive in no logical order, which frequently do not fit; some never arrive at all. In thanking everyone who helped make this possible I realise it is a cliché, but it is also the truth: I could not have done it without the help of other people. All the information, photographs, copies of documents, the diaries and records as well as the recollections were an essential part of building a coherent picture. Their generous support was invaluable.

I am indebted to my commissioning publisher, Jennifer Byrne, Publishing Director at Reed Books Australia who started the book, and for her vision, enthusiasm and commitment in the early stages. Margaret Connolly gave important advice when she suggested that I deal with Utzon's entire life – not merely the three years he spent in Sydney – and that it be a biography, rather than focus narrowly on the Opera House portion of the story. This was crucial and shaped my approach thereafter.

Writing a book such as this is an adventure that the author undertakes without the slightest assurance of success at the end. Only after it was done did I realise that I unconsciously had believed it was impossible. In the process I met some remarkable people who not only made the impossible possible, but also made the journey itself a joyous one. I am particularly indebted to Lisbet Balslev-Jørgensen, Tobias Faber, Ray Brownell, Peter Mandel Hansen, Kim Dirkinck-Holmfeld, Brita Beeston, Else Tholstrup, Yuzo Mikami and Evangelia Simos Ali.

The following individuals and institutions supplied me with pieces of the Utzon mosaic, advice, gave me shelter, took me to see Utzon's buildings, confided in me, and some even paid for lectures which enabled me to continue with my research:

Australia
Airforce Headquarters; Archives Office of NSW; Nigel W. Ashton; Ella Ashworth; Elsa Atkin; Australian Archives; Brita Beeston; Paul Bentley, Dennis Wolanski Library of the Performing Arts; Lady Gillian Bunning; Neil Burley; Hon. Mr Justice John Joseph Cahill; David Clark; Don Coleman & Tony Mitchell, Public Works NSW; Shirley Colless; Hon. Sir Charles Cutler; Frank D'Arcy; Joan Domicelj; Dr J.D. Donaldson, University of Tasmania; Denis T. Doonan; Elias Duek-Cohen; Pat Edgington; Elizabeth Ellis, State Library of NSW; Peter Georgiades; Jim Godard; Margaret Fulton; Jeff Harris, ABC Archive, Gore Hill; Owen Haviland; Hon. Sir Davis Hughes; Peter Kollar; Michael Lavers; E.C. Mack; Jack Martin; Angela McGing, Sydney City Council; George Molnar; National Library of Australia; Milton Moon; Philip Nobis; Alex Popov; Margaret (Moorcroft) Pritchard; Les Reedman; Dorothy Ryan; Rt Hon. Ian Sinclair; Joan Skibby; John Spence, ABC Radio Archives; Lionel Todd; Libby Turner; Josef Vissel; Bill Wheatland; Mrs Joan Winston; John Zaat.

Denmark
Marianne Asmussen, Karen Blixen Museet; Lisbet Balslev-Jørgensen, Martin and dog; Mads Bryld; Adrian Carter; Kaj Christensen; Gerda Corydon; Dr Poul Dedenrooth-Schou, Museet po Koldinghus; Kim Dirckinck-Holmfeld, *Arkitekten*; Tobias Faber; Albert Gehrke; Gilbert Hansen, *B* magazine; Prof. Hans Munk Hansen; Peter Mandal Hansen; Keld Helmer-Petersen, photographer; Jens

Hogaard; Prof. Gudmand Hoyer; Industriminestriet Patentdirectoratet; Kongelige Bibliotek; Knud W. Jensen, Lousiana Museum; Lars Jensen, Englesk Institut Århus University; Jacob Kielland-Brandt; Kunstakademiets Bibliotek; Birgit Flemming Larsen; Nils Madsen; Arne Magnussen; Ebbe Melgaard, Kunstakademiets Arkitektskole; Charlotte Paludan, Kunsthandværk Industri Design Museet; Aage Hartvig Petersen; Rigsarkivet; Bruce Clunies Ross; Birger Schmidt; Poul Schouboe; Fleming Skude, Kunstakademie Arkitekskole Library; Prof. Carsten Thau; Else Tholstrup, photographer, for research; Ole Winding, School of Architecture Århus; Lene Utzon; Lin Utzon.

England
Povl Ahm, OAP; Raymond P. Brownell, for his photographs and friendship; Michael Lewis, OAP; Sir Leslie Martin, Cambridge; Patrick Morreau, OAP; James R.G. Thomas, Rothermel Thomas; Prof. Ian Boyd White, University of Edinburgh; Sir Jack Zunz.

Finland
Joakim Hansson, Alvar Aalto Museum.

France
George M. Ibrahim, Hôtel de Lépante, Nice, who handled my Kuwait visit; Jon Lundberg; Mogens Prip-Buus.

Japan
Yuzo Mikami of MIDI Architects for giving his time, insights, photographs.

Kuwait
Mr Abdulaziz al-Hamdan; Mr Bader al-Qabandi, Chief Engineer, Ministry of Public Works; Mrs Wafa Al Majed, Ministry of Planning; Evangelia Simos Ali, my guide who showed me Kuwait City, Ministry of Planning; Aidan Broderick, The British Council; Geoffrey J. Pollitt; Mr Hamid Shuaib (original Advisory Committee) Pan Arab Consulting Engineers.

Norway
Helge Hjertholm, Bergen; Professor Christian Norberg-Schulz, Oslo.

Spain
Oriol Bohigas, who made my vist to Mallorca possible; Rafael Moneo, Madrid. Mallorca: Jørn and Lis Utzon for their kindest regards.

Switzerland
Dr Justus Daihinden; Hans Rudolf Rüegg.

USA
Federal Aviation Administration, US Department of Transportation; Abby Pevrvil, MOMA; Prof. P.C. Papademetriou, NJIT; Kevin Roche, Kevin Roche John Dinkell & Associates. Hawaii: Prof. Leighton Liu.

Notes

1: A Country Youth

1. A. Thiset to Lausen Utzon, 1907, in C. Chr. Lausen Utzon, *Familien Utzon: En Stamtavle Slaegten*, Konrad Jørgensens Bogtrykkeri, Kolding, 1907, p. xii.
2. The fame of Kolding in southern Jutland rests on its fifteenth-century castle which was originally Gothic. It lay a gutted ruin for 150 years prior to its splendid restoration in 1972 as a museum of cultural history by Inger and Johannes Exner. It was an important commercial centre in the Middle Ages because of its strategic location at a junction of north–south and east–west and its proximity to the German-speaking lands to the south. Kolding received its charter in 1321.
3. P. Eliassens, *Det Gamle og Nyere Kolding*, vol. 2, Trykt i Konrad Jørgensens Bogtrykkeri, Kolding, 1975, p. 255. Peder Udsen is described as a councillor, merchant, and church verger, 1659. He is depicted with his wife. A stone slab in the floor of Kolding church with a carved likeness of Ude Pedersen carries the inscription: 'Under the Lord, an honest and well respected man, Ude Pedersen and former citizen of Kolding, who passed on 14 November 1641, with his dear wife, Sl. Marine Sørensdatter, deceased on 10 June 1640 AD, in the hope of an honourable resurrection …'
4. Utzon, op. cit., 1907, p. ix. See also, Ra: J.C. Wog and K. Hirsch, *Danske og Norske Officerer 1648–1814*, vol. XI, 4, Tr-U, p. 361. Peder Udsen joined the Fynen Regiment in 1761 at the Kolding garrison. Reconstituted as the Dragon [dragoon] Regiment in 1763, it was dissolved in 1767 while in Schleswig leaving Udsen financially distressed. A year later, in 1768, the Dragoon Regiment moved to a new garrison at Randers, and from there to Gaarden in Kolding.
5. Ibid., preface, p. vi.
6. Ibid., p. vii. The address of the farver works is given as Gaarden No. 1, Søndergade at Kolding.
7. From the 1 February 1890 census. Ra. Hans Jørgen Utzon was a *Tælingskommissærens* for the 1890 census. H.J. Utzon stated his occupation as *opsynmand* (watchman or keeper). Nicolaj Peder Utzon, Aage Utzon's older brother, who was 17 years old at the time of the census, is described as *skovfagdeler* or a forester, possibly someone licensed to collect forest timber and sell it to the townspeople for firewood.
8. From 'Hellebæk' by Carsten Hauch in Jens Kruuse and Kristian Kjær, *Danmark i Digting og Kunst*, Thaning & Appel, Kobenhavn, 1967, p. 169. Translated by Brita Beeston.
9. National census 1 February 1890; Ra: M.15.681-#7.
10. Aage Oberg Utzon is listed in the 1890 census as aged four years which is consistent with him being born 16 November 1885. Hans Jørgen, his father, was 47 years of age, born at Ribe in 1843, and his wife Anette Marie Utzon's age is given as 44 years. Utzon's middle name commemorates the Anette Marie Christine Oberg connection from Sønderborg.
11. See Jan Ebert, 'The Utzon Legend', in *Danske Lystbade, Vol. 2: 1940–1986*, Cervius, Copenhagen, p. 68.
12. In his Gold Medal address to the Royal Institute of British Architects in London,

on 20 June 1978, Jørn Utzon said: 'I was brought up in the Danish colony of England: Denmark. In some ways our young days were very much formed by the English lifestyle. We took our Danish furniture from 1750; we took English quality in our lifestyle. My father, by the way, was trained in England.

'Professor Steen Eiler Rasmussen who wrote a marvellous book about London [*London: The Unique City*, 1934] influenced us with English quality, in the sense that Peter Smithson told us: that if you make something, it must be the best you can make of its time whatever the materials you may have ... This sense of English quality has influenced Denmark very much, and I am grateful for it.'

Allowing for the transparent flattery contained in Utzon's remarks, the significance of which was not lost on his English audience, it is evident that English lifestyle and quality were an important influence on Utzon which he received originally from his father. 'Jørn Utzon: Royal Gold Medallist 1978,' *RIBA Journal*, vol. 85, no. 10, October 1978, p. 427.

13. The forename Valeska is of Polish origin and provides a clue to her non-Danish roots. The name may derive from the 18-year-old Countess Marie Walewska who prevented a war between Poland and France at the beginning of the nineteenth century by agreeing to become Napoleon's mistress. Evangeline Bruce, *Napoleon & Josephine, An Improbable Marriage*, Weidenfeld & Nicolson, London, 1995, pp. 403–6.

14. See R. Hornby, *Danske Personnavne*, Gads Faglekskon, København, 1978, p. 114. Hornby states that Jørn is the new Danish form of Jørgen. Oberg is not listed. Jørgen is the Danish form of George from Georgius, after the Asiatic martyr St George the dragon slayer.

15. 'The Utzon Legend', op. cit. p. 68. *Kragejolle* means a crow-dinghy in Danish, which suggests it had a sharp pointed bow like a crow's beak. See also Jan Ebert, *Danske Lystbade*, vol. 1, 1866–1940, p. 164. Ebert states that George Berg created the first *kragejolle* or crow dinghy in 1914, and went on to design a clinker boat, or *kuling*, with a small 30 m² sail. Utzon and Berg later worked on a large 40 and 65 kvm boat together for which Berg claimed the credit of designing.

16. See Thomas C. Gillmer, *A History of Working Watercraft of the Western World*, 2nd ed., International Marine, Camden, Maine, 1994, pp. 51–63.

17. Ebert, op. cit., p. 68.

18. See Hans Steffensen, 'Aage Utzon', *Sejl og Motor* (Sail and Motor), Copenhagen, January 1971, p. 26. Molbach built the *Shamrock* and for many years he sailed it with considerable success between Ålborg and Århus.

19. Half-models have been around for several centuries – ever since common sense suggested that, as the hulls of most craft are symmetrical about the longitudinal centre line, it was unnecessary to model the complete vessel. Before any technical form of design was evolved, the hull shapes of many traditional boats evolved from a half-model alone, carved by a craftsman with an experienced eye. Peter Ward, 'Half Truths', *Classic Boat and The Boatman*, no. 103, January 1997, p. 66–71.

20. See Aage Utzon obituary by Hans Steffensen, op. cit., p. 26. Many hundreds of copies of Aage Utzon's Ålborg dinghy were built throughout Denmark and Sweden as a result of his sending out sets of plans from the 1940s on.

21. This was particularly the case with the Sydney Opera House and caused considerable problems with consultants when Utzon discontinued with a solution after he found a better approach. In a letter to Davis Hughes on 12 July 1965, p. 4, Utzon reiterated his commitment to perfection: 'It was mutually agreed with the Client, every time a better solution was evolved on

one point or another, it was necessary to incorporate the better solution. I have not compromised with either my previous client or the consultants in my search for perfection. This is what separates this building from any other building – that it is being perfected at the same time as it is being built.' AONSW.

22. See *Klostermarksskolen Yearbook* (Ålborg): 1 June 1925, p. 11; 1 June 1926, p. 14; 1 June 1927, p. 17.
23. Tobias Faber, *Jørn Utzon: Houses in Fredensborg*, Ernst & Sohn, Berlin, 1991, p. 6.
24. In a 1995 interview, Utzon remarked that he was both dyslexic and lacked the mathematical cognition necessary to be a good engineer. Henrik Sten Møller, 'Jørn Utzon in conversation', *LA*, no. 14, 1995, p. 115. It is unclear from these remarks how severe the reading impairment was.
25. Report Card, Immatr. No. 5242. Jørn Utzon was enrolled at Ålborg Katedralskole on 1 August 1929 and completed his studies on 31 July 1937 in eight years. His poorest average mark was 5.98 for 1935, and his best, 6.65, was achieved in 1933 when he repeated his fourth year. A handwritten note on the card states, 'ingenior [engineer] i Frankrig + april 1964', and presumably refers to the death of Leif Utzon in France.
26. See Faber, 1991, op. cit., p. 6.
27. In 1931, the manifesto of the Stockholm Exhibition was published in *acceptera (accept) – Gunnar Asplund, Wolter Gahn, Sven Markelius, Gregor Paulsson, Eskil Sundal, Uno Ahren*, Bokforlag Saktiebolaget Tiden, Stockholm, 1931, with illustrations of the exhibits and a text setting out the arguments for a distinctly Swedish, progressive functionalism. The aim of the social democrats was to create a culture for the nation in which there would be an acceptance and affirmation of the mass-produced article. Thirty-four years later, Jørn Utzon took up this theme in his search for a geometrical basis for mass-producing the elements of the Opera House roofs and interior Halls.
28. Henrik Sten Møller, 'Jørn Utzon on Architecture', *LA*, no. 8, 1989, p. 172.
29. The Scandinavian appreciation of natural beauty stripped of calculated artifice had a considerable impact internationally through Greta Garbo's American movies around 1931–2, when many Hollywood starlets adopted the new Nordic ideal of feminine beauty in imitation of Garbo. This was based on a simple naturalness. A natural acting style was typical not only of Garbo as an artist but had its roots in a broader Scandinavian ideal.
30. Møller, op. cit., pp. 172–3. Over half a century later, Utzon recalled, 'Kylberg constantly deals with the god in nature, the tree, the sea, heaven and glowing light.' The importance of nature as a theme is especially Scandinavian and to a considerable extent, in his architecture, Jørn Utzon manifests a similar fascination with nature that is typical of the Scandinavian approach to design. Barry Paris, *Greta Garbo: A Biography*, Sidgwick & Jackson, London, 1995, p. 43.
31. Møller, op. cit., no. 8, p. 173. Utzon became deeply interested in painting while Kylberg lived next door to Utzon's grandmother.
32. Conversation with Kai Christensen, 21 November 1995 at Vester Voldgade 100, Copenhagen.
33. Møller, op. cit., no. 8, p. 173.

2: Snow Sleeping

1. *Aalborg Vaerft Gennem 75 Ar* (Aalborg Country through 75 Years), ALHM, p. 15.
2. His sculptures are illustrated in *Billedhuggeren: Einar Utzon-Frank, I Tekst og Billeder*, Kobenhavn, N.C. Roms Forlag, 1945.
3. See Tobias Faber, op. cit., 1991, p. 6.
4. Poul Schouboe interview, 25 October 1995, at Hørring. September was the training period for all candidates. According to Schouboe, a hundred candidates presented themselves in 1937 and only 25 were accepted. Schouboe was second last, and Jørn Utzon was the last.
5. Aage Utzon's address in 1938 was 3 F, Orehoi, Nr. Sdr. Strandvej 42, Helsingør. In 1940 he is listed in *Rigstelefon Katalog*, vol. 1, *Navneregister: A Sjælland 1940*, column 3114, no. 734, Aage Utzon Ingenior at Troldhøj Stubbedamsvej, HELSINGØR, so he may have moved.
6. Klint's furniture is described in Rigmor Andersen, *Kaare Klint Mobler*, with Introduction by Gunnar Biilman Petersen and Bent Salicath, Kunstakademiet, 1979.
7. See Gunnar Biilman Petersen, *Traditionen, Naturen og Kunstneren*, Copenhagen, 1958.
8. My informant was Kai Christensen, interview 21 November 1995 at his flat at Vester Voldgade 100, Copenhagen. Christensen qualified as a carpenter after high school and enrolled at the Academy in 1939, completing his studies in 1943, a year after Utzon. Like many other students he worked as a carpenter for three summers, although other students worked two summers. He describes how: 'You should imagine how it is, if it is not right, you pull it down.' In 1953, while he was the Director of the Danish Building Centre in London, he met Ove Arup.
9. The date on Utzon's plans for the shed on Fra M. Olsen's property is 26 July 1939. HKTf, Espergærde.
10. Jens Hogaard (8260 Viby J) to author, 20 March 1996. Hogaard noted that he is the only one from the Århus group of 1942 still alive.
11. Mogens Fenger is listed in *Kraks Blaa Bog 1955*, Kraks Legat, Copenhagen, p. 401. Born in 1889, he qualified as a doctor of medicine in 1919, and died in 1955. Overkirurg Dr med M. Fenger's surgery address in 1940 was at Bolig Dronningensv. 12, KØBENHAVN.
12. See Hakon Ahlberg, *Gunnar Asplund Arkitekt 1885–1940*, Stockholm, AB Tidskriften Byggmastaren, 1943.
13. In an interview with Gavin Souter, 'Joern Utzon Discusses The Opera House,' *SMH*, 1 July 1964, p. 2.
14. HA. *Design 218*. ABC TV, Sydney, 4 April 1962. Interview JU and JZ.
15. TF kept Utzon's books. They include the following titles: J. Prip-Møller, *Chinese Buddhist Monasteries. Their Plan and its Exterior as a Setting for Buddhist Monastic Life*, G.E.C. Gads Forlag, Copenhagen, Oxford University Press, London, 1937; Karl Blossfeldt, *Wunder in der Natur*, Pantheon-Verlag für Kunstwissenschaft, 1942; Robert Christensen, *Kineseren i sit rige*, Det Danske Forlag, Kobenhavn, 1947 (when JU and TF were working together on the Crystal Palace competition); Lin Yutang, *Mit Lang og Mit Folk*, Gyldendalske Boghandel, Nordisk Forlag, 1938; Hans Ludwig Oeser, *Wunder der Grossen und Kleinen Welt, Ein Bild Werk von den Formen und Kraften der Natur*, Deutsche Buch-Gemeinschaft, Berlin, 1937 (gift 1944 one of the best early micro-photographic visual explorations of structure in nature); *Galeria della*

Mostra di Architectura Rural, Alla VI Triennale di Milan. Faber and Utzon read about Chinese philosophy and felt that Chinese architecture was more interesting than Japanese which they viewed as more degenerate. Utzon was not interested in Chinese architecture before he came to Stockholm. Before that, he was chiefly interested in original architecture and the forms of nature.

16. A plan was drawn up in 1965, and updated between 1975 and 1978, which established a financial framework to conserve selected buildings in Gamla Stan. See 'Stockholm: The Origins of the City: Gamla Stan', in *Abitare Annual 7*, Editrice Abitare Segesta, Milan, 1992, pp. 56–63.

3: Drawing Dreams

1. See Eero Saarinen on Utzon's Sydney Opera House Competition drawing submission in HA, *Opera House Competition – Discussion*, ABC Centre, Ultimo, Sydney, 29 January 1957. Saarinen commented to Ashworth that, 'When we found out that it [Utzon's submission] was a Scandinavian that explained why it is so [much] sketchier.'
2. See *Arkitekten* (Copenhagen) M, 1945, pp. 26–31. JU and Henning Helger each received a *mindre Guldmedaille* in 1945.
3. Curriculum outline attached to a letter, JU to HA, 4 July 1957. ANL: Ashworth Papers MSS 4500; box 1, f. 9, Correspondence – Joern Utzon to 1960.
4. The name Denmark, literally 'Field of the Danes', sums up the flat, small-scale, confined and essentially undramatic quality of Danish landscape with the sea never very far away.
5. Joachim Hansson (Alvar Aalto Foundation, Helsinki) letter to the author, 6 October 1995.
6. Ibid.
7. Résumé dated 27 July 1964, 2 pp. Held by Owen Haviland. In it, Utzon states that he studied Town Planning as a specialised field under Professor Steen Eiler Rasmussen for two years at the Royal Academy, Copenhagen.
8. 'Konkurrenceforslag til Crystal Palace i London: by architects Tobias Faber, Mogens Irming and Jørn Utzon', *Arkitekten*, (Copenhagen) U, nos. 8/9, 1946, pp. 70–3. The prize in the Crystal Palace competition is mentioned in a letter, JU to HA, 4 July 1957.
9. 'A New Crystal Palace', *The Times* London, no. 50,443, Saturday, 4 May 1946, p. 4.
10. See 'Crystal Palace Competition: First Three Premiated Designs', *AJ*, 16 May 1946, pp. 375–82.
11. *Architects' Year Book: 2*, London, 1947, p. 166.
12. 'Crystal Palace Competition', introduced by Le Corbusier, ibid., p. 158.
13. 'Maxwell Fry's Report on the Crystal Palace Competition', *AJ*, 23 May 1946, p. 396.
14. See *Arkitekten* (Copenhagen) U, 1946, p. 258.
15. Ibid., p. 232.
16. This is well illustrated and accompanied by a descriptive text in 'A New Personality: Jørn Utzon', *Z*, no. 5, 1959, pp. 70–1.
17. See Christian Norberg-Schulz, *Arne Korsmo*, Universitetsforlaget, Oslo, 1986, p. 66.
18. The photographs were reproduced in an article by Arne Korsmo, 'Til Unge

Arkiteksinn' (To young architects), *Modern Norske Arkitektur*, A 5, nos. 1–2, Regigeres af Arkitektstuderende i de Nordiske Land, Oslo, 1956, pp. 40–54. He also published several of the projects he had done with Utzon: Schoyen-Opsahl and Vestre Vika, Oslo; they are also illustrated in *Byggekunst*, no. 2, 1954.
19. The story was retold by Jørn Utzon in his introduction, 'About Arne Korsmo', in Christian Norberg-Schulz, op. cit., p. 8.
20. *Prize Designs for Modern Furniture*, The Museum of Modern Art, New York, 1950, documented entries in the international competition for low-cost furniture designs held in 1946. The catalogue was published afterwards and has an illustration of the chair designed by Arne Korsmo, Oslo, Norway, and JU, Copenhagen, Denmark.
21. TF and JU, 'Tendenser i Nutidens Arkitektur', *Arkitekten*, vol. 49, nos. 7+8+9 (July, August, September), 1947, pp. 63–9.
22. See Albert Frey, *In Search of a Living Architecture*, New York, 1939.
23. Figures 1 to 7 were taken from the Albert Frey book from pp. 68, 72, 73, 26, 27, 20 and 25 respectively. Illustrations were taken from other works including Hans Ludwig Oeser, *Wunder der Grossen und Kleinen Welt*, Deutsche Buche-Gemeinschaft, Berlin, 1937.
24. *Arkitekten* (Copenhagen) U, 1948, pp. 86–7.
25. Denmark is a small country, therefore it does not pay either to hold grudges, or to litigate. Knud Lautrup-Larsen (1919–90) later worked for JU in his Hellebæk office in 1959–60. This is typical of Utzon who rarely, if ever, behaved vindictively.

4: Architecture Without Signatures

1. See Christian Norberg-Schulz, *Arne Korsmo*, Universitetsforlaget, Oslo, 1986, p. 68.
2. *Opera House Competition, Panel Discussion of the Winning Design*, H. Ingham Ashworth interviewing Leslie Martin and Eero Saarinen. ABC Radio, Ultimo, Sydney, 29 January 1957. Acc. no. 635.
3. Hans Munk Hansen interview, Copenhagen, 27 September 1995. In a later interview with Henrik Sten Moller, *LA*, no. 14, May 1996, pp. 100, 104, JU gives a very different version of the meeting.
4. Christian Norberg-Schulz, 1986, op. cit., p. 68.
5. F.L. Wright, 'The Destruction of the Box', in E. Kaufmann & B. Raeburn (eds), *Frank Lloyd Wright: Writings and Buildings*, Meridian, Cleveland, 1960, pp. 284–9.
6. See Gavin Souter interview, 'Utzon and Andersson: "Bennelong Pointers" at work', *SMH*, no. 37,324, 3 August 1957, p. 2.
7. JU letter to Mr George Nelson, Zeeland, Michigan, 11 January 1960. Utzon wrote, 'Once I have talked with my friend Charles Eames of the possibility of designing furniture for Herman Miller: he asked me to contact you because you were the main critic in the firm.' ML. MSS. 2362/10, item 26.
8. Arthur Drexler, *Charles Eames: Furniture From the Design Collection, The Museum of Modern Art*, Catalogue, Museum of Modern Art, New York, 1973. In particular the Leg Splint of moulded plywood from 1942, p. 13, fig. 16; and p. 16 ff.
9. In his writings, Wright emphasised the horizontal which to his mind tended to

suggest harmony with nature, rather than opposition to nature. Peter Blake, *Frank Lloyd Wright*, Penguin Books, Harmondsworth, UK, 1963, pp. 32–3, also E. Kaufmann & B. Raeburn (eds), *Frank Lloyd Wright: Writings and Buildings*, Meridian, Cleveland, 1960.

10. See Henry Stierlin, *Ancient Mexico*, Living Architecture, Macdonald, London, 1968, pp. 132–3.
11. Henri Stierlin noted: 'Their artificial acropolises do not raise up the buildings so as to cut them off from the world. They form spring-boards whereby the eye passes unconsciously from the natural landscape to the built-up surfaces.' Henry Stierlin, *Mayan*, Benedikt Taschen, Lausanne, 1963, p. 177.
12. Henri Stierlin, 1968, op. cit., p. 133. The row of buildings on the west side of the esplanade are slightly offset from the general north–south line of the complex but the reason for this deviation, which does not exceed 6 degrees, has not been determined. At Teotihuacan, the 17-degree deviation from the north–south axis is related to the sunset on a particular date.
13. See Jørn Utzon, 'Platforms and Plateaus: Ideas of a Danish Architect', *Z*, no. 10, 1962, p. 115.
14. See ibid, p. 114. On p. 112 there is a photograph of Utzon at the car wheel in Mexico attired in a sports coat which appears incongruous for such a rough journey.

5: The Beech Forest

1. Peter Høeg, *The History of Danish Dreams*, trans. Barbara Haveland, Harvill, London, 1995, p. 125.
2. Erik Christian Sørensen's house at Smutvej, Ordup, Copenhagen was completed in 1955, followed three years later by Halldor Gunnløgsson's house on Strandvejen, Rungsted, in 1958. All three houses had open plans. T. Faber, *Danish Architecture*, trans. Frederic R. Stevenson, Det Danske Selskab, Copenhagen, 1978, pp. 210–13.
3. An application to develop the land on parcel no. 2, Hellebækgaard, was submitted to the Tikob kommune Bygningskommissioner on 4 February 1951 (ref. 5087-50), by JU who gave his address as Hornbæk. The trapezoidal-shaped site was approximately 110 m along the long south boundary next to the stream by 60 m deep.
4. The Helsingør Land Registry Office records show that Jørn Utzon purchased the first registry land nr. 2 EN of 5850 m^2 in 1952 for Kr 10,000 from Mrs Pullich, and the second registry land nr. 2 ES, of 6754 m^2, adjoining it in 1958, for Kr 15,000, giving him a total of 12,694 m^2. Before Mrs Pullich, the property was owned by F. Buchwaldt. The Hammermolleskoven (Hammermill Wood) was privately owned and only became public, but with no access for cars, a few years back.
5. The first set of drawings for Utzon's house at parcel no. 2, Hellebækgaard, is dated 1 February 1950. Utzon listed his address as Kystvej 51, Hornbæk. This first plan differs from the completed house in a number of important respects. The garage was linked by an underground connection to the main house and was open at the front and back; instead of the closed box which it later became, it consisted of two longitudinal walls, the longest of which was separated from the house proper by a porte-cochere space covered by a deck 3.24 m wide. The internal planning was also different with the two children's bedrooms

pushed much farther forward to within 1.2 m of the south glass wall, and the toilet and bathroom off the entry behind them along the back wall. There was no children's play area and the house was planned on a 120 cm module.

6. On 25 September 1950 Utzon submitted a revised scheme (ref. 5087-50) which was very different to the earlier February drawings. It was considerably smaller and consisted of three units: a long wing having three bedrooms and a toilet in a narrow pavilion with the kitchen and dining area opposite a large living room whose axis opposed it on the east. This common central pavilion was terminated by an equally sized outdoor terrace on the west. A garage and bicycle store was attached on the north side in a wing off the kitchen. The main entry was from the west into the living room. The elevations clearly reveal the influence of Frank Lloyd Wright in the extended horizontal brick walls that were carried on into the landscape and the composition of low stretched overhanging roof planes. All of this was typically Wrightian, as was the cruciform arrangement of the individual units around the chimney core. The final scheme moved away from this overtly Wrightian scheme and became more Miesian in its simplified sculptural arrangement of the principal planes.
7. Barbara Richards, 'Utzon Designs his own Bush Home', *WD*, 25 March 1963, p. 10.
8. JU to HA, 4 July 1957. Included as part of a short biographical résumé attached to the letter. NLA, Ashworth Papers, MSS 4500, box 1, f. 9: *Correspondence – Joern Utzon to 1960*.
9. See Christian Norberg-Schulz, *Nightlands, Nordic Building*, trans. Thomas McQuillan, MIT Press (Gyldendal Norsk Forlag A/S), London, 1996, p. 57. Norberg-Schulz cited as an instance of the Danish '*firlænge*' type, True at the Lyngby Museum, Copenhagen.
10. Tobias Faber, *Jørn Utzon, Houses in Fredensborg*, Ernst & Sohn, Berlin, 1991, p. 7.

6: A Cathedral in the Air

1. Gavin Souter, 'Joern Utzon Discusses the Opera House', *SMH*, 1 July 1964, p. 2.
2. Knud W. Jensen, *My Louisiana Life*, ms, Humlebæk, 1997.
3. From Utzon biography and résumé attached to letter, JU to HA, 4 July 1957. ANL, Ashworth Papers, MSS. 4500, f. 9: *Correspondence, Joern Utzon to 1960*.
4. See 12th Meeting, OHC, Thursday, 26 April 1956. ANL: MSS 4500, box 2, f. 14. The secretary reported that 881 competitors had been registered, 772 had paid their deposits and been supplied with copies of the detailed conditions. 45 countries were represented: UK, 232; Australia, 113; USA, 113; Germany, 78; Switzerland, 46; South Africa, 32; Canada, 25; France, 25; New Zealand, 20; South Holland, 19; Italy, 16.
5. E. Rasmussen interview with JU, 'Utzon talks; Why I built the Opera House this way …' *S-H*, 13 March 1966, p. 67.
6. *Idem*.
7. Ibid., p. 65.
8. Ibid., p. 69.
9. See V.L. Jordan, *Acoustical Design of Concert Halls and Theatres: A Personal Account*, Applied Science Pub., London, 1980, p. 13.

10. 'Utzon Explains His Designs', *SMH*, Wednesday, 30 January 1957, p. 3.
11. Rasmussen interview, *S-H*, op. cit., p. 67.
12. See *International Competition for a National Opera House at Bennelong Point: Assessors' Report*, January 1957, p. 2.
13. The set of 12 drawings submitted by Utzon in the competition were not the originals but prints. They are 72 cm x 101.4 cm and have since been mounted on linen paper. AONSW: SZ-112, National Opera House, Sydney, Australia. Competition Drawings, 1956.
14. Eric Ellis interview, 'Utzon: My Orange Peel Opera House', *GW*, 31 October 1992, p. 14.
15. See Wolf von Echardt, *eric mendelsohn*, George Braziller, New York, 1960, pp. 33–48, figs 1–45. A sketch from 1915 by Mendelsohn called 'hall' seems to anticipate Utzon's SOH concept.
16. Jørn Utzon, 'The Sydney Opera House', *Z*, no. 14, 1965, p. 49.
17. The stage area of the Major Hall was 33 m wide by 32 m deep with an area of approximately 850 m^2. It had two 12 m x 6 m stage lifts in a 18 m diameter revolving stage and a 7.8 m x 13.4 m stage lift at the back. The stage opening was 14 m wide by 9 m high. In the Minor Hall, the area was approximately 250 m^2 with the stage itself, measuring 28 m deep by 20 m maximum wide. There were two stage lifts each 10 m x 5 m in a revolve measuring 14 m diameter. The Minor Hall rear third lift was slightly larger than the revolve lifts at 10.4 m x 6.6 m. The stage opening was only 10 m wide. In both auditoria the orchestra pit was inadequate: the Major Hall pit was a maximum 4.2 m deep by 14 m wide; while the Minor Hall had a pit that was much smaller still.
18. By extraordinary coincidence, Sir Eugene Goossens visited the Vienna State Opera early in 1956 and subsequently described its stage in his *Report of Visit to Vienna State Opera House, Hamburg Opera*, H. Ingham Ashworth Papers, ANL, MSS 4500, box 2, f. 14, which was submitted to the Opera House Committee on 26 April 1956. In his report he glowingly described the stage mechanical appliances: 'Its size alone is staggering. The following gives some idea:- Height approx. 81½ ft (28 m); Breadth 137 ft (48 m); Depth 85½ ft (30 m).' Then he goes on to observe, 'The stage itself can be raised or lowered in eight different sections, by powerful hydraulic-electric machinery. During the progress of the opera a new setting can be built up in an adjoining dock and rolled into position while the previous scene is being dismantled. A visit to the enormous space below-stage with its lift mechanisms impresses by the sense of power and height, because of the stark functionalism of the machinery.'
19. The notes added to the drawings state the Main Hall could accommodate 3500 and the Small Hall 1200 people but these figures were open to doubt because the distance between the seats in the main auditorium was inadequate and varied from a minimum of 73 cm (28.75 in) to a maximum of 82 cm (32.5 in) at the middle. On an area calculation, the corresponding figures (without any allowance for aisles) was 2876 and 1253 persons. With three aisles in the Main Hall and a single aisle in the Minor Hall the audience capacity was reduced to 2200 and 1120 respectively.
20. See Morten Lund, 'Vilhelm Lauritzen's modern concept of space', in *Vilhelm Lauritzen: A Modern Architect*, trans. Martha Gaber Lindhe, Bergiafonden, Aristo, 1994, p. 290.
21. See Morten Lund, op. cit., p. 284.
22. See Drawing no. 10: Section [through the Main Hall]. Scale is not indicated but is 1:200 or approximately 1'0" = $\frac{1}{16}$".
23. This is identical to the jig-saw puzzle box of the Sydney Opera House by Utzon at Christmas 1963 which used a circular abstract design of red on a

white ground. This by itself does not prove anything.
24. See Christian Norberg-Schulz, *Arne Korsmo*, Universitetsforlaget, Oslo, 1986, p. 66.
25. 'Opera House funds talks expected to open this week', *SMH*, 19 June 1957. The little drawing was reproduced on the back of the business card, which Utzon enclosed with the pictures of the Opera House model he sent to Premier Cahill on 11 June.

7: Men of Vision

1. EG III to EG II, 13 July 1947.
2. Lionel Carley, *Delius: A Life in Letters*, Scolar Press, 1988, p. 163.
3. *Sydney Daily Telegraph*, 2 August 1947. Goossens believed there was a minimum size for the different kinds of musical performances: 3500–4000 for orchestral and choral concerts; 1800–2500 for grand opera; but to be effective, the presentation of drama called for much smaller audiences of 1500–1800. The correct approach, Goossens stressed, was an auditorium large enough to seat from 3500–4000 people but he allowed that opera and drama and other uses might require a smaller auditorium which he proposed could be accomplished using a simple mechanism.
4. Dr Langer's recommendation was contained in *The Planning Scheme for the County of Cumberland New South Wales*, Report of the Cumberland County Council to the Hon. J.J. Cahill, MLA, Minister for Local Government, 27 July 1948, p. 207, among the six institutions to be located in the City: '(b) A National Opera House and Theatre for performances of opera, ballet, drama and music.' The report made no mention of Bennelong Point. See also 'Opera House Plan for Sydney', *SMH*, 7 October 1947.
5. *Report of the Proceedings of a Conference Convened by the Premier and Held in the Lecture Room, Public Library, Sydney on 30th Nov., 1954, Concerning the question of the establishment of an Opera House in Sydney,* Government Printer, Sydney, 1954, p. 8.
6. *Circular Quay Replanning*, Report to Chief County Planner by Dr Karl Langer, 21 August 1947.
7. 'Conductor delivers ultimatum – An opera house – or no Goossens.' *Sunday Telegraph*, vol. XI, no. 13, Sunday, 19 February 1950, p. 4.
8. From Carole Rosen, *The Goossens: A Musical Century*, Andre Deutsch, London, 1993, p. 315.
9. Ibid., p. 246.
10. Eugene Goossens, 'How Long Before Our Opera House Dream Comes True?', *S-H*, no. 13, 17 April 1949, p. 2.
11. Goossens referred to this feature of the Malmö Opera House during his conference address, *Report of the Proceedings of a Conference Convened by the Premier ...*, op. cit., p. 8.
12. 'Another Opera House Plan', *SMH*, no. 36,276, Wednesday 31 March 1954, p. 2.
13. The choice of a site became a sort of lottery with people being asked to nominate their favourite sites. The *SMH* investigated a range of alternatives from March 1954, including the site above Wynyard ramp (*SMH*, Monday, 29 March 1954); Bennelong Point (*SMH*, Wednesday, 31 March 1954). Well before this, the *Sunday Sun,* Supplement, 23 November 1947, pp. 8–9,

nominated the Parliament House on Macquarie Street as the site of a National Opera House and Theatre.
14. The full text was published in *Report of the Proceedings of a Conference Convened by the Premier ...*, op. cit., 1954.
15. The first committee was comprised of Mr S. Haviland (chair), Professor Ashworth, Colonel Moses, Sir Eugene Goossens and Mr Hendy (Town Clerk). On 2 July 1957 it was extended to include Dr Nicolai Malko, Sir Bernard Heinze, Mr Hugh Hunt, and others representing the trade unions and business. On 19 August 1957, Mr Heffron, the Minister for Education, recommended Dr Wyndham be on the committee.
16. As CM explained, it was all a simple matter of arithmetic. Instead of holding five concerts in the Town Hall with 2000 per performance, giving a total audience of 10,000 seats; by increasing seat numbers to 3200 the new opera house concert hall would reduce the number of repeat concerts to four while catering for an extra 2800 subscribers, or a total of 12,800. Even the compromised 2000 seats later suggested by JU would have meant 1200 more people would be able to attend the ABC concert series. It was all a matter of numbers from the ABC's viewpoint; for Goossens it meant he would not have to work the SSO so hard.
17. *Report of the Proceedings of a Conference Convened by the Premier ...*, pp. 14-15.
18. *Memorandum on Siting of an Opera House for Sydney*, attachment to Chief Planner's Report to Council on Department of Local Government's letter, 9 December 1954.
19. *Report of the Opera House Committee Appointed by the N.S.W. Chapter of the Royal Australian Institute of Architects*, to Meeting, 4 February 1955 at Sydney University, chaired by HA.
20. *Draft Report Upon the Question of a Site for the Proposed Opera House*, OHC, May 1955.
21. Ibid., to J.J. Cahill, Premier of NSW, May 1955, p. 2.
22. Ava Hubble, *Sir Charles Moses*, Oral History, interview no. 2, 8 July 1986, p. 30. DWLPA.
23. *Report-on-Visit to Vienna State Opera House, Hamburg Opera House*, Sir Eugene Goossens submitted to the 12th meeting, OHC, Thursday, 26 April 1956, p. 3.
24. OHC meeting no. 8, 4 August 1956.
25. 'The maturing modern', *Time* magazine, Pacific ed., vol. 68, no. 1, 2 July 1956, pp. 32–9.
26. Ibid., p. 32. The story seems unlikely because the TWA Terminal had a difficult shape; it is far more plausible that the grapefruit was used to model the hemispherical shell of Kresge Auditorium of the MIT at Cambridge (1953–5).
27. At the 20 December meeting of the OHC, the total number of designs is given as 222, so some may have been rejected later for technical reasons.
28. This story was reported by Don Moser in 'A Far-out Opera Uproar Down Under', *Life* magazine, vol. 62, 6 January 1967, p. 64. John Yoemans, *The other Taj Mahal*, Longmans, London, 1968, p. 34, repeated this story.
29. 'Halls of Music', *Time* magazine, 25 February 1957, p. 30.
30. Ashworth to Robin Boyd, 8 October 1971. ANL. MSS 4500/f. 12. There were 230 or 222, not 270 submissions as Ashworth stated. One wonders how much else Ashworth got wrong.
31. This version was repeated in 1967 by Don Moser, op. cit., under the headline 'Dane's design rescued from the discards'. Moser did not say where he heard the story. In *The other Taj Mahal*, p. 34, John Yoemans dismissed the story as a 'piquant bit of gossip'.
32. 'Judges Choose Design – But It's Hush-hush'. *SMH*, no. 37,156, 19 January

1957, p. 2. The report and selection was handed over on Friday, 18 January at an informal ceremony in the Lands Department Building. The work of judging apparently finalised earlier, on Tuesday 15th, because on Wednesday the assessors were being entertained at a luncheon given by the Institute of Architects for Martin and Saarinen in addition to a civic reception on the same day.

33. From *Saarinen's Itinerary* from 7 January to 10 February 1957 for Eero and Aline Saarinen's 'Around The World Trip'. 2 pp. During their nine-day visit, the pair stayed at the old 1891 Hotel Australia in Martin Place. See also Walter Bunning, 'Key Role for Noted Architect In Opera House Design'. *SMH*, no. 37,147, Wednesday 9 January 1957, p. 2.
34. 'Dane's Controversial Design Wins Opera House Contest,' *SMH*, no. 37,165, Wednesday, 30 January 1957, pp. 1, 2, 3.
35. *Panel Discussion of the Winning Design, by Joern Utzon, in the Opera House Design Competition*, Sydney, 29 January 1957. ABC Radio, Ultimo Centre. RADA Acc. no. 635.

8: The Tough Political Questions

1. Eric Ellis, 'Utzon, my orange peel Opera House', *GW*, 31 October 1992, p. 15.
2. 'Phone talk to winner', *SMH*, no. 37,165, Wednesday, 30 January 1957, p. 1.
3. 'Poetry or Pastry? Argument on Opera House Plans', *SMH*, no. 37,165, Wednesday, 30 January 1957, p. 3.
4. A selection of opinions for and against after the competition announcement was presented in 'What Readers Think of the Design for Sydney Opera House', *SMH*, no. 37,167, Friday, 1 February 1957, p. 2, and 'Opera House Design Continues to be a Lively Topic', *SMH*, no. 37,168, Saturday, 2 February 1957, p. 2.
5. Gavin Souter, 'Utzon and Andersson: "Bennelong Pointers" at Work', *SMH*, no. 37,324, 3 August 1957, p. 2.
6. From *An International Competition for a National Opera House at Bennelong Point, Sydney, New South Wales, Australia: Assessors' Report*, 6 February 1957, p. 3.
7. The relative merits of each scheme are discussed in 'Sydney Opera House', in Haan, H. de & Haagsma, I, *Architects in Competition*, Thames & Hudson, London, 1988, pp. 136–46.
8. *Assessors' Report*, op. cit., p. 4.
9. Ibid.
10. Ibid.
11. Ibid. p. 3. The estimates give an interesting comparison: J. Utzon scheme, £3,667,231; 2nd prize, £5,900,00; and 3rd prize: £4,800,000. Utzon's scheme on this estimate was £1,132,769, or 31% cheaper than the next lowest entry 3rd prize, and 61% cheaper than the 2nd prize scheme. The estimated cost of the winning design was publicly announced as £3,500,000, to the nearest half-million. 25th meeting, OHC, 30 January 1959.
12. LM to HA, 12 February 1957. NLA. H.I. Ashworth papers: MS 4500, f. 6.
13. OA had been employed by Christiani & Nielsen from 1922 to 1934 in its Hamburg office, and later in London. See *Ove Arup 1895–1988*, London, 1988, p. 14, pp. 62–6.
14. OA wrote to JU on 3 February 1957 after reading about the competition in the

London *Times* newspaper. Arup Papers. This was a regular practice with him, in the 1951 Coventry Cathedral competition he assisted Peter Smithson, but when Basil Spence won, Arup quickly switched to Spence.

15. Document, 26 March 1963, OAP to NSW Minister of Public Works, with request to vary arrangement to free OAP from the responsibility for all consulting work except structural and civil engineering matters for which they were directly responsible. This was agreed and thereafter the other consultants were paid by JU.
16. JU to SOHC, 11 February 1957. ANL. H.I. Ashworth papers, MS 4500, f. 9, Correspondence – Joern Utzon to 1960.
17. JU to HIA, 4 March 1957. ANL. Ashworth Papers, MS 4500, f. 9.
18. Ibid.
19. Ibid. JU states 25 architectural magazines from Europe and USA and numerous newspapers had written for photographs of the model.
20. 'Opera House building still in doubt', *Daily Telegraph*, 7 March 1957.
21. 'Cahill now plugs homes – New Opera House view', *Truth*, 28 April 1957.
22. 'Recision – Opera House rebuff – Move in Caucus', *The Sun*, 8 May 1957; 'Cahill wins Opera House Vote', *SMH*, 9 May 1957.
23. 'Mammoth Lotteries planned to help build Opera House', *SMH*, 2 April 1957; 'Lottery for opera house', *Daily Mirror*, 2 May 1957.
24. 'State A.L.P. gives green light to Opera House', *SMH*, 17 June 1957.
25. 'Opera House funds talks expected to open this week', *SMH*, 19 June 1957.
26. JU to HA, 17 April 1957. NLA. Ashworth Papers, MS 4500, f. 9. JU described the model as rather big, making it impossible to include more of the surroundings. The showcase is given as 120 x 150 cm, glass thickness 6–7 mm.
27. Gavin Souter, 'Utzon and Andersson: "Bennelong Pointers" at work', *SMH*, no. 37,324, 3 August 1957, p. 2.
28. Ibid.
29. Hans Munk Hansen interview, Copenhagen, 27 September 1995.
30. Ibid.
31. '£235,500 Raised for Opera House in one hour after launching of appeal', *SMH*, no. 37,328, Friday, 8 August 1957, p. 1.
32. The main speeches and the music were recorded on a single gramophone disc, *Official Opening of Sydney Opera House Appeal*, 7 August 1957. Cahill papers, ML MSS: GR. 122.
33. *20th Meeting OHC*, Friday 16 August 1957. It decided such important matters as the size and usage of the halls, as well as hearing JU's request on Arton. For its answer in draft see OHC to JU, August 1957. H.I. Ashworth Papers, ANL MS 4500, box 2, f. 14.
34. *Statement of 26th March, 1963, by Messers Ove Arup and Partners*, p. 2.
35. The fee proposal is set out in OHEC to JU, 8 November 1957. H.I. Ashworth Papers, ANL MS 4500, box 2, f. 9: Correspondence – Joern Utzon to 1960. By this arrangement which followed the standard RAIA contract conditions Utzon would be entitled to be paid 4% of the cost of actual work for which the consulting engineers are engaged, plus 6% of the actual cost of the balance of the total work [where architectural services are directly involved], with a stipulation that the total fees payable should not be less than 5% of the actual cost of the whole work. This protected Utzon by setting down a minimum fee of 5%. In nearly every case, Utzon found it expedient to claim the 5% minimum fee calculated on the cost of the whole work, rather than a combination of the two rates for coordinating the engineering consultants and for architectural services.
36. The trip and Utzon's account provide a valuable insight into the design issues

	which preoccupied his attention at the time. He is concerned about scale, the detailing of the glass walls which he had left out of the Opera House model, and the problems of not destroying the clean structural expression of the shells, in particular, the shell effect and lightness by the glass walls and roofing. JU to HA, 3 October 1957. H.I. Ashworth Papers. ANL MS 4500, box 1, f. 9. JU visited the office of Kunio Maekawa while he was in Tokyo and this relationship was an important one. Maekawa worked for Le Corbusier in Paris.
37.	Henrik Sten Møller, interview with JU, *LA*, no. 14, May 1966, p. 106.
38.	Eero Saarinen, monthly desk calendar, Yale University Library. Peter C. Papdemetriou to author 8 September 1997.
39.	JU to HA, 19 November 1957. H.I. Ashworth Papers. ANL MS 4500, box 1, f. 9.
40.	G.E. Kidder Smith, *The New Architecture of Europe*, Penguin, Harmondsworth, 1961, p. 62.
41.	See OA, 'Philosophy and the Art of Building', in *Ove Arup 1895–1988*, op. cit., p. 13.
42.	HA to Mr P. Thomson, sec. OHC, 10 October 1957. H.I. Ashworth Papers. ANL MS 4500, box 2, f. 14. On the matter of acoustics, Ashworth suggested the Committee take a second opinion of the acoustics report.
43.	OHC: *Summary of developments since Nov. 19, 1957*. H.I. Ashworth papers. ANL MS 4500, box 2, f. 14. In its summary, the Secretary of the SOHEC refers to a letter from Mr Utzon, on 24 January 1958, in which he stated that he was financially embarrassed owing to the delay in meeting his claims for fees. He stated that he employed ten architects on drawing work alone, as well as model workers, engineers, theatre technicians and so on, on top of this. This resulted in action to authorise the A-G to pay Utzon £10,000 up to 1 February 1958. In fact the prize money was not received till 2 January 1958, and the further amount of £10,000, for work on behalf of the OHC, was paid on 25 February 1958.
44.	Secretary OHC to JU, August 1957. This letter also sets out the proposed terms of appointment and fees payable to the architect.
45.	22nd Meeting OHC, Friday, 11 November 1958. This amount was for the supply of copies of drawings, etc. at the order of JU. A payment of £4812 was authorised. The book was 580 x 390 mm, and 54 pages with a deep red cover and back board. AONSW: SZ 107. The OAP drawings 1112/sk 2,7 are dated 20 & 22 February 1958. The more recent drawings of the stage machinery by M.A.N. are dated 5 March 1958.
46.	The maximum width of the Main Hall seating was 120 ft; in length it was 180 ft for concerts and 115 ft for opera based on a seat 22 in wide by 36 in row to row. The same seat size was maintained until 1963.
47.	These figures were supplied by HA on 18 March 1958. A seat count by the author found the number of seats to be less: Concerts, 2617 (-383); Grand Opera, 1712 (+12); Theatre, 1099 (101 under the required 1200). The problem which emerged at a very early stage was the undersizing of the Main Hall. Yuzo Mikami in his May 1967 draft report for Ove Arup gives the seating capacity for concert as 2702 and 1826 for opera, with an approximate volume of the hall 1,100,000 ft^3 for concerts and 650,000 ft^3 for opera. The maximum length of the seating area for concerts is 180 ft, and 115 ft for opera. According to Mikami, this gave a reverberation time of 1.8–2.0 seconds for concerts and 1.6–1.8 seconds for opera. Compared to the original scheme, the volume and size for opera together with the overall dimensions of seating were considerably reduced and this would have led to an improvement in both the acoustics and visibility for opera.

48. See Yuzo Mikami, *Draft Report on Major Hall Auditorium Design, Sydney Opera House*, London, May 1967, p. III.
49. VJ estimated the volume of the Major Hall during concerts at 1,000,000 ft^3, corresponding to 390 ft^3 per seat; and 650,000 ft^3 for grand opera, or 360 ft^3 per seat. The Minor Hall, with a volume of 280,000 ft^3, was less satisfactory with only 265 ft^3 per seat, this being considerably lower than for the Major Hall. VJ commented that this was due to the lower ceiling height which he considered appropriate for a theatre where the stress is laid more upon definition than upon reverberation.
50. OA to HA, 12 December 1960. H.I. Ashworth Papers. ANL MS 4500, box 1, f. 2.
51. J. Prip-Møller was the author of *Chinese Buddhist Monasteries*, G.E.C. Gods Forlag and Oxford University Press, London, 1937, and established his Institute in Hong Kong in 1930–39.
52. JU to HA, 12 June 1958. H.I. Ashworth papers. ANL MS 4500, box 1, f. 9. JU enclosed a reprint of a 900-year-old Chinese building code for Ashworth that detailed a 'code' or system of standardisation for temples and castles, which later influenced his own ideas on standardisation and the application of colour to building elements before their assembly on the site.
53. JU to HA, 19 November 1957. H.I. Ashworth Papers. ANL MS 4500, box 1, f.9.
54. R.S. Jenkins (Ove Arup & Partners) to R.J. Thompson, sec., OHC, 25 November 1959. H.I. Ashworth Papers, ANL MS 4500, box 2, f. 15.
55. *Extract from report by Mr Fred Turner of Robertson and Marks, Architects, upon recent visit to Denmark and interview with Mr Utzon*. 23rd meeting OHC, Thursday, 28 August 1958. H.I. Ashworth Papers. ANL MS 4500, box 2, f. 14.
56. See discussion *M & DP*, 20 July 1964, arising from criticism by Roger Covell in the *S-H*, 26 June 1964. The blame rested squarely with the architect's advisers. The meeting concurred that in general terms, 'it seems symptomatic of the compromises that prevented comprehensive and leisurely planning of the building's use before construction started'. The Chair stated (p. 2 of report in 1964) that 'Mr Utzon complied with these requirements for the Minor Hall and has built an orchestra pit which will accommodate 34–37 players.' This was supported by an earlier *Report M & DP*, 27 July 1959.
57. The low tender led to many problems with Civil & Civic who endeavoured to recover their losses. The quantity surveyors estimate for Stage I was A£1,511,000, which was A£113,071 higher than Civil & Civic's tender figure, and A£211,778 below the next tender amount from John Holland.
58. JU to HA, 6 June 1958. H.I. Ashworth Papers. ANL MS 4500, box 1, f. 9.
59. Mikami designed the inaugural plaque over the week from 23–28 January and it was fabricated by 14 February in time for Utzon's departure on 18 February.
60. Stanley Haviland wrote to Mr C.B. Cutler the following day, 3 March 1959, thanking him: 'Only a short note to say a very genuine thank you for your substantial contribution to what I believe had been regarded as a very successful function.' To a degree, Cutler was speaking for himself, but there was not a lot of opposition to the Opera House within the Country Party, and what opposition there was came from a few individuals.
61. DH's winning margin on 21 March 1959 General Election was 2786, an increase of 1991 over the previous 3 March 1956 result, but was considerably less than the 1968 margin of 6171.
62. CM, Interview no. 2, by Ava Hubble, 8 July 1986, p. 78. DWLPA.

9: Following *Sputnik*'s Trajectory

1. Jørgen Saxild, an outstanding figure in the world of trade and industry who had been active as an engineer in the Middle East for many years, was on the committee of Danske Samvirke in 1962, when JU's Fredensborg Terraces ran into difficulties. He helped save the project by personally buying a few of the houses and then placing them at the disposal of members of Danske Samvirke. See T. Faber, *Jørn Utzon: Houses in Fredensborg*, Ernst & Sohn, Berlin, 1991, p. 9.
2. JU to G.L. Moline (Stephenson & Turner), 24 June 1960. ML MS 2362/10, item 25: 'Kampsax A/S [a Danish firm] is making a small bank in Teheran [Iran] with me at the time being.'
3. The letter from Bent Alstrup at Vallerod, to the Elsinore kommune office of teknisk kontor is dated 28 April 1958, and the date on the drawings is earlier, 25 April. Evidently Alstrup handled the work with dispatch.
4. The second east–west pavilion at the rear of JU's 1952 house consisted of a courtyard at the west end next to the old boiler room with office, toilet, a main drawing office 4.72 m deep x 10.08 m long, three smaller drawing rooms 3 m x 3 m, drawing archive in the hallway, plus two bedrooms, bathroom and toilet forming a guest area at the east end. This drawing office was connected by a narrow glazed gallery linking it to the dining area of the 1952 house. The entire single-storey north pavilion is 30.74 m long by 5.34 m deep.
5. The Confidential Cabinet Minute by the Premier is dated 7 September 1959, and was prefaced by notes for the proposed *Sydney Opera House Bill, 1960*, by R.J. Heffron.
6. The *Sydney Opera House Act*, No. 29 was assented to on 19 April 1960. Various amendments to the original act were passed to fix the maximum amount to be expended on the Sydney Opera House: Act No. 6, 1963; Act No. 5, 1965; Act No. 45, 1966; and *Sydney Opera House (Amendment) Bill, 1967*, *Sydney Opera House Act 1960–1967*.
   At the second reading debate on 5 and 6 April 1960, although the Opposition generally supported the bill, it criticised the Government's procedure. The Assembly passed the bill without amendment on 6 April, and it was passed on to the Legislative Council after a constructive debate during which the Government was urged to set up the Management Trust.
7. J.J. Cahill, Confidential Cabinet Minute, 7 September 1959, p. 1.
8. These matters were discussed by the OHC, at its 37th meeting on 17 January 1961, p. 2. Little came of this discussion and the powers provided under the Act to the Minister lay dormant until DH chose to exercise them to the full in 1966.
9. At its 30th meeting, 28 April 1960, the OHC was told that under the new arrangements the Minister for Public Works was the 'constructing authority' and the committee would be subject to his over-riding authority in the area of building, but it considered that in all other matters the committee was unaffected and would continue to have the same scope as it presently did.
10. 25th meeting, SOH Technical Panel, 22 January 1960.
11. JU to George Nelson, 20 March 1960. ML MSS 2362/10, item 25. JU thanked Nelson for a delightful evening.
12. JU to Mr G. Nelson (c/o Herman Miller Furniture, Zeeland, Michigan) 11 January 1960, Utzon wrote: 'First now I have designed some pieces of furniture which I think are really interesting for your firm to produce. They are completely different from anything you make and they do not [look] like any

other form of furniture. They are designed for the Sydney Opera House and will be produced in 2 years time for that house but I would like to have them out in production as standard furniture before that time. There are some parts in them, which can be patented, and I have already taken steps to do that. They are not expensive, I think very charming.' JU was being truthful in mentioning the patent; on 25 March 1960 he applied for Dansk Patent No. 93100 Mobel: *navnlig stol eller bord, med sarg or ben*. It was issued on 26 March 1962, and published 18 June, that same year. This is the same patent to which he refers in his letter to Nelson and related to his plans for the Opera House furniture.

13. Vodder arrived in JU's office on 1 February 1960.
14. JU's secretary mentions the office closing down from 27 June till 16 July, 1960, and listed his summer address as Uttra Burholmen, Strömstad, BOHUSLAN, Sweden. Ashworth papers, ANL MS 4500, f. 9.
15. The tender documents for stage machinery, light apparatus, electro acoustics, etc., were issued on May 1960. The increase was £1.2 million and this caused consternation as the budget had only just been established with the Sydney Opera House Act on 22 March 1960 by Parliament, which limited expenditure to A£4.8 million (A$9.6 million). *Annual Reports of the Sydney Opera House Executive Committee*. AONSW, PWD SOH 4-8069.
16. Poul Schouboe was six months younger than Utzon; he started his studies at the Royal Academy of Fine Arts at the same time as JU in October 1937 and graduated in 1943. He worked as a draughtsman in Mogens Irming's office, on competitions. In 1958–9 he called on JU for a job, however, it was not until he moved to Helsingør in 1960 that he joined the Hellebæk office and stayed for 3 years.
17. Meeting at OAP's office, London, 25 August 1960. Utzon was present with Poul Schouboe from his office. Ove Arup, Ronald Jenkins, R.N. Kelman, and H. Møllmann (listed as part time) were in attendance.
18. The full details of this trip are contained in: *Report to the Sydney Opera House Executive Committee from Professor H. Ingham Ashworth further to his tour overseas from August 17th, 1960, to September 21st, 1960*. NLA: H.I. Ashworth papers, MS 4500, box 7, f. 60.
19. In 1960, the number of staff employed by JU at his Fordamsvej 1, Hellebæk office comprised seven architects plus a secretary and model makers: Osmond Jarvis (expected to leave on 12 December 1960), Jacob Kielland-Brandt, Knud Lautrup-Larsen, Yuzo Mikami, Aage Hartvig Petersen, Poul Schouboe (on site) and Olaf Skipper Nielsen. ML MSS 2362/5 item 10, #769. The address of the OAP's office was 13 Fitzroy Street London W1, the same location as today. Utzon gives the Arups staff working on the SOH project as R.S. Jenkins, Hugo Møllmann, and R.N. Kelman with Ian MacKenzie and A. Levy on site.
20. Utzon related that the 'model shop was at that time rather famous and we had, for instance, members of the International Union of Architects coming from all over the world to a meeting in Copenhagen, and many other visitors. It was a unique but necessary way of finding the shapes and constructions of the various parts of the SOH. The model shop was very well equipped and we had a close connection with the pattern maker's shop in Helsingør [Elsinore] shipyards, and we could very quickly get any model of any shape made to illustrate new ideas.' *Report on Acoustical Research on Major and Minor Hall, Sydney Opera House*, June 1965, forwarded 21 June 1965. ML MSS 2362/21: Reports to the Minister for Public Works, item 37, p. 1.
21. The Elvira competition scheme is illustrated in *Z*, no. 10, figures 20–2. JU made the sea the dominating motif of the town plan to ensure that each

building had undestroyed contact with the sea, no matter how far back it was from the beach. Utzon noted that there were certain points in the terrain which stood out as distinctive, such as where the mountains met the plain. He selected this point for the commercial centre and the hotels and restaurants. The other important distinctive point he selected was high up in the mountains where there were some clearly defined natural plateaus which spread out like the fingers of a hand in a very dramatic way. He chose this as the setting for his humanistic centre. Elvira, perhaps inspired by its beautiful name, is one of JU's most poetic and natural designs. The town is expressed as a series of earth-sculptured platforms and excavated amphitheatre with roofs like flying teardrops that leap across the surface like wildly energetic dancers.

The Elineberg Shopping Centre is illustrated in *Z*, no.10, pp. 134–6 and in figures 36–40. It continues the platform and flying roof theme in a more concentrated way. In this scheme the shopping activity, in Utzon's words, takes place in the central crater in a low volcano-like section with the platform protected by a series of V-profile transverse beams set at different heights and different lengths stacked up on one another. It is reminiscent of the Sydney Opera House concourse with its folded slabs, but here they have been separated and lifted up so they stand free of each other as individual architectonic units.

22. Utzon wrote of Nielsen: 'Skipper [Nielsen] is not a social type and he dislikes that side of the life, so please do not televise and broadcast him and all these things.' Before this, Nielsen worked for four years in Kenya, East Africa. JU to HA, 2 November 1960. H.I. Ashworth papers. ANL MS 4500, box 1, f. 9.

23. Balslev & Partners were paid A$56,662 for their consulting services to September.

24. R.S. Jenkins to HA, November 24 1960. H.I. Ashworth papers. ANL MS 4500, box 1, f. 2.

25. Between August 1962 and August 1964, the estimate for Stage II jumped from A£2,253,077 (A$4,506,154) to A£4,201,564 (A$8,403,128), an increase of A£1,948,487 (A$3,896,974) or almost double. The cost impact of JU's indecision was considerable but in retrospect was well worth it. The new figures were presented to Minister Ryan in April 1964 who expressed amazement according to Robert Maclurcan, letter to JU, 17 April 1964. ML MS 2362/23, item 59, # 95, 97.

26. R.J. Jenkins (OAP) to JU, 27 January 1961. H.I. Ashworth papers. ANL MS 4500, box 1, f. 2.

27. Ove Arup, in an interview at Copenhagen, was unusually frank: 'The world has seen – a fantastic mathematical problem which Jorn Utzon had never dreamed about when he, with his vivid imagination in a somewhat unrealistic way, designed the great, graciously formed concrete shells which were an integral part of this Theatre and Opera House … Our best mathematical experts have been engaged in the project – many calculations have ended in the waste paper basket and a lot of work has been altered. I would guess that about 60 of our engineers have been busy on this job for the last four-and-a-half years.' One can understand Arup's chagrin because the cost of finding a solution was excessive and was not helped by Utzon's changes. Rather optimistically, Arup concluded the interview with the prediction that the project would be completed in three years, i.e. by 1966. 'Interview with Ove Arup', *BT*, Friday, 6 December 1963. A copy of the interview was sent to JU in Sydney which must have shocked him by its frank apportioning of blame for the delays.

28. See Yuzo Mikami, 'Sydney Opera House: Development of its design and its Leap', *The Journal of the Architectural Institute of Japan*, April 1994, p. 42.

29. Jenkins described the construction of the shells at the 13th fortnightly meeting

at the Hellebæk office of JU on 10 May 1961. The engineer anticipated a total dead load of 340 kg/m². Dr Jordan requested that a porous acoustical plaster be considered on the soffit of the inner shells and calculated a sound reduction for the construction of about 55 to 65 dB. ML MS 2362/4. On 20 April 1961, Jenkins wrote to the Secretary, OHC, with the description of a double skin only 7.6 cm (3 in) thick supported by a steel tubular latticework which he suggested could be produced by the Cockatoo Docks & Engineering Co. P/L.

30. OA to HA, 21 October 1961. H.I. Ashworth papers. ANL MS 4500, box 1, f. 2.
31. JU to OA, 10 February 1966. ML MS 2362/12, item #31.
32. JZ was born in Germany on 25 December 1923, worked at OAP's London office from 1950 to mid-1954, then he returned to South Africa, where he linked up with Michael Lewis who had started his own consulting firm and later linked up with Arups at about this time. OA approached JZ to come back to London and take over the running of the SOH project as an associate partner in 1960 following Jenkins's departure.
33. Ruth Thompson, Interview with Jack Zunz, 28–9 September 1987, p. 6. DWLPA.
34. Ibid., p. 15.
35. Ibid., p. 17.
36. Utzon explained his idea of expressing the concrete vaults as a load carrying structural medium the following way: 'I have treated the concrete in this building in its pure form and arrived at structures which express their load carrying function, (the ribs and the folds) and now I want to express truthfully, the plywood as a thin membrane which achieves its stiffness in bent form.' JU to Minister, Public Works Department, September 1964, ML MSS 2362/10, item 249.
37. JU to J. Yoemans, at Honolulu, Hawaii, 31 March 1967, quoted by John Yoemans in *The other Taj Mahal: What happened to the Sydney Opera House*, Longmans, London, 1968, pp. 90–1.
38. JU told Yuzo Mikami this after he had left to work as Ove Arup's architectural assistant in London. Mikami repeated the story on a visit to the writer on 8 November 1996. The progression through various geometries proceeded from 1) non-geometrical freehand curves in the original scheme, 2) parabola, 3) ellipse (which suited OAP because of its convenience), to 4) circle. This represented a steady progression to an ever more simple geometry based on conic sections. One of the ironies of all this is that Utzon probably could have kept the parabola if he had chosen to cut his shells from a parabolic surface of rotation which is like a sphere, except that it is generated by rotating a parabola.
39. Ibid., p. 91.
40. Eric Ellis, 'Utzon: My Orange Peel Opera House', *GW*, 31 October 1992, p. 13. It should be remembered that JU was 74 when he related the story, and was recalling an event that happened 31 years earlier. In an interview with Steen Eiler Rasmussen at Copenhagen in March 1966, Utzon explained the roof solution using the same orange analogy: 'We actually made a spherical plane by triangular ribs. All these ribs are exactly similar to each other, all having the radius of the ball. And they can be divided up again in smaller parts, so that the ball could be divided like the pieces of an orange.' In reality it was much more difficult than Utzon leads us to believe.
41. See Pi Michael's television documentary 'Clouds – Utzon and the Opera House', Denmark, for Danmarks Radio, TV Department of Culture, Current Affairs and Documentaries, 1994.
42. OA to HA, 20 October 1961. H.I. Ashworth papers. ANL MS 4500, box 1, f. 2.

43. Rafael Moneo to the author, 26 January 1996.
44. On his way back to Spain, Rafael Moneo made an excursion through the Scandinavian countries and was received by Alvar Aalto to whom he showed the *Yellow Book*. He spent one full day with Aalto which made him feel he was the happiest man alive in the world. Thirty-five years later, Moneo still retains the warmest memories of Utzon, whom he respects and loves even more as time passes. Moneo received the $100,000 Pritzker Prize in 1996, the world's most prestigious architectural honour. Ibid., p. 2.
45. See Mark Kauffman, ' Spectacular Structures for Olympic Games', *Life International*, vol. 29, no. 4 (15 August), 1960, pp. 44–51 for a profile of Nervi and account of his Rome Olympic stadium structures.
46. The Little Sports Palace (1955–7) seating 5000 spectators was completed in the autumn of 1957 at the remarkably low cost of $US425,000 or approximately A£250,000. *Life International*, op. cit., p. 47.
47. Mr Ian Nightingale wrote to the Lord Mayor of Sydney, 30 April 1962, and claimed that Utzon had engaged Pier Luigi Nervi to work out the structural problems of the Sydney Opera House. It was passed on to the Opera House Trust and denied. It was dated four months before a Cabinet sub-committee meeting on cost to reassure the client which JU, JZ, and OA had all attended that dealt with Mr Heffron, the NSW Premier, on 23 August 1962. The Government ended up asking for a second opinion from Yves Guion, a French expert on prestressing, who subsequently confirmed all the principles on which the design was based and Pier Luigi Nervi, who is referred to by Michael Lewis. Whatever the interpretation, it suggests that JU was having second thoughts about OAP. The letter says: 'A few days later my friend [an unnamed architect] was at a dinner [in London] attended by the Danish designer of the Opera House and he said that Mr Utzon wasn't very happy about all this and had engaged the services of the brilliant Italian engineer architect Pier Luigi Nervi to work out the structural side of the job so he is able to do the job at a cheaper cost than OVE ARUP and a *better* result. OVE ARUP'S hotly deny this of course …' OHC Records box A.1839/box 9.
48. R.S. Jenkins (OA & P) wrote to R.J. Thompson (Sec. & E.O. to OHC) 13 June 1961, 'It is important to realise that the most highly complex work of Nervi, Esquillan and Candela has been done without competition. In these three examples, we see the results achieved by the highest collaboration, since each has his own contracting organisation behind him.' Jenkins bemoans the fact that in Sydney, OA & P have to produce structures of even greater complexity by teamwork in a situation where the contractor has not even been decided upon. DWLPA, PWD: Stage 2 file, starting 16 April 1961.
49. The interim SOHT held its first meeting on 12 April 1961 following the passing of the Opera House Act with the Premier, the Hon. R.J. Heffron, as President and the Lord Mayor of Sydney, Alderman H.F. Jensen, as Vice-President. Mr S. Haviland remained as Chairman. At this meeting it was hoped that the building would be completed and in use by early 1964, only two years away.
50. See Richard Witkin, 'Cause of Crash a Mystery; Take-Off called Normal', the *New York Times*, vol. CXI, 38,023, Friday, 2 March 1962, pp. 1, 14–16; 'Control System Studied in Crash', vol. CXI, 38,024, Saturday, 3 March 1962, p. 1, 45. The United States Civil Aeronautics Board released its Aircraft Accident Report on 15 January 1963 into *American Airlines, Inc., Boeing 707-123B, N 7506A*, (File No. 1-0001; SA-366) which found the probable cause of the accident 'was a rudder control system malfunction producing yaw, sideslip and roll, leading to a loss of control from which recovery action was not

532   The Masterpiece

	effective.'
51.	Yuzo Mikami, in his May 1967 report on the Major Hall, Pt. V, estimated its seating capacity for concerts at 2700 and 1722 for opera. The approximate volume of the hall was 960,000 ft^3 for concerts and 680,000 ft^3 for opera, with a maximum width of seating of 126 ft, and length of 107 ft for opera. The length for concerts was unavailable. The whole seating area constituted one continuous space with a clear architectural simplicity which made it a favourite of Utzon's.
52.	From Summary of JU's Visit to Sydney, March 1962, ML MSS 2362/4, item 41, Monday, 2 April 1962. During the course of the Monday site meeting Mr Dusseldorp insisted that his aim was a figure of A£2,520,000 comprised of A£1,400,000 plus A£1,120,000 plus 10% overheads giving in total A£2,630,000. Civil & Civic's pricing for 'C' class formwork was low by about 50% and the area involved had increased by five times the area listed in the Bill, resulting in a substantial loss. Supervision was poor and this also caused problems with the concrete work. DWLPA: *PWD Stage I file*, A.1839-8, September 1965, p. 5.
53.	See OA per R.S. Jenkins to Sec. OHC, 20 April 1961. Report, Sydney Opera House – Stage II, The Main Contractor, p. 4.
54.	The matter was discussed at the 60th meeting of the OHC, 7 March 1963, p. 2, at which Ove Arup stated from his meeting on 5 March with the contractor that the claims were grossly inflated by the inclusion of numerous items that could not be substantiated. The exact sums involved in the negotiations were kept in the strictest secrecy and are not disclosed in the minutes.
55.	The thrust in the pairs of beams which form the concourse was adjusted after time-dependent distortions had taken place. The adjustments were carried out by ship jacks each of 2000 kN capacity. *Sydney Opera House*, Reprint Series, no. 1, 1988, p. 7.
56.	Ruth Thompson, Interview with Jack Zunz, 28–9 September 1987, at London offices of OAP, p. 9–10. DWLPA.

10: Terraced Sanctuaries

1.	Fatima Mernissi, *The Harem Within: Tales of a Moroccan Girlhood*, Transworld, London, 1994, p. 153.
2.	The general address for the Kingo houses is Kingosvej, Helsingør.
3.	Poul Schouboe lived there when he moved to Helsingør in 1960 to work for Utzon. Jacob Kielland-Brandt, who started with Utzon in October 1959, currently lives at Baggesensvej 3 in the south-eastern sector. Aage Hartvig Petersen recalled that the first of the Kingo houses were being finished when he came to the Hellebæk office in 1958.
4.	The Danish kroner amounts were calculated on the fixed exchange rate of 6.907 Danish kroner to $US1. The Australian pound was worth US$2.2, giving a direct rate of 15.1954 Kr to A£1 or 7.5977 Kr to A$1. After November 1967 the Kr rate was fixed at 7.5 to US$1.
5.	Ole Rafn gives the figure as Kr 38,000 (Kr 365.4/m^2) in a 1969 document forwarded to Professor Steen Eiler Rasmussen. This is roughly equivalent to Kr 427,000 today, or about A$92,720 at the current exchange rate. This was a very cheap cost outcome exclusive of the cost of the land, which was provided by the Helsingør Kommune. This is significant because Utzon was often

accused of financial extravagance in relation to the SOH and not being able to control his costs. The Kingo houses provide a perfect rebuttal of such charges against JU.

6. See T. Faber, *Jørn Utzon, Houses at Fredensborg*, Ernst & Sohn, Berlin, 1991, p. 8.

7. Utzon lived much of his later life away from Denmark. He spent three years in Australia, part of three more in Hawaii, and from 1970 on lived permanently in Mallorca. Henrik Ibsen alluded to the ambivalence many Norwegians (and possibly many Danes) feel towards their homeland climate; the fear of the darkness to come is at the back of their dreams of escape. In *The Lady from the Sea*, Ellida says: 'Oh no – that isn't true. Our joy is something like the joy we get in the long light summer days – it implies the darkness that is to come, and that by implication cast its shadow over all human joy, just as the drifting clouds cast their shadows over the fjord. It lies there so blue and shining, and then – ' Henrik Ibsen, *The League of Youth, A Doll's House, The Lady from the Sea*, trans. Peter Watts, Penguin Books, Harmondsworth, 1973, p. 281.

8. The use of water in this way has many precedents in Denmark, e.g. when Kay Fisker, C.F. Møller and Povl Stegmann jointly won the competition for the new University at Århus in 1931 that exploited the rolling terrain containing a valley with a little stream running the length of it, which they ponded in its upper reaches to heighten the landscape impact. In 1943, Viggo Møller-Jensen realised a group of linked Studio-Houses on Gronnemose Alle 21-49 at Utterslev, west of Copenhagen, for painters and sculptors which also used a small lake in a similar fashion that anticipated Utzon by a quarter of a century. In 1978, Bente Aud and Boje Lundgaard completed the handsome Sjolund/private housing estate at Hellebæk that takes the Kingo housing for its starting point.

9. Poul Erik Skriver (ed.), *Guide to Modern Danish Architecture*, Arkitektens Forlag, Copenhagen, 1969, p. 12. The introduction says that the Kingo houses were of enormous importance to the development of new types of housing estate in Denmark and observed that a large number of atrium houses were being built.

10. For his comment on the influence of Utzon's single-storey square courtyard see 'Echoes of Utzon', Kim Dirkinck-Holmfeld (ed.), *Danish Architecture 1960–1995*, vol. 2, Arkitektens Forlag, Copenhagen, 1995, pp. 53 (4-7). He gives Ved Stampedammen atrium houses in Usserod (1965), terrace house scheme in Overod (1963), Carlsminde park in Søllerød (1965), Altoften and Nivavænge (1966) as in some way indebted to Utzon. In the latter examples, planner Hans Hartvig also acknowledged his indebtedness to the Islamic city and the Casbah, models which also inspired Utzon.

11. The magnificent domed palace, which was designed by Johan Cornelius Krieger, was built by Frederick IV between 1720 and 1724 and has had numerous additions to it since. Most important, from the point of view of Utzon, because the site for his courtyard houses is immediately south-west of the palace and partly encroached on it, is the wooded park which is open to the public all year round. Its sophisticated layout, with vistas across Lake Esrum and lime-tree walks fanning out from the palace, was worked out by Nicolas-Henri Jardin in the 1760s.

12. T. Faber, op. cit., p. 9. Faber comments that the owner was an eccentric who sold the land for Kr 120,000 in 1959, the same price he had paid for it in the original purchase. Utzon faced a prior approval by the local authority for 20 detached houses in four rows with access by two parallel roads.

13. On completion of the housing Jørgen Saxild decided that the community building should be decorated with works of art and ethnographic crafts as a

reminder to the many years residents had spent in foreign countries. He and his wife Birthe Saxild presented a large beautiful Persian carpet that hangs in the party room to set the process in train. Many people use the community building for family celebrations or parties for friends.

14. When the project was completed in 1963 some people who did not fulfil the original conditions were allowed to move in. The Fredensborg Housing Estate is a freehold institution with a board on which Dansk Samvirke is represented. T. Faber, op. cit., p. 11, mentions that in 1990 new residents were required to pay a bond and an entrance fee each of Kr 100,000 (A$20,185) or Kr 200,000 (A$40,370) total. The rent in 1990 was Kr 55,000 (A$11,102 or A$213/week) for a 113 m^2 house, Kr 66,000 (A$13,322 or A$256/week) for a 129 m^2 house, including heating. The rent on a more modest 73.3 m^2 terraced house was Kr 36,000 (A$7267 or A$140/week). This is remarkably cheap for Denmark, which is about two to two-and-a-half times as expensive as Australia.

15. With its fresh lawns and occasional large boulders sticking out like rocks in the sea, it is suggestive of paradise and has all sorts of medieval connotations such as the tournament meadow of chivalric literature, and the magic meadow in Chrétien de Troyes's 1190 poem, 'The Tent in the Meadow'.

16. Steen Eiler Rasmussen, *Experiencing Architecture*, MIT Press, Boston, 1959, p. 5.

17. T. Faber reported that, on a visit to Fredensborg in 1990, all the residents thought that their courtyard was the best. All the people he ran into while he was walking around wanted him to visit their home because they were certain no one had a garden like theirs.

11: A Big Exotic Bird

1. JU to Mr A.R. Meyer, Architecture Lecturer, University of Sydney, 2 July 1962. ML MSS 2362-10, item 26.
2. Jørn Utzon, 'The Sydney Opera House', Z, no. 14, p. 48.
3. Because of their structural nature, the acoustic ceiling for the Concert Hall or studio 1 of Radiohuset was designed by V. Jordan in collaboration with Christian Nokkentved, the engineer responsible for designing the roof shell. Lisbet Balslev Jørgensen et al., *Vilhelm Lauritzen: A Modern Architect*, trans. Martha Gaber Abrahamsen, Bergiafonden Aristo, 1994, p. 268.
4. Ibid., p. 284.
5. See J. Utzon, Report on Acoustical Research on Major and Minor Halls, Sydney Opera House, June 1965. ML MSS 2362/21, item 37, p. 1.
6. See Vilhelm Lassen Jordan, *Acoustical Design of Concert Halls and Theatres*, Applied Science Publishers, London, 1980, p. 63. VJ's first model of the Major Hall, at 1:10 scale, was never tested due to a change of design by Utzon before it was ready.
7. Ibid., p. 63. VJ states that the first major project where model testing was considered was the early designs for the two large halls of the SOH.
8. The criticism was contained in a letter by Martin Carr, in a long letter to the *SMH*, 'Sydney Opera House Controversy', no. 38,834, Wednesday, 6 June 1962, p. 2. Martin Carr was stage director of the Royal Ballet Covent Garden, which, as Roger Covell afterwards pointed out, was one of the most primitively equipped opera houses in Europe. Utzon replied immediately in an interview 'Opera House stage is Adequate, Says Utzon', published the same day, on p. 1, and the *Herald* interview which followed on Saturday June 30, at

Hellebæk, was an attempt to settle any lingering doubts that still remained and obtain more detailed answers to Carr's points.

In 'And now for the Roof', *S-H*, 694, 10 June 1962, p. 39, Roger Covell, the *Herald* music critic, rebutted Carr's criticisms and concluded, 'Although it [the Sydney Opera House] will not have the depth of vista possible in the Vienna State Opera and other major European houses, the stage area required for all practical uses is more than adequate. Action taking place at a distance of more than 90 ft or so from the front of a stage (the approximate depth of the stage area in the Opera House) usually has small interest for anyone further back than the front rows of the auditorium.'

9. 'Opera House Architect Replies to Critics', *SMH*, no. 38,885, Tuesday, 3 July 1962, p. 2. The *Yellow Book* was published in much greater numbers than the *Red Book*. This in turn meant that many more people, such as Carr, knew what Utzon was planning in more detail than ever before. It is apparent from the Carr incident, and the Strand Lighting lobbying of the Minister for Public Works over the stage lighting contract, that English companies resented JU's sourcing of German and Austrian suppliers and contractors because they still regarded Australia as their colonial economic sphere, from which the Germans, as the enemy in World War II, were excluded from having economic access. Utzon admired the English, but he went to Siemens for the stage lighting because it had the most advanced and refined equipment. British companies had fallen behind technically after the war and now sought to hold on to their colonial markets by exploiting Australian loyalty to the 'Home Country' to compensate for their technical backwardness.

10. See Roger Covell, *S-H*, 694, Sunday, 10 June 1964, p. 39.

11. Interview with Jack Zunz by Ruth Thompson at OAP London office, 28–9 September 1987, p. 31. An account of the meeting is provided in a press statement issued by the NSW Government on 24 August 1962. SOH Press Statements, August 1962–March 1966. AONSW 4/8038. It noted that due to difficult site conditions, a heavy extra payment had been made to the Stage I contractor of A£1.2 million (A$2.4 million), and the stage machinery would now cost A£1,650,000 instead of the estimated A£470,000. Mr Heffron said that the conference had explored the possibility of reducing the estimated cost, but this could not be done without 'grave detriment to the efficiency and aesthetic appeal of the building'. He also stated that Stage III would be commenced while Stage II was still in progress. This, by implication, ruled out calling public tenders for Stage III as it would have to be treated as an extension of Stage II, under the same Head Contractor.

12. See TAP meeting 38, 3 April 1962, item 2. Revised Estimate. The amendment to the *Sydney Opera House Act*, which legitimised the new increased estimate of A£12.5 million (A$25 million), was not presented to Parliament until March 1963, almost a year later. By April 1963, the cost of the building had risen a further A£1.493 million (A$2.986 million) to A£13.993 million (A$27.986 million). At this meeting, JU advised the members of TAP of his decision to use precast exposed granite aggregate slabs for wall cladding instead of sandstone.

13. Interview with Michael Lewis, by Ruth Thompson at OAP London office, 28 September 1987, p. 32. DWLPA. Michael Lewis (OAP) mentioned that Pier Luigi Nervi was asked to carry out a check, but most likely he was confusing Nervi with Yves Guion at the time.

14. Cremer and Gabler were formally engaged in November 1962. Dr Jordan gave up when he came to a dead corner in the Minor Hall, at this point Utzon contacted Professors Cremer and Gabler in Berlin, whose halls he had studied

including the Berlin Opera House which Utzon admired very much. Jørn Utzon, *Report on Acoustical Research on Major and Minor Halls*, Sydney Opera House, June 1965, p. 5.

15. JU. Summary of Visit to Berlin and Vienna, 1–10 June 1962. ML MSS 2362/4.
16. JU stated that the substitution of convex for concave surfaces in Scheme II occurred October–November 1962, and coincided with the completion of models and drawings at $\frac{1}{4}$ in = 1 ft scale. He comments that at this time there was 'a fine collaboration between my office and the acoustical experts [Gabler and Cremer] in Berlin and it was soon evident that this solution was acoustically good.' J. Utzon. *Report on Acoustical Research*, op. cit., item 39, p. 2.
17. W. Gabler to JU, 20 August 1962. ML MSS 2362/17, item 44. Gabler calculated the volume of the Minor Hall at 6800 m^3 or 5.6 m^3 per seat for 1214 seats, and in the Major Hall as 17,600 m^3 or 9.7 m^3 per seat for opera with 1814 seats, and 25,800 m^3 or 9.5 m^3 per seat for an audience of 2715 for concerts.
18. Cremer to Lundberg, Comments on the Plans of the Sydney Opera House, 17 April 1962, p. 4.
19. Beckmann to JU, 26 October 1962. ML MSS 2362/32, item 469.
20. The evidence that Utzon consciously sought to apply the same method as the roofs to the interior acoustic shells of the halls is found in a letter to Professor Henry J. Cowan dated 13 September 1964: 'working on the development of the shell structure led me, through the years, into the idea of building no longer shells – but the whole house, – interiors and so on, by mass produced inter fitting units, of various materials. To master this, I have developed a number of geometrical systems which give my free form shells harmony between the different parts, enabling them to be mass produced from a few simple forms and erect them in a simple way, and we see the result today on the site ... For the interiors, a number of geometrical systems, based on spheres and cylinders and differently controlled movements gives us the inner free forms of the halls and the interiors in the same simple way, and we have complete control which we could not get by doing this job in the traditional way with craftsmen of different trades, because it is so big, so uniformity in quality from many groups of say – tilers, would not be possible. So the main situation today is that the architect has developed a number of geometrical systems in order to realise his idea of producing all the parts of this free form shaped building of mass produced components in a controlled harmonious way.' ML MSS 2362/4, item 23.
21. V.L. Jordan, op. cit., p. 39 ff.
22. In his May 1967 report, Yuzo Mikami examined the application of the convertible concept to the Sydney Opera House in part III, Various Approaches to Convertible Hall Design. He calculated that a model concert hall seating 2800 with dimensions 120 ft x 200 ft x 45 ft high and a volume of 1,080,000 ft^3 would give a R.T. of 2.0 seconds. If a different absorption coefficient for walls and ceiling was assumed this yielded a R.T. of 1.65 seconds. In his model opera hall, seating 1800 with dimensions 120 ft x 115 ft x 45 ft high and a volume of 632,000 ft^3 this would give a R.T. of 1.75 seconds. If a lower absorption coefficient was used this gave a R.T. of 1.45 seconds. From this he concluded that the target reverberation times of 2.0 seconds for concerts and 1.5 seconds for opera were achievable. Mikami was able to demonstrate that this was achievable in practice. The irresistible conclusion from this is that it was not only theoretically possible, but quite feasible, for Utzon to have designed the Major Hall of the Sydney Opera House within the restrictive profiles of the shells to suit both the concert and opera requirements.

23. JU to DH, Statement 1, 7 March 1966, p. 4.
24. Described by J. Utzon. op. cit., item 41, p. 3.
25. Yuzo Mikami dates the introduction of the 'wave' analogy for the Minor Hall on 27 July 1959, immediately after Utzon's meeting in Paris with Le Corbusier. A month later, on 27 August, a 1:60 scale wood model arrived from the Helsingør shipyard and Utzon took a photograph of it on Mikami's head. The discussion of the Major Hall took place separately early the following year on 22–24 February 1960. Work on the Major Hall started after the Minor Hall in November–December 1959 with the compilation of a small booklet on the uses of the Major Hall for the client.
26. J. Utzon, op. cit., item 41, p. 3.
27. Of the interiors of the halls, Utzon wrote: '… Ideally, a hall could be compared with the inside volume of a string instrument, i.e., a violin or a double bass, and many years' research into the problem shows that wood is the ideal material …' JU to Minister for PW, 29 September 1964. ML MSS 2362/4, item 249.
28. See Yehudi Menuhin, *The Violin*, Flammarion, Paris & New York, 1996, pp. 60, 63, diagram of parts on p. 28, and 'The Violin Maker', pp. 71–97.
29. In a short note to Mr Nutsch, Professor Cremer's assistant in Berlin, dated 12 December 1962, Jean Nielsen, Utzon's secretary, said the office is in the process of packing things and getting ready for the move to Sydney. ML MSS 2362/5, item 11, #379.
30. Jack Zunz interview, op. cit. p. 24.
31. Op. cit., p. 25.
32. Interview with Michael Lewis, 28 September 1987, London, by Ruth Thompson, p. 3. DWLPA. Lewis worked with OAP in London from February 1951 until the end of 1954 when he returned with his family to Johannesburg and opened a practice there with Jack Zunz.
33. Letter to the author from Yuzo Mikami, July 1996, p. 5.

12: Maturing the Vision

1. The Royal Inspection was reported in the minutes of the 60th Meeting of the OHC, 7 March 1963, p. 2, which Utzon, together with R.S. Jenkins and JZ from OAP attended, and ends with, 'This genuine interest and recognition by our Royal visitors during their brief stay in Sydney was extremely gratifying and we are indeed happy to record our appreciation.'
2. 'Utzon Guest in Britannia', *SMH*, 39,066, Tuesday, 5 March 1963, p. 1.
3. 'In the context of Architecture,' Interview with Lin Utzon, Andrew Ollie, ABC Radio, 17 January 1989.
4. Papeete and Tahiti have changed enormously since Utzon visited it in February 1963. See Luis Marden, 'Tahiti, "Finest Island in the World"', *National Geographic*, vol. 122, no. 1, July 1962, pp. 1–47, for a description of the Tahiti Utzon would have encountered.
5. See Patrick White, *Flaws in the Glass: a Self-portrait*, Penguin, Ringwood, Vic., 1981, p. 219. White appreciated Utzon's company sufficiently to allow him to show him and Manoly over the base structure later on, '… while it [Opera House] still looked like the ruins of Mycenae'.
6. When Ava Hubble spoke to Utzon at Mallorca in 1983, she found his English was 'very good', although not as fluent as it had been when she talked to him on the telephone. The accusation that was levelled by Davis Hughes, the

Country Party Minister for Public Works after May 1965, that the problems on the Opera House were due to Utzon's poor English appears to be wholly without foundation, since he never made any effort to have an interpreter present at their meetings. Ava Hubble, 'Utzon reveals the great Opera House wrangle', *Weekend Australian Magazine*, 31 December 1983–1 January 1984, p. 9.

7. White to Desmond Digby, 8 March 1963. David Marr (ed.), *Patrick White: Letters*, Random House Australia, Sydney, 1994, p. 221.
8. White to Desmond Digby, 15 March 1963, ibid., p. 223.
9. JZ's recollection is characteristically humorous and caustic: 'And lo and behold, God appears from Heaven. He [Utzon] flies into Sydney from Tahiti. And his plane lands at nine or ten o'clock and then of course he's wheeled into lunch with the Queen, you see. And in the afternoon he comes into the site and he starts complaining about some things he wasn't informed [about]. I mean, there was no one we could contact!' JZ was angry because Utzon could find the time to attend the royal lunch, but failed to tell his engineer where he could be contacted for over two months. It must have been galling for Zunz to find himself taken to task under such circumstances. Interview with Jack Zunz, by Ruth Thompson, 28–9 September 1987, London, p. 25. DWLPA.
10. JU purchased Lot 1, D.P. 27991, containing 4a. 3r. 10p. of land, Transfer no. HI 27938 (vol. 10916-120) in the Parish of Narrabeen, on 20 February 1961. He acquired it under a mortgage arrangement with A.C. Blumet, R.G. Blumet & A.J. Blumet on 14 April 1961, but discharged the mortgage on 16 August 1962. On 11 January 1965, JU registered a new subdivision no. 6180, which amalgamated D.P. 4010 and D.P. 27991 in D.P. 224856.

    On 24 April 1964, he sold Lot 1 of the new D.P. 224856 to a Mona Vale solicitor, Frederick McClure Edgington, and the following year disposed of Lot 3, D.P. 224856, on 1 June 1965, to Gervaise Churchill, a photographer. These sales left him with ownership of Lot 2, D.P. 224856, having an area of 5a. 3r. 11.5p. together with an adjoining Lot 62, D.P. 30648, of 1a. 0r. 0p. which he purchased from W.P. Gaha on 21 November 1962, for A£4145.0.0 (A$8290), entered 26 November 1963, after he settled in Australia permanently, on the west side of Lot 2 running down from Kara Crescent. This gave him a combined site of 6a. 3r. 11.5p. He subsequently sold the property on 21 August 1968 to Beacon Investments for A$83,000, A$13,000 for Lot 62 and A$70,000 for Lot 2.
11. See *Notes re 33 Alexandra Crescent and Subsequent Subdivision*, by Frederick McClure Edgington, a Bayview solicitor and adjoining neighbour. Utzon approached Edgington on or about 15 October 1963. The latter at that time owned Lot 1 on a Plan of Subdivision Lots 15, 16 and part 17 of Deposited Plan no. 4010. On 31 March 1964, Utzon sold a corridor of land beside 33 Alexandra Crescent (owned by Edgington) for A£5000 (A$10,000). Edgington died in April 1966 around the time Utzon left Australia.
12. The 8.9 m long, 2 m beam, *Yachting World* Diamond Class keelboat was designed by Jack Holt of the UK in 1961, and was a highly competitive build-her-yourself double chine plywood yacht. The example Utzon bought was built by Hans Ericson, and was the first one in its class at Pittwater. Utzon re-named it 'Kim' and later sold it to Dr Leigh Cooper, a Manly dentist.
13. Barbara Richards, 'Utzon designs his own bush home', *WD*, 25 March 1963, p. 10.
14. Margaret Jones, 'House "in sea of trees"', *S-H*, 10 March 1963, p. 15. The sea content in JU's imagery is strong in his Bayview house. He explained, 'The house I build for my family will be a ship in a sea of trees.' As a matter of

	priorities, JU wisely recognised he would be too busy at first and thought he would build it when the second stage of the OH was under way. JU wanted to plan everything himself including the furniture.
15.	The date on these sketches of the Bayview house at Kara Crescent is 21 May 1963. The Utzon Collection, ML.
16.	JU lodged Application No. 34,837/63 for AN IMPROVED ROOFING CONSTRUCTION AND BUILDING ELEMENTS THEREOF, Commonwealth Patent Specification no. 271062, for his system of plywood roof beams on 30 August 1963. The full application was lodged on 10 August 1964, published on 10 February 1966 and a patent was granted on 31 October 1966.
17.	JU was granted a patent under Danske Patent no. 93100 by the Direktoratet for Patent-og Varemaerkevaesenet, København, for *Mobel, navnlig stol eller bord, med sarg og ben* on 26 March 1962.
18.	For an explanation of the role of the industrial designer and a short history of the evolution of this important design professional see Ralph Caplan, *By Design*, St Martin's Press, New York, 1982, pp. 32–5. Historically, industrial design shapes objects that are manufactured by machine rather than crafted by hand. This was crucial to Utzon's approach to Stage III of the Sydney Opera House, because neither the NSW Government Architect, nor his Minister for Public Works, Norman Ryan, and his successor, Davis Hughes, understood his approach or its advantages on so large a project as the prefabrication of the halls from machine-made components finished in the factory to a uniformly high quality. Utzon's approach, wherever possible, was to use machine-manufactured elements in place of ones crafted by hand.
19.	The motif in the shield at the centre of the 88-year-old coat of arms of Sydney is a sailing ship which represents the First Fleet. *SMH*, 1 June 1996.
20.	When Ray Brownell returned to the Hellebæk office from a three week summer holiday in August 1961, he was told he was redundant, but a reprieve came soon afterwards. Knud Lautrup-Larsen, Aage Hartvig Petersen and Poul Schouboe all found new jobs and left. Interview with R. Brownell, 2 December 1995. Staff numbers obviously fluctuated depending on what other jobs were being done besides the Opera House, since not everyone was directly employed on it. A list of staff at the Fordamsvej 1, Hellebæk, office in late 1960 included Osmond Jarvis (to leave December 1960), Jacob Kielland-Brandt (1959–October 1965), Knud Lautrup-Larsen, Yuzo Mikami (1959–60), Aage Hartvig Petersen, Poul Schouboe, Olaf Skipper Nielsen (on site, Sydney). A number of additional staff were not included: Raymond Brownell was interviewed in May and joined in June 1961, Oktay Nayman (Turkey), Rafael Moneo (Spain), Herman Huber (Switzerland), James Thomas (UK), Charles Jacobs (USA), Helge Hjertholm (part time, Norway, joined same time as Lundberg), Hans Munk Hansen (Denmark) and Minoru Takeyama (Japan), 1962.
21.	JU wrote to Mr Ron Thomson, Secretary of the OHC on 21 November 1962, with a short statement on progress which also included details of his move and what he planned to do after his arrival. On p. 2 he stated he expected to arrive about 1 March 1963, and would stay the whole period of the construction until the building was finished. He then says he is sending his four top architects, Jon Lundberg, Mogens Prip-Buus, Oktay Nayman and Ray Brownell, and they will arrive in Sydney between 1 February and 1 March.
22.	A lunch-room staff list at Utzon's Bennelong Point office from 13 July 1965 listed: Mogens Prip-Buus (Denmark, 1959–66), Bob [Robert] McLurcan (Australia), Bill Wheatland (Australia), Paul Hopkins (Australia), Jacob

[Kielland-Brandt] (Denmark), Oktay Nayman (Turkey), Erik Fischel (Switzerland), Ian Breden (Australia), Rick Le Plastrier (Australia), Leslie Westman (Australia), Ron H. Devine (Australia), Clive Burich (Hungary/Australia), Jon Lundberg (Norway), Frank D'Arcy (Australia), Ray Brownell (Australia), Sergio Buzzolini (Switzerland). Of the 16, six or nearly 40 per cent are Europeans. Many of the staff had worked outside Australia. ML MSS 2362/27 item 82.

23. *NSWPD ser. 3, vol. 44*, Wednesday 20 February 1963, p. 2699 ff. Askin started by saying: 'I believe, from letters that I have received and from statements that have been widely made, that there is grave public disquiet rife in this community about the finance of this [Sydney Opera House] project.'

24. In 'We signed for it with our eyes shut …', *S-H*, 21 June 1964, p. 92, the writer argued convincingly that 'For one thing, the cost when finally worked out would not have been appreciably less than the £17.4 million now estimated, and no Government would have been willing to commit itself open-eyed to this expenditure, with or without Opera House lotteries.'

25. See *Sydney Opera House – Financial Review, Sep. 1963*. ML MSS 2362/23, item 59, #253. This report contained an estimate for September 1963 of A£14,799,529, that already exceeded by A£2,299,529 Parliament's A£12.5 million approved figure, so was outside the 10% amount of A£13.75 million financial envelope that was sanctioned under the legislation. One of the more obvious conclusions from this fiasco is that no one – except perhaps Utzon and Ove Arups, possibly Rider Hunt – had even the least idea what a building with the technical complexity and long-term cultural significance of the Opera House would cost.

    What politicians and newspapers failed to do was take into account the increased cost of building due to inflation in the years after March 1959. The Building Price Index rose from 79.2 in January 1960 to 176.7 by October 1973 when the Opera House opened. A final building cost of A$85 million in 1973 was equivalent to A$37 million in 1960 or A£18.5 million. The rise in the BPI to March 1966, when Utzon resigned, was 32.5 per cent. A cost of A$9.76 million in 1960 was the same as A$12.93 million in 1966. Politicians would have been acting responsibly had they revealed to the public the Opera House would cost A£40 million. Instead, they developed a practice of giving interim cost estimates which invariably were too low and had to be revised.

26. *NSWPD*, Legislative Assembly, ser. 3, no. 44, 6 March 1963, Second Reading debate, *Sydney Opera House (amendment) Bill*, p. 3109.

27. Interview with Michael Lewis, op. cit. In Johannesburg Lewis supervised a staff of 30 people. In London, the Arups' Sydney Opera House operation employed 50–60 people compared to a maximum of 16 architects on Utzon's staff. The ratio of engineers to architects was at least five to one. Lewis stated that: 'my responsibility was to take that prime agency role and to set up our unit on site to carry it through, and at the same time, if possible, to establish a practice, carrying out work other than the Opera House. So that's what I went out to do.' p. 4. It was Lewis's actions to establish a practice which later caused friction to develop between Utzon and Lewis, because Utzon considered Lewis had a conflict of interest that caused him to fail to distinguish between his two responsibilities in his dealings with the Minister for Public Works, at that time a major employer of engineering consultants.

28. JU to Chairman TP (SOHC), 14 August 1963. ML MSS 2362/24, #233.

29. The last precast roof segment was lowered into place on 17 January 1967, four years after the start of work on Stage II. This was not the end of this stage of the work because the tile lids still had to be fixed to the ribs.

30. *Z*, no. 14, p. 83.
31. See Erik Kolle to HA, 12 May 1958. H.I. Ashworth papers, NLA MS 4500, Ove Arup & Partners (13 October 1958–), f. 3. Symonds's factory was able to supply plywood formwork in sheets 15 m x 1.8 m (50 ft x 6 ft) wide with a plastic surface to ensure a perfectly smooth finish to the concrete.
32. JU to Minister for PWD, 29 September 1964. ML MSS 2362/10, item 24.
33. Ibid., #243.
34. Summary of Mr Utzon's visit to Sydney, March 1962. ML MSS 2362/4, item 41–. Utzon's first visit to the Ralph Symonds factory was on the afternoon of Wednesday, 28 March 1962; this was followed by a second visit on Monday, 9 April, at which the toilet cubicle mock-up was approved in principle. Utzon discussed a rough timing schedule with Mr Dwyer and Mr Ezra and asked that further mock-ups be ready for his next visit at the end of October. In the meantime, Olaf Skipper Nielsen, from the Utzon site office, was to arrange patents and photographs of the roof mock-ups. This must refer to Patent 271062 which was not lodged until the following year, on 30 August 1963. The report states that Ralph Symonds were to be paid, presumably by Utzon, for present and future experiments.
35. See drawing no. SOH 875: Minor Hall Reflecting Panels, dated 5 June 1963. ML PXD 492.
36. See drawing no. SOH 948: Minor Hall ceiling & Rear Wall Layout, dated 3 September 1963. ML.
37. JN to JU, 27 May 1964. ML MSS 2362/27. Nutsch comments to Utzon that he must first determine how to arrange the audience in the Major Hall and suggests that he consider the experience of the Berlin Philharmonic where it was necessary to form groups of listeners and to enclose these on all sides using the vineyard principle since there was not the space otherwise to overcome the sound energy losses.
38. The drawings referred to are nos. SOH 1092 to 1094 (13 July 1964), and 1101 to 1105 (15 August 1964) and measure 180 cm x 90 cm.
39. Frank D'Arcy, an experienced 37-year-old Australian architect, who had previously worked in Scandinavia for three years, left in November 1964, followed by a Swiss architect Sergio Buzzolini who did the early drawings for Utzon's Bayview house and the conversion of the boat shed at Snapperman's Beach, returned to Switzerland, and after him, the ex-Tasmanian, Ray Brownell.
40. Quite surprisingly in a letter to Stan Haviland on 27 September 1963, from New York, Bernard Heinze called Berlin 'a triumph of architectural design', and further stated that not one acoustician he consulted from Vienna to Berlin considered it was possible to use the Opera House for orchestral purposes in accordance with the original design, with the orchestra at the rear of the stage.
41. None of the 2218 seats in the Berlin Philharmonic hall was farther than 32 m from the podium. The Sydney Committee and Minister insisted on seats for 2800 in the Opera House concert hall, which appears somewhat ridiculous by comparison. The seats are grouped in four blocks in front of the orchestra, with three on each side and two behind. Its reverberation time lasted a full two seconds and the concert space was the largest in Europe, measuring 74.68 m x 68.58 m x 33.83 m high.
42. WG to JU, Sydney, 30 August 1963. ML MSS 2362/17, item 44. Gabler wrote: 'It just so happened that the new hall in the Philharmony here in Berlin has progressed so far in construction, that its final form and the arrangement of the seating on all sides of the orchestral podium are recognisable …' The Berlin Philharmonic had its first performance on 15 October 1963 with Herbert von

Karajan conducting Beethoven's Symphony no. 9. The vineyard system of seating terraces was first used in the Stuttgart Liederhalle in 1956.

43. Scheme II, with the orchestra in the middle of the Major Hall, had already been carried out in detail. Models were made by Gabler and Cremer in Berlin at 1:10 scale with various types of seating and orchestra arrangements and showed the possibility of making the ceiling from triangular plywood reflectors. This was gone into in great detail and many drawings and models were made to solve the problem of mass-production and also structural soundness. Sir Bernard Heinze's intervention was extremely costly and resulted in the abandonment of much valuable work by Utzon. Heinze was wrong about the position of the orchestra, which was eventually moved back to a more central location similar to the Berlin Philharmonic in the final redesign of the main hall. *Report on Acoustical Research ... June 1965*, p. 3. ML MSS 2362/23, item 41.

44. JU, *Report on Acoustical Research ... June 1965*. ML MSS 2362/21, item 55, # 37. Utzon wrote: 'Sir Bernard Heinze gave us a report from Berlin from his visits to the new Philharmonic Hall, where the orchestra is in the middle. Sir Bernard was unhappy because so many concerts in this hall will be soloists and 1/3 of the audience, which sits behind the orchestra, will not get 100% good sound. At the 67th meeting of OHC on 16 September 1963 Sir Charles Moses suggested discussion be deferred and in the meantime he discuss with Utzon the effect of a centrally placed orchestra and audiences generally. Sir Charles Moses afterwards asked that all 2800 seats, or nearly all seats, should be on one side of the orchestra. The scheme was therefore abandoned and we started afresh.'

45. See Vern O. Knudsen & Cyril M. Harris, *Acoustical Designing in Architecture*, John Wiley, New York, 6th ed., 1962, p. 12. Since the area of a sphere increases as the square of its radius, the intensity of free sound waves originating at a point source diminishes inversely as the square of the distance from the source.

13: A Hammer Blow

1. See JU to R. Maclurcan, from Hellebæk, n. d., ML MSS 2362/23, item 59. Written in April 1964, another letter to Maclurcan seems to indicate that JU probably left before April 17. Utzon mentions having meetings in Europe with W.B. Siemens, etc., then adds a personal note at the end: 'But the situation in my family is not too good but there is hope now. The doctors are positive and I anticipate to be able to be in Sydney by the end of May.' In the event he did not return until early June 1964.

2. 'We had a fairly [great] tragedy – my father's brother died suddenly – for some reason that became – the other thing was bad (the Opera House problems) – but that [the brother's death] became almost more important and it didn't, and suddenly everybody was very unified. My father worked hard so we didn't see much of him.' From 'In the Context of Architecture', Andrew Ollie interview with Lin Utzon, ABC Radio, Sydney, 17 January 1989.

3. Henrik Ibsen, *Rosmersholm*, 1886, Act 3, in Henrik Ibsen, *The Master Builder and Other Plays*, trans. Una Ellis-Fermor, Penguin, Harmondsworth, 1973, pp. 101–2.

4. *Z*, no. 14, April 1965, p. 88.

5. See Competition document, *Wettewerb fur einen Neubau des Schauspielhauses Zürich*, Bauamt II der Stadt Zürich, Direction des travaux de la ville de Zürich

Service d'Architecture, Zürich, July 1963. 35 pp.
6. Comparisons are difficult. At this time, the Australian pound was valued against the US dollar at the rate $2.24 to the A£, and the Swiss franc rate was pegged at S Fr 4.37282 to the US$, or 9.795 to A£.
7. 'Concours Pour L'Opera National, Madrid,' *L'architecture d'Aujourd'hui*, no. 116, September/November 1964, p. xv. JU's entry was project A.29 and did not receive any recognition. The jury included Pierre Vago (France); Egon Eiermann (West Germany); Gio Ponti (Italy).
8. 'Utzon wins Swiss Prize', *SMH*, 39,463, 11 June 1964, p. 11.
9. 'Likely Opera Cost £18 m, Says Askin', *SMH*, Monday, 4 May 1964, p. 4. R.W. Askin announced that the Liberal Party sub-committee set up to investigate costs had determined the year before (March 1963) that the final figure would be at least three times the Government estimate. Askin revealed that the committee's most recent estimate was £16.3 million (excluding parking) and he challenged the Government to deny this in Parliament.
10. 'Opera House Estimate Now £17.4m: Minister "Concerned"', *SMH*, 39,469, Thursday 18 June 1964, p. 1.
11. This was equivalent to a rise of $81.34 million in 1996 dollars, from $207.50 million to $288.84 million. The increase was substantial, and while the indignation of Askin and his supporters may have been justified, they failed to ask themselves what the state was getting, whether this represented value for money, or what was a reasonable and responsible cost for the complete project. Even at A$540.6 million in 1996 (A$102 million in December 1973), the SOH was a very cheap building in terms of its various functions, in boosting tourist visits, and as a world-famous symbol for Sydney and Australia. One new Collins class submarine, to take a recent example, costs A$800 million, half as much again, and there are few complaints.
12. This happened earlier on 19 May 1964 at the 30th meeting of the OHC. Utzon was away until early June, and did not attend. Mr Maclurcan, representing Utzon, was asked by the Minister for Public Works, Mr Ryan, not to divulge the new cost estimate.
13. 'Opera House Cost – Enough for Second Bridge ... experts say', *S-H*, 21 June 1964, pp. 9, 28.
14. See 'Opera House Estimate Now £17.4m: Minister "Concerned"', *SMH*, 39, 469, Thursday 18 June 1964, p. 1.
15. 'Report by Utzon: Opera House Cost Stands', *SMH*, 39,462, 10 June 1964, p. 1.
16. See JU to Director of PWD Johnson in response to Mr W.W. Wood's appointment, dated 24 March 1964. ML MSS 2362/4. In his letter, Utzon pointed out to the Director that Mr Wood was only to be considered as a carrier of information from his office to the Minister to keep the Minister informed and up-to-date at any time. Mr Wood was to take no part in the administration, supervision etc. of the Opera House project. Later, Utzon would change his view of Wood's presence and consider him more a spy.
17. 'Inquiry On Opera House Cost', *SMH*, 39,469, 19 June 1964, p. 5. The actual figure, as revealed in the *Budget Papers 1964–65*, was higher. It noted the expenditure at 30 June 1964 for Architectural fees including travel, printing, models, specialist consultants of A£431,289.3.9 (A$862,578.40). The total for architect, consulting engineers and quantity surveyor was A£1,057,107 (A$2,114,214). The press omitted to mention that the consulting engineer's fees exceeded the architect's fees by A£84,556.
18. 'Report by Utzon: Opera House Cost Stands', *SMH*, 39,488, 10 July 1964, p. 1.

19. 'Challenged by Renshaw on Opera House Cost Reported', *SMH*, 39,500, 24 June 1964, pp. 1, 15. The Government was reported as anxious to avoid having to announce an even higher estimate after declaring what has been offered as a final estimate. The Ministers engaged Utzon in what was described as 'plain talking', because it considered that a further reassessment of costs or a revival of doubts about costs closer to the State elections could cause it serious political harm. Before the meeting broke up, Utzon was asked to provide Cabinet with certain additional information by the end of August.
20. See *Conference at Premier's Department, 23 July 1964*, at 11 a.m. ML MSS 2362/3.
21. JU to NR, Minister for Public Works, 3 August 1964. ML MSS 2362/21, item, 55, #9, 11. Utzon in his letter makes two important points: the building must be designed to the requirements of the user if costly alterations are to be avoided later; the second point is more subtle for a politician to appreciate: 'I have been working with the Committee and the Panels and with you, on the presumption that everything that comes into this building in every detail, down to the last tea spoon and every piece of art going into the building was designed and controlled by the architect. I had full understanding of this from the Committee and I want to assure you that without your understanding on this, the building will not be a success, and not an organic whole.'
22. See Special Meeting OHC 30 June 1964. JU submitted alternative proposals for carparking on 16 June and, in addition, presented an overall scheme for the redevelopment. He made four suggestions: Domain carpark, new 4-level carpark under the gardens beside the Tarpeian Way, 2-section carpark to accommodate 1050 cars along Circular Quay East, and a underground carpark in front of the Opera House steps. The OHC Executive approved the plan for a 1000 vehicle parking station immediately adjacent to the Opera House at this meeting. Utzon promised to prepare the plans for the carparking station within three months.
23. JU correctly pointed out in a letter that, '… it is not possible to plan the Opera House without considering the near surroundings from Unilever House to the Botanical Gardens including Man-O-War Steps, because all objects in this district are seen together with the Opera House, and if they are wrongly formed, they will destroy this building.' JU to NR, Minister for Public Works, 3 August 1964. ML MSS 2362/21, item 55, #11, p. 2.
24. Gavin Souter, 'Joern Utzon Discusses the Opera House', *SMH*, 39,480, 1 July 1964, p. 2. In reply to critics at this time, Utzon pointed out that the Opera House with its three stages was still relatively cheaper than the corresponding facilities at New York's Lincoln Center and was no more expensive than the latest new theatre in Germany. He was talking to the deaf – no Opposition politician was remotely interested in hearing about the comparative cost of concert halls around the world because this meant nothing to the Australian public. The entire debate failed to take in the intangible contribution of the Opera House which can now be seen as simply immense and incalculable in terms of the benefit to NSW. As Utzon pointed out, the largely useless piece of crumbling sandstone the Opera House sat on was now valued at A£20 million (A$40 million).
25. 'Sniper Fires at Opera House', *SMH*, 39,258, 15 October 1963, p. 1. Ian Mckenzie left his desk to talk to someone when he heard two reports and looked up and saw the shattered window beside his desk. The bullet was later found lodged in the wall. A second bullet strike hit an office occupied by girls.
26. At the 77th meeting (34th Trust) of OHC, 15 September 1964, JU reported on his European trip and refers both to the Zürich visit, which he proposed to

	share the cost on an equal basis with the OHT, and visits to Waagner-Biro in Vienna and Siemens in Germany. This gives some idea of his hectic schedule.
27.	JU to WG, 23 December 1964. ML MSS 2362/8, item 21.
28.	VJ to JU, 3 February 1965. ML MSS 2362/9, item 79.
29.	From Jørn Utzon, *Report on Acoustical Research* …, 21 June 1965, p. 9. ML MSS 2362/21, item 55, #53.
30.	See Jørn Utzon, *Descriptive Narrative: Sydney Opera House*, January 1965, p. 13, also pp. 12, 15.
31.	LC to JU, 29 January 1965. ML MSS 2362/5, item 10, #167. Cremer wrote that Gabler was ready to start the production of the model at the end of January and was glad Utzon accepted the alterations to the ceiling of the Major Hall. In the meantime, Cremer announced the model of the Minor Hall was installed and ready for testing.
32.	Jørn Utzon, op. cit., p. 4.

14: A White Radiance Rising

1.	JU, 'The Sydney Opera House', *Z*, no. 14, 1965, p. 49.
2.	While JU was living in Australia he met the South Australian potter Milton Moon with whom he became friends. In a letter to Moon dated 2 September 1965, Utzon described the Opera House tiles: '… The matt ones [tiles] are the black colours on the drawing of the tile surface or the shell. You see that they are extruded and that the *chamotte* + engobe + glaze makes a very fine surface in the sun and they have a really fine quality about them. Not two of the tiles had the same colour, of course, within a very small range of different whites.'
3.	See Nader Ardalan & Laleh Baktiar, *The Sense of Unity: The Sufi Tradition in Persian Architecture*, University of Chicago Press, Chicago, 1973, p. 37.
4.	JU to Ron Thomson, Secretary to OHC, 29 November 1961 re: Ceramic tiling to shells. DWLPA, NBR: Sydney Opera House, box 1/ PWD: Stage 2 File beginning 26 April 1961.
5.	Professor O. Pettersson, *Calculations and Recommendations of the Outer Ceramic Wall Facings*, Stockholm, Sweden, May 1959. ML MSS 2362/5, item 10, #705–37.
6.	Rudolf Olssen (Höganäs), letter to JU, 17 May 1963. ML MSS 2362/5, item 5, #397–9.
7.	From an interview with JU on 31 March 1967. John Yoemans, *The other Taj Mahal: What happened to the Sydney Opera House*, Longmans, London, 1968, p. 91.
8.	I. Naslund (Höganäs), letter to Prip-Buus, 10 April 1962. ML MSS 2362/5, item 10, #523–5. Naslund mentions experiments with tiles having a completely black body and blue tiles, and asks Prip-Buus whether brown might be acceptable instead, since it seems there were problems with the very dark colours such as black.
9.	*Höganäs ceramic tiles for Sydney Opera House*, 14 August 1964. ML MSS 2362/5, item 10, #69. Utzon's specification is a masterpiece of brevity: 'Tiles for the main part of the lids should be of white stoneware and have a shiny transparent glaze so that the natural colour of the stoneware determined the colour of the tile. The stoneware clay was to be mixed with a rather coarse *chamotte* providing a living surface texture which could reflect the sun-rays in different angles. Tiles for the edges of the lids should be of white unglazed stoneware

with a rather smooth and dense surface. Both types of tiles should be of waterproof quality and have great compression and tensile strength. Tolerances must be kept to a minimum ...' The main dimension was 5 in x 5 in x 15 mm (G and M Types). Utzon relied on a sample and careful supervision to ensure the quality and uniformity of the tiles.

10. 48th Meeting OHC, 20 February 1962, item (k) Ceramic Tiling. At its previous meeting, Utzon told the Committee that, 'Some two years ago when inquiries as to local prices [Wunderlich Limited and Commonwealth Ceramics] had been made, Mr Utzon been surprised at the cost of the local product.'
11. JU to Ron Thomson, Secretary OHC, 28 March 1962. ML MSS 2362/5, item 10, #537. In it, JU recommended the acceptance by the Committee of the quotation submitted by Höganäs as theirs was the cheapest of the three quotations as well as a product of high and even quality which Utzon was confident would meet the requirements, architecturally as well as structurally.
12. Minutes of meeting at Hellebæk, 11 December 1962, attended by Utzon, H. Hjertholm, V. Florin and I. Naslund for Höganäs. ML MSS 2362/5, item 10, #481. Utzon advised Höganäs that Hjertholm would inspect the deliveries at Skromberga as his representative.
13. JU to I. Naslund (Höganäs), 2 July 1962. ML MSS 2362/5, item 10, #511. JZ would send the total quantities of tiles required in a week's time but JU still needed approval from Sydney to start manufacturing the tiles.
14. Michael Lewis, 'Roof Cladding of the Sydney Opera House', *Journal and Proceedings, Royal Society of New South Wales*, vol. 106, 1973, p. 18 ff.
15. Höganäs to JU, 14 June 1963. ML MSS 2362/11, item 30, #309.
16. Michael Lewis Interview, by Ruth Thompson, London 28 September 1987, p. 15.
17. JU to I. Naslund, Höganäs Billesholms A.B., 6 September 1965. ML MSS 2362/11, item 30.

15: Ballot-box Despot

1. Skipper Nielsen to Margaret Moorcroft, 6 June 1965, pp. 1–2.
2. The results were Liberal 807,868 votes (39.60 per cent) and 31 seats; Country Party 208,826 votes (10.23 per cent) and 16 seats, giving the Coalition a total of 47 seats – it required half as many votes to elect a CP member as it did a Liberal, so great was the gerrymander in favour of the CP – and ALP 883,824 votes (43.31 per cent) and 45 seats. *NSWPD*, 3 November 1965, p. 1689.
3. Only once during the entire 1965 campaign is there any reference to a 'Full inquiry into Opera House Costs', *AEx*, Wednesday, 14 April 1965, p. 10. A far greater priority was aid to the Armidale Council which leads in the advertisement on 30 April, followed by free school buses.
4. 'Cutler on decentralisation: Country Party Pledges a New Concept', *Central Western Daily* (Orange), Tuesday, 6 April 1965, pp. 1, 4, 9, 13.
5. SC (Utzon's secretary), to George & Lorraine, 3 May 1965, p. 2. SC writes: 'Feeling down here at the Opera House is that nothing could be worse, and most of the chaps seem to think that there will be an inquiry or a Royal Commission, so the Liberals can start off with a clean sheet ...' Utzon was away in Europe and did not return until 23 or 24 May.
6. See *Sydney Opera House – Report July 1968*: by Legal Office, Department of Public Works, ch. 3, p. 8. AONSW 4/7948. This report provides very

interesting details of the Government Architect's involvement behind the scenes as well as exposing the falsity of Hughes's later claims to be imposing new controls on the project. It states: dissatisfaction with the situation centred around the then Minister for Public Works, Mr Ryan, and the dissatisfaction affected the Premier [J.B. Renshaw] and his Deputy, Mr Hills, in view of the proximity of an election, and for other appropriate but unrelated reasons.' It goes on to state that, 'On 23.9.64 Premier Renshaw wrote to the Architect informing him in short that work would not proceed on Stage III until a comprehensive detailed report [i.e. *The Narrative Description* of January 1965] had been furnished to the Government. Other requirements in his letter were that the whole of Stage III should have been fully designed and all working drawings and specifications available to enable the calling of competitive tenders. It was further required that the Architect must obtain the approval of the Minister for Public Works for his proposals.'

7. NR, Address-in-reply, *NSWPD*, ser. 3, vol. 62, 25 August 1966, p. 582.
8. *NSWPD*, ser. 3, vol. 58, 3 November 1965, p. 1711.
9. During the Sydney Opera House Act, second reading debate DH said 'The Deputy Leader of the Country Party [Chaffey, Tamworth] has made a devastating case for the establishment of a trust to control and manage the opera house; it is unanswerable.' *NSWPD*, ser. 3, vol. 31, 6 April 1960, p. 3732. It was in the context of Country Party pressure that the Government set up the Trust a year later.
10. The deficiencies of the *Sydney Opera House Act, 1960* were discussed at a meeting of OHC #37, on 17 January 1961 following receipt of a letter from the Assistant Director, PWD, 16 December 1960, pp. 3–4. HA and Dr Parkes both expressed concern that several of the clauses could lead to considerable confusion in terms of the position and rights of the constructing authority and just how far the minister and his officers might exercise those rights. In 1966, DH cleared up the confusion – his powers were pre-eminent.
11. At a conference at the Premier's Department on 23 July 1964, between Utzon and the Premier J.B. Renshaw, P. Hills and P.N. Ryan (Minister for PW), Utzon pointed out that the Premier was head of the Trust and that the specialist panels were treated as the client on design matters. The confusion over the Trust's executive role existed prior to Davis Hughes, what was new was his usurpation of the Trust function, compared to the previous Labor administration which mixed up the two. At the 23 July meeting, Premier Renshaw told Utzon that 'the Minister for Public Works was the client'. When it was repeated that the Ministry of Public Works was the only authority, Utzon responded he had worked seven and a half years with one client – 'would he have the same conditions now as before? – or would he be prevented from designing or having the final say on all details of the building.' None of the politicians, Labor, Liberal or Country Party, seem to have properly understood the important distinction between the client role and that of constructing authority which were quite separate and very different in nature. ML MSS 2362/3. At an earlier PWD meeting in Utzon's office on 18 September 1963, Johnson for the PWD said 'He did not think that the minister, having appointed such an august body [Technical Advisory Panel of the Trust], would contradict their decisions.'
12. At a meeting with J.C. Humphrey (Director PWD) and S. Haviland (Chairman OHC) on 10 August 1965, DH conceded that since the building was being built for use by 'the Trust it must have the opportunity of stating its needs' but he insisted that, 'It remained the [sole] responsibility of the Minister, however,

to decide what actually was built.' What no one asked was how the Minister would know this? Something intervened to change Hughes's mind. Handwritten notes on the document ORIGIN OF MEMBERSHIP OF THE SYDNEY OPERA HOUSE EXECUTIVE COMMITTEE, EVENTUALLY THE SYDNEY OPERA HOUSE TRUST, read: 'The last meeting recorded of the SOH Executive Committee was in April 1966,' and below it is written, 'Since when Mr Haviland has said the "SOH Exec. C'ttee no longer exists," Davis Hughes has said "The SOH Exec C'ttee is defunct."' The *Sydney Opera House Act (Amendment) Bill*, introduced on 18 March 1969, provided that eligibility for membership of the Trust was subject to an age limit of 70 years, had the effect of abolishing the previous Trust.

13. See 'Askin: The verdict', *S-H*, 28 November 1993, pp. 14–19. There are two books on Askin: David Hickie, *The Prince and the Premier*, Angus & Robertson, Sydney, 1985, in particular, pp. 47–59, 71, 83, 87, 142, 177 and 208, argues the case for convicting the Premier of involvement in organised crime, the counter viewpoint and defence is provided less convincingly by Geoffrey Reading in *High Climbers: Askin & Others*, John Ferguson, Sydney, 1989. Denis Lenihan, former chief executive of the National Crime Authority concluded in the *S-H* article, p. 19, that, 'Taking all this together, it seems to me that the thrust of the allegations is made out, and there are reasonable grounds to believe Askin was corrupt ... I would have committed him for trial.'

14. 'The Sun-Herald Commission of Inquiry, Askin: The verdict', *S-H*, 28 November 1993, p. 14.

15. Geoffrey Bolton, *The Oxford History of Australia*, vol. 5: *1942–1988, The Middle Way*, MUP, Melbourne, 1990, p. 168.

16. John Yoemans, op. cit., p. 134.

17. See Heather Radi et al., *Biographical Register of the New South Wales Parliament 1901–1970*, ANU Press, Canberra, 1979, p. 138.

18. DH represented Tasmania in interstate football (Tasmanian League), intervarsity tennis in Adelaide (1935), and played A Grade cricket with the Newtown Cricket Club in Hobart till 1936.

19. Davis Hughes (253785) RAAF record, *Application for Position of Temporary Education Officer, Civil Staff*, dated 17 June 1940, item 56, p. 1. Hughes evidently gave careful thought to the exact wording of his statement. It is open to two quite divergent interpretations: one that he had read the listed subjects towards a degree, and two, that he had in fact been awarded the degree. By introducing the subordinate clause '... completing it in ...' and then listing subjects he implies he had satisfactorily completed the degree requirements. Later, when no RAAF official investigated his qualifications, he claimed to have the degree outright.

20. Further false claims crop up in RECORD SHEET – *Officer and Airmen Pilot* form completed by Hughes and in a RAAF *Application for a Commission in Administrative Branch*. Both are in Davis Hughes's handwriting. The list of graduates produced in 1970 by the University of Tasmania does not record DH as a graduate.

21. *RAAF Assessment Report*, pt. II, Assessing Officer's Statement, #15, dated 26 July 1945.

22. Hughes's election was not straightforward. The NSW Country Party was divided into separate regions: the north coast, the northern tablelands, the north west formed a northern block with 12 members; the central west and Riverina with three members, a second block. Davis Hughes was the northern candidate, Charles Cutler was the representative of the southern block. As reported by Sir

Charles Cutler, Hughes lost the first ballot to Cutler. Because three of the 12 members of the northern block of the party were absent from the vote, Colonel M.F. Bruxner called for a second ballot in which Hughes scraped in with a majority of one.

23. 'Mr Davis Hughes to leave Hospital on Sunday', *AEx*, #5065, Friday, 27 March 1959, p. 1. The announcement claimed DH would support the Leader of the Opposition Mr Morton develop the Liberal–Country Party Coalition speech at Mosman Town Hall on the following Tuesday evening.

24. *AEx*, #5067, Wednesday, 4 March 1959, p. 1. Denials of DH's impending resignation were repeated on 13 and 25 March.

25. *CAPD*, vol. H, R. 22 (NS), 17 February–14 May 1959, see 11 March 1959, p. 475 ff, p. 480. Mr Osborne, Minister for Air, gave his answer on 6 May, vol. H, R. 23 (NS) p. 1931. Osborne was clearly embarrassed by Mr Griffiths' question; to avoid a direct answer which would have exposed DH, he followed advice supplied by David Drummond: 'I refer the honorable member to the statement made by Mr Davis Hughes in the Legislative Assembly of New South Wales on Tuesday, 22nd April, 1959.'

26. 'Mr. Hughes' Appreciation', *AEx*, #5074, Friday, 20 March 1959.

27. The episode is described by Don Aitkin in *The Colonel: A Political Biography of Sir Michael Bruxner*, ANU Press, Canberra, 1979, n. 17, p. 270.

28. DH was elected Leader of the Country Party on 6 May 1958, with Charles Benjamin Cutler as his Deputy. In April 1959, after 11 months and 8 days as Leader, DH was replaced by Cutler as Leader with William Chaffey as the Deputy (1959–68). Cutler led the NSW Country Party until his resignation in 1975. In 1968 DH became the Deputy Leader replacing Chaffey who had proved unsatisfactory, and in January 1973 he resigned as the MLA for Armidale, two years before Cutler, to become the NSW Agent-General in London.

29. *NSWPD*, ser. 3, vol. 27, 21 April 1959, p. 14.

30. *NSWPD*, ser. 3, vol. 54, 3 November 1965, p. 1727. Earlier (p. 1712), during the same debate, Renshaw made another reference to Hughes's deception of the Parliament: 'It would seem that the Minister is the only honest man who has stepped into the House: he never tells a lie and never misleads anybody.' To which a flustered Hughes blurted out: 'You are terrific.'

31. Margaret Moorcroft joined Utzon's office at Bennelong Point in February 1963 and left in January 1965 to have a son. She was married to the architect John Moorcroft.

32. Sir Charles Moses interview, by Ava Hubble, no. 2, 8 July 1986, pp. 118–19. DWLPA.

33. SC to Gavin Souter (*SMH*) 19 May 1966. She writes: 'In spite of Mr Utzon's repeated invitations, Mr Hughes never had lunch on the site with Mr Utzon and never visited Mr Utzon's drawing office, met his staff or inspected the work they were doing on drawings and models. I think he inspected the site with Mr Utzon once, perhaps twice, and on several occasions at meetings held in the Department of Public Works, Mr Utzon's associate architects were not permitted to join the meetings but had to wait outside.'

34. In,'Sails unfurl on Harbour foreshore', *SMH*, #39,770, Saturday, 5 June 1966, p. 1, the *Herald* carried an impressive photograph on its front page from the west side of Circular Quay with an accompanying caption: 'The huge concrete sails of the Opera House are starting to unfurl …' and observed that the scale of the cranes and scaffolding dwarfed a ferry crossing in front of them. One of the things many people did not really understand was just how big the structure was. This in particular affected many politicians.

35. JU, *Report on Acoustical Research* ..., 21 June 1965, p. 4. ML MSS 2362/21, item 53, #51.
36. JU to WG, 2 September 1965. ML MSS 2363/8, item 5.
37. Mr W.W. Wood, confidential memo to Minister [DH], 12 August 1965, p. 8. AONSW 4/8070.
38. DH to JU, 25 August 1965, p. 9. AONSW 4/8070.
39. DH, Confidential Cabinet Minute, 25 August 1965. AONSW 4/8070.
40. See *TBPNSW, 1964-65*, p. 133. Total fees paid to Architectural consultants were estimated at A$1,480,000; appropriation A$1,100,000; expenditure A$1,448,280 with NR as the Minister. The following year, 1965–6, the figures rose to A$2,400,000; A$1,480,000; and A$2,000,000 respectively under DH, an increase of A$551,720.
41. NR, *Sydney Opera House (Amendment) Bill*, NSWPD, ser. 3, vol. 63, 29 September 1966, p. 1374–5.
42. *Ron Gilling Report on Negotiations on Behalf of J. Utzon*, RAIA (NSW Chapter), 14 March–14 June 1966, p. 6.
43. NR said, 'On 30th August in the same year people were put on alert in the Department of Public Works and elsewhere for a proposed Ministerial Statement on this question ... – but in fact he did not make the statement.' *NSWPD*, ser. 3, vol. 63, 29 September 1966, p. 1359. DH's actions in the matter compromised the Institute of Architects.
44. See JU to DH, 7 March 1966: 'If you look back again in history, you will see that I have been flexible and I have suffered enormously from constant alterations, but I have felt it my job and duty to satisfy my client 100%.' Statement No. 1, p. 4.
45. In Gitta Sereny, *Albert Speer: His Battle With the Truth*, London, 1995, p. 297–8, Speer, who was previously Hitler's architect, rejected rigid authoritarian industrial structures in his remarkably successful reorganisation of German wartime munitions production and put non-political technicians in charge, giving each factory considerable autonomy. Hughes, in contrast to Speer, was authoritarian, rigid, and tried to force Utzon to adopt Public Works's fundamentally outmoded nineteenth-century system of building crafts to produce the Opera House.
46. DH, Address-in-Reply, *NSWPD*, ser. 3, vol. 16, 22 May 1956, p. 132.
47. Ava Hubble, 'Utzon reveals the great opera house wrangle', *Weekend Australian Magazine*, 31 December 1983–1 January 1984, p. 9.
48. Julian Vincent, 'Tricks of Nature', *New Scientist*, vol. 151, no. 2043, 17 August 1996, pp. 38–40.
49. Meeting at Utzon's office 23 March 1965, with Mr Ezra, P. Miller, M. Lewis, J. Nutt with Prip-Buus, Kielland-Brandt and Nielsen from Utzon's office present. ML MSS 2362/12, item 32, #249.
50. See Forestry Commission of NSW to M. Lewis, 6 March, 1965. In its table comparing the properties of coachwood and white seraya, tension stress to proportionality is 4620 psi for seraya and 9477 psi for coachwood; modulus of elasticity 1,740,000 psi compared to 2,150,000 psi; in compression coachwood does much better at 7247 psi compared to 4410 psi for white seraya. The objection to coachwood was not structural but its variability and Utzon wanted a uniform appearance throughout the Opera House.
51. *Stability Tests on Plywood Beams*, by J. Raffaels (OA & P), 11 December 1964, p. 2. ML MSS 2362/25, item 76, #279.
52. Michael Lewis supplied the advice on maximum shell loading directly to the Secretary of PWD on 25 August 1965. ML MSS 2362/12, item 32, #157.
53. Kenneth O. Humphreys (Receiver) to JU, 19 July 1964. ML MSS 2362/12,

item 32, #373.
54. The Financial Committee looking at this anticipated a bank guarantee would be forthcoming from the Commercial Banking Company who had appointed the receivers and were prepared to go to a A£50,000 (A$100,000) performance bond – more than enough. ML MSS 2362/3, items 3–5.
55. See NR, 'Sydney Opera House (Amendment) Bill', *NSWPD*, ser. 3, vol. 21, 29 September 1966, p. 1366.
56. JU to Sec. PWD, 18 May 1965. ML MSS 2362/5, item 10, #87. This followed a letter from E. Ezra at Symonds stating, '… we are quite confident that all items can be successfully manufactured to the drawings.' The drawings referred to are SOH draw. nos 1211, 1212, 1213, 1214 and 1215.
57. Poul Beckmann wrote to Utzon on 26 October raising a number of objections to the proposed structure for the Minor Hall shown on Utzon's draw. no. 803 (ML MSS 2362/12, item 32, #469–73). As a result of this, Beckmann visited Utzon in mid-November. See report by P. Beckmann, *Design Principles for Windows and Auditorium ceilings following P. Beckmann's discussions in Mr Utzon's Office on the 14th to the 16th November 1962 inclusive*, dated 19 November, 7 pp. ML MSS 2362, item 32, #455–67. The consideration of the glass wall structure, admittedly only in principle, is quite crude at this point and suggests there was a long way to go before a fully workable solution would be found.
58. JU provided this explanation at a meeting in his office on Monday 17 February 1964, attended by J. Dwyer, E. Ezra (Ralph Symonds), M. Lewis & J. Nutt (OA & P).
59. Notes on meeting at JU's office on 28 July 1965, preparatory for Stage III. ML MSS 2362/3.
60. JU to Director PWD, 25 August 1965. ML MSS 2362/23, item 59, # 7. The commencement date of January 1966 was given by Michael Lewis in a letter to Rider Hunt & Partners, the quantity surveyors, on 16 July 1965, a month earlier.
61. *Estimate of Area of Plywood in Building*, Mr Ezra, 31 March 1964. ML MSS 2362/23, item 59. *The Analysis of Plywood Costs Included in Estimate Cc, April 1964* is dated 8 March 1965. The areas of plywood given for the Minor Hall is 19,000 ft^2 for ceiling and walls, with 12,800 ft^2 allowed for floor and seats; in the Major Hall 27,100 ft^2, with 22,800 ft^2 for floor and seats; other quantities include 8300 ft^2 and 10,700 ft^2 for the two stage towers.
62. *Estimate of Area of Plywood in Building*, by Mr Ezra (Ralph Symonds) to JU, 31 March 1964. ML MSS 2362/12, item 32, #259–61.
63. P.O. Miller to Elias Ezra (Ralph Symonds), 6 September 1965. ML MSS 2362/32, item 3.
64. Frank O'Neil, 'Utzon works in Solitude', *Sunday Mirror*, no. 332, 29 August 1965, p. 7. The O'Neil piece concluded its pathetic search for some sensational titbit with the startling announcement that Utzon, 'designer of the nation's most ambitious cultural project', had another problem – the owner of his house was about to return from overseas and Utzon would be forced to move elsewhere. That really was giving the *Sunday Mirror*'s readers their sixpence worth.
65. At this time Utzon's drawing office had produced 1278 drawings so it could not be said he was exactly lazy.
66. See *Report on visit to Melbourne by Mr D.S. McConnell and Mr W. Wheatland*, 3 November 1965. Subject: Critical Path Network and use of computers (8 pp.). ML MSS 2362/21 item 54, #3–17. Wheatland visited IBM at 173 Fitzroy Street in Melbourne to examine the use of Pert. Cost 2. This was the programme being used for the North-West Cape Naval Communications

67. station. On p. 6 it stated: 'It was agreed between the Consultants that the cost of producing Reports on the computer must be weighed against their costs, but stated that the most important feature of the use of a computer in connection with Network Diagram was the facility for quickly updating the programme in terms of the current status of the job.'
67. The interesting thing is that the total number in JU's office came to 23, counting staff in Denmark, just two less than the number required by the Government and considered necessary under its Wood Plan for a drawing office to replace Utzon's staff. This was further proof of just how badly muddled and confused was the Government and DH's thinking.
68. OHC meeting No. 88/OHT no. 45, p. 2.
69. NSWPD, ser. 3, vol. 28, 3 November 1965, p. 1714.
70. Ibid.
71. Ibid.
72. Ibid., p. 1697.
73. Ibid., p. 1728.
74. 'Not so much a fashion … more a way of life', Woman's angle, *Sunday Mirror*, 23 October 1965. Everything to do with the Utzons now attracted the attention of the press. In November, a *Sunday Mirror* journalist went to the art college where Lin Utzon was studying and got the principal to send for her in their attempt to dig up more family details.

16: A Conspiracy of Nobodies

1. See *Lin Utzon*, catalogue, Herning Kunstmuseum, July 1995, p. 7. Sketches of No theatre costumes from this trip are included in Adrian Carter, 'Kunsten Tilbage i Arkitikturen', *Arkitektur DK*, no. 5, 1990, p. 259.
2. Lis Utzon to SC, 19 January 1966, Nara Hotel, Hara Park, Japan.
3. This is confirmed by a card Utzon sent to the office from Honolulu on 1 February 1966, showing the Hozo Gate's Deva King figure at the Senso-ji Temple in Tokyo. The short message reads: 'dear friends, filled with energy like the fellow on front [of the post card] – am coming back soon – defending our work – look out! good greetings from Jørn.'
4. SC to mother and father, 8 February 1966. The king was Frederick IX who was succeeded by the present sovereign Margrethe II in 1972.
5. JN, SOH site, to LC, Berlin, 8 December 1965. ML MSS 2362/27, Utzon/Cremer & Gabler, trans. of correspondence by Philip Nobis, vol. 1.
6. JN, ibid.
7. See drawing SOH 1040 Major Hall, Internal Contours of Shells related to Radial Axes of Hall, 22 November 1963. ML. Lundberg and Utzon did the drawing to show the acoustic consultants the space that was available underneath the shells of the concrete roof as well as giving the minimum depth in which to fit all services, lighting, etc.
8. The model is held in the ML.
9. LC to JU, 11 February 1966. ML MSS 2362/17, item 43, #87–8. 2 pp. typewritten in English.
10. JU to Secretary PWD, 14 February 1966. ML MSS 2362/21, item 55, #3–5.
11. JU to OA, 10 February 1966. ML MSS 2362/12, item 32, #31.
12. Interview with OA, *BT*, Friday, 6 December 1963. ML MSS 2362/4, #351.
13. *Michael Lewis Interview*, by Ruth Thompson, 28 September 1987, OAP office,

	London, p. 22. The meeting Lewis mentioned at which Utzon presented his carparking scheme and was threatened by Pat Hills, the Labor Minister for Local Government, took place on 23 July 1964, not early February 1966.
14.	Ibid, p. 23.
15.	WW for JU to DH, Minister for PW, 15 February 1966: *Sydney Opera House – Further Recommendation for Mock-ups for Ceiling Elements for the Minor Hall.* ML MSS 2362/12, item 32, #5–21.
16.	SC to parents, Friday, 4 March 1966. The maximum ceiling for tax in Denmark was 70 per cent. In Australia the general rate of tax payable by persons other than companies was 160 pence for every pound above £16,000, 66.7 per cent. Utzon earned in an average year around £120,000 or more, less expenses and an allowance of £234 for a spouse and one child under 16 years. The combined tax amount would have come to something like 131.7–136.7 per cent, exceeding by more than a third his actual earnings.
17.	SC, diary entry 3 March 1966. JU showed these men P.O. Miller's report on the plywood, Michael Lewis's letter rescinding the report, Ove Arup's letter to JU dated 25 February, and JZ's memo to Lewis, 1963, including the tax assessment.
18.	See *Tax Treaties Concluded by European Countries, European Taxation* – International Bureau of Fiscal Documentation, Amsterdam, 1994, section C/2. This document is only useful in explaining the rules that applied after Utzon's time.
19.	See *Income Taxes Outside the United Kingdom*, vol. 1, Group 1, EEC, HMSO, London, 1976, re Denmark p. v.
20.	See *Sydney Opera House – Report July 1968*: by Legal Office, Department of Public Works, p. 9. AONSW 4/7948.
21.	The notices were sent under the authority of R.R. Gray, Deputy Commissioner of Taxation, to the Director of Public Works for 2 November 1967, for $91.310.70; 14 March 1968 for $80,130.95; and 24 May 1968 for $57,8355.45 after payment of a further $22,295.50 by Utzon under section 218 of the *Income Tax Assessment Act*. What is not made clear is how the Deputy Commissioner was justified in waiving Utzon's right to privacy by providing such sensitive information in the midst of a legal dispute with the Minister for Public Works over outstanding fees. This could only have been prejudicial.
22.	See Janne Ahlin, *Sigurd Lewerentz, Architect*, London, 1987, pp. 117–18. Possibly Utzon heard a version of the story about Lewerentz and Asplund from Hakon Ahlberg when he worked in his office in 1943, around the time when Ahlberg published his monograph on Asplund. It is also possible that Utzon heard the story about Lewerentz, whom he later confused with Asplund, although that seems unlikely.
23.	*Appendix A*: E.H. Farmer (Jan. 1965), pp. 1–2, included with *Sydney Opera House – Report July 1968* by the Legal Office, Department of Public Works. AONSW 4/7948.
24.	Ibid, p. 2.
25.	See 'The Government Architect's Office – Third Period 1947–1965', in G.P. Webber, *E.H. Rembert: The Life and Work of the Sydney Architect 1902–1966*, University of Sydney, Sydney, 1982, pp. 54–60. Rembert was placed in charge of a small section of the Government Architect's office known as the 'Design Room' which was established to promote and improve design for the large and more specialised projects. This ultimately became the nucleus for the resurgence of design when first Peter Webber in 1954, then Ken Woolley a year later, joined it as new graduates (pp. 58–9).
26.	See WW, 'Bennelong "Conspiracy" a tragedy at the opera', *A*, 9081, 1

	November 1993, p. 11. Wheatland suggested to JU that he seek a legal opinion before delivering the letter but Utzon replied, pointing to the Opera House: 'Bill, if I involve a solicitor in this project, the Opera House will suffer.' Either way the building was bound to suffer. DH effectively sacked JU.
27.	*Utzon v Minister, Correspondence*, AONSW 4/7893. Copies were sent to J.C. Humphrey (Director PWD), S. Haviland (Chairman, OHC), & Mr Turnbull (OHC). A note at the bottom reads 'Replied to D.H., 28 February 1966'.
28.	WW thought that the news reached the press at about 10.30 p.m. *WW, Diary 28 Feb-31 March, 1966*: 28 February 1966, pp. 18–19. Ron Gilling, President, NSW Chapter, RAIA, was contacted at 11.30 p.m. on the 28th for comment by the *Daily Telegraph*. R.A. Gilling, *The Institute and the Opera House*, report, p. 8.
29.	See *NSWPD*, ser. 3, vol. 60, 1 March 1966, p. 3672. Askin in reply to Questions Without Notice: 'My colleague telephoned me yesterday afternoon after some discussion with the architect about extra fees which were claimed back to 1960 …' In his report, DH stated JU had said 'Well I resign,' adding 'This is regrettable.' Michael Lewis stated he received a telephone call from DH the same afternoon, and Corbet Gore was also telephoned, to inform them that the Minister was accepting JU's resignation and asked for assurances of support which were forthcoming in both instances. *Michael Lewis interview*, London, 28 September 1987, p. 23. Lewis thought then that Utzon would not come back.
30.	WW mentions meeting Corbet Gore and Mick Lewis returning to the SOH site when he was leaving on the Monday night, 28 February; they both had sheepish expressions on their faces which led him to believe they were returning from a meeting with the Minister. WW, *Diary Notes*, Monday, 1 March 1966, p. 5.
31.	DH, *Cabinet Minute, Sydney Opera House – Resignation of Architect*, 28 February 1966, B. 3421. AONSW 4/7901, #23–7.
32.	John O'Hara, 'Utzon Quits Opera House, *SMH*, 1 March 1966, p. 1.
33.	JU, ITEMS TO BE DISCUSSED WITH THE MINISTER FOR PUBLIC WORKS 1 March 1966. AONSW 4/7901, #9. Hughes's copy of the list with his crabbed notation has survived. Points 2 to 6 inclusive are bracketed together as they related to conditions of work, 8 and 9 have squares drawn around them that suggest Hughes rejected outright the immediate approval of the plywood mock-ups and the replacement of W.W. Wood by two more experienced architects, with Utzon to have some say in their selection.
34.	See *Conditions of Engagement and Scale of Minimum Charges, 1963*, prepared by the RAIA to operate from 1 July 1963, especially, 4. Conditions of Engagement clauses (j) and (m). *RAIA Year Book 1964*, pp. 32–3.
35.	Geoffrey Bolton, *The Oxford History of Australia*, vol. 5: *The Middle Way, 1942–1988*, Oxford University Press, Melbourne, 1990, p. 160.
36.	*Atelier*, Journal of the Architecture Club (UNSW), April 1966, p. 1.
37.	'Support for Public Works Minister', *AEx*, Wednesday, 23 March 1966, p. 6.
38.	Letters to the Editor – Opera House from J.R. Ellis, Dept. of History, UNE, *AEx*, Monday, 28 March 1966, p. 8.
39.	*NSWPD*, ser. 3, vol. 60, 1 March 1966, p. 3680.
40.	'Compromise plan to bring back Utzon', *A*, 510, Friday, 4 March 1966, p. 1.
41.	The job of locking the materials away fell to SC. As the key did not work on the outside of the door, she tried to lock it from inside, whereupon it snapped in the lock leaving her trapped inside with the drawings. She was pulled out through the window after the louvre blades were removed. SC, *Diary*, Wednesday, 2 March 1966, p. 1.
42.	WW, *Diary Notes*, 3 March 1966, p. 9.

43.	'The Great Dane Hunt – part 320', *A*, 510, Friday, 4 March 1966, p. 16. This humorous piece made fun of the antics of the press to interview Utzon, but press harassment of Utzon and his family was not a laughing matter.
44.	'Compromise plan to bring back Utzon', *A*, 510, 4 March 1966, p. 1.
45.	R.A. Gilling to DH, Minister PWD, 4 March 1966. See in particular paragraphs 4–5, 9, 10, 11, 13. Gilling concurred with JU that 'The selection of the liaison architect [W.W. Wood] was an unsuitable choice and it appears he has caused discontent between the various parties.'
46.	R.A. Gilling, *The Institute and the Sydney Opera House*, p. 16. ANL MS 4500, f. 12. Gilling telephoned the Director PWD at 5.30 p.m. and the Minister at 6.00 p.m. The statement was broadcast on the 6.30 p.m. news bulletin.
47.	'Opera Designer Wants to Stay in Australia', *S-H*, 6 March 1966, p. 2.
48.	E.H. Farmer, *Sydney Opera House: matters to be considered if the Government Architect is to take responsibility to the Government for the satisfactory completion of the Building*, 15 March 1966. AONSW 4/7901, #41–7. This plan appointed C. Weatherburn as Architect-in-Charge representing the Government Architect. It named ten firms of private architects including Rudder, Littlemore and Rudder (3), and Hanson, Todd and Partners (10). On p. 4, Jack Torzillo was chosen as Architect to control the design drawing office (co-operating with Mr Utzon if he agrees to return) and David Littlemore as Architect in charge of construction. Torzillo wisely rejected the offer.
49.	There is a report on HA's negotiations on behalf of JU in 90th meeting of OHC (Trust No. 47), 14 April.
50.	*NSWPD*, 9 March 1966, p. 4021.
51.	WW, *Diary Notes*, Thursday, 10 March 1966, p. 15.
52.	Outstanding Architectural Fees for the Sydney Opera House, 18 March 1966. AONSW: *Utzon v The Minister*, 4/7896A.
53.	Giorgio Vasari, *Artists of the Renaissance*, trans. George Bull, Allen Lane, London, 1978, p. 283.
54.	E.C. Mack retained copies of the two-page 18 March 1966 petition to DH, as well as a counter statement consisting of seven sub-clauses prepared by the Director which the 14 rebel Department architects refused to sign. Mack comments that it ended in anti-climax because, although they did eventually sign a second short statement of their own, it was never handed back.
55.	'Govt. Employees Support Utzon', *SMH*, # 40,018, Saturday, 19 March 1966, pp. 1, 12. Some government architectural staff said the implication was that the signatories would refuse to work on the Opera House. The Assistant Government Architect (Design), Peter Webber, presented copies of the petition to E.H. Farmer at 3 p.m. on Friday.
56.	Les Reedman, *Notes on the Sydney Opera House Crisis*, 21 November 1993, pp. 10–12. Reedman was the Project Architect for the University of New England in DH's Armidale electorate. Neither he nor anyone else in his group suffered any penalisation to their careers as a result of this incident. In 1986–8, Reedman was appointed Assistant Government Architect.
57.	SC to George & Lorraine & Dianne Lynne, 22 March 1966, p. 2.

17: Tangles in the Web

1. NR, *NSWPD*, ser. 3, vol. 79, p. 4779.
2. Giorgio Vasari, op. cit., p. 289.
3. 'Utzon flies out under a false name', *A*, 558, Friday, 29 April 1966, p. 3.
4. 'Utzon: "I'll be on job again in 2 years"', *S-H*, no. 897, 1 May 1966, pp. 3–4.
5. Cables were received by the Utzon in Charge Committee from Louis Kahn, Richard Neutra, Walter Gropius's TAC group, Felix Candela, Sven Markelius, Aldo van Eyck, Andre Wogenscky and others. 'World architects back Utzon', *SMH*, 40,024, 30 March 1966, p. 6. Vincent Scully at Yale University wrote to the Australian Prime Minister pointing out the importance of avoiding making the glass walls appear load-bearing or seeming to compete with the shells. Scully noted: 'Saarinen, who so championed Utzon's project, was never able to solve these problems entirely in his somewhat similar structures ... Utzon's studies to date indicate that he was on the road to a solution. One can only urge that he be given the chance to find it.'
6. Utzon received the Gold Medal of the German Architects' Association from the Association's Chairman Mr Conrad Sage at Lübeck on 7 June 1966. 'Utzon bitter in interview', *SMH*, 40,084, Wednesday, 8 June 1966, pp. 1, 3.
7. JU to Chief Building Inspector, Warringah Shire Council, 14 July 1964.
8. JU, 'Platforms and Plateaus', *Z*, no. 10, 1962, pp. 130–3, figs 34, 35. The sketches presuppose a much more fluid and open interaction with the outside than is apparent in the final heavily contained inwardly directed spaces at Bayview.
9. Gavin Souter, 'Brave man, said Utzon', *SMH*, 40,044, 22 April 1966, p. 5.
10. E.H. Farmer interview with Ruth Thompson, 28 March 1988, at Glenbrook, NSW, p. 20.
11. Appendix A 1–3, by E.H. Farmer, p. 2, attached to *Sydney Opera House – Report*, July 1968, by the Legal Office, Department of Public Works, AONSW 4/7948.
12. E.H. Farmer interview, op. cit., p. 21.
13. 'P.A.A. Afraid of Fresh Hangar Fall', *SMH*, no. 37,151, Monday, 14 January 1957, p. 1. The collapse caused damage estimated at between A£50,000 and A£100,000 (A$200,000).
14. These are the words the former Minister, Davis Hughes, used to describe the nine years Labor was in charge at the SOH. Davis Hughes, *Twenty Years at the Sydney Opera House – May 1965 to January 1973*, p. 5. DH resigned in January 1973 nine months before the building was finished to take up the appointment of NSW Agent-General in London.
15. See *RAGNSW, Year Ended 30th June, 1966*, p. 105.
16. Item (7), *Confidential Cabinet Minute*, 25 August 1965, by DH. AONSW 4/8070
17. HTL, *Analysis of Costs of Production: Fees etc.* 22 April,1966. 1 p. The fee calculation was $38,000 for each of the principals.
18. HTL, *Report on Partnership Profits*, 31 December 1968, 2 pp.
19. 'Inquiry on Opera House refused', *SMH*, 40,083, Tuesday, 7 June 1966, p. 4. In a dispute with WW in which he accused DH of refusing permission ten months earlier to test mock-ups for the glass walls, DH responded: 'The dispute I had with Mr Utzon over mock-ups concerned the interior not the glass wall.' This was untrue because the mock-ups included the interiors and the glass walls.
20. 'Utzon claims seat plans "seen long ago"', *SMH*, 40,086, Friday, 10 June 1966, p. 3.

21. HTL, *Review of Programme*, 12 December 1966, 12 pp.
22. E.H. Farmer interview, op. cit., p. 24.
23. TP, Meeting 61, OHT, Friday 10 March 1967, p. 3.
24. Yuzo Mikami and MIDI, 'Orchard Hall, Shibuya, Tokyo', *Space Design*, no. 301, October 1989, pp. 88–96. It is certainly no coincidence that this splendid convertible hall was designed by Yuzo Mikami, the talented young Japanese assistant who worked in Jørn Utzon's Hellebæk office in 1959. The seating capacity of Orchard Hall for concerts is 2150 and is reduced to 1928 for opera by the using the pit for the orchestra. The convertible stage enables a reverberation time of 2.0 seconds for music, and a shorter one of 1.6 seconds for opera.
25. The figures are from Utzon to the Minister for Public Works, 9 November 1965, Re: Sydney Opera House – Architect's Fees. pp. 3, 2. AONSW.
26. Waagner-Biro, Vienna, *Sydney Opera House: Stage Machinery – Modification of Supply Schedule*. ML MSS 2362/24, item 63, #5.
27. *Design 218: Professor H. Ingham Ashworth interviews Jørn Utzon and G.J. Zunz*. Sydney, ABC TV, 1962.
28. Memo, *Sydney Opera House: Glass Walls – Concrete or Steel Mullions*, n.d, 2 pp.
29. See *Sydney Opera House, Stage 3*, report, February 1968, 21 APPENDICES (ii) p. 12.
30. HTL, *Sydney Opera House, Stage 3*, February 1968, 13 pp.
31. Since 1966 Australia's basic unit of currency has been the dollar, consisting of 100 cents. This decimal system replaced the 'sterling' pounds, shillings and pence inherited from Britain in 1826.
32. *NSWPD*, ser. 3, vol. 79, 18 March 1969, p. 4642.
33. These figures have been calculated using data from the *Government Architects' Branch Cost Manual* prepared by the Quantity Surveyor, John McCrae, 15 April 1986.
34. *NSWPD*, ser. 3, vol. 63, 29 September 1966, p. 1357. DH asked Parliament for approval of an appropriation of $37.5 million in the *Sydney Opera House (Amendment) Bill*. DH engaged in a semantic sleight of hand to do this as the further debate on 6 October, p. 1598, makes abundantly clear.
35. 'Bennelong blues', *SMH*, Saturday, 27 July 1968, p. 2.
36. See *Cabinet Minute, October 5, 1971 from DH*, AONSW: 10/42708.
37. See *RAGNSW*, 30 June, no. 47, 1974, p. 94.
38. *Report of the Department of Public Works*, NSW Parliament, 30 June 1963, pp. 36–7; also *Report*, 30 June 1964, pp. 43–4.
39. *NSWPD*, ser. 3, vol. 63, Wednesday, 28 September 1966, p. 1289.
40. List of HTL staff for Hong Kong flu vaccinations dated 5 January 1969. With the three partners, the total is 54. Lionel Todd was not included in the list as he was overseas.
41. '$150,000 paid to Utzon for Opera drawings', *SMH*, 40,666, 18 May 1966, p. 1. *The Report of the Auditor-General*, 30 June 1966, p. 105, gives the amount as $160,000 paid to Utzon, 'Without prejudice' in respect of a claim lodged by him in connection with his services. Bill Wheatland who held power of attorney for Utzon, said the drawings included working drawings for interior finishes, cladding and paving, glass walls, Major and Minor auditoria, rehearsal rooms and windows. In a memorandum prepared by L. Todd, H. Isele, D.S. Littlemore and B. Shaw, on 19 May, Todd and Littlemore stated by contrast: 'It is the considered opinion of all four architects present that there were no working drawings available, nor any complete detail drawings.' By 24 February 1966, Utzon's office had completed a total of 1454 drawings. The number handed over represented less than 8 per cent of the total.

42. In his <u>Statement No. 2</u>, to DH on 7 March 1966, JU stated: 'I charge you for what is built and some installation drawings ... The drawings which you have not received for Stage 3 I simply refuse to deliver to you for the above-mentioned reasons.'
43. Correspondence on the state of the pleadings, January 1970: Claims by Architect for Fees & Expenses. File B. 4515/23 PWD. *SOH: Utzon*, NBR box 2. On 17 December 1968, Nicholl & Nicholl to R.J. McKay, State Crown Solicitor re *Utzon-v-Minister for Public Works*, complained that the matter 'has already been very long delayed.'
44. JZ interview, op. cit., p. 43.
45. Charmian Clift, 'Pilgrimage to a possibility,' *SMH*, 40,079, Thursday, 2 June 1966, Women's sect. p. 2.

18: Back in Denmark

1. Steen Eiler Rasmussen, 'Australien fatter ikke Utzons værk', (Australians do not understand Utzon's work) *P*, 6 March 1996, p. 47.
2. Halldor Gunnløgsson, 'Ytringer om Utzon' (Comment on Utzon), *P*, 15 March 1966, p. 4.
3. Ove Arup, 'Utzon afslar for sig selv og stab', (Utzon refuses for himself and staff), *P*, 16 March 1966, p. 7.
4. 'Jørn Utzon's Projekt fur ein neues Schauspielhaus', *Neue Zürcher Zeitung* (Zürich), no. 2973, Tuesday, 9 July 1964, p. 4 (Zürcher Lokalchronik).
5. The comment was made by the late Sigfried Giedion in the 5th edition of *Space, Time and Architecture*, Harvard University Press, Cambridge, Mass., 1971, p. 689.
6. JU to Mr Wasserfallen, Stadtbaumeister der Stadt Zürich, 11 April 1969.
7. E. Frech, 'Die Kulturbauprojekte in Zürich: Schauspielhaus-Operahaus-Kunsthaus', *Neue Zürcher Zeitung*, 18 February 1970, p. 25. A summary of this article was shown to the NSW Minister for Public Works, DH, on 5 March 1970, accompanied by a translated excerpt, 'The story has also reached Zürich that Utzon has built a theatre in Sydney where the first estimate was multiplied several times. This fairy tale was played up during the change of Government in Australia. But the truth is that the theatre building is financed by lottery and every year some additional buildings were added to the project in connection with the money received from the lottery. At Zürich we are multiply safeguarded against surprises: the approved project is binding, the credit is fixed with the vote, the periodical financial reports allow a balance anytime and furthermore it is foreseen to let a contract for supervision of building to a very well known Zürich firm.'
8. See 'Grand Masters', *Architectural Review*, April 1967, p. 248; 'Uddrag af dommerkomiteens bemaerkninger til Jørn Utzons projekt', *Arkitekten*, no. 15, 1966, pp. 312–13.
9. See Jørn Utzon, 'Additive Architecture', *Arkitektur* (DK), no.1, January 1970, pp. 1–50.
10. See Nader Ardalan and Laleh Bakhtiar, *The Sense of Unity: The Sufi Tradition in Persian Architecture*, University of Chicago Press, Chicago, 1973, p. 105 ff.
11. See Richard Neville, *Hippie Hippie Shake: The drugs, the trips, the trials, the love-ins, the screw-ups ... the Sixties*, William Heinemann Australia, Melbourne, 1995, p. 72.

12. Susan Dunlop, 'See You in Australia', *WD*, October 1973.
13. Birger Schmidt to author, 14 May 1998: 'As far as the bonfire in Ålsgårde is concerned, I was not present, but Utzon told me about it. I have no recollection of any dates or details.' There are many stories about this happening which tie the event to the Midsummer Eve festival on 24 June weekend when bonfires are lit along the Danish coastline.

19: Laying Low

1. Robert Graves, *Collected Poems*, Cassell, London, 1975, p. 465.
2. 'Bad-sensation fra Jørn Utzon,' *Badnyt*, no. 3, 15 June 1971, p. 10.
3. Utzon's scheme was published in *B* magazine (Århus) no. 46, July 1989, pp. 12–13.
4. Interview with Henrik Sten Møller, '"Can Feliz", Jørn Utzon's own house', *LA*, no. 14, 1995, p. 98.
5. John Sergeant interviewed Utzon in April 1996, see, 'Utzonian Houses', *Architectural Review*, vol. 200, no. 1196, October 1996, p. 49, n. 2.
6. Palma receives 826.5 mm (33 inches) of precipitation annually, the bulk of it between September and April. In winter the average temperature falls to 11°C in January, but climbs to 26°C in July.
7. Henrik Sten Møller, '"Can Lis" Jørn Utzon's own house', *LA*, no. 8, 1989, p. 146.
8. Robert Graves, op. cit., p. 231.

20: Flowers of Light

1. Susan Dunlop, 'Opera House, Designer still has soft spot for us – SEE YOU IN AUSTRALIA', *WD*, 30 April 1973, p. 2.
2. See Ava Hubble, 'An interview with the architect of the Opera House, Joern Utzon', *Sydney Opera House Monthly Diary*, vol. 5, no. 9 (June) 1978, p. 1.
3. Ibid, p. 5.
4. Henrik Sten Møller, 'Inspiration; Naturen', *P*, Saturday, 9 April 1988, sec. 2, p. 1.
5. Jørn Utzon, 'En skoleby i Herning', *Arkitektur*, no. 1, 1970, pp. 12–17.
6. Martin Hartung, 'Han lavede Utzon-hus til sit eget musikhus,' *Berlingske Sondag*, 6 October 1985, sec. 5, p. 2.
7. See Peter Anker, *The Art of Scandinavia*, vol. 1, Hamlyn, London, 1970, pp. 201–12.
8. See Michael Swanston, *Beowulf*, Manchester University Press, Manchester, 1978, l. 81.
9. See Margaret E. Goldsmith, *The Mode and Meaning of Beowulf*, Athlone Press, London, 1970, p. 83.
10. Johannes Slok, *Kierkegaard's Universe: A New Guide to the Genius*, trans. Kenneth Tindall, Narayana, Copenhagen, 1994, p. 147.
11. Le Corbusier, *Towards a New Architecture*, trans. Frederick Etchells, Architectural Press, London, 1965, p. 222.
12. Svend Simonsen (ed.), *Bagsværd Church: I am inspired by clouds*, booklet,

Bagsværd Parochial Council, 1976, p. 3.
13. Pi Michael, *Clouds*, television documentary, Danmarks Radio, Soeborg, 1994.
14. *Exodus* 40: 34. In *Numbers* 9: 15, it states, 'On the day that the tabernacle was set up, the cloud covered the tabernacle, and the tent of the testimony; and at evening it was over the tabernacle like the appearance of fire until morning. So it was continually; the cloud covered it by day, and the appearance of fire by night.'
15. See *Lin Utzon*, exhibition catalogue 5 August–24 September 1995, Herning Kunstmuseum.
16. George Pedersen, a senior lecturer at Sydney's Conservatorium of Music, performed in a concert in Bagsværd Church in 1980 and remembered with delight: 'I shall never forget the extraordinary beauty and purity of its interior, its classical yet striking modernistic lines.' *SMH*, 49,764, Saturday, 1 March 1997, p. 40 (Letters). He said of the acoustics that they had a 'really lovely sound'.

21: 'It isn't necessary'

1. Christopher Walker, 'Triumphant return of troops tempered by torture stories', *The Times*, no. 63,951, Thursday, 28 February 1991, p. 4.
2. For a report on the effect of the second Gulf War on Kuwait City see Michael Kramer, 'Kuwait: Back to the Past', *Time Australia*, vol. 6, no. 31, 5 August 1991, pp. 14–22.
3. Ray Clancy, 'Jubilation as flag flies once more in Kuwait City', *The Times*, no. 63,952, Wednesday, 27 February 1991, p. 3.
4. The building cost is contained in a National Assembly document, *The National Assembly Building*, published after its restoration, which describes the current building and its facilities on p. 5. The work of restoration was carried out by the Corps of Engineers supervised by Diwan Engineering.
5. The work of restoring the interiors was carried out by the New York office of Hellmuth, Obata & Kassabaum (HOK) led by principal designer Juliette Lam. HOK had extensive prior experience in the Middle East in Cairo and Saudi Arabia since 1982.
6. See Dilip Hiro, *Desert Shield to Desert Storm: The Second Gulf War*, Paladin, London, 1992, p. 27. Hiro provides a detailed history and the background of the war as well as an overview of the politics of Kuwait and the role of the ruling Sabah family in Kuwaiti affairs. Of the 440,000 Kuwaiti nationals in 1975, fewer than 40,000 were eligible to vote. Kuwait's democratic record is better than most Gulf States and Saudi Arabia.
7. For a description of this plan and its effect on the development of Kuwait City see Stephen Gardiner, *Kuwait: The Making of a City*, Longman, London, 1983, p. 58. Buchanan, a Scottish expert on transport, born in 1907, is best known for his working-group study of the long-term development of motor traffic in urban areas in 1960–3. A shortened edition of the *Buchanan Report*, November 1963, was published as *Traffic in Towns*, Penguin, Harmondsworth, 1964.
8. Ibid., p. 66. According to LM, the panel of four advisers comprised Professor Franco Albini (Milan), Dr Leslie Martin (Cambridge), Dr Omar Azzam (Egypt) and Hamid Shuaib (Kuwait), then the Assistant Director of Technical Affairs in Kuwait. The advisory panel was chaired by Sheikh Jaber al Ahmed, Kuwait's Prime Minister who succeeded as ruler on the death of Sheikh Sabah III on 31

December 1977 as Sheikh Jaber III Al Sabah.
9. Interview with Abdulaziz al-Hamdan on 12 December 1995, a Kuwaiti architect trained at the University of Arizona, who served on the Advisory Committee which initiated the project in 1970.
10. The figures are from the National Assembly summary, op. cit., pp. 1–2. This gives the area of the basement carpark as 18,750 m^2, the ground floor of 18,750 m^2 and first floor of 18,750 m^2, making a total area of 56,250 m^2. Evidently this did not include the north-west shade canopy measuring approximately 82.5 m x 40 m, or 3300 m^2. Calculations give an even smaller total size: basement and ground floor each 11,187.5 m^2; a first floor of 9562.5 m^2; making a total of 31,937.5 m^2 (343,784 ft^2), or 35,237.5 m^2 (379,306 ft^2) including the shade canopy.
11. JU is quoted as saying, 'In this way it can grow like a tree. If it grows naturally the architecture will look after itself.' Unfortunately for Utzon the tree did not grow naturally and suffered a wide variety of insults along the way towards its realisation. *LA*, no. 5, 1986, p. 120.
12. A ground plan, sections and elevations of the preliminary scheme are illustrated in Poul Erik Skriver, 'Kuwait National Assembly Complex', ibid., 1986, pp. 119–20. Oktay Nayman, who joined Utzon on the Sydney Opera House in 1962–6, produced the drawings for the 1970 competition scheme.
13. This account was provided by Utzon on a visit to the 'Can Lis' house on Mallorca on 18 February 1990.
14. The *Blue Book*, so named because of its deep blue cover with floor plan in white, is dated November 1973. It contains 37 pages of drawings, text and photographs of the model, together with engineering studies on 840 mm x 595 mm sheets. For his engineering consultant, Utzon used Walt + Galmarini, Zürich, and J. Byskoc Ovesen, Copenhagen, as services consultant. Page 5 shows the Conference Hall mirroring the National Assembly. The mosque is freestanding in its own reflecting pool and is linked to the covered public square opposite the Gulf by a pedestrian bridge.
15. Susan Dunlop, 'Designer still has soft spot for us', *WD*, 30 April 1973, pp. 2, 3. The interview took place some time before its publication, and coincided with a celebratory dinner for the new building in Kuwait which Utzon did not attend but sent Jan Utzon in his place.
16. Interview with Hamid A. Shuaib (he was one of the four on the Advisory Panel chaired by Sheikh Jaber Al Sabah) on 12 December 1995. Shuaib is currently Technical Manager of Pan Arab Consulting Engineers in Kuwait.
17. Interview with Bader al Qabandi, Chief Engineer Planning and Development, Ministry of Public Works, Kuwait, 12 December 1995.
18. 'Special Report on Kuwait', *Middle East Economic Digest*, August 1977, p. 43.
19. Markku Komonen, interview with Jørn Utzon, 'Elements in the Way of Life', *Arkkitehti* (Finland), February 1983, p. 61.
20. Reference is made to this saying in the Pi Michael video documentary *Clouds*, Danmarks Radio, Soeborg, 1994. It is quoted earlier by Stephen Gardiner, op. cit., p. 2, in 1983, and it seems likely that this is where Utzon read it.
21. Utzon explained this in the Pi Michael video, ibid., 1994.
22. From my interview with Hamid A. Shuaib, op. cit.
23. Ibid., from the same Shuaib interview,
24. From Hamid A. Shuaib interview, op. cit. Shuaib started on the site in September 1978 and the drawings arrived in November 1978. It started as a 32-month project and should have been ready by August 1981, but took more than six years, and was only 90 per cent completed by October 1983. The

separate carpark structure on the east side of the Assembly building took a further two years.
25. Markku Komonen, op. cit., p. 60.
26. See S. Giedion, *The Beginnings of Architecture*, Princeton University Press, Princeton, 1981, p. 361 ff; ill. 238. There are a number of important similarities between the National Assembly internal street and the ancient Egyptian hypostyle hall: both form the core of the complex; both serve as a processional itinerary; and both are orientated on a north–south axis. The term 'hypostyle' denoted a hall with a roof borne on columns, which is precisely what Utzon has done in the National Assembly complex in Kuwait City.
27. Lisbet Balslev-Jørgensen to author, 10 January 1997.
28. The UNO-X service station at 2–4 Poulsgade, Herning, was completed in November 1986, but in 1992 it was sold to Texaco and re-named the Hydro-Texaco. Vitia Lysgaard (b. 1930–), the senior director who founded Tankskibsrederiet Herning A/S, has since retired and her place has been filled by her son Knud Lysgaard (b. 1948–).

22: Solitude

1. Herman Melville, *Moby-Dick; or The Whale*, Penguin Books, Harmondsworth, 1972, p. 593.
2. Melissa Roberts, 'Utzon Jnr forgives nation he loves', *A*, Tuesday, 24 April 1984, p. 3.
3. Ava Hubble, 'Utzon reveals the great Opera House wrangle', *Weekend A Magazine*, 31 December 1983–1 January 1984, p. 9.
4. Sir Denys Lasdun, 'Royal Gold Medallist 1978: Jørn Utzon', *RIBA Journal*, vol. 85, no. 10, p. 425.
5. Ibid., p. 427.
6. Peter Balslev-Clausen (ed.), *Songs from Denmark*, Danish Cultural Institute, Copenhagen, 1988, p. 102–3. Adam Oehlenschlager wrote the words of Denmark's National Anthem in 1819 and they were later set to music by H.E. Kroyer, c. 1835.
7. See Else Glahn, 'Chinese Building Standards in the 12th Century', *Scientific American*, vol. 244, no. 5, May 1981, p. 132–41.
8. 'Paustians Hus', *Arkitektur DK*, no. 8, 1989, pp. 353–69.
9. See Jon Stephensen, 'Jeg fortyder ikke et Sekund', *B Magasin*, s. 2, Friday, 1 January 1988, p. 1; Martin Hartung, 'Han har laert af naturen', *B Magasin*, s. 3, Saturday, 9 April 1988, p. 1; Henrik Sten Møller, 'Inspiration: Naturen', *P*, Saturday, 9 April 1988, s. 2, p. 1.
10. Kim Dirkinck-Holmfeld, 'Jørn Utzon 75 Ar', *Arkitekten*, vol. 95, no. 5, April 1993, p. 165.
11. The exhibition, *Jørn Utzon: Udvalgte Arbejder 1942–1988*, at the Skissernas Museum, Finngatan 2, Lund, Sweden, from 11 September to 23 October 1994. The catalogue contained a brief essay on Utzon with a valuable list of works and descriptions.
12. See Henrik Sten Møller, 'Ildhu er drivkraften: Studerende lykkedes med den forste Utzon-udstilling', *P*, s. 2, Friday, 22 April 1988, p. 6; and Martin Hartung, 'Smagsprove pa Utzon', *BT*, 27 July 1988. The exhibition at the Danske Arkitekturcentre, Gl. Dok, ran till 7 August.

13. 'Utzon bag byfornyelse til 1,5 milliarder kr', *BT*, 24 April 1988, and Søren Frank, 'Ny bydel i Kobenhavn: Weidekamp er begejstret for Utzons milliardprojekt ved Svanmollen', *P*, 27 April 1988.
14. Tina Blomgreen, 'Kongreshotel pa Langelinie', *P*, sec. 1, Thursday, 3 September 1985, p. 7.
15. Jørgen Holst, 'Utzon-projekt vakler', *Aktuelt*, 18 February 1987. Four harbour projects were under consideration in May 1998: the Utzon Kalkbrænderihavnen project; a congress centre at Langelinie also by Utzon; Peter L. Stephensen's glass hall for Vesterport Station; and a hotel and congress centre at Kalvebod by Bent Severin and Arne Meldgaard, all described in Nils Thorsen, 'København er projekternes by: Det vrimler med nye planer til mange milliarder kroner', *P*, sec. 3, Thursday, 12 May 1988, p. 7.
16. Nils Thorsen, 'Utzon-projekt far en ny chance', *P*, 23 March 1988.
17. Kaj Holm-Jørgensen, 'Byudvikling i Kalkbrænderihavnen-er det en realitet eller en utopi?', *Københavns Havneblad*, vol. 41, no. 9, November 1988, pp. 10–11.
18. Michael Varming, 'Københavns ny Havn', *Arkitekten*, vol. 90, no. 13, July 1988, pp. 297–300.
19. Henrik Sten Møller, 'En by for mennesker: Jørn Utzons havneprojekt kan vær klar til indflytning i 1996', *P*, sec. 2, Monday, 7 October 1991, p. 1.
20. Bo Trolle, 'Århus far sit Århus-tarn', *P*, sec. 1, Wednesday, 14 February 1992, p. 6.
21. Bo Trolle, 'Mod Stjernerne: Bygningen af et 155 meter hojt tarn diskuteres i Århus', *P*, sec. 2, Wednesday, 14 February 1990.
22. Jørn Utzon, '"Can Feliz", Jørn Utzon's own House', *LA*, no. 14, 1995, p. 100.
23. Pi Michael television documentary, *Clouds*, for Danmarks Radio, Soeborg, 1994.
24. T. Faber, 'To hus pa en middelhavs-o', *Arkitektur DK*, no. 2, 1996, p. 113.

Reflections

1. T. Faber, ibid., p. 111.
2. JU to Elias Duek-Cohen, 15 April 1997.
3. JU to Elias Duek-Cohen, 13 May 1997.
4. Olaf Olafsson, *Absolution*, Phoenix House, London, 1994, p. 132.
5. Henrik Sten Møller, 'Udsight til Stilheden', (View of the silence) *P*, kultur liv (Culture life), Saturday, 7 October 1995.

Index

A

Ålborg, xvii, 6–7, 11–14, 15, 18, 23, 34, 90, 195
Ålborg Katedralskole, 15
Ålsgårde, 5, 19, 30, 415
Ålsgårde cabin, 30
Aalto, Alvar (1898-1976), xv, xvii, 24–25, 51, 63–4, 107, 410, 444, 474, 480
Abben, Peer (1916-), 26, 45, 335, 352, 359, 373, 421
abbreviations, 502–4
Academy of Music, Østerbrogade, 46–7, 57
acoustics
    auditoria, 44, 49, 166, 222–5, 229–37, 284–6, 309–10, 312–13, 322–3, 328
    Greek theatre model, 223–4
    model testing, 44, 163, 225, 230–1, 262, 284, 286, 338
    Radiohus, 44, 166, 222, 224
    requirements for opera and concerts, 123, 133–4, 231–4
    reverberation time, different, 232–4, 266–7, 336, 387–9
    shoe-box concert halls, 135, 224
additive architecture concept, 60, 62, 410–14, 434–5, 465
Aerial Hotel, Heathrow Airport, 239–41
Ahlberg, Hakon, 34–5
Ahm, Povl, 240
Al-Boat Company, Helsingør, 418–19
Alberti, Leon Battista (1404-72), 60
Albini, *Professor* Franco, 449
Alexander, Robert E., 136
Allan, Norman, 304
Alstrup, Bent (1914-), 88, 96, 177
Alvar Aalto Medal (1982), 473
Ammon, *Lord,* 53
Andersson, Erik, 85, 97, 151–2, 154–5
Andrews, John, xiii
Århus, 31, 484–5
Århus School of Architecture, 480
Århus Sports Centre competition (1948), 67
Århus Town Hall, 43
Armstrong College, Newcastle, 5
Art Gallery of New South Wales, 136, 137
Arton (Utzon's business company), 154
Arup, *Sir* Ove Nyquist (1895-1940), 54, 147–8, 160–1, 163, 166–9, 177, 180–2, 188, 193–8, 201–2, 206–7, 228–9, 238–41, 295, 371–2, 396, 402
Ashworth, Henry Ingham, 36, 125–6, 128, 130–7, 143–4, 147–8, 159, 165, 167–8, 170, 182–7, 197, 225, 234–5, 334, 345, 360
Askin, *Sir* R.W., 149–50, 171–2, 253–4, 277–9, 281, 299–300, 304–5, 309, 320, 330, 352, 355, 357–61, 371–2, 432
Asplund, Gunnar (1885-1940), 35–6, 47–8, 70, 343, 346, 349
Asuussen, Erik, 39
auditoria design, 165–6, 229–37, 249, 260, 309–10, 312–13, 322–5, 328, 335–8
    convertible auditoria, 165, 232–4, 387–8
    history, 9, 72, 387–8
    multi-purpose auditoria, 165, 232–5, 386–7
    science of, 386–7
    Australian Broadcasting Commission (ABC), 121, 130, 186
Australian Elizabethan Trust, 128
Australian Labor Party, 432
    NSW Branch, 124–5, 148, 150–1, 173, 180
    Women's Organising Committee, 149
Azzam, *Dr* Omar, 449, 459

B

Bagsværd Church, Denmark, 28, 377, 437–45, 451
Baldwinson, Arthur, 143, 152
Balslev & Partners, 182, 187
Balslev-Jørgensen, Lisbet, 463
baramada (Hindi for veranda), 487
Barcelona Pavilion, 425
Bayview Heights, 246–7, 374
Bayview house designs (1963-5), 374–8, 406, 442
Beaumont, Steph, 471–2
Beckmann, Poul, 231, 325
Beckmarch Manor, 2
beech forest theme, 28, 80, 234–5, 475–6
Bellahøj Development competition, 45–6
Bellushi, Pietro, 134
Bennelong Point, 98–101, 103, 107–9, 112–3, 123, 125–6, 128, 144, 149, 152, 164–5, 171, 181, 204, 238, 252, 255, 451
Beowulf, 440

Berg, George of Flensberg, 8
Bergman, Ingmar, xvii
Berlin Opera House, 226
Berlin Philharmonic Hall (1956-63), 233, 264–7
Berning, Asger, 211
bibliography, 504–7
Birkehøj project, 209, 413
Birmingham, USA, 157
Blakeney, Ben, 431
Blixen, Karen, *Baroness* (1885-1962), 96, 475
Blue Book (November 1973), 454
Bo, Jørgen (1914-), 96
Bohr, Niels, xvii
Boissevain & Osmond, 144
Boras, Sweden, 57
Bøssemagergade, 4, 89–90, 158, 413
Bovis (UK), 459
Boyer, *Sir* Richard, 154
Brandt, Erik, 477
Brandt, Margit, 477
Brecht, Bertholt Friedrich (1898-1956), 406
Breuer, Marcel, 18
Brisbane, 121
Brown Book (February 1956), 98
Brownell, Raymond Preston, 251
Brun, Rasmus, 2
Brybmawr Rubber Factory, UK (1951), 160, 201
Buchanan, *Sir* Colin (1907-), 449
Bund Deutscher Arkitekten Prize, 373–4
Bunning, *Sir* Walter, 130, 136, 278
Burgtheatre, Vienna, 158, 184–5
Burmeister & Wain Shipyard, 5
Business School for Gothenburg competition (1948), 61

C
Cabellos, Manuel, 429
Cabin, Ålsgårde *see* Ålsgårde cabin
Cahill, John Joseph, 124–8, 129–31, 132, 137–9, 148–51, 166, 171–3, 178–80, 254, 279, 406
Cala Figuera, Mallorca, 426
Can Feliz house, Mallorca (1994), 485–91
Can Lis house, Mallorca (1972), 422–9, 433, 485–90
Candela, Felix (1910-), 113, 201
Capitol Theatre, Sydney, 122
Carl Rosa Opera Company, 119
Carr, Martin, 226
Castel de Santuari, Mallorca, 486
Cervantes, Miguel, 58
Chafey, W.A., 278

Charlottenborg Palace, Copenhagen, 24, 32
Chicago, 68–70, 155–6
Chichén Itzá, Mexico, 75
Chinese architecture, 37, 47, 49, 56, 63, 72, 90–2, 167, 410, 476–7
Christensen, Annie, 81
Christensen, Kai (1916-), 19–20, 26
Christian IV, 4
Christiani & Nielsen, 146, 161
Cincinnati, 121
Circular Quay, 98, 100, 102, 122, 283
Civic Centre for Falköping competition (1949), 61
Civil & Civic, 170, 202, 204–6
Clark, *Sir* Kenneth (1903-83), 53–4
Clemmensen, Ebbe (1917-), 40, 163
Clift, Charmian, 397
cloud theme, 225, 236–7, 378, 441–2
Coliseum Theatre, 184
Collard, Joanna, 330
Colless, Shirley, 334, 345, 349, 367
colour dyeing *(farver)*, 3–4
communism, 278, 354
competitions, architectural, 44–6, 49–58, 61–2, 67–8, 86, 88–9, 95–117, 162–3, 176, 187, 209–10, 272–7, 404, 410–12, 419
Compton, K.C., 281
Coombs, H.C. (Nugget), 128
Copenhagen, 23–34, 40, 43–65
Country Party, NSW, 149, 172, 255, 278, 299–301, 304–9, 371–2, 432
courtyard house type, 10, 90–93, 96, 209–19, 375–8
Crematorium Chapel at Sockenvågen, 35–6
Crematorium competition (1945), 49–51
Cremer, *Professor* Lothar, 229–30, 235, 238, 261–2, 266–7, 284–6, 310, 313, 328, 335, 338, 391
Crystal Palace, International Competition, London (1946), 51–7, 101, 475
Cumberland County Council, 121, 128
Cutler, Charles B., 172, 300, 307–8, 390

D
Dalerup, Vilhelm, 476
Damgaard, Aage, 435–6
Danforce Brigade, 40
Danish architecture, xv–xvi, 214–19, 272–6, 475–6, 494
Danish Union of Trade Unions (LO) competition (1957), 162–3
Danske Samvirke Committee, 210, 214–16
Darlinghurst Courthouse, 379

Descriptive Narrative (1965), 286
Design Room, 347–8
Detroit, 68, 157
Dirkinck-Holmfeld, Kim, 214, 479–80
diwan, 456, 467
Dominican Chapelle du Rosaire, Vence, Alpes Maritimes, 346
double-ender, 8–9
Drottingholm, 37
Drummond, D.H. (David), 306, 319, 397
Duck Island Resort project, Queensland, 470
Dusseldorp, Gerardus J., 205

E
Eames house, Pacific Palisades (1949), 69, 71–2
Eames, Charles (1907-69), 69, 71, 444
Eames, Ray, *née* Kaiser (1916-88), 69, 71
Eastman Kodak, 120
Eastman, George (1854-1932), 120
Edmonds, Reginald, 53
Eline Berge Shopping Centre, Halsingborg, Sweden, 187, 209
Elizabeth II (1926-), 243–5, 396, 431–2
Ellis, J.R., 355
Elvira, Spain, competition, 187, 209
Entwistle, Clive, 54–5
Espansiva timber component house (1969), 411–14
Estrup, 2
Ezra, Elias, 325

F
Faber, Tobias, xiii, 24, 26, 33–40, 44–6, 51–2, 55, 57, 62–5, 402, 475, 490–1
Falköping, Sweden, 57
Farmer, E.H., 280, 303, 331, 347, 356, 360, 363–6, 372, 379–82, 394
Farnsworth House, Plano, Ill., 69–70, 82–4
Farum Town Centre competition (1966), 411
farver, 3–4
Fenger, *Dr* Mogens (1889-1955) (father-in-law), 34
Fenger, Lis (1919-), 33
   see also Utzon, Lis
Festival Hall, Salzburg, 158, 185
Finland, 51
First Schleswig War (1848-50), 3
Fisker, Kay (1893-1965), 24, 71
Fordamsvej office, Denmark, 226
forest pavilion, Jutland, 58
Foster, *Sir* Norman (1935-), 473
Frampton, *Professor* Kenneth, xiii
Frankild, Otto, 45

Fraser, R.D.L., 128
Fredensborg, 477
Fredensborg courtyard housing, 46, 89, 210, 212, 214–19, 248, 489
Frederiksburg Town Plan competition (1959), 176, 209
Frey, Albert, 62
Frisch, Max Rudolph (1911-91), 276, 404, 406
Fry, Maxwell, 56
functionalism, 17–18, 19, 64, 480
Furniture competition (1946), 61, 72

G
Gabler, Werner, 230–1, 235, 262, 264–6, 284–6, 310, 313, 391
Gale, *Mrs,* 128
Gamla Stan, Stockholm, 38
Garbo, Greta, xvi
Genarp, Sweden, 39–40
Geneva, 49
geometry as a design tool, 188–201, 221–2, 230–2, 273
Giedion, Sigfried (1894-1968), 27
Gilling, Ron, 316–18, 358–60, 362–4, 373
Giurgola, Romaldo, 445
Gladsaxe Town Hall (1938), 438
Goldstein Hall, University of New South Wales, 379
Goossens, *Sir* Eugene (1893-1962), 119–128, 130–3, 370, 387
Gore, Corbert, 351
Gosmer, Denmark, 2
Göteborg (Gothenburg), Sweden, 23, 85, 295, 434
Grand Arche de la Defense, Paris, 470
Graves, Robert Ranke (1895-1985), 422–3, 427
Greek amphitheatre, 104–5, 109–10, 223–4
Gropius, Walter Adolph (1883-1969), 56, 248, 357
Grundvig Church, Copenhagen, 28, 440
Guggenheim Museum, New York, 273, 275
Guion, Yves, 229
Gunnløgsson, Celia (*née* Lund), 37–9
Gunnløgsson, Halldor (1898-), 26–7, 32–3, 34, 37–9, 80, 401

H
H. Hoffmann & Sonnen A/S, 481
Hall Todd & Littlemore (HTL) consortium, 393
Hall, Libby (*née* Bryant), 330
Hall, Peter Brian, xv, 318, 330–31, 354, 365, 372, 378–87, 394–6, 465–6, 472

Halling, Denmark, 2
Hamburg Opera House, 132
Hammershøj high house, Helsingør, 210
Hammershus on Bornholm, 419
Hammond, *Miss* Joan, 154
Hana Hedin house, Mallorca (1972)
Hansen, *Professor* Hans Munk (1929-), 158, 162, 176
Hanson, Fred, 304
Hauch, Carsten, 4
Havel, Vaclav, xvii
Haviland, Stanley, 137–9, 154, 345, 360–1
Heatherington, Bruce, 420
Hedquist, Poul, 35, 37, 59
Heffron, R.J., 178, 228, 260, 277
Heger, Jarl (1929-), 163
Heinze, *Sir* Bernard Thomas (1894-1982), 151, 233, 264–6
Helger, Henning, 46
Hellebæk, xiii, 3–5, 12, 35, 70–1, 79–92, 157–62, 169, 175–7, 186, 238
Hellebæk Fabrik, 3
Hellmuth Obata & Kassabaum (HOK)
Helsingbørg, Sweden, 85, 98, 104, 154, 210
Helsingør, 5, 12, 28, 67, 162
Helsingør Shipyard, 23, 159, 171, 195
Helsinki, 51
Hennessy, Jack, 183
Hergel, F., 152
Herman Miller Inc, Zeeland, Mich. (f. 1923-), 72, 182
Herning, 434–7
Herning Art Museum (1977), 436
Heron Island, Queensland, 310–11
High School, Helsingør, 406
Highpoint One, Highgate, London (1935), 161
Hills, Pat, 228, 281–3, 343
Hirschfeld, Kurt, 276, 406–7
Hjertholm, Helge, 295–6
Hjørring, 34
Hobro restaurant and community centre competition, 58
Hobro, Jutland, 58
Høeg, Peter, xv, 79
Höganäs, Sweden, 163, 194, 292–6
Holte house (1952-3), 86–8
Holte, Denmark, 86–8
Holweg, Ole, 39
Honolulu, 334–5, 369, 420–2
Hornibrook M.R. (NSW) Pty Ltd, 206, 229, 256–7
Huan, Joe, 239
Hughes, *Sir* Davis, 172, 180, 300–9, 311–24, 328–30, 333, 344, 346–59, 370–3, 380–401, 415, 417, 433, 472, 492

Humlebæk, Denmark, 96
Humphrey, J.C. (Colin), 279, 317, 325, 326, 351, 356, 358, 366
Humphreys, Kenneth O., 322
Hunt, Hugh, 169–70
Hvid, Valdemar, 214

I
Ibsen, Henrik, xvii
Idlewild Airport, 189
industrialisation of building, 286–7, 444,
Irming, Mogens (1915-), 26, 52, 55, 57
Islef, Christian, 481

J
J.F. Kennedy Airport, 135
Jackson, Herbert, 53
Jacobsen, Jens, 3
Jämtland, Sweden, 39
Japan, 155–6, 177, 334
Jeanneret, Charles Edouard (1887-1959) *see* Le Corbusier
Jeddah Stadium scheme (1969), 411–12
Jenkins, Ronald S., 160, 170, 177, 181–3, 187–93, 196, 202
Jensen, Johannes, 465
Jensen, Knud W., 96
Jepsen, *Professor* Gunnar, 485
Johnson, *President* Lyndon B. (1908-73), 305
Johnson, R.A.P. (Alan), 279, 347, 381
Johnson, R.N., 325, 326
Jordan, Vilhelm Lassen (1910-82), 44, 163, 166, 168–9, 178, 186, 187, 222–4, 229–30, 232–3, 235, 284–6
Jorn, Asger, 272–3, 275, 373
Jutland, xvii, 2–3, 7, 9, 12–13, 34, 50, 58, 90, 494–6

K
Kailua, Hawaii, 421
Kalkbrænderi south basin proposal, Copenhagen Harbour, 481–4
Kampax A/S, 175, 523n2
Kattegat, 5, 19, 30, 104
Kemp & Lauritzen U 4860 pendant lamp, 71
Kerr, *Sir* John, 206–7
Kielland-Brandt, Jacob (1923-), 251–2, 300
Kierkegaard, Søren Aabye (1813-55), 142, 440
Kingo courtyard houses, Helsingør (1957-60), 89–91, 210–14, 216
Kingsgate Footbridge, Durham (1963), 162, 238
Klint, Kaare (1888-1954), 28

Klint, Peter Vilhelm Jensen (1853-1930), 28, 440
Klostermarksskolen elementary school, 11–12
Kolding, 2–3
Kolle, Erik, 259
Kongens Nytorv, Copenhagen, 24, 31
Koppel, Nils (1914-), 39
Korsmo, Arne, 58–62, 68–70, 73, 85, 115
Korsmo, Grete, 60, 68–9
Korsmo-Utzon chair, 61
Kronborg Castle, 102–4, 152
Kuwait City, 447–65
Kuwait Prefabricated Building Company (KPBC), 458–9
Kylberg, Carl (1878-1952), 19–20, 24

L
La Cour, Charlotte, 182
Labour Organisation College, Helsingør, 209
Lambert Airport Terminal, St Louis, 156
Langaard, Ebbe, 211
Langelinie Pavilion, Copenhagen Port (1953), 86, 187
Langelinie Pier proposal, 480–3
Langer, Karl, 121–2, 130
Large Sports Palace, Rome (1960), 201
Larsen, Henning (1925-), 482
Lasdun, *Sir* Denys Louis (1914-), 473
Lauritzen, Vilhelm (1894-1984), 44, 49, 113, 187, 222–4, 438
Lautrup-Larsen, Knud (1919-90), 62–63, 181, 250, 402
Le Corbusier, 48–9, 53–4, 63, 346, 423, 440, 480
League of Nations Palace, Geneva (1927), 49
Leavey, W.M., 206–7
Lend Lease, 205
Lewerentz, Sigurd (1885-1975), 35, 346
Lewis, Michael, 239–41, 246, 256, 272, 322, 341–4, 351, 357
Liberal Party, NSW, 131, 149, 254, 432
Limfjord Sound, Denmark, 6
Littlemore, David Surrey, xv, 372, 382, 386
Liu, Leighton, 421
Liverpool, UK, 122
Lorenz, Erhard (1913-), 51
Louisiana Art Museum (1956-58), 96
Lübeck, Germany, 374
Lubetkin, Berthold (1901-), 161
Lundberg, Jon, 178, 187, 196, 231, 251–2, 266–7, 277, 295, 300, 336, 406
Lysgaard, Vitia, 465

M
Mack, Edward C. (Ted), 365
Maclurcan, Robert Geoffrey, 251, 317
Macquarie Street, 98, 122, 128–9
Maekawa, Kunio, 235
Mallorca, xiii, 420, 422–9, 485–92
Malmquist, Sandro, 163, 168, 177
Markelius, *Professor* Sven (1889-1972), 276
Martin, *Sir* J. Leslie, 133–4, 136–39, 144, 146, 161, 449
Marzella, Joseph, 144
Maschinenfabrik Wiesbaden GMBH (MAN), 182
Mattmar, Central Sweden, 39
Mayan architecture, 63, 73–6
McKay, R.J., 396
McKenzie, Ian, 284
Melli Bank, Teheran, 67, 158, 162, 175–6, 210, 216, 377, 442
Mendelsohn, Erich, 107–8
Menzies, *Sir* Robert Gordon (1894-1978), 171, 354
Metropolitan Opera House, New York, 183
Mexico, xii, 47, 65, 67–69, 73–7
Michael, Pi, 197
Michelangelo di Lodovico Buonarroti (1475-1564), 365, 369
Mies van der Rohe, Ludwig (1886-1969), 68–70, 82–4, 88, 156–7, 222, 346, 425, 480
Mikami, Yuzo, 171, 186–7, 234–5, 239, 256, 321, 388, 493
Miller Milston & Ferris, 261, 325
Miller, Peter O., 261, 325, 377
Missingham, Hal, 135, 357
MIT Auditorium, Cambridge, Mass., 135
Mitterand, Francois, 53
model making, 159–6, 169
modern architecture, xii–xiii, xv, 34, 45, 48, 53, 56, 62, 73, 77, 88, 161–2, 172, 222, 251, 286, 480
Mogelvang, Ib, 210
Molbach (Ålborg harbourmaster), 8–9
Mølgård, Kjeld, xvi
Møller, C.F. (1898-), 435, 484
Mollman, Hugo, 182, 192–3
Molnar, George, 126, 136, 137, 372
Moneo, José Rafael (1937-), 198–202
Monte Alban, 69, 73–77, 406
Montgomery, Bernard Law, *1st Viscount*, 40
Moon, Milton, 310
Moorcroft, Margaret, 310–11
Moro, Peter, 134
Morocco, xii, 67–8, 72, 92, 410
Moses, *Sir* Charles, 130–1, 133, 265, 312

Muirhead, Desmond, 470
Mulberry harbours, World War II, 54
Museum of Modern Art scheme (April 1988), 476–9, 489
Museum of Modern Art, New York, 61, 72, 172

N
Nara, Japan, 334
Næstved Sports Park competition, 58
National Assembly Building, Kuwait City (1971-83), 403, 420, 447–65, 467, 469–70
National Museum, Hammershus on Bornholm competition (1969), 419
National Opera, Madrid competition (1964), 277, 480
National Theatre of Mannheim, 184
Nayman, Oktay, 231, 261–2, 335
Nelson, George (1907-86), 182
Nervi, Pier Luigi (1891-1979), 146, 189, 197, 201–2
Neutra, Richard (1892-1970), 136, 152
Neville, Richard, 414
New Town Centre, Farum (1966)
Nexø, Bornholm, 58
Nicholl, R.W., 371, 395
Nielsen, Elsebeth Gerner, xvii
Nielsen, Olaf Skipper, 187, 205, 286, 300, 458
Norberg-Schulz, Christian, 61
Nordic style, 19
Nørresundby, 6, 12
Norway, 413, 439
Novo Nordisk Company, 438
NSW Conservatorium of Music, 127–8, 131, 264
NSW Parliament
  Cabinet, 129, 178–9, 228–9, 315, 351–2, 382
  Legislative Assembly, 127, 149
NSW State Government, 122, 162, 167, 184, 201, 260, 263, 270, 286–7, 296–7
  Askin administration, 299–330, 352, 355–67, 372, 378–97, 417, 492
  Cahill administration, 124–39
  Heffron administration, 178–181, 228–9, 253–5, 302
  Renshaw administration, 277–84, 309
Nutsch, Joachim, 261–2, 328, 335–8
Nutt, Dr John, 342, 352

O
Oberg, Anette Marie Christine (1846-1912) (grandmother), 4–5, 6
oil-shock (1973), 421–2, 434

Olafsson, Olaf, 494
Old Concert Hall, Tivoli, Copenhagen, 105, 187
Olivier, Sir Laurence, xvii
Olsen, Estrid Valeska Halina (1894-1951) (mother), 5, 81, 92
Olsen, Martha (grandmother), 19
Olssen, Rudolf, 292
Olympic Games, Melbourne (1956), 97
Olympic Games, Rome (1960), 200
Opera House, Malmö, Sweden, 123
Orchard Hall, Tokyo, 388, 493
Øresund, 4–5, 19, 85, 88, 96, 103, 159
organic architecture, 64, 70, 72–3, 92, 412
Organisation of Arab Oil Exporting Countries (OAPEC), 456
Oslo Central Railway Station competition (1947), 61, 115
Oslo plan (1952), 86
Oslo, Norway, 62
Östberg, Ragnar (1866-1945), 36–7
Østre Havn, 7, 16
Ove Arup & Partners, 10, 146–7, 155, 161, 177, 181–4, 191–3, 201, 206, 231, 238–41, 246, 252–3, 255–7, 294, 296, 316, 321–4, 336, 340–3, 352–3, 358, 390

P
Paddington, Sydney, 351–2
Palm Beach, Sydney, 137, 271–2, 433
Paper factory scheme, Morocco, 67–8
Paris, 53, 82, 270, 470–1, 480
Parkes, Cobden, 133, 137, 280
Paustian Furniture Showroom, North Harbour, Copenhagen (1987), 473–8, 481, 489
Paustian, Ole, 473–4, 483
Paxton, Sir Joseph, 52, 54
Peblinge Sø indoor swimming pool scheme (1979), 476–7
Peddle Thorp & Walker, 342
Pedersen Ude of Kolding (1578-1641), 1–2
Pedersen, Ude (d. 1707), 2
Penguin Pool, Regent's Park Zoo (1934), 161
Persian Gulf War (1991), 447–8
Petersen, Aage Hartvig (1927-), 250
Petersen, Gunnar Biilman, 28–9
Petersen, Tom, 483
Petersson, Associate Professor Ove, 292
Pietilä, Reima (1923-), 450
Pittwater, 246–8
platforms, 75–6, 83, 109, 187, 478–9
Players' Theatre, London, 168
plywood
  applications, 72, 259–61, 319–22

formwork, 259, 325
glass wall mullions, 321, 323–5, 390, 465–7, 493
hall ceilings, 231–2, 234–6, 248–9, 258–61, 285–7, 317, 322, 336, 340–1, 344, 492
patents, 260
structural uses, 259
police corruption in NSW, 304
Police Headquarters, Copenhagen, 23
Popov, Alex, 414–15, 471
Popper, Karl, xvii
Porto Petro, Mallorca, 374, 378, 420, 422–9, 485–92
Praxiteles, 36
precast concrete, 87–8, 161, 188–9, 197–8, 201, 203, 403, 411, 457–9
Prip-Buus, Mogens, 182, 196, 251–2, 256, 277, 352, 360
Prip-Møller, J., 36, 167, 522n51
Pullich, *Mrs*, 177

R
Rahiohus (Radio House), Copenhagen, 43–4, 49, 113, 166, 222, 224
Ralph Symonds factory, Homebush, 264, 285, 322–5, 377
Rasmussen, Steen Eiler (1898–), 25, 156, 217, 401
Red Book (March 1958), 163–5, 191, 193, 202, 234, 454
Rembert, E.H., 347
removable concert shells, 231–7
Renshaw, J.B., 127, 277–9, 281–2, 300, 309, 328–30, 361, 384, 391
Ribe, Denmark, 3–4
Ricci, *Mrs* Ruggeriero, 154
Rider Hunt & Partners, 185, 254, 294, 393
Riga, 5
Rochester Philharmonic Orchestra, 120–1
Rohrbandt, Knud, 32
Romer Husene see Kingo courtyard houses, Helsingør (1957–60)
Ronchamp Chapel, Belfort, France, 423
Rønne, Bornholm, 58
Royal Australian Institute of Architects (RAIA)
NSW Chapter, 128, 130, 316–17, 353, 358, 472–3
Royal Copenhagen Porcelain (1980), 445
Royal Danish Academy of Fine Arts, 19, 23–4, 28, 46, 156
Royal Festival Hall, London, 126, 133
Royal Institute of British Architects' Queen's Gold Medal for Architecture (1978), 473
Royal Opera House, Covent Garden, 184
Royal Theatre, Copenhagen, 23
Rungsted, Denmark, 88
Russell, Bertrand, xvii
Ryan, Philip Norman, 180, 228, 253–4, 260, 263, 281–2, 286, 300–1, 317–18, 347, 361–2, 372, 391

S
Saarinen, Eero (1910–1961), 68–9, 135–9, 146, 148, 157, 172
Sæby, xvii
San Francisco War Memorial Opera House, 123, 128, 387
Saxild, Jørgen, 162, 175, 216
Scania house competition (1953), 210
Scharoun, Hans (1893–1972), 230, 233, 265, 276, 410
Schlanger, Ben, 385
Schmiegelow, Anne Malthea (mother-in-law), 34
Schmiegelow, *Professor* Ernest, 34
Schouboe, Poul (1918–), 26, 183–5, 250
Schrøder, Poul (1899–1957), 19, 29
Scottsdale, Arizona, 69
sculpture, architecture as, 15, 50, 68, 82–3, 106–7
Seidler, Harry, 136, 143, 357, 364
Seiffert, J., 150
Shaffer, *Miss* Elaine, 154
Sheikh Abdullah III al Sabah, 448–9
Sheikh Jaber al Ahmed al Sabah (1928–), 450, 452–3
Sheikh Sabah III, 456
shell structures, 9, 47, 49, 57, 110–14, 146, 153, 156, 189–201, 293, 441–3
shipbuilding, 8, 23
Sicard, François, 129
Silkeborg Kunstmuseum (1963–4), 272–6, 373
Siren, Osvald, 37
Skaanske low-cost housing competition (1953), 89–90
Skagen Odde Centre proposal (1995), 494–5
Skagen, Denmark, 494–5
Skane, Sweden, 45
Skibby, Joan, 311
Skissernas Museum, Lund, 480
Skjern rowhouses commission (1956), 95–6
Skodborghus, 2
Skoyen, Upsala, 86
Skromberga, Sweden, 292, 295
Snapperman Beach, 271–2
Sønderborg, 3
Søndergade, 3

Sonning Prize (Denmark) (1998), xvi
Sørensen, Erik Christian (1923-), 39, 80
souk, 57, 451, 463, 465
Souter, Gavin, 283
Southampton University, UK, 181
Speer, Albert (1905-81), 53, 485
Spence, *Sir* Basil Unwin (1907-76), 134
Spidsgattere boat type, 8, 10
Spreckelsen, Johan Otto von (1929-), 470–1
Sputnik, 99, 175, 191, 195
St Louis, USA, 134, 155–6
standardisation in architecture, 10, 249, 286–7
Star-Tower, Århus, 480, 484–5
stavkirke, 439, 443
Steensen & Varming, 163
Stockholm, 34–41, 59
Stockholm Town Hall, 36
Stockholmsutstalingen Exhibition, Stockholm, 1930, 16–19
Strömstad, Sweden, 183
Styrsö, Sweden, 434
Svaneke, Bornholm, 58
Swift Torrents Samsø Island project (1995), 495–6
Sydney, 102, 243–53
Sydney City Council, 128
Sydney Harbour, 122, 152
Sydney Harbour Bridge, 102
Sydney Opera House, xi, xiv–xvi, 9–10, 44, 47, 49, 55–6, 61, 74–5, 85, 338–40, 450–1, 492–3
official opening, 396, 431–3
political opposition, 148–51, 167, 227, 253–5, 277–84, 299–320
project development, 157–170, 177–207, 221–40, 258–67, 284–7, 289–97, 309–331, 333–40
architectural and secretarial staff, 497–8
auditoria, 72, 100, 134, 159, 165–6, 202, 221–5, 229–37, 249, 258–67, 319–25, 328, 335–8, 344
Major Hall, 110, 134, 163, 165, 168, 170, 178, 181–2, 186–8, 201–3, 205, 221–5, 232–7, 261–7, 283–7, 312–13, 323, 328, 335–8, 339, 340, 344
Minor Hall, 163, 168–70, 182, 186–7, 203, 221–5, 230–2, 235, 257, 261–7, 285–7, 312–13, 323, 328, 337, 339, 340–1, 344
review plans, 384–90, 394–5
carpark, 282–3, 393–4
construction, 203–6, 252, 255–7, 283, 314–15
commencement ceremony, 171, 300
contracts, 170, 178, 202, 206, 229, 237–8, 256–7, 328–9
legislation, 178–80, 253, 302–3, 312, 390
staging of work, 329
tenders, 170, 184, 205–6, 257
cost estimates, 167, 179, 184, 228–9, 253–5, 278, 280–4, 329, 359–60, 383–4, 390–4
crisis, 354–67
critical path planning, 313–14, 327
design concept, 99–117
model, 151–4, 172, 185–7
Experimental Theatre, 168, 170, 203, 386
furniture, 182
glass walls, 36, 72, 105–6, 112, 154, 156, 202, 257–8, 310, 341, 465–7, 492–3
project proposal, 121–9,
alternative sites, 121–3, 126, 128–9
public donations, 152–4
Recording Studio, 386
Restaurant, 145, 154, 163, 168
shell roof
alternative designs, 159, 163, 169, 181, 188–202, 227–8
glazed tile surface, 289–97
sketch plans, 162–5, 167–8
stage areas, 225–8
stage lifts, 108, 132–3, 178, 184–5, 227
stage machinery, 170, 178, 181–5, 227, 310, 348, 388–9
stage tower, 101, 103, 184, 233, 388–9
tourist attraction, 358
Sydney Opera House competition (1956), 96–117, 123, 129–30, 132–8
announcement of the winning design, 137–9
Sydney Opera House Executive Committee, 127, 129, 131–3, 137, 142, 147, 154, 162, 164, 167–70, 179–81, 183, 187, 228, 265, 297, 327, 345, 350, 353, 363
see also Sydney Opera House Trust
Sydney Opera House Lottery, 150, 154, 164, 253
Sydney Opera House Trust, 202, 282, 302–3, 315, 360–1, 386
Sydney Public Library, 127

Sydney Symphony Orchestra (SSO), 121, 123, 127, 132
Sydney Town Hall, 121, 127, 152–3
Symonds, Ralph S., 168, 202, 259–61, 264, 285, 312, 318, 321–6, 344, 375

T
Taliesin East, 69, 71, 375
Taliesin West, 69, 71
Tankskrbsrederiet Herning A/S, 465
Tati, Jacques, 287
Tatischeff, Jacques *see* Tati, Jacques
tent theme, 186, 235, 453–4, 462
terrace, in architecture, 47–9, 55–7, 74–6, 83, 110, 214–19
Textile School, Herning (1967-68), 411, 434–5
Tingsryd, Sweden, 45
Todd, Lionel Milton, xv, 372, 382, 385
Torzillo, Jack, 366
total design concept (Ove Arup), 161
town planning, 25, 45–6, 51, 56, 57–8
tree theme, 412, 451
Tri-Tail yacht, 418–9
Truelsen, Niels Frithiof, 275
Turner, Fred, 169
TWA Terminal, 135, 157, 172, 189

U
Ud, 1
Udsen, Ane Birgitte, *neé* Høstmarch (1740-85), 3
Udsen, Lauritz, 2
Udsen, Morten, 2
Udsen, Peder (1616-59), 2
Udsen, Peder (1727-92), 2–3
UNESCO, 96–7
University of Hawaii, 420
University of Sydney, 143
UNO-X petrol station, Herning, 465–7
Unruh, *Professor* Walter, 177–8, 183, 186, 187, 226, 230
Utsep modular furniture system, 411
Utzon and Associates, 421, 471, 480–5
Utzon House, Hammermill Wood, Hellebæk, 80–5
Utzon Huset Museum (1970), 435–7
Utzon, Aage Oberg (1885-1970) (father), 11–13, 16–17, 28, 82, 88–9, 417–19
birth, 4
career, 5–6, 7–9, 23
contribution to Sydney Opera House, 9–10, 153, 159
death, 419
marriage, 5
world fame, 8–9
yacht design, 8–11, 15
Utzon, Anne Catherine (1845-1922) (aunt), 23
Utzon, Erik Oberg (1924-55) (brother), 12–13, 92–3
Utzon, Hans Jørgen (1845-1922) (grandfather), 3, 6
Utzon, Jan Oberg (1944-) (son), 41, 88, 247, 334, 401, 421, 459, 470–1, 481, 484–5, 488
Utzon, Jørn Oberg (1918-)
  Art and Thought
    drawings and architectural styles, xii, xv, 16, 27–31, 45–50, 55–8, 63–5, 67–8, 73, 77, 79–85, 86–92, 156, 159–60, 169, 274–6, 464–5
    influences, 9–11, 15–16, 18–20, 28, 34–6, 47–9, 59–61, 70–2, 104, 311–12
  Career
    architectural competitions, 44–6, 49–58, 61–2, 67–8, 85–6, 88–9, 95–117, 162–3, 176, 187, 209–10, 272–7, 404, 410–12, 419
    awards and prizes, xvi, 46, 51, 58, 95, 162, 176, 209–10, 272, 276, 373–4, 404, 472–3, 502
    Sydney Opera House competition, 142–7
    building projects, 29–30, 58, 79–92, 96, 210, 272–7, 412–14, 435–45, 447–67, 473–7 (*see also* Sydney Opera House)
    business companies (*see also* Arton; Utzon and Associates)
      office in Hellebæk, 157–62, 169, 175–7, 238, 250–1, 399–415, 434–45
      offices in Sydney, 238, 243, 250–3, 256–67, 271–2, 309–10, 372–3
      Copenhagen, 43–65
    Danish national legend, 479–80, 494
    government conspiracy against Utzon, 279–84, 299–331, 340–4, 346–67, 400, 492
    Hawaii, 420–2
    military training, 39–40, 45
    residence at Bayview Heights, Pittwater, 246–50, 374–8
    residence in Hellebæk, 79–92, 175–7

residences in Mallorca, 422–9,
    463, 485–91
retirement, 469–71, 491–6
Sweden, 34–41, 58–9, 85
travel, 65, 68–77, 155–7, 167,
    184–6
works and projects (1944-1988),
    496–502
Education
    Royal Danish Academy of Fine
        Arts, Copenhagen, 24–34
    schooling, 11–14, 14–15, 23
Life and Character
    ancestry, 1–5
    birth and early years, 6, 13–21
    children, 41, 51, 84, 88, 97, 371,
        374, 401, 414, 421, 438,
        444–5, 459, 470–2, 480–5,
        491
    crises, xv–xvi, 269–71, 345–73,
        384–5, 415, 420
    marriage, 37
    parents, 4–20, 81
    personality, xii, xiv–xvii, 6, 16,
        18–19, 20–1, 25–7, 310–11,
        399–401, 425, 433–4, 464–5,
        490, 492–4
    Utzon, Kim Oberg (1957-) (son),
        84, 142, 177, 196, 247, 333,
        335, 421, 471, 481, 483–4,
        488–9, 494
Utzon, Leif Oberg (1916-64) (brother), 6,
    11, 14, 19–20, 23, 28, 81, 104,
    269–71, 471
Utzon, Lin Oberg (1946-) (daughter), 51,
    141–2, 160, 247, 269, 334, 401,
    414–15, 438, 444–5, 471–2, 477, 481
Utzon, Lis (*née* Fenger) (1919-) (wife),
    38–9, 67, 170–1, 243–5, 330, 333–4,
    359, 491–2
    see also Fenger, Lis
Utzon, Michael Lausen, 3
Utzon, Nicolaj Peder (1805-80) (great-
    grandfather), 3
Utzon, Nicolaj Peder (uncle), 4–5
Utzon-Frank, Aksel Einar (1888-1955)
    (cousin), 23–4
Uxmal, Mexico, 76

V

Varming, J., 54
veranda, 376, 487
vernacular architecture, xii, 19, 36–7, 48,
    63–5, 73, 217, 221–2, 410, 422
Vestra Vika, Oslo competition (1948),
    61–2, 115

Vidal, Jaime, 424
Vienna State Opera House, 109, 132, 158,
    184–5
Vietnam War, 277–8, 305, 354
Villa Arnung, Nærum (1953), 88
Villa Frank, Vedbæk (1955), 88
Villa Lillesoe, Furesoen (1955), 88
Vodder, Knud, 182

W

Waagner-Biro, 184–5, 310, 389
Walk, Max, 458
Wanscher, Vilhelm (1875-1961), 32
Warringah Council, 374
Water tower and maritime signal, Svaneke,
    58
Waterhouse, B.J., 137
wave theme, 441–2
Weatherburn, Charles, 360, 363, 394–5
Westergaard, Bjorn, 371
Wheatland, W.W. (Bill), 327, 340, 348–9,
    352, 357, 360
White, Patrick, 244–6, 354, 357
Whitlam, Edward Gough (1916-), 432
Willer, *Reverend* Bernard, 440
Winston, *Professor* Denis, 167, 357
Wohlert, Vilhelm (1920-), 96
Wolf Prize (Israel) (1992), xvi
Wolfsburg Theatre competition (1965),
    410
Wood, W.W., 279–80, 313–15, 325, 340,
    350, 360
Woodland Cemetery, Sockenvägen (1917-
    40), 35, 346
Workers' Educational Association, 128
World War II (1939-45), 12, 20,
    39–40
    German Occupation of Denmark,
        31–40, 43, 222
Wright, Frank Lloyd (1867-1959),
    48, 63–4, 69–71, 73, 82, 86,
    111, 143, 176, 248, 274–5, 346,
    375

Y

yacht design, 8–11, 417–19
double-ender, 8–10, 418
    half-models, 9
    models, 10, 16, 418
    testing, 10
Yachting World Diamond Class Keelboat,
    247, 259
Yellow Book (January 1962), 199, 202–4,
    227, 236
Ying-tsao fa-shih, 477
Yom Kippur War (1973), 456

Z
Zeuthen & Sørenson, 187
Zunz, *Sir* Jack (1923-), 36, 193, 201–3, 205, 228–9, 240–1, 246, 341, 396
Zürich Hochbauamt (Board of Works), 407
Zürich Schauspielhaus Theatre (1964–70), 272, 275–7, 284, 402–10, 415, 463
Zürich, Switzerland, 276, 284, 402–10